MW01485740

MIPHAM'S DIALECTICS AND THE DEBATES ON EMPTINESS

This book explores a number of themes in connection with the concept of Emptiness, a highly technical but very central notion in Indo-Tibetan Buddhism. It examines the critique by the leading Nyingma school philosopher Mipham (1846–1912), one of Tibet's brightest and most versatile minds, formulated in his diverse writings. The book focuses on related issues such as what is negated by the doctrine of Emptiness, the nature of ultimate reality and the difference between 'extrinsic' and 'intrinsic' emptiness. These issues continue to be the subject of lively debate among contemporary exponents of Tibetan Buddhist thought. Karma Phuntsho's book aptly undertakes a thematic and selective discussion of these debates and Mipham's qualms about the Gelukpa understanding of Emptiness in a mixture of narrative and analytic styles. For the first time, a major understanding of Emptiness, variant to the Gelukpa interpretation that has become dominant in both Tibet and the West, is revealed.

Karma Phuntsho was trained to be a *Khenpo*, a Tibetan Buddhist monastic abbot, for about a dozen years during which he studied, practiced and taught Buddhism in several monasteries in Bhutan and India. In 2003, he received a D.Phil in Oriental Studies from Balliol College, Oxford. He currently works at the University of Cambridge and the Centre national de la recherche scientifique (CNRS), Paris as a post-doctoral researcher specializing in Buddhism and Bhutan. His main interest lies in the preservation and promotion of Buddhist and Bhutanese culture.

ROUTLEDGE CRITICAL STUDIES IN BUDDHISM

Edited by
Charles S. Prebish and Damien Keown

RoutledgeCurzon Critical Studies in Buddhism is a comprehensive study of the Buddhist tradition. The series explores this complex and extensive tradition from a variety of perspectives, using a range of different methodologies.

The series is diverse in its focus, including historical studies, textual translations and commentaries, sociological investigations, bibliographic studies and considerations of religious practice as an expression of Buddhism's integral religiosity. It also presents materials on modern intellectual historical studies, including the role of Buddhist thought and scholarship in a contemporary, critical context and in the light of current social issues. The series is expansive and imaginative in scope, spanning more than two and a half millennia of Buddhist history. It is receptive to all research works that inform and advance our knowledge and understanding of the Buddhist tradition.

A SURVEY OF VINAYA LITERATURE
Charles S. Prebish

THE REFLEXIVE NATURE OF AWARENESS
Paul Williams

ALTRUISM AND REALITY
Paul Williams

BUDDHISM AND HUMAN RIGHTS
Edited by Damien Keown, Charles Prebish and Wayne Husted

WOMEN IN THE FOOTSTEPS OF THE BUDDHA
Kathryn R. Blackstone

THE RESONANCE OF EMPTINESS
Gay Watson

AMERICAN BUDDHISM
Edited by Duncan Ryuken Williams and Christopher Queen

IMAGING WISDOM
Jacob N. Kinnard

PAIN AND ITS ENDING
Carol S. Anderson

EMPTINESS APPRAISED
David F. Burton

THE SOUND OF LIBERATING TRUTH
Edited by Sallie B. King and Paul O. Ingram

BUDDHIST THEOLOGY
Edited by Roger R. Jackson and John J. Makransky

THE GLORIOUS DEEDS OF PURNA
Joel Tatelman

EARLY BUDDHISM – A NEW APPROACH
Sue Hamilton

CONTEMPORARY BUDDHIST ETHICS
Edited by Damien Keown

INNOVATIVE BUDDHIST WOMEN
Edited by Karma Lekshe Tsomo

TEACHING BUDDHISM IN THE WEST
Edited by V. S. Hori, R. P. Hayes and J. M. Shields

EMPTY VISION
David L. McMahan

SELF, REALITY AND REASON IN TIBETAN PHILOSOPHY
Thupten Jinpa

IN DEFENSE OF DHARMA
Tessa J. Bartholomeusz

BUDDHIST PHENOMENOLOGY
Dan Lusthaus

RELIGIOUS MOTIVATION AND THE ORIGINS OF BUDDHISM
Torkel Brekke

DEVELOPMENTS IN AUSTRALIAN BUDDHISM
Michelle Spuler

ZEN WAR STORIES
Brian Victoria

THE BUDDHIST UNCONSCIOUS
William S. Waldron

INDIAN BUDDHIST THEORIES OF PERSONS
James Duerlinger

ACTION DHARMA
Edited by Christopher Queen, Charles Prebish and Damien Keown

TIBETAN AND ZEN BUDDHISM IN BRITAIN
David N. Kay

THE CONCEPT OF THE BUDDHA
Guang Xing

THE PHILOSOPHY OF DESIRE IN THE BUDDHIST PALI CANON
David Webster

THE NOTION OF *DITTHI* IN THERAVADA BUDDHISM
Paul Fuller

The following titles are published in association with the *Oxford Centre for Buddhist Studies*

Oxford Centre for Buddhist Studies
a project of The Society for the Wider Understanding of the Buddhist Tradition

The *Oxford Centre for Buddhist Studies* conducts and promotes rigorous teaching and research into all forms of the Buddhist tradition.

EARLY BUDDHIST METAPHYSICS
Noa Ronkin

MIPHAM'S DIALECTICS AND THE DEBATES ON EMPTINESS
Karma Phuntsho

MIPHAM'S DIALECTICS AND THE DEBATES ON EMPTINESS

To be, not to be or neither

Karma Phuntsho

Routledge
Taylor & Francis Group
LONDON AND NEW YORK

First published 2005
by Routledge
2 Park Square, Milton Park, Abingdon, Oxon, OX14 4RN

Simultaneously published in the USA and Canada
by Routledge
270 Madison Ave, New York NY 10016

Routledge is an imprint of the Taylor & Francis Group

Transferred to Digital Printing 2010

© 2005 Karma Phuntsho

Typeset in Times New Roman by
Newgen Imaging Systems (P) Ltd, Chennai, India

All rights reserved. No part of this book may be reprinted or reproduced or utilised in any form or by any electronic, mechanical, or other means, now known or hereafter invented, including photocopying and recording, or in any information storage or retrieval system, without permission in writing from the publishers.

British Library Cataloguing in Publication Data
A catalogue record for this book is available
from the British Library

Library of Congress Cataloging in Publication Data
A catalog record for this book has been requested

ISBN10: 0–415–35252–5 (hbk)
ISBN10: 0–415–59998–9 (pbk)

ISBN13: 978–0–415–35252–9 (hbk)
ISBN13: 978–0–415–59998–6 (pbk)

TO THE EXPONENTS OF EMPTINESS

yaḥ śūnyatāṃ pratītyasamutpādaṃ madhyamāṃ pratipadaṃ ca/
ekārthaṃ nijagāda praṇamāmi tam apratimabuddham//

Nāgārjuna

CONTENTS

ACKNOWLEDGEMENTS

When I look back on the day I embarked on the daunting project of writing the thesis, which culminated in this book, and the subsequent years of work, the first popular analogy that comes to my mind is Frodo's journey to the Land of Mordor. Like the little hobbit, my intellectual journey took me beyond the traditional 'shire' with which I was familiar and comfortable, to realms unknown and ingrained with academic nitty gritties, nuances and vicissitudes which I was ill-equipped to deal with. The journey has seen several high points filled with a sense of discovery and excitement as well as sad times when I was drawn into the dark forces of frustration and despondency. If it were not for the kindness and support of numerous teachers, friends and relatives, I would have discarded my 'ring' a long time ago.

Foremost among my *kalyāṇamitra*s in my traditional training are H. H. Penor Rinpoche, whose very presence imbues one with the spirit of a bodhisattva, H. H. the Dalai Lama, H. H. Khenpo Jigme Phuntsho, Nyoshul Khenpo, Khenpo Pema Sherab, Khenpo Namdol, Khenpo Tsewang Gyatsho, Khenpo Wangchuk Sonam, Khenpo Kātyāyana, Khenpo Tsering Dorji, Geshe Pema Gyeltsen, Geshe Gedun Choephel and over two dozen other masters whose words of wisdom and compassion have been an incessant source of inspiration and strength. I am equally grateful to my monastic colleagues, Khenpo Tsewang Sonam, Khenpo Tenzin Norgey, Lopen Dorji Wangchuk, Lopen Thinley Dorji, Lam Nidup and numerous others, for their sustained encouragement.

However, the credit of accomplishing the academic task primarily goes to my western academic gurus. Without their guidance, I would have never left my traditional domain and ventured out on an academic mission to deliver this 'ring'. Among them, my gratitude first goes to the late Michael Aris, my best friend, supervisor and guiding light. Michael's premature demise deprived me of Gandalf, whom I will miss in all the years to come. I am also deeply grateful to Prof. Richard Gombrich, who has, with a paternal affection and professorial acumen, shown unfailing support, both academic and otherwise, since the inception of this project until its publication. I thank Prof. David Seyfort Ruegg, a king in his field and my true mentor for this work, who has painstakingly spent hundreds of hours reading and discussing my work, and guided me through the byways of academic professionalism. This book is the achievement, albeit a modest one, of my training at the feet of these remarkable teachers.

Equally to be thanked is E. Gene Smith (my Tom Bombadil), the Godfather of Tibetologists, for the support he gave with his encyclopedic knowledge of Tibetan literature, for the provision of bibliographical resources and for his hospitality during my days in Harvard and New York. I also owe much gratitude to John Pettit whose help in the initial days of my research enabled me to embark on the doctoral research full of hope, and to Alak Zengkar Rinpoche and Karma Gelek for sharing their vast knowledge of Mipham and Tibet. I must also thank Robert Mayer, Burkhard Quessel, Franz-Karl Ehrhard and Matthew Kapstein, Michael Kowalewski, Douglas Duckworth and many others for their valuable feedback on my work, Ralf Kramer and others at the Indian Institute for their prompt assistance, and my comrades in the same Indo-Tibetological boat at Oxford (Isabelle, William, Peter to name but a few) for their solidarity, which has helped me avoid many pitfalls and overcome obstacles.

Mention must also be made of my days in Holywell Manor (my Rivendell), a hub of intellectual excellence and social exuberance, where I have enjoyed the company of many a bright and beautiful friend. In our fellowship, I not only found a window to the wide world outside my own but fulfilling repose from the pressure of Emptiness. At the same time, though not by the same token, I must also remember and thank my folks in the remote villages of Bhutan who wholeheartedly celebrated their 'son' at Oxford. Their affection and support can never be fully acknowledged and reciprocated.

I am deeply indebted to John and Polly Guth for their generosity in funding my work at both Oxford and Harvard, to Elizabeth Chatwin for looking after me like her own child, and to the Aris family for making me one of them. My gratitude also goes to *mon amis français* for their support during my time in Paris: to Françoise Pommaret for finding me a post-doctoral position in the CNRS and to Anne and Gerard Tardy for providing me a homely *habitation*. Through their generosity, I found the time and space to recast my thesis into this book.

Finally, I pay my respects to the subjects of my study, the Buddha, Nāgārjuna, Śāntideva, Tsongkhapa and Mipham and other masters of yore, whose sublime lives and stupendous works not only humble me beyond all measure but also inspire me to strive for higher ideals. Whether or not the 'ring' is cast successfully, the journey has reached its end and all those who I have met on the way have contributed their share. Therefore, whatever virtue and good there may be in this endeavour, I dedicate it to others; all errors, obfuscations and omissions are mine alone.

Karma

ABBREVIATIONS

AK	Vasubandhu, *Abhidharmakoṣa*
AN	*Aṅguttara Nikāya*
BA	Śāntideva, *Bodhicaryāvatāra*
DK	Derge Edition of the Tibetan bKa' 'gyur
DN	*Dīgha Nikāya*
Dogs sel	Mipham Gyatsho, *rDo grub pa dam chos zhes pas gzhan gyi zer sgros bsdus nas mkhas su re ba'i 'khyal ngag de dag mi mkhas mtshang phung du kho rang nas bskul ba bzhin nyams mtshar du bkod pa*
Drang nges	Tsongkhapa, *Drang ba dang nges pa'i don rnam par phye ba'i bstan bcos legs bshad snying po*
DT	Derge Edition of the Tibetan bsTan 'gyur
dGag lan phyogs bsgrigs	Khedrub Geleg Palzang *et al.*, *dGag lan phyogs bsgrigs*
dGongs pa rab gsal	Tsongkhapa, *bsTan bcos chen mo dbu ma 'jug pa'i rnam bshad dgongs pa rab gsal*
Grub bsdus	Mipham Gyatsho, *Yid bzhin mdzod kyi grub mtha' bsdus pa*
rGyal sras 'jug ngogs	Gyaltshab Je, *sPyod 'jug 'grel pa rgyal sras 'jug ngogs*
rGyan 'grel	Mipham Gyatsho, *dBu ma rgyan gi rnam bshad 'jam dbyang bla ma dgyes pa'i zhal lung*
IATS	*International Association for Tibetan Studies*
JIABS	*Journal of the International Association for Buddhist Studies*
JIP	*Journal of Indian Philosophy*
'Jug 'grel	Mipham Gyatsho, *dBu ma 'jug pa'i 'grel pa zla ba'i zhal lung dri med shel phreng*
Ketaka	Mipham Gyatsho, *sPyod 'jug sher 'grel ketaka*
Lam rim	Tsongkhapa, *Byang chub lam rim che ba*
LTWA	Library of Tibetan Works and Archives
MA	Candrakīrti, *Madhyamakāvatāra*
MGS	Mipham Gyatsho, *Mi pham rgya mtsho'i gsung 'bum*

MK	Nāgārjuna, *Mūlamadhyamakakārikā*
MN	*Majjhima Nikāya*
Nges shes sgron me	Mipham Gyatsho, *Nges shes rin po che'i sgron me*
Nyi snang	Mipham Gyatsho, *brGal lan nyin byed snang ba*
Prasannapadā	Candrakīrti, *Prasannapadā*
PV	Dharmakīrti, *Pramāṇavārttika*
Rab gsal	Pari Lobzang Rabsal, *'Jam dpal dbyangs kyi dgongs rgyan rigs pa'i gzi 'bar gdong lnga'i sgra dbyangs*
Rab lan	Mipham Gyatsho, *gZhan gyis brtsad pa'i lan mdor bsdus pa rigs lam rab gsal de nyid snang byed*
Rigs pa'i rgya mtsho	Tsongkhapa, *dBu ma rtsa ba'i tshig le'ur byas pa shes rab ces bya ba'i rnam bshad rigs pa'i rgya mtsho*
SN	*Saṃyutta Nikāya*
gSung sgros	Mipham Gyatsho, *gZhung spyi'i dka' gnad gsung gros phyogs bsdus rin po che'i za ma tog*

༄༅། །རིག་སྟོང་འཇམ་དཔལ་གཞོན་ནུའི་བྱིན་རླབས་ལས།།
དགོངས་པའི་ཀློང་ནས་སྤོབས་པའི་གཏེར་བརྒྱད་གྲོལ།།
ལུང་རྟོགས་ཆོས་མཛོད་རྒྱ་མཚོར་མངའ་དབང་བསྒྱུར།།
མི་ཕམ་འཇམ་དཔལ་དབྱངས་ལ་གསོལ་བ་འདེབས།།

Plate 1 Ju Mipham Namgyal Gyatsho (1846–1912).

INTRODUCTION

Of all Buddhist philosophical concepts, the theory of Emptiness has perhaps attracted the most curiosity in the Occidental world. The teachings of Emptiness, received *via* both the Sino-Japanese Zen tradition and Indo-Tibetan Buddhism, were at once philosophical, paradoxical, therapeutic and mystical, appealing to Western imaginations of Oriental religions. The only Oriental topic to rival Emptiness in this regard is perhaps the Taoist dyad of *Tao* and *Te*. Even they, however, cannot compare with the theory of Emptiness in the virtue of being grounded in rational argument, the true mark of philosophy.

The popularity of Emptiness in the West was no doubt due to its supreme importance in the tradition itself. Emptiness is not only the most important subject of philosophical study for its soteriological, doctrinal, ontological and hermeneutic significance, but is also the pivotal topic of meditation. Emptiness remains at the heart of the Buddhist system and, for this reason, it has often been dubbed the central philosophy of Buddhism. Because of its central position, a countless number of scholars and mystics have treated Emptiness in great depth and detail. Among them is Ju Mipham Namgyal Gyatsho (1846–1912), one of the brightest and most versatile minds to appear in Tibetan history. This book explores the theories of Emptiness that Mipham formulated in his diverse writings, focusing mainly on the debates he had with his opponents.

Emptiness and *what there is*

One of the most perplexing and perennial issues of philosophy has been the ontological problem of appearance and reality. Does everything that appears really exist and exist as it appears? Or, as Russell asks, 'Is there a real table at all? If so, what sort of object can it be?'[1] Quine puts this ontological problem into 'three Anglo-Saxon syllables: "What is there?" '[2] Throughout history, this problem of ontology has intrigued all philosophers. Every world philosophy can be considered in one way or other to have developed as a response to this question. The Buddhist philosophy of Emptiness is one such response, which deals with *what there is and the ultimate nature of what there is*, although it does so mainly through an apophatic approach by demonstrating *what there is not* rather than by pointing out *what there is*.

The question has received a wide array of answers ranging, from 'everything' to 'nothing'. The first one can be attributed to the realist schools although there is no general consensus even among realists as to what the term 'everything' covers. Within Buddhism, many early schools such as Sarvāstivāda, as its name suggests, can be considered to have given such an answer though their 'everything' would preclude, *inter alia*, a theistic God, Vedic soul or Cartesian Ego. Conversely, the Mādhyamikas would have said 'no-thing' in the context of existence in the ultimate sense. Between the two answers of 'everything' and 'nothing' can be included a range of other theories delimiting various sizes and kinds of existence. These divergent theories constitute the numerous schools of thought that we know as realism, substantialism, atomism, nominalism, conceptualism, idealism, monism, absolutism, scepticism, etc. The discrepancies in the ontological theories have also inspired some of the hottest philosophical controversies, exemplified by the debates between the realists and nominalists in the West, between the Buddhists and Nyāya thinkers in India, the Rangtongpas and Zhantongpas in Tibet, and the theists and atheists everywhere. The question, with its perplexity and persistence, continues to this day among philosophers and scientists, vibrant as ever.

The theory of Emptiness is a Buddhist philosophical schema which addresses this ontological issue. By demonstrating how things are empty and what they are empty of, it distinguishes the real from the false, the substantial from the imagined, the ontic from the apparent. It is an existential enquiry into *what there is* by searching for ontic reality behind the veil of appearance. Thus, the doctrine of Emptiness is the Buddhist ontological theory *par excellence*. However, this is not to say that all differences are resolved in the theory of Emptiness and a homogeneous ontology is accepted across all Buddhist schools. Despite the common acceptance of the theory of Emptiness, ontological differences persisted among Buddhist schools because they could not agree on what things are empty of.

The theory of Emptiness originated in the Buddha's teachings that the world is unreal, empty and without self.[3] His teachings, subjected to various interpretations, gave rise to a variety of ontological theories leading to the formation of various Buddhist philosophical systems. Most early schools such as Sarvāstivāda formulated a substantialist/realist ontology in which they understood Emptiness as an absence of self and what belongs to self. This theory of non-self, that is, that there is no person beside the psychosomatic composition, akin to Hume's bundle theory, is accepted by all Buddhist schools except the Vātsīputrīya-Saṃmitīya school who asserted an ineffable person. They are however said to have professed an Emptiness *qua* absence of an eternal self. These substantialists thus rejected an immutable person and maintained a substantialist pluralism, in which the world is composed of discrete entities. Associated with this are also Vaibhāṣika atomism, which holds that only indivisible atoms and moments of consciousness are ultimately existent, and Sautrāntika pragmatic dualism, in which the only real things, determined by their causal efficacy, are mind and matter.

Cutting across the essentialist/substantialist trend of the early schools, Nāgārjuna and his Mādhyamika school propounded a non-essentialist theory of Emptiness which negates any real, substantial, independent and hypostatic existence. Known as the Madhyamaka or Middle Way philosophy, this thought has been variously described in the West as nihilism (e.g. Burnouf, 1844; La Vallée Poussin until his last days when he changed to absolutism; Tola and Dragonetti, 1995), negativism (Keith, 1923), monism (Stcherbatsky, 1927), absolutism (Schayer, 1931; Murti, 1955), agnosticism (Lamotte, 1964), empiricism (Warder, 1971; Kalupahana, 1986), linguistic analysis (Robinson, 1967; Streng, 1967), scepticism (Matilal, 1986), etc. However, others such as May, Seyfort Ruegg, Schmithausen, Lindtner, Huntington and Garfield have chosen to let the Mādhyamikas speak for themselves.

According to this school, all things are empty because they lack self-existence; they lack self-existence because they originate in dependence on causes and conditions. Empirical things, though they appear, do not ontologically exist as they appear. Hence, the Mādhyamika thinkers explained the problem of appearance and reality by arguing that there is no ultimate objective reality corresponding to appearance. Appearance, as illustrated by the Buddhist analogies of illusion, dream, mirage, echo, falling hair, etc. is not evidence for real existence. To the Mādhyamikas, whatever appears is empty of reality, and were there anything real, such an entity could not even appear. Appearance is possible only for a thing for which Emptiness is possible; for that for which Emptiness is not possible, nothing is possible.[4] Thus, appearance does not affirm but it negates the real existence. It is not only short of being a criterion for a thing's real existence but is a token of its ultimate non-existence or Emptiness. Hence the Tibetan maxim: 'It appears because it is empty; it is empty because it appears' (*snang ste ci phyir stong pa'i phyir / / stong ste ci phyir snang ba'i phyir*). A major project of Mādhyamika philosophy, since the days of Nāgārjuna and Āryadeva, is to equate empirical appearance with ontological Emptiness.

Emptiness also found a mentalist interpretation as an absence of mind–matter duality in Yogācāra idealism, the rival Mahāyāna ontology to Mādhyamika thought. Some later thinkers belonging to the Mādhyamika and Vajrayāna traditions further advocated an absolutist theory of Emptiness, asserting an essential absolute nature empty of the accidental illusory world. Thus Emptiness, subjected to a rich hermeneutic enterprise, came to mean different things in different schools. Instead of designating an invariant unitary concept, it came to refer to a wide range of contextually varying ontological positions.

The concept of Emptiness, in this capacity, can be seen as a doctrinal mechanism or philosophical method employed variably to delineate divergent ontological theories rather than as an absolute concept with invariable denotation uniformly espoused by all Buddhist denominations. Like Ockham's razor, it is used as a tool to demarcate different ontologies. Even in Nāgārjuna's Mādhyamika, the school in which Emptiness found its greatest exponents and most thorough interpretation, there was no general agreement as to what constitutes Emptiness, and discrepant dialectical and ontological theories developed thereof. The discrepancies leading to the Svātantrika-Prāsaṅgika and *rang stong-gzhan stong* controversies are two examples of differences in understanding and approaching Emptiness among those who belonged to the Mādhyamika school.

The debates between Mipham and his Gelukpa opponents discussed here, which have hitherto hardly caught the attention of Western scholarship, are largely an ontological dispute among scholars adhering to the Prāsaṅgika and *rang stong* lines of Mādhyamika tradition. They deal with the issue of what things are empty of and the existential question of *what there is/is not* from the viewpoint of the analytical investigation employed by the Mādhyamikas to establish Emptiness. Although both parties, as Mādhyamika philosophers, agreed in negating a hypostatically established entity (*bden par grub pa*) and accepting things to be empty of hypostatic existence, conflicts arose as to whether or not things are empty of themselves and whether things are negated by the ultimate analysis employed to establish Emptiness.

Emptiness, to be and not to be

Intricately linked to the issue of *what there is* is the further puzzling question of what it is 'to be' or 'to exist'. A significant number of ontological disputes about what really exists and what is empty derive from the differences in defining 'existence', a word, which, like truth, nature, etc. defies any unitary and homogeneous application. A variety of ontological categories are used in Indian and Tibetan philosophies to explain various kinds and degrees of existence. One such system of categorization is the binary one of two truths, a dichotomous classification of things into ultimately or really existent (*paramārthasatya, don dam bden pa*) and conventionally or relatively existent (*saṃvṛtisatya, kun rdzob bden pa*). This typology is used to bifurcate existence into two kinds and distinguish the ontic and real from the apparent and false. The two truths, it must however be noted, are, like Emptiness, multivalent terms which designate a range of contextually varying categories. Thus, despite the use of the identical terms, the ultimate truth of Vaibhāṣikas, for instance, differs drastically from that of Yogācāra, and even within one school what is ultimate truth in one context can be conventional truth in another. We will see the latter case clearly in Mipham's hermeneutics which employ dual sets of two truths in Prāsaṅgika Mādhyamika.

The Mādhyamikas used the theory of two truths not to dichotomize all phenomena into two classes of entities but to distinguish two modes of existence applicable to every phenomenon: one corresponding to empirical appearance, associated with commonsense knowledge and linguistic and pragmatic transaction – the conventional truth – and the other pertaining to reality associated with the enlightened understanding and analytical finding – the ultimate truth. Every phenomenon, to gloss Candrakīrti, consists of two natures as apprehended by correct and false perceptions.[5] This contrasts with the use of two truths among other schools and with the use of other ontological categories, dichotomous ones such as the sets of the substantial (*bhāva, dngos po*) and the unsubstantial (*abhāva, dngos med*), of discrete substances (*dravyasat, rdzas yod*) and nominal abstracts (*prajñaptisat, btags yod*) mostly used by the Sarvāstivāda/Vaibhāṣikas, of individual characteristics/particulars (*svalakṣaṇa, rang mtshan*) and general characteristics/universals (*sāmānyalakṣaṇa, spyi mtshan*) employed mainly in Sautrāntika/Pramāṇa schools, and the trichotomous categories of the constructed (*parikalpita, kun btags*), the dependent (*paratantra, gzhan dbang*), and the absolute (*pariniṣpanna, yongs grub*) natures generally associated with the formulation of Yogācāra idealism.

In Madhyamaka, everything that exists, exists on the conventional level and it is on this level that ethical and soteriological systems are viable. No phenomenon exists on the ultimate level; all things are empty of ultimate existence. The thrust of Mādhyamika philosophy and the main issue between Mipham and his opponents is the negation of an ultimately existent entity *qua svabhāva*; conventional theories are secondary to this project.

From the general Mādhyamika viewpoint, to exist ultimately is to exist independently, hypostatically and inherently, and a thing is independently and hypostatically existent if that thing, subjected to a reductive analysis, can withstand such analysis. A chariot, to give the classic example, is ultimately existent if and only if it exists in its parts in the manner of being either identical or heterogeneous, possessive, the locus, the located, the shape or the collection of the parts. When it is not found in these manners after a full search, the chariot is declared to be without ultimate existence or *svabhāva* and therefore 'empty' or, as Mipham may prefer to put it: the chariot 'empties'.[6]

This reasoning perforce was not unique to the Mādhyamika school but it was they who applied the analysis rigorously to all phenomena to establish their ultimate non-existence. Similarly, when a sprout is analysed to see if it is at all produced by using the tetralemmic method of production from a cause that is identical, heterogeneous, both and neither (*ex nihilo*), no production is found to occur. The sprout is never produced, has never come into being and therefore is empty of reality. This lack of reality or Emptiness, paradoxically, is then the reality of all things.

The dichotomy of existence into two kinds and the claim that everything exists conventionally and nothing exists on the ultimate level, however, did not resolve all the problems but led to further questions concerning the nuances of dialectical procedure, hermeneutical approach and ontological commitment. What is negated by the Mādhyamika analysis? Is an empirical phenomenon, say a commonsense vase, negated in course of establishing Emptiness? If it is, does that amount to annihilation? If not, can it withstand the analysis? What bearing does either case have on soteriology? What determines the existential status of a thing: its ultimate non-existence or its conventional existence? Can one illusory empty thing prove another empty? Questions also include the application of the qualifying terms 'ultimate' and 'hypostatically existent' before the negandum (*niṣedhya/pratiṣedhya, dgag bya*), the negation of the tetralemma, the viability of logical rules and so on. These questions have intrigued Mādhyamika thinkers down the ages and have become the subject of volumes of scholastic literature and series of philosophical debates. The debates between the Gelukpas and non-Gelukpas such as Mipham, the former accusing the latter of over-broad delimitation of the Mādhyamika negandum and the latter's attack on the Gelukpa scholastic definition of the negandum and their theory that 'the vase is not empty of vase but of hypostatic existence' (*bum pa bum pas mi stong, bum pa bden grub kyis stong*), exemplify the treatment of these questions in Tibetan Mādhyamika philosophy.

A further vexing issue in the Mādhyamika enquiry into existence and reality is the nature and status of the ultimate *qua* Emptiness itself. The intriguing and perennial nature of the problem of the ultimate in Mādhyamika philosophy, and for that matter in all Indian philosophical systems, can be best compared to the question of Being in Western philosophy. Like the concept of Being in philosophy from Parmenides to Heidegger, the theory of the ultimate *qua* Emptiness holds the central place in Mādhyamika philosophy from Nāgārjuna to Mipham and is a topic broached by thousands of its proponents and their opponents. In being so broached, the theory of the ultimate has diverged significantly, giving rise to variant streams of thought mainly characterized by emphases and elaborations on a specific approach, application or understanding of the ultimate. These divergences include ramifications such as the Svātantrika and Prāsaṅgika division, which, according to Mipham, are based on their difference of emphasis on the dialectical approach to and the exposition of the ultimate *qua* Emptiness, the gradualist and simultaneist currents, which are based on their practical approach to and application of the ultimate, and the *rang stong* and *gzhan stong* thinking, which differs in the theory of the ultimate due to unequal emphases on the two themes of Emptiness and Buddha Nature presented respectively in the Mahāyāna corpuses of the Middle Turning and the Last Turning of the Wheel of Dharma.

Such disparities and divergences – although any responsible Mahāyāna hermeneutician such as Mipham would see them from a higher vantage point of religious inclusivism as complementary parts of a coherent soteriological whole and as theories and practices suitable and expedient for a person of corresponding calibre, temperament and interest in leading him/her toward enlightenment – appear inevitable given the seeming discrepancies even in the sources the Mādhyamikas consider to be authoritative. The *rang stong* and *gzhan stong* philosophical dissension, for instance, to no less a degree owes its origin to the two different approaches to the ultimate adopted by Nāgārjuna: that of a critical apophaticism in his scholastic corpus and a romantic cataphaticism in his hymnic corpus. What is even more puzzling is to find possibly conflicting ideas in a single work, as seems to be the case in MK, XV/2, which proposes a fundamentally absolutist theory of the ultimate *qua svabhāva*, defining it to be uncontrived and independent, and thereby diverges from the general refutation of any such *svabhāva* throughout the rest of the book. Such inconsistencies, whether *prima facie* or real, have indeed not been passed over in silence but have aroused much philosophical scrutiny involving a great deal of hermeneutic and scholastic effort.

The debates on the theory of the ultimate, which is treated in this thesis, however, concern a different contestation from those mentioned earlier, although those dissents, and the arguments and hermeneutics employed in them, strongly impinge on this. The controversy between Mipham and his Gelukpa opponents on the ultimate chiefly deals with the definition of the ultimate *qua* Emptiness as understood in the Prāsaṅgika and *rang stong* traditions of Mādhyamika thought. Other issues pertaining to the dialectical, epistemic, linguistic and meditative operations arise as corollaries to their disagreement on defining Emptiness. The Gelukpas understood the ultimate *qua* Emptiness to be an absence of hypostatic existence and therefore an absolute negation. Although it lacks hypostatic existence, the ultimate *qua* Emptiness, like any other phenomenon, exists and is an object of language and thought. Its basic existence, knowability and expressability are fundamental to Mādhyamika soteriology.

Mipham, on the contrary, argued that the ultimate *qua* Emptiness, in its highest form, is not merely an absence of hypostatic existence. He enumerated two kinds of ultimate, the notational ultimate (**paryāyaparamārtha, rnam grangs pa'i don dam*) and the non-notational ultimate (**aparyāyaparamārtha, rnam grangs min pa'i don dam*),[7] and relegated the mere absence of hypostatic existence to the level of notational ultimate, which, also known as the concordant ultimate (*mthun pa'i don dam*), eliminates only partial extremes and serves as a step to the non-notational ultimate. The non-notational ultimate *qua* final Emptiness, which is the *quidditas* and the ultimate nature of things, he argued, is reality free from all fabrications (*prapañca, spros pa*) and extremes (*anta, mtha'*). He also used names such as Great Coalescence (*zung 'jug chen po*), Great Middle Way (*dbu ma chen po*), Resultant Middle Way (*'bras bu'i dbu ma*) and Equality (*mnyam nyid*) to refer to this.

To be or not to be are both extremes, and Emptiness as the philosophical middle way, Mipham argued, must transcend the extremes of being and non-being, existence and non-existence, negation and affirmation, and even the empty and the non-empty. Even to perceive Emptiness itself would be wrong, for there is nothing (not even that nothing!) to be perceived. To conceive a thing called 'Emptiness' in discerning Emptiness is a gross reification, the incorrigible view and wrong understanding Nāgārjuna repudiated in MK, XIII/8 and XXIV/11.

'Seeing Emptiness' is a designation for not seeing anything. Conventional concepts and words such as 'Emptiness' are used for conveying the intuitive and ineffable experience of Emptiness but to stick to them beyond their transactional value is a sheer literalism like the remarks of the White King in Carroll's *Alice Through the Looking Glass*. The King tells Alice that he has sent all his horses and all his men, but two, to poor old Humpty Dumpty. Two of his messengers couldn't be sent because they'd gone to town. 'Just look along the road, tell me if you can see either of them.' 'I see nobody on the road', said Alice. 'I only wish I had such eyes', the King remarked in a fretful tone, 'to be able to see Nobody! And at that distance too!'[8]

Mipham's understanding of Emptiness thus contravenes the Gelukpa theory by taking the ultimate *qua* Emptiness beyond the absence of hypostatic existence to a reality which defies any notion of existence, non-existence, both or neither and transcends dialectical, epistemic and linguistic operations. The Gelukpas shunned such an understanding taxing its proponents with naïve literalism and nihilistic inclination.

The understanding of Emptiness in Mipham's thought and in the Gelukpa school represent two main currents of Mādhyamika philosophy in Tibet: one primarily driven by a strong sense of rationality set in the framework of dialectical and epistemological theories, the other inspired by a spirit of transcendence and mysticism, although both have these elements in them. In presentation and exposition, the Gelukpas have generally formulated the theory of Emptiness as a scholastic discourse with an intellectual orientation, making it fully rational and intelligible to its audience, while Mipham and other scholars in his tradition delivered it in a canonical style imbued with antinomical and paradoxical language and orientation to the ultimate experience of Emptiness. For this reason, Tibetan scholars often associate the Geluk with ground (*gzhi*), the Sakya with path (*lam*) and the Nyingma with result (*'bras bu*) in their expositions of Emptiness. In the West, the two currents are reflected in the writings of many such as Seyfort Ruegg, Hopkins, Thurman, Cabezón, Napper, Newland and Magee, who slant toward the Gelukpa understanding and few others like Pettit who offer a contrasting view.

Emptiness: a religious issue and the nature of the debates

It is perhaps clear from the questions and problems raised that the concept of Emptiness is a philosophical issue and not purely a theological or religious discourse, as may be assumed by Western philosophers, who often exclude from philosophy anything outside the Western philosophical tradition of Greek origin, and that the deployment of reasoning and argument in this debate count as proper 'philosophizing'. However, the importance of Emptiness in the Buddhist tradition lies mainly in its soteriological significance as an essential and expedient path to enlightenment. It is this soteriological role that places it at the heart of the Buddhist philosophy and gives urgency and weight to the debates on it. Thus, a proper assessment and understanding of issues raised can be reached only by seeing Emptiness in its religious context.

This approach does not apply only to Emptiness but to any major Indo-Tibetan philosophical topic as has been pointed out by Seyfort Ruegg:

> Let me emphasize from the outset that the philosophical side cannot usually be divorced and treated entirely separately from the religious without a certain more or less arbitrary compartmentalization, for no hard and fast dividing line can normally be drawn between the philosophical and the religious in either India or Tibet.[9]

The pursuit of philosophy without a soteriological vision, from an Indo-Tibetan Buddhist perspective, is mere ratiocination with no worthy purpose or benefit. Philosophy is a beacon to guide you through the byways of religious practice to the higher goal of liberation and enlightenment, and not an independent end in itself. It becomes meaningful when it has a soteriological cause to stand for. Emptiness, as the primary path to enlightenment, is a soteriologically rewarding subject of study and thus a worthy philosophical enterprise. Even people slightly curious about it, Āryadeva remarks, will destroy the bondage of *saṃsāra*.[10]

Now, to turn to the nature of the debates here, it is clear that the religious significance of Emptiness, more than its philosophical nature, has made Emptiness an urgent and sensitive issue of discussion and debate. However, it is also the religious nature of Emptiness, which confined the debates on it to a restricted perimeter bound by religious commitment and faithfulness to the tradition. Although it has led to frequent regeneration and development of ideas, philosophical investigation of topics such as Emptiness in traditional scholarship is not a fully open and innovative enterprise intended to reveal new findings, but a rather restricted hermeneutic endeavour to reinterpret and reassert the existent materials within the limits of a given tradition. Such practice of philosophizing in a traditional framework to defend and develop one's own position is, in Dreyfus' words, 'responsible philosophy'.[11]

Thus the debates recounted here are not to be seen as philosophical enquiries aimed at reaching a new truth but as efforts to reappropriate and reformulate theories of one's own school and to reappraise and refute those of others, using the shared authorities of reasoning and scripture. The debates are often vitiated by obdurate defence of one's position and criticism of the opponent's stance, and seldom result in a change of viewpoint or conversion. They can also sometimes digress from serious philosophical issues to pedantic nitpicking. However, this is not to suggest that the debates in question are pointless eristic, making no improvements whatsoever in the understanding of Emptiness. In general, debate, as one of the three scholarly activities of exposition (*'chad pa*), debate (*rtsod pa*) and composition (*rtsom pa*), is an expedient method of exchanging knowledge and furthering insight into the subject matter. It is used as a pedagogical and educational technique, as is best seen in the performative debates commonly witnessed in Tibetan debate courtyards.[12]

The debates recounted here, however, are not merely such educational exercises, though they no doubt serve an educational purpose. They are serious philosophical discourses undertaking systematic defences of one's own position and critical examination and calculated refutation of theories espoused by the opposing party. However, they are not debates, like political debates in a parliament, where arguments for and against are presented and weighed before a forum in order to reach a conclusion. Neither are these debates contests, like those said to have taken place in ancient India and Tibet between different religious schools, which culminate in the final verdict of victory for one side and defeat for the other, and the defeated party having consequently to face conversion or other punitive measures. These debates have no such immediate implications and often take the form of a critical dialogue.

The objectives of debates of this kind are frequently stated to be the purification and defence of the Buddhist doctrine and the stimulation of philosophical activity. Whether or not the debates cleanse the Buddhist doctrine of wrong views and defend the right ones is dependent on the even more debatable question of what constitute right or wrong views, but there is no doubt that the debates invigorate philosophical activity. The debates on Emptiness, a subject of critical importance, have particularly aroused extensive and deep discussions conducted with solemnity, earnestness and fervour.

These debates are religious contentions fought on philosophical grounds but mostly in a socially amicable atmosphere. It is considered a noble trait of the debater to couple intellectual acumen with social amicability and logical reasoning with scriptural citations. Mipham reiterates that philosophical debates must be carried out without sectarian prejudice or ill feeling but with sagacity and equanimity. A good example of the social spirit of amiability in the midst of philosophical and doctrinal disagreements is seen in the debates between Mipham and Pari Lobzang Rabsal (1840–1910) both of whom showed mutual respect and admiration for each other in spite of their ruthless philosophical attacks. However, it is also not very rare to find Tibetan polemics containing attacks on individuals, harsh language, censorious remarks, sarcasm and pedantic nitpicking. When he received such polemics, Mipham declined to write responses for fear of arousing sectarian conflict. He despairs that his writings have been sometimes misconstrued as sectarian attacks instead of philosophical investigations.

The debates between Mipham and his major opponents were carried out in the form of written works and did not normally involve direct encounters. As for the few direct encounters that took place, there is barely any record of what transpired during the debates. The written debates are generally well structured and contain arguments that are well thought out. However, the publication and circulation of these works seem to have taken much time, additionally hampered by Tibet's rough terrain and the isolated lifestyle of the debaters. The debates between Mipham and his opponents thus spanned many years.

While some polemical writings were written as specific criticism and sent to the opponent concerned, many appear to have been written without the aim of sending them to a particular person but as general discourses for people to read. In any case, these debates, like many other writings that belong to the polemical genre of Tibetan literature, are the stimulatory spices in the Tibetan literary feast. To a student of Indo-Tibetan Madhyamaka, these polemics prove a handy source for divergent theories in juxtaposition and help one to analyse the arguments through comparison and contrast.

Mipham: a polymath and his works on Emptiness

Mipham was a luminary of the nineteenth-century Nyingma renaissance and *ris med* ecumenical movement, which started in the Kham region of eastern Tibet.[13] He was born to the Ju clan in the Zachu valley, the north-western end of modern day Sichuan province of China and joined the local Jumo Hor Sa-ngag Chöling monastery at the age of twelve. A prodigious child, even in his early youth he became famous as a young monk scholar (*bstun chung mkhas pa*). He studied with Jamyang Khyentsei Wangpo (1820–92), his main guru, Kongtrul Lodoe Thaye (1813–99) and Paltrul Ugyen Jigme Chökyi Wangpo (1808–87), who in their days were leading figures of Buddhism in Kham. Except for his brief sojourn in central Tibet when he was eighteen, Mipham stayed all his life in Kham, teaching and meditation being his two main occupations. Most of his literary output, he claims, is extemporaneous composition written during the recesses of his meditation and teaching sessions.

Although his life and works began to attract the attention of Western scholars a few decades ago, his enigmatic life and monumental works have yet to be studied properly. Despite the brief discussions of Mipham's life and works by Gene Smith, Steven Goodman and John Pettit, and the rendering of the catalogue of his writings into German by Dieter Schuh,[14] no attempt has so far been made to gain a complete overview of his output, to reveal the assumptions which lie behind it, or to assess its significance as a whole. A more thorough study of his life and works will have to wait for another project.

Mipham is perhaps the greatest polymath Tibet ever produced. His writings comprise works on a wide range of subjects, covering almost every science known to his milieu. In traditional terms, he is a Mahāpaṇḍita, who has mastered the ten sciences of arts and crafts (*bzo*), health science (*gso ba*), language (*sgra*), logico-epistemology (*tshad ma*), soteriology (*nang don*), poetry (*snyan ngag*), lexicology (*mngon brjod*), prosody (*sdeb sbyor*), dramaturgy (*zlos gar*) and astrology (*dkar rtsis*). It is due to the polymathic nature of his learning and his exceptional ingenuity that Mipham today ranks amongst the leading religious and spiritual celebrities of Tibet such as Sakya Paṇḍita (1182–1251), Longchenpa (1308–63), Tsongkhapa (1357–1419) and Pema Karpo (1527–92) and is accorded the title, *'Jam mgon*, which identifies him with Mañjuśrī, the Buddha of wisdom and learning.

His oeuvre, compiled by his students and published at Derge Chözod Chenmo and other monastic printeries in Kham and reproduced in 1987 by Zhechen Monastery in Kathmandu in 27 voluminous *poti*s, consists of several hundreds of works ranging from elementary grammar to Dzogchen mysticism. About two thirds of his writings are on philosophical topics such as ontology, epistemology, phenomenology, logic, metaphysics, and on Buddhist soteriology, monastic discipline, doxography and mysticism. His works also include treatises on language, poetry, politics, medicine, art, geometry, astrology, yoga, divination, magic, sorcery, monastic rituals and dances. He also wrote many homiletic epistles, hymns, prayers, songs and satire. Some of these are short, often just a single page, while others are long, the largest being his commentary on *Kālacakralaghutantra*, which has close to two thousand pages.[15]

Mipham's interest went beyond the general religious fields that occupied most Tibetan scholars. He is one of the few scholars, who showed keen interest in anthropological matters so that he can be rightly considered an anthropologist and an antiquarian. His zest for popular culture, ethnography and antiquity is evident in his various writings on the epic and cult of Gesar, of which he was a prominent promoter and compiler,[16] and the Bonpo art of knot-sortilege known as *'Ju thig*,[17] which was being neglected and dying even among Bonpos, his *Kun gzigs dbyangs 'char chen mo*[18] on divination through vital air (*rlung*), zodiac positions (*khyim*) and syllables (*dbyangs gsal*), his *gTo sgrom 'bum tig*[19] collection of folk rituals, some of which are possibly connected to Confucian rituals and his *gZo gnas nyer mkho 'i za ma tog*.[20]

In this last one, he writes about graphology, calligraphy, painting, sculpture, metallurgy, carpentry, pottery, jewellery, ornamentation, knitting, sewing, embroidery and the art of making incense, ink, pens, colours, paints, paintbrushes, of dyeing, plating, decorating, alloying, carving, and of making herbal pills and religious relics. Talking about the art of making inks, he discusses what kind of materials, containers, temperature and methods should be used to concoct different varieties of inks. While writing on almost every science that was known to him, he displays great talent and expertise in them. Even the art of love making did not escape the imagination of Mipham, who became Tibet's first author of *kāmaśāstra*.[21]

However, of all his writings, his writings on Emptiness and Madhyamaka attracted the most attention from other scholars and bought him popularity and fame in religious and scholarly circles. Mipham showed great enthusiasm in Madhyamaka and came up with much novelty and also dissent. Both the popularity of the subject in Tibet and the innovative but controversial nature of his writings contributed toward making his works on Madhyamaka distinctive and famous. Perhaps the earliest work that Mipham wrote on Madhyamaka is his *Nges shes sgron me* written at an initial period of his intellectual career and set as a dialogue between a judicious sage and an inquisitive mendicant on seven crucial topics of Tibetan Madhyamaka scholarship.[22]

In what he claims to be an extemporary composition, Mipham cogently expounds various aspects of Madhyamaka, and unravels the cruxes of the philosophy, especially while answering the first question on whether the view is absolute or implicative negation (*lta ba dgag gnyis gang ltar smra*), and the last question on whether or not the Mādhyamika have a thesis (*dbu mar khas len yod dam med*). The coherence and consistency with which he provides answers to these questions, thereby elucidating the Nyingma doctrinal position, gives us an impressive picture of Mipham's erudition even at that early stage of his scholarship.

However, one sees Mipham's exposition of Madhyamaka growing more elaborate, profound and rigorous in his commentary on the *Madhyamakālaṃkāra* of

Śāntarakṣita, written in 1876. At the behest of his chief master, Khyentsei Wangpo, he composed, within only twenty-one days, a stupendous exegesis on this short treatise, previously to a great extent neglected by Tibetan scholars. In his detailed commentary on the main body of the text and the extensive, systematic introduction to the commentary, he formulated the Nyingma doctrinal position corresponding to both the Svātantrika and the Prāsaṅgika traditions of Mādhyamika. For posterity, this commentary was to become his most authoritative work on Madhyamaka and the most important source for his interpretation of several controversial topics.

Connected to this work is Mipham's short polemic entitled *Dam chos dogs sel*, written at the request of Dodrub Damchö, a Nyingma scholar who at first seems even to have challenged Mipham to a public debate. In 1878, two years after his commentary on the *Madhyamakālaṃkāra*, Mipham wrote *Sher le'u 'grel pa nor bu ketaka*, his exposition on the ninth chapter of the *Bodhicaryāvatāra* of Śāntideva, which, in the years to come, was to provoke several controversies and polemical discussions. This commentary, as Gene Smith has correctly said, turned into a tempest that triggered an intellectual commotion in Gelukpa circles.[23]

The Gelukpas retaliated by sending him several refutations of his work, which subsequently led to the writing of his two other polemical works, *rGal lan nyin byed snang ba* written in 1889 in reply to Drakar Trulku Paldan Tenzin Nyandrak (1866–1928) and *Rigs lam rab gsal de nyid snang byed* in 1903 in reply to Pari Lobzang Rabsal. These three works and three subsequent polemical tracts embody almost the entire contributions of Mipham in Madhyamaka philosophy and thus form the *magna opera* of Mipham's writings on Madhyamaka.

Major issues on which Mipham shed new light in these works are: the nature of Emptiness, its knowability and inexpressibility, the classification of the ultimate truth, the dual sets of the two-truth theory, distinction of Svātantrika and Prāsaṅgika sub-schools, the Mādhyamika stance on reflexive awareness and store-consciousness, the process of discarding the two obscurations, the degree of realization of Selflessness by Śrāvakas and Pratyekabuddhas, the viability of thesis in Prāsaṅgika system, the mode of reasoning and meditation on Emptiness, the validity of convention and the scrutiny of shared appearance (*mthun snang*) among the six realms of being.

Mipham covered in these texts philosophical, soteriological, gnoseological and ontological issues that most writers on Madhyamaka would deal within commentaries on Candrakīrti's *Madhyamakāvatāra* or Nāgārjuna's *Mūlamadhyamakakārikā*. One often wonders why Mipham, apart from his annotations that his students later compiled,[24] did not write a proper commentary on those two, but wrote on *Madhyamakālaṃkāra*. Could this be because of his greater faith in Śāntarakṣita, as he was a Nyingma master? Similarly, he did not write an extensive commentary on the *Abhisamayālaṃkāra* and *Mahāyānottaratantra,* as did other masters, but wrote on the other works of Maitreya. Perhaps, Mipham was deliberately avoiding comment on those popular texts that already had a great deal of scholarly work done on them, and was trying to bring, with his antiquarian bent of mind, some less known works to light. Or was Mipham trying to avoid the risk of more controversy, which would be inevitable if he undertook an elaborate exposition on those books that are widely studied in Tibetan monasteries?

One important characteristic of Mipham's writing is his inclusivistic and ecumenical spirit of reconciliation. Although his controversial contributions and the related polemics make him appear disputatious and provocative, Mipham was a master who fervently sought to reconcile and respect all conflicting views and systems as consistent parts of a soteriological whole. It was his liberal approach, interpreting dissonant teachings so as to bring them into harmony, which often annoyed and provoked opposition from orthodox groups. His effort to bring dichotomous systems, such as the profound view-tradition of Nāgārjuna (*Klu sgrub kyi zab mo lta srol*) and the vast praxis-tradition of Asaṅga (*Thogs med kyi rgya chen spyod srol*), the Svātantrika and Prāsaṅgika Mādhyamika, *sūtrayāna* and *vajrayāna*, the Sarma and Nyingma and even Tsongkhapa and his opponents, into agreement is evident in his Madhyamaka writings.

In the last case, despite the fact that most of polemical writings are critiques of Tsongkhapa's interpretation and the Gelukpa understanding of Emptiness, he even went as far as to eulogize Tsongkhapa and identify his final understanding of Emptiness with the Primordial Purity (*ka dag*) of Dzogchen thought.[25] He repeatedly argued that Tsongkhapa and other eminent Gelukpa masters like Changkya Rolpai Dorje (1717–86) held views consonant with the Nyingmapa and other Ngarabpa[26] viewpoints, although they taught a provisional understanding of Emptiness that their followers, the Gelukpas, mistook for definitive and final.

Mipham's reconciliatory approach can also be seen in his hermeneutics on the crucial and controversial topic of Buddha Nature (*tathāgatagarbha, bde gshegs snying po*), the pivot of *rang stong* and *gzhan stong* dissension in Tibet.[27] Mipham touches upon it in the above-mentioned works, although it is his annotative commentary on the *Mahāyānottaratantra*, and the supplementary exegesis, *bDe gshegs snying po'i stong thun senge'i nga ro* which deal with it in depth and detail. In this short work and his *Nges shes sgron me*, Mipham analyses and criticizes both the positions of *gzhang stong* absolutists and of *rang stong* espoused by Sakya and Geluk scholars and maintains a middle stance wherein the *tathāgatagarbha* is ultimately empty of its own being, as the Rangtongpas assert, but conventionally endowed with all the qualities of the Buddha, as the Zhantongpas maintain.

Mipham's synthesis of these two traits in his *tathāgatagarbha* theory, which is clearly a hermeneutic attempt to harmonize the purports of the Middle and Last Turning of the Wheel of Dharma, and his general theory of Emptiness have led to some degree of confusion among both traditional scholars and academics as to which of the two camps Mipham truly belonged to. In the West, Smith, Hookham and Stearns considered Mipham a Zhantongpa and Williams took pains to argue for this case.[28] On the other hand, Samuel took Mipham to be a Rangtongpa[29] while Pettit started treating Mipham's position as equivocal but verged toward considering Mipham as Rangtongpa in his criticism of Williams.[30] Yet, Kapstein[31] and Wangchuk[32] expressed caution in such doxographical classification but saw the two systems, like intellectual processes of affirmation and negation, as doxographical categories both of which Mipham, as Dzogchenpa, would ultimately transcend.

Part of the confusion was caused also by Mipham's defence of *gzhan stong* philosophy in his *gZhan stong khas len sen ge'i nga ro* and *Dam chos dogs sel* and his close association with Zhantongpas such as Kongtrul. Nonetheless, his repeated and systematic criticism of it in his Madhyamaka writings outweighs his rather meagre defence of *gzhan stong* in these two texts. Beside, he also remarks in *Dam chos dogs sel* that he is not obliged to defend the *gzhan stong* position and in his *gSung sgros*, he categorically declares, after discussing the two systems that his 'own tradition, as explicated in his *Rab lan*, is that of the exponent of *rang stong*'.[33]

Toward the end of his life, Mipham also composed three other works on *tathāgatagarbha* and Innate Mind (*gnyug sems*), entitled, *gNyug sems skor gsum*.[34] Unfortunately, Mipham did not live long enough to see a formal completion of this trilogy; his student, Zhechen Gyaltshab Pema Namgyal (1871–1926), finished it by augmenting miscellaneous notes by Mipham on the same theme. In this trilogy, he bridges the *tathāgatagarbha* in *sūtrayāna* and the Innate Mind in *vajrayāna* and goes on to show how this concept is fundamental and crucial to Mahāyāna philosophy and practice irrespective of what terms are used for it in different schools and vehicles. This, one could say, is one of his last attempts to harmonize not only the *sūtra* and *tantra* schools in their basic theory and ultimate goal but the positions of various Buddhist traditions and schools with respect to *tathāgatagarbha*.

Other works of Mipham on Madhyamaka include his commentaries on Nāgārjuna's *Pratītyasamutpādahṛdaya*[35] and the *Hastavāla*.[36] Mipham did not write anything on Āryadeva's *Catuḥśataka*, one of the major treatises of Madhyamaka in Tibet, but he wrote a commentary on the *Jñānasārasamuccaya*,[37] believed to be by the same Āryadeva. He composed around a dozen practical instructions for meditation on Madhyamaka and his quintets of Swords and Lilies[38] impinge heavily on Madhyamaka issues. His student Zhanphan Chökyi Lodoe (*c*.1890–1960) compiled his miscellaneous notes on Madhyamaka philosophy and created a collection entitled *dBu ma sogs gzhung spyi'i dka' gnad skor gyi gsung gros sna tsogs phyogs gcig tu bsdus pa rin po che'i za ma tog*.[39] Most of the notes in this and in his annotation of MA are refutations of the Gelukpa understanding of Emptiness as lack of inherent nature and the phrase 'vase is not empty of vase but of hypostatic existence'. It is also in this text that he uses the terms, *kun rdzob gzhan stong* and *don dam gzhan stong*, which in his *Nges shes sgron me*, he calls *tshig gi gzhan stong* and *don gi gzhan stong*, and accuses the Gelukpas of espousing the first type of *gzhan stong*.

In the West, John Pettit has produced a thorough study and translation of Mipham's *Nges shes sgron me* and its commentary by Throshul Jamdor (1920–60),[40] Kennard Lipman has worked on Mipham's commentary on *Madhyamakālaṃkāra*, and a voluminous translation of it by Thomas Doctor has come out while this work was being completed.[41] Franz-Karl Ehrhard has written on Mipham's theory of assertions in Prāsaṅgika school[42] and Katsumi Mimaki on Mipham's commentary on *Jñānasārasamuccaya*.[43] Two of Mipham's meditation instructions on Madhyamaka have been translated into English by Tibetan Nyingma Meditation Center[44] and Matthew Kapstein has made a paraphrastic presentation of *Don rnam nges shes rab ral gri*.[45] He has also written a thoroughgoing critique of Paul Williams' highly stimulating but slightly misguided account of Mipham's theory of reflexive awareness.[46] Translations of Mipham's annotation to the MA and his commentary on *Dharmadharmatavibhāga* have also been published recently.[47]

One of Mipham's last wishes was to write another extensive exegetical work on Madhyamaka. This wish however was not fulfilled, due to the deterioration of the illness that troubled him for the last decade of his life. From the nature of his works and the degree of his emphasis, it is clear that Madhyamaka was for Mipham a profound and crucial subject, deserving more attention than any other in the *sūtrayāna*. The correct understanding of Madhyamaka *qua* Emptiness was not only an indispensable soteriological factor in itself but a direct link to the knowledge of Dzogchen. In many of his works, Mipham stressed this connection between Dzogchen and Madhyamaka and went so far to deny that one could master Dzogchen without adequate knowledge of Madhyamaka.

In his *Nges shes sgron me*, he says: 'In order to scrutinize thoroughly the Primordial Purity, one has to perfect the view of Prāsaṅgika',[48] and also in his annotations to the MA, he states: 'The Great Perfection [view], which realizes the equality of appearance and Emptiness, could be seen only by means of the excellent treatises of Nāgārjuna.'[49]

This was a bold claim for him to make, especially as a Nyingmapa, because many yogic Nyingmapas in his milieu regarded themselves as Dzogchen adepts although they were not really versed in Madhyamaka philosophy. More disconcerting to such Nyingmapas was his opinion that full knowledge of Madhyamaka can be gained only in the light of sufficient *pramāṇa* understanding. Like the Gelukpas, Mipham argued that knowing *pramāṇa* concepts is a prerequisite for mastering Madhyamaka philosophical theories and propositions.

In his commentary on the *Madhyamakālaṃkāra*, he stated that Śāntarakṣita's text was particularly meant for a Mādhyamika who has a strong interest in and taste for *pramāṇa*. In the same text, he mentioned the concept of *dbu tshad sen ge mjing bsnol*, the coalition of Madhyamaka principle and *pramāṇa* logic, represented by two lions intertwining their necks to guard each other.[50] Thus, Mipham revolutionized Nyingma scholarship by not only encouraging philosophical learning and exposition but by emphasizing the rational and analytical approach of learning and pedagogy.

Through his writings on Madhyamaka, of all his contributions, he left for future Nyingmapas what they could consider as assertions of their own tradition (*rang lugs kyi 'dod pa*) or philosophical boundaries to hold (*gzhung gi 'dzin mtshams*). In this respect, Mipham fulfilled his goal in writing commentaries, for it was partly to make the Nyingmapas, who were then heavily dependent on other traditions, self-reliant in their doctrinal field that Mipham undertook the writing of his works. He repeatedly admonishes the Nyingmapas to stop relying on other schools for philosophical and doctrinal positions while so much goodness is stored in the Nyingma tradition itself.[51] With this message, he encourages the Nyingmapas and for that matter any other scholars and practitioners to develop twofold certainties in the teachings: a certainty through which one need not rely on others anymore (*gzhan dring mi 'jog pa'i nges shes*) and a certainty which cannot be invalidated by others anymore (*gzhan gyis mi 'phrogs pa'i nges shes*). These dual certainties form a common theme in many of his works.

Mipham's output in Madhyamaka redefined, for the Nyingmapas, their perspective on Madhyamaka scholarship and their scholastic modalities by pointing out both strengths and weaknesses, while it proved a stimulus for other traditions of Tibetan Buddhism to reassess and reconstruct their doctrinal positions. For general Tibetan scholarship, it rejuvenated the long history of polemical debate and thereby gave fresh life to the study of Madhyamaka in Tibet.

Sources and methodological considerations

This book is far from being an exhaustive treatment of Mipham's Mādhyamika thought or of the debates on Emptiness he had with his Gelukpa opponents. It is at best a selective discussion of the major themes in Mipham's writings that pertain to his understanding of Emptiness and his disagreements with that of the Gelukpas. In reconstructing the stimulating and complex dispute between Mipham and his Gelukpa opposition, I have juxtaposed here their theories, arguments and counter arguments pertaining to the three themes of (1) the dialectical/logical procedures for establishing Emptiness, (2) the nature of Emptiness so established and (3) the viability of epistemological and linguistic operations with regard to Emptiness.

This book is a revised version of my doctoral thesis for Oxford, entitled, 'The Position of Mipham in the Indo-Tibetan Debate on Emptiness'. I have left out the chapter on Mipham and his writings in the thesis with the hope of expanding it into a separate book, but information, vital to the present discussion, has been incorporated in the Introduction. The book undertakes primarily a thematic treatment, rather than a textual study, of the debates on Emptiness, although a large number of crucial texts are used for comparative analysis of their interpretations. It is therefore mainly an assortment of distinct arguments and counter arguments on the three themes from a wide range of sources, presented in the language and format of contemporary Western scholarship. My role in presenting this is no more than that of the commentator in a football match, giving both a narrative account and an analytic treatment of the philosophical contest that took place between Mipham and the Gelukpa opposition.

Among the primary sources I have used for Mipham's thought are his *Ketaka*, the *rGyan 'grel*, the *Nges shes sgron me*, the three polemical rejoinders (*Rab lan*, *Nyi snang* and *Dogs sel*), the *'Jug 'grel* and the *gSung sgros*. Other writings on Madhyamaka are also referred to and cited sporadically. For his opponents, I have used mainly Tsongkhapa's *Lam rim*, the *dGongs pa rab gsal*, the *Rigs pa'i rgya mtsho*, the *Drang nges*, Gyaltshab Je's *rGyal sras 'jug ngogs*, the polemical collection, *dGag lan phyogs bsgrigs* and the polemical rejoinders of Pari Rabsal and Drakar Trulku.

The first two chapters lay out the background for the debates. Chapter 1 discusses the significance of Emptiness in Buddhism through looking at its soteriological, ontological, doctrinal and historical importance. Chapter 2 sets the historical backdrop to the debates by recounting the debates on Emptiness that have occurred in India and Tibet and has led to the debates triggered by Mipham. The next three chapters deal with the main bones of contention between Mipham and his Gelukpa opponents in their understanding, interpretation, approach and application of Emptiness. Chapter 3 discusses the debates on the delimitation of the negandum and the dialectical procedures used to establish Emptiness. Chapter 4 is on the theory of the ultimate *qua* Emptiness. Chapter 5 discusses the viability of epistemic and linguistic operations with regard to the ultimate *qua* Emptiness and delves into the issues of the unknowability and ineffability of Emptiness. A summary of the three polemical writings of Mipham are appended to provide the textual context for the debates and to indicate the variety of topics he covered in his polemics.

For easy reading, Tibetan names are given in phonetical transcription keeping as close as possible to the orthographic form where there is no established standard. A list of these names and their corresponding form in Wylie's transliteration is included in the appendix. All dates provided here come from a number of sources including Seyfort Ruegg's *The Literature of the Madhyamaka School of Philosophy in India*, Gene Smith's database on the Tibetan Buddhist Resource Center website and *Bod rgya tshig mdzod chen mo*. All translations are mine unless otherwise stated and Tibetan and Sanskrit originals are provided where appropriate. Throughout the work, I have also touched on Mipham's consideration of the *ris med* outlook and the inclusive nature of Dzogchen, both of which have significant influence on his philosophical outlook and polemical approach.

It was one of Mipham's dying wishes to write a definitive exegesis on Madhyamaka but his failing health did not permit him. This work, being a digest or a compilatory treatise (*thor ba sdud pa'i bstan bcos*) in nature, can be seen as a humble attempt on my part to actualize, as it were, this unfulfilled wish. It is my modest hope that through this selective discussion of Mipham's qualms about the Gelukpa understanding of Emptiness, we will be able to capture Mipham's philosophical mood and improve our knowledge of this extraordinary polymath, who still remains a personal enigma.

Plate 2 Ju nyung hermitage above Jumo Hor Sang-ngag Chöling monastery.

Plate 3 Mipham's birthplace near Ju nyung.

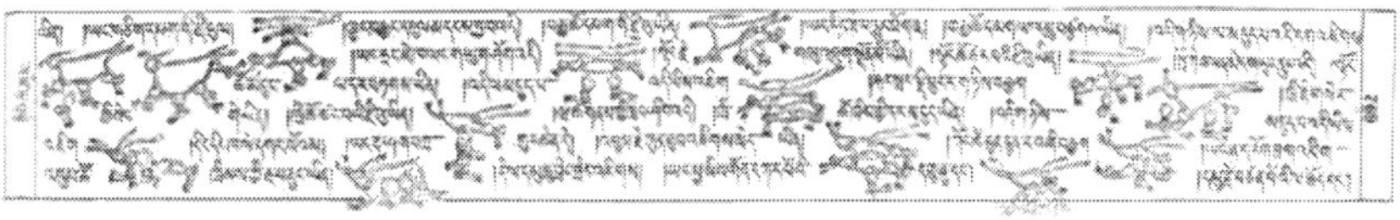

Plate 4 A page from Mipham's illustrations of knot-sortilege.

Plate 5 Woodblocks of Mipham's writings, Derge Chözod Chenmo (main shelves).

Plate 6 Woodblocks of Mipham's writings, Derge Chözod Chenmo (side shelves).

1

EMPTINESS

Its soteriological, doctrinal, ontological and historical significance in Buddhism

Deliverance comes from the view of Emptiness,
All other religious practices lead to Emptiness.
(Dharmakīrti,
Pramāṇavārttika, Prāmaṇasiddhi/255)

Mipham's reputation among Tibetan scholars, as mentioned earlier, was largely an outcome of his contributions on Madhyamaka. There is no doubt that the importance of Emptiness in Mahāyāna Buddhism and the zeal with which Tibetan scholars generally undertook the study of Madhyamaka had a great deal to do with the rise of Mipham's popularity. Tibetan scholars, following their Indian precursors, considered Madhyamaka *qua* Emptiness as the primary path to Buddhahood, and therefore the most important topic in Mahāyāna philosophy. This notion was conducive for the propagation of Mipham's innovative and often controversial interpretations that earned him much notoriety. It is also this that influenced Mipham, like many other scholars, to emphasize and elaborate on the Madhyamaka doctrine.

Hence, the significance of any discussion or debate on Emptiness can only be fully appreciated in the light of the pivotal place Emptiness occupies in the Mahāyāna system. It is the centrality of Emptiness, in relation to other concepts and practices in Buddhism, which makes debate on Emptiness a serious issue. In this chapter, I shall briefly discuss how and why the theory and practice of Emptiness are essentials of Mahāyāna Buddhism. A great number of ancient and modern scholars have written on Emptiness appraising it as the central concept of Buddhism.

If we look at Mahāyāna soteriological taxonomy, Buddhist paths to enlightenment are often classified into view (*dṛṣṭi/darśana, lta ba*),[1] the philosophical understanding of the nature of all things, and praxis (*caryā, spyod pa*), the moral and ethical principles. This roughly corresponds to the other binary classification of Buddhist practice into wisdom (*prajña, shes rab*) and skilful method (*upaya, thabs*) and to the two kinds of accumulations (*saṃbhāra, tshogs*) of gnosis (*jñāna, ye shes*) and merits (*puṇya, bsod nams*) commonly known in the Mahāyāna tradition. Similarly, Buddhist practice, since its inception, is also divided into calm abiding (*śamatha, zhi gnas*) and insight (*vipaśyanā, lhag mthong*).

In Mahāyāna soteriology, the view, wisdom, gnosis and insight in these binaries all pertain to Emptiness *qua* Non-self while under praxis, skilful method and accumulation of merit are assorted a diverse range of precepts and practice including calm abiding. This typological bifurcation of Buddhist paths and the distinct place it accords to the understanding of Emptiness therefore clearly demonstrate the importance of Emptiness.

Emptiness *qua* Non-self: the heart of Buddhist soteriology

The crucial role of Emptiness *qua* view, wisdom, gnosis and insight perhaps can be better appreciated by placing it in the context of the concept of *spang gnyen* – the things to be eliminated and their antidotes – which constitutes the second and the fourth of the four noble truths and sums up the entire process of transforming an ordinary individual into an enlightened being. A proper treatment of this concept is beyond the range of this book, hence, mention will be made here only of what is relevant to and sufficient for the present purpose citing primary Indian sources, which Tibetan scholars such as Tsongkhapa and Mipham profusely used.

In all schools of Buddhism, the world is a result of actions (*karma, las*) and these actions are generally induced by defiling emotions like attachment, hatred and ignorance. These, in turn, arise from grasping the 'I' or self (*ahaṃkāra/ātmagraha, ngar/bdag 'dzin*). In other words, the mistaken grasping of 'I' gives rise to the notions of 'my/mine' (*mamakāra/ātmīyagraha, nga yir/bdag gir 'dzin pa*) and, in contrast, to notions of you, he, she, they, etc. From these notions arises impulses such as likes and dislikes, attachment and hatred, and from them actions, and from actions this world full of dissatisfaction. It is this process that Candrakīrti has in mind when he laments at the beginning of his MA:

> First, [the beings] grasp at 'I' thinking 'this is me',
> Then, [they] grasp at things thinking 'this is mine'
> And sway without self-control [in the world] like a paddlewheel.[2]

Similarly Dharmakīrti explains through this causal theory the conditioned genesis of the world:

> If [the notion of] self exists, the [notion of] other is conceived.
> From discriminating the self and other arise attachment and
> hatred.
> [It is] through being in connection with these two
> [That] all the defects come into being.[3]

He equates I-grasping with the view of substantiality (*satkāyadarśana, 'jig lta*) and identifies it with the ignorance in the Buddha's twelve link of dependent origination:[4] 'All defects are rooted in this [ignorance] and this is also called the view of substantiality.'[5] He goes on to give three reasons as to why the view of substantiality is ignorance.[6] Āryadeva before him observed that this ignorance or delusion pervades all defiling emotions just as tactility pervades the body and that defiling emotions can only be overcome by removing this I-grasping.[7] The I-grasping thus forms the root of all evils and the core of what is to be eliminated (*prahatāvya, spang bya*). The antidote (*pratipakṣa, gnyen po*), which can uproot this I-grasping, is then the discriminating wisdom discerning Emptiness *qua* Non-self (*anātman, bdag med*) or unsubstantiality of a person as Candrakīrti has it:

> Seeing through wisdom that all defects of defiling emotions
> Arise from the view of substantiality,
> And knowing the 'I' to be its object,
> The yogis negate the 'I'.[8]

Dharmakīrti too reasons that without negating its referential object, 'I', the I-grasping cannot be eradicated. It is the view of Emptiness (*śūnyatādṛṣṭi, stong nyid lta ba*), which acts as the counteracting force to eliminate the I-grasping because, in spite of having the five aggregates as the common object of focus (*ālambanaviṣaya, dmigs yul*), the view discerning Emptiness sees the aggregates void of 'I', whereas ignorance *qua* I-grasping superimposes an 'I' on them.[9] They are therefore in their mode of grasping (*'dzin stangs*) directly opposed to each other (*virodha, 'gal ba*) and incompatible (*sahānavasthāna, lhan cig mi gnas pa*). Other practices such as loving-kindness, discipline, calm abiding do not contradict I-grasping directly. Therefore, they lack the capacity to work as direct antidotes themselves but help the cultivation of insight into Emptiness and temporarily suppress the defiling emotions. Dharmakīrti formulates this in the following:

> Loving-kindness and so forth do not contradict ignorance,
> Therefore they cannot exterminate the defect [of ignorance][10]

and

> From the view of Emptiness comes liberation;
> All the other practices are for [generating] that.[11]

So far, we have seen the portrayal of the I-grasping and the grasping of 'my/mine' (collectively known as view of substantiality) as the ultimate roots of *saṃsāra* and Emptiness *qua* unsubstantiality of a person, as its direct antidote. This, according to Tibetan hermeneuticians, is a Mahāyāna viewpoint shared by other Buddhist schools. It is in this capacity that the view of Non-self came to be known as the Sole Entrance to Peace (*zhi sgo gnyis pa med pa*) as Āryadeva puts it:

> [That which is] the sole entrance to peace,
> The destroyer of all evil views
> [And] the scope of all Buddhas,
> Is designated as the Non-self.[12]

It also became a common concept that the person who gains direct knowledge of such Non-self is a sublime being (*ārya, 'phags pa*) and is no more in the domain of ordinary world (*pṛthagjana, so so skye bo*). Hence, direct knowledge of Emptiness *qua* Non-self is the criterion which distinguishes for Buddhist soteriologists the domain of *nirvāṇa* from *saṃsāra*.

Let us now look at the role of Emptiness from the Mādhyamika viewpoint or what Tibetan hermeneuticians call the unique Mahāyāna viewpoint (*theg chen thun min gyi lugs*). The problem of I-grasping and its counterforce is not as straightforward in Nāgārjuna's Mādhyamika as in general Buddhism. In his *Ratnāvalī*, Nāgārjuna argues that I-grasping is dependent on the aggregates just as the reflection is on mirror. As long as there is grasping of the aggregates, the I-grasping will endure, and from it arise actions and from actions rebirth.[13] He depicts a vicious circle comparable to a firebrand in which the I-grasping relies on the aggregates and aggregates in turn rely on I-grasping. The end to this vicious circle, he argues, can be found in knowing the aggregates to be empty and unreal:

> By seeing the aggregates to be unreal in this way,
> The I-grasping will be eliminated.
> Having eliminated the I-grasping,
> The aggregates will subsequently cease to arise.[14]

On a similar note, he writes in his *Mūlamadhyamakakārikā*:

> When grasping at internal and external objects
> As 'I' and mine ceases to exist,
> The cause [for rebirth] is stopped,
> And with its cessation, rebirth ceases.[15]

In his *Śūnyatāsaptatikārikā*, he mentions that the ignorance in the Buddha's twelve links of dependent origination, refers to the notion of conditioned things as real. Only through understanding the Emptiness of things can such ignorance and the subsequent chain of dependent origination be broken.[16] In his philosophy, it is not merely I-grasping but also grasping other things as substantial, real or hypostatic which gives rise to defiling emotions. In his MK, Nāgārjuna attributes the origin of defiling emotions to discursive thoughts (*vikalpa, rnam rtog*) and discursive thoughts to mental elaborations (*prapañca, spros pa*). It is only through negating mental elaborations by understanding Emptiness that discursive thoughts and the resultant defiling emotions, actions and rebirth can be eliminated. He writes:

> Through extinction of defiling emotions and actions, one is liberated.
> Defiling emotions and actions arise from discursive thoughts.
> They in turn arise from mental elaborations.
> Mental elaborations are overcome by Emptiness.[17]

The Mādhyamikas shunned any sense of substantiation or reification as a distorted mental elaboration. Āryadeva, in his *Catuḥśataka*, even refers to the consciousness itself as the seed of existence and observes that through discerning the unsubstantiality of objects on which the consciousness feeds, this seed of existence can be discontinued.[18] Śāntideva remarks that the mistaken notion of hypostatic existence (*satyataḥ kalpanā, bden par rtog pa*) of things is a cause of suffering and that such a notion is to be eliminated.[19] Thus, we see the range of what has to be eliminated expand in Mādhyamika encompassing thoughts and notions which pre-Mādhyamika Buddhism did not consider as obstacles to enlightenment. The term *ātman*, which denoted a personal self, was extended to substance or inherent nature of things thus becoming equivalent to own being or aseity (*svabhāva, ngo bo/rang bzhin*). The Mādhyamikas applied the reductionist arguments such as 'the chariot reasoning' used for negating the personal *ātman*, to all phenomena and negated substantiality in them.

This led to an extension of antidotes. Mere knowledge of Emptiness of personal self was not sufficient to lead a person to enlightenment. The understanding of all phenomena as empty and unsubstantial became a necessary condition for liberation. A salient feature of this extension of antidotes is the division of Emptiness into Non-self of persons (*pudgalanairātmya, gang zag gi bdag med*) and Non-self of phenomena (*dharmanairātmya, chos kyi bdag med*). The usage of the term *anātman/nairātmya* was no more limited to the lack of personal self but came to refer to the unsubstantiality of all things although it was used more frequently to denote the former just as Emptiness was used to denote the latter.

The formal division of these two kinds of *nairātmya*s appears to have developed after Nāgārjuna although he implicitly delineates both of them in his MK. Candrakīrti comments that the Non-self of person is taught primarily for the liberation of Śrāvakas and Pratyekabuddhas while the Non-self of both person and phenomena are taught for the emancipation of Bodhisattvas seeking omniscience. Mipham treats the relationship between the two *nairātymas* as one of a universal and particular (*spyi bye brag*). Just as personal self is a particular of the universal phenomena, *pudgalanairātmya* is a particular of the universal *dharmanairātmya*.[20] The first served primarily as an antidote to eliminate the obscuration of defiling emotions (*kleśāvaraṇa, nyon mongs pa'i sgrib pa*) and attain liberation (*mokṣa, thar pa*) while the latter is mainly to overcome the obscuration of the knowable (*jñeyāvaraṇa, shes bya'i sgrib pa*) and attain omniscience (*sarvajña, thams cad mkhyen pa*).

Although the Non-self of phenomena was primarily taught for the Bodhisattvas to overcome the obscuration of the knowable, Candrakīrti strongly maintained that Śrāvakas and Pratyekabuddhas too realize the Non-self of phenomena. In his auto-commentary on MA, Candrakīrti argues in length providing three arguments and seven citations that in order to eliminate defiling emotions and reach enlightenment, Śrāvakas and Pratyekabuddhas must realize the Non-self of phenomena.[21] However, he describes their realization of Non-self of phenomena as an understanding of 'this mere conditioned nature' (*imaṃ pratyayatāmātra, rkyen nyid 'di pa tsam*) and remarks that they do not perfect the practice of such realization.[22] The realization of Mahāyāna Bodhisattvas surpass the Śrāvaka and Pratyekabuddha understanding both in quality and variety; they fathom the complete depth and range of *dharmanairātmya* presented mainly in Mahāyāna corpus in categories such as the sub-divisions of Emptiness into sixteen, eighteen and twenty types.[23]

I shall not digress into the complex topic of Śrāvaka and Pratyekabuddha realization of *dharmanairātmya*, which is one of the highly debated issues with a long and vast hermeneutic and polemical tradition. Here, my objective is to demonstrate that in Nāgārjuna's Mādhyamika school, especially as understood by Candrakīrti and his followers, the understanding of Emptiness of both kinds of *nairātmya*s is *sine qua non* to attaining the state of liberation. I have thus far shown how Mādhyamika masters have held Emptiness to be the chief factor in the soteriological process as the direct antidote to the mental fabrications, which conditions existence and obstructs enlightenment. The following verses in Nāgārjuna's *Lokātītastava*, 27 and Śāntideva's *Bodhicaryāvatāra*, IX/55 further substantiate this:

> Without realizing the lack of characteristics,
> You [the Buddha] have taught there is no liberation[24]

and

> Emptiness is the antidote for the darkness
> Of the obscurations of defiling emotions and knowable.
> Why would [one] not meditate on it
> If one wishes to quickly attain Omniscience?[25]

Candrakīrti went even further with this Mādhyamika assertion of Emptiness as the indispensable and primary path to liberation to claim a form of soteriological monism. To him, it is specifically the understanding of Emptiness as it was delineated by Nāgārjuna, which is crucial to the Buddhist enlightenment. Those who are outside the path prescribed by Nāgārjuna, he declares at the end of his criticism of Cittamātra, have no means to reach enlightenment.

> Those who are outside the tradition of Master Nāgārjuna
> Do not have the means to peace.[26]

Those who fall outside Nāgārjuna's system, he reasons, are impaired in their vision of ultimate and conventional truths and for those who are so impaired, there is no hope for liberation. This sufficiently demonstrates how central the correct understanding of Emptiness is in the thought of Candrakīrti and his followers in Tibet.

Emptiness *qua* Prajñāpāramitā: the primary path

Emptiness also occupies a central place in Mahāyāna soteriology under the name of Prajñāpāramitā or perfection of wisdom, the last of the six perfections, which form the mainstream Bodhisattva practice. Prajñāpāramitā seems to initially figure as a genre of Mahāyāna *sūtra*s dealing with the exposition of Emptiness. These *sūtra*s, it is generally believed, took the name *Prajñāpāramitāsūtra*s after their content. Indo-Tibetan commentators speak of two levels of content of the *Prajñāpāramitāsūtra*s: the explicit teaching of Emptiness (*dngos bstan stong nyid*) and the implicit or hidden topic of experiential knowledge (*sbas don mngon rtogs*). In the first case, Prajñāpāramitā is equated with Emptiness, the objective reality whereas in the second case, it is understood as experiential knowledge or gnosis discerning Emptiness.

Most of the commentators argued that actual Prajñāpāramitā has to be a subjective experience just as the other five perfections are and maintained direct knowledge of Emptiness to be the genuine Prajñāpāramitā. Dignāga even argued that authentic Prajñāpāramitā is restricted to the gnosis of the Buddha and that paths and texts merely bear the name.[27] These two levels of content or aspects of the objective reality and subjective cognition however are not seen to be different from the viewpoint of the gnosis experiencing Emptiness because such subject–object distinction do not exist on that level.

In transmission, the first one is considered to have been formulated and systematized through the profound view-tradition of Nāgārjuna (*Klu sgrub kyi zab mo lta srol*) and the second revealed to us through the vast praxis-tradition of Asaṅga (*Thogs med kyi rgya chen spyod srol*). Nāgārjuna's tradition placed emphasis on the Prajñāpāramitā *qua* the philosophical concept of Emptiness and Asaṅga's tradition stressed the Prajñāpāramitā as the experiential knowledge of that Emptiness. Thus, the whole Mahāyāna tradition can be seen to revolve around Prajñāpāramitā.

The importance of Prajñāpāramitā in Mahāyāna soteriology is also most interestingly illustrated in the metaphorical epithet of Prajñāpāramitā as the mother of the Buddhas. Like the depiction of the Buddha as the father to Śrāvakas and Pratyekabuddhas, who are children of his speech, and Bodhisattvas who are children of his heart/mind, the Prajñāpāramitā is portrayed as the mother of the Buddhas. The following eulogy attributed to Rāhulabhadra, so commonly recited in Tibetan monasteries, encapsulates this:

> Homage to the mother of the Victorious Ones of three times,
> The Prajñāpāramitā, which is ineffable, inconceivable and inexpressible,
> Unborn, unceasing [like] the nature of space,
> And is the scope of intuitive gnosis.[28]

From the Mahāyāna viewpoint, Prajñāpāramitā is the mother of all Buddhas because the Buddhas are born from the realization and practice of Prajñāpāramitā coupled with expedient methods.

The *Prajñāpāramitāsūtra*s such as the *Saṃcayagāthā* and *Aṣṭasāhasrikā* further claim that those who are undergoing training to attain the enlightenment of the Śrāvakas, Pratyekabuddhas and Bodhisattvas must all train in the Prajñāpāramitā.[29] Based on these passages, Maitreya, in the salutary verse in his *Abhisamayālaṃkāra*, avouch that the Prajñāpāramitā is the mother of all saints including Śrāvakas, Pratyekabuddhas, Bodhisattvas and the Buddhas.[30] This concept of Prajñāpāramitā as mother of all saints is perhaps the origin for the Mādhyamika designation of Emptiness as the Sole Entrance to Peace and the assertion made by Mādhyamikas such as Candrakīrti that even Śrāvakas and Pratyekabuddhas have to understand Emptiness *qua* Non-self of phenomena in order to reach enlightenment.

This role of Prajñāpāramitā as the origin of all saints and primary path to enlightenment led to the glorification of Prajñāpāramitā and subsequently gave rise to the cult of Prajñāpāramitā in which both the Prajñāpāramitā scriptures and the deified embodiment of Prajñāpāramitā as a female Buddha are worshipped. Emptiness as Prajñāpāramitā stands out among the principles and philosophies of Buddhism as perhaps the only one that is represented in a personified deity in the entire Sūtrayāna Buddhism.

The assertion of the centrality of Prajñāpāramitā *qua* Emptiness in Mahāyāna Buddhism that brings us closest to the polemical theme of this book is however the opening verse to the ninth chapter of Śāntideva's BA. After an elaborate treatment of Bodhisattva practice which fall within the first five perfections or the skilful method, Śāntideva begins to expound Emptiness and wisdom stating how all the other practices are subsidiaries leading to wisdom:

> The Sage taught all these subsidiaries
> For the sake of wisdom.
> Therefore, one must generate wisdom,
> Wishing to pacify sufferings.[31]

In spite of the agreement that wisdom is the end of skilful means – giving, morality, patience, effort and meditation – a few debates occurred over the interpretation of this verse. Some scholars commented that the phrase 'these subsidiaries' here refer only to the perfection of meditation discussed in the preceding chapter. Tsongkhapa and his followers explained that wisdom is the product of the first five perfections, which arise in a sequential order.[32] They argued that the phrases 'these subsidiaries' and 'for the sake of wisdom' imply that each of the five perfections of method generates the next, culminating in meditation, which acts as the immediate cause for generating wisdom. Thus, wisdom is seen as the immediate goal and Buddhahood as the ultimate goal in the process.

Mipham rejects the first interpretation and argues that 'these subsidiaries' should refer to all other perfections.[33] However, he objects to any obdurate reading of the two phrases. To him, the two phrases simply make explicit the eminence of wisdom among spiritual practices. He agrees that the importance of wisdom could be indicated through the gradual process of how the former perfections lead to the cultivation of the latter culminating in wisdom but that is not the only possible explanation or the one implied by the two phrases. Wisdom is not paramount merely because it is at the end of the line of cultivation and is the end of all skilful means. Even if we do not view wisdom as a subsequent result of the other perfections, but as synchronous to them, wisdom is still the chief, for without it other perfections would not be able to lead the practitioner to enlightenment or even qualify themselves as perfections.

This, Mipham adequately proves by citing a number of passages from the *sūtra*s. He quotes the passage from the *Śatasāhasrikāprajñāpāramitāsūtra*, which compares wisdom to the river Ganges and the other perfections to its tributaries that join the Ganges to reach the ocean of enlightenment. He also compares wisdom to the universal monarch and the other perfections to the entourage of four regiments following the monarch. He uses the verse from *Saṃcayagāthā* to compare the five perfections of method to blind travellers and wisdom to the sighted guide.[34] Pari Rabsal, one of his opponents, attacked him for taking this position but, to Mipham, the whole point of the verse is to stress the essentiality and prominence of wisdom *qua* cognition of Emptiness on the Mahāyāna path.

Emptiness *qua Pratītyasamutpāda*: the central doctrine

Having briefly explored the soteriological significance of Emptiness, let us now turn to see how Emptiness, conflated with the theory of *Pratītyasamutpāda*, is the key doctrinal topic in Buddhism. *Pratītyasamutpāda*, the Buddhist law of dependent origination, is no doubt recognized by Buddhists of all creeds and ages as the hallmark of the Buddha's doctrine and as the fundamental tenet which distinguishes the Buddhist tradition from the non-Buddhist. It is the Buddhist explanation for the way things are, the *modus existendi* of the world in the absence of an absolute creator or soul. It is the philosophical 'slogan of the Buddha' as the current Dalai Lama puts it.

I have already discussed the indispensability of the knowledge of the unsubstantiality of persons and phenomena in the Buddhist path to enlightenment. It must be noted here that in order to understand such unsubstantiality, the knowledge of conditioned and dependent nature of things is essential. That is because the understanding of unsubstantiality and the understanding of the interdependent nature of things presuppose each other. Thus, it is through insight in the *Pratītyasamudpāda*, or in other words, through profound understanding of the dependent, relative and conditioned nature of existence that the absence of an absolute self or own being is discerned. Similarly, the knowledge of the unsubstantiality of things reaffirms the interdependent mode of existence. Unsubstantiality negates what does not belong to reality and *Pratītyasamutpāda* affirms the genuine state of things.

In the Mādhyamika system, we see the treatment of *Pratītyasamutpāda* develop even further. At the very outset of his MK, Nāgārjuna describes *Pratītyasamutpāda* as neither ceasing, nor arising, neither nihilistic nor eternal and neither unitary nor plural and neither going nor coming.[35] He identifies *Pratītyasamutpāda* as the reality free from all elaborations. Nāgārjuna further conflates *Pratītyasamutpāda* and Emptiness while observing that 'that which is dependently originated is said to be Emptiness'.[36] In his works, he repeatedly equates *Pratītyasamutpāda* with Emptiness and hails the Buddha as a supreme teacher for expounding it.

Prior to Nāgārjuna, *Pratītyasamutpāda* was mainly, if not exclusively, understood through the twelve limbs of dependent origination. Particularly for the *abhidharma* realists, the theory of dependent origination did not preclude the discrete existence of mind and matter as building blocks of the twelve links. Therefore, conditioned and unconditioned entities – the *dharma*s – existed really in spite of being dependently originated. Nāgārjuna underscored the understanding of *Pratītyasamutpāda* as Emptiness by denying any substantial and discrete entities that are dependently originated. To be dependently originated and to be substantial or discrete through possessing own being (*svabhāva*) are mutually exclusive. His rationale is that things are empty of own being or substantiality because they lack independence. 'There is nothing whatsoever that is not dependently originated, therefore there is nothing whatsoever that is not empty',[37] and 'That thing which is dependently originated is known as empty'[38] went his famous arguments. He argued that everything, including the components of dependent origination which the realists claimed to be real, is empty and unreal.

Nāgārjuna's treatment of Emptiness and *Pratītyasamutpāda* continued with his followers such as Āryadeva, Bhāvaviveka and Candrakīrti. In Tibet, scholars such as Tsongkhapa and Mipham championed the exposition of Emptiness *qua Pratītyasamutpāda*. To this day, the study of *Pratītyasamutpāda* remains as a major topic of scholarship. These masters have also praised the Buddha as an unsurpassable and infallible teacher specially for teaching the doctrine of *Pratītyasamutpāda*.

Emptiness *qua nitārtha*: the ultimate topic

Another striking way in which Emptiness is demonstrated to be the paramount topic in Buddhism is the bifurcation of the Buddha's teachings into *sūtra*s with provisional content (*neyārthasūtra, drang don gyi mdo*) and those with definitive content (*nitārthasūtra, nges don gyi mdo*). It is a common Buddhist idiom to describe the Buddha as a skilful teacher, who has prescribed a wide range of teachings corresponding to the needs of his audience. To the Mādhyamikas, the Buddha's skill-in-means is particularly remarkable in delivering a progressive range of discourses leading to the final understanding of Emptiness. In his MK, *Yuktiṣaṣṭikākārikā* and *Ratnāvalī*, Nāgārjuna mentions this systematic progression of Buddha's pedagogical approach.[39] Āryadeva compares the provision of diverse teachings delivered by the Buddha to medicines prescribed for certain diseases and explains how they all culminate in Emptiness free from all views.[40] Śāntideva even calls the Buddha the omniscient physician (*sarvajñavaidya, sman pa tham cad mkhyen pa*) for his skill in progressive dispensation.[41]

Both Nāgārjuna and Āryadeva are explicit that the ultimate message of the Buddha is Emptiness free from all mental elaborations, and all other theories and practices are provisory methods leading to the realization of Emptiness. However, the formal designation of discourses on Emptiness as teachings with definitive content appears to occur only later. Candrakīrti, keeping in line with his

Mādhyamika precursors, declares the discourses on Emptiness to be understood as definitive teachings, and the rest, including *sūtra*s such as those on *tathāgatagarbha* which belong to the third turning of the wheel and was held by many Mahāyāna philosophers to be definitive, to be of provisional significance.[42] Thus, the topic of Emptiness defines for Candrakīrti and his followers the teachings with definitive content (*nitārtha, nges don*).

Emptiness *qua* the ultimate: the ontological truth

The prominent role of Emptiness in soteriology and doctrinal exegesis is directly linked to the ontological status of Emptiness. Indo-Tibetan thinkers often evaluated the ontological status of things by using the philosophical apparatus of the two truths: the conventional truth (*saṃvṛtisatya, kun rdzob bden pa*), which is the relative and conventional level of existence, and the ultimate truth (*paramārthasatya, don dam bden pa*), which is the absolute and the ultimate. To the Mādhyamikas, this dichotomy represents two modes of being: the conventional appearing mode (*kun rdzob snang tshul*) and the ultimate ontic mode (*don dam gnas tshul*). Emptiness, for them, is the ontic mode, the actual way the things are and therefore the ultimate truth. It is, like the Kantian noumena and Schopenhauer's will, the quiddity of the apparent phenomenal world.

According to the Mādhyamikas, Emptiness is the ultimate nature of all things and to view things as empty is the most objective and veridical view. All other modes of understanding and discerning things are mistaken in relation to the view of Emptiness. Emptiness, as the ultimate truth, is then the most important philosophical topic to be delineated and all other dialectical, philosophical and epistemological theories are only steps leading to the theory of Emptiness. Just as the first five perfections are considered to be the means to perfection of wisdom, the conventional truth inclusive of all conventional theories and concepts is treated as a means to the realization of the ultimate truth. Candrakīrti states this in his MA:

> Conventional truth is the means
> And ultimate truth the outcome of the means.
> Those who do not know their difference
> Engage in the wrong and evil path of discursive thoughts.[43]

Candrakīrti was most likely only rephrasing in this verse what Nāgārjuna has stated in his MK, XXIV/8–10. Nāgārjuna systematically argues that the Buddhists teach their doctrine through relying on the theories of two truths of the conventional and the ultimate. Those who are ignorant of this binary concept of truth, he goes on to say, would not understand the profound reality taught by the Buddha. That, he reasons, is because without depending on the conventional truth, the ultimate cannot be shown and without discerning the ultimate, *nirvāṇa* cannot be attained.

The delineation of Emptiness as the ultimate truth and a *sine qua non* of *nirvāṇa* led to the ascription of another notable role to Emptiness. Emptiness came to be the philosophical determinant in ranking the Buddhist schools. Indo-Tibetan doxographers used the understanding of Emptiness of a particular school or tradition as the main criterion to determine its place in the Buddhist religious hierarchy. The philosophical status and soteriological efficiency of a Buddhist school were judged by the quality and degree of their understanding and delineation of Emptiness. Such ranking of schools in an ascending mode can be found in *Jñānasarasamuccaya* and many later doxographical works. Śāntideva also mentions how intellectuals with higher understanding of Emptiness outshine those with lower ones.[44] In this way, the understanding of Emptiness became the yardstick to determine the philosophical ranking of a particular school or tradition.

The Mādhyamika doxographers perforce considered themselves as the best exponents of Emptiness and thus placed themselves on the top of the religious hierarchy. The adherents of Cittamātra were given the position next to them and the Sautrāntika were placed higher than the Vaibhāṣika realists but lower than the Cittamātra idealists. Thus, all schools are accorded their place corresponding to their understanding of Emptiness as judged from the Mādhyamika point of view. Difference within Mādhyamikas, as is the case with other schools, led to the formation of sub-schools, each of which claimed to be higher than their rivals. Later Vajrayānists claimed that their realization of the Emptiness is even greater than that of the Mādhyamikas and considered themselves higher than Mādhyamikas.

To the general Tibetan Mādhyamikas, Candrakīrti's Prāsaṅgika Mādhyamika presents the most thorough and complete delineation of Emptiness and is therefore considered the highest of the Sūtrayāna schools. Even Vajrayāna traditions do not surpass this school in its understanding and delineation of Emptiness although certain esoteric methods used in tantric practice to incite the experience of Emptiness qualify Vajrayāna to be classified as a higher school than the Prāsaṅgikas on the doxographical ladder. However, certain followers of Vajrayāna in Tibet contended that the Sūtrayāna schools including Prāsaṅgika Mādhyamika can reach Buddhahood without having recourse to Vajrayāna.

I shall not delve into this debate. What is notable for the current purpose is the relevance of the understanding of Emptiness as the determining factor to the position of a school in the doxographical hierarchy. The parties involved in the debates on Emptiness equally assert philosophical rectitude and superiority over others through claiming their understanding of Emptiness to be correct. They criticize and despise their opponent's understanding of Emptiness as nihilistic or eternalistic. To the Indo-Tibetan Mādhyamika schools, the understanding of Emptiness forms the basis of their claim to philosophical rectitude and religious superiority.

Emptiness *qua nirvāṇa*: the religious goal

In the previous sections, we have seen how Emptiness as the content of wisdom and definitive teachings is regarded as the purpose of other religious practices and doctrinal teachings, and as the ultimate truth is considered the end to which conventional truth leads. Now, we shall see Emptiness treated as the soteriological goal by equating it with *nirvāṇa*. In Mādhyamika, Emptiness is not merely a path leading to a religious goal but is itself identical with the goal to be achieved. Emptiness, to use the dual meaning of the English verb 'realize', is not only an objective nature of things which has to be realized in an epistemological sense but the *summum bonum* to be realized or attained as a soteriological goal.

Generally speaking, the Buddhist soteriological goal is understood as a state where all negative things, which characterize *saṃsāra*, are eliminated through realizing the true nature of things. It consists of the dual traits of the attainment of the gnoseological realization and other positive qualities, and the elimination of delusion and other factors of *saṃsāra*. These two properties presuppose each other and respectively represent the fulfilment of the salvific force – the third and fourth of the noble truths – and the elimination of defiling elements – the first and second noble truths. It is also through these two essential properties that the Buddhist soteriological goal received its names enlightenment (*bodhi, byang chub*) and liberation (*mokṣa, thar pa*).

Although these two terms are often used co-referentially, enlightenment is used to denote the positive realization attained while liberation denotes the freedom achieved through that realization. Vasubandhu, for instance, identifies enlightenment with the realization. He writes that 'enlightenment is the gnosis of non-arising and exhaustion',[45] that is, the knowledge that all defiling emotions are exhausted and will not arise again. In comparison, liberation, as Maitreya puts it, 'is the extinction of merely the faults', which conditions this *saṃsāra*.[46] It refers to the freedom from the bondage of defiling emotions and actions as Nāgārjuna observes: 'Liberation comes from the extinction of defiling emotions and actions.'[47]

The other very common appellation of the Buddhist religious goal is *nirvāṇa* (*myang 'das*), literally 'blowing out', which according to Gombrich is a metaphor used for the elimination of the fires of passion, hatred and delusion.[48] It denotes the soteriological state of transcendence encompassing both aspects of enlightenment and freedom from suffering. *Nirvāṇa* is a goal to be realized through inner transformation of the mind and therefore does not have a physical dimension as a place existing 'out there'. Many Mahāyāna philosophers also denied a temporal dimension to *nirvāṇa* by asserting that *nirvāṇa* is not a new state to be attained. They argued that sentient beings are in the state of *nirvāṇa* and are by nature Buddhas whether or not they are aware of it. They rejected the ontic reality of *saṃsāra* holding *saṃsāra* to be a mere illusion. Śāntideva, for one, remarks that sentient beings are by nature fully liberated (*sattvāh prakṛtyā parinivṛtāh, sems can rang bzhin mya ngan 'das*).[49]

I have already pointed out that Nāgārjuna understood *nirvāṇa* in a unique way by equating it to Emptiness. In his MK, XXIV/3, he gives a description of *nirvāṇa*, which is similar to the description of *Pratītyasamutpāda* in his opening verse of the same text:

> That which cannot be given up or attained,
> Is without annihilation or eternity,
> And without cessation or arising
> Is designated as *nirvāṇa*.[50]

'*Nirvāṇa*', Nāgārjuna further declares 'is unconditioned [while] both being and non-being are conditioned'.[51] *Nirvāṇa* transcends the dichotomy of being *qua* substantiality and non-being *qua* unsubstantiality and to attain *nirvāṇa* is to be free from such dichotomizing notions. He also writes in his *Ratnāvalī*: 'That which is the extinction of grasping at being and non-being is known as *nirvāṇa*.'[52]

Nāgārjuna calls *nirvāṇa* the unitary truth (*bden gcig pu*) and holds all other things to be false (*log pa*).[53] Thus, *nirvāṇa* is the ultimate reality, that is, Emptiness free from all elaborations. Nāgārjuna's conflation of *nirvāṇa* with such reality is also shown in his description of peace, an epithet of *nirvāṇa*. Nāgārjuna defines peace (*śiva, zhi ba*) as 'the utter pacification of all apprehension and mental elaborations'.[54] Peace is to be free from notions of tetralemma such as impermanence, permanence, both, neither, etc. In this way, Nāgārjuna repeatedly defines *nirvāṇa* as the reality free from all extremes and elaborations, the same way he defines the ultimate truth.

However it is his student Āryadeva, who directly conjoins the terms *nirvāṇa* and Emptiness in his summarized presentation of the Buddha's dharma.

> The Tathāgatas have taught that
> Dharma, in brief, is non-harming
> [And the] Emptiness *qua nirvāṇa*.
> In this [tradition,] these are the only two.[55]

Śāntideva, after establishing the unviability and non-occurrence of analysis without the analysed object, also observes such non-occurrence (*nodeti, mi skye ba*) is termed as *nirvāṇa*.[56]

One of Nagarjuna's most remarkable points made on the theory of *nirvāna* is his formulation of the identity of *nirvāṇa* and *saṃsāra*, which now wittily translated into a Western idiom goes: Nāgārjuna has good news and bad news. The good news is *saṃsāra* is *nirvāṇa* and the bad news is *nirvāṇa* is *saṃsāra*.[57] Nāgārjuna was very emphatic in his rejection of a dualistic existence of *saṃsāra* and *nirvāṇa* as disparate states of bondage and freedom. *Saṃsāra*, Nagarjuna argues, is not even slightly different from *nirvāṇa* and the *vice versa*.[58] He continues:

> That which is the limit of *nirvāṇa*
> Is the limit of *saṃsāra*.
> There is not even the slightest
> Of the subtlest difference between the two.[59]

In his thought, *saṃsāra* and *nirvāṇa* are not two polar existences but rather different perspectives of the same thing. Hence, to attain *nirvāṇa* is to fully realize the nature of *saṃsāra* for 'the knowledge of *saṃsāra* is known as *nirvāṇa*'.[60] *Nirvāṇa*, Stcherbatsky thus observes, is *saṃsāra* viewed *sub specie aeternitatis*.[61] This concept of the sameness of *saṃsāra* and *nirvāṇa* is also termed as the equality of existence and peace (*srid zhi mnyam nyid*). Thus, *nirvāṇa*, in Nāgārjuna's thought, is not merely a soteriological goal, which has to be attained by escaping from *saṃsāra*. It is the nature of *saṃsāra*, the ultimate state of Emptiness, the realization of which forms the primary soteriological goal.

Emptiness conflated with *nirvāṇa* thus combines both functions of an ontological truth and a religious goal. *Nirvāṇa*, as the unitary truth, represents the ultimate ontological value and as the state of liberation and enlightenment, constitutes the ultimate soteriological value. It plays the double role of reality, which has to be realized *qua* understood, and the result, which has to be realized *qua* attained.[62] Emptiness *qua nirvāṇa* is paradoxically both the state we are in and we aspire to be in. It represents both the ontological ground (*gzhi*) and resultant goal (*'bras bu*) fusing them as one and the same state.

Emptiness *qua* Mādhyamika philosophy: a historical milestone

While most traditional scholars have appraised the importance of Emptiness from a soteriological, doctrinal and ontological viewpoint, modern scholars have ventured to consider its significance historically. This was mainly done taking Emptiness as the central tenet of the Mādhyamika school. Although the concept of Emptiness was professed by all Buddhist schools, it was undoubtedly the Mādhyamika school pioneered by Nāgārjuna which championed the exposition of Emptiness. Due to this, the philosophy of Emptiness is often, and indeed rightly, associated with the Mādhyamika school. This association is undeniably reflected in the very name of this school.

I shall not attempt to list here the numerous scholars who have acknowledged the importance of Emptiness in Buddhist philosophy. Among them, T.R.V. Murti naturally comes to one's mind for the title of his book, *The Central Philosophy of Buddhism*. In it, he writes: 'Considering the role and importance of the Mādhyamika, I have ventured to appraise it as the Central Philosophy of Buddhism.'[63] He considered Emptiness central because it was 'a system which created a revolution in Buddhism and through that in the whole range of Indian philosophy'. To him, as to other scholars such as Stcherbatsky, the development of the doctrine of Emptiness through the Mādhyamika school was a revolutionary trend in Indian philosophy in general and Buddhism in particular. Stcherbatsky observes: 'It has never been fully realized what a radical revolution had transformed the Buddhist church when the new spirit, which however was for a long time lurking in it, arrived at full conclusion in the first centuries AC.'[64]

Whether or not this was radical revolution, it was a change and the change was to a large degree due to Nāgārjuna, the founder of Mādhyamika school.

His philosophy and his dialectical approach brought a considerable shift to Indian philosophical paradigm and initiated what became later one of the most important philosophical systems in India, China and Tibet. Speaking about Nāgārjuna's important role, Seyfort Ruegg writes:

> In sum, in view of his place in the history of Buddhist thought and because of his development of the theory of the non-substantiality and emptiness of all *dharmas*, it seems only natural to regard Nāgārjuna as one of the first and the most important systematizers of Mahāyānist thought.[65]

Nāgārjuna's introduction of the Mādhyamika school happened at a time when *abhidharma* substantialism was flourishing and Buddhist hermeneutics were at its acme. Mahāyāna teachings were also beginning to proliferate bringing considerable alteration in the soteriological paradigm through redefining both the nature and the goal of Buddhist practice. Brāhmanism at the same time was undergoing change with systematization and elaboration of the Upaniṣads and Vedic sources and development of partisan schools such as Naiyāyika, Vaiśeṣika, Vedānta, Mīmāṃsā and Sāṃkhya.

It was at such a historical juncture and philosophical climate that Nāgārjuna's foundation of Mādhyamika began. For the growing Mahāyāna current, it gave the greatest impetus to establish Mahāyāna as a prominent school. For other Buddhist and non-Buddhist schools, his philosophy, the dialectical approach he adopted and his refutation of the substantialist standpoints triggered serious philosophical contentions. It was received with strong scepticism and its critics did not refer to it as the Middle Way school, as its proponents do, but considered it a nihilistic trend. Even Vasubandhu, prior to his conversion to Mahāyāna, is said to have remarked that Nāgārjuna is a manifestation of *Māra* and his brother, Asaṅga, is following him.

Among the non-Buddhist schools too, the Mādhyamika critique was received with distaste and strong criticism. Stcherbatsky sums it up in the following:

> Kumārila accuses the Mādhyamika not only of denying the existence of external objects, but of denying the reality of our ideas as well. Vācaspatimiśra is full of respect towards Buddhist logicians, but for the Mādhyamika he has only remarks of extreme contempt; he calls them fools, and accuses them of reducing cognition to nothing. Śankara accuses them of disregarding all logic and refuses to enter in a controversy with them.[66]

Whatever their reaction to Mādhyamika dialectic may have been, it certainly invigorated Brāhmanical scholarship.

Thus, the birth of Mādhyamika had a considerable impact on all existing philosophical traditions. To the Mahāyānists it was a systematic formulation of

Mahāyāna philosophy, while to other philosophical schools it came as a sharp critique of their tenets. The criticism by Mādhyamika marked the beginning of the decline of the Buddhist substantialism in India. Even new systems such as the Yogācāra and Mantranāya could not escape the influence of Mādhyamika philosophy. T.R.V. Murti illustrates this impact by using the analogy of Kant in Western philosophy.[67] He compares the *anātman* system of Buddhist substantialists, which developed from the denial of Brāhmanical *ātman* theory, to empiricism, which grew from a rejection of rationalism and Mādhyamika dialectics to Kant's *Critique* of empiricism. Yogācāra is considered an offshoot of Mādhyamika just as Hegel's idealism is an outcome of Kant's *Critique*. The rise of the philosophical exegesis of Emptiness thus happened at a critical time and left an immense impact on the Indian philosophical setup.

We have so far seen the soteriological, gnoseological, doctrinal, ontological and historical importance of Emptiness in Sūtrayāna by looking at terms and concepts associated with Emptiness. Other epithets of Emptiness such as *dharmadhātu*, *dharmatā*, *dharmakāya*, *tathatā*, *tattva*, *niṣprapañca*, etc. also reflect the importance. However, Emptiness is not only important in Sūtrayāna but forms an indispensable feature of Mantrayāna. The following words of Hopkins sum up the significance of Emptiness in tantric Buddhism:

> Emptiness is the very heart of Buddhist practice in Tibet. In tantra even visualized gods, goddesses, channels, suns, moons, and so forth are qualified by emptiness. Without an understanding of emptiness the practice of Buddhism, be it sutra or tantra, cannot be complete.[68]

Thus, from a Mahāyāna viewpoint, there is no topic on a par with Emptiness. The importance of Emptiness in traditions adhering to Mahāyāna Buddhism is evident in the emphasis laid on it both in terms of scholarly output and meditative practice. However, what exactly Emptiness meant became a hot issue very early on and was to result in a series of debates and polemics. I shall now turn to discuss some of those polemics.

2

THE BIG FUSS ABOUT EMPTINESS

An outline of the history of debates on Emptiness

> Wonderful, profound, illustrious,
> Hard Thou art to recognize.
> Like a mock show Thou art seen, and
> Yet Thou art not seen at all.
> (Rāhulabhadra,
> *Prajñāpāramitāstotra*, 16)

The centrality of Emptiness in Buddhist theory and practice naturally made Emptiness a topic of considerable study and discussion. This gave rise to variant understanding and interpretations of Emptiness turning it into a highly controversial topic and the controversies in turn contributed to the rise of divergent philosophical schools. In this chapter, I shall draw an outline, albeit a sketchy one, of the history of controversies on Emptiness in India and Tibet in order to place Mipham in the right historical context. These controversies over the understanding of Emptiness and hermeneutics arising therefrom form the historical backdrop against which Mipham's role must be seen as well as the scenes which precede, and to an extent lead to, his active participation in the debates.

Controversies in India before Nāgārjuna

Very little, if anything at all, can be said for sure about the controversies on Emptiness before Nāgārjuna. However, the teachings on Emptiness were certainly known and seem to have played an important role. The canonical Nikāyas of the Theravādin order preserved in Pali and Āgamas of the Sarvāstivādin order now largely extant in Tibetan and Chinese translations contain whole *sūtra*s as well as passages on Emptiness.[1] Later Mahāyāna and Vajrayāna corpuses also contain large collections of teachings on Emptiness, strongly claimed to have been dispensed by the historical Buddha.[2] The *Prajñāpāramitāsūtra*s are the most important and elaborate ones among them.[3] These Mahāyāna *sūtra*s, particularly the *Prajñāpāramitāsūtra*s, often draw disparate distinctions between the Śrāvaka and Bodhisattva understanding of Emptiness and contain refutations of the *abhidharma* substantialism.[4]

Sparse information is available on the difference between various *nikāya*s in understanding Emptiness. The Theravādin school, from what their canon suggests, mainly understood Emptiness as philosophical negation of the substantial self or person. Things are described as being empty (*suññaṃ*) of the self and what belongs to the self (*attena vā attaniyena*).[5] The other variant interpretation of Emptiness as ontological absence of what is permanent or everlasting or eternal or not subject to change (*nicenna vā dhuvena vā sassatena vā avipariṇāmadhammena suññaṃ*) is relatively closer to the Mādhyamika understanding of Emptiness as absence of inherent nature (*svabhāva, rang bzhin*) or hypostatic existence (**satyasiddha, bden par grub pa*).[6] The *Kathāvatthu*, which could be considered a polemical treatise of the Theravādins, also treats among numerous other issues of debate the topic of person and Emptiness.[7] It also mentions a certain Vetulyaka group who, according to its commentary, is also known as Mahāsuññatāvādin.[8]

The Sarvāstivādin school, later associated with the philosophical system of Vaibhāṣika,[9] also seems to have understood Emptiness as negation of self and what belongs to self.[10] The *Vibhāṣā*, the *locus classicus* of Vaibhāṣika philosophical and soteriological system, mentions ten Emptinesses.[11] Both Theravādin and Sarvāstivādin scholars apparently professed *abhidharma* theories of ontological pluralism and do not seem to have accepted the insubstantiality or essencelessness of all phenomena.[12] In contrast, the Mahāsāṅgika school and its branches are said to have professed the non-substantiality of all mundane phenomena.[13] To them is attributed the understanding of Emptiness which is in line with, and sometimes considered as prototypical of, the later Mahāyāna concept of Emptiness.

Among the early monastic orders, the adherents of Vātsīputrīya–Saṃmitīya school, who were known as the Pudgalavādin, occupied a notorious place for their assertion of an 'ineffable person', basing their stance on the Buddha's discourse of 'the burden and burden-bearer'.[14] All other *nikāya*s attacked their theory of 'ineffable person' accusing them of advocating the non-Buddhist concept of *Ātman* in disguise.[15] Their understanding of Emptiness thus could be considered to be different from other *nikāya*s in that they did not accept phenomena to be without person or what belongs to a person.

The Sautrāntika, as harsh critics of Sarvāstivāda–Vaibhaṣika realism, played a distinguished role in doctrinal controversies among early schools but their position on Emptiness, like their very history, is not quite clear.[16] Mipham argues that the Sautrāntikas are philosophically superior to the Sarvāstivāda–Vaibhaṣikas in realizing the non-substantiality of the unconditioned entities, non-associated conditioned factors (*viprayuktasaṃskāra, ldan min 'du byed*) and past and future existences, all of which the Sarvāstivāda–Vaibhaṣika accepted as real and discrete.[17] From the Mādhyamika viewpoint, the Sautrāntika have certainly understood the Emptiness of more things than the proponents of *abhidharma* realism have.

Mention must be made of the doctrinal conflicts, or of at least a growing tension, between the adherents of Śrāvaka and Mahāyāna ideas which seem to have developed as the Mahāyāna *sūtra*s came to light. The polemical tendency in some Mahāyāna *sūtra*s and the defence of Mahāyāna by Nāgārjuna and later by Maitreya, Asaṅga, Bhavya/Bhāvaviveka and Śāntideva against the non-Mahāyānists who considered Mahāyāna *sūtra*s as aphocrypha[18] clearly indicate that there was by Nāgārjuna's time, or perhaps even before him, some degree of controversy concerning Mahāyāna *sūtra*s and their content.[19] Of particular relevance are the *Ratnāvalī*, IV/86 and BA, IX/41, both of which suggests discrepancies over Emptiness between the Śrāvakas and Mahāyānists.[20]

Nāgārjuna's critiques and subsequent controversies

Nāgārjuna was without doubt the greatest theorist of Emptiness.[21] The exposition of Emptiness as a systematic philosophy can be regarded as having started with him. His MK, as a critique *par excellence* of the *abhidharma* substantialism, can be certainly considered a polemical work on Emptiness. Throughout the work, Nāgārjuna uses numerous reasonings to negate aseity or own being (*svabhāva, ngo bo/rang bzhin*) in all phenomena, his criticism mainly targeted at Buddhist schools such as Sarvāstivādin, Vaibhāṣika, Sautrāntika and Sammitīya.[22] We find specially in chapter 24, a strong objection that were all things empty and without production and cessation as he expounded, there would not be the four noble truths, and consequently the four stages of sainthood, the Three Jewels, the law of cause and effect and the entire empirical existence. Nāgārjuna refutes this in detail explaining his concept of two truths and the understanding of Emptiness as another term for interdependent origination (*pratītyasamutpāda, rten 'brel*) and Middle Way (*madhyamā pratipat, dbu ma*).

Among his other works, the *Vigrahavyāvartanī,* as a rebuttal of objections concerning dialectical and epistemological implications of his theory of Emptiness, and *Vaidalyasūtra*, as critique of sixteen categories (*padārtha, tshig don*) of Naiyāyikas, are clearly polemical in nature.[23] In the hymnic writings which tradition attributes to Nāgārjuna, we also see a shift in his understanding and delineation of Emptiness, from a negational concept of Emptiness delineated through an apophatic approach of dialectical criticism to an absolutist theory of Emptiness as a substratic reality of all phenomena, sought through a cataphatic approach of romantic mysticism.[24] Although this shift or discrepancy in his writings seems to have not caused any philosophical controversy in India, it was to become a major issue of debate between the two currents of Mādhyamika thought in Tibet.

The rise of the Mādhyamika school of thought pioneered by Nāgārjuna revolutionized the study and understanding of the concept of Emptiness. Āryadeva (AD *c*.200–250), Nāgārjuna's foremost disciple, wrote the *Catuḥśataka* among other works attributed to him.[25] Despite its strong orientation toward practice, this work contains succinct refutations of various Buddhist as well as non-Buddhist theories and beliefs.[26] Traditional historians also mention his debate with a certain Brahmin who challenged the Buddhist to a debate.[27] The polemical verve in the Mādhyamika exposition of Emptiness continued with the writings of Buddhapālita (*c*.500), Bhavya/Bhāvavevika (*c*.500–70?), Candrakīrti (*c*.600–50), *et al.* who reinforced the critical approach of the founding fathers. Although their works were not polemics *per se*, they continually used Nāgārjuna's schema of analytic reasoning, and delineated the Mādhyamika system primarily through criticizing the assertions of other philosophical schools.

The systematization of the Cittamātra philosophy by Maitreya,[28] Asaṅga (fourth century), Vasubandhu (*c*.400–80) and their followers, started a tradition of yet another interpretation of Emptiness, the idealist understanding. The Yogācāra or Vijñānavada thinkers, based on a number of *sūtra*s later grouped as '*sūtra*s teaching mind-only',[29] formulated a distinct theory of Emptiness as the absence of ontological duality set in the parameters of their philosophical idealism. They divided phenomena into the three natures of the constructed (*parikalpita, kun btags*), the dependent (*paratantra, gzhan dbang*) and the absolute (*parinispanna, yongs grub*)[30] and, in the framework of this triadic presentation, established how the external world is a projection of subjective mind and mind, as luminous innate awareness, existed ultimately as the substructural basis of all empirical phenomena.[31]

Thus, they understood by Emptiness and the ultimate, the non-substantiality of external things and the absence of mind–matter dichotomy.[32] This introduced a new, and indeed a rich, hermeneutic tradition in the understanding of 'the lack of own being' (*niḥsvabhāva, ngo bo nyid med pa*) and Emptiness.[33] They even commented on Nāgārjuna and Āryadeva using such interpretation.[34] Many Mādhyamikas such as Bhāvaviveka, Candrakīrti and Śāntideva refuted the Yogācāra idealism attacking especially their reification of the self-conscious awareness,[35] while others like Śāntarakṣita (eighth century) and Kamalaśīla (*c*.740–95) synthesized the Yogācāra idealism and Mādhyamika Emptiness by maintaining the Yogācāra theories on the conventional level.[36]

A very significant development in the history of debate on Emptiness in India is the division that began to form within the Mādhyamika school led by Buddhapālita on one side and Bhavya/Bhāvaviveka on the other. Their main discrepancy was over the logical methodology employed in establishing Emptiness in their commentaries on MK, I/1. Bhāvaviveka criticized Buddhapālita's logical establishment of Emptiness through apagogic reasoning (*prasaṅga, thal gyur*) and endorsed the logical method of autonomous inference (*svatantra, rang rgyud*) to establish Emptiness.[37] Candrakīrti later rebutted Bhāvaviveka's refutations of Buddhapālita and criticized Bhāvaviveka over his logical operation and a few other issues.

Tibetan doxographers called these two streams of Mādhyamika Rang rgyud pa (Svātantrika) and Thal 'gyur pa (*Prāsaṅgika) after the logical procedure they mostly adopted to establish the theory of Emptiness.[38] The issue of disagreement between these two, according to Mipham, was not the nature of Emptiness because their final understanding (*dgongs pa mthar thug*) of Emptiness was identical;

it was rather the exegetical emphasis and the logical procedure, which they adopted to delineate Emptiness. The Svātantrika line of thought was passed down through masters such as Jñānagarbha, Śāntarakṣita, Kamalaśīla,[39] of whom the last two became well known as synthesizers of the Yogācāra and Mādhyamika thoughts and also as pioneers of the Mādhyamika thought in Tibet. The Prāsaṅgika line thrived through the writings of Candrakīrti, Śāntideva *et al.*[40] and in the second millennium, it widely spread in Tibet through its famous advocates such as Atiśa (982–1054), the apostle of Later Propagation of Buddhism into Tibet, Jayānanda, Kanakavarman and their Tibetan counterparts.

Controversies during Early Propagation in Tibet

The earliest major religious conflict recorded in Tibetan history is perhaps the great contest between the advocates of Bon religion and the Buddhists during the Early Propagation of Buddhism in that country.[41] However soon after that there took place another debate of remarkable significance between the Chinese simultaneists/quietists led by Hwashang Mohoyen and the Indian gradualists/intellectuals headed by Kamalaśīla.[42] Now commonly known as the Samye debate, the controversy had as its main issue of debate, the viability of quietist non-mentation and non-conceptuality as a path to enlightenment.[43]

The debate, unlike most later debates through polemical writings, was supposedly held in the presence of King Trisong Detsan and had a final verdict whereby Hwashang Mohoyen, who represented the simultaneists, was defeated and his teachings banned while his opponent Kamalaśīla, who represented the gradualists, was given the victory and his system of thought decreed to be Tibet's national tradition.[44] Not only was it significant as the first controversy among Buddhists, particularly among the advocates of Emptiness, in Tibet, this debate left far reaching implications for the future of Tibetan Buddhism. However, not long after that, Buddhism declined in Tibet for a while following the assassination of Tri Ralpachen around AD 842.

Early debates in the Later Propagation

The beginning of the Later Propagation of Buddhism from the middle of the tenth century saw renewed scholarly activity on Emptiness and Mādhyamika school through luminaries such as Atiśa Dipaṃkaraśrījñāna (*c*.982–1054), Kanakavarman (eleventh century), Jayānanda (late eleventh century) Rinchen Zangpo (958–1055), Nagtsho Tshultrim Gyalwa (b. 1011), Ngog Loden Sherab *et al.* (1059–1109).[45] It was however Patshab Nyima Drak (b. 1055), a pioneering exponent of Candrakīrti's thought in Tibet, who brought out the explicit distinction of Prāsaṅgika and Svātantrika schools of Mādhyamika. While Patshab and his disciples followed Candrakīrti's Prāsaṅgika, Ngog Loden Sherab and his followers in Sangphu Neuthog College were said to have professed Svātantrika position.[46] Among them, Chapa Chökyi Seṅge (1109–69),[47] the famous logician is said to have, in a debate, challenged Jayānanda, the Indian master who was an active exponent of Candrakīrti's thoughts,[48] and to have composed a polemical work refuting Candrakīrti's position.[49] His students, Tsangnagpa Tsöndrü Seṅge (twelfth century) and Maja Jangchub Tsöndrü (d. *c*.1185) however followed Candrakīrti and are said to have opposed Chapa on the Madhyamaka viewpoint.[50]

Despite the differences and debates, the exposition and practice of Emptiness flourished during the Later Propagation and the Mādhyamika current formed a major subject in the various traditions that began to emerge.[51] Another major religious dispute that occurred in the early part of Later Propagation, though it does not impinge on Emptiness, was the controversy on the authenticity of certain Nyingma tantras. A few Sarma figures such as Gö Lotsāwa Khugpa Lhatse (eleventh century) and Chag Lotsāwa Chöje Pal (1197–1264) rejected them as spurious tantras which are Tibetan forgeries lacking Indian origin and wrote refutations of spurious tantras (*sngags log sun 'byin*)[52] provoking defence of the tantras from many scholars, particularly from the Nyingma.[53]

In the beginning of the thirteenth century, Sakya Paṇḍita Kunga Gyaltshan (1182–1251) attacked the quietist practice of non-mentation (*amanasikāra, yid la mi byed pa*) and White Single Means (*dkar po gcig thub*), which became popular in the Kagyu tradition.[54] He branded it Neo-Mahāmūdra (*da lta'i phyag rgya chen po*) or Chinese style Dzogchen (*rgya nag lugs kyi rdzogs chen*) and dismissed it as mere revival of quietist doctrine of Hwashang except for the name.[55] He also refuted Machig Labdön's *gCod* and Pha Dampa's *Zhi byed* practice and is said to have made critical remarks about Kadampa practices.[56] This master also criticized the logico-epistemological theories of Tibetan logicians such as Chapa. His criticisms and interpretations in his *Tshad ma rigs pa'i gter* marked a new era of logico-epistemology in Tibet known as the Later Pramāṇa (*tshad ma phyi rabs pa*) in contradistinction to Earlier Pramāṇa (*tshad ma snga rabs pa*) before him.[57]

Scholarship on Emptiness thrived throughout the Later Propagation forming a crucial component of Madhyamaka, Prajñāpāramitā, Maitreya's *dharma* and Vajrayāna studies. Major scholarly centres included Sangphu Neuthog, founded by Ngog Lekpai Sherab in 1073, and Thangsag seminary, founded by Zhangthang Sagpa Jungne Yeshe (eleventh century), the former mainly for Svātantrika and the latter for Prāsaṅgika.[58] Leading figures in the twelfth and early thirteenth centuries include Chapa, his students, Patshab's students and Chomdan Rigpai Raldi (late thirteenth–early fourteenth century) for the Kadampa tradition, Gampopa Sonam Rinchen (1079–1159), Phagmo Drupa (1110–70) and Karmapa Düsum Khyenpa (1110–93) for the Kagyupa, Sapaṇ and Sonam Tsemo (1142–82) for the Sakya and Kathogpa Dampa Desheg (1122–91), Śākya Dorje (twelfth century) and Nyangral Nyima Özer (1124–92) for Nyingma.[59] A certain *Zhi byed* scholar, Nyedo Mrawai Seṅge alias Tsöndrü Seṅge (1186–1247), student of one Naljor Seṅge, is also said to have taken great enterprise in Madhyamaka and defeated many scholars in debate.[60]

The fourteenth century witnessed a great burst of Buddhist scholarship in Tibet through a large number of the exceptional minds that Tibet ever produced.

Among them were Butön Rinchen Drub (1290–1364) of Zhalu, Dolpopa Sherab Gyaltshan (1292–1361) of Jomonang and Yagde Paṇchen (1299–1339). Butön, as mentioned earlier, is said to have refuted certain Nyingma tantras and also written tracts on Mādhyamika viewpoint[61] while Dolpopa became the champion of *gzhan stong* theory.[62] His formulation of *gzhan stong* absolutism not only became a notoriously contentious issue provoking considerable criticism and debate in his time and in successive generations after him but also split the Mādhyamika tradition in Tibet into exponents of absolutist *gzhan stong* and of negational *rang stong* viewpoint.[63]

Longchenpa Drime Özer, an alumnus of Sangphu Neuthog and student of Rigzin Kumārarāja (1266–1343) revolutionized Madhyamaka scholarship among the Nyingmapas. Special mention must be made of his exceptional systematization of Dzogchen into a highly complex and coherent philosophy firmly grounded on the Mādhyamika theory of Emptiness.[64] He criticized the viewpoints of Tsangnagpa and Maja on the assertion of thesis by the Mādhyamikas.[65] Since his days, he was accorded the highest place in Nyingma scholarly tradition and his works influenced subsequent Nyingma authors including Mipham, who held him and Rongzom Chökyi Zangpo as two great authorities in the Nyingma school. Other Mādhyamika adepts at the beginning of the fourteenth century were Barawa Gyaltshan Palzang (1310–91), Lama Dampa Sonam Gyaltshan (1312–75) and Nya Ön Kunga Pal (1345–1439).

Yagtrugpa Sangye Pal (1348–1414), though himself a Sakyapa, is said to have criticized the Sakyapas on certain doctrinal points and Bodong Paṇchen Chogle Namgyal is said to have rebutted the criticisms.[66] Bodong Paṇchen is also known to have rebutted the refutations of Candrakīrti by Rongtön Sheja Kunrig alias Śākya Gyaltshan (1367–1449), a Sakya pa master who, although linked to Prāsaṅgika, is known to be one of the last masters to espouse Svātantrika position.[67] The most outstanding Mādhyamika philosophers in the second half of the fourteenth century were however the Sakya master Redawa Zhönu Lodoe (1349–1412) and his student Tsongkhapa Lobzang Drakpa. Redawa apparently was the foremost exponent of Prāsaṅgika tradition in his days and a reinvigoration of Mādhyamika exegesis is credited to him.[68]

Tsongkhapa, the founding father of Gadanpa/Gelukpa[69] school, was no doubt one of the greatest masters in Tibetan history. With the help of his teachers and partners in the investigation, Redawa and Lama Umapa Tsöndrü Seṅge alias Pawo Dorje, and through visionary consultation with Mañjuśrī, Tsongkhapa arrived at an understanding and interpretation of Emptiness which differed from what was current until then.[70] His interpretation and exposition of Emptiness,[71] which his disciples ardently continued, started a new chapter of Mādhyamika studies in Tibet and led to the division of Tibetan Mādhyamikas into the Ngarabpas and their followers on the one hand and the Gelukpas on the other.[72] He and his followers refuted the understanding of Emptiness of the Ngarabpas such as Ngog and Thangsagpa as well as the quietist tendency among Kagyupas and Nyingmapas, and the absolutist *gzhan stong* theory of the Jonangpas.

Among his disciples were Gyaltshab Dharma Rinchen (1364–1432) and Khedrub Geleg Palzang (1385–1438), also known as Gyaltshab Je and Khedrub Je, who, formerly Sakya scholars, became his chief spiritual heirs.[73] Gyaltshab Je debated with both Yagtrugpa and Rongtön, and Khedrub Je is recorded as having defeated Bodong in a debate but his debate with Rongtön is supposed to have not happened although a date was set.[74] Among other active Mādhyamika scholars of this period are Je Sherab Seṅge (1383–1445), Müchen Konchog Gyaltshan (1388–1469), Paṇchen Gedun Drub, the first Dalai Lama (1391–1474) and the historian Gö Zhönu Pal (1392–1481). An interesting but obscure figure is Gungruwa Gyaltshan Zangpo (1383–1450), a student of Tsongkhapa, who nonetheless is said to have dissented from the Gelukpa understanding and preferred the view of Rongtön.[75]

Debates after Tsongkhapa

The rise of the Gelukpa school with the establishment of its three seats in the first quarter of the fifteenth century marked a new phase of Buddhist scholasticism in Tibet. The young Gelukpa school stood out distinctively from all other schools especially in the understanding of Emptiness and other Madhyamaka theories. Most debates on Emptiness to take place since then were polemical exchanges between the Gelukpas and the exponents of other schools. The earliest critics of the Gelukpa school, besides Rongtön, perhaps were Sazang Lotsāwa Mati Paṇchen (fourteenth century) and Dagpo Tashi Namgyal (1398–1458).[76]

Immediately following the generation that established the Gelukpa school in the fifteenth century, there arose a generation of outstanding Sakyapa scholars who strongly criticized Gelukpa Madhyamaka interpretations. Among the refuters was Tagtshang Lotsāwa Sherab Rinchen (b. 1405), who, formerly a pupil of Jamyang Chöje, converted to Sakya and attacked Tsongkhapa accusing him of the eighteen great burdens of contradiction (*'gal ba'i khur chen bco brgyad*) that his theory of validly established conventions entailed.[77] Gorampa Sonam Seṅge (1429–89) and Serdog/Zilung Paṇchen Śākya Chogdan (1428–1507), both students of Rongtön, were the two other refuters, making the trio of Sakyapa critics known as the *Go śāk stag gsum*.

Gorampa, in his *lTa ba'i shan 'byed theg mchog gnad kyi zla zer*, attacked the Zhantongpas and Gelukpas for espousing respectively an eternalistic extreme as Madhyamaka (*rtag mtha' la dbu mar smra ba*) and a nihilistic extreme as Madhyamaka (*chad mtha' la dbu mar smra ba*).[78] He also criticizes Tsongkhapa harshly in his commentary on the MA, *lTa ba ngan sel*.[79] Zilungpa Śākya Chogdan wrote his *rTsod yig tshigs bcad ma* and the *dBu ma rnam par gnes pa'i chos kyi bang mdzod lung dang rigs pa'i rgya mtsho*, a highly refined and elaborate exegesis of Madhyamaka intended as a polemic to refute the interpretation of the Gelukpas.[80] He is also said to have written an answer to *Dri ba lhag bsam rab dkar* on behalf of the Kagyupa meditators.[81]

The Sakyapa criticism certainly did not go unnoticed but attracted a series of replies from the Gelukpa scholars. Jamyang Gawai Lodoe, also known as Jamyang Legpa Chöjor (1429–1503), wrote a rebuttal of Gorampa's criticism in *lTa ba'i shan 'byed*,[82] and Sera Jetsün Chökyi Gyaltshan (1469–1546), the *yig cha* writer of Sera Jay College, composed elaborate replies to both Śākya Chogdan and Gorampa although the work was finished only later by Paṇchen Delek Nyima.[83] Nyaltön Paljor Lhundrub of Sera is said to have defeated Śākya Chogdan in debate.[84] Paṇchen Sonam Drakpa (1478–1554), the *yig cha* writer of Drepung Loseling, was another great scholar who refuted the criticisms against Tsongkhapa.[85]

The sixteenth century saw the rise of two major Kagyupa adepts in Madhyamaka exposition: Karmapa Mikyod Dorje (1507–54) and Drukpa Pema Karpo (1527–92). The eighth Karmapa, Mikyod Dorje, critcized in his commentary on MA, *Dwags brgyud grub pa'i shing rta*, the Madhyamaka views of Jonangpas, Śākya Chogdan, Bodong and Tsongkhapa.[86] Prior to this, he also wrote a commentary on Haribhadra's *Sphuṭārtha* interpretating the ultimate intent of Prajñānapāramitā literature to be that of Alīkākāravādin Madhyamaka (*rnam rdzun pa'i dbu ma*)[87] and solicited comments and criticisms. In reponse, Sera Jetsün composed his critique, the *gSung lan klu grub dgongs rgyan*, attacking Karmapa's understanding of Emptiness[88] and Paṇchen Sonam Drakpa is said to have also written a *gSung lan*.[89]

Pema Karpo, the prodigious Drukpa Kagyu hierarch, wrote as defence of the Mahāmudrā, Single White Remedy and *amanasikāra* practices the *Phyag chen rgyal ba'i gan mdzod*, a definitive work on Mahāmudrā. In it he rebutted both Sapaṇ's criticisms in *sDom gsum rab dbye* and Tsongkhapa's in *Dri ba lhag bsam rab dkar*.[90] He has also authored over a dozen polemical tracts including the *Klan ka gzhom pa'i gtam*, which rebuts the criticism that Kagyupa Mahāmudrā is identical with Hwashang's teachings.[91] These tracts contain his responses to queries and criticisms on a wide range of subjects from contemporary scholars, including his reply to Gomde Namkha Gyaltshan Zangpo (1532–92), who wrote a refutation of his *Phyag chen rgyal ba'i gan mdzod*.[92]

Among the leading Gelukpa scholars of this period was Paṇchen Lobzang Chökyi Gyaltshan (1570–1662), a master known for his ecumenical outlook. He reckoned the views of all Tibetan Buddhist traditions to be ultimately the same.[93] However, he wrote a reply to Tagtshang's refutation of Tsongkhapa, the *sGra pa shes rab rin chen pa'i rtsod lan*, and also the *Dris lan blo bzang bzhad pa'i sgra dbyangs*, a response to Śākya Chogdan's reply to Tsongkhapa's *Dri ba lhag bsam rab dkar*.[94] Another remarkable figure of this generation was Jonang Tāranātha Kunga Nyingpo (1575–1634), in whom the *gzhan stong* philosophy found a chief exponent but his efforts did not last long as the Jonang tradition was expunged with the fall of Tsangpa government in 1642.[95]

The fall of Tsangpa dynasty and the establishment of Gadan Phodrang government under the fifth Dalai Lama Ngawang Lobzang Gyatsho (1617–82) was the most significant event in the seventeenth century, which, although a political shift, had considerable impact on the religious setup. The Karma Kagyupas and

Jonangpas who enjoyed royal support during the Rinpungpa and Tsangpa rule faced persecution and the Gelukpa school rose to the status of a state religion in Tibet. The great fifth, like his Gelukpa contemporary Shar Kaldan Gyatsho (1607–77), was an ecumenical leader except for his reservations against the Jonangpas and Karma Kagyupas who suffered severely during his reign.[96] By contrast, the Nyingmapas and Sakyapas and some Kagyupas flourished immensely through his support.[97] Jamyang Zhadpa Ngawang Tsöndrü (1648–1721/2) was perhaps the most distinguished Gelukpa exponent of Madhyamaka in his days. He wrote a refutation of Tagtshang[98] and also attacked him in his doxographical work.[99] In 1709, he founded the Labrang Tashikhyil, which became since then a hub of Gelukpa scholarship in eastern Tibet.

Thuken Chökyi Nyima mentions a certain Lobzang Rinchen, a disciple of Jamyang Zhadpa who later went to Mindrolling and became a Nyingmapa, to have criticized Norzang Gyatsho's *Phyag chen gsal sgron* which is purported to establish the ultimate intent of Kagyupas and Gelukpas as one (*bka' dge dgongs pa gcig*). He is also said to have considered Maitrīpāda as Alīkākāravādin of Cittamātra school and Paṇchen Lobzang Chögyan's treatment of Mahāmudrā as untenable if not merely a provisional method to lead the ignorant.[100] Changkya Rolpai Dorje (1717–86) remarks that such comments should be discarded like a 'toilet-stone' (*'phongs phyis pa'i rdo*), and Thuken dismisses it as verbiage motivated by sectarian prejudice.[101]

Rolpai Dorje, the second Changkya and his predecessor Changkya Ngawang Lobzang Chödan (1642–1714) were both important Gelukpa Mādhyamika scholars.[102] Rolpai Dorje wrote numerous works on Madhyamaka including the Mādhyamika chapter in his *Grub mtha' thub bstan lhun po'i mdzes rgyan*, and his *dBu ma lta ba'i gsung mgur*, on which Mipham has commented.[103] The first one contains a lot of polemical remarks while the latter with a strong poetic fervour questions the view of scholars of all traditions including the Gelukpas. His students Konchog Jigme Wangpo (1728–91) and Thuken Chökyi Nyima (1737–1802) were both doxographers and eminent Mādhyamika scholars. The latter of the two authored the *Grub mtha' shel gyi me long*, an interesting doxographical work not only on Indo-Tibetan Buddhist traditions but on all creeds known to the author.[104]

Other Gelukpa savants of this century include Sumpa Khenpo Yeshe Paljor (1704–88),[105] Yongzin Yeshe Gyaltshan (1713–93),[106] Longdol Lama Ngawang Lobzang (1719–94/5), Gungthang Konchog Tanpai Drönme (1762–1822/3) and the ecumenical scholar, Balmang Konchog Gyaltshan (1764–1853), whose reconciliatory approach to the Madhyamaka view of the four major traditions is expressed in his *Bya gtong snyan sgron bdud rtsi'i bsang gtor*.[107] The Gelukpa school, under the auspices of Gadan Phodrang, was thriving undeterred and its scholasticism, embodied in the *yig cha* curriculum and upheld by pedagogical regime of training in debate, reached its climax.[108]

During this century, the *gzhan stong* 'heresy' banned under the great fifth also found new advocates in the persons of Kathog Rigzin Tshewang Norbu (1698–1755), the famous Nyingma historiographer, and Situ Paṇchen Chökyi

Jungne (1699–1774), the famous Sanskritist and grammarian.[109] Gene Smith observes that the latter was converted to *gzhan stong* philosophy through the efforts of the former.[110] This period also saw the birth of one of the most important Nyingma hierarch, Jigme Lingpa (1730–98),[111] the *gter ston* who wrote several works related to Madhyamaka and the Nyingma defence, *sNga 'gyur rnying ma la rgol ngan log rtog bzlog pa'i bstan bcos*. It was due to him and through the institutions associated with his students and three incarnations that there came about a great renaissance of the Nyingma tradition in the nineteenth century.

The renaissance unlike other major revivals in Tibetan history took place mainly in the Kham region and the leading virtuosi of this renaissance were Paltrul Ugyen Jigme Chökyi Wangpo, Jamyang Khyentsei Wangpo, Kongtrul Lodoe Thaye, Getse Paṇḍita Gyurme Tshewang Chogdrub (nineteenth century), Gyalse Zhanphan Thaye (b. 1800), Khenchen Pema Vajra (nineteenth century), Tertön Chogjur Lingpa (1829–70) and Mipham. Not only did this period see a massive burst of new scholarship and *gter ma* revelation but extant Nyingma literature was compiled, classified and reproduced. Simultaneously, there also occurred a revitalization of the Nyingma monasticism and the development of scholastic activity which Gene Smith called the Gemang movement.[112] The literary and institutional legacies left by these masters revolutionized for Nyingmapas the nature of Buddhist scholarship in general and of the Dzogchen system in particular.

However, the most significant development for Madhyamaka thought and Tibetan Buddhism as a whole in this century was the rise of the *ris med* movement, which occurred parallel to the Nyingma renaissance.[113] With figures such as Paltrul, Khyentse, Kongtrul and Mipham taking its lead, this movement came into being primarily to counteract the sectarian disputes and violence that frequently marred Tibetan Buddhism. In the past, there were violent clashes during the conflicts between the Sakyapas and Drigungpas in the thirteenth and fourteenth century, during the repression and reprisals between Kagyupas and Gelukpas in the seventeenth century, in the Jungar war of the eighteenth century to give few examples.

However, the immediate conflict, which inspired the *ris med* movement, were more local to Kham, particularly to Derge. First, there was the civil rebellion caused by Ngorpa envy of the Nyingmapa dominance of the Derge royal patronage through Jigme Lingpa's reputation, which resulted in the defeat of the Nyingmapa side and the imprisonment of the Queen of Derge and her Guru, the first Dodrub Jigme Thinley Özer in 1798. Then there was the war between Gelukpa monastery, Ba Chöde and Palpung affiliate, Pungri Gönnang, which Kongtrul worked hard to calm down, followed by the Nyagrong invasion under Gönpo Namgyal in 1863. The Lhasa army intervened and exterminated Gonpo Namgyal's forces only to take side with the Gelukpa factions in Kham and settle old scores against other traditions leading to prolonged religious feud. These successive religious violence saddened the to-be-promulgators of the *ris med* movement and the Derge royal household, the staunch patron of *ris med* masters, and veered them toward a religious ecumenism.[114]

In addition, the Gelukpa tradition was spreading in more parts of Kham and the Gadan Phodrang was extending its power over Derge.[115] The *ris med* masters were worried that the growing missionary influence of the Gelukpa school was leading to more religious prejudice and proselytization. In addition, they also had reservations against the Gelukpa scholasticism, which as codified in individual college *yig cha*s and professed through eristic study of formulaic argumentation, from their viewpoint, consisted largely of a narrow and linear understanding of Buddhism through a scholastic pursuit that is practically inept. Mipham particularly expressed such concern about the rigidity, verbosity and aridity of Gelukpa scholasticism founded on their *bsdus grwa* logic.

To stem this scholastic trend and the doctrinal controversies arising from partisan interpretations, the *ris med* teachers promoted the reorientation of religious study to the Indian originals and an eclectic approach of professing the essential teachings of all Tibetan traditions in spite of one's religious affiliation.[116] This perforce led to a new structure of scholarly curricula among the non-Gelukpa schools and to some degree of interdenominational learning and teaching. The *ris med* movement was thus the flower of the rich cultural and religious bonanza, which the nineteenth century saw.

Mipham and the later debates

Mipham's emergence among the Tibetan literati as a great scholar took place at the peak of this *ris med* movement, the Nyingma renaissance and the proliferation of Gelukpa scholasticism, each of them having considerable impact on the formation of his thoughts and the composition of his literary output in general and polemical writings in particular. The intellectual ferment and socio-religious milieu of this era especially shaped his writings on Emptiness and Madhyamaka. It was through the religious climate prevailing in his time that Mipham obtained both his ecumenical bent of mind and the polemical verve, which made him notorious as a refuter of the Gelukpa tradition.

However, Mipham's arrival at his understanding of Emptiness *per se* was not influenced by the religious developments in his time any more than by the inspiration he received from past masters such as Longchenpa and Rongzom.[117] Mipham generally tends to rely more on the Indian sources than on later interpretations insofar as understanding topics such as Emptiness is concerned. Therefore, apart from minor influences from his masters such as Paltrul, his milieu appears to have contributed nothing very significant to his understanding of Emptiness.[118] In this respect, Mipham is an original hermenuetician and an independent thinker working freely within the limitations set by the authoritative literatures.

Nonetheless, the nature of his exposition of Madhyamaka in depth and detail with a reconciliatory attitude as well as the polemical verve, can be seen as a direct outcome of the intellectual climate of his days. The element of the reconciliatory attitude in his Madhyamaka writings is no doubt as much an influence of his milieu – the sectarian strife, the *ris med* gurus and his involvement in the movement – as of his belief in Mahāyāna/Dzogchen inclusivism.[119] The reconciliatory approach was also a skilful, not to mention the best Buddhist, way of counteracting the growing conversion and domination of other denominations by the Gelukpa school.

In spite of being a sincere advocate of *ris med*, Mipham remained a staunch propagator of the Nyingma tradition. He championed the cause of advancing the petrified Nyingma scholarship, particularly in the domain of *sūtra*, to a highly sophisticated system *vis-à-vis* dialectical enquiry and philosophical exposition. His enthusiasm in doing this service to his school and the polemical verve he expressed in his writings, notwithstanding his *ris med* attitude, had ample justification. Mipham was discontent with the proliferation of Gelukpa scholasticism embodied in their *yig cha*s and their eristic mode of study. He also seems to have been disturbed by the disparity between the philosophical presentation of Emptiness in Indian sources and in the scholastic text books and by the over-systematization of profound topics to fit into the framework of ordinary minds. His qualms about Gelukpa scholasticism was all the more acute because certain Nyingmapas depended heavily on the Gelukpa *yig cha*s for their study.[120]

We find Mipham, in his commentary on *Madhyamakālaṃkāra*, exhorting the Nyingmapas to enjoy and be satisfied with the spiritual wealth that the Nyingma tradition enshrines and not mimic others.[121] Mipham's composition of philosophical works frequently drawing a clear-cut Nyingmapa stance on controversial issues, and the encouragement of those at whose behest he wrote, were motivated by these circumstantial reasons. Thus, his works gave Nyingma a *yig cha* of their own, although in their style of presentation and pedagogical approach, they are distinct from the Gelukpa scholastic text books. According to Mipham's claims, he has no intention to be argumentative and polemical but it was in the stride of building and defending his own system that his opponents got offended leading both sides into polemical controversy.

Causes for the polemical nature of his writings also include, *inter alia*, his zest for rationality and philosophical discussion as pedagogic instrument, intellectual training and purificatory investigation. Mipham is unequalled among the Nyingmapas in his logico-epistemological fervour and like Tsongkhapa, he took great pride in synthesizing the epistemology of Dharmakīrti with the ontology of Candrakīrti. Through writing elaborate commentaries, Mipham was also trying to bring to light specific texts whose significance in the Buddhist scholarly arena was being sidelined due to emphasis on other texts. This is reflected in his extensive commentaries on *Madhyamakālaṃkāra*, *Sūtrālaṅkāra* and chapter 9 of BA.

Mipham's efforts to revitalize Nyingma scholarship and build a philosophically strong and self-reliant Nyingma system did not go unnoticed. His commentary on *Madhyamakālaṃkāra* attracted criticism even from Nyingmapas such as Dodrub Damchö, for whom he wrote the *Dam chos dogs sel*.[122] However, it was the comments in his exposition of chapter 9, *sPyod 'jug sher 'grel nor bu ketaka*, which provoked fierce criticism from all corners of the Gelukpa world.[123] Among the Gelukpa refutations he received, he rebutted those of Pari Lobzang Rabsal and Drakar Trulku Tenzin Nyandra.[124] One scholar Japa [Alag] Dongag is said to have challenged Mipham in a direct debate on this commentary.[125] They are said to have debated again on Ngari Paṇchen's *sDom gsum rnam nges* I/1 dealing with the concept of Dzogchen being the general embodiment of gnosis (*rdzogs pa chen po ye shes spyi yi gzugs*) with Paltrul as witness. Khenpo Jigme Phuntsho also reports a debate with Mongolian Gelukpa scholar Lobzang Phuntsho in the presence of Jamyang Khyentsei Wangpo, Nyingma scholar, Dodrub Tanpai Nyima, Sakya scholar, Loter Wangpo and Minyag Kunzang Chödrak.[126] Kapstein mentions a debate between Mipham and Bada Gelek Gyatsho (1844–1904), the great synthesizer of Gelukpa and Jonang traditions and an important contributor to the Jonangpa curriculum.[127]

The polemical element pervades throughout most of Mipham's major Madhyamaka writings. In his *Nges rin po che'i sgron me*[128] and *bDe gshegs snying po'i stong thun seṅge'i nga ro*[129] Mipham criticizes both *gzhan stong* absolutism and Gelukpa Emptiness *qua* negation of hypostatic existence (*bden stong*). Other works laden with criticism of the Gelukpa understanding of Emptiness are the *gSung sgros*[130] and his commentary on MA, *'Jug 'grel zla ba'i zhal lung dri med shel phreng*[131] although both of these are compilations of his notes.

Among his opponents, Pari Rabsal was a senior Gelukpa figure of his day. He wrote elaborate criticism of Mipham in the *'Jam dpal dbyangs kyi dgongs rgyan rigs pa'i gzi 'bar gdong lnga'i sgra dbyangs*[132] composed in 1897 and few subsequent responses to Mipham's replies.[133] The polemical exchanges of Pari Rabsal and Mipham epitomized the intellectual encounter of this period so that it became known as 'the encounter of Sarma and Nyingma tiger and lion' (*gsar rnying stag seng gdong thug*).[134] Both Mipham and Pari Rabsal were accomodating masters in that they could agree to disagree and undertake sharp philosophical criticism in a socially amicable manner. They became great polemical partners exchanging presents as much as polemics and shared mutual admiration.

Drakar Trulku, Mipham's other main Gelukpa opponent but also a practitioner of *sNying thig* teachings, was a scholar from Drepung monastery and started writing rejoinders to Mipham's *Ketaka* at the age of twenty-three. He wrote three works rebutting Mipham. The first *Zab mo dbu ma'i gnad cung zad brjod pa blo gsal dga' ba'i gtam* written in 1888/9(?) inspired Mipham to write the rebuttal, *brGal lan nyin byed snang ba.*[135] The second, *'Jam dbyangs rnam rgyal gyis 'dod tshul la klan ka bgyis pa zab mo'i gtam*[136] is a selection of arguments from the first and the third, *Mi pham rnam rgyal gyi rtsod pa'i yang lan log lta'i khong khrag 'don pa'i skyug sman,*[137] was written in response to Mipham's reply to the first. This last response, a large piece of work, is not dated but seems to have not reached Mipham or to have been ignored by Mipham for its shallow arguments and abusive language as the title suggests. The other scholar known to have written a refutation of Mipham is Danma Lobzang Chöying, who authored the *Mipham rtsod lan* and also the *brGal lan legs pa'i gtam 'byed.*[138] There is a short rebuttal of his arguments in the *gSung sgros.*[139] Among others who seem to have engaged in a debate or discussion with Mipham were Bumsar Geshe,

Gunthang Jampaiyang, Ngaban Kunga, Norbu Tenzin and Khangmar Rinchen, some of whom later became admirers of Mipham.[140]

Among numerous other scholars of Madhyamaka in the late nineteenth century were Geuteng/Giteng Lobzang Paldan (1881–1944), who wrote many polemical tracts including the *rTsod yig 'jigs med rigs pa'i gad rgyangs* and *dGag lan chu yi 'phrul 'khor*[141] and Lubum/Dobi Geshe Sherab Gyatsho (1884–1968), a staunch defender of Gelukpa system who authored the *brTsod yig rigs pa'i rgad rgyangs la rnam par dpyad pa bskal pa'i me dpung,*[142] a criticism of Geuteng Lobzang Paldan's work and the *Klu grub dgongs rgyan la che long du brtags pa mi 'jigs seng ge'i nga ro,*[143] a response to Amdo Gedun Chöphel.

As a result of the intellectual revival mentioned earlier, the Nyingma school saw the rise of a large number of scholarly monks, mostly entitled Khenpos, at the turn of the twentieth century. These Khenpos continued the spiritual and intellectual legacies of previous masters such as Mipham. Among them were Khenpo Kunzang Paldan, Mipham's student and literary executor, Khenpo Zhanga, the ecumenical teacher who introduced the Dzongsar *yig cha* of thirteen Indian classics with annotated commentaries, Khenpo Yonga or Yontan Gyatsho (late nineteenth century) and Khenpo Ngaga or Ngawang Palzang (1879–1941), the great Dzogchen adept. However, the most distinguished advocates of Mipham's philosophical thoughts were Zhechen Gyaltshab Pema Namgyal, and Bodtrul Dongag Tanpai Nyima, whose *lTa grub shan 'byed gnad kyi sgron me* is a systematic exposition of Mipham's Madhyamaka thought.[144]

A revolutionary Tibetan thinker and a writer of the twentieth century was Amdo Gedun Chöphel, the renegade Gelukpa scholar-traveller who criticized the Gelukpa understanding of Emptiness.[145] Amdo Gedun Chöphel's composition of his *dBu ma'i zab gnad snying por dril ba legs bshad klu grub dgongs rgyan* ignited the last round of controversy on Emptiness provoking serious reprisals from the dominant Gelukpa school.[146] Among the rejoinders is the *Mi 'jigs seng ge'i nga ro* by Geshe Sherab Gyatsho, his erstwhile teacher and colleague from Gadan monastery. More recently a volume edited by Chukye Samten has come out from Tibet rebutting Gedun Chöphel's criticisms.[147]

Since the Chinese occupation in the 1950s, the debates on Emptiness, like other religious and intellectual activities in Tibet, have faced almost complete annihilation. The brutal and calculated destruction of religious and cultural life during the cultural revolution brought the whole Tibetan religion close to extinction inside Tibet although there is now a restricted regeneration of religious scholarship. Among the Tibetan diaspora, 'the debates on view' (*lta ba'i rtsod pa*) has been overshadowed by urgent political imperatives and other religious controversies such as the Dorje Shugdan issue.[148] However, Emptiness remains a hot topic for intellectuals of Tibet, the country which has been, as Newland describes, 'the only country governed by Mādhyamika philosophers'.[149]

3

WHAT IS NEGATED BY ULTIMATE ANALYSIS?

Debates on the delimitation of the Mādhyamika negandum

I do not negate anything for there is nothing to be negated.
(Nāgārjuna, *Vigrahavyāvartanī*, 63)

Emptiness, in the Mādhyamika system, is generally understood to be an apophatic concept. The delineation of Emptiness involves a process of negation using reductionist analyses and a philosophical procedure that is a *via negativa*.[1] Mādhyamika masters, from Nāgārjuna and Āryadeva through Candrakīrti and Śāntideva to Tsongkhapa and Mipham, widely employed in their writings sharp reasonings and arguments, which are highly analytical, reductionist and negational in their mode of investigation, to establish Emptiness. These reasonings are known as the Mādhyamika reasoning (*dbu ma'i rigs pa/gtan tshigs*) or the reasoning scrutinizing the ultimate (*don dam dpyod byed kyi rigs pa*). For brevity, I shall call them 'the ultimate analysis' here.[2]

The Mādhyamika thinkers employed the ultimate analysis to delineate the theory of Emptiness and eliminate the philosophical extremes (*anta, mtha'*) and elaborations (*prapañca, spros pa*), which are considered to be the main obstructions to enlightenment. We have already seen how, according to Nāgārjuna, these elaborations give rise to conceptualization and conceptualization breeds evil actions and thoughts, which lead to rebirth in *saṃsāra*.[3] In order to attain enlightenment and eradicate elaborations, one must realize Emptiness, which in turn is achieved through the negation of elaborations by an investigative analysis. Thus, the practice of establishing Emptiness through a negational and reductionist analysis remains at the heart of Mādhyamika philosophy and is the most fundamental method of Mādhyamika investigation into the reality of things.

Mādhyamika scholars generally agreed on the purpose and need of such negational *modus operandi* for delineating the theory of Emptiness, and the analytic and apophatic dialectical approach to Emptiness formed a salient characteristic of the Mādhyamika school. However, discrepancies developed among Mādhyamika scholars as to what exactly is being negated by the ultimate analyses. They could not agree on what things are empty of in the philosophy of Emptiness. The identification of what is being negated by the ultimate reasoning and the verification of the grasping, apprehension and elaboration that are obstructive to enlightenment turned into a highly controversial issue and gradually developed into a major topic of philosophical debates. It is these different identifications of what it is that is being negated – the negandum of ultimate analysis – and the debates on it between Mipham and his opponents that will form the subject matter of this chapter.

The delimitation of the negandum

The debates on the negandum, in a prototypical form, can be seen in the hermeneutic discrepancies among Buddhist scholars in understanding the doctrine of Emptiness and what is negated in the process of establishing Emptiness. The Buddha claimed that the world is dissatisfactory and impermanent and taught the path leading out of this *saṃsāra* to the tranquil and blissful state of *nirvāṇa*. Yet, he also declared that this world is empty and without substantiality.[4] These two forms of teachings, the first an empirical theory of the world presented, for instance, in the apparatus of the four noble truths and the chain of dependent origination and the second an ontological theory of the world as empty, can be seen as conflicting in that the latter theory of Emptiness appears to negate the former. In addition, the Buddha's teachings on the world as empty also seem to contradict the empirical experience and the common sense knowledge of the world as an evident reality.

The various hermeneutic endeavours shown by the Buddhist thinkers to resolve these *prima facie* contradictions between the existential teachings and empirical experiences on the one hand and the ontological theory of Emptiness on the other, and other interpretations to accommodate the various teachings of the Buddha into one coherent religio-philosophical system can be seen as different forms of delimitation of the negandum insofar as they are verifications of the real and the unreal, the true and the false, and the negated and the affirmed. In this respect, the identification of the negandum is not exclusively a Tibetan Mādhyamika issue; it pertains to the general Buddhist hermeneutics concerning Emptiness and reality. It comprises the disagreements among various schools and thinkers on the interpretation of what is negated by statements such as 'the world is empty' and 'there is no matter, sound etc.', in the *sūtra*s such as *Prajñāpāramitā*s and, in the Mādhyamika context, by the numerous dialectical arguments formulated by the Mādhyamika philosophers.

Although the debate on the identification of the negandum reached its culmination only in Tibet, the identification of the negandum, as a verification of what is negated in the philosophy of Emptiness, thus forms a key doctrinal point among Indian thinkers and contributed to the formation of diverse ontological schools. Among the Mādhyamikas, one would find in the criticisms of Buddhapālita by Bhāvaviveka and the latter by Candrakīrti, a precedent to the Tibetan debates on negandum. Their debates, which gave rise to the Prāsaṅgika and Svātantrika Mādhyamika bifurcation, were mainly on dialectical procedures and methodological issues but their arguments impinge on the issue of identifying the negandum of Mādhyamika reasoning.

In Tibet, the debate on Mādhyamika negandum reached its peak through Tsongkhapa. It seems that there was no major debate, except for some discrepancies, on the identification of the negandum until Tsongkhapa's days. Since then, the identification of the negandum has become, among Tibetan scholars, one of the most debated issues with profound religious and social implications. Tsongkhapa, as Magee notes,[5] gave it an unprecedented impetus by underscoring the importance of delimiting the negandum and by launching a rigorous criticism of the position held by most of his predecessors in Tibet. The emphasis on the importance of the identification of the negandum is certainly one of the outstanding contributions Tsongkhapa has made to the Mādhyamika study. It can be seen repeatedly in all his major writings on Mādhyamika philosophy. In his famous *Lam rim*, Tsongkhapa writes:

> For instance, in order to ascertain that a person is absent, one must know the person who is not there. In the same way, in order to ascertain the absence of self and absence of inherent nature, the self and inherent nature that is not existent must be properly identified, because unless the universal [image] of the negandum appears vividly, its negation cannot be correctly ascertained.[6]

The need to envisage the picture of the hypostatic existence in order to realize the lack of hypostatic existence is also reiterated in his *Drang nges*.[7] Without the clear picture of negandum, one would not grasp the concept of Emptiness although one may present several arguments on what does not exist and why. Similarly, in his commentary on *Madhyamakāvatāra* (MA), the *dGongs pa rab gsal*, he observes:

> If the picture of the hypostatic existence, which does not exist, and the negandum, of which [things] are empty, does not appear accurately in the scope of [one's] mind, it is impossible to ascertain properly the nature of the lack of hypostatic existence and Emptiness. Furthermore, because merely identifying the hypostatic existence which is contingently speculated by proponents of tenet systems, and the grasping of [such] hypostatic existence is not sufficient, it is very essential to properly identify the grasping of hypostatic existence, which persisted from beginningless time and is innate in both those who are and who are not converted by tenet system, and the hypostatic existence grasped by it. Without identifying that, even if [one] negated the negandum with reasoning, it would not do any harm to the grasping of hypostatic existence which persisted since beginningless time and the relevant purpose would be lost.[8]

Tsongkhapa and his followers insisted that correct definition of the negandum is of utmost cruciality to the delineation of Emptiness. He argued that over-wide delimitation of the negandum would lead to the extreme of nihilism just as over-narrow delimitation of the negandum would lead to the extreme of eternalism.[9] It is only through the correct definition of the negandum that one would understand Emptiness and be able to establish the Middle Way. After his death, his followers continued the emphatic treatment of negandum and to this day the identification of the negandum remains a fundamental procedure of Mādhyamika learning and pedagogy in the Gelukpa tradition. Studies of the Gelukpa exposition of the identification of the negandum has been done in the West by Hopkins, Thurman, Waymen, Napper, Newland, Magee and Lopez among others.[10] Yet the recent translation of the entire *Lam rim* makes by far the most significant contribution to the study of Gelukpa Madhyamaka. The Gelukpa theory that ascertainment of the negandum is a prerequisite to understanding Emptiness has been also seriously challenged by critics such as Śākya Chogdan and Amdo Gedun Chöphel.[11]

It is also Tsongkhapa's Gelukpa tradition to which Mipham devoted most of his refutation and from whom he received most opposition. Thus, the debate on the negandum, and for that matter on other Mādhyamika issues, which involves Mipham is largely between him and the Gelukpas. Sakyapas and Kagyupas, except those who are Zhantongpas, by and large hold the same position as Mipham on the subject of Emptiness. The Zhantongpas, most of whom are Jonangpas and some Kagyupas, Nyingmapas and Sakyapas, are attacked by Rangtongpas including Mipham although he also defended *gzhan stong* philosophy, on behalf of the Zhangtongpas, against the intensive attack from the Gelukpas.[12]

Let us now briefly look at what constitutes a negandum in Tibetan dialectics and the Mādhyamika system. The Tibetan word for the negandum is *dgag bya*, a rendering of the Sanskrit *niṣedhya* and/or *pratiṣedhya.* Literally 'a thing to be stopped', it is the gerundive of the verb *dgag,* to stop, refute, negate, etc. Tibetan scholars classified *dgag bya* into two kinds: the dialectical negandum, which is to be negated by dialectical reasoning (*rigs pa'i dgag bya*) and the cognitive negandum, which is to be eliminated by practising the path (*lam gyi dgag bya*).[13] In spite of the binary classification, the term *dgag bya* in a philosophical context is used mainly for the dialectical negandum and the verb *dgag* and its conjugations (*'gog, bkag, khegs/khog*) generally denote 'to negate'. Mipham divides the dialectical negandum into self/substantiality of person and of phenomena.[14] The cognitive negandum, which includes a wide range of defiling emotions and their impressions, is generally known as the thing to be eliminated (*prahāṇa, spang bya*) and/or obscurations (*āvaraṇa, sgrib pa*), and constitutes the cognitive impulses that a person must eradicate to achieve enlightenment in Mahāyāna soteriology.[15] It is generally agreed that the elimination of the latter can only be actualized through the elimination of the former by means of analytical reasoning.

Tsongkhapa, however, includes the mistaken grasping at inherent existence alongside inherent existence as the dialectical negandum and remarks that the latter is the primary negandum because the elimination of the cognitive grasping depends on the negation of its object.[16] This inclusion of cognitive grasping within dialectical negandum has, however, posed hermeneutic problems to some Gelukpas, particularly when juxtaposed with their theory that dialectical negandum cannot be existent even conventionally. In fact, Tsongkhapa himself states immediately after his division of dialectical negandum into subjective grasping and objective inherence that 'this negandum has to be non-existent' (*dgag bya 'di shes bya la med pa zhig dgos*). Magee discusses the binary concept of negandum presented in the *Lam rim* but completely ignores this problem by assuming every subjective negandum to be a cognitive or path negandum.[17]

Many Gelukpas like Sera Jetsün and Changkya, based on Tsongkhapa's division, argued that not every dialectical negandum has to be non-existent[18] while others maintained that every dialectical negandum as negandum of valid reasoning is necessarily non-existent or else it cannot be negated. Jamyang Gawai Lodoe, for one, contends in his rebuttal of Gorampa that the negandum of ultimate analysis cannot even exist conventionally. He accuses Gorampa of misreading Tsongkhapa in classifying the cognitive grasping under the dialectical negandum.[19] Thus, the Gelukpas are divided on whether or not the cognitive grasping to hypostatic existence, which is conventionally existent, is a dialectical negandum.

Now, the dialectical negandum can also be understood in two slightly different ways. In a strictly technical sense, which we find in the Tibetan *bsdus grwa*[20] and *rtags rigs*[21] textbooks, it refers to the combination of the subject (*chos can*) and the property negated (*dgag bya'i chos*) in a syllogistic formula (*prayoga, sbyor ba*). For example, in the argument:

> the subject *x*, is without hypostatic existence, because it is dependently originated

the negandum is the subject *x* put together with the property negated, hypostatic existence. 'Dependently originated' is the mark or reason. The negandum in this context is the subject of debate (*rtsod gzhi chos can*) conjoined with the property negated; it is the opposite of the probandum (*bsgrub bya*) or inferendum (*rjes su dpag bya*), that is, the lack of hypostatic existence of *x* which is proved and inferred by this formulaic presentation. Thus, this argument negates the 'hypostatically existent *x*' and establishes *x* without hypostatic existence or empty of hypostatic existence, that is, the Emptiness of *x*. According to the Gelukpa *bsdus grwa* logic, any such negandum should be non-existent for no existent entity can be negated by a valid reasoning.[22] Equally, through the rule of excluded middle, the negandum must be non-existent where the inferendum is existent and *vice versa*. These rules and such other principles of *bsdus gwra* logic persistently influence the Gelukpa reading, understanding and exposition of Emptiness.

In a more broad and less technical usage, a negandum is any property that is negated. It need not be strictly understood as the compound of the subject and the property negated presented through a syllogistic formula. For example, in the statements '*x* is without hypostatic existence' and 'there is no matter', hypostatic existence and matter are the neganda. Such statements on the Emptiness of all phenomena are commonly seen in the *sūtra*s such as the *Prajñāpāramitāsūtra*s, just as the formal dialectical arguments to delineate Emptiness are employed profusely in the *śāstra* literature of the Mādhyamika school.

While the Gelukpas mostly treated the negandum in a strictly dialectical sense, Mipham, like other Nyingmapas, saw the negandum more in this broad sense although he and Longchenpa frequently made use of syllogistic presentation and was well aware of the dialectical definition.[23] Both statements and syllogistic arguments such as the ones mentioned earlier are negational in their mode of enquiry, and establish Emptiness by nullifying the negandum. Therefore, the negandum is presented by both; the difference is one of methodology and syntax. Mipham, unlike the Gelukpas, was inclined to the latter use and construed all phenomena to be negated by Mādhyamika analysis whereas the Gelukpas mostly understood the negandum in a strict dialectial context and thus asserted that no existent thing can be negated by Mādhyamika analysis.

BA, IX/140 and negandum

The imperative to identify the negandum in order to establish its absence, from the viewpoint of the Gelukpas, is not a novel approach. They traced the need for the identification of the negandum to authoritative Indian sources. The source most frequently cited by the Gelukpas to substantiate their emphasis on the identification of the negandum is the following verse from chapter 9 of Śāntideva's *Bodhicaryāvatāra* (BA):

> Without contacting the constructed entity,
> Its non-entity cannot be grasped.[24]

According to them, the term entity (*bhāva, dngos po*) in the first line corresponds to hypostatic existence or hypostatically established entity (**satyasiddha, bden* [*par*] *grub* [*pa*]), and this verse shows how one cannot understand the non-entity or absence of hypostatic existence, in other words Emptiness, without knowing what hypostatic existence is. They further explain that in order to grasp the Emptiness of things, one must first have a clear mental picture or universal image (*arthasāmānya, don spyi*) of the negandum, the imaginary hypostatic existence, of which phenomena are empty. Without the clear idea of the negandum, one would not know what to negate and, without any conviction, fall into the metaphysical pitfalls of either excessive negation or inadequate negation. Hence, using this verse as support, they argue that ascertainment of the negandum *qua* hypostatic existence is very fundamental to understanding Emptiness.

Mipham, like many other Indian and Tibetan commentaries on the BA, however, understood the verse differently. He did not take the verse to show the importance of identifying or delimiting the negandum so as to understand Emptiness correctly.

Instead, he took it as an argument to prove how ultimately both entity and non-entity or existence and non-existence cannot be apprehended. Let us place the lines within the preceding and following verses and study it in its context. BA, IX/139–41 reads:

> If correct cognition were not correct [ultimately]
> Would not what it cognizes be false?
> Therefore, in the ultimate level
> Meditation on Emptiness would not be viable.
>
> Without contacting the constructed entity,
> Its non-entity cannot be grasped.
> Thus, for that which is a false entity,
> Its non-entity is also clearly false.
>
> Therefore, if in a dream a child dies,
> The thought that it did not exist
> Annuls the thought that it exists.
> That [thought it did not exist, however,] is also false.[25]

A detailed and critical study of these verses, appraising both philological and philosophical aspects, has been done by Paul Williams collating major Indian and Tibetan commentaries.[26] Hence, it shall not be repeated here. However, a brief study of Gelukpa and Mipham's commentaries on this verse will be instrumental in highlighting the contrast between their interpretations. All commentaries, including those by Gelukpa scholars and Mipham, take these verses as a proleptical discussion, in which Śāntideva answers a criticism levelled against the Mādhyamikas on the authenticity of meditation on Emptiness. The criticism made in stanza 139, ascribed to the Sāṃkhya, contends that if the correct cognition which discerns Emptiness were not valid in the ultimate sense, Emptiness could not be validated. In that case, it would follow that Emptiness is epistemologically unviable and meditation on it pointless because it is also a false concept. The next two verses present Śāntideva's reply, the first one being the actual answer and the second analogical.

Commenting on these verses in his commentary on chapter IX of the BA, the *Ketaka*, Mipham writes:

> Here, we [the Mādhyamikas] are not positing a tenet of a hypostatically established object of apprehension [in] maintaining Emptiness as a fact established by correct cognition. That is because without recourse to or dependence on the entities such as the vase, which are to be examined,[27] the 'non-entity' of those entities such as the absence of vase can never be grasped on their own. Therefore, because the notational or inferior Emptiness such as the absence of vase or Emptiness of vase is the aspect of those entities having been negated or eliminated, [we] assert the non-entity of any entity, which by nature is false, to be also clearly or definitely false. [If he says:] In that case, what is the point of meditating that 'all

> phenomena do not exist' because both entity and non-entity are equally false and untrue? For the time being, it is just [for] getting accustomed to the absence of inherent entity as an antidote to the attachment to entities, which, wonted since beginningless [time], fettered [us] to the worldly existence. Because both entity and non-entity are false, [meditating on the absence of entity] is just like the way in a dream, while dreaming of mourning over a son who was born and dead, the thought that the son did not exist is an antidote to the thought that the son did exist. That [thought the son did not exist] is also false.
>
> Thus, just as the fire created from scrubbing the two twigs together would burn both twigs, the fire of wisdom, which analyses all entities [and proves them] to be without hypostatic nature, will burn the entire thickets of all points of apprehension [we] posit as entities and non-entities. Thereby, when [one] abides in the [state of the] gnosis, which is pacified of all elaborations, such [state] is the great middle way, free from all assertions.[28]

Mipham clearly takes these verses to show that Emptiness *qua* absence of hypostatic existence is not absolute and therefore the notion of it must also be ultimately given up. It is not logical, after negating the concept of entities, to hold onto non-entity *qua* Emptiness of hypostatic existence. Without recourse to the concept of the existence of *x*, where *x* denotes an entity, the non-existence or Emptiness of *x* is not tenable and apprehensible for the latter is just an absence of the former. His theory is that the concept of non-*x* is entirely dependent on and relative to the concept of *x* that if *x* did not exist, the non-*x* cannot exist. Because the entity *x* (*bhāva, dngos po*) is proved to be false and untenable (*mṛṣa, rdzun*), the non-entity of *x* (*tadabhāva, de'i dngos med*) is also definitely false and untenable. Thus, to him the second verse shows how ultimate Emptiness presupposes the negation of all elaborations of entity, non-entity, existence, non-existence, production, non-production, etc., which is exactly the position the Gelukpas criticize as nihilistic because of over-wide delimitation of the negandum.

This can be further elucidated in the light of the connection that Mipham makes between this and Śāntarakṣita's *Madhyamakālaṃkāra*, 71ab:

> Because there is no production and so forth
> There cannot be non-production and so forth.[29]

While commenting on these and the lines following these,[30] Mipham cites BA, IX/140–1 and argues that because no negandum, be it existent, non-existent, both or neither, remain ultimately, their negation, that is their absence and the reasoning, words and thoughts used to delineate the absence would not remain either. As Williams has correctly noted,[31] Mipham interprets these verses, both in *rGyan 'grel* and *Ketaka*, in line with his binary concept of ultimate truths which he repeatedly expounds in most of his treatises on Madhyamaka. The mere absence of hypostatic existence (*bden med tsam*) is only a notational or relative ultimate and one must transcend this to reach the final ultimate free from elaborations (*spros bral*), the Great Madhyamaka (*dbu ma chen po*). We shall return to this bifurcation in Chapter 4.

Commenting on the verse 141, Mipham argues that it is not however pointless to meditate on mere absence of hypostatic existence. Notwithstanding the fact that the notion of Emptiness of hypostatic existence is itself unreal and must be discarded ultimately, it can help overcome the strong sense of wonted attachment to existence and substances if one meditates on it. If one has a dream in which one's child dies, and then one thinks in the same dream that the death is a mere dream and unreal, this thought, despite being as false as the thought of the child's death, would nevertheless help quell the suffering. The absence of hypostatic existence, like the second thought, is a provisional antidote but ultimately it is also false and untenable just as the other phenomena are. Mipham remarks that in spite of its provisional value, the notion of non-entity *qua* Emptiness, just like the notion of entity, must be ultimately abandoned to reach the gnoseological state where all elaborations, theses and apprehensions are stilled.

The Gelukpa interpretation on verse 139 does not differ from that of Mipham. However, the interpretation of the last two takes a different course. I shall cite Gyaltshab Je on the Gelukpa side here as his commentary is the most authoritative Gelukpa work on the BA representing the mainstream Gelukpa interpretation. Commenting on verses 140 and 141, he writes:

> It is very appropriate for us to have a false correct cognition which discerns Emptiness and also false Emptiness posited by it because the ascertainment of the negation, [in which] hypostatic entities are negated by the conceptual mind, is dependent on the appearance of the [mental] picture of the negandum. That eventuates because without having recourse to the entity conceived, that is, hypostatic existence, or [in other words] without the appearance of the [mental] picture of hypostatic existence, the lack of hypostatic existence cannot be grasped by the conceptual mind as the nature of Emptiness of hypostatic [existence]. Therefore, because the negandum, which is a false entity, is impossible, the negation of such negandum, [which is] the non-entity, is clearly false.
>
> The example for the previous case [of not apprehending non-entity without picturing entity]: [It is] like [how] without the appearance of the picture of the son of a barren woman to the conceptual thought the picture of the demise of the son of a barren woman will not appear. . . . The Emptiness of hypostatic existence, [which is established] after having negated it (i.e. hypostatic existence) is also false and not hypostatically existent. That shows the content of [the verses] such as 'If there is anything little that is not empty' in the *Mūlamadhyamakakārikā* (XIII/7).
>
> Because the Emptiness of hypostatic existence cannot be ascertained correctly unless the universal [image] of the hypostatic existence appears,

> it is necessary to be an expert in delimitation of the negandum in order to ascertain Emptiness. Owing to this reason, for example, when in a dream the death of a son is perceived, the thought that the son does not exist is an antidote to the thought that the son exists. However, the object to be eliminated and the antidote in the dream are false. In the same way, it is not contradictory for a false antidote to overcome a false object to be eliminated and a false correct cognition to perceive a false object. . . .[32]

Gyaltshab, like Tsongkhapa and many other Gelukpa masters, considers the first two lines of verse 140 as an important source highlighting the need to correctly identify the negandum in order to realize Emptiness. Unlike Mipham who took the verses more directly and reasoned that entity – existence – and its non-entity – lack of existence – are equally false in the ultimate because non-entity cannot exist without entity, Gyaltshab interprets the verses differently to argue that without the proper identification of the entity *qua* hypostatic existence, its non-entity, the absence of hypostatic existence, cannot be understood.

One of the striking differences between Gyaltshab and Mipham's positions seems to be the understanding of the word 'entity' (*bhāva, dngos po*) in this context. A similar discrepancy occurs while interpreting this word in verses 34 and 35 of the same chapter.[33] Although the meaning of *bhāva* vary according to contexts, it is clear that Mipham takes it to mean any entity here whereas the Gyaltshab and other Gelukpas equate it with hypostatic existence or hypostatically established entity. Hence, Mipham argues that a non-entity, say vaselessness or non-cupness, is ultimately untenable because such a concept depends on the concept of the entity, the vase or cup. To him, there cannot be a vaselessness or non-cupness without the vase and cup. Gyaltshab takes *bhāva* as hypostatic existence and *abhāva* to be lack of hypostatic existence and argue that without having the picture of entity *qua* hypostatic existence, the non-entity *qua* absence of hypostatic existence cannot be properly understood.

Similarly, Mipham paraphrases contacting or recourse (*spṛṣṭvā, reg pa*) as depending, hence 'without contacting entity' as without depending on entity, whereas Gyaltshab interprets contacting as picturing and understand 'without contacting entity' as without picturing the universal image of entity *qua* hypostatic existence. Gyaltshab thus argues that the non-entity *qua* Emptiness or absence of hypostatic existence cannot be understood without grasping the negandum, hypostatic existence through picturing its universal image. The main thrust of Gyaltshab's interpretation of the verses is therefore clearly the identification of the negandum or setting the target of negation but his arguments sound rather unconvincing and seem to deviate from Śāntideva's thought.

His reasoning in the first line of his commentary that both false cognition and false Emptiness are tenable in the Mādhyamika tradition because the understanding of negation of hypostatic existence is dependent on the picture of negandum lacks logical pervasion (*vyāpti, khyab pa*) between the reason and the thesis that they seem irrelevant. Similarly Gyaltshab's interpretation of the reasoning in 140ab does not connect coherently to the Śāntideva's conclusion in 140cd. There is the problem of pervasion in arguing that the non-entity of a false entity is clearly false because the non-entity *qua* Emptiness cannot be grasped without picturing the universal image of entity *qua* negandum. Gyaltshab's commentary focuses on proving two main points: (1) the picturing of the negandum is required for understanding Emptiness and (2) because of that, both entity *qua* hypostatic existence and non-entity *qua* absence of hypostatic existence are false but the points do not seem adequately connected to work as reason and conclusion.

Gyaltshab's interpretation of verse 140 faces further problems in connecting to the analogy in verse 141. Thus he does not directly apply the analogy of the death of the child and the thought that it did not exist to the notion of entity and non-entity as Śāntideva does. Instead, Gyaltshab supplies a different analogy of the barren woman's child and its demise to illustrate his point concerning the identification of the negandum. He then uses the analogy in verse 141 to demonstrate that false antidote can overcome false obstructions and false cognition can perceive objects, thereby rewinding the argument to answer the criticism in verse 139.

Another problem is in understanding Śāntideva's equation of both entity and non-entity as false. The Gelukpas generally accepted that entity *qua* hypostatic existence is even conventionally non-existent while the non-entity *qua* absence of hypostatic existence is the ultimate truth. Thus, there is a vast difference in the ontic status of the two. To resolve this, Gyaltshab reasons that the absence of hypostatic existence is false because it is not hypostatically existent whereas the hypostatic existence is false because it is not existent. Mipham does not encounter this problem as both entity and non-entity, according to him, are conventionally existent but ultimately false and unobtainable.

The Gelukpa interpretation of verse 140–1, diverging from most other commentaries, seems to have been influenced by their theory of limiting Mādhyamika negandum to hypostatic existence. If entity were understood as an existent phenomenon, as Mipham and several other commentators do, it would lead to the acceptance that existent phenomena are also negated by Mādhyamika analysis – a position which they ascribed to the Ngarabpas and considered nihilistic. Entity in this context, therefore, has to be understood as hypostatic existence. Now, according to the Gelukpas, such hypostatic existence does not exist even conventionally and therefore it would be wrong to consider Emptiness or lack of hypostatic existence to be dependent on it. Thus, the understanding of Emptiness is not dependent on the entity *qua* hypostatic existence but rather on the proper understanding of this hypothetical hypostatic existence. To this effect, they bring in the mental picture or universal image, and reason that without a clear picture of the negandum, that is, hypostatic existence, its absence or Emptiness cannot be apprehended fully.

Gyaltshab and the Gelukpas, as Williams observes,[34] seem to cite 140ab to support the importance of identifying the negandum merely because it is from an authoritative source. The verse does not explicitly or even implicitly show the identification of the negandum if read independently of the commentaries. Mipham does not take this verse to imply such imperatives. According to him, it is just a reasoning that non-entity cannot be apprehended without recourse to entity, and because the entity is false, its non-entity should be false. Why would identification of hypostatic existence be a difficult philosophical point and why would it have to be said so emphatically? After all, it is what sentient beings are accustomed to from time immemorial. Thus, the whole emphasis on identifying the negandum, from Mipham's viewpoint, is superfluous.

Mipham must have been fully aware of the emphatic use of this verse by Gelukpas as an authority stressing the need of identification of the negandum. He was also definitely aware of Gyaltshab's commentary on this and the disparity between Gyaltshab's and his own interpretations. However, Mipham surprisingly does not refute Gyaltshab's interpretation here as he did in the case of many other verses in his commentary. Nonetheless, it is clear that Mipham took the opportunity to underline his position as regards the ultimate understanding of Emptiness.

Some Gelukpa criticisms of the Ngarabpa position

The stark difference between the Gelukpas and proponents of the Ngarabpa viewpoint is the delimitation of negandum, to only hypostatic existence by the former and to all phenomena by the latter. The thrust of the Gelukpa stress on the negandum is to point out that the Mādhyamika dialectical negandum is a hypostatic existence and not all phenomena as most of the non-Gelukpa thinkers understood. Tsongkhapa, in his *Lam rim,* mentions two groups of opponents: those who profess an over-wide delimitation of the negandum and those who profess an over-narrow delimitation of it. He devotes most of his criticism against the first category. The non-Gelukpa thinkers who asserted that the ultimate analyses negated all phenomena fall within the first category.[35] According to the Gelukpas, it is sheer nihilism to claim that the ultimate reasoning negates all phenomena.

Tsongkhapa mentioned two main problems that this theory entails. First, negating all phenomena destroys the whole spirit of Mādhyamika philosophy by hitting its central concept of dependent origination.[36] If conventional phenomena such as matter, sound, production, cessation, etc. were negated by the ultimate analysis, the theory of dependent origination would not be tenable. Denial of dependent origination is not only a nihilistic view philosophically, but it also destroys the fundamental practice of seeking enlightenment through the knowledge of the true nature of things, namely, dependent origination. Second, if the words and reasoning utilized in the ultimate analyses were empty, how can they ever be able to establish the Emptiness of other things?

Tsongkhapa and his followers strongly proclaimed that the whole point of conducting the ultimate analyses is to prove that everything is empty of inherent and hypostatic existence and therefore dependently originated. The ultimate analyses that establish Emptiness must not harm dependent origination but reinforce it. It is the unique characteristic of the Mādhyamika tradition to deny existence of even a speck of inherent entity established by its own being (*rang gi ngo bos grub pa'i rang bzhin rdul tsam yang med pa*) and at the same time assert all concepts of *saṃsāra* and *nirvāṇa* (*'khor 'das kyi rnam gzhag thams cad khas blangs pa*) such as production, affirmation, negation, etc.[37] Hence, an ultimate analysis should not negate all phenomena but only hypostatic existence, inherent nature and own being. Let us take a sample of the ultimate analysis to study this more closely. Nāgārjuna in the first verse of the chapter of his *Mūlamadhyamakakārikā* (MK) reasons:

> Neither from itself, nor from other[s]
> Nor from both or from without cause
> Does any entity anywhere
> In any time arise.[38]

This reasoning, known as 'the Analysis of Cause: the Diamond Splinter (*rgyu la dpyod pa rdo rje zegs ma*)', which I call here 'the production analysis', is one of the most well-known analyses used by the Mādhyamika scholars to delineate Emptiness, and has become subjected to different interpretations and subsequent debates both in India and Tibet. The reasoning proves the negation of arising or production from different causes through the use of tetralemma (*catuṣkoṭi, mtha' bzhi*) method. It is commonly seen in the following syllogistic format in many commentaries:

> All entities, the subject, are without production because they do not arise from themselves, others, both or neither (*ex nihilo*).

The Gelukpas argued that an ultimate analysis of this kind does not refute production *in toto*, but only hypostatically existent production (*skye ba bden par grub pa*), inherent production (*rang bzhin gyis skye ba*) or production at the ultimate level (*don dam par skye ba*). Thus, instead of taking the reasoning directly, they paraphrased the predicate of the reasoning, 'without production' as 'without hypostatically existent production' and argued that what is negated by this is a hypostatic production and not production as such (*skye ba tsam*).

Citing the MK and other texts profusely, Tsongkhapa accused those who accepted the production analysis to negate production, of misunderstanding the scope of Mādhyamika reasoning and the meaning of Emptiness as the substantialists have done.[39] The substantialists such as the Vaibhāṣikas are said to have taken the Mādhyamika concept of Emptiness as a nihilistic theory, which defies empirical realities and thus debase the Buddha's teachings of the middle way. Tsongkhapa comments that they have misconstrued Mādhyamika negation of inherent production as the negation of production itself and have thus accused Mādhyamika of nihilism. All contradictions raised by the substantialists in chapter 24 of the MK would befall those who negate general production.[40] Tsongkhapa is here referring to the argument in which Nāgārjuna's opponents argue that if everything is empty, there would not be any production and cessation, and without them, there cannot be dependent origination, and that consequently theories of the four noble truths, the paths and stages, the three jewels, the law of cause and effect and all worldly conventions would become untenable.

In his rebuttal of this criticism, Nāgārjuna expounds his theory of two truths and the co-referential nature of Emptiness and dependent origination. He explains how the Buddha dispensed his teachings relying on the two truths, how the conventional truth leads to the realization of the ultimate truth, how profound and subtle Emptiness is and how the Buddha was reluctant to teach it, how everything that is empty is dependently originated and the *vice versa*, and how features such as production and so forth are possible to that to which Emptiness is possible. He reverses the refutations used by his opponents against themselves by arguing that if things were absolute and hypostatically existent, they cannot be produced, and hence dependent origination, etc. would not be possible in their system.[41]

What Tsongkhapa and his followers want to underline is that conventional phenomena are not negated by Mādhyamika reasoning. He observes that it is a simplistic understanding to think that conventional phenomena such as vase are negated merely because they cannot be found in their parts when being investigated.[42] Were all phenomena negated, the most fundamental concept of dependent origination would be at stake. Not only is it possible to deny inherent existence and accept phenomena such as production, cessation, etc. the combination of such denial and acceptance is the unique feature of Mādhyamika philosophy. Using the reasoning, which delineates the lack of inherent existence to negate the dependent phenomena of production, etc., is like reducing a divine deity to a devil. Such an act will only obstruct the correct understanding of Madhyamaka.[43]

Both the Gelukpas and Mipham accept the two levels of existence, and that in the ultimate ontic mode (*gnas tshul don dam par*) everything including production does not exist and in the conventional appearing mode (*tha snyad snang tshul la*) things exist. According to both parties, the contradictions mentioned in chapter 24 are inevitable if one either asserts production and so forth to exist ultimately or to not exist even conventionally. Holding either of the positions is clearly an extremist viewpoint. They have no disagreement inasmuch as the conventional existence of phenomena or lack of the ultimate existence is concerned. The main issue of disagreement here is what is actually negated by an ultimate analysis such as the production analysis, and what, from the viewpoint of the ultimate analysis, is non-existent.

Mipham, adhering closely to Ngarabpa philosophers, took the ultimate analyses such as the production analysis to negate all phenomena without exception because nothing can withstand the scrutiny of such analysis. If there is anything that remains when being investigated by the ultimate analysis, it ought to be by nature absolute and inherently existent. Since nothing can resist the reductive analysis employed to establish the ultimate truth, no entity, and for that matter even non-entity, can exist on the level of the ultimate truth. Like most of the Nyingma, Sakya and Kagyupa thinkers, he took the negation of existence, non-existence, matter, sound, smell, taste, etc. in the *sūtra*s and Mādhyamika literatures literally.

Thus, it is not just hypostatic existence that is negated but all phenomena ranging from matter to omniscience (*gzugs nas rnam mkhyen bar gyi shes bya'i chos thams cad*).[44] However, because one asserts the dependent existence of things on conventional level, one is free from the contradictions mentioned in chapter 24 of MK. Thus, the theory of dependent origination, the four noble truths, the paths and stages, the three jewels, the law of cause and effect and the worldly conventions can work perfectly on the conventional level, when no such ultimate analysis is conducted, although they are untenable at the ultimate level.

The second problem, which the Gelukpas raised, has to do with the validity of the words and reasoning used in the ultimate analysis if they are empty and to be negated themselves. One of the frequent arguments of the Gelukpas is that if all phenomena are negated and not existent at the level of the ultimate analysis, words and reasons used in the analysis would also have to be negated. How can such words and reasons then analyse or negate other things? The refutation made by substantialists that were all things without inherent nature, the Mādhyamika words or reasoning would also be without inherent nature and therefore incapable of negating the inherent nature in other things would befall the Mādhyamikas. Here, they are referring to the first verse of *Vigrahavyāvartanī* where Nāgārjuna's opponents argue that if everything is without the inherent nature, words such as 'the vase is empty' would also be without the inherent nature.[45] Consequently, all such statements and reasons would be false and incapable of negating inherent existence.

According to Tsongkhapa, the substantialists misunderstood the Mādhyamika negation of inherent nature of phenomena such as vase, production, etc. as the negation of phenomena themselves. As a result, they argued that words and reasoning utilized to negate inherent existence and establish Emptiness would not be capable of doing so.[46] However, from Tsongkhapa's viewpoint this criticism does not affect the Mādhyamika because only inherent nature is negated and conventional reasoning, words and persons exist and Emptiness can be established by them. The dependently originated words, although they may be without inherent nature, can effectively negate inherent existence. From his perspective, the contradiction raised by the substantialists definitely fall on those proponents who assert the ultimate analyses to negate all phenomena.

However, Tsongkhapa's reading of the *Vigrahavyāvartanī*, verse 1 although it sounds very coherent, seems to diverge from the original argument presented in the verse. The verse clearly raises the contradiction that if everything, including the Mādhyamika words, is without inherent nature, how can words which are without inherent nature possibly negate inherent nature. It does not explicitly question the negation of all phenomena as Tsongkhapa interprets. The fear of the substantialist is that if words did not have inherent existence, although they are existent, such words would not be able to negate inherent existence in other things. Nāgārjuna replies by saying that his words are without inherent nature but dependently originated and that they can, like one magical illusion overcome the other, negate inherent nature notwithstanding their lack of inherent nature.[47]

To Mipham, such acts of negation and delineation are possible on the conventional level where the theory of dependent origination is tenable. The act of establishing all things as empty is a conventional phenomenon and is a valid function from the conventional viewpoint. On the ultimate level, nothing is found, nothing exists and all acts of negation, affirmation, etc. are not tenable. Hence, even the delineation and realization of Emptiness cannot be accepted on the ultimate level.

What is 'hypostatically existent' and when does one negate?

It is not a unique tenet of the Gelukpas that a hypostatic or inherent entity is not existent and negated by Mādhyamika reasoning. The Gelukpas and their opponents such as Mipham generally agreed insofar as the negation of hypostatic existence is concerned. They also had no great discrepancies over the hypothetical description of hypostatic existence as an absolute, permanent, independent, inherent, reified substance, and that were such a thing to exist, it would resist the ultimate analysis. Mipham remarks in his *rGyan 'grel:* 'For instance, what is hypostatically existent is generally known as that which can withstand ultimate analysis and most people understand it likewise' and 'if there is anything that is not repudiated or negated after being analysed by ultimate analysis, that would be hypostatically existent'.[48] He elaborates that, speaking hypothetically, if an atom were hypostatically existent as a singular entity, it cannot be relative to any other thing and nothing could be derived from it. Were anything hypostatically existent, it cannot be known and no other thing except 'it' can exist.[49]

In his *'Jug 'grel* and *gSung sgros* he says, when the conventional phenomena, scrutinized by the ultimate analysis, cannot resist the analysis, they are said to be without hypostatic existence, and if they can withstand the analysis, they are considered hypostatically existent.[50] He writes in his *'Jug 'grel*:

> When the ultimate analysis examines the conventional vase of shared appearance, nothing, which can withstand the analysis, is obtained or apprehended. Then, [it] is termed as 'not apprehended by the correct cognition of ultimate analysis, ultimately non-existent, empty of own being and without hypostatic existence that can resist analysis'. There is no other definition of hypostatic existence and definition of lack of hypostatic existence apart from that.[51]

In his exposition of the negandum in his *dGongs pa rab gsal*, *Drang nges* and *Lam rim*, Tsongkhapa treats in detail the definition of what is hypostatically existent in both Svātantrika and Prāsaṅgika. I shall only present the gist here. In the Svātantrika system, a thing is considered to be hypostatically existent if it exists in its objective mode (*rang gi sdod lugs su*) without being posited because of its appearance to subjective thought (*yul can blo la snang ba'i dbang gis bzhag pa min pa*). Explaining this, he writes in his *dGongs pa rab gsal*:

> Taking it thus, that which exists by the way of abiding objectively and not by appearing to thought or by being posited by thought is hypostatically, ultimately and truly existent and the apprehension of such is the innate grasping to hypostatic existence.[52]

He equates what is hypostatically existent (*bden par yod pa*) with the ultimately existent (*don dam par yod pa*) and truly existent (*yang dag par yod pa*), and defines the ultimately existent or truly existent as 'that which exists as ontic reality without being posited by thought' (*blo yis dbang gis bzhad pa min par don gyi sdod lugs su yod pa*) and as resistant to analysis (*rigs pas dpyad bzod*).[53] The Svātantrikas, according to Tsongkhapa, understood a thing to be hypostatically existent if it existed independent of subjective cognition. Whatever is posited by subjective cognition is conventional and what is ultimately existent is the reverse.[54] However, he argues that the Svātantrikas accepted a degree of objective reality in what is posited by subjective cognition. Although there is no objective reality independent of subjective cognition, there is yet some objectivity as posited by cognition, which is not purely a nominal construction. Thus, there is some hypostatization. The Prāsaṅgikas, on the contrary, rejected such objectivity posited by subjective cognition.

The Prāsaṅgikas surpassed the Svātantrikas in negating all kinds of reality or objectivity. If there is anything that exists apart from being merely posited through its designation by a label (*ming gi tha snyad kyi dbang gis bzhag pa*), it would be hypostatically existent. He writes in his *dGongs pa rab gsal*:

> Apprehending [something] to exist, not as posited merely through the designation of a label, as mentioned before, but apprehending [something] to exist hypostatically, ultimately, truly, and by its own being, own characteristics and inherent nature is innate [grasping]. The object conceived by it is hypothetically the definition of hypostatic existence.[55]

It is a unique Prāsaṅgika perspective to see everything as posited by conceptual thought (*rtog pas bzhag pa*); to assume otherwise is reification or hypostatization. In Prāsaṅgika system, what is hypostatically, ultimately and truly existent is equivalent to what is established (*grub pa*) by own being (*ngo bos*), by own/individual characteristics (*rang mtshan gyis*) and by inherent nature (*rang bzhin gyis*). While in the Svātantrika thought, only the first three are equivalent, as they accept conventional existence of the last three, the Prāsaṅgikas treated all six as equivalent, thus rejecting all six even on conventional level.[56] Discussing what is established by its own characteristics in the Prāsaṅgika, he explains in his *Drang nges* that a thing is established by its own characteristics if the referent of the designation used for it is found when thoroughly searched by ultimate analyses (*tha snyad btags pa'i btags don btsal ba'i tshe na rnyed pa*).[57] An entity established by its own being and own characteristics must exist through its ontic mode (*rang gi gnas lugs kyi dbang gis yod pa*) and would resist analysis (*dpyad bzod*).[58] On the definition of what is inherent nature, Tsongkhapa writes in his *Lam rim*: 'Therefore, that which is established not through being posited by internal thought but objectively through its own being is that [which is] called self or inherent nature.'[59]

Drakar Trulku repeats Tsongkhapa's definition of what is hypostatically existent and the corresponding innate grasping in Svātantrika and Prāsaṅgika thought. He says, that which is established from the point of ontic reality without being posited through appearing to an unmistaken cognition (*blo gnod med la snang ba'i dbang gis bzhag pa ma yin par don gyi sdod lugs kyi ngos nas grub pa*) is hypostatically existent in Svātantrika system. In Prāsaṅgika thought, a thing is hypostatically existent if it is established from the point of objective nature and not merely imputed by conceptual thought (*rtog pas btags pa tsam ma yin par yul rang ngos nas grub pa*).[60]

Mipham attacked this distinction arguing that all Mādhyamika scholars accept all things to be imputed by conceptual thought insofar as they lack any inherent objective truth.[61] It is a sheer mistake to consider it a unique Prāsaṅgika understanding. Although it may be argued that there is a difference because Svātantrikas accepted conventional entities with their own characteristics, which Prāsaṅgikas rejected, that assertion, he says, is only on the level of delineating the relative or notational ultimate. Citing MA, VI/25, Mipham also contends that Prāsaṅgikas too accept conventionalities on the basis of being posited through appearing to the unmistaken cognition.[62] The distinction of conventionality *qua* what is posited through appearing to unmistaken cognition and conventionality *qua* what is imputed by conceptual thought between Svātantrika and Prāsaṅgika does not solve any problems. In addition, if conventionality in the Prāsaṇgika system is defined by being imputed by conceptual thought, even conceptual constructs such as the creator Īśvara and Prakṛti would be conventionally existent.[63] Mipham further queries whether or not the conceptual thought in question is a mistaken thought which superimposes what is not objectively existent. If it is, the Buddha would not know any conventional phenomenon as he does not have such mistaken conceptual thought. If not, it would follow that things are not entirely superimposed by subjective thought. He continues his criticism asking which of the three types of conceptual thought[64] constitutes the conceptual thought in question.[65]

Tsongkhapa and Mipham concur in the description of the inherent nature and equally deny the existence of such inherent nature. They explain that the lack of such inherent or hypostatic substance in a person is the Non-self of person (*pudgalanairātmya, gang zag gi bdag med*) and its absence in other phenomena is the Non-self of phenomena (*dharmanairātmya, chos kyi bdag med*).[66] One must, however, note that both Tsongkhapa and Mipham in their commentary of MK, XV/2 present an antinomical treatment of reality *qua* Emptiness as the inherent nature with tripartite attributes. Hence, they did not always understand inherent nature as synonymous to hypostatic existence, which has to be entirely negated.[67]

In spite of the agreement in defining what is putative hypostatic existence, the Gelukpas and Mipham differed in asserting what is being negated by the ultimate analysis and what is empty. To the Gelukpas, the dialectical negandum is strictly limited to hypostatic existence and no empirical phenomena, such as production, is or could be negated. Both Tsongkhapa and Mipham agree that all conventional phenomena are unfindable (*ma rnyed pa*) under the scrutiny of the ultimate analysis, and that what is unfindable is also considered non-resistant or non-immune to the analysis (*rigs pas dpyad mi bzod pa*).[68] The point they differ on is whether or not all that cannot withstand the analysis are negated by such analysis. To Mipham, an ultimate reasoning such as the production scrutiny investigates the nature of things and does not find them; therefore, he regards all things as being negated. Nonetheless, its being negated does not mean it is found to be non-existent. Thus, although from the purview of ultimate analyses, things do not exist, and therefore are considered negated, they are certainly not proved to be non-existent.

Tsongkhapa makes an explicit difference between not being capable of withstanding/resisting the scrutiny (*rigs pas dpyad mi bzod pa*) and being assailed/negated by the reasoning (*rigs pas gnod pa*).[69] He argues that the mere reason that production, etc. is not found under the scrutiny of the ultimate analysis, or the fact that production, etc. cannot withstand the ultimate analysis does not mean that production, etc. are entirely negated by it. A thing is negated only when it is not found by the analysis, which should find it were it existent.[70] Ultimate reasonings such as the production scrutiny are investigations seeking ultimate reality or absolute nature of things, and as such, they are called ultimate reasoning and they exclude conventional things from their scope of investigation. The inferential cognition based on an ultimate analysis would not apprehend conventional phenomena because conventional things are not objects which are sought by such analysis. One could say that they cannot withstand the analysis because they are not found by the ultimate reasoning, but they are not negated as they are not confirmed to be non-existent. Tsongkhapa says it is just like sound and visual perception; it cannot be said sound is negated by visual perception just because it is not heard by it.[71]

The ultimate reasonings are investigations looking into the absolute or inherent nature; they ought to find such inherence in production, etc. if there exist any. Because they do not find any such inherent or absolute nature, such a nature is said to be negated. Tsongkhapa compares it to searching for a vase in the east.[72] If one is supposed to find out whether or not a vase is there in the eastern direction, then one can rule out the existence of a vase in the east when one does not find it. However, that does not negate the general existence of a vase. Other vases could exist elsewhere beyond the range of the search. Existence of conventional things, to Tsongkhapa, is like the vases elsewhere, outside the scope of the investigation. Not finding them during and at the level of the ultimate analysis does not negate their existence, for such analysis is only focused on finding inherent or hypostatic existence, not *mere* existence.

Thus, Tsongkhapa and Mipham clearly differed in asserting what the object of investigation (*dpyad don*) is. Tsongkhapa took only inherent and hypostatic nature of production to be the subject of the ultimate analysis, while Mipham included both production and its inherent or hypostatic nature within the scope of the ultimate analysis.[73] To negate (*dgag*) something in Tsongkhapa's thought is to confirm it to be non-existent while Mipham considered a thing negated when it is not found by the analysis searching for it. Thus, only inherent or hypostatic production is negated according to Tsongkhapa whereas even general production, like all other phenomena, is negated according to Mipham.

Furthermore, to assail something with correct cognition (*tshad mas gnod pa*) in Tsongkhapa's thought is to invalidate that point or thing and prove the cognition of it wrong even conventionally, like the notion of a snake is assailed by the knowledge of the rope. To Mipham, every phenomenon is prone to be assailed by the ultimate cognition as their existence can be refuted by it. Ultimate cognition is superior to conventional cognition; thus, the former can logically assail the latter. Invalidation of phenomena on the level of ultimate analysis does not however terminate the conventional status of things. Tsongkhapa held phenomena to be only empty of hypostatic existence but not of themselves. On the contrary, Mipham argued that everything is empty of itself on the level of the ultimate analysis. He refuted the Gelukpa thesis that 'the vase is not empty of vase but of hypostatic existence' because, to him, the vase is not merely empty of hypostatic existence but empty of vaseness on the ultimate level.

Figures 3.1 and 3.2 may clarify the difference between Tsongkhapa's and Mipham's usage and equations of different terms. They show that both Tsongkhapa and Mipham accept what is found (*rnyed pa*) under ultimate analysis as immune to analysis (*rigs pas dpyad bzod*) and what is not found as not immune. The same

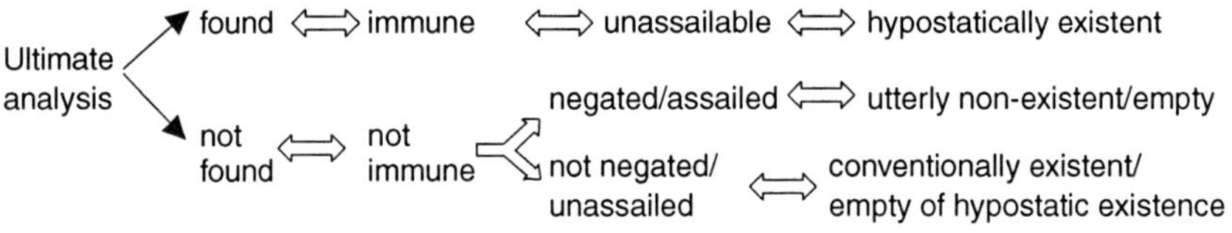

Figure 3.1 Tsongkhapa's equation.

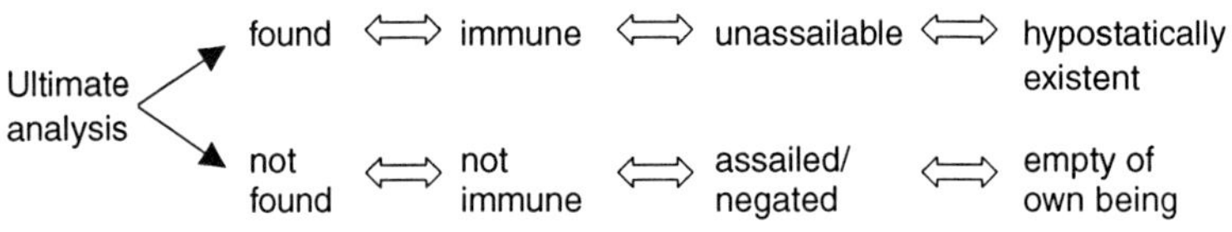

Figure 3.2 Mipham's equation.

applies *vice versa*. What is immune cannot be assailed or negated by ultimate reasoning and thus is hypostatically existent, to both of them. However, it is clear that Mipham understands whatever is not found and not immune as being assailed and negated by ultimate reasoning and therefore empty. To Tsongkhapa, lack of immunity does not necessarily lead to being assailed or negated. Of those that are not immune, only the utterly non-existent (*gtan med/med nges*) are assailed and negated by reasoning. Conventionally existent phenomena are not negated although they are not immune to the ultimate analysis. Hence, they are not empty of themselves but only of inherent or hypostatic existence.

On insertion of the qualifiers

Tsongkhapa and his followers made it explicit that what is negated by the ultimate analysis is hypostatic existence and not mere conventional phenomena, which are objects of our experiences. To them, the crux of Madhyamaka philosophy is that things lack hypostatic or inherent nature and, by the virtue of that, they exist conventionally. If conventional things are negated by the ultimate analysis, it would follow that they are non-existent because no negandum of a valid reasoning can be existent.[74] Thus, they add the qualifier 'hypostatically existent' or 'truly established' to production and paraphrase statements such as 'there is no production' as 'there is no hypostatically existent production'. This tradition of using the qualifier 'hypostatically existent' is a salient feature of Gelukpa Madhyamaka hermeneutics, and has come under rigorous attack from their opponents. The Gelukpa gloss of 'neither existent nor non-existent' as, 'neither hypostatically existent, nor conventionally non-existent' and the statement that 'the vase is not empty of vase but of hypostatic existence',[75] are frequently quoted by their opponents as a Gelukpa dictum of Madhyamaka understanding.

Most Sakya, Kagyu and Nyingma critics of Gelukpa refuted this paraphrasing as a superfluous and encumbering effort while some such as Amdo Gedun Chöphel even rebuked it as a self-serving interpolation.[76] According to them, it is redundant to add the qualifier 'hypostatically existent' for it is not just hypostatic existence that will fail to exist under the scrutiny of the ultimate reasoning but all phenomena. Mipham comments that application of such a qualifier is not an error *per se* and, if correctly done, could sometimes be helpful for beginners. However, if the qualifier is applied in order to distinguish an isolated hypostatic existence as the negandum, it is *malapropos* and it would deter the correct understanding of Emptiness.[77]

He attributed the insertion of such qualifiers to the Svātantrika Mādhyamikas[78] and argued that Candrakīrti's refutation of Bhāvaviveka's interpretation of Madhyamaka reasoning, and the reason why they consider Svātantrikas to be substantialists would equally apply to those who use such a qualifier to exclude the conventional truth from being negated.[79] Bhāvaviveka, in his commentary on the MK, interpreted Nāgārjuna's ultimate reasoning such as the production analysis by adding the qualification 'ultimate' to the predicate. He argued that the

Madhyamaka reasoning is employed only to negate the ultimate or absolute nature of things and not their conventional status. Thus, he paraphrased negation such as 'no production' as 'no ultimate production'.

Candrakīrti, siding with Buddhapālita whose dialectical procedure and methodology Bhāvaviveka refuted, attacked Bhāvaviveka's position and accused him of misinterpreting Nāgārjuna. He reasoned that the insertion of such a qualifier is unnecessary as no production in terms of the tetralemma exists even conventionally.[80] The Gelukpas however argued that Candrakīrti was not against the application of the qualifier in general but only refuting Bhāvaviveka for applying the qualifier 'ultimate' to production from oneself which is superfluous as production from oneself does not exist even conventionally.[81] Tsongkhapa cites several verses from the *sūtra*s and Mādhyamika works to demonstrate that the use of qualifier 'ultimate' is not restricted to Svātantrika works. He also observes that other qualifiers such as 'hypostatically existent' (*bden par grub pa*), 'truly' (*yang dag pa*), 'inherently existent' (*rang bzhin gyis grub pa*), 'existent with own being' (*ngo bos grub pa*), 'existent with own characteristics' (*rang mtshan gyis grub pa*) are common in both traditions of Mādhyamika and widely used in the *sūtra*s, MK, *Buddhapālita*, *Prasannapadā*, etc.[82] Where it is left out, it is mainly with the intention to avoid the text becoming wordy, so, one must infer its application from other cases where the application is explicit.[83]

Further, in his *Lam rim*, he explains the different cases when the insertion of such qualifier is crucial and when it is not necessary. Such qualifiers are not needed while refuting non-existent things such as a rabbit's horn, or non-existent concepts which are imputed by the substantialists. Neither is it applied while negating a particular thing in a particular place. That is because, the negandum in these do not exist even conventionally. It is very crucial, according to Tsongkhapa, to apply such qualifiers to the negandum if it is a conventionally existent phenomenon in the Mādhyamika system. Negating a conventional entity without inserting a qualifier would mean denying its general existence in which case the reasonings used for negating it would also have to be denied.[84]

Mipham disagrees and says that it is clear from the *Prasannapadā* and *Madhyamakāvatāra* and its *bhāṣya* that the issue of using the qualifier 'ultimate' is the main point of debate between Bhāvaviveka and Candrakīrti.[85] When the ultimate analysis scrutinizes production, it must negate both ultimate or inherent production and conventional or relative production. If it fails to negate any production, then it would follow that such production is not empty of its own being and immune to the ultimate analysis. Besides, if the negandum were just hypostatic or inherent existence, such hypostatic or inherent existence or own being does not exist according to Candrakīrti at both ultimate and conventional levels.[86] Therefore, there is no point in adding the qualifier 'ultimate' to the negandum.

Again, to both Gelukpas and Mipham, the purport of 'existing ultimately' (*don dam par yod pa*) is to exist under scrutiny of the ultimate analysis (*don dam pa'i rigs pas dpyod ngor grub pa*) and from the viewpoint of ultimate correct cognition (*don dam tshad ma'i ngor*). When phenomena such as production are under the scrutiny of the ultimate analysis, they are being investigated to see whether or not they exist ultimately. Ultimate analysis *per se* is the investigation searching for anything ultimately existent. Thus, while one is in the course of such investigation by using the Mādhyamika reasoning, there is no need for the insertion of the qualifier 'ultimate'.

It is redundant to add such qualifiers while one is in the philosophical context of the ultimate analysis. Mipham criticizes the Gelukpa formulation of Madhyamaka as being superfluous in words.[87] He criticizes the Gelukpa paraphrase, 'the vase is not empty of vase but the vase is empty of hypostatic existence', as tautological. It is sufficient to say that the vase is empty of hypostatic existence; the first clause 'vase is not empty of vase' is unnecessary. The second clause sufficiently shows us that the vase is without hypostatic existence and indirectly implies, through the qualifier, that it is conventionally existent.

A similar refutation appears in the first question in his *Nges shes sgron me*, where Mipham criticizes the Gelukpas of being ignorant of semiotics (*brda la rmongs*).[88] He argues that if one is saying the pillar is not empty of the pillar in the conventional context, why cannot one just say the pillar is existent or the pillar is not empty instead of saying 'the pillar is not empty of pillar but the pillar is empty of hypostatic existence'. Saying the pillar is not empty of pillar gives a misleading connotation of one pillar placed on/in the other, and the repetition of the word 'pillar' is needless as the same purport could be rendered by just saying 'the pillar is not empty'. If the phrase is to be understood in an ultimate context, in which case the pillar is not perceived, then why would not the pillar be empty of the pillar?

According to Tibetan scholars including Tsongkhapa and Mipham, Bhāvaviveka accepted that things were empty of an ultimate nature but not of their conventional own being even under the scrutiny of ultimate analysis. They attributed the acceptance of conventional existence of entities with own characteristics (*tha snyad du rang mtshan gyis grub pa*) to all Svātantrikas.[89] Candrakīrti denied the existence of things with own characteristics even at the conventional level[90] and refuted Bhāvaviveka rigorously in his works on this point.[91]

Thus, acceptance and denial of entities with own characteristics on the conventional level, like the insertion of the qualifier 'ultimate', is one of the major differences between the Prāsaṅgika and Svātantrika school in Mipham's thought.[92] Hence, Mipham argues in his *Rab lan* that the Prāsaṅgika accusation of the Svātantrikas of holding a substantialist position (*dngos [por] smra ba*) would also apply to the Gelukpas[93] because the refutation of the Svātantrika insertion of qualifier 'ultimate' would also equally affect the Gelukpa paraphrasing. Such insertions are unnecessary as nothing, in either ultimate or conventional manner, can exist under the scrutiny of the ultimate analysis.

Mipham also points out the hermeneutic complications the persistent insertion of such qualifiers can cause. If negation of phenomena in relation to their empty nature were to be understood as negation of hypostatic existence, one will have to read phrases such as loving kindness without apprehension (*dmigs pa med pa'i byams pa*) as loving kindness without hypostatic apprehension,[94] not having thesis (*khas len med pa*) as not having hypostatic thesis, being without elaborations (*spros pa med pa*) as being without hypostatic elaborations.[95] Non-apprehension of the triad factors (*'khor gsum mi dmigs pa*) of donor, beneficiary and the act of giving, will have to be understood as non-apprehension of the hypostatic triad, which would imply that the pluralistic notion of the three are not overcome.[96] Every negative phrase or sentence denoting Emptiness in the *sūtra*s and later treatises has to be paraphrased likewise. In addition, insertion of such a qualifier to all neganda implies that it is only hypostatic existence, which is negated. Were such the case, why would Mādhyamikas have to negate two, four or eight kinds of extremes? Simply negating hypostatic existence should do.

However, the Gelukpas not only glossed the negation of existence with the qualifier 'hypostatically existent', but also glossed negation of non-existence with the qualifier 'conventional' thus reading, for example, 'neither existent nor non-existent' as 'neither hypostatically existent nor conventionally non-existent'. They used the two qualifiers to avoid the extreme of eternalism and nihilism respectively. Mipham argues that such interpretation clearly suggests that one can only negate the extreme of eternalism *qua* existence through the ultimate *qua* Emptiness and one has to rely on the conventional existence to dispel the extreme of nihilism *qua* non-existence. This would imply that Emptiness *qua* reality is not capable of eliminating all extremes and dogmatic views on its own.[97]

In Mipham's opinion, the parenthetic insertion of qualifiers complicates the reading of *sūtra*s and Mādhyamika texts and creates more hermeneutic problems than it solves. Emptiness *qua* reality is defined to be without the extremes of self and non-self (*bdag bdag med*), appearing and non-appearing (*snang mi snang*), empty and non-empty (*stong mi stong*) and so forth. If all dichotomies negated in defining Emptiness *qua* reality were to be supplied with these qualifiers, several complications would arise.[98] Statements such as 'reality is neither with self (*bdag yod pa ma yin*) nor without self (*bdag med pa ma yin*)' will have to be read as 'reality is neither with hypostatically existent self nor without conventional self'. Similarly, reality being neither appearing nor non-appearing would be 'neither appearing hypostatically/ultimately nor non-appearing conventionally', and neither empty nor non-empty 'neither hypostatically/ultimately empty nor conventionally non-empty'. Reading with such insertions will sometimes fit but at other times entail contradictions. More problems, particularly those relating to the tetralemma, will be appraised later.

Referring to this Gelukpa hermeneutics, Gedun Chöphel states that when the Gelukpas encounter statements such as 'neither existent, nor non-existent', they first see who said the verse.[99] If it is composed by a Ngarabpa scholar, they criticize the author as nihilistic and ignorant so that they can be seen as a heroic scholar. If it is the Buddha or an authoritative Indian master, for the fear of being seen a cynic, they do not defy it but interpret as 'neither hypostatically existent, nor conventionally non-existent'. He shuns such biased double standards and calls the parenthetic insertions 'nice patches' (*lhan pa mdzes po*). To scholars such as Mipham and Gedun Chöphel, these glosses are cumbersome and unnecessary efforts, which hinder the proper reading and correct understanding of the concept of Emptiness in the Indian treatises.[100]

Mipham's main criticisms

Among the various polemical topics, the Gelukpa delimitation of the Mādhyamika dialectical negandum to hypostatic existence and their application of qualifiers to that effect received by far the strongest criticism from Mipham. In his *rGyan 'grel, 'Jug 'grel, gSung sgros, Nges shes sgron me, Ketaka, Rab lan* and *Nyi snang*, Mipham undertakes rigorous criticism of this Gelukpa position. He devotes dozens of pages to refuting this position and the paraphrase, 'the vase is not empty of vase but of hypostatic existence' in these works and also touches on it in many other works.[101] A detailed study of all of his arguments cannot be contained in this book. I shall discuss a few major criticisms he hurls at the Gelukpas in the form of apagogical arguments (*prasaṅga, thal ba*).

Emptiness will become an implicative negation

Mipham refutes the Gelukpas by arguing that their concept of Emptiness, on contrary to their claim, would not be an absolute negation (*prasajyapratiṣedha, med dgag*) but an implicative negation (*paryudāsa, ma yin dgag*).[102] Mipham and the Gelukpas, following Indian masters such as Candrakīrti,[103] claim that Emptiness is an absolute negation.[104] However, Mipham contends that understanding Emptiness as mere lack of hypostatic existence without negating the subject in question would make Emptiness an implicative negation as the existence of the subject in question is implied after negating hypostatic existence.[105] For instance, adding the qualifier 'hypostatically existent' to the statement 'there is no production' and reading it as 'there is no hypostatically existent production' negates hypostatic existence, but it implicitly affirms that there is a production albeit without hypostatic existence. Thus, Emptiness becomes an implicative negation and to say so contradicts their claim that Emptiness is absolute negation.

Emptiness will become an Emptiness of other

One of the main criticisms in his *'Jug 'grel, Nges shes sgron me* and *gSung sgros* is the argument that, because vase is not empty of vase but only of a separate entity – hypostatic existence – which is other than the vase, the Emptiness of vase would become an extrinsic Emptiness contradicting their claim.[106] The Gelukpas claim to be proponents of *rang stong* or Emptiness of one's own being and strongly criticized the advocates of *gzhan stong* or Emptiness of other, who maintained that the ultimate reality *qua tathāgatagarbha* is not empty of its own being but of other adventitious things.[107] Mipham's argument is that in establishing the Emptiness of the vase, if the vase is not empty of itself, the thing of which it is empty has to be other than the vase. If the vase is only empty of an entity other than itself, such Emptiness is an extrinsic Emptiness. Such Emptiness, according to Mipham, is Emptiness of one thing lacking another (*itaretaraśūnyatā, gcig la gcig med pa'i stong pa*) like the yak's horn being empty of rabbit's horn. He associates this with the ephemeral Emptiness (*prādeśikaśūnyatā, nyi tshe ba'i stong pa*) mentioned in the *Lankāvatārasūtra.*[108] He also calls it the worldly form of Emptiness (*'jig rten pa'i stong tshul*) and not the ultimate, which is the scope of yogis (*don dam rnal 'byor pa'i spyod yul*).[109] Other terms he uses for it are the extrinsic Emptiness of conventional things (*kun rdzob gzhan stong*) and the extrinsic Emptiness of the verbal (*tshig gi gzhan stong*) in contrast to the extrinsic Emptiness of the ultimate (*don dam gzhan stong*) or the extrinsic Emptiness of the objective (*don gyi gzhan stong*) professed by the Jonangpas.[110]

This criticism has been raised even before or at the time of Tsongkhapa as, in his *dGongs pa rab gsal*, Tsongkhapa dismisses such refutation as invalid.[111] He says that if vase is empty of vase then vase would be without the nature of vase, and consequently vase would become utterly non-existent (*gtan med*) because nothing else can be the vase. Similarly, everything would become empty and non-existent and even the person who delineates Emptiness would not exist. Such an understanding is totally nihilistic and is outside the teachings dispensed by the Buddha and his followers. All four Buddhist philosophical schools in India have eschewed such a position as nihilistic. Hence, the delineation of the vase to be empty must be understood as establishing the vase, which is the basis of negation (*dgag gzhi*), to be empty of hypostatic existence, the negandum. The fact established by the ultimate analysis is the lack of the hypostatically existent vase, in other words, the basis of negation, not being, by nature, the negandum (*dgag gzhi dgag bya'i ngo bor med pa*).

Mipham states that the fear of the vase becoming utterly non-existent if it is empty of itself is due to the lack of understanding that the vase does not exist ultimately and at the same time exists conventionally. It is a substantialist tendency to think what is negated by the ultimate analysis as conventionally non-existent and what is conventionally existent as unassailable by the ultimate analysis.[112] For the Mādhyamikas, even if the vase does not exist under ultimate analysis, its dependently orginated appearance (*rten 'brel gyi snang ba*) is undeniable (*bsnyon med*) on the conventional level. The ultimate non-existence and conventional existence of the vase are not contradictory and can coexist, and what is negated and proved empty by the ultimate analysis are these very evident conventional phenomena. Those that are conventionally non-existent such as a rabbit's horn and barren woman's son are not scopes of the ultimate analysis and do not need to be negated by the ultimate analysis. They can be negated by conventional reasoning. Hence, the purpose of an ultimate analysis is not merely to negate a conventionally non-existent hypostatic and inherent nature.[113]

Mipham denies that the negation of a non-existent entity on an existent entity can qualify to be Emptiness of own being. He repeatedly points out that the mere absence of a non-existent hypostatic existence on an existent conventional phenomenon is not sufficient to be considered Emptiness of own being. Understanding conventional phenomena to be without an isolated hypostatic existence is like knowing the vase to be without cloth or the yak's horn without a rabbit's horn. Such absence is not Emptiness of one's own being.[114] In addition, how could the absence of non-existent thing, that is, hypostatic existence, be the reality (*dharmatā, chos nyid*) of all conventionally existent things?[115] Although the yak's horn lacks rabbit's horn and the vase lacks cloth, the lack of rabbit's horn and of cloth are not the reality of the yak's horn and the vase respectively. Similarly, the absence of hypostatic existence which is separate from the vase cannot be the reality or the nature of the vase.

Mipham adds that not only does this position go against the scriptures such as 'matter is empty of matter' or 'eye is empty of eye', it is logically contradictory to say that the basis of Emptiness (*stong gzhi*) remains after having negated hypostatic existence.[116] If the pillar and hypostatic existence were one, negating hypostatic existence would also negate the pillar, and if they are different, even if hypostatic existence is negated, the pillar would remain immune to the analysis, which would mean it is hypostatically existent.[117] To an ordinary mind, there is no isolated hypostatic existence other than the non-empty vase itself, so it is the vase, which has to be established as empty in order to establish the Emptiness of hypostatic existence.[118]

Moreover, if the vase were not empty of its own nature, the vase cannot be established to be illusory even if it is known to be without an isolated hypostatic existence. Knowing the rope to be without the snake would not help one realize the rope to be illusory and unreal.[119] He continues that understanding the absence of a thing other than the subject itself, like knowing the absence of a cow on a horse, is of no relevance in establishing the concept of Emptiness. An analysis of whether or not an entity is present or absent in another entity would not contribute toward fathoming the profound nature of Emptiness.[120] The absence of an extrinsic entity such as a cow on the horse is not sufficient to be considered the Emptiness of horse. One cannot realize a horse to be empty just by knowing that it lacks the nature of a cow.[121] Emptiness of horse has to do with lack of its own nature and not with the lack of some other entity. If Emptiness of vase is merely the absence of hypostatic existence, an imputed quality distinct from the vase, it would be so simple. It is like saying the horse is empty because it is without the cow, or the reflection of the moon is empty because it is not the sky-moon; everyone can understand such Emptiness and fathom the coalescence of such absence and appearance. Why would the great masters proclaim that understanding of Emptiness is exquisite?[122]

Emptiness will become segregated from appearance

Mipham argues that if the negandum is hypostatic existence which is not identical with the vase but other than the vase, then the lack of such hypostatic existence would also be other than the vase. He claims the two cases of the vase being different from hypostatic existence and different from the lack of hypostatic existence are similar.[123] It would be an isolated hypostatic existence and isolated absence of it only being added to the vase. In that case, it would follow that the vase is not by nature void of hypostatic existence just as it is not by nature empty, but only attributed with a separate absence of hypostatic existence.[124] Consequently, one would have to accept that Emptiness, which is considered to be the nature of the vase, is separate from the vase. Such a position is unacceptable as it segregates Emptiness from the conventional appearance of the vase.

Were the vase empty of hypostatic existence and not of itself, Emptiness of the vase would not be of one nature with the vase, for it is not the vase, which is empty. Rather, it is the hypostatic existence which is empty. Mipham understands the term 'empty' in the statements such as 'form is empty' in the same manner as the adjective 'red' in the statement 'the flower is red'. In both cases, the adjectives describe a natural quality. As such, it does not semantically require one to add what the form is empty of or the flower is red of. Form is empty *per se*. It is wrong to construe the concept of being empty as one thing (e.g. vase) lacking another (e.g. water or hypostatic existence). Mipham's idea of being 'empty' can be better understood by equating it to 'being not found' under ultimate analysis. To say 'vase is empty' is to say the vase is not found by the ultimate analysis just as one could say 'hypostatic existence is empty' when it is not found. Thus, 'vase is empty' need not be interpreted as 'vase is empty of hypostatic existence'. Both vase and hypostatic existence are equally empty instead of the vase being empty of hypostatic existence.

In this respect, Mipham even tends to use the term 'empty' (*stong*) as if it were a verb in active voice. The vase is empty means that 'the vase empties' (*bum pa stong*) just as the vase is existent means the vase exists (*bum pa yod*). The act of emptying here should not be understood in a tripartite framework of agent–container–content model of an agent (e.g. a dustman) emptying a container (e.g. a dustbin) of some content (e.g. rubbish). Just as the vase exists and changes conventionally, it 'empties' ultimately because it is without its own being. Thus, to be empty is to lack own being and to be unfindable on the ultimate level. Both the vase and the hypostatic existence lack own being and are unfindable and are therefore empty. Now, for those who accept the vase to be empty of itself, such Emptiness can coalesce with the interdependent and the illusory appearance of the vase for, inspite of its empty nature, the empirical appearance of the vase is evidently experienced. The Emptiness of the vase thus reinforces the interdependent nature of the illusory vase.

However, for those who accept the vase to exist as it is and argue for the Emptiness *qua* absence of hypostatic existence, the vase which empirically appears is not empty, hence, its appearance is separate from Emptiness. Because hypostatic existence is even conventionally non-existent, there is no empirical appearance of hypostatic existence for the Emptiness *qua* absence of hypostatic existence to coalesce with. Thus, the absence of hypostatic existence becomes an isolated Emptiness (*stong pa rkyang pa*). The appearance of the vase and the absence of hypostatic existence fails to form the necessary coalescence of appearance and Emptiness (*snang stong zung 'jug*). The Gelukpas however explained such coalescence by conjoining Emptiness *qua* absence of hypostatic existence with the appearance of the vase. Mipham rejected that such absence of hypostatic existence, which is different from the vase, can coalesce with the appearance of the vase. How could the Emptiness *qua* absence of non-existent rabbit's horn, for instance, coalesce with appearance of the yak's horn?[125]

He goes on to say, the coalescence of two truths or equality of *saṃsāra* and *nirvāṇa* cannot be applied to such Emptiness of hypostatic existence, and understanding such Emptiness would not do any benefit to spiritual practice of eliminating negative thoughts and enhancing virtuous thoughts.[126] It would not do any harm to the root of worldly existence and not induce the realization of the reality free from mental elaborations but block such realization. Without meditating on the Emptiness, which is free from apprehension, how can contemplation on the Emptiness of hypostatic existence lead to the non-dualistic meditative equipoise?[127] One is only deceiving oneself by stressing on such verbal distinction in identifying the negandum, for such verbiage only undermines the understanding of essential points.[128]

The absence of hypostatic existence will not be established

As long as the entity such as the vase is not known to be empty of its own nature, it cannot be known to be without hypostatic existence. If things were not empty of their own being, how could they be ascertained to be empty of hypostatic existence? Establishing conventional phenomena to be empty of hypostatic existence is to analyse them and not find any own being in them. If such things as the vase are not thoroughly analysed or their own being or nature not negated but found under analysis, even if one claims to have established them to be without hypostatic existence, one actually does not establish the lack of hypostatic existence.[129]

Thus, Mipham says that even understanding the lack of hypostatic existence involves investigating the vase itself and not just an isolated hypostatic existence, and as long as the phenomena under investigation is not negated, even the understanding of lack of hypostatic existence cannot be acheived. A similar argument is made in *gSung sgros* where he argues that when the vase is not apprehended under the ultimate analysis, the designation 'lack of hypostatic existence' is given. Were the vase apprehended under the analysis, its lack of hypostatic existence could not be established. So, proving the vase to be empty of itself is *sine qua non* of establishing its lack of hypostatic existence. He observes:

> If ultimate analysis does not prove the vase to be non-existent, how would it negate hypostatic existence. If [it] proves [the vase] to be non-existent, it [proves the vase] to be ultimately empty. What is [the point of] the reasoning which negates an isolated hypostatic existence other than it (i.e. the vase).[130]

Hence, he even questions the Gelukpa claim that they have understood the Emptiness of hypostatic existence.

Conventional things will become hypostatically existent

Mipham further attacks the Gelukpa position arguing that if the vase were not empty of vase, the vase would become hypostatically existent. He writes:

> Thus, according to this system, [which claims] vase to be empty of the hypostatic existence other [than the vase], because [they] accept that very [thing which] appears as vase to be not empty of its own being, the vase will become hypostatically existent. [That is so] because there is no hypostatic existence other than that which is not known to be without its own being when analysed by the ultimate analysis.[131]

To Mipham, to be not negated by the ultimate analysis is tantamount to being immune to the analysis and being immune to the ultimate analysis qualifies a thing to be hypostatically existent. Were the vase not negated, it would follow that it is actually hypostatically existent.[132] Thus, by asserting that conventional phenomena are not negated but their hypostatic existence is, one would only establish a verbal negation of the hypostatic existence. One would not establish the correct form of Emptiness, but consequently be forced to unwillingly accept hypostatic existence.[133]

Conventional things will have their own characteristics

In another argument, he argues that if conventional production, cessation, abiding are not negated by the ultimate analyses, it would follow that they exist by their own characteristics (*rang mtshan gyis yod par 'gyur*). Were they to exist so, deluded emotions such as attachment cannot be eliminated because phenomena existing by their own characteristics are objects conceived by such delusions, and as long as they persist, the subjective emotions would not cease. Prāsaṅgika refutation of Svātantrika Mādhyamika assertion that conventional things exist by their own characteristics would befall this interpretation.[134] The same argument is repeated verbatim in *gSung sgros*.[135] He also mentions that the same form of reasoning that Tsongkhapa used in attacking and categorizing the Svātantrika Mādhyamikas as substantialists would also apply to the proponents of the dictum, 'the vase is not empty of vase but vase is empty of hypostatic existence'.[136]

Tsongkhapa and his Gelukpa followers accused the Svātantrika Mādhyamika of a substantialist orientation for their assertion of inherent nature (*prakṛti, rang bzhin*), own being (*svabhāva, ngo bo*) or own characteristics (*svalakṣana, rang tshan gyis grub pa*) on the conventional level.[137] Although they are Mādhyamikas because they assert the absence of even a particle of hypostatically existent thing, according to Gelukpas, they denied that the ultimate analysis negated the inherent nature, own being and own characteristics on the conventional level. Tsongkhapa reasoned that if there were an inherent nature, own being or own characteristics which resists the ultimate analyses, it would become hypostatically existent. According to them, the Prāsaṅgikas negated all three even on the conventional level.[138] Mipham adds that the same criticism could be made against the Gelukpas for asserting that conventional things are not negated by ultimate analyses.

The varieties of Emptiness will become unnecessary

Again in *'Jug 'grel*, Mipham refutes the Gelukpa interpretation with reference to the twenty kinds of Emptinesses.[139] Because grasping and attachment arise in us through conceiving the external and internal things, Emptiness of the external, Emptiness of the internal, etc. were taught in order to destroy the grasping and attachment to the external and internal things by establishing them to be empty of own being. If these external and internal phenomena are not negated and proved empty, and Emptiness of external, etc. refer to Emptiness of hypostatically existent external, etc. the objects conceived by the grasping and attachment would still continue. Citing the *Ratnāvalī*, I/35[140] Mipham argued that without realizing the aggregates to be empty, the negation of hypostatic existence merely cannot overcome the grasping at aggregates and the subsequent notion of 'I'. It is obvious that grasping to the aggregates as 'I' arise merely through apprehending the aggregates.[141]

Mipham also questions in his *Rab lan* that, were hypostatic existence the only thing to be negated, why would it be taught that the different neganda of two, four, eight and thirty-two extremes are overcome by Emptiness? If hypostatic existence were the only negandum, absence of hypostatic existence should alone be sufficient to eliminate all extremes.[142] It would then follow that the various kinds of Emptinesses are unnecessary. However, it was clear from the Gelukpa exposition of middle way that absence of hypostatic existence is not capable of eliminating all extremes. They took conventional existence to dispel the extreme of nihilism. Mipham repeatedly criticizes this Gelukpa delineation of the middle way through clearing eternalism by Emptiness and nihilism by conventional existence. This will be discussed in Chapter 4.

Lack of hypostatic existence cannot be Emptiness

Mipham also questions whether the absence of hypostatic existence on the conventional phenomena can be considered as Emptiness. Emptiness *qua* reality, he argues, is applicable only to things that conventionally appear, and not to non-existent entities such as a rabbit's horn. He states:

> Generally, it is not possible for the appearance of *saṃsāra* and *nirvāṇa* to ever cease. If there is appearance, [the fact of] it being empty is designated as Emptiness. Those without appearance such as rabbit's horn are not bases of Emptiness. Because [it] is conventionally non-existent, even if the designation 'empty of horn' is given to the rabbit's horn, it [just] means it is utterly non-existent. Emptiness is the reality of all things conventionally existent, . . . Therefore, this Emptiness is to be delineated

> as the nature or ontic mode of all things conventionally existent. It is not at all to be delineated as the reality of that which is conventionally non-existent.[143]

This, Mipham mentions, is because the dependently originated things which are conventionally existent are the objects of grasping and the basis of liberation and bondage. 'Thus, what is called Emptiness', he continues, 'is the reality of things which exist conventionally. There cannot be an isolated Emptiness on [any] thing'.[144] Emptiness must be seen as the unfindability of phenomena under ultimate analysis. Specifying hypostatic existence as the negandum and holding Emptiness to be a mere absence of hypostatic existence is at best a propaedeutic method. It is not the Emptiness, which is the reality of all things. Emptiness, he goes on to say, is primordially coalesced with dependent origination, and the nature of such coalescence is free from all elaborations and can be experienced intuitively by sublime gnosis.

Things will not be inherently pure (viśuddha, rnam dag)

Referring to the Mahāyāna concept of all things being pure by nature (*rang bzhin rnam dag*), he argues that were conventional things not empty of themselves or Emptiness not their nature, they would not be pure by nature.[145] Things are pure by nature because they are empty of their own being. It would follow from the Gelukpa argument that conventional phenomena are not pure by nature but only hypostatic existence is. If grasping at hypostatic existence is deception and being without it qualifies things to be pure by nature, then grasping the rope as snake and dummy as man would also be deception and the fact that the rope is without snake and the dummy without man would qualify the rope and the dummy to be pure by nature. This is not acceptable as things such as the vase are pure by nature because they are void of own nature, and thereby of any innate adventitious reifications and afflictions of the *saṃsāra,* not merely because they are void of another entity.

Mipham's criticisms of the Gelukpa identification of hypostatic existence as the negandum are intensive, diverse, subtle and sometimes repetitive. He raises against them problems and contradictions of a hermeneutic, ontological, semantic, dialectical and soteriological nature. I shall now summarize another one of his attacks of the Gelukpa position presented in his *gSung sgros.*[146] Mipham reasons that the Gelukpa statement, 'the vase is not empty of vase but of hypostatic existence' is a flawed speech (*ngag skyon can*) because it is untenable on levels of both truths. He elaborates on how it is not tenable on the level of both truths providing four reasons each. The statement in question is not tenable on the level of conventional truth for the following reasons:

1 It does not fit into the context (*skabs su ma babs pa*). The discussion of the vase to be empty is an issue pertaining to the ultimate level. It is not being determined whether the vase is empty or not conventionally. Neither is the

issue of whether the vase is empty of itself or of some other thing scrutinized on the conventional level.

2 On this level, such clarification would be needless (*dgos pa med pa*) for even the ordinary people know that the vase is not empty of itself and is empty of other things such as cloth, which it lacks.

3 This statement entails contradiction of one's words (*rang tshig 'gal ba*) for if the vase is not empty of vase conventionally, it would mean the vase exists as it appears thereby implying that it is hypostatically existent in a conventional sense.[147] This implication contradicts with the claim that it is empty of hypostatic existence.

4 The statement is irrelevant (*'brel med*) on the conventional level for the same reasons provided for 1 and 2.

He then contends that such statement is untenable on the ultimate level:

1 It entails internal contradiction of assertions (*khas blang nang 'gal*) to claim that the vase is not empty of vase and at the same time that it is empty of hypostatic existence. From the viewpoint of the ultimate, the vase is not found when searched by the ultimate analysis. The unfindability or non-establishment under ultimate analysis is what 'the vase is empty of vase' means. It is also described as the lack of hypostatic existence. There is no other form of absence of hypostatic existence. Thus, to be ultimately non-empty is synonymous to being hypostatically existent. If the vase is without hypostatic existence, it is also empty of itself.

2 It contradicts the scriptures (*lung dang 'gal ba*) because in the *sūtra*s and *śāstra*s, when eighteen Emptinesses are taught, things are said to be empty of themselves in phrases such as eye is empty of eye, matter is empty of matter, etc.

3 It makes the Gelukpa proponents deviate from their assertion that Emptiness is an absolute negation (*stong nyid med dgag tu khas blang pa las nyams pa*). We have already discussed this criticism earlier. Mipham succinctly presents both problems of Emptiness becoming an implicative negation and Emptiness of other and remarks that such Emptiness of other, like a monastery being empty of monks, is a petty Emptiness among the seven Emptinesses taught in the *Laṅkāvatārasūtra*. If things are not known to be empty of themselves, knowing them to be empty of hypostatic existence would not overcome grasping at substantiality of person and phenomena and dualistic appearance.

4 It deviates from the point of viewing Emptiness as dependently originated. (*stong pa rten 'brel du 'char ba'i don las nyams pa*). Mipham remarks that it is the heartfelt intent of the Mādhyamika masters including Tsongkhapa to see Emptiness as dependently originated (*pratītyasamutpāda, rten 'brel*). However, this statement closes down the understanding of the coalescence of Emptiness and dependent origination. It is possible to see the meaning (*don*) of Emptiness and dependent origination as one (*gcig*) if one understands that

things are empty, just as fire is hot and water is wet, and yet appearing. If the thing, which is not empty of its own being, is seen to appear from the Emptiness *qua* lack of some other thing, that is, hypostatic existence, why cannot the whole world appear from the lack of rabbit's horn? How can Emptiness and dependent origination be reconciled as having one nature by merging an Emptiness of a non-existent rabbit's horn with the appearance of yak's horn? In addition, such conjoining of yak's horn with the lack of rabbit's horn is evident even to the yak herder. If such were the case, why would coalescence be difficult for the scholars?

Emptiness will lose its soteriological efficacy

Mipham's main refutation of the Gelukpa interpretation of Emptiness seems to be the one in connection with the soteriological role of Emptiness. If the negandum of Mādhyamika reasoning is not an existent phenomenon but hypostatic existence and Emptiness is mere absence of hypostatic existence, it cannot overcome attachment and grasping.[148] Emptiness *qua* absence of hypostatic existence of the vase must be understood as the lack of vase under the scrutiny of the ultimate analysis and not just the lack of some impossible entity, hypostatic existence, that is different from the vase.[149] Negating an isolated hypostatic existence on the vase and leaving the vase unscathed by the analysis will not do any harm to the attachment to the vase because attachment to the vase arise from apprehending the vase and not from apprehending an isolated hypostatic existence.

Moreover, to the ordinary experiences of the worldly beings, the vase and the hypostatic existence imputed on it are inseparable. Not even ordinary beings grasp a hypostatic existence separate from the vase.[150] Sentient beings cling to the vase itself as real rather than grasp at a hypostatic existence apart from the vase. Hence, without deconstructing the object of our daily experience through ultimate analyses, we cannot overcome clinging and attachment to these objects merely by refuting the metaphysical concept of hypostatic existence.

In *'Jug 'grel*, Mipham asks who actually would need to negate the hypostatic existence, the ordinary people who do not know Madhyamaka philosophy or yogis who know it.[151] The ordinary people do not need to negate such hypostatic existence because they would not have conceived philosophical abstracts such as the hypostatic existence. They only conceive empirical things as real and would not have the concept of an isolated hypostatic existence. The yogis would not need to negate such hypostatic existence because they would have overcome the reification of things and have no more apprehension of hypostatic existence. Mipham also asks whether the negation of hypostatic existence is meant for people grasping the vase as hypostatically existent or people who grasp the vase as lacking hypostatic existence. It is obvious that the latter do not need to negate the hypostatic existence as they have already eliminated the grasping of it. The former group would not have to negate because they have no grasping of the hypostatic existence other than phenomena such as vase, pillar, etc.[152]

In addition, if such hypostatic existence were not the own being of the vase, negating it would neither help us understand the Emptiness of the vase nor overcome misconception about the vase. If it is, negating it would simultaneously negate the vase too.[153] Were the hypostatic existence totally different from the empirical appearance, understanding the absence of such entity would have no impact on the usual experience of the empirical things. To show the irrelevance between the need – the eradication of attachment, etc. – and the antidote – lack of hypostatic existence – he cites this verse from MA:

> Seeing the snake remain in the hole in the wall of one's house,
> If one proceeds to dispel even the fear of the snake
> By ascertaining that 'there is no elephant there',
> Alas! [how] bizarre would it be to others.[154]

To the same effect, Mipham also quotes this hymn from Changkya's *lTa mgur*, on which he wrote a commentary, to argue that even Gelukpa masters saw this Gelukpa inconsistency in theory and practice:

> Leaving the fleeting appearance as they are,
> Some of our scholars, nowadays,
> Seek an object with horn for negandum.
> But the old mother seems to be running away [from them].[155]

Mipham takes Changkya to be insinuating in this verse that Gelukpa scholars generally are moving away from understanding Emptiness being caught in negating a non-existent negandum – hypostatic existence. Bodtrul Dongag Tanpai Nyima and Amdo Gedun Chöphel, two main refuters of the Gelukpa understanding of Emptiness after Mipham, also cite this hymn.[156]

Amdo Gedun Chöphel argues in his *Klu grub dgongs rgyan* that because ordinary sentient beings are accustomed to grasping at hypostatic existence, the moment an object is apprehended, there arises spontaneously the grasping at it as hypostatically existent. Thus, whatever one may verbally distinguish as the negandum, it is the empirical object which requires to be negated in order to give up grasping at it because ordinary experiences cannot differentiate between the conventional object and the superimposed hypostatic existence. This, he says is not just the understanding of Ngarabpa scholars but also of several Gelukpa masters such as Changkya Rolpai Dorje, Gungthang Tanpai Drönme and Paṇchen Lobzang Chögyan.[157] He also says that the Gelukpa claim to identify the negandum in order to realize the view is dissonant with Tsongkhapa's words that ordinary people cannot distinguish between what is hypostatically existent and existent and what is without hypostatic existence and non-existent.[158] He does not however comment on how this claim relates to or contradicts Tsongkhapa's emphasis on the importance of identifying the negandum in order to understand Emptiness correctly.

Mipham, followed by Bodpa Trulku and Amdo Gedun Chöphel, also comments that if the existence of an empirical object such as the vase is refuted by

Mādhyamika reasoning and established to be false, there is no need to define hypostatic existence as the negandum. Even without negating hypostatic existence, Emptiness of the vase can be realized by seeing it as false and illusory. Amdo Gedun Chöphel further argues that if the fear is that negating an empirical object such as vase would annihilate the existence of conventional vase, it is unnecessary. He observes:

> The fear in some [people] that a nihilistic view seeing everything as non-existent would arise [in oneself] if vase, pillars, so forth were negated by the reasoning is a needless worry. How can it be possible for a nihilistic view that 'the vase visible in the front is utterly non-existent' ever arise in an ordinary person? Were such a thought to arise, because [one] knows directly that the vase is visible and tangible, a thought that 'this vase, although appearing to me, is utterly non-existent while it is appearing' would arise spontaneously. Such a thought is Madhyamaka view of coalescence of appearance and Emptiness which comprehends appearance to be not existing as it appears. How could it be a nihilistic view?[159]

Some problems with this Gelukpa identification of the negandum to be hypostatic existence and not empirical objects have also been raised in Western scholarship on Gelukpa Mādhyamika in recent times. Hopkins dicusses both Amdo Gedun Chöphel and Tandar Lharampa's viewpoints and remarks that Gelukpa 'emphasis on the valid establishment of conventionalities might merely fortify the habitual sense that things exist the way they appear'.[160] Napper states that there is

> a danger that, because Dzong-kha-pa chose to emphasize a verbal distinction between existence and inherent existence which cannot be realized in ordinary experience, people will miss the Mādhyamika message altogether. They will not understand that Mādhyamika is attacking and refuting our very sense of existence and, misled by the verbal emphasis on inherent existence, will see Mādhyamika as refuting something merely intellectual, 'out there', not immediate . . .[161]

Similarly, Newland comments:

> (It) is clear that 'Tsong-ka-pa's system', as institutionalized in the monastic textbooks (*yig cha*), supplies pat answers to many Ge-luk-bas and close down their reading of Nāgārjuna, Candrakīrti, and even Tsong-ka-pa himself. At worst, the result is a defanged Mādhyamika whose insistence upon the valid establishment (*tshad grub*) of conventional reality serves only to confirm the samsaric (and social-political) status quo. Cutting against this tendency, and thus revealing it, Jang-gya, Den-dar-lha-ram-ba (b. 1759) and other Ge-luk-ba writers warn their fellows against taking 'these concrete appearance as givens'. Inherent existence,

> they say, is not some horn-like or hat-like protuberance ready to be lopped of, leaving our world unscathed.[162]

On the tetralemma methodology

Carrying on the criticism, Mipham says that the Gelukpa understanding of Emptiness as mere lack of hypostatic existence does not cohere with the description of Emptiness as a reality which is not existent (*asti, yod pa*), non-existent (*nāsti, med pa*), both (*ubhaya, gnyis ka*) and neither (*anubhaya, gnyis min*).[163] He observes that the Gelukpa application of the qualifier 'hypostatically existent' would not work with the use of tetralemma method whereby all extremes of existence, non-existence, both and neither are negated. This methodology, either with all four lemmas or with two or three, occur in many *sūtra*s and *śāstras*.[164] The same method of tetralemma applies to the denial of reality as other tetrads formed from lemmas such as permanent/impermanent, one/many, is/is not, self/non-self and their combinations. The tetralemma analysis, as Seyfort Ruegg says, 'constitutes one of the basic methods used by the Mādhyamikas to establish the inapplicability of any imaginable conceptual position – positive, negative or some combination of these – that might be taken as the subject of an existential proposition and become one of a set of binary doctrinal extremes (*antadvaya*)'.[165]

Translating this method into symbolic logic, one could say Emptiness is taught to be $\sim x$, $\sim(\sim x)$, $\sim(x \,\&\, \sim x)$ and $\sim\sim(x \,\&\, \sim x)$ where the proposition x denotes the first extreme, existence. Mipham took this denial of the four extremes in the Indian sources literally and thus understood Emptiness to be without the extremes of x, $\sim x$, $(x \,\&\, \sim x)$ and $\sim(x \,\&\, \sim x)$. The Gelukpas however argued that it is full of logical contradictions to take the application of tetralemma literally and thus supplied qualifiers to the extremes negated. Holding Emptiness to be $\sim x$ is not valid as it annihilates conventional existence, conventional self, etc. In addition, $\sim(\sim x)$ contradicts with $\sim x$ because by the rule of double negation it becomes positive, thus, implying x; the third denial, $\sim(x \,\&\, \sim x)$, is tautologous to $\sim x$ and $\sim(\sim x)$, and $\sim\sim(x \,\&\, \sim x)$ contradicts with $\sim(x \,\&\, \sim x)$ because it implies $(x \,\&\, \sim x)$. Sera Jetsün argues:

> If it were not so, then it would follow that all *dharma*s, the subject, are existent, because they are not non-existent . . . Furthermore, it would follow that all *dharma*s, the subject, are existent, non-existent, both and neither, because all *dharma*s are not existent, non-existent, not both nor neither. [This is because of] the reason [you] hold.[166]

Using the law of double negation, the Gelukpas criticized the Ngarabpa position of 'neither existent, nor non-existent' (*yod min med min*) as being full of contradictions and logically untenable. Pari Rabsal, for instance, writes:

> Here, although [one] might claim the reasoning of the wise of India and Tibet that double negation is understood to be affirmation, one is [only]

> sharpening the weapon [which would] kill oneself. For if [it is] without lack of hypostatic existence, [it] would become hypostatically existent and even if [it is] not non-hypostatic existence, [it] would be hypostatic existence. [This shows] one's case of being unfamiliar even with the *bsdus tshan* (=*bsdus grwa*) of 'reversion of is and reversion of is-not'[167] which are [within curricular] scopes of beginners. [Hence] maintaining a tenet system, it appears, would be very difficult [in your case].[168]

Pari Rabsal is saying that Mipham's assertion is self-destructive given the logical contradictions it entails through the rule of double negation. Mipham denied, the contradictions mentioned in the earlier passage would arise because the negation of the tetralemma is a non-implicative or absolute negation and nothing is implied. The negations merely refute the lemmas of existence, non-existence, both and neither to help discard the corresponding apprehension and notions.

Unlike his followers such as Sera Jetsün and Pari Rabsal, Tsongkhapa himself did not raise the contradiction through the rule of double negation. Instead, he stressed that Mādhyamika negation of extremes is absolute and non-implicative.[169] However, he used the law of non-contradiction and excluded middle to refute the Ngarabpa understanding of Emptiness as neither existent nor non-existent. He reasoned that in an analysis where one investigates whether or not there is inherent existence, there cannot be something that is neither with inherent nature nor without it.[170] Everything must fall within either the category of things with inherent nature or without inherent nature, just as everything should be either existent or non-existent. Because there is no middle between the two, he observes in the *dGongs pa rab gsal*, a thing has to be without inherent nature if it is not with inherent nature and the *vice versa*.[171] Further, he says in his *Drang nges*, of the two: hypostatic existence of sprout and lack of hypostatic existence of sprout, if one is conceptually eliminated (*rnam par bcad*) the other will be fully affirmed (*yongs su gcod*). Both cannot be negated at the same time.[172]

Tsongkhapa goes on further to say that such analysis can negate the hypostatic existence of sprout and the hypostatic existence of lack of hypostatic existence of sprout simultaneously but not hypostatic existence and lack of hypostatic existence of sprout because in the latter case one will be automatically affirmed when the other is negated.[173] The same is argued with regard to ultimate existence. Ultimate existence and ultimate existence of lack of ultimate existence can be negated at the same time, whereas ultimate existence and lack of ultimate existence cannot be negated at the same time. Tsongkhapa remarks that the understanding that in establishing Emptiness, existence, non-existence, hypostatic existence, lack of hypostatic existence, etc. are all negated is a misconception based on phrases such as 'neither existent nor non-existent' in the Mādhyamika treatises.[174] Because these laws of excluded middle and non-contradiction applies to the Mādhyamika analyses just as they apply to other reasoning, naively claiming Emptiness is neither existent nor non-existent, etc. would lead to a host of contradictions. Thus, statements such as 'neither existent, nor non-existent' in the Mādhyamika works have to be understood with reference to inherent existence.[175] To support this argument, he and his followers frequently cited this verse from *Vigrahavyāvartanī*:

> If the lack of inherent nature are negated
> By [a thing] without inherent nature,
> With the negation of lack of inherent nature
> Inherent nature will be established.[176]

Mipham does not comment on this verse although his opponent Pari Rabsal cites this against him. He argues that the rules of logic such as the law of double negation, non-contradiction and excluded middle are not applicable on the level where Emptiness, free from all elaborations (*niṣprapañca, spros bral*), is established and all assertions of tetrad extremes (*mtha' bzhi'i khas len*) are refuted. Such rules are valid on the level of conventional truth, but not on the ultimate level just as it would be pointless to expound a theory of 'neither existent nor non-existent' on the level of worldly transaction.[177] The refutation in *Vigrahavyāvartanī*, cited by the Gelukpas, does not affect the delineation of Emptiness beyond all elaborations.

If one were truly refuting the lack of inherent nature, it would lead to the consequence of accepting inherent nature as is said in the verse. But in delineating the ultimate Emptiness transcending all limited elaborations (*spros pa nyi tshe ba*) such as existence, non-existence, Emptiness and non-Emptiness, etc. one is not really negating the lack of inherent nature, but delineating the lack of inherent nature fully by overcoming even the notion of lack of inherent nature itself. Mipham brings up the concept of relative and final ultimates by stating that lack of inherent existence can have two referents: one which is a mere negation of inherent existence and the other which transcends both notions of inherent nature and lack of inherent nature. Hence, negating the first, that is the lack of inherent nature *vis-à-vis* inherent nature, would lead to the proper understanding of lack of inherent nature *qua* ultimate Emptiness and bring about a culmination to its understanding and experience.[178]

In course of his rebuttal, Mipham despises the Gelukpa use of *bsdus brwa* logic as the standard means of argumentation to fathom the subtle topic of Emptiness. If Emptiness could be delineated and understood through the medium of profane *bsdus grwa* logic, which is taught in order to help beginners with articulation in debates (*blo gsar bu ba dag gi thal ngag kha byang gi ched du bstan pa*), why should the philosophy of Emptiness be considered profound and subtle and why would the Buddha be reluctant to even dispense it? If it were just as easy as understanding impermanence, all of us would be able to understand it quite easily and there would be no point in describing Emptiness as profound and abstruse.[179] Mipham asks, 'Is not [one] going too far if [one] refutes the doctrine of the Buddha (i.e. concept of neither existence nor non-existence) with the [reasoning from] *bsdus tshan* texts?'[180]

Furthermore, what is there to be so proud of knowing these life-consuming (*mi tshe 'phul byed*) exposition of mere words (*tshig tsam gyi smra ba*) such as 'reversion of what is existence is non-existence and reversion of what is non-existence is existence'? Although these rules could be easily understood at mere glance (*bltas pa tsam gyis rtogs sla ba*), most of them, apart from being interesting ways of finishing long days (*mtshar mtshar nyi ring 'phul byed kyi ched*) are of not much benefit to understanding the main philosophies of the books even if they are learnt and mastered. Not only that, if one adheres obstinately to such expositions dependent on words (*tshig la rton pa'i chad tshul la tha gcig tu zhen na*), one's assertions would also be at stake.[181]

In this way, Mipham discredits the *bsdus grwa* reasoning at the level of ultimate analysis, and dismisses them as profane sophistry and rebukes the use of purely verbal and intellectual casuistry and reasoning such as the rule of double negation to appraise the profound philosophy of Emptiness as *malapropos*. Gedun Chöphel joins Mipham in showing disapproval of profane reasoning to delineate such profound topics as Emptiness. However, one must not overstate Mipham's denial of *bsdus grwa* arguments in establishing Emptiness as an outright denial of every rational argument. Mipham is perhaps the most rational of all Nyingma adepts and his contribution to logic and epistemology in general and his ratiocinative approach in Madhyamaka exposition should not be overlooked.

In Mipham's thought, the domain of logic and reasoning is the realm of conventional truth, where worldly transactions occur. In establishing the relative Emptiness, the mere lack of hypostatic existence, principles such as double negation, logical bivalence, excluded middle and non-contradiction are valid and tenable.[182] That is because, this lack of hypostatic existence, which corresponds to the Gelukpa concept of Emptiness, is, according to him, a conventional truth in Prāsaṅgika tradition although it is an ultimate truth in Svātantrika system. But, in establishing the final Emptiness, which is free from all elaborations, profane reasoning (*tshur mthong rigs pa*) such as double negation and excluded middle do not work. Such reality, also called the Great Madhyamaka, transcends intellectual ratiocination (*tarka, rtog ge*). Hence, the Gelukpa criticism based on these rules will not affect his position. Mipham does not say explicitly but he seems to also suggest that the law of double negation, excluded middle and non-contradiction would not apply to the Mādhyamikas themselves on the level of ultimate analysis because they do not hold any thesis on that level.[183] However, such logical tools may be used as long as they prove instrumental in delineating Emptiness for other. The use, however, would not incur any assertion on the part of Mādhyamika himself.

Both Tsongkhapa and Mipham undoubtedly incorporated Dharmakīrti's dialectical and epistemological theories into their Mādhyamika exposition albeit to different degrees and at different levels. Tsongkhapa and his followers not only explicitly endorsed the use of Dharmakīrti's method of reasoning in Madhyamaka philosophy – even in Candrakīrti's Prāsaṅgika tradition which is supposed to be not quite in favour of Dignāga – but also goes to the extent of considering it fundamental to Madhyamaka. This has been carefully studied by Seyfort Ruegg in his *On pramāṇa-Theory in Tsoṅ kha pa's Madhyamaka Philosophy*.[184] Mipham, in his commentary on *Madhyamakālaṃkāra*, frequently applauds the unification of the Nāgārjuna's Madhyamaka dialectics, which delineates ultimate reality, with

Dharmakīrti's logico-epistemology, which delineates conventional reality. This may be due to the fact that this work is a Svātantrika Mādhyamika text by a scholar coming directly from Dharmakīrti's tradition. He does not however make any direct connections between Candrakīrti's Prāsaṅgika and Dharmakīrti's system in any of his works which are considered to be mainly Prāsaṅgika in approach. Moreover, he frequently dismisses, citing even Dignāga and Dharmakīrti, the validity of pure intellectualism (*tarka, rtog ge*) in fathoming ultimate Emptiness.

Yet, in his general works such as the *Nges shes sgron me* and *Don rnam nges shes rab ral gri*, Mipham presents a systematic philosophy where Dharmakīrti's logico-epistemology forms the rudiments of conventional truth and Mādhyamika Emptiness embodies the ultimate reality. We do not know whether Mipham is underplaying the role of Dharmakīrti's rationalism in expounding Candrakīrti, because Candrakīrti showed some reservation against Dignāga, the founder of Dharmakīrti's tradition or because of his own Nyingma-Dzogchen orientation or both. In spite of his careful distinction of Candrakīrti's Madhyamaka from Dharmakīrti's rationalism, the influence of Dharmakīrti's thoughts on his writings cannot be denied as Dharmakīrtian terms and technique permeate throughout his exegesis of Madhyamaka philosophy. This may be partly because Dharmakīrti's logico-epistemological tradition has become a medium and method of Madhyamaka discussion in Tibetan scholarship.

The Gelukpa interpretation of 'neither existent nor non-existent'

The Gelukpas, with the aim of avoiding the contradictions allegedly faced by those who took the tetralemma negation literally, not only supplied the qualifier 'hypostatically' to the first negandum – existence – but also added the qualifier 'conventionally' to the second – non-existence – thus reading the negation of tetralemma as 'neither hypostatically existent (*bden par grub pa'i yod pa ma yin*), nor conventionally non-existent (*tha snyad du med pa ma yin*), both (*gnyis ka ma yin*) and neither (*gnyis min ma yin*)'. They did not use the negation of tetralemma as a method to exhaust all logical possibilities of being, as the Ngarabpas have. In fact, the negation of the second lemma, according to them, affirmed the conventional existence. However, with these glosses, the tetralemma method becomes inapplicable to other tetrads formed from production from self/other, permanence/impermanence, self/non-self, is/is not, etc.

Mipham's criticism is that if this method of tetralemma is seen to negate merely hypostatic existence and conventional non-existence, it is redundant and pointless to have the negation of the third lemma – both hypostatic existence and conventional non-existence – because the negation of the first two lemmas sufficiently proves that. In addition, the application of the law of double negation, which the Gelukpas consider to be applicable here, would lead to the ridiculous conclusion that Emptiness is both hypostatically existent and conventionally non-existent because the negation of the fourth lemma annuls the hypostatic non-existence and conventional existence. If both and neither are not to be glossed but taken literally as both existence and non-existence, and neither existence and non-existence as the Ngarabpas did, then Mipham asks whether this existence and non-existence refer to having existence and non-existence either ultimately or conventionally. Either way, the negation of the third lemma will be tautologous to the negation of first two lemmas and that of fourth lemma will lead to the ridiculous acceptance of both existence and non-existence for those who accept the validity of the law of double negation in this context.[185]

In order to escape this contradiction, Sera Jetsün goes on to make further interpretations saying that one must understand the negation as denials of the hypostatic existence of the four propositions, that is to say, (1) the fact that all phenomena are ultimately non-existent is not hypostatically existent (*chos thams cad don dam par yod pa ma yin pa bden par ma grub*), (2) that they are conventionally not non-existent is also not that (i.e. hypostatically existent) either (*tha snyad du med pa ma yin pa yang der ma grub*), (3) that being both ultimately existent and conventionally non-existent is also not hypostatically existent (*don dam par yod pa dang tha snyad du med pa gnyis ka yin pa yang bden par ma grub*) and (4) that being neither is also not hypostatically existent (*de gnyis ka ma yin pa yang bden par ma grub*).[186] According to him, the tetralemma analysis negates hypostatic existence of the fact of being neither hypostatically existent, nor conventionally non-existent, both and neither. However, this does not just make the reading of this method sophisticated, but leads, through the rule of double negation, to the host of contradictions that Sera Jetsün himself raised against his opponents.

Furthermore, Mipham argues that if the hypostatic existence of the four propositions is the sole negandum, then it is sufficient to just negate hypostatic existence. Why negate the four extremes?[187] In addition, if one accepts the Gelukpa paraphrasing, the denial of the tetralemma can no more be an exclusive characteristic and definition of Emptiness or ultimate reality as the Indian sources state, but of all phenomena even conventionally. A vase, for example, is even on the conventional level neither hypostatically existent, nor conventionally non-existent, both and neither. It would follow that every phenomenon can be attributed with the negation of tetralemma even on the conventional level. This deviates from the thrust of original Mādhyamika usage of the tetralemma in ultimate analysis to delineate Emptiness.

We have also seen Mipham argue in his *Rab lan* and *gSung sgros* that an understanding of mere negation of hypostatic existence cannot dispel the misconceptions of two or four extremes (*mtha' gnyis/bzhi*), eight elaborations (*spros pa brgyad*) and the thirty-two superimpositions (*sgro 'dogs so gnyis*).[188] Whereas Emptiness is supposed to eliminate all conceptual thoughts and their projections, the negation of hypostatic existence can only eliminate hypostatic existence and the grasping at it. Thus, refuting a negandum of just hypostatic existence is not sufficient to understand Emptiness fully and eliminate all misconceptions. He writes in his *rGyan 'grel*:

> In this way, if the reasoning of ultimate analysis negated only such 'hypostatic existence' and did not negate any of the subjects (i.e. phenomena)

> or repudiate any of their subjective cognitions, Emptiness would not be negating all subject–object elaborations. Beside, the three apogogical arguments[189] such as the meditative equipoise of the exalted beings becoming the cause of destruction of things would apply, and if there is a thing which is not repudiated or negated after being analyzed by ultimate analysis, it will become hypostatically existent. Therefore, with terms such as 'absence of production' [one] must engage in the pacification of all elaborations.[190]

Mipham also mentions in his *Rab lan*, *gSung gros* and *'Jug 'grel*, how Emptiness *qua* lack of hypostatic existence cannot even overcome the two extremes of eternalism and nihilism in the case of Gelukpa interpretation.[191] Adhering closely to the Ngarabpa stance, Mipham took Emptiness to be the negation of all entities including existence, non-existence, matter, sound, smell, etc. From the perspective of person conducting the ultimate analysis, everything is negated, not just hypostatic existence, and everything is empty of itself. Such Emptiness is free from all mental apprehension and elaborations and is the final form of the ultimate truth. It is, dialectically speaking, an absolute negation. It is this kind of Emptiness or Primordial Purity (*ka dag*), Mipham claims, that has been unanimously delineated by Candrakīrti in India and Rongzom in Tibet.[192] This interpretation perforce was the main target of Gelukpa refutation and the first opposition mentioned in Tsongkhapa's *Lam rim*.

Tsongkhapa says that using the analyses such as the scrutiny of whether the whole and parts are one or different mentioned in the Mādhyamika texts, some people examine the nature of things such as a vase in relation to their parts and come to conclude that there is no vase and so forth. Similarly, they apply the same to the investigator and conclude that there is nothing which exists and consequently hold the mistaken view of 'neither existent nor non-existent'. If such were the case of understanding Emptiness, instead of seeing Emptiness as dependent origination, the Madhyamaka view would be one of the easiest.[193] This is similar to the later argument made by the opponents of Gelukpas that if profound Emptiness were mere lack of hypostatic existence and not free from all elaborations, such Emptiness would be very easy to understand.

Tsongkhapa says, the Ngarabpas could not distinguish the non-existence of inherent sprout from the non-existence of sprout and existence of sprout from the inherent existence of the sprout. Unless one knows this distinction, one is bound to negate the existence of sprout while negating inherence in sprout and thus fall into nihilism, or assert inherent sprout while asserting sprout and end in eternalism, like the substantialists. The middle way is to view the sprout as existent but without inherent nature.[194] Further, Tsongkhapa elaborates on the identification of existence and non-existence of the *catuṣkoṭi*:

> If these phenomena are asserted to be existent by their own being, [one] falls into the extreme of substantialism or existence; accepting them to be

> merely existent is not substantialism or an ism of existence. Similarly, if the internal and external phenomena are asserted to be insubstantial [in the sense of] being void of capacity to function, [one] falls into the extreme of non-substantialism or non-existence; accepting them to be without inherent nature will not [make one] fall into extreme of non-existence. In this way, without distinguishing [what is] utterly non-existent from [what is] inherently non-existent, and [what is] established by [its] own being from [what is] mere existence, while preventing from falling into the extremes of existence and non-existence, if [one] relies upon stating, 'we say [things] are not existent but we do not say [they] are non-existent [and] we say [things] are not non-existent but do not say [they] are existent', [one] expounds solely contradictions and not even a bit of Madhyamaka message is revealed.[195]

The distinction between existence and inherent existence, production and inherent production, etc. is absolutely crucial in the Gelukpa system to identify the right dialectical negandum and establish the Emptiness that is beyond all extremes. To Mipham, such a distinction was relevant and tenable only on the conventional level but not applicable at the level of the ultimate analysis, which establishes the final Emptiness.

The nuances of inferential arguments

At the very beginning of the refutation of the Gelukpa position in the *'Jug 'grel*, Mipham presents the logical reasons why and how Gelukpas thought only hypostatic existence of the vase is negated by the reasoning but not the vase. The logical procedure of the ultimate analysis is juxtaposed and compared with that of the famous syllogistic argument, '*sound, the subject, is impermanent, because it is conditioned*' (*sgra chos can/mi rtag ste/byas pa'i phyir*).[196] In this probative inference, sound is the subject (*chos can*); impermanence, the property to be affirmed (*bsgrub bya'i chos*); being conditioned, the reason (*rtags*); permanent sound, the negandum (*dgag bya*) and impermanent sound, the probandum (*bsgrub bya*). According to the rules of *rtags rigs* logic, sound is not negated by this reasoning because it is the subject and not the negandum. The negandum, hypothetically, is the subject characterized by the property to be negated (*dgag bya'i chos kyis khyad par du byas pa'i chos can*), permanent sound in this case. Thus, it is non-existent and it would be a gross mistake in logic to take the subject and the negandum as identical.

The Gelukpas applied the same rules and procedures to the ultimate analysis such as the reasoning of dependent origination (*rten 'brel chen po'i gtan tshigs*) and production analysis mentioned earlier. In the argument, '*vase, the subject, is without hypostatic existence, because it is dependently originated*', the vase is the subject of the inference and therefore cannot be the negandum. A valid reason does not negate the subject. Mipham remarks that following this dialectical procedure, the Gelukpas firmly believed that vase, the subject of the ultimate reasoning, just as sound in the case of the reasoning proving sound to be impermanent, cannot be negated. It is the hypostatic existence which is the property to be negated and a hypostatically existent vase, which is the negandum. With this dialectical scenario in mind, they made the hermeneutic gloss 'vase is not empty of the vase but of hypostatic existence'. Mipham states:

> Considering that, although there arose the assertion that ultimate analysis does not negate the vase but negates hypostatic existence, [such an assertion] can be established likewise only if, without negating the vase by ultimate analysis, there exists a reasoning which negates an isolated hypostatic existence. Nevertheless, until [one can] establish [that] the vase is not apprehended ultimately, its lack of hypostatic existence cannot be established either. When the ultimate analysis examine the conventional vase [which] appears commonly, nothing, which can withstand the analysis, is obtained or apprehended. Then, [it] is termed as [that which is] not apprehended by the correct cognition of ultimate analysis, ultimately non-existent, empty of own being and without hypostatic existence that can resist analysis. There is no other definition of hypostatic existence and definition of lack of hypostatic existence apart from that.[197]

Mipham argues that although the distinction between the subject and negandum of the inference should be made while debating with the substantialists, it is a mistake if one considers only an isolated hypostatic existence as the negandum and assumes to realize Emptiness merely by negating it. The reason why vase is without hypostatic existence is because it cannot withstand the ultimate analysis and is not apprehended under the scrutiny. If the ultimate analysis does not negate the vase, there is no other way to prove the vase to be without hypostatic existence, and it would become hypostatically and ultimately existent.[198] Although one could make the verbal distinction that the vase is the subject and hypostatic existence is the negandum and that the former exists and the latter does not, in reality there is no such distinction as the latter is just a reification of the former.

This is also the case with the autonomous inference proving sound to be impermanent. Despite the verbal distinction, there is no separate permanent sound to be negated other than the reification of the sound as permanent.[199] In the case of the ultimate analysis, the Gelukpas held the subject to be the basis of Emptiness and not itself empty. In the *gSung sgros*, Mipham argues that this distinction is purely nominal and cannot be made ontologically.[200] He resorts to another analogous inference, '*rabbit's horn, the subject, is non-existent, because it is not perceived by correct cognition*' and argues that in spite of the nominal plurality of the basis of negation, the subject, and the negandum, they are not separate ontologically. The subject, predicate and reasoning are stated separately but they are not ontologically distinct. In the same way, in the reasoning, '*vase, the subject, is without hypostatic existence, because it is dependently originated*', the basis of the empty and the empty are not different (*stong pa dang stong gzhi tha dad du ma grub pa*).[201]

Mipham reiterates in *'Jug 'grel* that in the cases of both inferences, that is, the reasoning proving sound to be impermanent and the reasoning proving the vase to be without hypostatic existence, they eliminate the reification of the object; the misunderstanding of sound as permanent in the former and of the vase as hypostatically existent in the latter. There is nothing added or reduced ontologically with the sound and the vase. They are the same as before objectively irrespective of the different dialectical analyses and subjective cognition.[202] The main purpose of the reasoning, therefore, is to eliminate the subjective reification by negating the objects conceived (*zhen yul*) by such misunderstanding. In the case of the former, apprehending sound as permanent is the subjective misunderstanding, therefore, the object conceived, which requires negation, is the permanent sound. In contrast, the misunderstanding in the latter case is apprehension of the vase itself, not particularly of a hypostatically existent vase.

Sound and permanence are two distinct conventional entities even to the ordinary cognition, but the vase and its hypostatic existence are almost always identical to the ordinary mind. Hence, just as the vase cannot be separated from the hypostatically existent vase from the viewpoint of the ordinary thought, it cannot be separated under the scrutiny of the ultimate analysis. One cannot really apprehend the vase to be without true existence until the vase is itself negated. Thus, the vase has to be negated in order to eliminate the reification of the vase as hypostatically existent, for what needs to be negated is the object conceived by mistaken grasping.[203] The negation of such reification can be achieved by examining the vase itself with the ultimate analysis. Forsaking that, if one argues that the vase is not negated but an isolated hypostatic existence is, and thus advocates an Emptiness of other, it would not take one too far. Mipham says such negation of an isolated hypostatic existence is not expounded anywhere in the *sūtra*s and the Mādhyamika *śāstra*s.

Another distinction that the opponents of the Gelukpa make between the two inferences is their mode of reasoning. The inference proving sound to be impermanent is a probative inference (*sgrub rtags*) and as such it is logically not feasible according to *rtags rigs* logic to negate the subject of the inference. However, the ultimate analysis is a negative reasoning (*dgag rtags*) and negation of the subject would not render them invalid. The subject of a negative inference need not even be existent. Mipham however does not mention this.

Mipham repeatedly acknowledges that there is no Mādhyamika scholar who accepts anything to be hypostatically existent or who negates the shared appearance (*mthun snang*) *qua* empirical world.[204] Anyone doing so would be falling into the extreme of reification or annihilation. Negating the vase of shared appearance is to deny it even on a conventional level because the vase of shared appearance is the conventional vase (*mthun snang gi bum pa de ni kun rdzob kyi bum pa de yin*). In this view, the subject, reason, etc. in the aforementioned reasoning are all things conceived at the conventional level, and on that level one cannot deny their existence.

Hence, the subject, the vase of shared appearance, is not negated in the purview of conventional thinking in which the rules of inference function. Nonetheless, from the perspective of the ultimate analysis, the vase, which is the subject, is negated as much as the negandum, hypostatic existence. It is not the case that the ultimate analysis only negates non-existent entities.[205] Mipham reiterates that the ultimate analysis is not required to prove an utterly non-existent thing such as hypostatic existence to be non-existent.

The verification of contexts

To Mipham, it is of paramount importance in Mādhyamika hermeneutics to distinguish two different contexts of the conventional and the ultimate mode of thinking, and to place the discussion of negandum in the right context. Differentiating these two philosophical contexts in the Mādhyamika system, he states:

> Therefore, what is meant by 'empty/not empty' in this context is not [about being] conventionally empty/non-empty. It is the context [where the terms] non-empty and empty are assigned to [what is] ultimately existent and non-existent. Thus, [one must] understand that there is utterly no phenomenon whatsoever [that is] not ultimately empty. In conventional sense, [one] asserts the vase to be not empty of vase, [because] if it is empty conventionally, it would become non-existent.[206]

All things are empty on the ultimate level, but conventionally, things exist and are not empty. Conventionally speaking, he says that we can even claim things to be *bden par grub pa*, truly existent,[207] although *bden par grub pa* in this case would not have the same purport as the *bden par grub pa* discussed in the context of the ultimate investigation. From a conventional perspective, the vase, he argues, has to be truly established as vase, just as the law of cause and effect and the Three Jewels are true (*bum pa bum pa nyid du bden par grub dgos te las 'bras bden pa dang dkon mchog gsum bden pa bzhin no*).[208] However, in the context of the ultimate level, these very things that we experience in life are what are empty and negated by the ultimate analysis. It is the dependently originated phenomena, which are proved to be empty. The union of dependent arising and Emptiness would not be possible if the dependently originated things were not themselves empty.

The fact that all these empirical appearances are empty in one context and yet inevitably existent in the other is what makes Emptiness and appearance coalescent. This coalescence is what the Buddha proclaimed with his lion's roar of reasoning (*rigs pa'i seng ge'i sgra*), which no one in the world including gods can refute. Mipham criticizes the Gelukpas saying that some commentators, not being able to grasp this coalescence, have inserted words that do not appear in the *sūtra*s and *śāstra*s in order to interpret as it suits their understanding.[209] Failing to understand that what is not existent ultimately can perfectly exist conventionally, and thinking that existence and non-existence are mutually exclusive, they could not see existent things empty and negated on the level of the ultimate analysis.[210]

In the *gSung sgros* and *Rab lan* he presents the various positions held in Tibet concerning the theory of existence in these two contexts.[211] The Ngarabpa argued that whatever is the case in the ultimate context is more veridical and the true case. The Rangtongpas among them expounded that being ultimately non-existent suffices to be non-existent, whereas being conventionally existent is not a sufficient reason to be existent because conventional existence cannot assail the fact of being non-existent ultimately, whereas the fact that things are ultimately non-existent can assail conventional existence. The Ngarabpa who are Zhantongpas also gave precedence to the ultimate context and argued that whatever is ultimately existent is existent and ultimately non-existent is non-existent. According to them, the ultimate truth comprised Emptiness as well as all pure phenomena of the enlightened state, and conventional truth included the impure phenomena of *saṃsāra*, which are not really existent but are illusory projections of the deluded mind. The former existed in reality and the latter only as illusions.

Most Chirabpas, he comments, accepted that being existent conventionally qualifies a thing to be existent but being ultimately non-existent does not qualify to be non-existent. This is indeed the Gelukpa position. The Gelukpa scholars argued that general existence is defined by conventional existence, hence being non-existent ultimately does not suffice to be non-existent but being existent conventionally suffices to be existent (*don dam par med pas med go mi chod tha snyad du yod pas yod go chod*).[212] Citing this Gelukpa theory, Mipham remarks that this theory implies whatever is existent from the veiwpoint of the dualistic misconception qualifies to be existent whereas lack of duality discerned from the viewpoint of the sublime gnosis does not suffice for the non-existence of duality.

It would then follow that the dualistic mind of ordinary people and the objects it perceives are real and authentic, and the non-dual gnosis of the enlightened beings and its objects such as Emptiness are false. As such assertions are ludicrous insults to the gnosis of the *ārya*s and Emptiness, Mipham warns the Gelukpas to reconsider such philosophical stance.[213] Amdo Gedun Chöphel makes the same criticism accusing the Gelukpas how such position entails that what is not apprehended by the gnosis of the *ārya*s is not really non-apprehensible and what is ascertained by the imagination of ordinary folk is really existent.[214]

Regarding his own position, Mipham says, 'my/our tradition, clarified in the *Rab lan*, is the tradition of exponents of intrinsic Emptiness (*rang stong*)'.[215] However, Mipham's tradition is not the same as that of other Rangtongpas. We have seen his stance as regards *tathagātagarbha* in the Introduction. On the existential theory related to the two truths, he writes in his *Rab lan*:

> Most of the Ngarabpas observed that being conventionally existent does not suffice for being existent but being ultimately non-existent suffice for being non-existent. Most of the Chirabpas say that being conventionally

> existent suffices for being existent but being ultimately non-existent does not suffice for being non-existent. We do not expound like either of them. Being conventionally existent suffices for being conventionally existent but not for being ultimately existent. Being ultimately non-existent suffices for being ultimately non-existent but not for being conventionally non-existent. We expound the understanding of [how] the two [aspects] – ultimately non-existent and conventionally existent – in things can be seen without contradiction as one by nature.[216]

According to Mipham, what is negated in the context of the ultimate analysis is negated ultimately; it does not invalidate the conventional existence. Similarly, what is affirmed by the conventional mode of thinking exists conventionally, and not ultimately. The negation and affirmation are valid in their own contexts and at their particular levels. It is the substantialists, who equated the two and [mis]understood what is existent conventionally as existent ultimately and what is not existent ultimately as not existent even conventionally.[217] Thus, in Mipham's thought, the two modes of looking at things are equally important and their findings are valid in their own contexts that neither can repudiate the findings of the other. He also discusses the equal significance of the two truths in detail in his *Nges shes sgron me*.[218]

Mipham's bifurcation of human plane of thinking into that of the ultimate and the conventional mode clarifies his position on Mādhyamika assertion.[219] He emphatically shows that, with full knowledge of the two levels, one must negate all things on the ultimate level of thinking, and accept the existence of conventional realities on the other level. Because establishing Emptiness concerns the ultimate level and the ultimate analysis is carried out from such a viewpoint, there is no logical contradiction in negating all phenomena, and there is no need for the qualifiers. Thus, the negandum of ultimate reasoning must not be limited to hypostatic existence. However, to the Gelukpas, not finding phenomena on the ultimate level does not suffice for the negation of phenomena. Only hypostatic existence is required to be negated because only the apprehension of things as hypostatically existent caused the defiling emotions and subsequent bondage in *saṃsāra*. Mipham and other non-Gelukpa scholars disagreed. It is to this dispute on the cognitive negandum that we shall turn now.

An analysis of the cognitive negandum (*lam gyi dgag bya*)

The discrepancies in identifying the dialectical negandum between non-Gelukpa scholars such as Mipham, Gorampa, Gedun Chöphel *et al.* and the Gelukpas is directly linked to their disagreements in the identification of the cognitive negandum. Generally, Tibetan scholars enumerated the two obscurations (*āvaraṇa, sgrib pa*) of defiling emotions (*kleśa, nyon mongs*) and of the knowables (*jñeya, shes bya*) as the cognitive negandum, which has to be relinquished by practising the Buddhist path. In the current study, one kind of thought is discussed, namely, the subjective apprehension which causes negative impulses such as attachment. Because the debate on this is directly related to or a corollary of the identification of dialectical negandum, the persons involved and the nature of arguments are not different from the debate on dialectical negandum.

In his *Lam rim*, Tsongkhapa underlines the importance to identify, among all conceptual thoughts, the thought which is the root cause of all negative impulses, and relinquish it through negating its object.[220] The thought, he says, is ignorance or stupidity in contradistinction to the knowledge of Non-self or Emptiness. It is also known as the apprehension of hypostatic existence.[221] It is the grasping of an inherent nature or self, which he describes as that which is established by the way of its own nature objectively without being posited by the mind.[222] In this way, Tsongkhapa and other Gelukpas explicitly argued that it is grasping to hypostatic or inherent existence that obstructs the realization of Emptiness and that requires removal, and not all kinds of thoughts such as the apprehension of vase, pillar, etc.[223] Because the grasping of the conventional things such as vase and pillar did not obstruct enlightenment, it is not necessary to negate the objects of such grasping.

Pari Rabsal used the analogy of the projection of snake onto a colourful rope to demonstrate this point.[224] The misconception in the analogy is the superimposition of the snake on the rope and thus, it is the absence of snake on the rope that has to be realized in order to overcome the fear of snake. It is sheer annihilation to refute the existence of rope; one only has to negate the existence of the snake on the rope. In the same way, apprehension of things as hypostatically existent is what has to be eliminated, not the apprehension of things themselves, and in order to do that one need not negate the conventional things, but only the hypostatic existence in them. Tsongkhapa categorizes all conceptual thoughts into three categories depending on their mode of grasping (*'dzin tshul*): (1) those that engage with grasping of hypostatic existence (*bden par 'dzin pa*) when they hold an object, (2) those that engage with the grasping of lack of hypostatic existence (*bden med du 'dzin pa*) and (3) those that engage with grasping characterized by neither of them (*de gnyis gang gis kyang khyad par du ma byas par 'dzin pa*) thus being neutral.[225]

Presenting this triad, Tsongkhapa explains that not all thoughts which do not see things as lacking hypostatic existence are thoughts which grasp things as hypostatically existent and the *vice versa*. There is the third set (*phung sum pa*) which contains numerous thoughts that are neither.[226] In his *Lam rim*, he elaborates on how the persons in whom the view of lack of inherent existence has not arisen possess the first and the third but not the second. Were there no such third cateogory and all conceptual thoughts in people who have not achieved the view of Emptiness grasping at hypostatic existence, Tsongkhapa argues that there would not be a common ground of conventional standard or transactional means for the substantialists and the Mādhyamikas to have meaningful discussion and debate. This is because the phenomena conceived by the substantialists, that is, hypostatically existent world, would not be acceptable to the Mādhyamikas and the Mādhyamika world, that is, illusory existence, will not be acceptable to the substantialists.

By the same token, the unmistaken conventional theories delineated by the ordinary world, which the Mādhyamikas ought to accept, will be invalidated. This will result in a chaotic system, in which even Īśvara, existence and non-existence cannot be conventionally differentiated. Such a view is seriously detrimental to the understanding of Madhyamaka. He says that a lot of people seem to have forsaken many teachings, in the manner of Hwashang, through misunderstanding all conceptual thoughts to be defective and [mis]construing the religious praxis undertaken prior to obtaining the view of lack of hypostatic existence as involving grasping of characteristics and as fetters of *saṃsāra*, and consequently reducing them to provisional values taught for beginners who have not obtained the definitive view.[227] Thus, in Tsongkhapa's thought, it is a sheer mistake to view all thoughts, which do not discern lack of hypostatic existence, as flawed and negative. Only the first type of thoughts is epistemologically wrong and has to be negated.

Mipham and Gedun Chöphel *et al.*, dissented from this view holding all ordinary thoughts and concepts such as the notion of vase, etc. to be mistaken and obscuring in relation to the understanding of the ultimate reality. Mipham divides the cognitive negandum into grasping at the self of person and the self of phenomena and the obscurations of defilement and of knowable, which arise from them respectively.[228] He says through negating the self of person, one overcomes grasping at 'I', and subsequently, the defiling emotions and actions thus reaching the cessation of suffering, and in Mahāyāna, through negating both self of person and phenomena, one overcomes the subjective grasping and subsequently the two obscurations. Of the cognitive neganda, the manifest (*mngon gyur*) is overcome on the path of preparation, the seed (*sa bon*) on the first seven sublime stages, and the impressions (*bag chags*) finally on the three pure Bodhisattva stages.[229] According to him, there is no cognitive negandum which is not a dialectical negandum because if the path eliminates what was not negated by reasoning, it will be a nihilistic path.[230] However, not everything which is dialectical negandum is a cognitive negandum, for spiritual values such as compassion are not eliminated by the path.[231]

Mipham criticizes the Gelukpa identification of cognitive negandum with the notion of the hypostatic existence, which is separate from the empirical objects. He argues that the apprehension of the five conventional aggregates, without the need to hypostasize a separate self, gives rise to the notion of 'I'. Likewise, the notion 'this is a vase' is grasping the vase as phenomenon (*chos su 'dzhin pa*) and such grasping can give rise to defiling emotions, which can lead to accumulation of *karma* and consequently to suffering. Thus, if the notions of the aggregates and vase are not to be negated, what need is there to negate the notion of a separate hypostatic existence, which like a rabbit's horn does not even exist conventionally, and would not give rise to defiling emotions or lead to accumulation of *karma*.[232]

Continuing the argument, he says that as long as the five aggregates are grasped as aggregates of the internal continuum (*nang rgyud kyi phung por bzung ba*), the grasping at 'I' (*ngar 'dzin*) will evidently continue to exist.[233] As long as the five aggregates are not empty of their own nature, negating some hypostatically existent aggregates would not stop grasping at 'I' because grasping at 'I' arises in reference to the five aggregates. Thus, to Mipham, the notion of or grasping at the five aggregates must be eliminated in order to eliminate the grasping at 'I' and merely negating the notion of the hypostatic existence of five aggregates would not stop that. To support his arguments, Mipham cites the following lines from *Ratnāvalī*:

> As long as there is grasping to the aggregates,
> So long grasping at 'I' on them will arise.[234]

Tsongkhapa, followed by other Gelukpa scholars, however interpreted this verse by paraphrasing it with a qualifier thus reading it 'as long as one apprehends the aggregates as hypostatically existent'.[235]

In his annotative commentary on MK, Mipham makes another criticism of the Gelukpa theory in connection with the meditative equipoise of the *ārya*s, which, he observes, is free from all kinds of mental notions and elaborations. As long as all conceptual thoughts are not eliminated, although the notion of hypostatic existence is overcome, the meditative equipoise would not be free from all concepts and elaborations. The notion of hypostatic existence is just one of the numerous mental elaborations. Furthermore, if there is grasping at the absence of hypostatic existence, that is itself a mental elaboration.[236] He uses the same argument in *Rab lan* and reasons that in spite of overcoming the notion of hypostatic existence, gnosis free from all notions and elaborations will not be attained because the grasping at the lack of hypostatic existence is also a notion.[237]

In a similar argument in *gSung sgros*, he argues that if lack of the hypostatically existent dualistic appearance suffices for the lack of dualistic appearance in meditative equipoise of *ārya*s although other things such as the vase and notions of vase may still appear to the gnosis, it follows that minds of all sentient beings abide in reality without dualistic appearances.[238] That is because no one has the hypostatically existent dualistic appearance as such a thing is utterly non-existent. Hence, freedom from mental elaborations (*niṣprapañca, spros bral*) is to be without any notion, conception and apprehension,[239] not just to be without notion of hypostatic existence. He also says in *Nyi snang* that notions of characteristics are not free from the elaboration of dualistic appearances (*gnyis snang*) and Emptiness *qua* ultimate truth can be actualized only if one is free from all such dualistic thoughts.[240]

Amdo Gedun Chöphel followed Mipham in criticizing the Gelukpa theory that ordinary notions and thoughts other than the grasping at hypostatic existence are not to be negated. He sarcastically notes that according to the Gelukpas, the notion of a vase is correct whereas the notion of hypostatically existent vase is a delusion, and that these two thoughts can arise simultaneously in a person and are so alike that they cannot be easily distinguished.[241] He asks how bizarre it is that a correct cognition, which leads to enlightenment and deluded cognition, which hinders enlightenment are so alike. He goes on to say that if they arise simultaneously, the thought of the vase must be eliminated as much, and at the same time, as the thought of the hypostatic existence of the vase.

He continues further arguing that if the thought of the vase is not mistaken, other thoughts such as 'it is dawn', 'I am waking up', 'I am eating this food', etc. will also have to be unmistaken. In that case, it follows that most of the thoughts we have in a day are unmistaken and not to be negated. When does the clinging to hypostatic existence arise then? He says that it would be strange if this clinging to hypostatic existence to which we were wonted since beginningless time arose only occasionally in us. Are not the thoughts that we are most habituated with supposed to arise first and frequently? 'Because we are accustomed to this thought of hypostatic existence from beginningless time', he reasons,

> when we see a vase, [we] must confirm that the first thought [which] rises [in us] is the clinging to the vase as hypostatically existent. Hence, however [we] may distinguish the dialectical negandum verbally, in reality the negandum [we] must negate is the vase. [We] must negate the pillar, [we] must negate existence, [we] must negate non-existence. How can there be a separate negandum called hypostatically existent vase, leaving the vase aside?[242]

In the eyes of his Gelukpa colleagues, Gedun Chöphel's refutation, however sharp and satirical, is a tool of annihilation. To them, negation of conventional phenomena and ordinary thoughts is sheer nihilism.

On BA, IX/26

It is perhaps appropriate at this point to look at the differences between Gyaltshab Je's and Mipham's commentaries on the following verse, which Gelukpas often cited to support their interpretation:

> What is seen, heard or known
> Is not what has to be negated here.
> Here, the conceptual thought of [something] to be hypostatically [existent],
> Which is the cause of suffering, is to be eliminated.[243]

Both Mipham and the Gelukpas take this verse as a reply to the questions raised by the proponents of Cittamātra whose concept of reflexive awareness Śāntideva is refuting at this stage. The proponents of Cittamātra argue that if the consciousness is without reflexive nature, it would not be conscious of itself and if it is not conscious of itself, it would not be capable of knowing other things. Thus, all accounts of visual, auditory, mental and such other consciousnesses will have to be denied. It is as an answer to this refutation that most commentators of Śāntideva construed this verse.

Gyaltshab Je wrote an elaborate commentary on this verse, explaining the problems that the negation of empirical phenomena entails. He comments:

> Were [the proponents of Cittamātra] to say that if there was no reflexive awareness, there would not be memory, and therefore, all experiences of the objects, and seeing, hearing, etc. would become non-existent, [the answer is,] the conventional things which are seen by visual consciousness, heard by auditory consciousness, known by the mind and so forth are not the negandum here. They need not be negated because suffering is not caused merely by them and even the *arhat*s have such conventions. [They] cannot be negated because were [one] to negate them, [they] must be negated by scriptural citations and reasoning, and were they so negated, the same [negation would] also [apply] to the scriptural citations and reasoning. There is a fault if [they are] negated for [one will] become [a person] with nihilistic view. Therefore, in here, the conceptual thought of those objects to be hypostatic, which is the cause of suffering, is to be stopped because that is the root of *saṃsāra*. If the root of *saṃsāra* is not reversed, *saṃsāra* cannot be stopped, and because the grasping at form, sound, etc. as hypostatic is taught to be the root of *saṃsāra*, [Śāntideva] clearly accepts that *śrāvaka* and *pratyekabuddha* realise the Non-self of phenomena. Kharagpa *et al.*, say that mere appearance [of things] to the sensory cognition is not the negandum, but holding it as permanent/impermanent, existent/non-existent, etc. is the negandum. This [indicates] the return of the Chinese abbot.[244]

Negating the empirical experiences and conventional phenomena, according to Gyaltshab Je, leads to a host of problems. It is logically wrong to negate them as the same logic would apply to the reasoning and words used to negate them. Philosophically, negating the conventional phenomena entails a nihilistic view. Both of these criticisms have already been discussed. Soteriologically, the negation of conventional phenomena is unnecessary as they are not causes of suffering in *saṃsāra*. Referring to the position of Kharagpa and other on the cognitive negandum, Gyaltshab Je ridicules it as the doctrine of the Chinese abbot Hwashang. Let us now juxtapose it with Mipham's commentary on the same verse. He observes:

> If [one] speaks from the perspective of mere non-analytical gaiety,[245] these [experiences] of seeing, hearing and knowing are not negated here, for they cannot be negated and there is no need to negate [them]. If asked what is negated then, here the conceptual thought of hypostatic existence, [which] clings to every entity as being it[self] and is the cause of suffering, is to be eliminated. In this case, the commentary explains the term seeing as direct perception, hearing as [learning] from scriptures or other persons and knowing as establishing through correct inferential cognition. In brief, the negation of reflexive awareness is negation on the

> ultimate [level], and the concept of designating reflexive awareness to [the mind] for just being isolated from insentience is not negated. . . .[246]

Mipham designates the context in which empirical experiences such as seeing, hearing, knowing and other conventional phenomena are not negated as the level of frivolous gaiety, where analysis into the nature is not conducted but existence of things is taken for granted. Both Mipham and Gyaltshab point out that they cannot be negated; on the conventional level in Mipham's case, and generally in Gyaltshab's. Neither is there any need to negate them according to both. However, Mipham and Gyaltshab's descriptions of the negandum, the conceptual thought grasping something as hypostatically existent (*satyataḥ kalpana, bden par rtog pa*), are disparate. To Gyaltshab, this thought is the grasping at objects as hypostatically existent whereas Mipham deliberately interprets this thought as a clinging to an entity as itself. It is not just imagining the vase with an additional hypostatic existence but grasping the vase as the vase, which is the negandum in Mipham's interpretation.

Mipham held all such ordinary notions to be misconception obscuring the ultimate reality. Even the thought of reaching enlightenment is a form of ignorance that must be ultimately given up.[247] Were one to view that these ordinary thoughts and notions such as apprehending the vase as vase exist in a state of enlightenment, it would be a great insult to the Buddha for he has eliminated all ordinary thoughts and has actualized the non-dual gnosis.[248] Both Mipham and Gyaltshab exploits the verse to support their other assertions. Mipham uses it to authenticate his distinctive position that the Prāsaṅgika scholars such as Candrakīrti and Śāntideva refuted reflexive awareness only on the ultimate level and accepted it conventionally. Because the verse appears immediately after the refutation of Cittamātra concept of reflexive awareness, it is contextually appropriate for Mipham to interpret this as Śāntideva's assertion of reflexive awareness on the conventional level.

Gyaltshab uses the verse to support the Gelukpa assertion that *śrāvaka* and *pratyekabuddha arhat*s must realize Emptiness and eradicate grasping of hypostatic existence like the Bodhisattva in order to reach *nirvāṇa*. Both the issues of reflexive awareness and *śrāvaka* and *pratyekabuddha* realization of Emptiness are intricate topics and beyond the scope of this book. Some work on Mipham's theory of reflexive awareness and his position on whether or not *śrāvaka* and *pratyekabuddha arhat*s realize Emptiness has been done by Paul Williams and John Pettit respectively.[249]

Resemblances and reciprocal comparisons

According to the Gelukpas, denying all notions and thoughts and the understanding of Emptiness as 'neither existent nor non-existent' not only undermines the theory of dependent origination and faces many logical contradictions, but is also misleading in terms of meditative practice. Contemplation on Emptiness that is neither existent nor non-existent without any thoughts and apprehension, is a nescient meditation with no philosophical conviction. The Gelukpas accused Nyingmapas and other followers of the Ngarabpa tradition of taking up the viewpoint of Hwashang Mohoyen, the Chinese master involved in Samye debate between the simultaneists and gradualists.[250] They consider that Hwashang held a nihilist understanding of reality as neither existent, nor non-existent, neither is, nor is not, etc. and that all conceptual thoughts, including the virtuous ones, are hindrances to enlightenment.

To them, the Hwashang became a stereotype of the nihilists, and the Ngarabpas, the Nyingmapas in particular, are constantly ridiculed for their close similarity with Hwashang's system. Earlier, we saw Gyaltshab making critical comments on the position of Kharagpa and other Ngarabpa scholars who apparently held all notions such as 'the vase is existent' or 'the vase is impermanent' to be cognitive negandum. He remarked in passing that such interpretation is the return of the teachings of the Chinese abbot. Pari Rabsal, in his refutation of Mipham, observes with sarcasm:

> In this way, you say [that one] falls by holding the self to be non-existent to the extreme of non-existence and by holding the self to be existent to the extreme of existence. In that case, holding [it] as non-both, [one would] fall into the extreme of neither. Therefore, there is no doubt that [you] follow Hwashang Mahāyāna by not having grasping at anything. I do not blame you for you have inherited as [your] share, the shoe that was left behind.[251]

He also states:

> Although you seriously pretend to despise the view of Hwashang, [you] rely on the citations, which he quoted to support [his view], as a matter of credence, and because [you] assert [what] is existent and non-existent, to be adopted and to be given up, cognition and knowable [objects] and whatsoever [we] think of is clinging to self and obscurations hindering the path, you are undoubtedly the one from China who has come in a monastic garb.[252]

Similar accusations were made by other Gelukpa scholars including Tsongkhapa.[253] Referring to the story that the Hwashang left his shoe and prophesied that his tradition will come back to Tibet in future, the Gelukpas alleged that the Ngarabpa understanding of Emptiness is Hwashang's prophecy coming true.[254] This accusation was no surprise to the Nyingmapas as many of their prominent masters accepted the authenticity of simultaneist approach of Chan, the tradition propagated by Hwashang. Mipham's view however is different and is discussed in Chapter 5.

While the Gelukpas accused Ngarabpas, particularly Nyingmapas, of following Hwashang in defining the cognitive negandum, Mipham observed that the Gelukpa understanding of Emptiness and Mādhyamika dialectics are close to that of the Svātantrika Mādhyamika against their strong claim that they are Prāsaṅgika

Mādhyamikas. In the eyes of Mipham, the Gelukpas resembled the Svātantrika Mādhyamika in many philosophical and dialectical issues. It is not the aim of this book to discuss in detail the similarities Mipham pointed out. Suffice it to make a brief comparison. As mentioned earlier, the Gelukpas supplied the qualifier 'hypostatically existent' just as the Svātantrikas added the qualifier 'ultimate'. The Gelukpas defended by saying that both Prāsaṅgikas and Svātantrikas use the qualifier and that it is not a practice exclusive to Svātantrikas.[255] In both Svātantrika and Gelukpa schools, they argued that conventional truths such as vase and production, even from the purview of the ultimate analysis, are not negated by reasoning. It is to this effect that the qualifiers are used.

This led to another philosophical resemblance between the Svātantrikas and the Gelukpas, namely, the position that Mādhyamikas even at the level of ultimate analysis have theses and assertions. The other striking similarity between the two is the assertion of status of conventional existence, described as the convention established by own characteristics (*tha snyad rang mtshan gyis grub pa*) in the Svātantrika system and convention established by correct cognition (*tha snyad tshad mas grub pa*) by the Gelukpas. The Gelukpas argued that despite the fact that nothing exists ultimately, existence of conventional phenomena is confirmed by correct cognition. As such, their ontological status and the corresponding subjective cognitions are not mistaken or assailable even by the ultimate analysis. The cognitions are authorities in what they perceive and therefore not delusions which one must eliminate.

Mipham and the Ngarabpas refuted this theory arguing if the conventional things, as apprehended by worldly beings, are existent and established by correct cognition, and such ordinary cognition of conventional phenomena are not mistaken but authorities in what they apprehend, there is no reason to cultivate the transcendental gnosis of the exalted beings. The whole point of cultivating the gnosis of the *ārya*s through spiritual practice is to transcend the matrix of ordinary thoughts, which are mistaken and deluded. They argued using the following verse from *Samādhirājasūtra* that cognition of conventional things through the visual, auditory, olfactory, gustatory, tactile and mental faculties are not authorities in determining the ontological status of their objects. *Samādhirājasūtra*, IX/23 states:

> Eyes, ears and nose are not authority,
> Tongue, body and mind are not authority.
> Were these faculties authoritative,
> What use is the path of the exalted ones to anybody.[256]

Gyaltshab in his *rGyal sras 'jug ngogs* and Tsongkhapa in his *Lam rim*, interpreted this verse as showing that ordinary cognitions are not authorities in apprehending the reality[257] although they are generally correct cognitions. Were they authorities in defining reality, the gnosis of *ārya*s would become useless. In another case, Tsongkhapa commented that these cognitions are not authorities in connection with the apprehension of the own characteristics (*rang gi tshan* *nyid*), because they perceive their objects with own characteristics although the objects lack own characteristics.[258] Mipham makes sparse rebuttal of this Gelukpa concept of convention established by correct cognition, but other scholars such as Tagtshang and Gedun Chöphel made intensive criticism.

Of all the philosophical, dialectical and hermeneutic similarities between the Svātantrikas and the Gelukpas, the most outstanding perhaps is the definition of Emptiness. Although the Svātantrikas, according to Mipham, professed two kinds of ultimates, the topic to which we shall return in Chapter 4, they emphasized the notational ultimate (*rnam grangs pa'i don dam*), the Emptiness which is mere absence of the first of the tetralemma. The Gelukpa interpretation of Emptiness as lack of hypostatic existence but not free from all elaborations and apprehension, from the view point of Mipham, corresponds to this Svātantrika concept of notational ultimate. We shall return to this briefly in the next chapter. Referring to this, Mipham makes an insinuating and satirical remark in his *rGyan 'grel*, that perhaps the reason why in Tibet the understanding of Emptiness among even those who claim to be Prāsaṅgika Mādhyamikas is inclined toward the Svātantrika understanding is because of the auspices of having Svatāntrika Mādhyamika initially through Śāntarakṣita and his disciples.[259]

The resemblance and association of Nyingmapas with Hwashang and the Gelukpas with Svātantrika can both be explained as a result of their religious affiliations, philosophical priorities and practical orientations. The influences of the studies and practices, which constitute the primary components of their religious life, on their Madhyamaka understanding and exegeses are evident in both cases. While the Nyingmapas, on the one hand, expounded Madhyamaka with frequent overtones of the subitaneous and mystical Dzogchen thought, even considering Madhyamaka as synonymous to it, on the other, the Gelukpas, like Bhāvaviveka, Śāntarakṣita and their followers, formulated a highly systematic Madhyamaka tenet system with a heavy dose of Dharmakīrtian logic and epistemology, and *bsdus grwa* dialectics. The Nyingmapas, though not anti-rational, looked down on pure intellectualism and prioritized the exposition of Emptiness that is neither existent nor non-existent while the Gelukpas championed the rationalizing of Emptiness *qua* absence of hypostatic existence and disdained quietism. Both Gelukpas and Mipham provided ample reasons and scriptural citations to substantiate their positions and both adroitly interpreted the scriptural quotations which are *prima facie* different from their tenets and cited against them by their opponents. It is to the discussion of these Emptinesses and their theories of ultimate that we shall turn now.

4

THE FULLY EMPTY

Mipham's theory of the ultimate reality

He cannot say what the Absolute is, but he can say what it is not.
(J. W. de Jong, *Buddhist Studies*, p. 57)

A direct consequence of the difference in the identification of the negandum between Mipham and his opponents, which we have seen in Chapter 3, is the disagreement between them in defining the ultimate reality in Prāsaṅgika Mādhyamika thought. Both parties, like most other Mādhyamika thinkers, accept the absence of the negandum (*dgag bya med pa*) established by a negative Mādhyamika analysis to be the ultimate reality *qua* Emptiness. Unlike the exponents of *gzhan stong* who espoused an absolutist theory of the ultimate reality in the form of inherent Buddha Nature, both the Gelukpas and Mipham maintained the ultimate reality to be a pure apophatic and negational concept (*pratiṣedha, dgag pa*). However, due to the discrepancies in identifying what is negated by the analysis, and therefore is absent or empty, they differ in defining the nature of such an absence or Emptiness, which, to both parties, constitutes the ultimate reality.

In this chapter, I shall discuss the differences in the theories of ultimate reality between Mipham and the Gelukpa masters. Several scholars including Seyfort Ruegg, Hopkins, Thurman, Newland, Wayman and Cabezón[1] have written on the presentation of the Gelukpa theory of ultimate reality in the West. In contrast, John Pettit's doctoral dissertation entitled 'Theory, Practice and Ultimate Reality in the Thought of Mipham Rinpoche', which was published as *Mipham's Beacon of Certainty*, is the only major work on Mipham's theories of ultimate reality in Mādhyamika thought so far. Based mainly on Mipham's *Nges shes sgron me*, Pettit provides a stimulating study of Mipham's thought by juxtaposing them with those of Tsongkhapa and Gorampa, and highlight Mipham's concept of coalescence as being the ultimate reality. Nonetheless, he does not make use of many other major writings of Mipham in which several crucial issues pertaining to ultimate reality are discussed. Hence, the aim of this chapter is to further elaborate on Mipham's theories of ultimate reality by using all his major writings on Mādhyamika philosophy and thereby draw distinctions between the mainstream Gelukpa position and Mipham's stance on the philosophy of the ultimate reality in Prāsaṅgika thought.

The ultimate and two truth theories

It is a general Mādhyamika assertion that every phenomenon possesses the binary natures of the conventional and the ultimate, which can be seen from two varying perspectives of the correct and false perceptions.[2] Like most other Indian scholars, the Mādhyamikas divided existent things into two degrees of reality. Commonly known among Buddhist scholars as the conventional truth (*saṃvṛtisatya, kun rdzob bden pa*)[3] and the ultimate truth (*paramārthasatya, don dam bden pa*) for being true and valid in their own specific contexts, these two aspects comprise the objects of a mistaken worldly view and a correct enlightened view of things. According to the Mādhyamikas, the conventional nature of the vase, for instance, is the physical vase we see, touch and make use of in holding water, etc. while the ultimate nature of the vase is the way it actually is (*yin lugs*), its ontic mode (*gnas lugs*), reality (*chos nyid*), *quidditas* (*de kho na nyid*) and true nature (*rang bzhin*) as seen by the unmistaken gnosis of sublime beings and as established by the Mādhyamika analysis. Hence, ultimate reality, ultimate truth and ultimate nature here denote the same thing. In the Mādhyamika system, Emptiness is the ultimate nature of the vase because the vase, from the perspective of the gnosis of sublime beings and under the scrutiny of the Mādhyamika analysis, is not found and therefore proved empty of hypostatic existence according to the Gelukpas and of even its own existence according to Mipham.

However, to many Tibetan Mādhyamika scholars, Emptiness is not the only ultimate reality in Mādhyamika thought. As mentioned earlier, Zhantongpa thinkers such as the Jonangpas included the *tathāgatagarbha* and all aspects of Buddhahood within the category of the ultimate truth. Further, others such as Longchenpa, Karmapa Mikyod Dorje and Śākya Chogdan included the non-dual gnosis which discerns Emptiness within the category of ultimate nature. The Gelukpas, strictly following Candrakīrti, accepted only Emptiness to be the authentic ultimate nature (*don dam mtshan nyid pa*) in the Mādhyamika system. Mipham underscored the importance of distinguishing the different philosophical contexts within Mādhyamika in order to verify what is ultimate reality in a particular context. He argued that even within the Mādhyamika system, there are two different concepts of two truths: the two truths of abiding/ontic and appearing/phenomenal modes (*gnas snang bden gnyis*) and the two truths of appearance and Emptiness (*snang stong bden gnyis*).

In his *rGyan 'grel, gSung sgros, Rab lan, Don rnam nges shes rab ral gri* and *Nges shes sgron me*, he reiterates this distinction of two different theories of two truths stressing on its crucial significance in understanding the *sūtra*s and *śāstra*s. He writes in his *Rab lan*:

> In the great treatises two different ways of delineating the two truths are explained. The first case is that in which the ontic nature of non-production (= Emptiness) is termed as the ultimate and the transactional mode of appearance as the conventional. The second, maintained with

> regard to transactional [mode], is [in which] both objects and subjects of which the ontic and appearing [modes] conform are termed as the ultimate, and both objects and subjects [of which the ontic and appearing] do not conform as the conventional. According to this system, whether in *sūtra* or *mantra* [tradition], the term ultimate also applies to the subject. It is also possible to designate even persons, who realize, as notational and non-notational sublime persons. Although the terms 'ultimate' and 'conventional' are the same [in both], the two systems vary in understanding the meaning. Hence, if [one] does not know how to explain through distinguishing the intentions of individual traditions, hopes to fathom the great treatises would be in vain for [it would be like] a needle's eye-like-narrow mind measuring the space.[4]

Mipham formulates the binary theories of two truths and the corresponding cognitions in order to explain varying concepts of the ultimate in Mādhyamika and the nuances involved in the usage of the term. The two truths of ontic and appearing modes of the two different theories pertain to the dichotomy of ontic existence and phenomenal appearances taught in the *sūtra*s categorized as the Last Wheel (*'khor lo mtha' ma*) and later formulated in treatises such as Nāgārjuna's *Dharmadhātustotra* and Maitreya's *Ratnagotravibhāga*. According to Mipham, a thing which is objectively existent so that its phenomenal appearance and its ontic state are consistent (*gnas snang mthun pa*) are ultimate whereas phenomenal appearances, such as the illusion of *saṃsāra*, which do not conform with the ontic reality, are considered to be conventional or worldly. The pure realm of the Buddha, for instance, exists as it appears and is thus ultimate in this sense whereas the infernal ground in the hell is an illusion and thus termed conventional. According to Mipham, all things which fall within the domain of *nirvāṇa* or enlightenment are ultimate truths in this context because they are ontic as opposed to the adventitious appearances of the *saṃsāra*, which form the conventional truths.

Corresponding to these two truths are the two subjective cognitions of the correct cognition of mundane seeing (*tshur mthong tshad ma*) and the correct cognition of pure discerning (*dag gzigs tshad ma*).[5] Although both fall within the category of entirely conventional cognition (*kun tu tha snyad pa'i tshad ma*)[6] because they are not analytical and investigative cognition as it is in the case of the ultimate cognition apprehending ultimate *qua* Emptiness, the former is mainly a sense experience or dependent on sense experience and is characterized by a limited scope (*nyi tshe'i yul*) while the latter is a product of some transcendental insight and has greater scope (*rgya che'i yul*) in terms of both depth and magnitude.[7] Thus, the latter is considered closer to objective reality than the former. It is through the theory of ontic and appearing truths and corresponding cognitions that Mipham explains the varying degrees of pure and impure, mistaken and non-mistaken, ontic and superficial, permanent and transient conventional existences. Both ultimate and conventional in this case are still within the domain of non-analytical transaction. Analyses such as the scrutiny of production are not undertaken at this level. Thus, both are conventional truths if viewed from the perspective of the Mādhyamika analytical cognition.[8]

In contrast, the two truths of appearance and Emptiness pertain to the theories of conventional phenomena and the ultimate reality as taught in the *sūtras* of the Middle Wheel (*'khor lo bar pa*) and later systematically formulated in the Mādhyamika treatises. In this case, ultimate reality constitutes Emptiness, the absence of own being as established by the Mādhyamika analysis whereas conventional truth consists of all phenomena other than the ultimate truth apprehended on a non-analytical level of transaction. Thus, conventional truth in this context encompasses the conventional and also the ultimate truths of the previous theory except for Emptiness. Conventional cognition encompasses all empirical experiences and conceptual thoughts, which apprehend their objects without investigating their nature while the ultimate cognition is the analytical insight or gnosis experiencing the empty nature of things. It is this theory that is more commonly known as the two truth theory and Mipham also uses the terms 'conventional' and 'ultimate' in most cases to denote the two truths in this context.

The theory of these two truths in Mādhyamika thought forms a topic of extensive study in Tibet. I shall not deal here in great detail with the theory of these two truths. However, I shall briefly juxtapose a few Nyingmapa and Gelukpa definitions of the two truths to illustrate the difference which is crucial to their understanding of the ultimate truth. Longchenpa, in his *Grub mtha' mdzod*, defines the two truths as follows:

> As for definitions: of the two, the definition of the conventional [truth] is the appearance in the form of elaborations of object and subject. . . . The nature free from elaboration of object and subject is the definition of the ultimate truth.[9]

Similar definitions are also given in his *Yid bzhin mdzod*.[10] Longchenpa understood Emptiness as the nature free from the duality of subject and object. As long as it appears in the form of either a subject or an object, it is still within the domain of conventional truth. Tsongkhapa, a few decades after him, provided a different understanding of the two truths in Prāsaṅgika thought. In his *dGongs pa rab gsal*, he glosses Candrakīrti's verse and explains that conventional truth is that which is obtained by incorrect perception; that is to say, the objects obtained by conventional correct cognition which discerns deceptive and false objects. The ultimate is the object obtained by the reasoning consciousness, that is, the Mādhyamika analytical mind, which discerns the correct nature.[11] He also explains the same in his commentary on MK[12] and BA. He comments on BA, IX/2:

> Therefore, the object of the correct cognition which discerns the ultimate is the definition of the ultimate. . . . 'Is said to be conventional' is [showing] the thing to be defined. Thought is the definition, that is to say the object of transactional thought as implied by the earlier.[13]

He explains that there are three kinds of thoughts: basic, transactional and ultimate thoughts. Ultimate truth being beyond thoughts refers to the first two types of thoughts and the thought described as conventional truth refers to the second. The first two are not free from a dualistic appearance and no dualistic cognition can discern the ultimate directly. Thus, it is the ultimate thought which discerns the ultimate truth and it is through the subjective non-dualistic thought that the ultimate truth is distinguished from other entities.

Tsongkhapa's description of the two truths is a vicious circle in that the understanding of the definition of the two truths depends on verifying their subjective cognitions and the subjective cognition in turn can only be verified by understanding the two truths. Hence, Tsongkhapa remarks that for someone to know if something is conventional, he will have to discern the Madhyamaka view.[14] Tsongkhapa's circular definition of two truths is continued by most of his Gelukpa followers. Sonam Drakpa in his commentary on MA writes:

> This treatise [MA] bifurcates, in the case of every phenomenon, objects through which correct cognition investigating convention becomes a correct cognition investigating convention and objects through which correct cognition investigating the ultimate becomes a correct cognition investigating the ultimate. The former is shown to be the definition of conventional truth and the latter to be the definition of the ultimate truth.[15]

Sera Jetsün also defines in a similar way:

> That which is the object obtained by reasoning consciousness investigating the ultimate and to which the reasoning consciousness investigating the ultimate engages as reasoning consciousness investigating the ultimate is the definition of that which is ultimate truth. . . . That which is the object obtained by conventional correct cognition and to which that [conventional correct cognition] engages as conventional correct cognition is the definition of that which is conventional truth.[16]

Similar definitions are given by Khedrub Je, Jamyang Zhadpa, Changkya Rolpai Dorje and Ngawang Paldan. Newland discusses these definitions in detail in his *Two Truths* and also comments that these definitions would seem to involve circular elements but are not circular.[17] However, he does not give any reasons as to why they are not vicious circles. Among the Gelukpa scholars, Gyaltshab Je, in his *rGyal sras 'jug ngogs*, is rather unique in his definition of the two truths. He presents the definitions putting them in a special *bsdus grwa* format known among the Gelukpas as the 'perfect formula of defining' (*mtshon sbyor rnam dag*):

> The lack of inherent nature in person and aggregate, the basis of definition, is defined to be the ultimate truth, for it is not known by the correct perceptual cognition which directly discerns it by the way of appearing

itself dualistically to that, but is [still] knowable by the perception which perceives it. . . .

The person and aggregate, the basis of definition, are termed as conventional truths, for they are to be known by the correct perceptual cognition which directly discerns them by the way of appearing themselves dualistically to it.[18]

Gyaltshab explicates that the ultimate truth is that which appears to direct the perception but without the appearance of subject–object dualism. He is clear in his statement of the second part of his definition of ultimate truth that ultimate truth is knowable. This he clarifies in order to argue against his opponents who interpret BA, IX/2 directly and maintain ultimate truth to be beyond the scope of the mind. We can say that to Gyaltshab, the ultimate is determined by its appearance to its subjective cognition in a non-dualistic way. This is quite similar to Longchenpa, at least in presenting the difference through subject–object duality. Closely following Gyaltshab, Drakar Trulku also distinguishes the two truths with regard to subject–object duality in his criticism of Mipham.[19]

Mipham does not give terse definitions in his commentary on the BA, IX/2. Instead, he explains that conventional truths are the illusory appearance of production and so forth resembling dream and magic which appear even as they are void of inherent nature. The ultimate is the lack of production when the nature of such an appearance is analysed properly.[20] However, in his *Grub bsdus*, he presents verbatim the definitions of the two truths which Longchenpa formulated in *Yid bzhin mdzod*:

> The definitions are: Conventional [truth] is the phenomenon which is not beyond the scope of thoughts and which cannot withstand analysis. Ultimate [truth] is the reality beyond the scope of thoughts and utterly pacified of apprehensions.[21]

We can see that according to Mipham a major distinction between the two truths is that of being within and beyond the scope of thoughts. The status of being within and beyond the scope of the thoughts is determined by whether or not they lack elaborations and apprehension. One of Mipham's direct disciples, Khenpo Kunzang Paldan also puts it in a similar way:

> That which is beyond thought, ineffable and inconceivable is the definition of the ultimate truth. The deluded thought and its objects is the definition of conventional truth.[22]

Bodpa Trulku, a staunch follower of Mipham and an outstanding Nyingma scholar however puts it in a slightly different way which resembles the Gelukpa style. He writes in his *lTa grub shan 'byed gnad kyi sgron me*:

> In our tradition the definition of two individual truths is asserted in [this] way: The reality *qua* ontic nature which is the object of the gnosis of

> equipoise which transcends thoughts and the phenomena *qua* appearance which is the object of empirical conventional thoughts are respectively the definition of ultimate and conventional truths.[23]

He goes on to say that Candrakīrti in his MA expressed the definition of the ultimate truth in a cataphatic manner whereas Śāntideva in his BA taught it in an apophatic manner. Both present the definition of the conventional truth in an cataphatic manner.[24] In this book, Bodpa Trulku also undertakes an elaborate treatment of Mipham's Madhyamaka position including the binary theories of two truths. In Bodpa Trulku, Mipham's theory of the ultimate and the two sets of two truths found a staunch advocate. Passed down through masters such as him, these theories of Mipham remain central to the understanding and exposition of Mādhyamika in the Nyingma school. Let us now return to Mipham's arguments for the assertion of the two sets of two truths.

Delineating the two different theories of two truths, Mipham argues that the verification of the two is vital to the proper understanding of the concept of the ultimate and in dealing with the nuances of the term 'ultimate'. He writes in his *gSung sgros* that not all conventional appearances have to be deceptive and mistaken and not everything termed ultimate have to be mere Emptiness; there are two ways of understanding the two truth theories in the *sūtra*s and *śāstra*s.[25] Like Plato's myth of the cave, Mipham presents several degrees of reality corresponding to the different subjective cognitions. The impure worldly existence apprehended by the cognition of mundane seeing is the lowest level of reality, a mere illusion and the most conventional of conventions.

By comparison, the appearances apprehended by the cognition of pure seeing which is free from delusion are objectively existent according to Mipham. Notwithstanding their Emptiness or absence from the viewpoint of Mādhyamika analysis, they are ontic entities evident to some higher plane of thought albeit only in a transactional capacity. According to Mipham, things such as *tathāgatagarbha*, gnosis and qualities of the Buddha belong to this category of the ultimate. However, even these ontic entities are not found if thoroughly investigated using the Mādhyamika analysis. Thus, from the viewpoint of the ultimate cognition, only Emptiness *qua* absence of own being is tenable. Furthermore, even ultimate *qua* Emptiness is divided into notational and non-notational ultimates, the classification to which we shall come back later.

It is evident in his writings that this persistent formulation of the two sets of two truths and different gradation of realities to Mipham is a hermeneutic attempt to coherently accommodate in one Mādhyamika tradition, the concepts of the deceptive and non-deceptive or the pure or impure conventions, and the theories of ultimate *qua* Emptiness and ultimate *qua* ontic existence that appear in different Mādhyamika treatises. Among various contributions of Mipham in Mādhyamika scholarship, this formulation of the two-truth theories stands as an important one of his philosophical exposition as well as his hermeneutic enterprise to bridge the two major traditions of profound and vast Mahāyāna Buddhism passed down from

Nāgārjuna and Asaṅga respectively. I shall not elaborate here on his endeavours to bring the two traditions into one coherent system. Instead, I shall revert to the disputes between Mipham and his opponents concerning the understanding and the definition of ultimate *qua* Emptiness, the ultimate of the two truths of appearance and Emptiness (*snang stong bden gnyis*).

The ultimate and the nature of negation

Emptiness, when described in dialectical terms by Tibetan scholars, is generally accepted to be a negation and most Tibetans agree on the definition of negation and its subcategories of implicative or pre-suppositional negation and non-implicative or absolute negation.[26] However, Tibetan scholars varied in asserting as to which of the two categories of negations Emptiness belonged. Some Tibetan scholars such as Jonangpas, Karmapa Mikyod Dorje and Śākya Chogdan took Emptiness to be a pre-suppositional or implicative negation because an affirmation of ultimate gnosis or absolute *tathāgatagarbha* is implied after the negation of transient worldly things. Both Mipham and the Gelukpas accept Emptiness to be an absolute negation. However, as seen in the previous chapter, Mipham accused the Gelukpas of having to assert a theory of Emptiness that is implicative in nature.

What became more contentious than the question of which negation is Emptiness is the dispute on the very nature of Emptiness, which both Mipham and his Gelukpa opponents considered to be absolute negation. The Gelukpas explicitly equated Emptiness with the absence of hypostatic existence or the inherent nature and maintained such absence to be the ultimate truth. Thus, in their theory, the view that Emptiness is an absence of hypostatic existence is an unmistaken understanding, which cannot be invalidated or surpassed by any further understanding in its ontological rectitude. However, to Mipham, as to many other non-Gelukpa scholars, the view of Emptiness *qua* mere absence of hypostatic existence is also to be ultimately given up. Just as hypostatic existence does not exist under the scrutiny of the Mādhyamika analysis, the absence of hypostatic existence cannot exist under such scrutiny either. Ultimate Emptiness must transcend the dualism of hypostatic existence and its absence, of existence and non-existence, one and many, empty and non-empty, self and non-self, permanence and impermanence and so on. Ultimate Emptiness, in Mipham's thought, is free from all mental elaborations (*niśprapañca, spros bral*), and the view of Emptiness *qua* absence of hypostatic existence is an inferior and provisional understanding. It has to be negated in order to reach the ultimate Emptiness free from all elaborations. Although both absence of hypostatic existence (*bden med*) and lack of elaborations are, in dialectical terms, absolute negations, they differed vastly in their philosophical description and it is over this difference that the two parties continue to attack each other considering their own interpretation as the correct way of understanding the ultimate Emptiness.

Tsongkhapa and his followers attacked the Ngarabpa position that the absence of hypostatic existence or inherent nature has also to be negated in order to realize the ultimate Emptiness. They repeatedly asserted that what is negated by ultimate analysis is the hypostatic existence or inherent nature but not mere absence of hypostatic existence. Tsongkhapa writes in his *Lam rim*:

> When an inherent nature which is established by its own being is negated, we ascertain that there is no inherent nature in the sprout. Then, even when another thought holds such absence of inherent nature to exist, its object (i.e. the absence of inherent nature) is not negated by the analysis. If that Emptiness is asserted to be established by its own being, then [that object] is negated.[27]

According to him, what is negated is a reified absence of hypostatic existence or inherent nature, which is itself established hypostatically or inherently, and not a mere absence of hypostatic existence. He maintained that the absence of hypostatic existence, like other conventional phenomena, is the object of a correct cognition, and therefore cannot be negated. Gyaltshab and Pari Rabsal, closely following Tsongkhapa, reasoned that it is the hypostatic existence which one needs to negate because it is the apprehension of hypostatic existence (*bden 'dzin*), which is the root of *saṃsāra*. Apprehension of the absence of hypostatic existence is a correct view and does not bind one to *saṃsāra*.[28]

In his *Drang nges*, Tsongkhapa also refutes certain earlier Tibetan scholars who observed that, in the case of Mādhyamikas, there are only reasons and inferential cognitions which negate inherent nature but not those which establish the absence of inherent nature.[29] These scholars held the view that Mādhyamika reasoning negates inherent nature but does not establish the absence of inherent nature and thus a mere absence of inherent nature is not its probandum. Mipham clearly espouses this position in his Mādhyamika works. Tsongkhapa argues that Mādhyamika reasoning and inferential cognition must establish the absence of inherent nature as the probandum, because without a probandum, the reasoning and inference would not be valid. Furthermore, he reasons that negating inherent nature with the help of scriptural citations, reasoning and by discerning it through inferential cognitions is in itself proving the absence of inherent nature. Although no other separate positive entity is affirmed, Mādhyamika reasoning is not without probandum. He elaborates that when we say or know that there is no smoke on the lake, smoke is negated but the smokeless nature of the lake is automatically established. Likewise, when we say or know that there is no inherent nature in the sprout, the inherent nature is negated while the absence of inherent nature in the sprout is simultaneously established. Thus, negating inherent existence is the act of affirming the absence of inherent existence.[30]

Tsongkhapa remarks in the *Drang nges* that maintaining 'inherent nature is merely negated by the reasoning but the absence of inherent nature is not affirmed' is an argument neither of Mādhyamika nor of Pramāṇa tradition.[31] Arguments against these opponents appear also in his *Lam rim* and *dGongs pa rab gsal*.[32] The two positions of the Ngarabpa scholars (a) that all phenomena, not merely hypostatic existence, are negated by Mādhyamika reasoning and (b) that ultimate Emptiness is not a mere absence of inherent nature which is affirmed by Mādhyamika reasoning but a reality transcending existence and non-existence, etc. form the two main targets of the Gelukpa criticism. Tsongkhapa devotes dozens of pages in his *Lam rim* and several passages in his other works to the refutation of the first stance and many pages in his *Lam rim* and *Drang nges* besides passages in other writings arguing against the second. His refutation of these two positions has been rigorously continued by his followers in most of their Mādhyamika works.

Using the laws of logical bivalence, excluded middle and non-contradiction, they argued that if absence of hypostatic existence were negated, hypostatic existence would be implied. Negating the absence of inherent nature would lead to an absurd consequence of reversing the absence of inherent nature to existence of inherent nature. Similarly, if Emptiness were empty of itself, it would become non-empty. Thus, to the Gelukpas, when a vase is analysed by an ultimate analysis, an inherent or hypostatic nature of the vase is negated. That negation or absence of inherent or hypostatic nature in the vase is the ultimate reality of the vase and apprehending such negation or absence is a correct view. Such negation and absence need not be negated to reach a greater reality free from all elaborations.

We have already seen in the previous chapter, how according to Tsongkhapa, things have to be either with or without hypostatic existence, with or without inherent nature and empty or non-empty.[33] These dichotomies, according to the Gelukpas, are contradictory in a mutually exclusive manner (*phan tshun spang 'gal*) and, as mentioned in the *bsdus grwa* texts, there cannot be a third option (*phung sum pa*) in the case of such mutually exclusive contradictions. Moreover, in the case of such dichotomies, when one is positively affirmed (*yongs su gcod*), the other is negatively eliminated (*rnam par bcad*) simultaneously. Tsongkhapa explains in his *Drang nges* that hypostatic existence and the lack of hypostatic existence are such a dichotomy.[34] However, what one must note is that hypostatic existence and a hypostatic absence of hypostatic existence (*bden med bden grub*) are not such a dichotomous pair and both can be negated at the same time.

Sera Jetsün, in his rebuttal of Gorampa, states that the use of these principles of double negation, excluded middle and simultaneous affirmation and elimination originate from the teachings of the Buddha and masters such as Nāgārjuna. He and other Gelukpas often cite this line from the *Saṃcayāgātha*, 'What is not existent is said to be non-existent',[35] to argue that in the case of mutually exclusive pairs what is not existent has to be non-existent, and what is not empty non-empty. There cannot be a middle which is neither existent nor non-existent. Thus, one cannot define Emptiness as neither existent nor non-existent or as neither empty nor non-empty. Similarly, Emptiness has to either possess hypostatic existence or lack hypostatic existence. Were Emptiness understood to be without the lack of hypostatic existence, it would then revert to being hypostatically existent. The Gelukpas consistently used the *Vigrahavyāvartanī*, verse 26 to support this argument.[36]

As mentioned in the previous chapter, Mipham maintains that the Mādhyamikas employed such dialectical principles only on a conventional level. He rebukes the Gelukpa for applying their profane *bsdus grwa* casuistry to fathom the profound philosophy of Emptiness.[37] He argues that on the level of the ultimate analysis, negation of absence of inherent nature would not imply inherent nature, but further reaffirm the concept of absence of inherent nature by transcending the dualism of the substantial and non-substantial, empty and non-empty.[38]

Mipham does not give an explanation of the verses cited by the Gelukpas. However, we can perhaps infer Mipham's interpretation of the verse by putting it in the light of his general position on the subject of having theses in Prāsaṅgika Mādhyamika. Mipham, following Longchenpa,[39] classifies Prāsaṅgika Mādhyamika perspectives into three different levels of (1) understanding the ultimate reality free from elaborations corresponding to the gnoseological experience in meditative equipoise of the sublime beings, (2) theorizing the experience of such ultimate in post-meditative state and (3) delineating the conventional theories.[40] In the first two cases, Longchenpa and Mipham deny that Mādhyamikas have any thesis of their own. It is in these two contexts Mipham reads Nāgārjuna's *Vigrahavyāvartanī*, 29–30, *Yuktīṣaṣṭikā*, 51, Āryadeva's *Catuḥśataka*, XIV/25, Candrakīrti's *Madhyamakaprajñāvatārakārikā*, 1 and Śāntarakṣita's *Madhyamakālaṃkāra*, 68. In the context of the third perspective, that is to say on the conventional level, Mādhymikas make their assertions and it is here that Mādhyamika must maintain the theories of ground, path and result of their tenet system.

The act of establishing ultimate Emptiness through reasoning and refutations falls within the second category of the three and from that perspective, the Mādhyamikas do not have any assertions of their own but only destroy assertions of their opponents. On this level, rules of logic such as that of excluded middle and double negation are used for the purpose of refuting the tenets of their opponents because the opponents accept the validity of such rules.[41] The Mādhyamikas do not accept the validity of such principles in establishing the ultimate, thus, the rules are not applicable to the Mādhyamikas. According to Mipham and Ngarabpa scholars, Nāgārjuna and other Mādhyamika masters used these principles, which are accepted by their opponents, only to destroy the positions of their opponents by showing internal contradictions in their systems. Because the Mādhyamikas did not have such an assertion and position themselves, the arguments using the rules of excluded middle, double negation and non-contradiction do not apply to them. This kind of argument of *reductio ad absurdum*, whereby the assertions of the opponents is used to dismantle their own system, is commonly used as a polemical technique of Mādhyamika to refute their opponents and establish Emptiness.

In his *Ketaka*, *rGyan 'grel* and *Nges shes sgron me*, Mipham also marks a distinction between the delineation of final ultimate lacking all elaborations and the partial ultimate *qua* mere absence of hypostatic existence and explains that the former is beyond any theories of negation and affirmation, existence and non-existence while the latter is still within the domain of intellectual theories such as negation and affirmation. He thus argues that the Mādhyamikas have assertions and accept the viability of principles such as excluded middle and non-contradiction on the level of establishing the partial Emptiness *qua* absence of hypostatic existence. Hence, at this level even the use of autonomous inference to establish this ultimate is appropriate.[42] However, this level of delineation of Emptiness is still a conventional level when compared to the ultimate Emptiness free from all elaborations.[43] On the level of ultimate Emptiness, no such principles would be tenable. Thus, Mipham accepts the validity of principles such as excluded middle and non-contradiction inasmuch as establishing the mere absence of hypostatic existence is concerned but categorically denies that such an absence is the ultimate Emptiness and that these principles of logic are applicable to the ultimate Emptiness.

One verse that some Ngarabpa scholars are reported to have cited in order to argue against the viability of rules of excluded middle and double negation is the following from *Lokaparīkṣa*:

> Here, existence is being negated,
> Non-existence is not being maintained.
> While saying '[it is] not black',
> [one] does not mean '[it is] white'.[44]

Ngarabpas argued that negating existence does not necessarily imply affirmation of non-existence or not being non-existent need imply being existent. Tsongkhapa quotes this verse in his *Drang nges* and goes on to argue that this does not show that the absence of hypostatic existence is not affirmed. Just as saying 'it is not black' denotes the mere absence of black and does not imply a separate white thing, saying, for instance, 'the sprout is ultimately without inherent nature' affirms the mere negation of the lack of inherent nature ultimately but does not imply a separate absence of hypostatic existence that is other than the sprout. Thus, he interprets the verse by arguing that it is an isolated lack of hypostatic existence that is not implied after negating hypostatic existence but a mere absence of hypostatic existence is definitely affirmed.

Closely following Tsongkhapa and citing Bhāvaviveka and Avalokitavrata, Sera Jetsün, in his rebuttal of Śākya Chogdan, reasons that this verse just shows the absence of inherent nature to be an absolute negation. He argues that the verse just negates inherent nature, just as black is negated by saying 'this is not black', but does not imply the existence of the absence of inherent nature, just as white is not implied by saying 'this is not black'. Were negation of inherent nature to imply the existence of an absence of inherent nature, it would become an implicative negation. The verse, according to him, just shows that the absence of hypostatic existence is not an implicative but an absolute negation.[45] It does not prove that the absence of an inherent existence is not affirmed or that rules of double negation and excluded middle are not applicable.

However, from Mipham's viewpoint, the Gelukpas are mistaken in affirming (*sgrub*) the absence of hypostatic existence as the final ultimate. According to him, ultimate Emptiness cannot be affirmed, delineated or discerned in the normal sense of the word. Words such as establish, affirm, discern are used only for the sake of convenience. They are like a finger pointing to the moon. The moon is not on the finger tip and it would be childish and wrong to think so.[46] Similarly, words are also misleading. Although the terms such as prove, establish or delineated are used, there is nothing that can be proved, affirmed or delineated to be the ultimate Emptiness. He frequently cites the following verse by Maitreya to describe this state.

> Herein, there is not a thing to be negated,
> And not a thing to be affirmed.
> View the reality as it really is;
> One who views the reality is emancipated.[47]

In answer to whether the view is implicative negation or absolute negation, he says in his *Nges shes sgron me*:

> Both of them are imputed by the mind,
> In reality, [we do] not accept it to be either.
> The primordial reality is beyond thought
> Without any negation or affirmation.[48]

If there were something affirmed or proved on the ultimate level, there would still be a cataphatic entity, a substance or being. 'As long as [it] is in the apprehensive mode of negation and affirmation', Mipham writes in his *rGyan 'grel*, 'it is not the nature which is void of four extremes of conceptual elaborations'.[49]

Mipham often compares delineating the ultimate Emptiness to pointing out space; there is nothing that can actually be pointed out.[50] As described in BA, IX/33 there is not anything (*kiṃcin nāsti, ci yang med*) that is apprehended on the level of ultimate Emptiness. In his *rGyan 'grel*, he cites the *sūtra* saying, 'Emptiness is a term denoting "there is not perceiving anything".'[51] However, he says that it is not like Hwashang's concept of not thinking of anything. Hwashang's lack of thinking is not totally free of thinking and without any reifying notions, but it is only a suppression of emotions and thoughts through thinking of 'nothing'. Being in such a state does not even avoid the extreme of existence, let alone all extremes.[52] More shall be said on Mipham's viewpoint of Hwashang in the next chapter.

In many of his Mādhyamika works, Mipham argues that establishing the absence of inherent nature is not what is of main concern. It is the negation of inherent nature and other mental elaborations that characterizes the ultimate Emptiness. The following aphoristic statement in his commentary on MK sums up his position.

> In brief, the existence of inherent nature is negated, a mere absence of inherent nature is not being established.[53]

This is exactly the same as the Ngarabpa position which Tsongkhapa refutes toward the end of his *Drang nges*. In the same passage, Mipham compares clinging to inherent existence and understanding the absence of inherent existence to disease and medicine, and remarks that the medication of absence of inherent nature would be only necessary and suitable when there is the illness of clinging to inherent nature. If the illness is cured, what use is the medicine? Thus, the theory of absence of inherent nature should also be given up after the attachment to inherent nature is remedied. As long as there is an absence or a negational entity which is an object affirmed by the mental apprehension, substantialization of some sort will persist and a proper understanding of things being neither empty nor non-empty, as taught in the MK will never be reached. Thus, to Mipham, the Mādhyamika reasonings do not ultimately prove anything, not even the absence of hypostatic existence, but only negate the presence of hypostatic existence and any extremes of mental elaborations for that matter.

Like many Ngarabpa scholars, Mipham cites from Candrakīrti's *Prasannapadā* to support this understanding:

> We are not proving this to be non-existent. What then? [We] are negating the conception of this as existent by others. Likewise, we are not proving this to be existent. What then? [We] are negating the conception of this as non-existent by others, because we wish to establish the middle way having dispelled the two extremes.[54]

Tsongkhapa quotes this in his *Drang nges* as one of the scriptural citations of his Ngarabpa opponents and seems to comment that this verse shows that Mādhyamika reasoning does not positively prove the non-existence of the ultimate production but merely negates the ultimate production, and it does not prove the existence of the ultimate production but negates the hypostatic absence of the ultimate production[55] and Sera Jetsün, in a slightly different interpretation, observes:

> The meaning of [the passage from] *Prasannapadā* is that we do not prove [things] to be ultimately existent or conventionally non-existent. Clearing the hypostatic existence which others impute in terms of existence and conventional non-existence which others imputed in terms of non-existence, [we] wish to establish the middle way free from these two extremes.[56]

Thus, unlike the Ngarabpas who most of the time read such passages by Indian authors without any interpretation, Tsongkhapa and his followers consistently interpreted them as negating inherent nature or hypostatic existence and affirming the absence of such inherent nature or hypostatic existence supplying qualifiers such as 'hypostatically existent', 'ultimate' and 'conventional'. One striking example, which shows the application of such qualifiers and the Gelukpa interpretation of Emptiness as negation of hypostatic existence and reflects the dissonant understanding between the two parties is the negation of the tetralemma (*catuṣkoṭi, mtha' bzhi*). This has already been dealt with in the previous chapter in the context of the negandum.

Mipham, like the Ngarabpas, took the negation of the four extremes of existence, non-existence, both and neither directly and maintained that the ultimate Emptiness is beyond intellectual elaboration of existence, non-existence, etc. To him, the ultimate Emptiness is free from all elaborations and to be free from elaborations is to transcend all objects of mentation and conceptualization. The Gelukpas disparaged such understanding as a nihilistic view and ascribed it to Hwashang. According to them, the negation of tetralemma cannot to be taken literally; doing so would lead to a host of internal contradictions. I have already discussed the logical problems alleged by the two sides to their opposition in the previous chapter. The following gloss of Sera Jetsün in his refutation of Śākya Chogdan on the interpretation of *Jñānasarasamuccaya*, 29 shows a typical Gelukpa reading of the negation of the tetralemma:

> Now, I shall explain the meaning of the lack of elaborations of four extremes, taught in *Jñānasarasamuccaya* and *Madhyamakāvatāra*, etc. in accordance with the intent of Je Tsongkhapa. That is to say, 'all phenomena are not existent' means all phenomena are not ultimately existent, 'all phenomena are not non-existent' means all phenomena are not utterly non-existent, 'not both' means all phenomena are not both existent and non-existent, and 'not neither' means not neither of the existent and non-existent. . . . In brief, if [one] expounds the content of those citations in brevity, the point is that all phenomena are not ultimately existent, not utterly non-existent, not both existent and non-existent, and not neither existent nor non-existent.[57]

Jetsün's gloss clearly shows that the tetralemma in his thoughts are not merely existence, non-existence, both and neither but hypostatic existence, utter non-existence, both existence and non-existence and being neither. The reality of the vase, for instance, is thus not characterized by transcendence from existence, non-existence, both and neither but by the lack of hypostatic existence, utter non-existence, being both existence and non-existence and being neither.

Mipham's main qualm concerning the Gelukpa theory of the ultimate is their assertion of the lack of a hypostatic existence as the ultimate Emptiness. He does not deny that the absence of hypostatic existence is a perfectly valid and tenable theory inasmuch as the understanding of provisional ultimate is concerned.[58] He repeatedly mentions in his works that it is a step to reach the final ultimate free from all elaborations.[59] However, to maintain that the lack of hypostatic existence is the final Emptiness *qua* ultimate truth in Prāsaṅgika thought entails many philosophical problems.

First, it is logically incoherent to argue that mere absence of hypostatic existence remains after hypostatic existence itself is negated by the Mādhyamika analysis.

As discussed in the previous chapter, nothing including the absence of hypostatic existence can withstand the Mādhyamika analysis. From the perspective of the Mādhyamika analytical mind, the absence of hypostatic existence, like hypostatic existence itself, cannot be found. This is because the notion of the absence of hypostatic existence is dependent on the hypostatic existence that if the latter is negated, the former would not be viable, as shown by Śāntideva's analogy of the death of a child in a dream.[60] He strongly argued for the interdependent and the ultimately untenable nature of dualistic notions such as existence and non-existence, production and non-production, empty and non-empty, self and non-self, investigation and the investigated in his commentary on MK, IX/7, BA, IX/111, 141 and *Madhyamakālaṃkāra*, 71.

Besides, if the absence of hypostatic existence were found on the level of the ultimate reality, ultimate cognition would have to apprehend it. Apprehending the absence of hypostatic existence as Emptiness on this level, according to Mipham, is a mental elaboration. From the ultimate perspective, apprehending any entity or non-entity constitutes objectification and reification. To view that there is Emptiness or absence of hypostatic existence on this level is thus reification. It is clinging to Emptiness (*stong pa nyid la zhen pa*) and it amounts to having the incorrigible view (*gsor mi rung ba'i lta ba*). If Emptiness itself were to remain after negating everything else, why would the Emptiness of Emptiness have to be taught? Mipham repeatedly cites MK, XIII/8 and XXIV/11 in his works insinuating that the Gelukpa understanding of the absence of hypostatic existence as ultimate Emptiness, and it being present from the viewpoint of the ultimate cognition is a misunderstanding. We shall return to a more detailed study of this accusation later.

He also argued that if all that the Prāsaṅgikas had to establish as ultimate was the absence of hypostatic existence, why would they have to abandon all views and have no thesis? There would not be any point for Candrakīrti to reject the use of autonomous inference to delineate Emptiness. If the ultimate *qua* final Emptiness were merely the absence of hypostatic existence, why would it be regarded as difficult to fathom, profound and ineffable? Mipham alludes to the story in *Vimalakīrtinirdeśasūtra* in which Mañjuśrī enquires Vimalakīrti about reality and Vimalakīrti remains silent to indicate that it is profound and ineffable. Mañjuśrī applauds him for the unuttered answer.[61] Mipham remarks, 'How could it be that Vimalakīrti did not know how to say "the quiddity [of things] is absence of hypostatic existence"?'[62] If the mere absence of hypostatic existence were the ultimate Emptiness understood by ordinary beings and discerned by the sublime ones, it would not be any more difficult than the understanding of subtle impermanence.[63] Mipham also questions how the ultimate *qua* absence of hypostatic existence can be understood to be the sphere of reality (*dharmadhātu, chos dbyings*), which is embodied in the Svābhāvikāya (*ngo bo nyid sku*)?[64]

Furthermore, Mipham argued that understanding a mere absence of hypostatic existence as the final ultimate goes against the objective nature of all things.[65] The ultimate nature of all phenomena is coalescence of Emptiness and appearance. Things are simultaneously empty as they appear. Emptiness and appearance are not separate parts but one and the same thing. Understanding Emptiness as absence of hypostatic existence and holding the conventional entity to be different from Emptiness defies the nature of coalescence. The Gelukpa understanding of the ultimate non-existence as one truth and conventional existence as the other splits the two truths into separate entities. Mipham termed this Gelukpa understanding, whereby one asserts the ultimate non-existence and conventional existence of things, as leaving two truths unaffected in their individual states (*bden gnyis so so rang sa na ma nyams par bzhag pa*) and went on to say that this is a provisional Svātantrika understanding of Emptiness. This and the topic of coalescence will be discussed in more detail in the following sections.

He also asks how the absence of hypostatic existence alone could eliminate all elaborations which it should eliminate if it were the ultimate Emptiness?[66] In his *Nges shes sgron me*, VII/17 he argues that if there is no ultimate reality other than the absence of hypostatic existence which is an absolute negation obtained after negating the negandum, then the discernment of the ultimate would not involve any appearance. It would be purely a negative modal apprehension of non-existence of hypostatic existence. If so, would not one become an advocate of the view of non-existence (*med par lta ba*) and one's view, meditation and conducts be influenced by an utterly negative approach because the understanding of reality is what one must adopt across all practises?[67]

Using various arguments, Mipham, in most of his writings on Madhyamaka, undertakes intense refutations of the Gelukpa position that Emptiness is the absence of hypostatic existence and sets out to delineate the Emptiness free from all elaborations to be the final ultimate in Madhyamaka philosophy. In addition to the arguments, Mipham cites from a wide range of *sūtra*s and *śāstra*s to show that the Gelukpa understanding contradicts the classical definition of Emptiness as transcending all notions and elaborations. Mipham devotes numerous pages to quoting these sources in his *rGyan 'grel* while commenting on *Madhyamakālaṃkāra*, 69 and over 40 pages in his *Rab lan* in his rebuttal of Pari Rabsal, who, like most other Gelukpas, dismissed the understanding of Emptiness free from elaborations as a legacy of Hwashang.[68]

It is to counteract this dismissive treatment of the Ngarabpa position, as the residue of Hwashang's doctrine and to prove that the concept of the ultimate reality *qua* Emptiness free from all elaborations is an authentic Buddhist teaching and is in tune with the Mādhyamika exposition of Emptiness, that Mipham undertakes an extensive quotation of the passages from the *sūtra*s and Mādhyamika literature to support his stance. Through the citations Mipham mainly demonstrates (a) that what is negated in establishing Emptiness is not merely hypostatic existence or inherent existence and (b) that the ultimate Emptiness is not merely the absence of such hypostatic existence. The Gelukpas, from his viewpoint, are not only wrong in limiting the negation to only hypostatic existence but mistaken in affirming (*sgrub*) the absence of hypostatic existence as the ultimate.

The Gelukpas, however, tactfully interpreted the citations applying qualifiers to the negandum. They shunned the negation of existent things in order to establish

Emptiness and the theory of the ultimate, which is free from all elaborations, as resilient leftovers of the teachings of the Hwashang. The Gelukpas further argued that it is taught that things are empty of inherent nature (*rang bzhin med pa*), without own being (*ngo bo nyid med pa*), without hypostatic existence (*bden med*), etc. or that things are ultimately or in reality not existent, in the *Prajñāpāramitāsūtra*s and other Mādhyamika literature.[69] Reified entities such as inherent nature, own being, hypostatic existences and ultimate existence, as shown in the previous chapter, are negated and the negation of such neganda is proper Emptiness. Therefore, the concept of Emptiness, as the terms indicate, should be negation or absence *per se*, of inherent nature, own being, hypostatic existence and so forth. The negation need not be negated to reach an ultimate reality that is free from all elaborations. They argued that if things, on the ultimate level, were not merely empty or lacking inherent nature but are free from all elaborations whereby they are neither empty nor non-empty, neither existent, nor non-existent, etc. the *sūtra*s and Mādhyamika treatises would not teach all phenomena to be empty and lack of inherent nature.

Mipham interpreted the terms, absence of inherent nature, etc. differently. According to him, these terms can mean two different things in different contexts. In the process of Mādhyamika analysis to negate inherence, hypostatic existence, own being, substantiality, etc. the terms absence of inherent nature, etc. are generally used to refer to the mere negation of inherent nature, etc. However, they are not restricted to just these meanings. While delineating the ultimate reality, which is non-notational, these terms are also used to refer to the ultimate Emptiness free from all elaborations. Thus, in this latter case, the absence of inherent nature (*rang bzhin med pa*) refers to the reality where both inherent nature and the absence of inherent nature are not viable. The same applies to other terms such as the absence of hypostatic existence, absence of own being, absence of production (*skye med*) and so forth. He writes in his *rGyan 'grel*:

> In this way, terms such as 'absence of production' show the whole scope of perceptions to be empty. [They] show the lack of perception because whatever phenomenon is empty, grasping of it is eliminated. Therefore, the word, lack of hypostatic existence, indicate that things are simply not perceived when analysed. It is not such that vase, etc. are empty of a separate negandum called 'hypostatic existence'.... With terms such as 'absence of production', [one] must engage in the pacification of all elaborations.[70]

In the same text, he mentions that words such as the lack of inherent nature and Emptiness can refer to both notational and non-notational ultimates and in the latter case, it indicates the lack of all elaborations. As noted earlier, he refers to the *sūtra* describing Emptiness as 'the term denoting not seeing anything'.[71] Therefore, one must not cling onto the mere absence as the sole referent of term 'lack of inherent nature'. Here, he quotes the dialogue from *Prasannapadā*, where a person says,

'There is no good (*paṇya, zong*) whatsoever that I can give you' to a customer and the customer demands 'the whatsoever good which is not there' (*na kiṃcin nāma paṇyam, ci yang med pa zhes bya ba'i zong*) be given to him. In such a case, how can one make the customer realize what 'there is no good whatsoever' means?[72] Holding onto Emptiness, which is supposed to denote lack of all elaborations, as an entity that is a mere negation, is exactly like this. Thus, it is very important to distinguish what the term, lack of inherent nature, refers to: either to the notational ultimate, the understanding which involves modal apprehension of a mere absence of inherent nature, or to the non-notational ultimate. One should not merely follow the literal picture of such words.[73]

Mipham was a pragmatist in the use of language emphasizing the contextual usage of the word than its literal meaning. The Gelukpas, for instance, strictly interpreted the term lack of production (*skye med*) as an absence of hypostatic production by supplying a qualifier. Mipham, in contrast, understood the absence of production depending on the context: as the lack of hypostatic production, as the absence of general production or as the reality transcending the tetralemma of production, absence of production, both and neither. He argues in his *rGyan 'grel* that one must understand words and phrases such as the absence of inherent nature, Emptiness, established by correct cognition and established by individual characteristics according to the various contexts.

In the same way, he argues in his *rGyan 'grel* and *gSung sgros* that terms such as *bden grub* (here better rendered as truly existent), although generally used for hypostatically existent entity, can be rightly used in the conventional sense to refer to things that genuinely exist in conventional terms. He says,

> Even true existence (*bden grub*) can conventionally mean those that are unmistakenly evident to a conventional correct cognition. And own being (*ngo bo*), individual characteristics (*rang mtshan*) and inherent nature (*rang bzhin*), etc. can conventionally mean the own being, etc. of a vase appearing with bulging belly.[74]

The fire, for instance, can be on the conventional level correctly described as truly and inherently hot.

Thus, he emphatically remarks that tenet systems should be delineated through content rather than obstinate usage of words, and words should be understood according to their contexts. He nonetheless adds that it may sometimes help understand the meaning easily in certain cases by supplying the qualifiers.[75] He took the terms absence of inherent nature, absence of production, etc. to refer to the mere absence of inherent nature or hypostatic production, etc. while establishing the notational Emptiness and to denote the ultimate Emptiness free from all elaborations while establishing the final Emptiness. He argued that these terms are used in both ways in the *sūtra*s and the Mādhyamika treatises.

On BA, IX/33–5

Let us further study the difference in understanding the ultimate Emptiness between Mipham and the Gelukpas by juxtaposing their commentaries on BA, IX/33–5, which encapsulates Śāntideva's understanding of the experience of ultimate Emptiness. After his reasoning against his opponents to prove all phenomena to be empty and illusory, Śāntideva presents an argument which he ascribes to his opponents. In the argument, his opponents question the efficacy of knowing things to be illusory for the purpose of overcoming attachment to things. They argue that the magician who knows the magical woman to be an illusory magic is still attracted by her. His knowledge of her illusory state does not help him to overcome his passionate attachment to her. Śāntideva answers saying that the attraction of the magician to the magical woman is due to his resilience of attachment in normal life. Because he has not given up the attachment to woman and other things in normal life and his inclination to see things as empty is poor, such attachment arises toward a magical woman.[76] Śāntideva then goes on to say:

> Through being inured to the propensity of Emptiness
> The propensity of substantiality will be overcome.
> Through being inured to the [thought] that there is not anything
> That too will be subsequently overcome.
> When that entity, of which one thinks 'it does not exist',
> Is not apprehended
> Then how would the non-entity, without any support [of entity],
> Remain before the mind?
> When neither entity nor non-entity
> Remain before the mind,
> Then, because there is no other aspect [to apprehend],
> The [mind] is pacified without any apprehension.[77]

Tradition has it that Śāntideva, while reciting this famous work, at this point, levitated into air and disappeared.[78] To Mipham, this passage summarizes the ecstatic realization of ultimate Emptiness free from all mental elaborations such as existence, non-existence, is and is not. He takes these verses as a reply to another proleptical query, in which the opponent asks how one can escape mental elaborations because both clinging to substantiality and clinging to Emptiness are within the range of conceptual elaborations. Even if one gives up clinging to substantiality, apprehending Emptiness would land oneself in another clinging. It would be like an elephant's bath, getting into another muddy water to cleanse the mud from the previous bath.[79] This question however is not in the root verses.

Mipham interprets the above-mentioned verses as an answer to such a question and goes on to say that whoever gets accustomed to Emptiness *qua* lack of inherent nature of all substances will overcome the propensity of clinging to substantiality, as apprehension of Emptiness and of substantiality are contradictory. However, the apprehension of the non-substantiality is also merely a mental construct and does not exist in reality. Hence, by getting accustomed to the fact that both substantiality and non-substantiality are not hypostatically existent, clinging to non-substantiality is given up.

He inserts yet another proleptic question arguing that if Emptiness *qua* negation of substance or existence were negated, would it not revert to affirmation? Emptiness *qua* absence of substantiality cannot be negated for such absence of substantiality is being proved here and being delineated as the antidote. This is exactly what the Gelukpas say to argue against the negation of Emptiness. Mipham is perhaps implicitly citing a Gelukpa position in this question. To this query, Mipham replies:

> For the time being, in the face of clinging to substances as existent, [to which one is] accustomed from beginningless time, [one must] prove [substance] to be non-existent and familiarise [oneself] with [it], because unless [one] knows substances to be without inherent nature, there is no chance at all of generating certainty about the ontic nature free from extremes. However, such mere non-existence is not the ultimate ontic nature. If, in claiming 'the substances such as matter and so forth are not existent', those substance under scrutiny are not perceived to be conventionally produced and so forth by their own nature, then, even the non-substantiality which depends on them turns out to be without the base of a substance. Hence, how can it remain before the mind as an object of apprehension? It cannot possibly remain so, just as the death of a barren woman's son is not perceived as its birth does not exist. Therefore, non-existence is merely imputed in dependence on existence; it does not exist independently by its nature. If [he] asks: what is the point of alternating the two: negating existence to prove non-existence and again negating non-existence to prove existence? [The answers is:] It is very true that thoughts such as this, which resembles an elephant's bath, arise to those who are dependent on worldly speculation and are relying on [ordinary] consciousness. The inconceivable reality is the best of great topics which frightens those with inferior fortune. [They] would not understand it. When taught to be non-substantial, [they] hold it to be a nihilistic Emptiness, when taught to be with appearance, [they] hold it to be hypostatically existent. When described as coalescence, [they] hold it to be like white and black threads twisted together. When described as inconceivable, nothing but an utter non-existence and nothingness like that of Hwashang's view is visualized. If this ultimate of the profound dharma can be easily understood by all, why would it be said to be transcending all worlds, the scope of sublime beings, difficult to view, difficult to understand and inconceivable.[80]

Mipham then cites MK, XXIV/11–12 and goes on to say that in order to realize the reality, one must follow a qualified teacher, accumulate merits and familiarize oneself with the profound topic of Emptiness. Being puffed up with pride of one's learning and adopting profane forms of logic would not bring forth even a partial understanding of this reality even if one strives for aeons. He continues:

> Therefore, when none of the substances and non-substantiality remain before the mind, because there is no other hypostatically existent aspect, all elaborations are pacified without any point of fixation for the clinging to hypostatic existence. [Such] is the equality like the centre of space, inconceivable, inexpressible and characterised only by the intuitive gnosis.[81]

Thus, Mipham makes it clear that a mere absence of hypostatic existence is not the final ultimate in Prāsaṅgika thought. He argues that holding onto the understanding of all phenomena to be empty is ultimately wrong. He cites the *Saṃcayagāthā* I/9, 'If the Bodhisattva thinks "this aggregate is empty," even so, he is engaging in phenomenal features and is not being attentive to the unborn state.'[82] He also quotes the MK, XIII/8, which states that the Buddha taught Emptiness to overcome all views and those who view Emptiness itself are irredeemable.

Let us turn to Gyaltshab's commentary on these verses. His commentary on BA, IX/33–5 in his *rGyal sras 'jug ngogs* is an almost verbatim reproduction of Tsongkhapa's notes on the wisdom chapter of BA which he probably compiled into a commentary entitled *Spyod 'jug sher le'u'i ṭīkā blo gsal ba*.[83] In their commentaries on the preceding verse answering why a magician gets attached to the magical woman he created in spite of his knowledge that she is illusory, Tsongkhapa and Gyaltshab states that it is because the magician has not given up clinging to hypostatic nature of the magical woman. Although the magician sees the magical woman as empty of woman, the propensity to see her as such is very poor and the propensity to cling to it as real is strong having been habituated with it since time immemorial.

They refute the interpretation of some earlier masters who claim that seeing the magical woman as empty of real woman is an understanding of partial Emptiness (*nyi tshe ba'i stong nyid*) and an understanding of pervasive Emptiness (*khyab pa'i stong nyid*) is required to overcome attachment.[84] They argue that understanding the magical woman to be empty of real woman is not an understanding of partial Emptiness. The reason why the attachment arises is because the inclination to cling is strong. Merely understanding the magical woman to be empty would not eliminate the attachment. One must get inured to the propensity of Emptiness. Tsongkhapa, Gyaltshab and Mipham agree that the magician cannot give up the attachment to the magical woman because he has not given up attachment generally and his sense of Emptiness is very weak. There is no antidote in him which can counteract the power of defiling emotions by directly contradicting it in its mode of apprehension (*dngos su 'dzin stangs 'gal ba*).

However Tsongkhapa and Gyaltshab's commentary on verse 33 vary from Mipham's. Gyaltshab writes:

> By getting accustomed to the propensity of Emptiness, i.e. if one understands substances to be empty of inherent nature, the propensity of clinging to substances as hypostatic will be eliminated. By getting inured to what is called 'there is not anything', i.e. the understanding that even the absence of hypostatic existence is itself without hypostatic existence, the clinging to absence of hypostatic existence as hypostatic is also subsequently given up. . . . When, saying 'substance is without hypostatic existence', the object under scrutiny, which has to be perceived if hypostatically existent, is not perceived and thus understood to be without hypostatic existence, then how could a hypostatic negation remain before the mind because the hypostatic non-substantiality is without the basis of hypostatic existence? Because there is no reality (*chos nyid*) without subject (*chos can*), the absence of hypostatic existence, if hypostatically existent, has to exist as the nature of that subject. The existence of such [subject] as hypostatically existent by nature has been negated early on. Therefore, when no hypostatic substance or non-substantiality remain before the mind, then, because there is no other aspect of hypostatic existence, [one] realizes the non-existence of all points of focus of clinging to hypostatic existence, and all elaborations are pacified. For those persons who discern Emptiness directly, even the elaborations of duality are pacified in the reality of Emptiness. For those who realize the reality of Emptiness through a universal [image], the elaboration of hypostatic existence of the object is negated although the dualistic appearance is not negated.[85]

The most striking difference between Mipham's and Gyaltshab's commentary is in the use of the qualifying phrase, 'hypostatic existence'. By glossing all negations with such a phrase, Gyaltshab makes it explicit that what is negated is not mere existence but a hypostasized entity. According to him, one first negates hypostatic existence by proving absence of hypostatic existence and subsequently the absence of hypostatic existence is also proved to be without hypostatic nature. Thus, ultimate Emptiness in his thought does not transcend the absence of hypostatic existence. Although the sublime beings discern this absence without dualistic appearance (*gnyis snang*) and ordinary beings realize it without the sense of hypostatization (*bden 'dzin*) but with dualistic appearance, the Emptiness they understand is the same.

Mipham, in contrast, takes the passages more directly without applying the qualifier. He holds Emptiness *qua* absence of hypostatic existence as a provisional antidote to overcome the strong inclination to cling to things as substantial and real. Once such clinging is overcome, the thought of absence of hypostatic existence must also be given up through the knowledge that there is not anything. The absence of hypostatic existence is a provisional Emptiness, which is a step to the ultimate Emptiness that transcends both existence, non-existence, emptiness, non-emptiness, etc. The former is known as the notational ultimate and the latter non-notational ultimate. Let us now turn to discuss the binary ultimates in Mipham's thought.

The two ultimates

The theory of the ultimate in Mipham's thought can be best understood through his typology of ultimates in his diverse writings. However, I shall not attempt to discuss the types of ultimates that do not directly impinge on the current topic of varying degrees of ultimates and Emptinesses in the Mādhyamika school. Such ultimates include the ultimates in the Vaibhaṣika, Sautrāntika and Cittamātra philosophical systems,[86] the three ultimates discussed in *Madhyāntavibhāga*,[87] and others such as the seven-fold ultimate (*don dam skor bdun*) discussed in the Vajrayāna literature.[88] We have also briefly discussed the two types of ultimates corresponding to the two theories of two truths of appearance *vis-à-vis* ontic mode and of appearance *vis-à-vis* Emptiness. Here, what concerns us is the theory of two ultimates *qua* Emptinesses in Mādhyamika thought, which forms the crux of Mipham's understanding of the philosophy of Emptiness and of his hermeneutical theories thereof.

The classification of ultimates *qua* Emptiness into notational (*rnam grangs pa'i*) and non-notational (*rnam grangs min pa'i*) ultimates[89] is a very frequent theme in Mipham's writings on Mādhyamika philosophy. Mipham attributes the origin of this classification to Svātantrika masters such as Bhāvaviveka, Jñānagarbha and Śāntarakṣita. He says that the Prāsaṅgikas do not accept the bifurcation of the ultimate.[90] What is termed as notational ultimate by Svātantrika thinkers would be a conventional phenomenon in the Prāsaṅgika system. It is clear that the concept of a provisional and ultimate understanding of Emptiness definitely goes back to Indian scholars such as Bhāvaviveka, Jñānagarbha and Śāntarakṣita although the technical use of the terms, concordant ultimate (*mthun pa'i don dam*), notational ultimate (**paryāyaparamārtha, rnam grangs pa'i don dam* or *saparyāyaparamārtha, rnam grangs dang bcas pa'i don dam*) and non-notational ultimate (**aparyāyaparamārtha, rnam grangs min pa'i don dam*) do not appear in their works. However, a clear mention is made of the nature which is concordant with the ultimate (*dam pa'i don dang mthun pa*) and therefore called ultimate.[91] The technical terms seem to have come to use much later, perhaps only in Tibetan works. Moreover, the reference of the term concordant ultimate seems to vary among the scholars.

Bhāvaviveka, while explaining the etymology of *paramārtha* in his *Madhyamakahṛdayavṛttitarkajvālā*, mentions the concordant ultimate as the discriminating wisdom which accords with the realization of the ultimate. Lopez translates the passage as follows:

> Regarding ultimate (*paramārtha, don dam*), with respect to 'object' (*artha, don*), it is an object because of being that which is to be known; this is synonymous with 'that which is to be examined (*parīkṣaṇīya, brtag par bya ba*)' and 'that which is to be understood (*pratipādya, go bar bya ba*)'. 'Highest' (*parama, dam pa*) is a word [meaning] supreme. With respect to the compound *paramārtha*, because it is an object as well as being highest, it is the highest object. Or [it means] the object of the highest (*paramasya artha, dam pa'i don*); because it is the object of the highest non-conceptual wisdom (*nirvikalpajñāna, rnam par mi rtog pa'i ye shes*), it is an object of the highest [consciousness]. Or, it [means] that which accords with the highest object [that is, the highest consciousness]. Since the ultimate exists for a wisdom that accords with a realization of the ultimate, it accords with [that which directly realizes] the highest object.[92]

Thus, in Bhāvaviveka's thought, concordant ultimate refers to the reasoning consciousness or the conceptual understanding of Emptiness in the ordinary state or the post-equipoise state (*rjes thob kyi skabs*) of the sublime beings. This is further supported by Bhāvaviveka's binary classification of ultimates in the same text. He writes:

> The ultimate is of two types. One is that which operates without contrivance, supramundane, undefiled and free from elaborations. The second operates with contrivance, accords with the accumulation of merit and gnosis, is with elaborations and called the pure mundane gnosis.[93]

Bhāvaviveka clearly asserts two kinds of ultimates and connects the first to the ultimate free from all elaborations and the latter to mundane understanding. This latter one, thus, clearly corresponds to the concordant ultimate described in the earlier passage. Lopez takes this classification to be that of ultimate consciousnesses and thus glosses the first line likewise: 'one is a supramundane non-contaminated [consciousness] free from elaborations which operates without activity'.[94] The insertion of 'consciousness' here however is interpolated into the reading and goes against Bhāvaviveka's assertion that the final ultimate, as opposed to concordant ultimate, is the reality and the object of the consciousness but not consciousness itself. It is clear from both passages that, in Bhāvaviveka's thoughts, the first ultimate is reality *qua* Emptiness free from elaborations and the provisional ultimate or concordant ultimate is the conceptual understanding of such Emptiness.

His successors such as Jñānagarbha and Śāntarakṣita understood the concordant ultimate differently. To them, concordant ultimate is the objective absence of entities such as production, existence, etc. and is not the subjective consciousness which discerns the absence as Bhāvaviveka maintains. The concordant ultimate does not involve negation of all extremes but is merely a negation of the first extreme. Thus, it is not an ultimate but a conventional phenomenon from the perspective of the final ultimate.[95] However, it is called ultimate because it is concordant with the final ultimate *qua* Emptiness which is free from all elaborations such as production, non-production, existence, non-existence, etc.[96] To support the argument that the mere absence of production, existence, etc. is not the final ultimate, both of them reasoned that if no neganda such as existence, production, etc. were found during the Mādhyamika analysis, there cannot ultimately be the negation or absence of such neganda. Śāntarakṣita states:

> Because there is no production and so forth
> There cannot be non-production and so forth.[97]

Jñānagarbha too puts in a similar way:

> Because the negandum is not existent
> It is clear that in reality, there is no negation [of it].[98]

They maintained that the final ultimate is the reality free from all extremes and elaborations whereas concordant ultimate is a notional negation of the neganda such as inherent nature, production, existence, etc. Although both the concordant and final ultimates are in dialectical terms absolute negations, they are vastly different concepts. On the ultimate level, the concordant ultimate must also be negated in order to reach the final Emptiness *qua* ultimate free from all elaborations. Mipham understands the above mentioned verses in the same manner as BA, IX/140 that we have discussed in the previous chapter.

Tsongkhapa while explaining what 'ultimately' means in the phrase 'ultimately non-existent' in his *Lam rim* cites both passages from Bhāvaviveka's *Madhyamakahṛdayavṛttitarkajvālā* and thus holds concordant ultimate to be subjective cognition of Emptiness including the understanding of Emptiness on the ordinary level as well as the experience of Emptiness in the post-meditative equipoise of sublime beings.[99] He also interprets that what is taught to be concordant ultimate in Śāntarakṣita's *Madhyamakālaṃkāra* and Kamalaśīla's *Madhyamakāloka* refers to the object of the reasoning consciousness (*rigs shes*).[100] Thus, Tsongkhapa appears to have bifurcated the objective realities into actual and concordant ultimates and accepted the conceptual understanding of Emptiness to be a subjective form of concordant ultimate.

His followers such as Changkya and Ngawang Paldan formulated a theory which could incorporate the bifurcation of both the objective and subjective ultimates. Both Napper and Newland have discussed the Gelukpa interpretation of concordant and actual ultimates although they have not clarified the problems posed by the bifurcation of objective Emptiness.[101] Changkya maintained there are cases of both objective reality and subjective cognition being referred to as ultimates and each is further classified into actual and concordant ultimates. The Emptiness that is free from the elaboration of duality which is discerned by the meditative equipoise of the sublime beings is the actual objective ultimate whereas the Emptiness understood by conceptual thought, which is not free from the elaboration of duality although it is free from the notion of hypostatic existence, is concordant ultimate.

In the same way, the gnosis of meditative equipoise, which engages into reality without any elaborations, is the actual subjective ultimate and the conceptual reasoning consciousness which infers Emptiness through a logical reasoning, is only a concordant ultimate because it cannot overcome the dualistic appearance although it can overcome hypostatic appearance.[102] He summarizes in the following passage in his *Grub mtha' thub bstan lhun po'i mdzes rgyan*:

> In brief, although the objective reality is the actual ultimate truth and the subjective cognition is not the actual ultimate truth, in textual exegesis, it [the latter] is also said to be ultimate. One should know that for each of them, there is the concept of two forms of the actual and the concordant.[103]

Tsongkhapa and Changkya's bifurcation of objective Emptiness is very similar to Mipham's understanding of the concordant and the actual ultimate. However, their bifurcation of ultimate into the concordant and the actual ultimate raises a serious problem among the Gelukpas, most of whom strictly maintain that Emptiness *qua* absence of hypostatic existence or inherent nature is the only actual ultimate truth and the rest are merely nominal. If Emptiness *qua* absence of hypostatic existence, the object of reasoning consciousness, were the actual ultimate, some other form of Emptiness would have to constitute the concordant objective ultimate. This is not feasible because the Gelukpas do not accept any objective ultimate other than the absence of hypostatic existence. If the absence of hypostatic existence, the object of reasoning consciousness, were a concordant ultimate, there will have to be an Emptiness superior to the absence of hypostatic existence, which is the actual ultimate. Besides, both Tsongkhapa and Changkya distinguish the actual and the concordant ultimate by their subjective cognitions whereas most Gelukpas and also scholars of other schools agree that the ultimate reality discerned during the meditative equipoise of sublime beings and understood by inferential cognition of ordinary beings are the same. Ngawang Paldan, to contain this problem, accepts the objective concordant ultimate, that is, the Emptiness that is the object of inference, as an actual ultimate.[104]

Mipham does not make the bifurcation of subjective cognitions into two ultimates in this context. He says that the bifurcation of subjective cognitions into concordant and actual or notational and non-notational ultimates can be made in the context of theory of two truths of appearing and ontic modes (*gnas snang bden gnyis*). It is in the context of such two truths that the non-dualistic cognition of Emptiness, free from all elaborations, is called non-notational ultimate and the dualistic cognition called notational ultimate. In that context, one could even make distinctions of non-notational and notational persons.[105] In his *Ketaka*, Mipham refutes a certain position that the meditative equipoise of the sublime beings, which is free from all elaborations, is the actual non-notational ultimate and that meditation on Emptiness among ordinary beings is a meditation only on the concordant ultimate, which is an absolute negation. He states that in the context of delineating Emptiness, negation of things such as matter is always an absolute negation. An ultimate which is an implicative negation will eventually lead to clinging to substantiality and would not fulfil the requirements of Emptiness. Thus, he implies that all ultimates are objective states of Emptiness, which in dialectical terms are absolute negations.[106]

Mipham formulates the theory of two ultimates along the lines of Śāntarakṣita and Jñānagarbha's arguments relating it purely to the two different objective states of Emptiness. In his thought, the Emptiness which is free from all elaborations is the non-notational ultimate and Emptiness which is the partial negation of extreme/s, that is, existence, production, etc. is the notational ultimate. He writes in his *Rab lan* that the difference between the two ultimates is being beyond the scope of limited elaborations and being beyond the scope of all elaborations.[107] Speaking on the two ultimates, he writes in his *Nyi snang*:

> The ultimate, then, is twofold: notational and non-notational ultimates. The first one is in every aspect an object of thought for it is the mere aspect of Emptiness of hypostatic existence. So, it is just an object of the conceptual mind, which is a particular kind of thought. It is not the genuine ultimate, however, it is designated as concordant or notational ultimate in the treatises because it is the door to realizing the [genuine] ultimate.[108]

Explaining the notational or concordant ultimate further in his *Ketaka*, he states:

> As for the ultimate, Emptiness, which is a mere negation such as non-production, non-abiding, etc. [reached] after negating production, abiding and so forth, is a mere entrance to approach the great Emptiness free from four extremes. Hence, [it] is called notational ultimate or concordant ultimate.[109]

In his *rGyan 'grel*, he defines the final ultimate in the following manner:

> Therefore, the lack of all extremes [reached] by the way of Emptiness of the External, etc. taught in order to overcome the clinging to existence (*yod par zhen pa*) and Emptiness of Emptiness, etc. taught in order to overcome clinging to non-substantiality (*dngos med la zhen pa*) is this non-notational ultimate.[110]

It is clear that according to Mipham, the latter is final and the former is provisional and only a step to the latter. We can also see that he holds the concordant and notational ultimate to be synonymous. In both *Ketaka* and *rGyan 'grel*, he explains that those who are intensely accustomed to clinging to substantiality cannot generate the gnosis free from all four extremes and must first strive to understand the absence of hypostatic existence, substantiality, etc.[111] Having understood the absence of hypostatic existence, etc. one must then transcend the absence by negating all extremes of elaborations. The concordant ultimate is thus a temporary understanding and not the proper ultimate. In the context of the final ultimate, this concordant or notational ultimate is a conventional phenomenon. He writes while commenting on *Madhyamakālaṃkāra*, 70:

> In this way, this utter non-existence from the dichotomy of existence and non-existence, [which is obtained] after the negandum – hypostatic existence – has been negated, in the definitive sense falls within the conventional or transactional [truth] and is not the final ontic nature. Nonetheless, *because it is concordant with the ultimate reality* or the ultimate which is the authentic final ontic nature, in the manner of giving the name of the result to the cause, *this* utter absence of hypostatic existence, the antithesis of hypostatic absence, *is also known as ultimate reality*. However, [this] is [only] the notational ultimate or nominal [ultimate]. For the authentic ultimate is not merely an utter non-existence but the lack of elaborations of the four extremes. Nevertheless, were this notational ultimate, the mere absence of hypostatic existence of things, which remain within the mental scope of the exclusionary conceptual mind, not to exist, there is no [other] means of understanding the great ultimate. Because it is the means or cause of understanding that [great ultimate], and is within its category, [it] is given the term ultimate.[112]

In his refutation of Mipham, Pari Rabsal refers to these expositions in *Ketaka* on the bifurcation of ultimates and accuses Mipham of following Hwashang by espousing such interpretation of the final ultimate. He accepts that there are concepts of subjective and objective ultimates taught in the *sūtra*s and tantras and the three ultimates mentioned in Bhāvaviveka's works.[113] Mipham, in his *Rab lan*, reiterates that there are two ways of understanding Emptiness.[114] One is to understand all conditioned and unconditioned things to be without inherent nature and hypostatic existence. The other is to transcend all extremes of elaborations and apprehensions. It is through the former that the latter is contacted. It is not his intention to argue that the lack of hypostatic existence is not a certain grade of ontological truth. It is in fact a well-founded reality. However, he says that it is nothing new that he is claiming to state that such understanding of partial Emptiness, where not all elaborations are done with, is not the final ultimate. He remarks, 'The Blessed Teacher and his followers have taught this and we claim in accordance with the Teacher',[115] and then goes on to cite over forty pages of scriptural sources.

In his *rGyan 'grel* too, he states that some *sūtra*s teach the non-notational ultimate which is free from all extremes whereas others teach notational ultimate of mere negation with phrases such as 'there is no matter, no consciousness' and so forth. Nāgārjuna correctly first proved all things to be without hypostatic existence, the notational ultimate, and finally established the Emptiness free from all elaborations, the non-notational ultimate. I have already discussed Mipham's liberal usage of terms and their varying referents. In his *Nges shes gron me*, Mipham provides a few other terms that he uses to refer to the notational and non-notational ultimate. He calls the notational ultimate the Madhyamaka of discriminating path, the gross, the causal and the lower Madhyamaka, which is delineated on the level of consciousness. On the contrary, non-notational ultimate is the actual Madhyamaka of the meditative equipoise, the subtle, the resultant and the Great Madhyamaka, which is delineated on the level of gnosis.[116]

The two ultimates and the two schools

One of the most outstanding characteristics of Mipham's exposition of the two kinds of ultimates is the connection he makes between the two ultimates and the Svātantrika and Prāsaṅgika school of Mādhyamika. This is clearly formulated in the following definition of the proponents of these two schools he provides:

> Therefore, it must be known that the definition of a Svātantrika is [one who] emphatically expounds the notational ultimate with assertion of theses while a Prāsaṅgika is [one who] emphatically expounds the non-notational ultimate without assertion of any thesis.[117]

Mipham argues that the differentiation of the Svātantrikas and Prāsaṅgikas through other criteria such as the acceptance and denial of the viability of individually characterized objects conventionally, the acceptance and non-acceptance of thesis, the use of autonomous inference and apagogic reasoning to establish the lack of inherent nature and the application of the qualifier 'ultimate' to the negandum are all secondary differences dependent on the major difference of emphasis on the two kinds of ultimates.[118] According to him, the Prāsaṅgikas stress on delineating the non-notational ultimate, which is free from all elaborations, and therefore do not take any philosophical stance or thesis. Espousing no philosophical assertions of their own, they destroy the positions of their opponents using apagogic reasoning (*prasaṅga, thal gyur*). Hence, they came to be called Prāsaṅgika. The Svātantrika, on the other hand, emphasizes on the delineation of the notational ultimate distinguishing even in the context of the ultimate analysis that things are ultimately non-existent and conventionally existent. Maintaining such assertions, they prove the lack of ultimate existence of things by using autonomous inference (*svatantra, rang rgyud*). Thus, they are called Svātantrika. However, eventually even the Svātantrikas delineate the non-notational ultimate and come to the point where they would have no assertions and realize the ultimate free from all elaborations. As demonstrated in *Madhyamakālaṃkāra*, 70/71 and *Satyadvayavibhāga*, 9 they first negate the first extreme by establishing the lack of hypostatic existence, inherent nature, ultimate production, etc. and finally, negate even the absence of hypostatic existence, etc. to fathom the Emptiness free from all elaborations of negation and affirmation.

To Mipham, the difference between Prāsaṅgika and Svātantrika therefore is one of methodology and pedagogy rather than that of a philosophical and ontological understanding. The Prāsaṅgikas emphasize the exposition of Madhyamaka corresponding to the intuitive experience of Emptiness by sublime gnosis in the meditative equipoise, which discern the two truths as of one single flavour (*bden gnyis ro gcig*) while the Svātantrikas emphasize the exposition of Madhyamaka from the viewpoint of post-equipoise understanding where the two truths are distinguished as separate entities (*bden gnyis so sor 'byed pa*).[119] He takes the Svātantrikas as persons of inferior calibre and as gradualist in their mode of approach to final Emptiness and Prāsaṅgikas as persons of superior calibre and as simultaneists in their approach to final Emptiness. Apart from their difference in emphasis and approach, both Prāsaṅgika and Svātantrika ultimately understand and expound the final Emptiness free from all elaborations. Thus, he warns that the Svātantrika understanding should not be seen as a mistaken or distorted interpretation of the *sūtra*s and *śāstra*s.[120]

To elaborate further, individuals such as Śāntideva and Candrakīrti have lesser degrees of attachment to things as substantial and sharper faculties which make them capable of comprehending Emptiness free from all elaborations by eliminating all extremes simultaneously in one session. They do not establish the mere absence of hypostatic existence to be the ultimate truth and do not bifurcate the ultimate into two categories. The terminologies 'concordant ultimate' or 'notational ultimate' do not appear in their works. It is due to this reason that Mipham categorically states that there are no two ultimates in Prāsaṅgika thought.[121]

In contrast, individuals of the Svātantrika category have a greater degree of attachment to things as substantial and real, and thus need to first establish all things to be without any hypostatic existence, substance or inherent nature. Although both the Prāsaṅgikas and Svātantrikas negate the four extremes one after the other, the Prāsaṅgikas do not hold the partial negation of the extremes as an ultimate whereas the Svātantrikas do. Basing themselves in the philosophical position that all things exist but lack hypostatic existence, etc. and that lack of hypostatic existence, etc. is an ultimate truth, they make use of autonomous reasoning and supply qualifiers to the negandum while negating the four extremes. Once they have fully understood the lack of hypostatic existence, etc. in this manner, they then eliminate the subsequent extremes of the absence of hypostatic existence, etc. of both and of neither just as the Prāsaṅgikas, thus approaching the Emptiness free from all elaborations and extremes gradually.

In this way, the delineation of the absence of hypostatic existence, etc. forms a necessary preliminary step to the understanding of the final ultimate in the Svātantrika system. To support this, Mipham uses the arguments of Jñānagarbha and Śāntarakṣita cited above and also frequently cites the following verse from Bhāvaviveka's *Madhyamakahṛdaya*:

> Without the stairs
> Of the correct conventional [truth]
> It is not possible for the wise
> To climb upto the mansion of the [ultimate] truth.[122]

Mipham, like Śāntarakṣita, takes the 'correct conventional truth' in the verse to refer to notational ultimate *qua* lack of hypostatic existence.[123] Bhāvaviveka in his auto-commentary however does not seem to specifically take it to denote such lack of hypostatic existence but seems to refer to all conventional phenomena and argue that conventional truth is a crucial means to understand the ultimate reality.[124] Mipham also cites the following from MK and MA and argues that conventional truth in these verses does not merely mean the conventional truth *vis-à-vis* notational ultimate:

> Without depending on the conventional,
> The ultimate nature cannot be shown,[125]

and

> The conventional truth is the means
> And the ultimate truth is that which results from the means.[126]

He says that conventional truth in this context encompasses the entire domain of language and conceptual thoughts (*sgra rtog gi spyod yul*) and includes all things transacted through knowing, speaking and engagement (*shes brjod 'jug pa'i tha snyad*). It is for this reason that Śāntarakṣita in his auto-commentary on *Madhyamakālaṃkāra* holds that even the notational ultimate falls within the category of conventional truth.[127] Ultimate, in these verses, denote the Great Madhyamaka, which is coalescence free from all elaborations.[128]

One could say that Mipham understands the Svātantrika philosophical world with three tiers: the worldly transactional level of conventional truth, the level of notational ultimate and the level of non-notational ultimate. From the viewpoint of the first two, there are two kinds of ultimates: the notational or concordant ultimate *qua* partial negation of extremes and non-notational or final ultimate free from all elaborations. From the perspective of the third level, that is, non-notational ultimate, the lower two are both conventional and that is why the notational ultimate comes to be called 'correct conventional truth'. However, it is on the level of the second, that is, notational ultimate, where they expound most of their doctrine of Emptiness asserting their own stance and carry on the Mādhyamika analysis and refutation of the opponents.

In contrast, the Prāsaṅgikas have only two tiers: conventional and ultimate. On the ultimate, there exists neither existence nor non-existence, neither production nor non-production and so forth. It is the level of final ultimate and no mental elaborations are viable and therefore no thesis is tenable. On the level of the conventional, the flow of interdependent appearance is uninterrupted and thus various kinds of worldly transactions are possible. Mipham is fully aware that even the Prāsaṅgikas such as Candrakīrti and Śāntideva, like the Svātantrikas, carry out a gradual negation of the four extremes using different arguments. This is clear in their works such as MA and BA. However, the Prāsaṅgikas do not base themselves at an intermediate state of partial negation, that is notational ultimate, but rather move on to the total elimination of extremes within one session. The Svātantrikas not only negate the extremes gradually but find an interim philosophical base on the level of notational ultimate and propound their philosophy from that state. Although they would finally move on to the third tier of ultimate Emptiness, they temporarily base themselves on the second tier and it is this graduated development that distinguishes them from the individuals of Prāsaṅgika category.

From Mipham's viewpoint, the Gelukpa understanding of Emptiness as a mere lack of hypostatic existence is similar to the understanding of the notational ultimate in Svātantrika system. We have already seen him remark that perhaps in Tibet the understanding of Emptiness of even those who claim to be Prāsaṅgika incline towards the Svātantrika understanding due to the auspices (*rten 'brel*) of the Svātantrika spreading first in Tibet.[129] According to him, the Svātantrikas see the clinging to substantiality or hypostatic existence as the main cause of *saṃsāra* and thus stress upon the delineation of the notational ultimate, that is, the absolute negation of substantiality, hypostatic existence, etc. on the ultimate level. Although they tend to negate all extremes on this level, they do so by supplying qualifiers such as 'ultimate' or 'hypostatically existent' thus only negating the first extreme of hypostatic existence, etc. In this way, they claim to dispel the extremes of existence (eternalism) and non-existence (nihilism); that of existence by the fact that things are without ultimate or hypostatic existence and that of non-existence by the fact that things are existent conventionally or in worldly transaction.

However, by negating only hypostatic existence and leaving the conventional existence unscathed, the two truths become dichotomous and consequently there arises apprehensions of non-existence while thinking 'it ultimately does not exist' and of existence while thinking 'it conventionally exists'. It is in this manner that the Svātantrikas view the two truths separately and it is due to this that they assert the individually characterized phenomena on the conventional level and also use autonomous inference in delineating Emptiness.[130]

Mipham argues that if ultimate truth is understood to be the non-existence of hypostatic property and conventional truth the existence of conventional property, the two truths become ontologically two different properties. This not only leads to diversion from the coalescent nature of the two truths, which we shall discuss later, but also entails fabricating apprehensions. Mipham says that it is this dualistic apprehension of the two truths as dichotomous entities (*bden gnyis so sor 'dzin pa*) which is the most subtle flaw of the Svātantrika understanding. Were they to overcome this, there would not be any difference between the Svātantrikas and Prāsaṅgikas in terms of understanding Emptiness.[131] Thus, he argues that as long as one asserts the ultimate to be a mere absence of hypostatic existence and the conventional phenomena to exist quite apart from such absence, one would have a dualistic understanding of two truths and never touch upon the non-notational ultimate, which is coalescence free from all elaborations.

The Prāsaṅgikas at the very beginning delineate the Emptiness free from all elaborations and eliminate the notion that although things do not have hypostatic existence they have individually characterized existence conventionally. Thus, they destroy the dualistic clinging that holds the two truths as if they were isolates (*bden gnyis so sor rang sa na 'dug pa lta bu'i tha dad du zhen pa zhig*), coalesce the two truths into one taste (*bden gnyis ro gcig tu 'dres*) and destroy all modal apprehensions grasping existence, non-existence and so forth (*yod pa med pa la sogs par 'dzin pa'i 'dzin stangs thams cad zhig*).

In this way, they do not have to supply the qualifiers regarding the two truths such as hypostatic existence and ultimate to the four extremes (*mtha' bzhi por bden grub dang don dam sogs kyi bden gnyis so so'i khyad par sbyar mi dgos*) but negate the conceived objects of the four extremes (*mtha' bzhi'i zhen yul khegs*) and reach the great Emptiness free from all apprehensions and theses of the subjective mind (*yul can blos dmigs pa dang khas len thams cad dang bral ba'i stong pa chen po*), the ultimate ontic nature (*mthar thug pa'i gnas lugs*) which corresponds to the gnosis of the equipoise of sublime beings (*'phags pa'i mnyam gzhag ye shes dang rjes su mthun pa*). Nonetheless, on the non-analytical and post-meditative state, it is very much appropriate to assert the theories of path and result as ascertained by the correct cognitions.[132]

Thus, in Mipham's thought, the Gelukpas are very similar to the Svātantrikas in understanding the absence of hypostatic existence to be the ultimate and in holding it separate from conventional phenomena. However, unlike the Svātantrikas who ultimately reach the final Emptiness free from all elaborations through understanding the concordant ultimate, the Gelukpas hold onto the concordant or notational ultimate as the final ultimate. This, from Mipham's viewpoint is the main flaw of the Gelukpa understanding of final Emptiness. Understanding the ultimate reality of all things as mere absence of hypostatic existence, which is different from the conventional appearance, faces rational inconsistencies and defies the ontological way in which all things exist as coalescence of appearance and Emptiness.

In many of his works on Madhyamaka, Mipham touches on the topic of binary ultimates and reiterates that the understanding of Emptiness *qua* notational ultimate is not final but only a propaedeutic method. It is a step to the ultimate Emptiness and is an antidote to strong attachment to things as substantial and real. Claiming that the lack of hypostatic existence is the notational ultimate and that it is not final Emptiness in his Mādhyamika writings, he criticises the Gelukpa understanding, at least that of most Gelukpas in the three seats, of being an incorrect and partial understanding of the final ultimate.

Mipham however specifically mentions that Tsongkhapa provisionally propounded such an interpretation of Emptiness to help his disciples, who have strong attachment, along the path to discern the final ultimate, which is free from all elaborations. The ultimate understanding of Tsongkhapa, like most other great scholars and saints of Tibet, accords with the ultimate Emptiness free from all elaborations. This, he demonstrates in *rGyan 'grel* by citing Tsongkhapa along with other luminary figures from the four traditions.[133] Mipham takes the following verse from Tsongkhapa's *Lam gtso rnam gsum* to show his final understanding of the ultimate Emptiness, which is coalescence free from all elaborations and apprehensions.

> As long as the unfailing interdependent appearance
> And the understanding of Emptiness without any assertions
> Appear [to him] as separate
> [He does] not understand the intent of the Buddha.
> When without having to alternate if [he can] simultaneously destroy
> All modal grasping of objects through certainty,
> With the mere seeing of interdependent [appearance] as unfailing,
> Then, [he] perfects the investigation of the view.[134]

Mipham uses this passage to argue that Tsongkhapa, unlike most of his followers, understood the final ultimate as coalescence of appearance and Emptiness from all elaborations but merely emphasized the exposition of Emptiness *qua* absence of hypostatic existence to help his disciples overcome their strong sense of reification. Arguing against Pari Rabsal, he also writes in *Rab lan*:

> In the scroll that Je Tsongkhapa offered to Redawa, [he] says that sublime beings in the Prāsaṅgika tradition, absorbed in the non-notational ultimate free from all theses, during meditative equipoise, envisage unobstructed the notational ultimate truth of interdependence, which is like a reflection, in their post-meditative state. Because the non-notational ultimate, the actual lack of elaborations is said to be the scope of sublime beings, it is therefore clear that [he] accepted the lack of elaborations to be the ultimate ontic nature.[135]

It thus appears from the earnestness with which Mipham presents Tsongkhapa's understanding in the passages mentioned above and his other remarks in his *rGyan 'grel* and *Rab lan* that Mipham genuinely believes that Tsongkhapa understood the ultimate Emptiness but emphasized the exposition of the notational ultimate which his followers misunderstood to be his ultimate thought.

The exposition of the bifurcation of ultimates into notational and non-notational forms one of Mipham's most significant hermeneutic enterprizes in Madhaymaka philosophy. By formulating the two levels of ultimates and explaining the Svātantrika and Prāsaṅgika discrepancies as differences in emphasis and approach, Mipham brings together the two Mādhyamika traditions to a harmonious phase, where both, in spite of their different methods, arrive at a single goal of the final ultimate. The bifurcation and gradation of the ultimates, according to him, is an outstanding way to harmonize the two traditions and thereby fathom the ultimate essence of Madhyamaka.[136] In this and in his understanding of Tsongkhapa through the passage cited above, we clearly see in Mipham the *ris med* spirit of reconciliation. Even at the heart of polemical disagreements, there is room for *ris med* attitude, with which he expresses profound respect to and admiration of Tsongkhapa, whose interpretations he strongly refutes.

The ultimate and the coalescence

Mipham clearly considered the Gelukpa understanding of Emptiness *qua* absence of hypostatic existence as an understanding of partial Emptiness (*nyi tshe ba'i stong pa*) which is utter absence (*med rkyang*). This, he argued, is because (1) such absence of hypostatic existence is not free from all elaborations and (2) is not consistent with the ontological state of the coalescence of appearance and Emptiness. Thus far, we have seen how Emptiness *qua* absence of hypostatic existence is not final Emptiness because it is a mere absence, which is itself one of the extremes that has to be negated in order to reach the ultimate free from all elaborations. Let us now turn to see how the absence of hypostatic existence is not the final ultimate because it is not the coalescence of appearance and Emptiness.

In Mipham's thought, the final ultimate, which is free from all elaborations (*spros pa thams cad dang bral ba*), is also described as coalescence of appearance and Emptiness (*snang stong zung 'jug*). The vase, for instance, is ultimately utterly free from elaborations for, when investigated by the Mādhyamika analysis, it can neither be found to be existent, nor non-existent, produced, non-produced and so forth. Not only does it lack hypostatic existence, it lacks any conceptual qualifications. The vase, on this level, is simply not anything, not even nothing. Yet, the appearance of the vase, that is, its interdependent existence, undeniably exists as long as its causes and conditions are present. Mipham uses the words *bslu med*, unmistaken or unfailing, and *bsnyon med*, undeniable to describe the interdependent appearance and show its inevitable and irrefutable presence. He also repeatedly claims that the Mādhyamika does not negate the mere appearance.[137] Whether or not the Mādhyamika analytic mind sees it, the appearance of vase exists simultaneously and inseparably with its state of being empty. The interdependent appearance of the vase is nothing intrinsically different from the empty nature of the vase. Therefore, the vase is described as a coalescence of appearance and Emptiness or of two truths (*snang stong/bden gnyis zung 'jug*).

Both in his *Ketaka* and *rGyan 'grel*, Mipham reasons that because Emptiness is an absolute negation, coalescence is possible. Coalescence is the ontological state of being where the appearance, which is utterly empty and not existent, is yet evidently appearing. Were Emptiness an implicative negation, coalescence would not be possible. Mipham writes in his *Ketaka*:

> Here, in the context of expounding Emptiness, the negation of matter and so forth is solely an absolute negation. Even if [one] negates

implicatively, [it will] ultimately result in clinging to substantiality and would not be suitable for the concept of Emptiness. [As] an absolute negation, even while being [so], the dependently originated [phenomenon] appears unfailingly. Hence, [it] is coalescence of appearance and Emptiness and therefore, one must be free from any modal apprehension of negation and affirmation. It has been said:

> Having known this [fact that] phenomena are empty,
> [Yet one sees] that the action and result are dependent,
> This is [more] amazing than [other] amazing things,
> This is [more] exquisite than [other] exquisite things.

And in the *Pañcakrama*,[138] it is said:

> That in which Emptiness and appearance,
> After [one] has realized their individual aspects,
> Are combined correctly,
> Is called coalescence.[139]

A similar argument appears in the *rGyan 'grel* stating that coalescence is the amazing state of being where appearance, while being non-existent, still appears.[140] Thus, in Mipham's thought, the ultimate is Emptiness free from all elaborations inseparably intertwined with appearance, and it is understanding as such that is the ultimate understanding of the ultimate. He explains this ultimate nature *qua* coalescence in all his Madhyamaka works equating it with concepts such as ultimate truth, lack of elaborations, selflessness, *quidditas*, ontic mode, etc. Following Nāgārjuna's point in MK, XXIV/18,19 Mipham reasons that whatever is empty is pervaded by appearance and whatever is appearance is pervaded by Emptiness. The two cannot be without each other for they are concomitant (*yod mnyam med mnyam*), inseparable (*'du bral med pa*) and indivisible (*dbye ba med pa*). They are only different aspects (*ldog pa tha dad*) of the same nature (*ngo bo gcig*).[141] If one has a thorough conviction in this indivisible nature of appearance and Emptiness, from which even a thousand Buddhas cannot convert one otherwise, then one reaches the bottom of the Mādhyamika analysis.[142]

However, ordinary people cannot comprehend the empty nature and appearance in this way because appearance, due to their attachment to it, obscures the empty nature. Hence, one must first establish the Emptiness in order to get rid of the attachment to appearance. For the sublime beings who have no attachment to appearance and are accustomed to Emptiness, appearance reminds them of its interdependent nature and thereby activates the experience of Emptiness and does not obscure it. For them, understanding of interdependent appearance helps them invigorate the experience of Emptiness and the experience of Emptiness helps stabilize their conviction in the interdependence of all phenomena. The two truths turn into some sort of a reciprocal catalyst for each other (*bden gnyis gcig la gcig grogs su shar ba*) in strengthening the conviction in Emptiness and interdependent appearance. However, as long as one is an ordinary being, one can only have the experience of Emptiness and appearance alternatively. On cannot view the two truths simultaneously.[143] The Buddhas with their omniscient gnosis see the Emptiness and appearance of things simultaneously and thus have constant direct experience of coalescence.

In his *rGyan drel*,[144] Mipham presents a graduated way of cultivating the understanding of coalescence and approaching the non-conceptual gnosis through four stages of Madhyamaka experiences[145] (*dbu ma'i 'char rim bzhi*).

1 First, the beginners, using the Mādhyamika reasonings such as that of lack of one and many (*gcig du bral*), must analyse conventional entities and establish them to be empty. Through this, one realizes that things, which exist when unanalysed, do not really exist when properly analysed. This is the experience of appearance as Emptiness (*snang ba stong par 'char ba*).
2 Then, one must prove that even non-existence or Emptiness is not tenable and contemplate on how all things, while being utterly empty, still appear, just as a reflection of the moon in the river. At this point, an exceptional certainty about how things are empty and at the same time appear and how things appear and are the same time empty will arise. This is known as the experience of lack of inherent existence and interdependent origination as non-contradictory or the experience of Emptiness as coalescence (*stong pa zung 'jug tu 'char ba*).
3 Because of the conviction in the indivisible coalescence of the two truths, which nonetheless are referred to by different words, the conceptual thought which artificially couples appearance – the basis of negation – and Emptiness *qua* negation of negandum, and holds them together, will automatically cease. An experience of lack of elaborations which is spontaneous and free from negation, affirmation, elimination and delineation will arise. This is the experience of coalescence as free from elaborations (*zung 'jug spros bral du 'char ba*).
4 By getting inured to such lack of elaborations, the discriminating thought which sees the subject (*chos can*) and its reality (*chos nyid*) as different will become free from any such partial and discriminatory objectification. One will gain conviction in the equality (*mnyam pa nyid*) of all things thus culminating in the experience of lack of elaborations as equality (*spros bral mnyam nyid du 'char ba*).

'In this way', Mipham summarizes, 'through getting used to the preceding ones of the four Madhyamaka experiences – Emptiness, coalescence, lack of elaborations and equality – conviction in the subsequent ones will arise. These are very important and sacred quintessence of instructions.'[146] Thus, as suggested by these four stages, a beginner must start by delineating Emptiness *qua* negation of things but that is not final. He must at some point see Emptiness coalescent with appearance for that is the objective truth and the way things are.

Mipham refutes two groups of Tibetan Mādhyamikas in his *Nges shes sgron me* saying that their understanding of ultimate Emptiness do not conform with the concept of coalescence. Against the Gelukpas, he argues that if Emptiness were understood to be just the negation of hypostatic existence, then the ultimate would merely be an absence. Such absence which is not appearance itself can never coalesce with appearance properly. He writes:

> An Emptiness *qua* negation of the [hypostatic] pillar
> And appearance that remains afterwards
> The two empty and non-empty [entities],
> Cannot coalesce, just as twisting threads together.[147]

Mipham uses the simile of spinning white and black threads also in his *Ketaka*.[148] To him, trying to coalesce the ultimate which is a mere absence of hypostatic existence with an existent conventional appearance is like conjoining two polar things and it would not work. Coalescence is the inseparable oneness of Emptiness and appearance by their nature and not a contrived syncretization of two different things, like twisting white and black thread together. Mipham says it is a misunderstanding of the coalescence of the two truths to see it as arbitrary unification.

Tsongkhapa, on the contrary, emphatically mentions in his commentary on MK and MA that the two truths are to be understood as two natures (*ngo bo gnyis*): of the ultimate and of the conventional. They are not just one nature seen differently from the perspectives of ordinary and sublime beings.[149] However, conflicting with this position, he and his followers also accept that the two truths are of one nature (*ngo bo gcig*) and different isolates or aspects (*ldog pa tha dad*). To Mipham, the two truths are seen as two different isolates only on the level of conventional transaction. On the ultimate level, the appearance and Emptiness of an object do not remain separate forming a dichotomy but coalesce into one nature. He states:

> However, in the context of the final ontic nature, the binary characteristics of existence and non-existence do not remain separate and polarised, termed as 'conventionally existent' and 'ultimately non-existent'. For whatever matter and so forth appear, that itself is empty and whatever is empty, that itself appears as matter and so forth. Therefore, until one actualises the sphere of reality which is the coalescence of appearance and Emptiness and free from thirty-two superimpositions, [one's understanding of Emptiness] is not authentic *Prajñānapāramitā*.[150]

Mipham clearly attacks the Gelukpa paraphrasing of 'neither existence nor non-existent' as 'neither ultimately or hypostatically existent nor conventionally non-existent'. According to such an interpretation, Emptiness *qua* ultimate truth becomes a negative absence of ultimate or hypostatic existence in contrast to conventional truth, which forms positive existence. Such understanding polarises the two truths instead of fusing them in coalescence.

The Prāsaṅgikas, Mipham says, not only negate hypostatic existence but also reject all elaborations thereby also denying the notion that although things do not have hypostatic existence they, in mere conventional context, possess individually characterized existence (*bden grub med kyang kun rdzob tsam du rang gi mtshan nyid kyis grub pa yod snyam pa*). By doing so, they destroy the clinging to two truths as different (*bden gnyis tha dad du zhen pa*) and coalesce the two truths into a single taste (*bden gnyis ro gcig tu 'dres*).[151] Attacking the position of those who propound only Emptiness of hypostatic existence as ultimate, he further argues under question 7 of *Nges shes sgron me*:

> The path which takes as its object
> Only the Emptiness is a partial view,
> Because it falls to one side of two truths.
> It is not coalescence and free from elaborations.
> While coalescence is equality
> Of existence and non-existence or appearance and Emptiness,
> This [view] is the subjective [cognition]
> Of only the ultimate sphere of Emptiness.
> Elaboration [includes] all kinds of perception
> Of existence, non-existence and so forth.
> This is not free from the elaboration of non-existence
> Because [this] perceives it.[152]

Thus, according to Mipham, the proponents of absence of hypostatic existence as ultimate do not comprehend the correct ultimate *qua* coalescence of appearance and Emptiness. Their concept of ultimate falls to the side of utter Emptiness (*stong cha kho na'i phyogs su lhung*) and the subjective cognition of such ultimate cannot possibly transcend conceptual thoughts (*rnam par rtog pa las 'da' ba mi srid*). Because there is a subject leftover after negating hypostatic existence, it will undeniably have to be an individually characterized entity. In that case, Candrakīrti's three reasonings against the Svātantrikas will apply to the proponents of such an ultimate.[153] In this way, Mipham repeatedly refutes the Gelukpa understanding of the absence of hypostatic existence as ultimate and goes on to prove that ultimate reality is coalescence free from elaborations.

Mipham's second opponents are the advocates of the *gzhan stong* theory, who claim that *saṃsāra*, including all the world within and without are illusory and ultimately not existent while the state of *nirvāṇa qua* enlightened nature is absolute and inherently existent. Such a state of enlightenment exists truly and is not empty of its own being but only of fortuitous and accidental delusions of *saṃsāra*.

Mipham refutes the *gzhan stong* theory reasoning that such Emptiness, where x is empty of y does not qualify to be Emptiness and the absence of non-existent *saṃsāra* in a absolute *nirvāṇa* would not make coalescence. He explains:

> Generally speaking, the Emptiness of other
> Does not qualify to be Emptiness.
> Although a cow is not perceived in a horse
> How can one [through that] perceive a horse to be empty?

> What kind of benefit or harm
> Will seeing a horse be to the [concept of] cow?
> Thus, it is improper for the non-empty *nirvāṇa* and [empty] *saṃsāra*
> To be *dharma* and *dharmatā*.
> The concept of coalescence of appearance and Emptiness
> And the equality of existence and *nirvāṇa* cannot be applied to this.
> Saying '[the reflection of] the moon in water is not moon'
> If the appearance of the moon in water itself
> And [the fact that it is] empty of sky-moon is [considered] coalescence,
> Coalescence would be so easy to understand.
> Everyone knows a cow is not a horse
> For the appearance is evidently seen.
> Why would the Great Sage say
> That it is amazing to realize it?
> Therefore, in our own tradition,
> If [the reflection of] the moon in the water is analysed,
> Nothing is found or [nothing] exists, and yet simultaneously
> The moon in the water appears; when [that is] evident,
> Although [it is] absolute negation, [it is still] possible to appear
> Although Emptiness and existence are contradictory
> To the mind of ordinary persons, here [they] evidently coalesce.
> The learned hail [this] with words of amazement
> Calling this [coalescence], 'the exquisite'.[154]

Refuting the theory of the ultimate in these two schools, Mipham declares the theory of his own tradition, Nyingma, to be that of coalescence. He claims in *Nges shes sgron me*:

> Therefore, following the assertion of the Omniscient One,[155]
> Our own tradition is to be known as follows.
> If [it] is the authentic middle
> [It] must be the Great Madhyamaka of coalescence
> Or the Madhyamaka free from elaborations.[156]

This understanding of the ultimate as the sphere of reality *qua* coalescence in which every elaboration is negated, he says in his *Ketaka*, is the special category of Mahāyāna realization and is given the name Great Madhyamaka.[157]

The ultimate, middle way and elimination of extremes

As the name indicates, the Mādhyamikas claim to delineate a theory of the ultimate that is the middle (*madhyamaka, dbu ma*) free from fabricating extremes (*spros pa'i mtha' dang bral ba*). Generally speaking, all Buddhist schools consider themselves to be both ethically and philosophically middle by avoiding the extremes. From an ethical viewpoint, the historical Buddha is said to have taught his followers to adopt the middle path where the extremes of self-indulgence in worldly enjoyments and of austere physical penance are both to be eschewed. Philosophically, all Buddhist thinkers claim their schools to be on the middle path by avoiding the ontological extremes of eternalism (*śāsvatavādin, rtag par smra ba*) and nihilism (*ucchedavādin, chad par smra ba*) although the understanding of what is eternalism and nihilism vary from school to school and from topic to topic.

The Mādhyamikas equated their theory of Emptiness with the philosophical middle way and refuted other Buddhist philosophical schools such as Vaibhāṣika, Sautrāntika and Cittamātra alleging their ontological theories of falling to the extreme of eternalism or substantialism (*ngos [por] smra ba*). Others in turn criticized the Mādhyamika theory of Emptiness as nihilism. Among the Mādhyamikas in India, Candrakīrti attacked Bhāvaviveka's interpretation of Nāgārjuna's middle way and his method of eliminating extremes. In Tibet, the understanding of the middle way and the elimination of extremes attracted rigorous debates. The Gelukpas and their opponents – the Ngarabpas and later scholars such as Mipham – differed considerably on the understanding of the middle way and the verification of philosophical extremes and alleged each other of falling to extremes. The Ngarabpas accepted that any mental elaboration is a philosophical extreme. On the ultimate level, not only are extremes such as existence, non-existence, both existence and non-existence and neither negated, but even the concept of the middle is to be negated. Any cataphatic apprehension amounts to reification and is an extreme to be eschewed. An affirmative determination of the middle is also a fabricating extreme.

Mipham understood the ultimate middle along the same lines. He presents several degrees of elimination of extremes and understanding of the middle way in an ascending order culminating in the non-abiding middle way (*rab tu mi gnas pa'i dbu ma*) corresponding the non-notational ultimate.[158] First, he gives the realist method of eliminating the extreme of eternalism through the fact that conditioned things are impermanent and eliminating the extreme of nihilism through the fact that conditioned things are produced through dependence on causes and conditions. Presenting the idealist tradition, he says that they eliminate the extreme of eternalism through understanding the Emptiness of subject–object duality and eliminate the extreme of nihilism through understanding the substantial existence of dependent nature *qua* mind.

In the Mādhyamika school, he says that on the level of delineating the notational ultimate, one eliminates the extreme of eternalism *qua* existence by understanding things to be without hypostatic existence, and eliminates the extreme of nihilism *qua* non-existence by understanding things to be conventionally existent. However, such elimination of extremes and understanding of the middle is not final but only a provisional step to enter the non-notational ultimate. While delineating the non-notational ultimate, all extremes inclusive of even subtle notions of existence and non-existence must be abandoned. If there are no extremes of any sort, how could there be a middle? Hence, it is a mistake to conceive a philosophical middle as a point of focus after eliminating the extremes.[159]

The Gelukpas generally understood the Mādhyamika middle way to be free from the extreme of eternalism through the lack of hypostatic existence and free from the extreme of nihilism through the conventional existence of things. Asserting hypostatic existence is espousing an eternalistic view. Similarly, denying the conventional existence of things is a nihilistic view. The rejection of hypostatic existence and the acceptance of conventional existence are both correct and do not need to be negated as extremes.[160] The middle way, thus, is to abide in the middle by avoiding the eternalistic view of reification of things as hypostatically existent and the nihilistic view of denying the conventional existence of things. However, mention must be made of the unique case in the *Lam gtso rnam gsum*, where Tsongkhapa proclaims the elimination of the extreme of existence by appearance and the extreme of non-existence by Emptiness.[161]

Mipham attacked the general Gelukpa theory of middle way contending that Emptiness *qua* lack of hypostatic existence cannot be the middle way which eliminates all extremes. Were it capable of eliminating all extremes, what is the point of using conventional existence to avoid nihilism? The Gelukpas, as mentioned, assert that Emptiness *qua* lack of hypostatic existence eliminates the extreme of existence and conventional existence the extreme of nihilism. They paraphrased 'neither existence nor non-existent' as 'neither hypostatically existent nor conventionally non-existent'. Mipham argued that this paraphrase indicates that Emptiness *qua* lack of hypostatic existence alone cannot eliminate all extremes and one must rely on conventional existence to negate the extreme of non-existence or nihilism.[162] It is further evident that there has to be a combination of the Emptiness *qua* absence of hypostatic existence and conventional existence to form the middle way. Without either component, one cannot abide in the middle.

Were such the case, he argued that such middle way could not be realized by gnosis of a sublime being in an equipoise. In the event of a person on the path remaining in an appearance-free equipoise (*mnyam gzhag snang med*), when all appearance are stilled, would the two thoughts that things do not exist hypostatically and that things exist conventionally arise in him simultaneously or gradually? The two thoughts cannot arise simultaneously because the objects of the thoughts, the two truths, are not perceived simultaneously in an appearance-free equipoise. The thoughts cannot arise gradually either because no thought of conventional existence alone can arise in the meditative equipoise characterized by the discernment of Emptiness.

Besides, the understanding that things do not exist hypostatically and that things exist conventionally involves conceptual thought (*zhen rig*) process and conceptualization do not occur in the meditative equipoise of sublime beings. It thus ridiculously follows that sublime beings in meditative equipoise do not abide in the middle because they lack conceptual thoughts to synthesize the two components of hypostatic non-existence and conventional existence whereas the ordinary person reflecting that things do not exist hypostatically and exist conventionally abide in the middle way.[163]

Objecting to the Gelukpa theory of the middle arrived through a syzygy of conventional existence and lack of hypostatic existence, Mipham conflates the middle free from extremes with the Emptiness free from elaborations. He argued that the philosophical middle of the ground (*gzhi dbu ma*) is the ontic nature which is free from all elaborations and which does not belong to any extremes or aspects of apprehension. The understanding of such a philosophical middle is the cognitive middle of the path (*lam dbu ma*).[164] The middle way free from all extremes (*mtha' thams cad dang bral ba'i dbu ma*) is not an excluded middle (*phung sum pa*) that is apprehended after negating extremes such as existence, non-existence, self, non-self, etc. A middle with regard to which mental apprehension persists cannot be found even conventionally.[165] The middle way is not an object of apprehension like a point between two pillars; it does not abide in any form as an apprehensible point of focus.[166]

Refuting Mipham's understanding of the middle, Pari Rabsal presents the following arguments:[167]

1 Mipham cannot be a Mādhyamika because he does not abide in the middle way because abiding in the middle free from the extremes of existence and non-existence, as per Mipham's own reasoning, would still lead to being on the extreme of neither existence nor non-existence.
2 Even abiding in the absence of all extremes would be abiding in the extreme of non-existence because such absence is the lack of hypostatic existence, and the lack of hypostatic existence is considered as the extreme of non-existence and negated according to Mipham.
3 Anything lacking hypostatic existence, has to be an extreme of non-existence in Mipham's theory because he considers whatever is conceived to be existent as extreme of existence and whatever is conceived to be non-existent as extreme of non-existence.

Pari Rabsal goes on to argue that there is a middle which exists free from the extremes and that abiding in such middle way is not negated.[168]

Mipham, in his rebuttal of the first objection, differentiates between the delineation of the middle on the level of notational ultimate and that on the level of non-notational ultimate. On the level of notational ultimate, he agrees that one eliminates the extreme of eternalism by understanding the absence of hypostatic existence and the extreme of nihilism by accepting conventional existence. This way of eschewing the extremes through using the binary factors of absence of hypostatic existence and conventional existence is valid on the level of discriminating wisdom in the post-equipoise state. Hence, on this stage, one need not formulate the middle free from existence, non-existence, self, non-self, etc. but in fact establish the lack of hypostatic existence and non-self.

However, when compared to the ultimate middle way, this is still on the conventional level and not all elaborations are overcome at this stage.[169] On the level of non-notational ultimate, both existence and non-existence, self and non-self are superimpositions of our conceptual thoughts and there is not even a middle that can be apprehended after eliminating all four extremes. Furthermore, Mipham argues that Pari Rabsal's accusation that he would be abiding in the extreme of neither existence nor non-existence does not apply because there is no abiding as such in this context. Abiding in middle merely indicates not being in any extremes; there is not any real action of abiding anywhere.[170]

Replying to the second argument, Mipham states that to abide in the absence of hypostatic existence is to cling onto the negation of hypostatic existence with the notion of characteristics (*mtshan ma'i rtog pa*). How can understanding the reality free from all extremes be abiding in such a negative extreme of non-existence, for reality free from elaborations is without any notion of positive and negative characteristics?[171] Mipham does not deny outright the purpose of understanding the lack of hypostatic existence. On the level of notational ultimate, it is a right view and crucial for beginners training in Emptiness. Alluding to the Kagyupa and Sakyapa criticism[172] of the Gelukpa understanding of Emptiness *qua* absence of hypostatic existence as nihilistic view, Mipham clarifies in *rGyan 'grel* that it is not a nihilistic view.[173] To him, the main mistake of the Gelukpas is holding the provisional absence of hypostatic existence as the ultimate Emptiness or the middle way.

In response to the third objection, Mipham denies saying out of context that whatever is conceived to be existent to be the extreme of existence and whatever is conceived to be non-existent to be the extreme of non-existence.[174] Conventionally speaking, absence of hypostatic existence and conventional existence are not extremes but antidotes to corresponding extremes of hypostatic existence and conventional non-existence. However, mere understanding of conventional existence and of the absence of hypostatic existence cannot overcome all conceptual elaborations. Instead, they themselves become subtle extremes. Hence, on the level of non-notational ultimate when reality free from all elaborations is established, even subtle extremes such as the notion of existence and non-existence are to be dispelled and no middle is cataphatically established.[175] To support his interpretation, Mipham cites the following verses:

> What is 'existence' and 'non-existence' are both extremes;
> So are 'purity' and 'impurity' extremes.
> Therefore, abandoning the extremes of both,
> The wise surely would not abide even in the middle.[176]

> How could there be a middle for that which has no extremes?[177]

> Therefore, one should not take the things to exist
> And should avoid the thought of the non-existence of things.
> Those who wish the state of omniscience
> Should not abide in the middle either.[178]

Mipham remarks that were one to understand the middle as his opponents did, the fourth verse of *Samādhirājasūtra* should read 'the wise surely would abide in the middle'. Pari Rabsal refers to the following from *Kāśyapaparivarta* to argue that a middle is established after negating the two extremes:

> Kāśyapa! This which is called 'permanence' is one extreme. Kāśyapa! This which is called 'impermanence' is a second extreme. The middle of the two extremes is what cannot be examined, cannot be taught, is not a basis, is without appearance, without cognition and without abiding. Kāśyapa! This is what is called the middle way, the understanding of phenomena correctly.
>
> Kāśyapa! This which is called 'self' is one extreme. This which is called 'non-self' is a second extreme. The middle of the two extremes is what cannot be examined, cannot be taught, is not a basis, is without appearance, without cognition and without abiding. Kāśyapa! This is what is called the middle way, the understanding of phenomena correctly. . . . Kāśyapa! This which is called 'existence' is one extreme. This which is called 'non-existence' is a second extreme. The middle of these two extremes is what is called the middle way, the understanding of phenomena correctly.[179]

In his response to Pari Rabsal, Mipham mentions that the *sūtra* does not teach a middle way that is established as an object of apprehension after the extremes are refuted. He points out that the middle in the *sūtra* is described as 'what cannot be examined, cannot be taught, is not a basis, is without appearance, without cognition and without abiding', and goes on to say how that contradicts the Gelukpa interpretation of the middle but suits his understanding. He writes: 'those treatises do not point out, as you do, a middle which is apprehensible and an object on which to abide, like the middle between two pillars placed [next to each other]' and 'therefore, middle refers to not apprehending [anything] in any extremes. If one were to hold [it] as an object on which the apprehensive [thought] can abide, one would never be able to transcend conceptual thoughts and elaborations, in whatever way Emptiness may be taught.'[180]

The concept of the middle way in Mipham's thought, like that of Emptiness and ultimate, is divided into the provisional middle between the extremes of hypostatic existence and conventional non-existence and the final middle which is free from all extremes of elaborations. The authentic middle in the Mādhyamika tradition, according to Mipham, is the latter and the former is a step to the latter. He explicates in his *Nges shes sgron me* the Nyingma stance on middle way:

> Therefore, following the assertion of the Omniscient One,
> Our own tradition is to be known as follows.
> If [it] is the authentic middle
> [It] must be the Great Madhyamaka of coalescence

> Or the Madhyamaka free from elaborations,
> Because [it is that, which] having been delineated
> In accordance with the gnosis of equipoise of sublime beings,
> Is the nature in which all extremes
> Such as existence and non-existence are pacified.[181]

Mipham refers to the two tiers of the middle way as the lesser and great middle way. He also calls them the causal and the resultant, the coarse and subtle, the middle way of the discriminatory path and the middle way of the stage of actual equipoise. They correspond to the cognitive middle ways of consciousness and gnosis.[182] Mipham refers to the gnosis of the equipoise as the resultant middle way (*mnyam gzhag 'bras bu'i dbu ma*) and to the discriminating wisdom on the path of ordinary persons as the causal middle way (*shes rab rgyu yi dbu ma*).[183] Describing the lesser middle way, he states:

> Therefore, the middle way with the assertions
> Of the two truths distinctively
> Is the lesser middle way, involving alternation,
> For which the name of the result is given to the cause.[184]

In the case of this middle way, the discriminating mind can comprehend the nature of Emptiness and appearance only alternately and cannot perceive them simultaneously. Speaking on the resultant or great middle way, Mipham points out that the gnosis which do not abide on the two extremes through alternating the two truths but is beyond the scope of mind is the great middle way. Unless one reaches this stage of gnosis, it is not the great middle way, which is the essence of the intent of all Buddhas.[185] He describes further:

> The great gnosis of coalescence,
> Induced by wisdoms comprehending the two truths,
> Pacified of all elaborations of four extremes
> Such as existence, non-existence, is and is not,
> The very gnosis of equipoise of sublime beings,
> Is asserted to be the resultant middle way of coalescence.[186]

On MK, XIII/8

Throughout this chapter I have discussed, looking from various angles, how Mipham accuses his Gelukpa opponents of misunderstanding Emptiness by holding the concordant or notational Emptiness *qua* absence of hypostatic existence to be ultimate Emptiness. We have also seen how the Gelukpas reasoned that Emptiness is absence of hypostatic existence *per se* and to see Emptiness either as a hypostatic absence or as reality transcending existence, non-existence, etc.

is a misunderstanding of Emptiness. Let's now turn to briefly look at their commentaries on the verses dealing with the misunderstanding of Emptiness such as MK, XIII/8:

The Victorious Ones have taught Emptiness
In order to expel all views.
Those who have the view of Emptiness,
They are said to be incorrigible.[187]

Nāgārjuna clarifies that the Emptiness is also not tenable after all other things are proved to be empty. He argues that if there is anything that is non-empty, there could be something empty. Because there is nothing which is not empty, how can there be anything that is Emptiness.[188] Then, he goes on to say that the Buddhas taught Emptiness to overcome all kinds of views and those who hold the view of Emptiness are incorrigible. All other kinds of views and clinging can be overcome by the antidote of Emptiness, but there is no other remedy to the view of clinging to Emptiness itself.

Closely following the commentaries of Bhāvaviveka and Candrakīrti on MK, Tsongkhapa and Mipham do not differ much in interpreting the verse in their commentaries on MK. Both interpret 'the view of Emptiness' as the view holding Emptiness to be with its own being. They cite the passage from *Kaśyapaparivarta* on how Emptiness does not make a thing empty but things are empty by nature or own being and both allude to the analogy of how a patient who, being treated with a medicine for a certain disease, cannot be remedied if that very medicine left inside him turns into a disease. They also both uses Candrakīrti's example of good.[189] If a person asks for a piece of good and is told there is no good whatsoever but if he still insists on 'the good that is not there', how can one communicate with such a person and make him understand what 'there is no good' means? Holding onto the view of Emptiness is like asking for 'that which is not there'.

Tsongkhapa however clarifies in his commentary that it is not wrong to hold all things to be empty of hypostatic existence. The view of Emptiness that is rejected in this verse is to hold Emptiness itself as hypostatic absence possessing some form of aseity. He also mentions this emphatically in his *Lam rim*.[190] He argues that it is clear from the analogy of the good. Knowing that there is no good is not wrong but grasping onto the lack of good as something substantial is mistaken. He elaborates on how the view of Emptiness is correct and crucial to the enlightenment. It is the view of Emptiness as hypostatic or substantial entity that is being shunned by Nāgārjuna.

Mipham in his *Rab lan, rGyan 'grel and Ketaka*[191] conflates the incorrigible view of Emptiness with the misunderstanding of lack of hypostatic existence as the ultimate Emptiness. The mistaken view of Emptiness is to view Emptiness *qua* the absence of hypostatic existence and hold it as the final ultimate. According to him, such a view of Emptiness is a provisional antidote to clinging to substance and is instrumental for beginners. However, to hold onto such a view of Emptiness, after having overcome the clinging, is redundant and can become a problem that cannot be remedied. It is clear that both Tsongkhapa and Mipham take the Emptiness in this verse to mean the absence of hypostatic existence. To Tsongkhapa, viewing it as hypostatically existent is wrong whereas, in Mipham's thought, to hold onto it and view it as ultimate Emptiness and not transcend it is wrong. Another verse on wrong understanding of Emptiness is MK, XXIV/11:

> An Emptiness wrongly understood
> Could ruin a person of inferior intelligence.
> It is like handling a snake incorrectly
> And cultivating a *mantra* knowledge wrongly.[192]

This verse appear in Nāgārjuna's reply to the objection by his opponents that if everything is empty and there were no production and cessation, the four noble truths, the three jewels, the Buddhist path would not be possible. Nāgārjuna replies by presenting the theory of two truths and explaining how Emptiness is not to be construed as sheer annihilation of the empirical and evident phenomena. He goes onto to say how Emptiness is subtle and difficult to fathom:

> Thus, knowing that the inferior ones
> Would have difficulty fathoming this dharma,
> The Sage has withdrawn his mind
> From teaching the dharma.[193]

Both Tsongkhapa and Mipham comment that to view Emptiness either as sheer annihilation of things or as a hypostatic absence of inherent nature is an incorrect understanding of Emptiness. Mipham comments that there are two ways of clinging to Emptiness: Emptiness as substantial and as insubstantial.[194] He takes Emptiness in this context to refer to the final Emptiness *qua* non-notational ultimate which is the coalescence of appearance and Emptiness free from all elaborations and insinuates that the Gelukpa understanding of Emptiness as the mere absence of hypostatic existence is incorrect clinging to Emptiness as insubstantial negation. He also adds in *Ketaka* and *rGyan 'grel* that to view the nature of Emptiness to be neither substantial nor insubstantial but as a blank state of indeterminacy just as Hwashang did is also a wrong understanding.[195]

He reasons that if Emptiness were so easy to understand, as it is in the case of Emptiness *qua* absence of hypostatic existence espoused by the Gelukpas or blank non-thinking propagated by Hwashang, why would the masters of antiquity proclaim it to be abstruse, profound and difficult to fathom?[196] Thus, he uses the profundity, inconceivability and ineffability attributed to Emptiness by earlier masters to argue that Emptiness in its ultimate form is not merely an absence of hypostatic existence but an ultimate reality transcending all fabricating extremes such as existence and non-existence. Let us now turn to the discussion of the inconceivable and ineffable nature of Emptiness that forms a major strand of Mipham's polemics on Emptiness.

5

IS EMPTINESS KNOWABLE AND EFFABLE?

As long as one keeps expressing it, it is not really expressed.
(Candrakīrti, *Madhyamakāvatārabhāṣya*, p. 139)

The discrepancies between Mipham and his opponents on the knowability and expressibility of Emptiness, the topic for this chapter, comes as an immediate corollary to their differences in their ontological understanding of the ultimate *qua* Emptiness, which we have discussed in the previous chapter. The ontological theory of *what* is the ultimate is invariably interwoven with the epistemological and semasiological issue of how it is known and expressed or whether it is knowable and expressible at all in the normal sense of the words. Thus, ontology, language and epistemology are closely linked together. We have seen this intricate link, in the preceding chapter, in the way the ultimate is defined through its epistemic subject and its mode of cognition. In this chapter, we shall see how the proponent's understanding of the nature of the ultimate determines his epistemological and semasiological position pertaining to the ultimate.

It is a common Mādhyamika theme that the linguistic exposition of the ultimate is conducive to the cognitive understanding of the ultimate, and the cognitive knowledge *qua* correct view, leads to enlightenment. All Mādhyamika thinkers accept the linguistic communication and cognitive realization of the ultimate *qua* Emptiness to be indispensable to the attainment of enlightenment.[1] However, they differ on the issues pertaining to the form of communication and the nature of the realization; on the type of thoughts, the efficacy of words in communicating the ultimate, the viability of apprehension and grasping and the role of conceptual thoughts in the cognition of the ultimate. Followers of the Mādhyamika tradition, in this regard, can be said to belong to two divergent trends: one inclined to passive quietism, as it were rejecting the involvement of all words, thoughts, apprehensions and concepts in the experience of the ultimate and the other emphasizing active rationalism and holding the ultimate to be an object of language and thoughts.[2] In this chapter, I shall discuss the debates between these two trends in the light of Mipham's interpretations and assess his own stance on the knowability and effability of the ultimate *qua* Emptiness.

On whether Emptiness is knowable (*jñeya, shes bya*)

The issue of whether or not the ultimate is a knowable (*jñeya, shes bya*) is one of the most salient topics of debate between the Gelukpas and their opponents on Emptiness. A knowable thing, in Tibetan dialectics, is generally defined as that which can be an object of thought (*blo yul du bya rung ba*). It is equivalent (*khyab mnyam*) to what is existent (*yod pa*), phenomenon (*chos*) or object (*yul*). Hence, whatever is existent, a phenomenon or object is knowable and *vice versa*. More specifically, it can refer to the object (*yul*) of the subject–object dichotomy (*yul dang yul can gyi zlas phye ba*) but in the context of the debates in question, it is understood primarily with the first denotation.

Tsongkhapa and his followers strongly opposed their Ngarabpa opponents to whom they ascribed the position that Emptiness *qua* ultimate truth is not a knowable entity. It is unclear whom exactly Tsongkhapa was refuting as he does not name his opponents. Hopkins and Napper report respectively that Jamyang Zhadpa and Zhamar Tenzin identify one of Tsongkhapa's opponents in this case as Ngog Loden Sherab.[3] Gyaltshab gives the name of Tölung Jamarwa, the most likely Jangchub Drak, the teacher of Chapa Chökyi Seṅge, in his commentary on the BA.[4] These Ngarabpas, including others such as Sapaṇ,[5] held the standpoint that ultimate truth *qua* Emptiness is not knowable, perhaps based on the direct reading of the *sūtra*s and the *śāstra*s such as the *Vajracchedikāprajñāpāramitāsūtra*,[6] MA, XVIII/7[7] and BA, IX/2. Were Emptiness knowable and the ultimate cognition such as the gnosis of meditative equipoise able to apprehend it, they thought it would be hypostatically existent – for only a hypostatically existent entity can withstand the ultimate analysis and remain before the ultimate cognition. We shall return to this discussion later. A more compelling reason for the unknowability of the ultimate truth is the delineation of Emptiness in the Mādhyamika literature as neither existent, nor non-existent, both or neither. Whatever is knowable is existent and what is not existent is not knowable.

The Gelukpas, as we have seen in the previous chapters, did not accept the literal reading of the negation of the four extremes presented in the Mādhyamika treatises. To them, the ultimate truth is existent; the two truths are divisions of existent things. Tsongkhapa and his followers attacked the Ngarabpa stance mostly in the discussion of the basis of the classification of the two truths (*bden pa gnyis kyi dbye gzhi*).[8] In his *dGongs pa rab gsal* Tsongkhapa emphatically points out that the basis of classification of the two truths is knowable things. That is to say, knowable things are classified into conventional and ultimate truths. The denial of the ultimate truth to be knowable, he mentions, is not the intention of Candrakīrti and Śāntideva.[9] He writes, 'Although there are various assertions of the basis of classification of two truths, here, it is knowable thing[s].'[10] He cites the following passage from *Āryapitaputrasamāgamanasūtra* cited in *Śikṣāsamuccaya* to support his stance that both truths are knowable things:

> In this way, the Tathāgata fathoms both conventional and ultimate, and all knowable things are included in the conventional and ultimate truths.

> They are clearly seen, known and properly actualized by the Blessed One to be empty. Therefore, [the Buddhas] are known as the omniscient.[11]

Tsongkhapa and his followers use the phrases 'knowable things' and 'clearly seen, known and properly actualised' in this passage to argue that the ultimate truth is knowable according to both the *sūtra* and Śāntideva who cited it. In his commentary on MK, XV/2,[12] Tsongkhapa also argues that Emptiness is existent and knowable because it is the inherent nature (*svabhāva, rang bzhin*) of things. Paradoxically, the lack of inherent nature is the inherent nature of things, the ontic mode, reality, *quidditas* and ultimate truth. They are all equivalent to Emptiness and they exist and can be known.[13]

Tsongkhapa's main qualm about the Ngarabpa position is that, were ultimate truth not knowable or existent, the understanding of the ultimate truth would not be tenable. Without the epistemological understanding, the soteriological efficacy of Emptiness as right view would be entirely lost. Thus, ontological theories of Emptiness, its epistemological understanding and the soteriological purpose would become isolated. Moreover, Tsongkhapa is worried that Tibetan thinkers, maintaining the ultimate as unknowable, misunderstand the Mādhyamika theory of Emptiness as a philosophy of non-thinking, as an indeterminate quietist approach that 'there is not anything at all' instead of a gradual and systematic development of a well founded certainty (*nges shes*) about the ultimate through rationalism. This 'philosophical naivety' as Jinpa calls it,[14] thus undermines the rational approach to understanding the ultimate and subsequently leads to neglect of moral and ethical values, which we shall discuss briefly later.

Mipham adopts a middle stance between the Ngarabpas and Gelukpas. He acknowledges that the ultimate truth is described as unknowable and like the Ngarabpas, often takes the texts describing the ultimate truth as unknowable without any interpretation. Yet he also presents the ultimate truth as an object of knowledge, the right view, which forms the central pillar of Mahāyāna soteriology. The cultivation of such a view or certainty about Emptiness forms a major theme in his writings on Madhyamaka. He resolved the apparent contradiction, which he considered as *prima facie*, through some hermeneutic devices of placing the variant understandings in their specific contexts and perspectives.

In his *Ketaka* and *Nyi snang*, he clarifies that one must verify the specific perspectives through which one looks at the topic of the knowability of Emptiness in order to say anything definite. From the perspective of the knowledge of the ultimate truth such as the gnosis of meditative equipoise, Emptiness is not knowable or existent. He writes:

> Reality, in this context, is said to be unknowable because reality transcends all elaborations, and therefore it is not apprehensible by [any] thought. How can that which is neither object nor subject and does not exist with any characteristics be really called a knowable?[15]

From the viewpoint of the non-dualistic thought, which discerns the ultimate, there is no object to be known or subject which knows; all such fabrications are fully pacified. Otherwise, if it has a sense of the subject knowing the object, how would it be free from the subject–object dualism?[16] If one argues that the subject–object duality does exist in reality but does not appear to the thought discerning the ultimate, then it would follow that the thought discerning the ultimate is wrong with regard to ontic reality as it is not consistent with the ontic reality.[17] Furthermore, Mipham reasons that if they insist that the inferential cognition or gnosis, which discerns the ultimate, obtains or sees Emptiness as such, Emptiness, one would have to say, is affirmed or ascertained positively. Asserting such positive Emptiness is equal to espousing the absolutist extrinsic Emptiness attributed to the Zhantongpas.[18] We shall come back to this argument.

Thus, what is meant by 'the gnosis discerning the ultimate' is the experience of Emptiness free from all extremes without any sense of duality and apprehension. Mipham cites *Saṃcayagāthā*, XII/10 and illustrates that claiming to know reality *qua* Emptiness is like claiming to see space.[19] If properly examined, there is nothing being seen and it is merely a term designating the seeing of a lack of matter. Similarly, there is nothing to be known or discerned in Emptiness in the normal sense of the word.[20] He remarks, 'Would not the claim be inconsistent in [its] direct and implied [meanings] if one says that in reality this [ultimate truth] is the object apprehended or known by the equipoise, which is without any apprehended object or apprehending subject.'[21]

However, from the perspective of conventional truth, it is appropriate to say that ultimate truth is knowable because the gnosis in the meditative equipoise of exalted beings is subjective experience which takes the ultimate truth as its object.[22] He cites the following verse from MA to show how conventionally one could speak of discerning the ultimate truth although there is no actual discerning of an object by a subject:

> Since unborn nature is reality and mind too is devoid of arising,
> Then that [mind], through depending on the aspect of [the unborn], [seems] as if it knows reality.
> Just as the mind [is said to] know an object when it acquires the aspect [of that object],
> So is reality [said to be] known, relying fully on convention.[23]

He adds in his *Nyi snang*, 'There is no need to mention that there is, on the conventional [level], a thought which discerns the ultimate according to all traditions.'[24] The whole point of delineation of the ultimate is to realize it. So, there is no need for special discussion on whether the ultimate is knowable or not on the conventional level. It is understood from the context. Were it not even knowable on the conventional level, there would be no purpose in delineating it. Hence, when the ultimate is described to be unknowable, one need not even doubt that it is denying the knowability from the viewpoint of the ultimate cognition and not mere convention.[25]

Mipham reiterates that the verification of the perspective from which the ultimate is discussed is crucial to the understanding of knowability of the ultimate. He writes:

> Therefore, with regard to the conventional, the ultimate is taught several times in all *sūtras* and *śāstras* to be knowable, object and so forth, and in accordance with the manner in which it is realized by the non-conceptual gnosis of equipoise, it is taught to be the abstruse, ineffable reality which is to be experienced by the intuitive awareness and without any net of elaborations such as knowing and knowable, object and subject, etc.[26]

Mipham warns that taking the description of the ultimate as knowable or unknowable out of context and having a partial understanding of the scriptures will lead to extreme conclusions. One would either be forced to accept that the ultimate is utterly unknowable and cannot be delineated, thus rejecting the soteriological role of the ultimate, or corrupt the essential teachings of the Buddha by claiming the profound ultimate, which is the reality free from all fabrications, to be within the domain of ordinary ratiocination. Any elaborations on a partial understanding is like ornamenting a corpse. However beautifully it is said, it will destroy the spirit of Mahāyāna. Showing the *ris med* side of him, Mipham adds that the understanding of the earlier and later Tibetan scholars, should be seen as non-contradictory, placed in their right perspectives. Let us continue to look at the debates on knowability of the ultimate through the commentaries on the BA, IX/2.

On BA, IX/2

The second verse of the ninth chapter of Śāntideva's BA is perhaps the hottest topic of debate among Tibetan scholars on the subject of the nature of the two truths. After stating the purpose of cultivating wisdom in the first verse, Śāntideva presents the concept of the two truths and describes their natures likewise:

> The conventional and the ultimate
> Are asserted to be the two truths.
> The ultimate is not within the scope of thought;
> Thought is asserted to be conventional.[27]

What has become highly controversial is the understanding of the description of the ultimate in the third line. There are two systems of interpretation which stand out on this: one which adheres to the direct reading of the line and espouses the unknowability of the ultimate and the other which interprets the reading and asserts the knowability of the ultimate.

The Ngarabpa thinkers such as Ngog Loden Sherab and Tölung Jamarwa are reported to have understood it in the first way by taking the third verse as a thesis and the fourth as reasoning, thus phrasing it 'the ultimate is not within the scope of thoughts because all thoughts are conventional'.[28] Ngog in fact argues in his *Theg chen rgyud bla ma'i don bsdus* that the ultimate is not an object of conceptual thought because conceptual thought is conventional.[29] As we have seen in the previous chapters, the ultimate *qua* Emptiness according to them transcends the dichotomies of existence and non-existence, subject and object, is and is not; it is beyond thought because all thoughts and objects in the scope of thought are conventional. Several later thinkers from the Nyingma, Kagyu and Sakya schools including Mipham and Karmapa Mikyo Dorje understood the above verse along these lines.

The Gelukpas from Gyaltshab, through Jamyang Zhadpa to Pari Rabsal and Drakar Trulku refuted the direct reading of the third and fourth lines as thesis and reasoning. Gyaltshab argues that, were the ultimate truth beyond the reach of all thoughts and were there no thoughts in the meditative equipoise of the exalted beings, one would have to accept that a person would cease to have thoughts when he becomes a sublime being absorbed in the meditative equipoise, just like Cārvākas believe thoughts to cease after death. Beside, if one does not accept a knowable reality, the knowledge of which would help eliminate the defilements, the elimination of defilements would not be possible and consequently there would be no distinction between the Buddhas and sentient beings. If one accepts a knowable reality, it would contradict the assertion that the ultimate is unknowable. Furthermore, if whatever is conventional does not apprehend the ultimate, there would not be anything that apprehends the ultimate for the ultimate does not apprehend itself. What is the point of having two truths, then?[30] He remarks that those, who hold the ultimate to be unknowable, defy ontic reality and belong to an evil tradition deprived of the soteriological purpose for their religious observance.[31]

Khedrub Je and Jamyang Zhadpa made similar refutations which Guy Newland presents in the following translation:[32]

> Borrowing from Kay-drup-jay's *Thousand Doses*, Jam-yang-shay-ba hurls four *reductio ad absurdum* arguments at those who maintain that emptiness is unknowable:
>
> (a) Śāntideva must have contradicted himself because his *Compendium of Instructions* cites a sūtra indicating that objects of knowledge are the basis of the division of the two truths, while his *Engaging in the Bodhisattva Deeds* teaches that the ultimate is unknowable.
> (b) Since the ultimate cannot be known, Buddha taught the ultimate without knowing it. Therefore, the sūtras that say that the Buddha knows emptiness are incorrect.
> (c) Emptiness does not exist because it is not an object of knowledge. Since sūtra and śāstra sources state that if emptiness did not exist

there would be no point in making great sacrifices on the path, other sūtras that say that such sacrifices should be made are incorrect.

(d) All sentient beings are already liberated from suffering because the mode of subsistence of phenomena has been clear to them for countless aeons. This must be the case because if emptiness is non-existent, phenomena have no mode of subsistence apart from the way that they appear.

The first argument, about an inconsistency that would arise between Śāntideva's two works, the *Śikṣāsamuccaya* and the BA, if the third line were taken directly and the ultimate understood to be unknowable, appears in several Gelukpa refutations and we have briefly touched upon this earlier. Using the passage cited in the *Śikṣāsamuccaya* from *Āryapitaputrasamāgamasūtra* on how all knowable things are included within the two truths, the Gelukpas argued that it goes against Śāntideva's intention to take the third line of BA, IX/2 directly and claim that the ultimate is unknowable. Tsongkhapa writes in his *dGongs pa rab gsal*: 'Therefore, expounding that ultimate truth is not a knowable and is not realized by any thought to be the intent of BA['s author] is an incorrect exposition.'[33]

The Gelukpas unanimously interpreted 'thought' in the third and fourth lines as thought with dualistic appearance (*gnyis snang can gyi blo*). They took the third line to show the definition of the ultimate and the fourth to show the definition of the conventional truth. Tsongkhapa understood thought in these three ways: the mere thought (*blo tsam*), the transactional thought (*tha snyad pa'i blo*) and the ultimate thought (*don dam pa'i blo*).[34] The thought in the context of BA, IX/2, he says, belongs to the first two. In the case of mere thought, one must attach a qualifier (*khyad par sbyar dgos*), that is, with a dualistic appearance. This is because no thought with fabrication of a dualistic appearance can directly discern the ultimate. With regard to the transactional thought, no thought other than Buddha's gnosis and Emptiness-discerning wisdom of those on the path of learning can properly apprehend the ultimate. It is clear that according to Tsongkhapa, and subsequently to all Gelukpas, the ultimate is not an object of thought with a dualistic appearance but is definitely an object of the non-dualistic thought or the ultimate thought, as he calls them in his tripartite understanding of thought.

Mipham was fully aware of the Gelukpa criticism of the Ngarabpa understanding of the verse. He lists in his *Ketaka* the following oppositions against the stance that the ultimate is unknowable.[35] If the ultimate truth were not an object of thought, (a) it would not be appropriate for the empirical qualities of elimination and realization (*spangs rtogs*) to arise from apprehending Emptiness, (b) gnosis of the sublime beings in meditative equipoise would not be the subject cognizing reality, (c) reality would have to be accepted like an inconceivable creator and (d) the basis of classification of two truths would not be knowable things. Notwithstanding these refutations, he followed the Ngarabpa system insofar as the direct reading is concerned and criticized the Gelukpa specification of 'dualistic thoughts' as an ado with mere words (*ming tsam gyis ngal ba*). In his commentary on the last two lines, he writes:

> Therefore, the ontic mode of things, the ultimate, is not within the scope of thought because [it] is free from all extremes of existence, non-existence, both and neither. [That is so] because thought and words are conventional, not ultimate. Whatever is apprehended and constructed as 'this and that' by thought and whatever is communicated as 'this and that' through words, such phenomena which are within the scope of mind and speech, are empty like a magical illusion, because they are not found if analysed. [A thing] which can withstand the analysis can never be possible.[36]

Then he goes on to cite the following passage from a *Āryasaṃvṛtiparamārthasatyanirdeśasūtra*:

> Devaputra! If the ultimate truth were within the scope of body, speech and mind, it would not fall within the category of the ultimate, but turn into conventional truth. Devaputra! However, the ultimate truth is beyond all conventions, undifferentiated, unborn, unceasing and void of [being] the expressible and expresser and the knowable and knower. [The ultimate truth] is that which is beyond the scope of even the omniscient gnosis endowed with the supreme of all aspects; [it] is not like [when one is] saying 'the ultimate'.[37]

Mipham cites this in most of his major Mādhyamika works to prove that the ultimate is not only beyond the scope of dualistic thoughts but is unknowable even by the non-dualistic thoughts such as the Buddha's omniscient gnosis.[38] Because the ultimate reality is without any elaborations, there is nothing to be apprehended. How could the ultimate be knowable without any form of subjectivity or objectivity?[39]

Tsongkhapa knew about the use of this passage to support the ineffability of the ultimate. He cites this to object the reading that the ultimate is beyond the scope of even the omniscient gnosis.[40] According to him, the first line shows that if the ultimate falls within the scope of body, speech and mind as the five aggregates do, it would not be free from elaborations and would then turn into an elaborative conventional truth. The second line demonstrates how the ultimate from the perspective of ultimate cognition is undifferentiated, unborn, etc. Commenting on the third line, he argues that the ultimate is not an object of the omniscient gnosis involving a dualistic appearance. He comments that the first half of the sentence mentions that the ultimate is not an object of the omniscient gnosis and the second half states in what sense it is not an object. Unlike in the case of the conceptual thought of the ultimate derived from hearing 'the ultimate', the realization of the ultimate by the Buddha's gnosis does not involve dichotomising appearance of subject–object duality (*yul yul can gnyis so sor snang ba*). Thus, this line shows the lack of a dualistic appearance to the Buddha's gnosis and the lack of conventional appearance to the gnosis directly discerning the reality (*de kho na nyid mngon sum du gzigs pa'i ngor*); it does not prove the ultimate to be unknown to the Buddha. He goes on to argue that the Buddha is the Buddha because he realizes the ultimate fully.

Mipham, as we have already discussed, distinguishes the two perspectives and argues that from the perspective of ultimate cognition, the ultimate is unknowable, even to the Buddha. However, from a conventional perspective, one can consider it as knowable, hence, the contradictions raised by Gelukpas against the Ngarabpas do not affect him. He cites MA, IX/13 to demonstrate how we can speak of knowing the ultimate as a mere nomenclature although there is no real knower and the known.

Another interesting hermeneutic device he uses in his *Ketaka* to resolve the inconsistency of the ultimate being described as knowable sometimes and unknowable at other times is the dialectical explanation through the mode of determination. There are two ways of determining an object or a fact: positive determination (*yongs gcod*) and negative determination (*rnam bcad*). Negative determination is a process where 'the nature of a thing is known [indirectly] through the elimination of what are not the thing' and positive determination is where 'the nature of a thing is [directly] affirmed and by doing so, what are not the thing are eliminated'.[41] The ultimate is not a positively determined object and therefore it is not knowable in a positive sense. It is a pure negation, established by negative determination. Hence, like space, it can be said to be a knowable thing apophatically, but not even the gnosis of the Buddha can discern the ultimate via positive determination.[42]

Rebutting his refuters

Mipham's commentary on the BA, IX/2 lead to a series of debates between him and the Gelukpa opponents. His opponents accused him of numerous contradictions in following the Ngarabpa tradition of reading the verse directly. A thorough treatment of the refutations and the elaborate replies of Mipham will require a more detailed presentation. Here, I shall summarize the debates between him and his two Gelukpa opponents.

Pari Rabsal states that by denying the ultimate to be the object of thoughts and words, Mipham contradicts his own words and the scriptures.[43] He demonstrates how Mipham contradicts his words by putting forth several apagogic reasonings:

(a) The ultimate, it follows is knowable, because there is the wisdom, which discerns it. This is so because Mipham says in his own commentary that 'one should persevere to cultivate the wisdom, which discerns the ultimate'.[44]
(b) The ultimate, it follows is not the object of yogis because the yogis are conventional truths. The pervasion (*vyāpti, khyab pa*) is established as Mipham holds that whatever is conventional cannot discern the ultimate.

This contradicts with his presentation of the persons who understand the two truths.[45]

(c) The ultimate, it follows cannot be approached through words and conceptual thought because they are conceptually constructed (*btags pa*). That is so because they are not established with their own characteristics (*rang mtshan gyis ma grub pa*). Pari Rabsal seems to think that Mipham would accept that whatever is conceptually constructed and without its own characteristics cannot point to the ultimate because Mipham states in his *Ketaka* that the ultimate is beyond the scope of language and thoughts and anything within the scope of thoughts and words cannot withstand the ultimate analysis.[46] If the thesis is accepted and there is truly no thought or word which point to the ultimate, Pari Rabsal argues that it would contradict his statement that Emptiness is known inferentially and through the power of the Buddha,[47] because inference involves conceptual thought and the latter involves words.

(d) The ultimate, it follows is an object of thought because Mipham mentions in several cases that it is an object of the thought of ordinary and exalted beings.

He goes on to point out numerous other instances where Mipham talks about the realization, understanding or the discernment of the ultimate and argues that all such descriptions are inconsistent with his assertion that the ultimate is unknowable.[48] Then, he refers to quotations from different *sūtra*s and *śāstra*s on the knowability of the ultimate and accuses Mipham of contradicting them.

Drakar Trulku makes a similar refutation of Mipham attacking the reading of the third line as a thesis and the fourth line a reasoning to support it.[49] He objects the stance that whatever is the conventional truth cannot apprehend the ultimate. Were it the case, the ultimate would become utterly non-existent because it cannot be an object of any thought. It would then follow that the two truths are not 'of one nature two aspects' (*ngo bo gcig ldog pa tha dad*) as taught in the *Bodhicittavivaraṇa*.[50] 'Furthermore', he writes, 'it [i.e. the ultimate], the subject, it follows is object of thought, because it is the object apprehended by the gnosis of equipoise of the sublime beings'.[51] He goes on to quote a few texts stating that the ultimate is realized by the exalted beings. Commenting on the citations Mipham used to support his argument that the ultimate is unknowable, Drakar accused Mipham of not properly distinguishing the provisional teachings from the definitive and not verifying thoughts with and without a dualistic appearance.[52]

Mipham responds to both Pari Rabsal and Drakar Trulku in great depth and detail citing their objections fully in each case. He denies that the ultimate is utterly unknowable, speaking from a conventional viewpoint. Responding to Pari Rabsal's refutation that the ultimate cannot be an object of yogis, of any word and thought because they are constructed and lacking individual characteristics, he rejects claiming that all things which are constructs and lacking individual characteristics cannot know or show the ultimate.[53] Following up his arguments in *Ketaka*, he reiterates, in both *Rab lan* and *Nyi snang*, the need to verify the perspectives from which the ultimate is discussed in order to properly understand the divergent description of the ultimate as knowable and unknowable. He remarks that the objections they raised against him are *prima facie* contradictions, which can be solved through verifying the specific perspective and context and accuses them of making pointless refutations without distinguishing the philosophical contexts in which the ultimate is discussed.[54] He rebuts Pari Rabsal:

> Thus, you are skilled in showing your faults through reckless words of opposition without verifying the assertions dependent on the two cases: the ultimate not being knowable within the scope of apprehension and being known in the context of conventional transaction.[55]

We have already discussed Mipham's way of resolving the seeming contradictions by verifying the contexts. This is one of Mipham's main ways of reconciling the variant teachings on the knowability and effability of Emptiness. His Gelukpa opponents however did not find his explanation convincing and sufficient.

Pari Rabsal, using a *reductio ad impossible*, asks if the ultimate, which is being delineated on a conventional level as one of the two truths, is free from all extremes of existence, non-existence, etc.[56] If it is, he argues that the ultimate then cannot be an object of thought and words because it is free from all extremes. This would contradict the assertion that it is knowable on the conventional level. Were the ultimate not an object, the delineation of two truths would be impossible even on the conventional level. There would not be an ultimate on either the ultimate level or the conventional level. Hence, Mipham's interpretation of the ultimate being unknowable from the perspective of ultimate cognition does not resolve the issue of the ultimate being unknowable in the context of the delineation of two truths such as the one in the BA, IX/2.

Drakar Trulku complains that Mipham overlooked the difference between 'the analysis of whether or not the ultimate is knowable' and 'the analysis of whether or not the ultimate exists ultimately' and assumes his opponents to accept the ultimate to exist as a knowable entity ultimately.[57] It is undisputed that the ultimate, like all other things, is not knowable on the ultimate level. The question of unknowability of the ultimate is thus a conventional issue. According to him, the delineation of both truths is conducted from a conventional perspective. He goes on to say that there is no doubt that conventional truth is delineated on the conventional level and cites a commentary on *Yuktiṣaṣṭikā*, to argue that even the delineation of the ultimate truth is conducted on the conventional level.

Replying to Pari Rabsal, Mipham says the middle way without any extremes is the reality of all things; such a middle way exists conventionally and is designated as the ultimate. He sees no philosophical inconsistency in accepting that the ultimate, which is free from all fabrications, is an object of thought on the conventional level. He does not assert from the viewpoint of a conventional outlook that the ultimate is beyond the scope of all thought and words. The ultimate is known by certain thought such as the intuitive gnosis of the sublime beings.[58] He also stresses on this point in his reply to Drakar Trulku.[59] Mipham would readily agree with Drakar Trulku that the theory of two truths is delineated on the conventional level and, on that level, they are of one nature and two aspects. However, he does not seem to read all the lines of the BA, IX/2 in one single context.

Whereas the Gelukpas understood the entire verse in the context of the delineation of the two truths, which is necessarily from the viewpoint of a conventional thought, Mipham read the last two verses as showing the perspective of the ultimate cognition such as the gnosis in the meditative equipoise. This difference in perspectival standpoints from where they delineate their theories of the ultimate, which pervades their writings, appears to be the main reason for discrepancies in their delineation of the ultimate. To Mipham, the ultimate can be best presented through describing how their subjective cognitions discern them, not by constructing an intellectual image that fits into the philosophical apparatus of ordinary understanding. The delineation of the final ultimate must strictly correspond to the gnosis directly discerning it and not be subjected to the constraints of intellectual theorization to fit the limited scope of the ordinary mind.

He fears that the Gelukpa exposition, in the course of building an intellectually coherent system, degrades the profound and transcendent nature of the ultimate by relegating it to the domain of ordinary thought. This viewpoint is also shared by Hopkins, a prominent advocate of Gelukpa Emptiness in the West:

> Sometimes, it seems as if the Ge-luk-bās deliberately disregard the more fantastic, relegating it to the realm of exceptions rather than attempting to blend the outlooks of higher experiences with their presentation. It seems as if they occasionally lose sight of the goal during their highly intricate philosophical maneuverings whereas other interpreters seem more content to keep the goal in mind and risk some apparent difficulties in presenting conventional objects.[60]

Newland also raises the problem of 'the predominant Gelukpa approach of speaking in terms that make sense in relation to where we are now' and discusses the way they reconcile this with the ultimate gnosis of the Buddha.[61]

With regard to Drakar Trulku's accusation of misunderstanding 'the analysis of whether or not the ultimate is knowable' and 'the analysis of whether or not the ultimate exists ultimately', Mipham explains that claiming the ultimate not to be an object in this context is essentially the same as saying it is not an object after having been analysed thoroughly by an ultimate reasoning. Whatever is established by the ultimate reasoning is discerned by the ultimate cognition because they must correspond. Hence, Mipham equates being an object from the viewpoint of the ultimate perspective to being an object ultimately, that is, in the face of ultimate reasoning. Because there is no object which is found when searched through ultimate analysis, there is no object from the viewpoint of the ultimate perspective. The third line is a statement made from the viewpoint of an ultimate perspective, thus, there is no object apprehended in that context.[62]

It is in this same context that Mipham reads the description of the ultimate as surpassing even the scope of gnosis of the omniscient Buddhas, such as the citation from *Āryasaṃvṛtiparamārthasatyanirdeśasūtra* we have seen earlier. Because the ultimate is beyond all fabrications, the Buddha taught it to be beyond the scope of even the omniscient gnosis.[63] He writes that when one expounds the ultimate which is free from all the apprehensions and the duality of subject and object, it is not contradictory to claim that the ultimate is not an object of even the gnosis of the sublime beings.[64] It is in reference to this that some *sūtra*s describe it to be beyond even the gnosis of the omniscient Buddhas. The ultimate should not be understood to be beyond the Buddha's scope of knowledge, conventionally.

Pertaining to the direct reading of the BA, IX/2, Mipham argues that there is no fault in taking the third line as the thesis and the fourth as the reasoning, just as the Ngarabpas did, and mentions in his *Nyi snang* that this is how the Indian commentators also understood the two lines.[65] Mipham presents a unique and striking interpretation of the verse by taking it to be an exposition of the two truths of appearing and ontic mode (*gnas snang bden gnyis*) rather than the two truths of appearance and Emptiness (*snang stong bden gnyis*).[66] He warns that the conventional truth in this verse is not to be understood as the conventional *qua* appearance, which includes all phenomena except Emptiness. It would be contradictory to argue that nothing conventional *qua* appearance can know the ultimate because the ultimate is discerned by the gnosis and the inferences, which are conventional truths.

He states that the two truths in this verse refer to the ultimate, which are things whose appearing and ontic modes conform, and the conventional, which are things whose appearing and ontic modes do not conform. He writes in his *Rab lan* while answering Pari Rabsal's objection that yogis would not discern the ultimate because they are conventional truths:

> In this way, the thought without apprehension is the subject of the ultimate because [its] appearing and ontic [modes] conform [with each other]. The thought with apprehension is the subject of the conventional because [its] appearing and ontic [modes] do not conform. Therefore, it is appropriate to reason that the conventional subject discussed in this case cannot know the ultimate because the thought, [whose] appearing and ontic [modes] do not conform, can never know the ultimate directly. Thus, although the yogis, from the point of being objects, are conventional truth [in the context where] the appearance aspect is delineated to be conventional truth, it is not being reasoned that no such [conventional truth] knows [the ultimate]. Of the two forms of delineation of two truths, which has been discussed earlier, context proves [this case] to be the latter form of delineation through the conformity and non-conformity between appearing and ontic [modes]. Not knowing [this] subtle key point, the objection

proves to be about the mere label 'conventional' without verifying the meaning.[67]

According to Mipham, 'thought' in the third and fourth lines is to be understood as thoughts with apprehension, which fall under the category of conventional truth of the two truths of appearing and ontic mode. As long as there is an apprehension and sense of subject–object duality, the thought will fall within the domain of the conventional truth. The ultimate, whether subjective or objective, is free from apprehensions and is therefore not within the scope of apprehensive thoughts. Given the context, it is appropriate to argue that the ultimate is beyond thoughts because thoughts are conventional.[68]

Mipham formulated the same argument in *Nyi snang* in his reply against Drakar Trulku's refutation of his direct reading of the verse following the Ngarabpa thinkers. He states that the Ngarabpa thinkers whom the Gelukpas refuted also accepted the reading in the context of the two truths of appearing *vis-à-vis* ontic modes, rather than appearance *vis-à-vis* Emptiness as the Gelukpas assumed.[69] He argues that in their tradition no conventional thoughts can discern the ultimate. Nonetheless, the ultimate and the subjective cognition of the ultimate is not unknown and non-existent because the ultimate is discerned by the subjective gnosis, which goes by the name of ultimate in the context of two truths of appearing *vis-à-vis* ontic modes. This way of understanding the ultimate and the conventional in the current context as the ultimate and the conventional of appearing and ontic modes is also perfectly in tune with Candrakīrti's classification of two forms of discernment: the correct seeing (*mthong ba yang dag pa*) and false seeing (*mthong ba rdzun pa*).

Thus, the Gelukpa refuters, Mipham remarks, the have not understood the Ngarabpa position properly and adds that narrow mindedness and bigotry like that of a pond-frog, with which they refute the Ngarabpas, does not suit learned persons. Mipham seems to see the Gelukpa criticism of the Ngarabpa position as mainly a denouncement motivated by sectarian prejudices rather than scholarly discussion. However, Mipham does not level his attacks against Tsongkhapa, who, he seems to think, was in agreement with the Ngarabpas in his ultimate intent. Mipham claims that Tsongkhapa clearly asserts the binary set of two truth theories in his *Lam rim*, but he does not provide the precise reference or citation, and he commends that other Gelukpas also profess an interpretation along the lines of Ngarabpa stance.[70] It is perhaps a *ris med* gesture on the part of Mipham to exclude Tsongkhapa from the Gelukpas he attacked.

Verifying subjective thoughts

In the discussion above, we have not only seen Mipham verify the perspectives of the two truths and contexts related to the binary theories of two truths, but also the verification of two kinds of subjective thoughts. This is a salient interpretation that Mipham adopts concerning the knowability of the ultimate in his *Rab lan* and *Nyi snang* which he did not properly explicate in his *Ketaka*. His verification of the thoughts into those with apprehension and without apprehension presents us with another form of major hermeneutic device he uses to understand the paradoxical teachings in *Prajñāpāramitāsūtra*s and Mādhyamika treatises. Let us, therefore, look at the distinction of thoughts with apprehension and without apprehension, which runs throughout his replies to the Gelukpa refutation on the subject.

In his works, Mipham repeatedly mentions that the ultimate should not be understood as utterly unknowable. He reiterates that the ultimate is not an object of thoughts with apprehension (*dmgis pa can gyi blo*) but is an object of thoughts, which are free from apprehension (*dmigs pa med pa'i blo*). Would not the acceptance that the ultimate is an object of thought then contradict the delineation of the ultimate as being beyond the scope of thought? He clarifies:

> The thought with regard to which [the ultimate] is proved to be not an object of language and thought is [thought] with apprehension. The thought which discerns the ultimate is without any apprehension. Therefore, [such objection] is purely a dispute of words relying merely on the word 'thought' without understanding the meaning.[71]

It is very important to verify which kind of thought is being referred to in the particular context. As long as there is apprehension, such thoughts will never discern the ultimate, hence, the ultimate is taught not to be an object of language and thought. Then, the ultimate is also taught to be the object of intuitive gnosis which is free from all apprehensions and elaborations. One must understand these two teachings as non-contradictory (*'gal med*) and showing the same point (*don gcig*). Trying to prove the ultimate to be in every respect (*rnam pa kun tu*) within the scope of language, thought and range of ordinary speculation serves only the purpose of corrupting the profound teachings of the Buddha.[72]

Mipham, we can see, is very emphatic about the distinction of subjective thought. According to him, it is clear from the context that 'thought' in the third and fourth lines refer to thought with apprehension. No one is claiming the ultimate to be beyond the scope of thought without apprehension on the conventional level. Hence, the Gelukpa fear of the ultimate being unknowable by all kinds of thought if the verse is taken directly is needless and their objections concerning this uncalled for. This, he acknowledges, is in fact not different from the Gelukpa distinction of dualistic and non-dualistic thoughts.[73]

He relates the Gelukpa inclination to interpret the ultimate as an object of language and thought, and their refutation of the Ngarabpa position to their intellectual incapability to comprehend the ultimate Emptiness. He insinuates that the Gelukpas are scared of losing all apprehensions if the apprehension of the absence of hypostatic existence were given up, and thus out of fear turn to refute those espousing the reality free from all extremes. With the intention of insisting on proving an Emptiness, which is apprehensible, they oppose the scriptures, reasoning and assertions supporting the position that the ultimate is not an object of language and thought. Such oppositions, Mipham rebuts, are futile endeavours and cannot even stir a hair of the Ngarabpas but instead make evident the refuter's own shortcomings of seeing all teachings as contradictory. He notes:

> In whatever way one may raise contradictions by using as counter-arguments the scriptures, reasonings and the opponent's assertions on [the ultimate] being an object of language and thought in order to assail [the opponents], [they] will never be more than pseudo-confutations. The ultimate truth can never be proved to be something within the scope of an apprehending [subject]. [However] for knowing the reality free from apprehension and elaboration, which is the object of the intuitive gnosis that transcends the scope of language and thought, even the previous party accepts that conventionally the ultimate truth is known. The intended purport of these two can be distinctly explained and there are valid reasons to prove them to be non-contradictory in content.[74]

To insist on the objective ultimate *qua* mere absence of hypostatic existence and the subjective cognition of purely conceptual understanding, Mipham comments, is showing one's opposition to the objective reality free from all extremes and subjective gnosis which is non-conceptual.[75]

Mipham mentions in his *Nyi snang* too that the Gelukpa critics, bereft of the understanding of reality free from all the elaborations, contend that there would not be any knowing of the ultimate if there were no apprehension.[76] By doing so, they demonstrate how they 'turn their back' on the profound understanding inspite of their claim that they uphold the profound teachings. Patching every phrase such as 'without apprehension' and 'without elaboration' with qualifiers such as 'hypostatic existence' and 'ultimate', and reducing all abstruse topics of Mahāyāna to comprehensive subjects of ordinary speculation and ratiocination is not doing service to the Buddha and his teachings because it destroys the depth of transcendental gnosis and validates the findings of ordinary consciousness. He adds that a variety of interpretations occurs to him too but it is of paramount importance to stick to the teachings of the sublime masters of the past while commenting on such vital issues.

Mipham also explains that of the two ultimates of notational and non-notational, the notational ultimate *qua* absence of hypostatic existence is a projection of conceptual mind and therefore within the scope of language and thought with apprehension.[77] The non-notational ultimate *qua* lack of all elaborations, on the contrary, is the objective reality which transcends conceptual notions and abides whether the Buddhas have revealed it or not; the nature described in the MA, XV/2 as uncontrived and non-dependent on another. Because it is free from all elaborations such as production and cessation, it is without any point of apprehension. Thus, the discernment of the ultimate is proved to be without apprehension from the point of both the object discerned and the subject discerning. Perhaps it would be appropriate to look at the role of apprehension and grasping in the theory of the ultimate in little more detail.

Apprehension, grasping and the ultimate

One of the most outstanding topics of controversy between the Ngarabpas and scholars such as Mipham, who adhered to their line of understanding, on one hand, and the Gelukpa scholars, on the other, is the issue of whether there is apprehension (*ālambana, dmigs pa*) and grasping (*grahaṇa, 'dzin pa*) in the cognition of Emptiness. While the former strongly denied any element of apprehension and grasping in the experience of Emptiness, the Gelukpas accepted that apprehension and grasping are constitutive of the proper knowledge of the ultimate and for that matter of any cognition. Some treatment has already been given to this in the discussion on cognitive negandum in the third chapter. Unlike in that case, the discussion here will focus on the nature of the epistemic subject which discerns the ultimate so as to investigate what is involved in the empirical cognition of Emptiness rather than what is negated by it. Thus, the issue we are concerned here with is an epistemological or more specifically a gnoseological rather than a dialectical one.

The Ngarabpas seems to have argued that if something is apprehended or grasped by the ultimate cognitive subject (*don dam pa'i yul can*) such as the gnosis of the meditative equipoise, it would follow that such a thing is found (*rnyed pa*) during the ultimate investigation and therefore it would withstand (*bzod*) the ultimate analysis. This amounts to the apprehended object being hypostatically existent. Thus, accepting apprehension in the cognition of the ultimate entails an ontological absolutism where the ultimate is itself ultimately existent. This was the concern of the Ngarabpas such as Ngog Lotsāwa. Discussing Ngog Lotsāwa's worry about the ultimate becoming absolute if it is apprehended or cognized by ultimate thoughts, Hopkins writes:

> Ngok's idea is that if an analytical consciousness cognized an emptiness, then that emptiness would necessarily inherently exist. For, an analytical consciousness is searching to find whether an object inherently exists or not, and if it 'finds' or cognizes an emptiness of inherent existence of that object, then it would seem that the emptiness must inherently exist since, according to him, it would be able to bear the ultimate analysis.[78]

Although this does not appear to be the main reason why Mipham rejects apprehension in the cognition of the ultimate, he mentions this reasoning in his works. In his *Rab lan*, he argues that if the ultimate *qua* Emptiness is apprehended by the ultimate cognition such as the gnosis of the meditative equipoise, then it would exist ultimately.[79] This is because in Mipham's thought what is ultimately existent is defined by what remains in the face of the ultimate cognition and analysis. In such event, it would not be logically incorrect to assert the ultimate to have hypostatic existence because it can withstand the ultimate analysis by remaining before the ultimate cognition. In this way, accepting apprehension in the cognition of Emptiness, Mipham reasons, will lead to an absolutist ontology.

The fear of the ultimate becoming absolute and resistant to the ultimate analysis for being apprehended by its subjective cognition is unnecessary according to the Gelukpa scholars. The ultimate cognition such as the gnosis of the equipoise ought to apprehend and perceive the ultimate because it is the subjective knowledge of the ultimate. The subject has to ascertain its object. The Gelukpas explained that when the ultimate analysis investigates an entity such as a vase, the vase is not found but the Emptiness of the vase (*bum pa'i stong nyid*) is found. If the vase were found, it would have to be hypostatically existent. However, although the Emptiness, although it is found, does not have to be hypostatically existent and resistant to the analysis because the analysis was seeking the vase, not the Emptiness of the vase. Were the ultimate or Emptiness found when the ultimate analysis was searching for it, then it would be hypostatically existent and resistant to the analysis. Hence, to the Gelukpas, apprehending the ultimate by thought does not entail an absolute existence of the ultimate. The ultimate can be apprehended by the ultimate cognition without having to exist ultimately or to resist the ultimate analysis.

Tsongkhapa, while commenting on the two truths in his *dGongs pa rab gsal*, states that the scholars, who argued that the ultimate would be hypostatically existent if the gnosis of sublime beings perceived it and therefore claimed that the ultimate is unknowable, completely missed the point that in Candrakīrti's system the ultimate could be obtained by the gnosis and yet be without the hypostatic existence. He charged them with degrading the tradition of the wise through their lack of understanding.[80] Mipham however contends that a thing found and apprehended by the ultimate cognition ought to be ultimately existent because it is the viability before the ultimate cognition that determines existence on an ultimate level. As mentioned already, to be ultimately existent, to him, is to be found on the ultimate level and to be apprehended from the viewpoint of the ultimate cognition. These are synonymous to existing hypostatically and withstanding the ultimate analysis. Thus, claiming the ultimate to be apprehended and obtained by subjective thought would only push one to the extreme of ontological absolutism.[81] Just like the accusation made pertaining to the negandum, Mipham also in this case incriminates the Gelukpas of espousing some sort of crypto-*gzhan stong* position despite their strong claim to be Rangtongpas and harsh rebuttal of the Zhantongpa tradition.

The Gelukpas, as we have already seen, made the distinction of thoughts with a dualistic appearance (*gnyis snang dang bcas pa'i blo*) and those without it, and propounded that the ultimate cannot be known by the former. There is no sense of subject–object duality in the ultimate cognition but they insisted that there is apprehension and grasping because it is a correct knowledge of its object. This perhaps is influenced by their interpretation in *tshad ma* literature that all correct cognitions, conceptual and non-conceptual, can and must apprehend (*dmigs*), grasp (*'dzin*) and ascertain (*nges*) their objects. Mipham agrees that the ultimate could not be known by a dualistic thought and went on to say that the classification of dualistic and non-dualistic thoughts is the same as his classification of thoughts with and without apprehension.[82] However, he dissents from the Gelukpas on whether there is apprehension and grasping or not in a non-dualistic cognition by strongly rejecting that non-dualistic thought can possess apprehension and grasping. 'A non-dualistic thought, then', he goes on to say, 'has to be described as [that which] has no object apprehended and no subject with apprehensive grasping'.[83]

Mipham's attribution of non-apprehension to the cognitive experience of the ultimate seems to be based on textual sources such as the BA, IX/35.[84] But in spite of his repeated distinction of thoughts with apprehension and without it in his *Rab lan* and *Nyi snang*, Mipham does not explicate as what defines the two. It is clear from his discussions that not all perception and cognition involve apprehension. Neither is apprehension merely a feature of a sense of gross hypostatization and reification such as clinging to a hypostatic existence. It appears that even a subtle sense of objectification and conceptualization amounts to apprehension and grasping. Perceiving anything to exist, not to exist, both or neither and to have an idea of anything is apprehension and grasping. If there is anything for the mind to hold on to, that amounts to an elaboration (*prapañca, spros pa*) and perceiving it involves apprehension. To be free of apprehension is to dissolve all notions and thoughts, to give up all contrivance, conception, fixation and focus, and to perceive nothing, not even nothing itself. Thus, the seeing of Emptiness is described as not seeing anything (*ci yang mi/ma mthong ba*)[85] or seeing without seeing (*ma gzigs pa'i tshul gyis gzigs pa*).[86] It is a mere convention to say that Emptiness is known by a subjective gnosis.

Tsongkhapa, however, understood it differently. In his *dGongs pa rab gsal* and *Rigs pa'i rgya mtsho*, he argues that the cognition of the ultimate is not merely 'not seeing anything'.[87] Statements such as 'Non-seeing is supreme seeing' (*mthong ba med pa ni mthong ba dam pa'o*) and 'seeing without seeing', Tsongkhapa comments, do not negate seeing altogether; they negate seeing elaborative objects but affirm seeing a lack of elaborations. He cites *Saṃcayagāthā*, XII/9–10 to contend that what is not seen by the ultimate cognition are conventional phenomena such as the five aggregates. The ultimate cognition discerns the reality itself. Applying the analogy of seeing space, he says, spatially obstructive things are not seen in the act of seeing space but space itself is seen.

Thus, Tsongkhapa objected to the understanding that seeing Emptiness is qualified by the lack of seeing or apprehending anything and asserted in the cognition of the ultimate in an active sense of seeing or apprehension of Emptiness itself. Mipham denies any such active or positive sense of seeing. According to Mipham, to say the reality is seen by the cognition of the ultimate is merely a positive way of saying it does not see anything. ' "Not seeing anything" (*ci yang ma mthong*)' he remarks, 'is the negative way of presenting the seeing whereas "seeing nothing" (*ci'ang med pa mthong*) is, as it were, a positive phrase. There is no difference between the two'.[88] He also takes 'not being the object of thought' and 'being the object of non-conceptual gnosis' in a similar manner. Thus, Mipham rejects even a subtle sense of seeing or apprehension in the gnosis discerning the ultimate.

Both the Gelukpas and Mipham use an apophatic approach to establish Emptiness in the Mādhyamika context and agree on Emptiness being known only by *via negativa*. Although they both advocate an apophaticism in as much as no positive entity is claimed to be known in the cognition of Emptiness, further scrutiny reveals difference in their apophaticism. The Gelukpas emphatically assert the ultimate cognition to be the subject which discerns the ultimate *qua* absence of hypostatic existence, which exists objectively. There is a direct cognition and discernment of the object by the subject. Mipham, in contrast, denies the ultimate to be an objective point which could be grasped or affirmed. The gnosis is termed as knowing the ultimate when it remains without any fixation, conception and objectification having eliminated all elaborations. Thus, from his viewpoint, the cognition of the ultimate as the Gelukpas understood, despite the claim of being the cognition of a pure negation, still involves positive determination and their subject–object apparatus, despite their claim to be non-dualistic, still involves dualism. They have reified the negation itself.

In Mipham's theory of the ultimate, apprehension is equivalent to grasping. Both terms, in this context, have a connotation of objectification, reification and contrivance. As long as there is a mode of grasping (*'dzin stang*), one is in the domain of conventional thought. In his answer to the third question in *Nges shes sgron me* on whether or not the gnosis of meditative equipoise is without any mode of grasping, he explicates that the experience of the ultimate, like seeing clear space, is free from any mode of grasping because there is nothing to be grasped in the reality free from all extremes after having pacified the grasping of the four extremes. All modes of grasping disappear because there is nothing which remains before the gnosis of the equipoise.[89] If something is obtained and found by the ultimate investigation, it could be apprehended or grasped. However, nothing is found and the ultimate is characterized by such non-finding. Thus, his gnoseological understanding is grounded on his ontological theory of Emptiness *qua* lack of all elaborations, and connected to his doctrinal position of no-thesis and the dialectics of unrestricted negation of tetralemma from the vantage point of the ultimate. The gnosis is free from apprehension and grasping because there is nothing to be apprehended or grasped in reality. Were there any mode of grasping, it would only obscure the ultimate. Thus, like the famous saying of the Sakyapa masters that 'it is not [right] view if there is grasping',[90] Mipham saw apprehension and grasping as obstructions to proper knowledge of the ultimate.

The Gelukpas, on the contrary, saw this denial of apprehension and grasping in the ultimate cognition as a very disturbing epistemological trend. According to them, rejecting apprehension and grasping deprives the ultimate cognition of the functional qualities of knowing and ascertainment, which are constitutive of wisdom and the right view. Maintaining such nescient view based on the philosophical understanding of Emptiness as neither existent, nor non-existent and the doctrine of no-thesis, from the Gelukpa viewpoint, destroys the philosophical essence – dependent origination – and the soteriological purpose – cultivation of wisdom/insight – of the Mādhyamika system. It deviates from Mādhyamika rationalism, and debases the analytic philosophy of the middle way to an indeterminate quietism, or even worse, to an ontological nihilism and epistemological scepticism. Tsongkhapa, Jinpa observes, was deeply concerned with this tendency of anti-rationalism inculcated by, what Jinpa puts as, philosophical naivety and epistemological skepticism, which was pervasive in his days, for its profound religious and ethical consequences.[91]

Let's look at these Gelukpa qualms about the lack of apprehension and grasping in the ultimate cognition in a little more detail. The Gelukpas saw Mādhyamika tradition as a highly analytical philosophy at the heart of which is featured the concept of Emptiness *qua* dependent origination. Understanding Emptiness as the lack of all elaborations such as existence and non-existence was shunned as a simplistic understanding based on the literal reading of the Mādhyamika texts. From their viewpoint, such understanding of Emptiness and the rejection of apprehension in the cognition of Emptiness would not go with the theory of Emptiness *qua* dependent origination.

The salvific capacity of Emptiness depends on developing the proper certainty (*nges shes*) about Emptiness, also known as discriminative knowledge of discerning Non-self (*bdag med rtogs pa'i shes rab*), through the process of zetetic enquiry using Mādhyamika analysis. At the very outset of the chapter on the insight of his *Lam rim*, Tsongkhapa explicates the role of this discriminative knowledge.[92] Further down, when he identifies the uniqueness of Mādhyamika tradition, he again stresses the soteriological role of certainty on the nature of two truths in order to achieve the two bodies of the Buddha.[93] We have already discussed in the chapter on negandum how, according to the Gelukpas, the clinging to hypostatic existence is the root of all evils and the primary defiling emotions to be eliminated. The Gelukpa logic is that in order to overcome the clinging to hypostatic existence, one must negate hypostatic existence and ascertain its absence *qua* Emptiness. It is apprehension of the lack of hypostatic existence that can counteract clinging to hypostatic existence and thereby all negative emotions.

Mere withdrawal of apprehension, grasping and other activities of mind without any conviction or confident knowledge of Emptiness derived from correct reasoning, cannot eliminate the defiling emotions. To the Gelukpas, apprehension of Emptiness is not a negative thing but the right view and the true antidote. Without the apprehension of Emptiness, certainty on and knowledge of Emptiness would not be possible. Tsongkhapa remarks that many people appear to assume wrongly that they obtained the quiddity of Madhyamaka in denying all theses such as 'this is' and 'this is not' and claim to meditate on correct view for contemplating on the 'non-grasping of anything' (*cir yang mi 'dzin pa*).[94] Such claims are ignoble words instigating wrong views and would only estrange the persons from the correct understanding.

While discussing the actual practice of insight meditation, Tsongkhapa elaborates further on the fallacies of those who reject apprehension in the cognition of the ultimate and profess various forms of non-conceptuality as the experience of Emptiness. He refutes four variations of this position in detail. I shall only summarise them in the following.

(1) The first group claims that even if one has not realized Non-self, holding the mind from conceiving anything is correct meditation on the nature of Emptiness as Emptiness is beyond any conceptual notions. Because nothing exists objectively, to have no grasping of any sort is in agreement with the reality. The crux of Tsongkhapa's refutation is that if such meditation is based on analytical investigations through which all phenomena are negated, it is contemplation on an annihilationist theory characterized by an over-broad definition of the negandum, not the correct meditation on Emptiness. If it is not inspired by analytical enquiry but merely in the non-conceptual state, one would have no conviction in the meditation. Beside, if mere non-conceptuality constitutes insight, all non-conceptual thoughts, such as some meditative experience of the non-Buddhists and even sensory consciousnesses, would turn out to be insight. Citing Kalamaśīla, he reasons that such practice undermines both the wisdom and method facets of the Mahāyāna path by undervaluing the instrumentality of discriminating wisdom and the practice of moral and ethical principles such as giving, and by discouraging discursive and zetetic thinking. There is also an internal contradiction in viewing all concepts as obstructions to enlightenment and at the same time encouraging altruism and morality, which are pursued by a conceptual mind. He remarks that the practice of withdrawal from all conceptual thoughts and abiding in the state of non-thinking as an insight-meditation is a legacy of the Chinese monk, Hwashang.

A follower of this group further argues that the elimination of grasping of self by realizing the Non-self through rational enquiry is only an elimination of the external problem, like the dog chasing the stone. To exterminate the grasping of characteristics entirely, one must hold one's mind from grasping anything, thereby overcoming the source just like the dog biting the hand, which throws the stone. Tsongkhapa rebukes this as a pathetic understanding which goes against the tradition of the Buddha and all great masters because they expounded the negation of the object of grasping using numerous reasoning and scriptures. If one were able to eliminate the grasping at self by merely withdrawing all thoughts and with no certainty in the absence of the self derived from analytical investigation, even in the state of sleep and unconsciousness one would realize the Non-self and eliminate the grasping at characteristics. He compares this to advising a person, who is scared because he is uncertain about whether there is a ghost in an unknown dark cave, to hold his mind from having conceptual thoughts of a ghost, instead of dispelling the fear by ascertaining whether it is there or not by using a lamp. He also cites the similes of a cowardly person closing his eyes when confronted by his enemy and a brave one confronting it with a weapon, and the analogy of a snake and a rope to illustrate how one must know the rope is void of snake in order to eliminate the fear.

(2) The second party argues that it is necessary to ascertain Emptiness before remaining in the state of non-conceptuality. Having ascertained Emptiness, all instances of abiding in the state of non-conceptuality after that qualify as meditation on Emptiness. Tsongkhapa questions that all the instances of non-conceptuality

even after gaining certainty about Emptiness can be meditation of Emptiness. Maintaining the flow of the certainty is the meditation on Emptiness; merely being in a non-conceptual state does not suffice to be meditation on Emptiness. If this were the case, why would not the practice of Bodhicitta also be meditation on view?

(3) The third group rejects both of the abovementioned and maintains that if analytical wisdom is generated at the beginning of meditation sessions with the aim of cultivating non-conceptuality, the subsequent state of non-conceptuality becomes the meditation on Emptiness. This, Tsongkhapa maintains, is also unacceptable for even the non-conceptual state in deep sleep preceded by the analytical investigation at the time of falling asleep would count as the meditation of Emptiness. He agrees that it is meditation on Emptiness as long as it is focused on Emptiness but a mere non-conceptual state, where the mind has lost its focus on Emptiness, not meditation on Emptiness.

(4) The fourth opponent professes a graduated combination of analytic and contemplative meditations. Unlike the first three, who ascribe an intrinsic gnoseological value to non-conceptuality, this one says that when meditating on Emptiness, one must initially generate certainty about Emptiness and then consistently retain one's mind on it. This is similar to the graduated approach that Mipham adopts in his *Nges shes sgron me*. Tsongkhapa objects that to retain the mind on Emptiness in a contemplative manner, in the meditation on Emptiness, is still partial meditation. Although there is the calm-abiding of contemplative meditation on Emptiness, it lacks the insight through analytic meditation, thus lacking the syzygy of the two.

These arguments clearly depict Tsongkhapa's concern about the practice of non-mentation (*yid la mi byed pa*), non-conceptuality (*mi rtog pa*) and not grasping anything (*cir yang mi 'dzin pa*). Not only did Tsongkhapa fear the misunderstanding of the view (*lta ba*) and the decline of intellectual rigour and discursive thinking at the hands of quietist anti-rationalism but he was also worried about the impact such practices have on religious praxis (*spyod pa*). Emphasis on such quietist and contemplative meditation and viewing it as a self-sufficient soteriological tool were causing laxity in moral and ethical practices among the religious practitioners. He was concerned that some of the Ngarabspas, complacent with the quietist trend of non-mentation and non-conceptuality seen as a single remedy to all negative emotions, overlooked or neglected the method aspect of the Mahāyāna soteriology.

Mipham believes that it was with these worries in mind and with the intention of promoting the rational and ethical side of Buddhism that Tsongkhapa made a concerted effort to refute the quietist trend and advocate the analytic approach to meditation on Emptiness. From his viewpoint, Tsongkhapa prescribed the rational approach with strong emphasis only to counteract the quietist trend. He persistently argues that ultimately, even Tsongkhapa accepted the lack of apprehension and the mode of grasping in the cognition of the ultimate.[95] This, he demonstrated by citing the verse from *Lam gtso rnam gsum*[96] which we have already seen during the discussion of the ultimate. Mipham here in particular refers to the second verse, which explicitly mentions the dissolution of all the modes of grasping during the complete understanding of the view *qua* Emptiness. He comments:

> When, without having to grasp appearance and Emptiness alternately, the unfailing interdependent [nature of] appearance is discerned, [then] merely through [that], because of the fact that the two truths are primordially inseparable, certainty in the ontic mode of coalescence free from extremes will arise. If [one] understands such homologous lack of elaborations, [where] all modes of grasping objects or points of apprehension such as Emptiness and non-Emptiness have ceased, the investigation of the view is complete. There is nothing higher than that to be investigated because the meaning of the ontic mode *qua* coalescence is understood. [I] think there is no doubt that [Tsongkhapa] taught that by getting used to being in such [state], the gnosis of the sublime beings is brought forth.[97]

Mipham then goes on to say that his understanding of Tsongkhapa, viewed by the contemporary followers of Tsongkhapa as an interpolation, came under attack from all directions. Although several instances of Tsongkhapa's writings support his understanding, he says that it would be unbecoming of him to claim that he understands Tsongkhapa better than the followers of Tsongkhapa. Elaborating on Tsongkhapa's thoughts to them, he remarks, would be as improper as selling a needle to the needle factory.[98]

Thus, in Mipham's understanding, Tsongkhapa's advocacy of rationalism and the apprehension and grasping in the cognition of the ultimate is only a provisional antidote to the aforementioned quietist tendency. It is wrong to avoid all thoughts at the very beginning before one has cultivated a firm certainty in Emptiness as one may misunderstand a blank state of non-thinking with genuine meditation on Emptiness. In the *sūtra* tradition, it is crucial to gain certainty by the means of a thorough analysis. Without such certainty, one would get lost into a nescient state of nothingness with a mere claim of being in the state free from all extremes and non-mentation. In this way, Mipham attributes an indispensable propaedeutic value to apprehension and grasping of Emptiness, to conceptual understanding of Emptiness and to certainty, which paves the way for direct experience of Emptiness. Let us now turn to look at the discussion concerning the role and status of conceptual thoughts in cognition of the ultimate.

Conceptuality, non-conceptuality and Emptiness

Tsongkhapa in his refutation of the four positions on non-conceptuality mentioned earlier refuted the theory that knowledge of Emptiness is necessarily without any conceptual thought. As per his opponents, Emptiness cannot be apprehended by thought. Since conceptuality involves apprehension of universal image (*don spyi*) of the conceived object (*zhen yul*), cognition of Emptiness can only be non-conceptual. It is implausible that all the Ngarabpas subscribed to the view that non-conceptuality is *sine qua non* of all forms of cognition of Emptiness, but as for those who did, Tsongkhapa and his followers made painstaking refutations. If all conceptual thoughts bind a person in *saṃsāra* and if meditation on Emptiness *qua* Non-self has to be without them, then, Tsongkhapa enquires whether Emptiness is an evident (*mngon gyur*) or a hidden (*lkog, gyur*) object to the ordinary person who is meditating on it?[99] If it is the first that is evident, the meditator cannot be an ordinary person. He has to be a sublime being because he discerns Non-self evidently. If he discerned Non-self but did not know that he did so and requires to be instructed by a teacher, it would be absurd that the student having discerned Non-self evidently still has to be taught by a teacher using inference.

If the object, the Non-self, is hidden to the meditator, then it is a laughable thing to claim that a hidden object is grasped by a non-conceptual thought. Tsongkhapa further explains that when the ordinary meditator on Emptiness meditates, his mind has to engage in the Non-self *qua* Emptiness. If it is not engaged, it cannot be meditation on Emptiness. If it is engaged, it has to engage either directly with the object being evident or inferentially with the object being hidden. Because he would be a sublime being if the Non-self is evident to him, the object has to be hidden to him. But to say a hidden object, which is known only through its universal image, is perceived by a non-conceptual thought is contradictory. A non-conceptual cognition of Non-self will have to be a yogic perception, exclusive to the sublime beings. Therefore, arguing without any certainty that all knowledge of Emptiness is without conceptual thought is an exposition full of contradictions.

Explaining the combination of analytic and contemplative meditations, Tsongkhapa writes that it is impossible to generate insight without a proper conviction in the view of Non-self.[100] In order to cultivate insight, one must delineate the view using various channels of reasoning and scriptures (*lung rigs kyi sgo du ma*) and the delineation must involve repeated analysis through the discriminative knowledge (*so sor rtog pa'i shes rab*). He shuns the position that once Emptiness is established through study, one must focus on it without further analysis because analysis involves notional grasping. If conceptual thoughts were to be negated in meditation because they involve grasping to hypostatic existence, then they would have to be negated even at the time of delineation through study. Furthermore, it would follow that conceptual thought would have to be negated during exposition, debate, composition and other activities, which are executed by conceptual thought. Were conceptual thought intrinsically grasping or clinging to hypostatic existence, they should be eliminated at all times.

Tsongkhapa is very emphatic that meditation on Emptiness should not just be contemplative and quiet. He goes on to explain how after attaining single pointed concentration, one must couple it with analytical meditation to form a syzygy of the two. Experience of Emptiness is not merely quiescence of thoughts and concepts but a dynamic and active awareness of the insubstantial nature of things. A non-analytic quiescent meditation would not be soteriologically effective because it cannot eradicate clinging to hypostatic existence through the knowledge of lack of hypostatic existence. Citing Kamalaśīla, he argues 'those who do not meditate by analyzing the nature of things with discriminative knowledge but rather meditate on mere dissolution of mentation can never overcome their conceptual thoughts and never realize the lack of own being, because [they] lack the light of wisdom'.[101]

Tsongkhapa reports that his opponents used the homologous nature of cause and effect to reason that the knowledge of Emptiness even at the level of ordinary persons has to be non-conceptual in order to give rise to a non-conceptual gnosis.[102] A conceptual knowledge, according to them, cannot give rise to a non-conceptual gnosis. Tsongkhapa considered the application of such homology superfluous. If such were the case, a pure path would not arise from an impure path, a green sprout would not arise from a yellow seed, smoke would not arise from fire and man would not be born to woman, because the cause and effect are not entirely similar. According to Tsongkhapa, the conceptual understanding of Emptiness by an ordinary person and the gnosis of a sublime being are homologous because they both cognize Emptiness. The analogy of two twigs rubbing and turning into flames in the *Kāśyapaparivarta* is illustrative of how a conceptual thought can lead to a non-conceptual gnosis.[103] Thus, for Tsongkhapa, homology of discriminative knowledge and gnosis did not necessarily require both to be non-conceptual.

Pettit, during his discussion of modal apprehension, juxtaposes Tsongkhapa's arguments with Yontan Gyatsho's exposition and comments that Nyingmapas, influenced by Vajrayāna Buddhism, specially Dzogchen, accepted one degree or another of formal homology of cause and effect whereas Tsongkhapa used the word 'homologous' (*mthun pa*) in a different way, in the sense of 'conducive', which implies a figurative or temporal understanding of the term and means a cause conducive to the desired result, not necessarily a cause that resembles the result. Pettit's distinction however smacks of reading between lines excessively and overstating the minor differences.

Tsongkhapa certainly would not accept all causes conducive to the desired result to be homologous cause and all effects produced from such a cause to be homologous effects of that cause, which is what Pettit's understanding implies. Homologous effects (*rgyu mthun pa'i 'bras bu*) in Tibetan dialectics, as explained in the *abhidharma* and later in Tibetan *bsdus grwa* textbooks, form only one of the five kinds of effects and are relative to the characteristics determining the homology. Generally, a homologous effect is determined by the continuity of properties and characteristics, which are the major constituents of the cause. A rice sprout is a homologous effect of a rice seed, not of moisture, earth and heat according to both the Nyingmapa scholars and Tsongkhapa. Tsongkhapa accepts that the seed and the sprout are homologous despite the differences in their colour and shape. In his thought, the non-conceptuality of the gnosis is like the green colour of the sprout; it is not an intrinsic property which defines the experience of Emptiness. Hence, it need not be present in both the ordinary cognition of Emptiness and the gnosis of sublime beings. However, the characteristic of being a subjective cognition of Emptiness, like being rice, is a constitutive characteristic. In so far as both have this characteristic, they are homologous. Thus, non-conceptuality is not the trait which determines the ordinary cognition of Emptiness and gnosis of sublime beings to be homologous.

Tsongkhapa's opponents however understood non-conceptuality as an intrinsic characteristic of cognition of Emptiness, like the property of being rice is intrinsic to both seed and sprout, and went on to say that the gnosis would not have a homologous cause were there no non-conceptual experience of Emptiness before the Path of Seeing. Hence, the two parties disagreed in defining what characteristics constitute the defining properties of the cognition of Emptiness which have to be intrinsic to both ordinary understanding and gnosis for them to be homologous, rather than in the general understanding of the term 'homologous'.

Mipham, like Tsongkhapa's opponents in *Lam rim*, raises the problem of the homology between ordinary understanding and gnosis of sublime beings in his writings.[104] However, instead of discussing homology with regard to non-conceptuality, he argues that the gnosis of the sublime beings would not have a homologous cause if there were no proper meditation on or understanding of Emptiness free from all apprehensions and elaborations in the state of ordinary beings. According to him, the gnosis discerning Emptiness free from all elaborations arises from the homologous cause of meditation on such Emptiness prior to the Path of Seeing. The cultivation of the understanding of a mere absence of hypostatic existence cannot lead to the generation of gnosis, which discerns Emptiness free from all elaborations. He writes:

> If the ordinary persons only meditate on [reality] with apprehension and elaboration, and through that the gnosis of the sublime beings free from apprehension and elaboration arises, such gnosis would not have the cause of preceding practice during the Paths of Accumulation and Preparation. [It] will be like rice arising from barley.[105]

Mipham argues that if meditation on Emptiness among ordinary beings, as the Gelukpas claimed, were only cultivation of conceptual understanding of the mere absence of hypostatic existence, the non-conceptual gnosis which is free from all elaborations and dualistic grasping would not have a preceding cause homologous to it. The Gelukpas however assert the non-conceptual gnosis of the sublime beings also to discern the absence of hypostatic existence, and not an Emptiness free from all elaborations, therefore, the gnosis is homologous to the ordinary understanding. On this, Mipham contends that it is untenable even conventionally to say an absolute negation such as the absence of hypostatic existence is cognized by a non-conceptual awareness.[106]

Mipham makes it quite clear that the ordinary practitioner on the Paths of Accumulation and Preparation understand and experience Emptiness *qua* lack of all elaborations albeit in a gradual manner by a conceptual thought, through the mediation of a universal image.[107] The non-conceptual understanding of Emptiness, for which one does not depend upon the mediation of a universal image, does not occur before the attainment of the gnosis of sublime beings. However, if there were no proper understanding of Emptiness free from all elaborations in the state of ordinary beings but only of the mere absence of hypostatic existence, the direct experience of Emptiness free from all elaboration at the stage of sublime beings would not have a homologous cause.

Thus, Mipham professed a different kind of homology from the Ngarabpa position, which we have discussed *vis-à-vis* the Gelukpa stance. He explained the homology between the cognitions of Emptiness of ordinary beings and gnosis of sublime beings through the content of the cognitions and not merely through non-conceptuality as raised by the Ngarabpas. Mipham's exposition of such a homology, further adds to his refutation of the Gelukpa equation of Emptiness to the absence of hypostatic existence. Through this argument, he intends to underline the point that understanding of the mere absence of hypostatic existence is not a sufficient and a homologous cause, which can give rise to the non-dualistic gnosis of the sublime beings.

It must nonetheless be noted that there are instances in Mipham's writings where he discusses the homology in terms of non-conceptuality and also seems to accept what Pettit calls 'formal homology of cause and effect'. This is clear particularly in his citation of the following verse from *Vajragarbhaṭīkā*, which states that a cause which is a conceptual cognition cannot give rise to a resultant gnosis which is non-conceptual:

> From the seed of *kodrava*,
> Rice grains would never grow.
> The result that arises from the seed,
> Which is conceptual, will be conceptual.
> The result that arises from the non-conceptual
> Will also be non-conceptual.[108]

It is plausible that this theory of formal homology of a conceptual cause giving rise to a conceptual result and a non-conceptual result requiring a non-conceptual cause, according to Mipham, is viable, as Pettit understands, only in the context of Vajrayāna soteriology, where the emphasis is on revealing the innate non-conceptual gnosis, rather than in Sūtrayāna where the emphasis is on transforming the ordinary conceptual mind into an enlightened non-conceptual gnosis of the Buddha. I shall not go into Mipham's theory of cognition of Emptiness and the role of conceptuality in the Vajrayāna system. What is striking and worth mentioning here is Mipham's theory of non-conceptuality (*rnam par mi rtog pa*).

Mipham's theory of non-conceptuality

Mipham did not understand the non-conceptuality of the gnosis discerning Emptiness only in terms of the absence of the generally known conceptual thought, that is, thoughts which Tibetan epistemologists classify as *zhen rig* because they cognize their conceived objects (*zhen yul*) through a universal image (*don spyi*) as their direct object. Merely being free of such conceptual thought, is not a unique characteristic of the cognition of Emptiness; all direct perceptions are free from this kind of conceptuality.[109] In his works on epistemology,[110] Mipham presents three different kinds of thoughts referred to by the term *rtog pa*:

(1) Conceptual thoughts grasping mixed word and object (*sgra don 'dres 'dzin gyi rtog pa*): This is the most common understanding of *rtog pa* in Tibetan Buddhist scholarship and is primarily known through the epistemological theories of Dignāga and Dharmakīrti.[111] This corresponds, according to Mipham, to *abhinirupaṇavikalpa* in Asaṅga's and Vasubandhu's classification of *vikalpa*.[112] Conceptual thought in this context include thoughts which comprehend the object through the mediation of a universal image. They mix the generic conceptual image – the universal – which is often the picture of word, with the actual object – the particular – thus grasping the mental picture and the object as one. This kind of conceptuality involves mental conceptualization and construction and therefore would not occur in the sensory consciousnesses.

(2) Notional thought of the own being (*ngo bo nyid kyi rtog pa*): This is defined in treatises such as *Madhyāntavibhāga* and *Satyadvayavibhaṅga*[113] and includes all the ordinary minds and the volitions of beings in the three realms. All cognitive processes, whether sensory or mental, involving dualistic grasping, reification and even a subtle notion of the own being fall within this category. Thus, some sensory and mental cognitions which are non-conceptual in terms of the first type of conceptuality would still fall under conceptual thought of this category.

(3) Thought [grasping gross features] of the gross and subtle (*rtsing zhib kyi rtog pa*): This concept of *rtog pa* is known in *abhidharma* phenomenology as *vitarka* in contradistinction to *vicāra* (*dpyod pa*) and forms one of two aspects of a subjective cognition.[114] In this case, *rtog pa* denotes the aspect of cognition with which the cognition has the general picture, the gross image and the sense of the whole of its object in contrast to *dpyod pa*, the aspect with which the cognition has the specific details in a meticulous manner. It is the tendency of cognition to apprehend the outline and the whole of the object as opposed to the tendency to apprehend the particulars and the details.

Of the three kinds, the Gelukpas, like most other Tibetan scholars, generally understand conceptuality in the first sense and non-conceptuality, to them, presupposes the lack of conceptualization by the mental consciousness. It is the conceptuality of this kind that the Gelukpa thinkers argue is present in the cognition of Emptiness among ordinary practitioners and is absent in the gnosis of the sublime beings. Pari Rabsal cites *Pramāṇasamuccaya*, I/3 and *Pramāṇavārttika*, Pratyakṣa, 281 to identify this conceptuality which the gnosis discerning Emptiness is free of and argues that the sublime gnosis, being free from such conceptuality, discerns Emptiness directly.[115] In fact it is this direct experience *qua* yogic perception free from the conceptuality of the first type, which characterizes the sublime gnosis and sublime person. It is in this respect that the Gelukpas argued that were cognition of Emptiness by ordinary persons non-conceptual as the Ngarabpas claimed, the ordinary persons will have to discern Emptiness directly, in which case they would already be sublime beings.

Mipham would certainly agree with the Gelukpas that conceptuality in the first sense is present in the cognition of Emptiness by ordinary beings and that the non-conceptual gnosis transcends such conceptuality. However, he contends that the Gelukpa theories of the middle way and the ultimate are not compatible with their understanding of the non-conceptuality.[116] In Mipham's thought, the non-conceptuality of the gnosis is not merely the lack of conceptuality in the first sense. Such non-conceptuality is present in all perceptions and is not a special trait of sublime gnosis.[117] He understands the non-conceptuality of the gnosis as the absence of notions of all three kinds of *vikalpa*s, not merely of the first type.

According to Mipham, non-conceptual gnosis is not merely a cognitive process without mental concepts but a profound and mystical experience of Emptiness without any apprehension, grasping and mentation. To be in the state of non-conceptuality is to be in the state of Emptiness, where all the mental activities and conceptual elaborations are stilled. The Gelukpa scholars, however, viewed such understanding as the quietist doctrine of Hwashang Mohoyen and rejected it as a nihilist practice. Mipham, in response, argues that his understanding of the non-conceptuality is far from Hwashang's practice of non-thinking and goes on to explain, both in his *rGyan 'grel* and *Rab lan*, how non-conceptuality in Mahāyāna soteriology presupposes the dissolution of all conceptualization and mentation.[118]

He cites the following verse from Maitreya's *Dharmadharmatavibhāga* to demonstrate how non-conceptuality must surpass the mere lack of conceptual thoughts as understood by the Gelukpas, as well as the non-thinking that Hwashang propagated:

> [The non-conceptual gnosis] is the individual characteristic
> Which precludes the five kinds [of cognitive states]:
> Non-mentation, transcendence, pacification,
> Essential nature and grasping at features.[119]

While commenting on this verse in his *Rab lan*, Mipham states that the non-conceptual gnosis cannot be pointed out cataphatically. Therefore, it is shown apophatically through the elimination of the five absorptive states.[120] (1) Explaining the five states, Mipham says that the state of non-mentation here implies the lack of conceptual thoughts which mixes word and object, that is, the first of three types of *rtog pa* discussed earlier. Non-conceptuality of the gnosis discerning Emptiness is not merely absence of such conceptuality for this type of non-conceptuality can occur even in babies who have not developed any linguistic tendency. (2) Nor is non-conceptuality of the gnosis merely a cognitive state which transcends the notion grasping at gross feature, the third type discussed above. The consciousness of sentient beings above the second *dhyāna* of the form realm lack this notion but the non-conceptuality of their consciousness is not paramount to the non-conceptuality of a gnosis discerning Emptiness. (3) Non-conceptuality of the gnosis is not mere pacification of mental concepts for that occurs even in the unconscious states such as the meditative absorption of *nirodhasamāpatti*. (4) The absence of any notion, thought and cognitive activity alone does not amount to the non-conceptuality discussed here. Non-conceptuality is more than the lack of the notion of essential nature or own being, the second type discussed above. Even the physical faculties such as the eyes and insentient objects are free from such a notion. (5) Non-conceptuality of the gnosis is not just a grasping at the feature of non-thinking, that is, the state of non-thinking where the mind is busy thinking about 'not thinking', for such a meditation is itself grasping at characteristics (*mtshan mar 'dzin pa*). Tibetan scholars accused Hwashang of mistaking non-conceptual meditation with this false state of non-thinking.

The description of the non-conceptual gnosis by Maitreya in this verse and the explanation Vasubandhu provided in his commentary, Mipham says, indicate that the non-conceptual gnosis is without any grasping (*cir yang mi 'dzin pa*) and without any conceptual thinking (*cir yang mi rtog pa*) and yet transcendent to these five non-conceptual states. If the non-conceptuality of the gnosis involves grasping and apprehension, why would Maitreya have to differentiate it from these states? There would not be any need for such clarification. Mipham then goes on to discuss the unique qualities and functions of the non-conceptual gnosis.

Mipham also argues that the understanding of mere absence of hypostatic existence is an ordinary wisdom or discriminative knowledge (*shes rab*) and does not qualify to be non-conceptual gnosis (*rnam par mi rtog pa'i ye shes*):

> The thought understanding the absolute negation *qua* absence of hypostatic existence is wisdom, an aspect of mind (*caitasika, sems byung*) whereas it is the gnosis without [duality of] subject and object which realizes the *dharmadhātu qua* indivisibility of two truths.[121]

He observes that the application of the terms wisdom and gnosis however may not always be restricted to this understanding. In his *Nges shes sgron me*, Mipham argues in yet another manner that the understanding of the absence of hypostatic existence is only an ordinary wisdom, which falls within the category of *caitasika*s. He reasons that an understanding which cannot comprehend the coalescence of two truths but only perceive the two truths separately and alternately is not non-conceptual gnosis.[122] Non-conceptual gnosis is marked by the dissolution of the duality of two truths; it transcends the concepts of negation and negandum, subject and object, and appearance and Emptiness. Discriminating wisdom apprehends the two truths separately and verifies them as such. As long as one is in the realm of such apprehension and discrimination, one's understanding is still within the domain of discursive wisdom and not of the gnosis free from apprehension and grasping.

Thus, while the Gelukpas understood non-conceptual gnosis discerning Emptiness as a cognitive process, which consists of epistemological features such as subjectivity, apprehension and grasping, Mipham saw it as a profound and mystical experience, which went beyond the norms of regular knowledge, understanding and perception. Normal epistemological definitions did not apply to the experience of non-conceptual gnosis, which is characterized *per se* by the dissolution of the subject–object duality and the cessation of all mental activities. From Mipham's viewpoint, the Gelukpa understanding of non-conceptual gnosis as a direct cognition of the absence of hypostatic existence is a naïve and simplistic theory and the association of Nyingmapa concept of non-conceptuality *qua* lack of mentation with Hwashang's view, a presentation made out of preconceived bias.

On Hwashang and meditation on Emptiness

We have seen throughout the discussions on negandum, ultimate and cognition of Emptiness how the Gelukpas accuse the Nyingmapas of espousing Hwashang's quietist system. They allege that the Nyingma exposition of tenets such as the negation of all phenomena, delineation of the ultimate which is neither existent, nor non-existent, both or neither and the rejection of apprehension and grasping in cognition of Emptiness is a repetition of Hwashang's nihilistic doctrine. This is not surprising as most Nyingma scholars did not outright reject Hwashang's philosophical positions and practical orientations. In fact, many Nyingma scholars such as Nub Sangye Yeshe, Nyangral Nyima Özer, Longchenpa and Jigme Lingpa accorded Hwashang's simultaneist system a high status in the Buddhist doxographical hierarchy placing it above Sūtrayāna gradualism and sometimes even taking it as akin to the Dzogchen thought.[123]

Mipham's viewpoint of Hwashang is different from both the Gelukpas and his Nyingma precursors. Unlike the Gelukpas, he does not contemptuously dismiss Hwashang as a contemplative nihilist and nor anywhere in his works does he attribute to Hwashang an eminent place in the Mahāyāna tradition like some of the Nyingma masters. Mipham repeatedly disapproves the figure of Hwashang who represents the practice of excessive contemplation and anti-rationalism but at the same time he is very scrupulous about refuting the historical figure, Hwashang Mohoyen, who took part in the great Samye debate.

Showing his reluctance to approve or disprove Hwashang Mohoyen, he writes in his reply to Pari Rabsal's allegation that his view is repetition of Hwashang's position:[124]

> Therefore, apart from a mere popular hearsay that in order to support [his point on] not thinking of anything the Chinese monk of yore [cited] eighty *sūtra*s as the source [of his view], none of [his] treatises citing the *sūtra*s and delineating the contents of those [*sūtra*s] are extant today. Hence, how can [we] say whether or not others are similar to his [system]? [One cannot,] because the basis of comparison is not known. If [he has] delineated the non-conceptual gnosis as said in the *sūtra*s and the great *śāstra*s, then this hearsay told these days claiming [that he] professed a complete negation of the aspects of skilful means such as giving is definitely untrue. If he correctly delineated the practice of skilful means and reasoning as

> a way to develop the non-conceptual gnosis and [delineated] the Emptiness attributed with the supreme of all aspects – i.e. attributed with aspects of skilful means such as giving, which are coupled with non-conceptual gnosis – the sole path trodden by the Buddhas and their [spiritual] heirs, then it is not proper that bad-mouthing against him as a holder of such an evil tradition [i.e. nihilism] should occur. Nor is it proper for Kamalaśīla et al. to refute him for there cannot possibly be a Buddhist scholar who refutes the correct path of the Buddha. If he, in spite of quoting the *sūtra*s as sources, explained [them] wrongly without understanding the contents of the *sūtra*s correctly, how can all those [people] seeking support in those citations today be considered to be [following] his tradition merely because he cited [the same citations] to support [his point]? Even if he contaminated the content of the teachings of the Buddha with his mental impurities, the Buddha's teachings would not become teachings that are not [the Buddha's] . . .[125]

This shows how Mipham, with no sufficient historical sources and evidence to ascertain what exactly Hwashang Mohoyen taught and practised, is not willing to form a determinate opinion of Hwashang Mohoyen's system. In response to Pari Rabsal's accusation that he is relying on the same sources as Hwashang, he argues that even if Hwashang were mistaken in his understanding and practice of Emptiness, it does not imply that all those who cite the same sources are also wrong. Moreover, it is a mistake to associate those *sūtra*s, which Hwashang cited, with his doctrine and dismiss them in their entirety.

Mipham states that not all teachings on 'not grasping anything' are Hwashang's doctrine. Those who consider every [concept] of 'not grasping anything' as Hwashang's tradition, Mipham remarks, are only revealing their own flaws of being totally ignorant of the ultimate freedom from all elaborations and of being opposed to the profound truth.[126] He clarifies that there are two forms of non-grasping: one on the ultimate level where the certainty derived from ultimate analysis does not apprehend anything and the other which is of a conventional kind. Without verifying the two, it would be an utter mistake to equate the non-mentation of the Buddha, where no elaborations are apprehended, with Hwashang's non-mentation, which involves grasping of features (*mngon rtags su 'dzin pa*).

He succinctly defines the two kinds of 'not grasping anything' in the *Nge shes sgron me* in answer to the question of whether there is a mode of grasping in the meditative equipoise of the sublime beings. The first and correct one is the experience of reality free from all elaborations, whereas the second and erroneous one is thinking of non-thinking as espoused by Hwashang. He writes:

> At the time of maintaining the actual state of view,
> Some say that one should not grasp anything.
> [But], there is a proper understanding and a wrong notion

> As to the meaning of 'not grasping anything'.
> The first is to be free from the elaborations of four extremes.
> It is the natural dissolution of mode of grasping
> Through seeing that nothing remains
> Before the gnosis of the sublime beings
> It is like looking into the empty clear sky.
> The second is Hwashang's tradition of lack of awareness.
> Through abiding idly without any analysis,
> [One], without the aspect of clarity of insight,
> Will remain ordinary like a rock on the seabed.[127]

Mipham distinguishes the two types of not grasping anything through the presence of philosophical conviction. In the first case, the meditator does not grasp anything because he cannot find anything to grasp when thoroughly searched using the means of Mādhyamika rational enquiry. It is an experience instilled by a philosophical understanding derived from rational analysis. Hwashang's practice, on the contrary, lacks such rational foundation and philosophical conviction or certainty. It is contemplation based on an unjustified assumptive thinking (*mos pa*) that there is nothing to grasp. Mipham further illustrates the difference by contrasting the Mādhyamika seeing (*mthong ba*) that things do not exist (*ci yang med*) and assumptive thinking of the beings of fourth formless realm that things do not exist. Although they are described in same words, they are vastly different like the heaven and earth.[128]

In his *rGyan 'grel*, he compares these two kinds of not grasping anything to a thief and an innocent person, both avowing that they did not steal.[129] Although both, in expression, deny stealing in the same manner, they nonetheless differ vastly in content as one speaks the truth and the other lies. Hwashang's concept of not grasping anything is not a non-thinking derived from not seeing any object of apprehension through the negation of all substantiation and reification. It is a mere suppression of mental discursivity through contemplation on non-thinking. As such, Hwashang's meditation is not one without thought as it was claimed, but a contemplation on the thought of non-thinking. It does not even eliminate the extreme of existence, let alone all extremes.[130]

Hwashang's tradition of not grasping anything is thus an unwarranted contemplation on non-thinking. According to Mipham, it does not surpass the realm of notions (*'du shes*) and the grasping of features or characteristics (*mngon rtags su 'dzin pa / mtshan mar 'dzin pa*) but falls within the category of notion and thought. It is a pseudo-practice of non-conceptuality and is at best a good calm abiding. He mentions that such practices of non-thinking is taught in Vajrayāna treatises as a method of maintaining (*bzhag thabs*) the mind on focus but not as a view or gnosis discerning the reality. Citing Saraha's *Dohakośa*, he shows that maintaining the mind in such mode of non-mentation can be the right mental setting to generate non-conceptual experience of gnosis provided there is a proper application of an effective instruction of a master.[131]

Apart from the uncertainty he showed about Hwashang in the passage in *Rab lan* cited earlier, Mipham presents Hwashang as a teacher of blank contemplation, thinking about non-thinking. He depicts Hwashang as an archetype of one who expounded the doctrine of 'not grasping anything' and yet grasped the thought of non-thought and practised a meditation of indeterminacy and blankness without any philosophical insight. While the Gelukpas took Hwashang as a nihilist for denying existence, non-existence, is, is not, both, etc. and for the corresponding meditation, Mipham doubts that Hwashang was even close to realizing such freedom from extremes and being without apprehension and grasping. Were he truly without any apprehension and grasping, he would have achieved the non-conceptual gnosis, which discerns the ultimate Emptiness.

He observes that Hwashang, from ancient descriptions appears to be a proponent of the White Single Remedy (*dkar po gcig thub*) which involves blank contemplation without any thought and without the requirement of skilful means.[132] According to such sources, Hwashang is said to have argued that as both white and dark clouds cover the sun, every good and bad thought obscures the reality, thus, all thoughts are to be eliminated. One has to remain only in the meditation of non-thinking. Such practice of non-mentation, Mipham comments, was refuted by Kamalaśīla because it would not lead to certainty about reality. Rejecting such a practice, Kamalaśīla clearly set, in his three *Bhāvanākrama*s, the procedures of reaching the non-conceptual gnosis free from all elaborations through developing certainty derived from analysis.

Taking this depiction of Hwashang and such doctrines that are ascribed to him by Tibetan scholars, Mipham adds that his path is not conducive to spiritual practice as it is overtly contemplative and deliberately ignores the practice of skilful means. As such, Hwashang's system is considered nihilistic for neglecting the aspects of skilful means but not, as the Gelukpas argued, for upholding the position of not apprehending anything.[133] A nihilistic view, properly understood, is to see existent things such as the law of cause and effect as non-existent. Not grasping anything, therefore, is not a nihilistic view and Hwashang is not a nihilist with regard to the view, but considered as nihilistic with respect to praxis as he overlooked the requirement of skilful means such as giving.

According to Tibetan scholars, Hwashang adopted a simultaneist approach, which emphasized inducing an instantaneous enlightenment through the elimination of all thoughts rather than a gradual path of cultivation and development. Hence, Hwashang did not profess a school of systematic theory and practice but stressed solely on not grasping anything. The Gelukpas, as we have seen earlier, argued that such approach is not only the wrong way of engaging in the ultimate but is also a dangerous practice leading to the negligence of moral and ethical values. They strongly denied that enlightenment is possible through following such a path.

Mipham does not deny that enlightenment is possible through a simultaneist approach. However, he is clear that even the simultaneist path involves the initial development of certainty on Emptiness and does not seem to associate simultaneism with Hwashang's quietism. He mentions in *Nges shes sgron me* that some students of high spiritual calibre, through the blessings of their master, can generate the understanding of Emptiness merely by the means of the analysis of arising, abiding, coming and going.[134] Such students are very rare and not everybody can discern Emptiness so easily. He also claims both in his *Nges shes sgron me* and *Ketaka* that simultaneous elimination of all elaborative extremes is difficult for ordinary practitioners. Hence, ordinary beings must negate the elaborative extremes gradually through the use of the Mādhyamika analysis.[135]

Mipham states with ample stress that in order to understand the ultimate truth, one must first master the understanding of lack of hypostatic existence through rational enquiry and that even the Primordial Purity (*ka dag*) of Dzogchen can be understood only through mastery over the Prāsaṅgika view.[136] Throughout his answer to the third question in *Nges shes sgron me*, Mipham shuns the quietist contemplation as a spiritual deadlock. All sentient beings, he remarks, have been roaming in the *saṃsāra* due to spiritual inactivity and there is no need to encourage them further into such anti-rational practice of spiritual torpor.

In connection with the quietist contemplation, Mipham also refutes certain Dzogchenpas, who claim that Emptiness is understood when one does not find the colour, shape, arising, abiding, going, etc. of the mind. He contends that such practice involves the great risk of mistaking naïve understanding for the right view. Mind is immaterial and therefore cannot be seen with colour and shape and it is a grave mistake to assume that one realized Emptiness just because one did not see the colour and the shape of the mind. Were that the case, understanding Emptiness would be so simple. The correct way of seeing the Emptiness of mind is to have by way of rational enquiry, the certainty that one's mind, even while flashing like an illusion, lacks the hypostatic existence.

He questions the Dzogchenpa concept of total liberation through a single knowledge (*gcig shes kun grol*) in which they claim to know, without much study, the luminous *dharmakāya* (*'od gsal chos sku*) *qua* nature of mind which is neither existent, nor non-existent. He remarks that the Dzogchen reality, which is neither existent, nor non-existent, is the lack of elaboration of the four extremes whereas their understanding of it tends to be of a mind which is within the options of both (*gnyis yin*) and neither (*gnyis min*). To conceive the mind as a base, which is neither existent nor non-existent, and as an object of thought is equivalent to conceiving the inconceivable self (*bsam gyis mi khyab pa'i bdag*).

He goes on to say that sentient beings are caught in this *saṃsāra* because of clinging to substantiality and such clinging can only be uprooted by the antidote of the well founded grasping of Non-self, not merely by blindly assuming it. Using the analogy frequently used by Gelukpa, Mipham argues that merely thinking 'there is no snake' would not help eliminate the misconception of the rope as a snake. The misconception must be overcome by seeing no snake through investigation. Therefore, in Mipham's thought, it is crucial for beginners to develop through investigation, the modal grasping of the lack of hypostatic existence and meditate on it in order to counteract the habituation of clinging to the substantiality. To teach that all grasping should be eschewed from the very early stages is a word of evil because grasping at the lack of hypostatic existence is the right path for a beginner. However, after the certainty about the lack of hypostatic existence has become firm, the practitioner must give up grasping and develop certainty on the lack of all the elaborations with no mode of grasping.

In the answer to the fourth question in *Nges shes sgron me*, Mipham elaborates on the three stages of how a practitioner should first stress on analytic meditation (*dpyad sgom*) to inculcate certainty. Then, having gained certainty, the practitioner has to maintain it through fixed meditation (*'jog sgom*) and if the concentration wavers, repeat analytic meditation to re-stabilise certainty. Thus, he has to alternate between analytic and fixed meditation (*dpyad 'jog spel ma*) to familiarise himself with certainty, and finally, when the certainty is firm and one needs no more of analysis to inculcate it, he maintains the certainty with purely fixed meditation.

Mipham thus adopts a gradual zetetic approach with strong emphasis on the rationally inculcated certainty (*dpyad pas drangs pa'i nges shes*), a theme which permeates throughout his Mādhyamika writings. Although he does not dismiss simultaneism altogether, he despises the subitaneous approach of Hwashang's quietism and of some Dzogchenpas, who practiced along those lines, as an ignorant meditation, which will not induce elimination (*spangs pa*) and realization (*rtogs pa*). Their contemplation on 'not grasping anything' without any certainty will instead obstruct the achievement of spiritual qualities, increase defiling emotions and undermine faith in the law of cause and effect.[137]

Hence, to Mipham, the figure of Hwashang came to epitomize the proponents of the quietist practice of the non-thinking who are ironically lost in the thought of non-thinking. It is difficult to say whether Mipham really took the historical Hwashang Mohoyen to be such a master. His depiction could as well be hypothetical but it is the most suitable interpretation of Hwashang he could provide to both denounce Hwashang, who emblematized quietist contemplation and simultaneist approach among the circles of Tibetan scholars, and at the same time maintain his theories of Emptiness free from the extremes of existence, non-existence, both and neither and of the apophatic knowledge of Emptiness which is free from grasping and apprehension.

Is Emptiness effable?

The controversy on the effability of Emptiness is not very different from the one on the knowability of Emptiness, which we have discussed so far. The Ngarabpa scholars such as Ngog Loden Sherab maintained that the ultimate *qua* Emptiness is ineffable (*avācya, smrar med pa*) and inexpressible (*anabhilāpya, brjod du med pa*). Ngog writes in his *Theg chen rgyud bla ma'i don bsdus*:

> The ultimate is not an object of speech for conceptual thought is conventional and the ultimate is not an object of conceptual thought. What is meant here by 'being inexpressible by speech' is to say [it] is not the referential object (*zhen yul*)[138] of word and conceptual thought.[139]

Ngog links the ineffability of the ultimate to its transcendent nature of being unknowable by conceptual thought. The ultimate is not expressible because it is not within the scope of conceptual thought; linguistic expression is feasible only to objects of conceptual thought. He reasons that 'the ultimate is not the referential object of language or conceptual thought because it is without any defining characteristic'.[140] Tsangnagpa and Butön, Seyfort Ruegg reports, also held the position that the ultimate is beyond words and discursive thought.[141] These scholars seem to have taken the description of the ultimate as ineffable and the inexpressible in texts like MK, XVIII/7 and the famous verse from Rāhulabhadra's *Prajñāpāramitāstotra*[142] directly without any interpretation.

The Gelukpas, in contrast, espoused a different position, which Seyfort Rueggs sums up in the following:

> En revanche, les dGe lugs pa soutiennent que le Sens absolu (*paramārtha*) peut faire l'objet de l'expression verbale, encore que le contenu de cette expression (*abhidheya*) ne pénètre évidemment pas dans l'essence même de son charactère propre (*svalakṣaṇa*). Et comme la Réalité absolue peut donc être l'objet de la pensèe et de la parole, elle est un connaissable (*jñeya*).[143]

They criticized the position maintained by Ngog and other Ngarabpas as rationally and practically untenable. Were it the case that Emptiness cannot be taught and expressed, the whole soteriological role of Emptiness would be lost and the entire range of teachings on Emptiness would be pointless. Thus, they interpreted the teachings describing Emptiness as ineffable. Commenting on Candrakīrti's remark that 'the ultimate will be illustrated through analogy because it cannot be shown directly (*dngos su bstan*) as it is not effable and an object of thought based on language'[144] Tsongkhapa argues the ultimate is described as ineffable because it cannot be expressed directly; it should not be understood to be ineffable and unknowable. He uses the analogy of a falling hair to explain that the person who has opthalmia can be told about the non-existence of falling hair he sees and he can also understand they are mere illusion and that they do not exist but nonetheless he cannot see the non-existence of falling hair as fully and clearly as a person who is not suffering from opthalmia.[145] Gyaltshab interpreted the teachings describing the ultimate as ineffable in similar manner. He writes in his *Theg pa chen po rgyud bla ma'i ṭīkā*:

> [By 'the ultimate is ineffable'] is meant that the reality, in whatever way [it is] expressed and pondered by language and conceptual thought, [it] cannot be [expressed or understood] as realised by the equipoise of sublime beings. It does not mean that the ultimate truth cannot be made the object of language and conceptual thought at all.[146]

Providing such interpretations to teachings describing Emptiness as ineffable, the Gelukpas argued that Emptiness is effable for it can be taught and understood.

To maintain that Emptiness, a crucial subject of Buddhist teachings, cannot be expressed in words is a contradiction in terms. Thus, there developed among Tibetan Mādhyamika scholars, as Seyfort Ruegg points out, two different currents of thought: one held by Ngarabpa scholars such as Ngog, Sapaṇ and Butön maintaining the ultimate to be ineffable and the other held by the Gelukpas asserting the ultimate to be effable.

To his Gelukpa opponents, Mipham's position was a repetition of the Ngarabpa stance and it entailed a host of internal contradictions. To demonstrate how Mipham is contradicting his own words, Pari Rabsal cites the instances in Mipham's *Ketaka* where he explicitly or implicitly mentions that Emptiness is taught or expressed. He begins by making this sarcastic remark: 'If [I] impose, in addition to the unbearable load of contradictions for not accepting [the ultimate] to be knowable, further [the load of] contradictions, the size of which only a *gandhahastin* can bear, for not accepting [the ultimate] to be effable, this pupil might die [from the weight] and I might lose my monastic vows. However, many learned and ignorant people in the world today seem to assist [him] carry the load of [such] great evil. So hoping that it would not damage [so much], I take the courage to speak.'[147] Pari Rabsal points out how Mipham mentioned that Śāntideva *et al.* expounded the ultimate *qua* Emptiness, referred to Emptiness and Mahāyāna doctrines as expressed and expresser, accepted that *Prajñāpāramitāsūtra*s teach Emptiness and that Emptiness may be taught to those sentient beings impoverished by apprehensions.[148]

Further attacking Mipham's remark that Emptiness is inexpressible, Pari Rabsal hurls at Mipham the following hermeneutic problems:

1 Claiming Emptiness to be ineffable will contradict the *sūtra*s such as the *Lalitavistarasūtra*, which mentions how the Buddha initially did not want to teach because the dharma he discovered was so profound and subtle that no one may understand but later taught at the request of Brahmā and Śakraḥ.
2 He argues that the statement in *Ratnakūṭa* that the Buddha did not utter even one word between the night he got enlightened and his *Mahāparinirvāṇa* would have to be taken literally if Emptiness was not taught.[149]
3 *Prajñāparamitāsūtra*s, which are regarded as the king of *sūtra*s for teaching Emptiness through extensive reasoning cannot be regarded as such if Emptiness is not effable.
4 If Emptiness is ineffable, there cannot be the distinction of provisional and definitive teachings as the bifurcation is based on the teaching of the two truths and there cannot be any *sūtra*s teaching the two truths. Because there are no teachings on Emptiness, Candrakīrti's statement that 'those teachings on Emptiness should be known as definitive'[150] would not be acceptable.
5 Nāgārjuna's description of the Buddha as the exponent of dependent origination *qua* Emptiness at the beginning of his MK would be wrong. He goes on to quote many other verses from Maitreya and Āryadeva to prove that Emptiness is effable and therefore taught in many treatises.

Mipham replies in great detail accusing Pari Rabsal of misunderstanding the texts and manipulating them to fit his own understanding.[151] Whereas Pari Rabsal, and the Gelukpas generally, delineated Emptiness as effable and interpreted the *sūtra*s and the *śāstra*s describing Emptiness as ineffable to agree with this understanding, Mipham maintained a flexible position employing a liberal use of the descriptions. Emptiness free from all apprehensions is intrinsically ineffable, nonetheless it is perfectly feasible to talk about it and attempt to describe it as best as one could for transactional purposes. Conventional expression of Emptiness for worldly transaction is compatible with the otherwise inexpressible nature of Emptiness. To Mipham, expressing the inexpressible is not a contradiction of terms but an expedient way of approaching the ultimate. Thus, he did not consider it contradictory to view Emptiness as ineffable and yet at the same time treat it as a subject of discourse, discussion or exposition.

In response to Pari Rabsal's first refutation, Mipham cites further passages from *Lalitavistarasūtra* to demonstrate that Emptiness is in fact described in it as inexpressible and difficult to understand. If the ultimate were merely the lack of hypostatic existence, as the Gelukpas understood, there would not be much reason to describe it as profound, unfathomable and ineffable. However, it is undeniably clear that the ultimate is taught to be free from all elaborations and as such it is taught to be beyond the scope of language and thought. He cites many more passages from major Indian sources describing the ultimate as ineffable and warns Pari Rabsal that he is antagonizing them through his refutations.

In his reply to the second question, Mipham denies saying that Emptiness was not taught. Instead, he categorically asserts that the Buddha delivered teachings on Emptiness which is free from apprehension.[152] If the statement in the *Ratnakūṭa* were understood in the conventional sense, it need not be taken literally because many conventional topics were taught even if Emptiness was not. How can it be the case that the Buddha did not utter even a word when he delivered the three wheels of dharma? The statement, he thus argues, is to be taken in reference to the reality free from apprehension, in which no teacher, teaching, or mode of teaching are apprehended. He seems to take the statement as viable in the context of the delineation of the reality, the way Tsongkhapa does in his commentary on MK, XVIII/7 and XXV/24.[153] However, he contends that if the statement is understood as implying that the Buddha did not utter any hypostatically existent word, then no sentient beings, it would logically follow, utter any word either.

Mipham's position on effability, like the one on knowability we have discussed earlier, is determined by contexts. In the context of conventional transaction, Emptiness is effable and expressible lest all *sūtra*s and treatises on Emptiness become pointless. Mipham does not deny the fact that teachings on Emptiness were delivered. Responding to Pari Rabsal's refutation, Mipham clearly mentions that Emptiness free from apprehension is extensively taught in the *Prajñāpāramitāsūtra*s and therefore the same are considered as the king of definitive *sūtra*s. It is in this respect that the Buddha is described as the greatest exponent of Emptiness *qua* dependent origination.[154] However, on the level of the ultimate free from all apprehension, no subject, object, expresser and expressed are viable. How could the ultimate then be effable in the normal sense of the word?[155] Mipham thus understands the statement that the Buddha did not teach anything in the context of the ultimate truth.

In reply to Pari Rabsal's question about bifurcation of *sūtra*s into provisional and definitive, he makes a clear-cut distinction between the two stating that 'those *sūtra*s which teach Emptiness free from apprehension are definitive and *sūtra*s which teach the conventional phenomena involving apprehension are provisional'.[156] Thus, from Mipham's viewpoint, Pari Rabsal's criticism that there would be no *sūtra*s teaching the two truths is unwarranted as there is no opponent holding such a stance. Furthermore, Mipham refutes the Gelukpa understanding that the *sūtra*s which teach Emptiness *qua* absence of hypostatic existence to be the definitive *sūtra*s. He reasons that were the *sūtra*s teaching Emptiness which involves apprehension definitive, it would then follow that the teachings, which negate apprehension and transcend the dualities of substance and non-substance, etc. will have to be provisional. In that case, only the hypostatic existence will have to be negated and the Buddha would not have taught of Emptiness dispelling diverse dualistic appearances of substance, non-substances, etc. Beside, thoughts with the subject–object duality will be correct and those without will have to be mistaken, and the description of the ultimate as a sphere transcending the subject–object duality will not be tenable.

Mipham also argues that it would be wrong to understand ineffability of Emptiness merely in the sense, as known in the general semasiological context, of linguistic incompetence in expressing the referent directly. Formulating his systematic theories of semasiology, which he attributes to Dignāga and Dharmakīrti, Mipham explains how language relates to its referent through the universal characteristics (*spyi mtshan*) of concepts and not through the direct expression of the individual characteristics (*rang mtshan*). According to Mipham, no individual characteristic can be expressed by words directly without the mediation of concepts.[157]

In several of his philosophical writings, Mipham presents a fourfold concept of the expressed (*brjod bya*) and expresser (*rjod byed*): the object directly expressed (*dngos kyi brjod bya*) and the object intended to be expressed (*zhen pa'i brjod bya*), the subject which is the direct expresser (*dngos kyi rjod byed*) and the subject which is intended to be the expresser (*zhen pa'i rjod byed*).[158] The object directly expressed, according to Mipham's theory, is the mental picture of the object, that is, the universal image of the object (*arthasamanya, don spyi*), and the object intended to be expressed is the specific object, the individually characterised thing (*don rang mtshan*). The conceptual picture of the word, the linguistic universal (*śabdasamanya, sgra spyi*), is the direct expresser and the individually characterised word (*sgra rang mtshan*), the sound of the word, is the intended expresser. In the instance of saying 'vase', the mental image of vase is the first, the actual vase, the second, the mental picture of the word 'vase', the third and the sound 'vase', the fourth respectively.

Language, in Mipham's thought, is intricately interwoven with conceptual thinking. When a word such as 'vase' is uttered, the speaker conceives the conceptual picture of vase and apprehends it as one with the actual vase. Similarly, he conceives the conceptual picture of the word 'vase' and apprehends it as one with the sound 'vase'. Mipham calls this process the mixing of the presented and the constructed (*snang brtag gcig tu bsres pa*), the presented being the specific object and sound, and the constructed being their conceptual images. It is through conceptually linking the mental image of vase with the mental image of the word 'vase' as the expressed and expresser and conceiving the mental image of vase as one with the actual vase and mental image of word 'vase' with actual word 'vase' that the actual vase and sound 'vase' are also connected as the expressed and expresser. Without this, the speaker, or the listener, would not be able to link the linguistic expresser with the object expressed. Now, when we say 'vase', vase is existent and therefore the object which is intended is found. In other words, the word vase has a referent. In the case of saying 'rabbit's horn', the object which is intended cannot be found. There is no referent of the word. Nonetheless, the expression is feasible and the message is also conveyed because there is the direct object, the conceptual image mentally generated. Thus, anything is expressible in this sense.

Like other Tibetan dialecticians, Mipham followed Dharmakīrti (and also Candrakīrti) in claiming that words and their referents have no natural relationship. The relationship between the expressed and the expresser (*brjod bya rjod byed kyi 'brel ba*) is a constructed one, forged by the conceptual mixing mentioned earlier.[159] Thus, it is a pure convention founded on our conceptual thinking to call a vase 'vase' and not 'pillar'. Were it the case that we are accustomed to calling vases 'pillars', it would be perfectly rational and pragmatic to call them 'pillars'. Words are devoid of inherent meaning and thus are not capable of expressing any referent automatically. They merely follow the intention of the speaker in referring to an object and their purpose is achieved when the intended referent is expressed or the message conveyed.

Thus, in Mipham's theory, no expresser can express any referent directly without the mediation of conceptual thoughts and intentions. Not only is Emptiness ineffable but all individually characterized entities are ineffable in this respect.[160] Mipham thus rebukes the interpretation that Emptiness is described as ineffable because it cannot be expressed directly by language as a naïve understanding. He remarks that such ineffability would be applicable to even conventionally existent things and Emptiness would not be the ultimate, which is uniquely described as transcending language and speculation.

However, it is not quite clear whom Mipham is criticizing here or if his argument, rather than being a general clarification, is targeted at anyone in particular at all. Even the Gelukpas accepted that the description of Emptiness as ineffable has to be understood differently from the linguistic theory that individual characteristics are ineffable by words directly. Gyaltshab clearly distinguishes the two:

> The two cases of individual characteristics not being objects of language and the ultimate being ineffable are different. Although language does not

> penetrate the nature of individual characteristics, they are fully cognised through [conceptual] dichotomization. The reality, in whatever way [it is] expressed and pondered by language and conceptual thought, [it] cannot be [expressed or understood] as realised by the equipoise of sublime beings.[161]

Thus, Gyaltshab argues that the ultimate is not termed ineffable merely because its individual characteristics cannot be directly expressed by language. Although the nature of individual characteristics is not penetrable by language, one can gain a full understanding of the individual characteristics depending on the words but in the case of the ultimate, one cannot gain a full understanding through words and conceptual thoughts. Ngog too makes the distinction:

> What is meant here by 'being inexpressible by speech' is to say [it] is not the referential object (*zhen yul*) of word and conceptual thought. It is not [about] merely being non-evident to linguistic cognition (*sgra'i shes pa*). If this were the case, it would follow that even conventional things such as vase are likewise [ineffable].[162]

Mipham then goes on to explain how he understands the description of Emptiness as ineffable:

> What then? All phenomena which fall within the substantial and non-substantial things – substantial things such as vase and the non-substantial such as space – or those which are known either negatively or affirmatively are within the scope of conceptual thoughts, because their particular natures can be apprehended and expressed. The definitive ontic nature *qua* Emptiness cannot be thought or said to be on the extremes of either substantiality and non-substantiality, negation and affirmation, or both and neither [of these]. Therefore, it is said to be inexpressible and beyond the scope of conceptual thought.[163]

In Mipham's thought, the ultimate *qua* Emptiness, unlike other phenomena which can be said to be substantial, non-substantial, negatively existent, positively existent, etc., cannot be truly said to be anything because it transcends being anything. The ultimate is to be free from all the elaborations; it cannot be apprehended by thought or expressed by language.[164] Citing the MK, XVIII/7 and *Vigrahavyāvartanī*, 29, he remarks that Pari Rabsal's arguments reveal no additional loads of contradictions but are pointless criticisms like attempts to cut space with a sword. The ultimate cannot be expressed as empty or non-empty, existent or non-existent, is or is not. He comments that this is exactly what is meant by 'the unspeakable, inconceivable, inexpressible perfection of wisdom', in the verse from *Prajñāparamitāstotra* by Rāhulabhadra,[165] which everyone is so used to chanting, and by the statement 'the Bodhisattva [Vimalakīrti] remained silent when Mañjuśrī asked him about reality'.[166]

Nonetheless, Mipham does not deny that as a propaedeutic method, the ultimate is given names such as Emptiness, *dharmadhātu*, etc. and described as the reality which is not a partisan appearance or Emptiness but beyond the extremes of existence and non-existence.[167] Such conventional designations and definitions are used and through them conceptual understanding of the ultimate is also cultivated. However, these conventional expressions and the conceptual understanding are merely ways to the actual experience of the ultimate. Although they are used to delineate the ultimate, they do not affirm or express the ultimate *per se* in the manner of an apprehensible entity. Delineation of the ultimate is not like delineating other phenomena where a positive or negative determination and apprehension are involved. The ultimate transcends being a linguistic referent in that it cannot be described or pointed out either cataphatically or apophatically, the way conventional things can be. Cataphatic and apophatic delineations, like the finger pointing to the moon,[168] are only distant signs leading to it. The ultimate, by its nature, is beyond linguistic description and therefore the delineation of the ultimate is known as the delineation of the inexpressible.

Then, Mipham draws a clear distinction between the understanding of effability/ineffability merely in the sense of being verbally enunciable and being subject of meaningful expression. Emptiness is definitely effable in the first sense as it can be verbally uttered and mentioned. Ineffability of Emptiness discussed in the *sūtra*s and *śāstra*s do not merely mean that the word 'Emptiness' cannot be uttered or mentioned by the mouth. Emptiness is ineffable in that it cannot be communicated properly even through meaningful expression. Without verifying the two forms of effability, it would be laughable to argue that Emptiness is expressible because it can be uttered by the mouth and is within the scope of thought because it can be thought of.

In another hermeneutic approach, Mipham distinguishes between the direct and the indirect engagement of language and thought and argues that the ultimate is not a direct object of language and conceptual thoughts because there are no words or conceptual thoughts which can engage in the ultimate directly. In this respect, the ultimate is said to be beyond being taught or illustrated (*bstan pa dang dper bya ba las 'das pa*). However, there are words and thoughts, which engage in the ultimate indirectly. The ultimate is directly discerned after cultivating and habituating the certainty about it with the help of analyses and scriptural quotations. He observes:

> Because there is no language or conceptual thought which directly engages with the ultimate, [it] is not a direct object of language and thought. [It] is taught to be beyond demonstration, analogies and so forth and so it is. However, language and conceptual thoughts which engage indirectly are not non-existent for it is appropriate to discern directly the

> ultimate through the force of practising the certainty about the ineffable nature of intuitive self awareness gained through flawless scriptures and reasoning delineating the ultimate, which is free from elaborations.[169]

Mipham in this case seems to use an argument based on the graduated soteriological stages of engaging in Emptiness. From this viewpoint, Emptiness is considered ineffable because words cannot directly engage in it; they can only lead the meditator to the cultivation of the intuitive gnosis of the sublime beings, which engages in it directly. Mipham's interpretation of ineffability of Emptiness here – that Emptiness is ineffable because words cannot engage in it directly – appears identical with the semasiological argument discussed earlier – that Emptiness is ineffable because words cannot express it directly – which he rejected to be a correct explanation of the ineffability of Emptiness. In fact, they are both based on the same principle of Emptiness not being a direct object of language. However, Mipham takes them differently. The previous one, which Mipham rejected, is a semasiological argument that Emptiness is inexpressible because it cannot be expressed by language directly. That does not hold because other individually characterized objects such as vases and pillars cannot be expressed directly either. The latter one is a case of linguistic pragmatism, where language can convey the meaning of objects such as vases and pillars but cannot convey the concept of Emptiness because it is transcendent. This explanation is viable. In this case, Mipham also takes into account soteriological gradualism, where word and conceptual thought, although bereft of the capacity to engage in Emptiness directly, leads to the generation of the direct experience of Emptiness.

In yet another instance,[170] Mipham quotes from the *Akṣayamatinirdeśasūtra*[171] and the *Āryasaṃvṛtiparamārthasatyanirdeśasūtra*[172] and Candrakīrti's *Madhyamakāvatārabhāṣya*[173] to prove that the ultimate is inexpressible. Then, he adds that although the inexpressible ultimate cannot be demonstrated exactly or accurately (*ji bzhin du*) by language and conceptual thought, it can nonetheless be delineated through dependence on them. Thus, Mipham interprets the ineffability of Emptiness in the sense of not being exactly, accurately or fully effable. This interpretation, it may be noted, is similar to Gyaltshab's theory that the ultimate cannot be realised fully (*yongs su rdzogs pa*) through language and conceptual thought alone.[174] The similarity is even more striking with other Gelukpa scholars who use the same terminology as Mipham and argue that the ultimate is not expressed and known accurately or exactly (*ji bzhin du/ji lta ba bzhin du*) by language and conceptual thought.

Mipham's usage of a variety of hermeneutic methods indicates the intriguing nature of the problem that the description of Emptiness as the inexpressible poses. He does not approve of the Gelukpa description of Emptiness as effable and their viewpoint that the description of Emptiness as ineffable is untenable if taken directly and thus requires interpretation. From his viewpoint, understanding Emptiness as unilaterally effable debases Emptiness to the realm of ordinary speculation and language.[175] Besides, persistence in such interpretation implies direly that the master of the past who described Emptiness as ineffable was inept at describing Emptiness.

There are few salient features of Mipham's hermeneutic approach to the problem of ineffability. Mipham adheres as closely as possible to the original sources both in use of linguistic description and philosophical presentation, thus preserving the often paradoxical and antinomical style of teachings on Emptiness which the Gelukpas, in the process of presenting a highly scholastic formulation of Emptiness, seem to have lost. Similarly, he favours a liberal use of terms by not obdurately following the literal meaning of words. An outstanding feature is also his enthusiasm to rationalize the paradoxical and antinomical values of Mādhyamika without reducing them to objects of mundane speculation. In his hermeneutic endeavours to accommodate the ineffability of Emptiness, its intrinsic characteristic, and the verbalization and the exposition of Emptiness for transactional purposes in one coherent system, we also see the typical Mipham, who is the champion of reconciling all divergent trends through an inclusivistic approach.

SOME CONCLUDING REMARKS

The three issues discussed here – the delimitation of the negandum, the theory of the ultimate and the knowability and the effability of Emptiness – represent the dialectical, ontological and epistemological aspects of the philosophy of Emptiness and form the main themes of Mipham's discussions. The arguments presented under these topics comprise Mipham's main criticisms of the Gelukpa understanding of Emptiness and his own distinctive contributions to the philosophy of Emptiness, although the discussion undertaken in this book is far from being either an exhaustive treatment of his polemics or a complete study of his theory of Emptiness.

Mipham's first and foremost qualm about the Gelukpa understanding of Emptiness, as we have seen, concerns their emphatic identification of hypostatic existence, which is distinct from the commonsense objects, as the negandum. The disputes on the nature of the ultimate and the knowability and effability of Emptiness arise as corollaries to this. Like many other opponents of the Gelukpa school, Mipham argues that by exegetic emphasis on negating an 'isolated' negandum and leaving the empirical world unscathed, Emptiness will be misconstrued as an absence of 'extrinsic' hypostatic existence, both in theory and practice. Consequently, people will miss the whole Mādhyamika point of discerning all things as Emptiness in order to eliminate attachment to empirical phenomena, thus destroying the main purpose of the philosophy.

The Gelukpas, however, have a different concern. They fear that the overbroad delimitation of the negandum involving the negation of all conventional phenomena by the ultimate analysis would annihilate even the conventional status of things. If all phenomena were negated, Emptiness would be misunderstood as a sheer denial of everything. Such a nihilistic view would destroy the coexistence of Emptiness and dependent origination, the philosophical essence of the Mādhyamika school. Practically, people would engage in the meditation of non-mentation without developing any insight. This would lead to indulgence and complacence in non-mentation, and undermine the moral and ethical aspects of the path. Thus, they formulated a Madhyamaka philosophy with a strong sense of rationality, and identifying the exact negandum formed a fundamental part of this rational approach.

Mipham is aware of this problem and he distinguishes the correct philosophical understanding of Emptiness through ratiocinative enquiry and meditative insight from the indeterminate view and contemplation of non-mentation. Identifying his own position with the former, he ascribes the latter to Hwashang. However, according to him, the Gelukpa fear that even the conventional status of things will be annihilated if things are negated by the ultimate analysis is an unnecessary worry, because the conventional phenomena, in spite of being negated under the ultimate analysis, will exist undeniably on the non-analytic transactional level. Nothing can resist the scrutiny of the ultimate analysis; therefore, everything is negated and proved to be empty. Were the things themselves not negated, negating a separate hypostatic existence would not overcome attachment to them.

Moreover, the identification of hypostatic existence exclusively as the negandum leads to the delineation of the mere absence of hypostatic existence as Emptiness *qua* ultimate. This is the view of a biased Emptiness (*stong pa phyang chad*), a mere absence of hypostatic existence. Mipham no doubt attributes a propaedeutic value to the absence of hypostatic existence, but strongly denies that such absence is the ultimate Emptiness. Positing an absence of hypostatic existence is also ultimately a reification like positing hypostatic existence. He relegates the absence of hypostatic existence to a relative status and argues that such Emptiness is only a provisional antidote for those who are enmeshed in a strong sense of substantiality but is ultimately to be given up to reach the final Emptiness free from all elaborations. He terms it the notational ultimate (*rnam grangs pa'i don dam*), which is free from only the partial extremes in contrast to the non-notational ultimate (*rnam grangs min pa'i don dam*), which is free from all extremes.

Thus, Mipham's understanding of Emptiness and the ultimate differs from the Gelukpa theory of Emptiness and the ultimate in an important way. This difference entails many other logical, epistemological and linguistic discrepancies. With the ultimate *qua* absence of hypostatic existence in mind, the Gelukpas accept the ultimate to be dialectically an absolute negation (*med dgag*). Ontologically, the ultimate, according to them, is an existent phenomenon, epistemologically, a knowable object and linguistically, an effable content. They also assert the viability of the rules of logic such as the non-contradiction, the excluded middle and the logical bivalence in delineating Emptiness.

Mipham agrees that all these are applicable to the notational ultimate *qua* absence of hypostatic existence. However, he professes the final ultimate to be Emptiness free from all elaborations (*spros pa thams cad dang bral ba'i stong nyid*), and argues that the ultimate is neither existent nor non-existent and therefore neither knowable nor effable in the normal sense of the words. The final Emptiness in Mipham's thought, as in the Gelukpa system, is an absolute negation, but he dissents from the Gelukpas in negating all the mental elaborations including, he specifies, the absence of hypostatic existence. Ontologically, it is the state where nothing can be apprehended, perceived or pointed out, and yet interdependent appearance presents itself unfailingly. The ultimate nature of things is the coalescence of Emptiness and appearance. Epistemologically, this

Emptiness is beyond the domain of language and thought but within the scope of the intuitive gnosis.

It is this non-notational ultimate that Mipham proves to be unknowable and ineffable. The Gelukpas do not accept this interpretation of the higher ultimate and dismiss the Ngarabpa understanding of Emptiness characterized as neither existent nor non-existent (*yod min med min*), as a naïve understanding with a nihilistic inclination. Thus, the debate on the knowability and effability of Emptiness is not on an Emptiness which is mutually accepted. Mipham readily agrees with the Gelukpas that the ultimate *qua* absence of hypostatic existence is knowable and effable. The main bone of contention, to him, is the Gelukpa assertion of such absence as the final Emptiness *qua* non-notational ultimate. He uses the description of the final ultimate as unknowable and ineffable to argue that such an ultimate is not mere absence of hypostatic existence but reality free from all elaborations.

The Gelukpas formulate their theory of the ultimate *qua* absence of hypostatic existence with a strong sense of rationality, drawing on Dharmakīrti's logico-epistemology and their *bsdus grwa* dialectics. The Nyingmapas generally are known to expound their theory of Emptiness under profound influence from Dzogchen. Hence, while the Gelukpas, with strict adherence to rules of logic, profess a highly coherent ontological theory of the ultimate, which neatly fits into their general dialectical and epistemological framework, the Nyingma ontological exposition is full of paradoxes and antinomies, often transcending the rules of logic. For this, we have seen the Gelukpas tax the Nyingmapas with naïve literalism and anti-rational quietism while the Nyingmapas rebuked them for excessive intellectualism and profane reasoning. These disparate trends are no doubt due to the religious education and the general religious orientation in the two traditions: the intensity of *pramāṇa* and *sūtra* studies among the Gelukpas and the dominance of *vajrayāna* and Dzogchen teachings in the Nyingma tradition.

Against this general background, Mipham stands out as unique in being both a committed rationalist and a staunch exponent of the theories of Emptiness with a mystical flavour. Mipham recognizes the need for rationality, but is always selective and cautious of its limitations. It is the excessive and the inapposite application of intellectual reasoning (*rtog ge'i rigs pa*) and verbal hair splitting (*tshig gi 'then khyer*) that enshrouds the proper view of Emptiness in the case of the Gelukpa exegeses. The identification of an isolated negandum, different from conventional phenomena, for one, is such a verbal and intellectual distinction. Mipham despairs that if one thinks introspectively about Emptiness, such specious arguments and reliance on words will only obstruct the realization of Emptiness and will not help overcome clinging and attachment to anything but only lead to mere quibbling.

Mipham, as we see throughout his writings, is trying to strike a balance between intellectual rationalism and transcendental mysticism, which he derives from his love of logico-epistemology and Dzogchen teachings. He presents both rational arguments and paradoxical and antinomical descriptions of Emptiness and links conceptual/rational understanding and non-conceptual/mystical experience, treating them as crucial and consistent parts of a systematic soteriological process. An outstanding feature in his thought is his rationalization of even the paradoxical, antinomical and the mystical through what may be termed Mahāyāna *surrationalism*. Even on the level of establishing the non-notational ultimate, where he rejects the viability of the ordinary rules of logic, he does not discard logic and rationalism altogether but endorses a transcendental form of rationalism. He distinguishes profane reasoning (*tshur mthong rigs pa*) from what he calls the reasoning of reality (*chos nyid kyi rigs pa*), and rejects that the rules of profane reasoning such as the law of double negation, non-contradiction, excluded middle and logical bivalence are viable on the level of the ultimate. In fact, on that level, it is logical and rational to defy these ordinary rules of logic and to argue that the ultimate is neither existent nor non-existent, etc. It would be irrational to maintain that the ultimate is one-sidedly existent or non-existent. This kind of *surrationalism* is also the logic behind Mahāyāna concepts such as the existence of a billion worlds in an atom and an aeon in a moment, and behind statements such as MK, XXIV/14 stating that everything is possible for that, for which Emptiness is possible.

Mipham's exposition of Emptiness is also marked by distinctive hermeneutic skills such as the binary sets of the two truths, the bifurcation of the conventional correct cognitions, the theory of the two ultimates, the verification of philosophical contexts, the distinction between thoughts and words with apprehension and without apprehension and above all by his inclusivistic approach and *ris med* outlook. These hermeneutic endeavours and religious approaches play a significant parts in building his philosophical edifice, the pinnacle of which is the theory of the final ultimate *qua* Emptiness free from elaboration and apprehension.

Mipham inherited the inclusivistic approach from his Nyingma predecessors such as Rongzom and Longchenpa, who were propagators of the Dzogchen inclusivism, which proclaimed that all other schools ultimately led to, and all theories and practices culminated in, the Dzogchen school of Atiyoga, the *ne plus ultra* of Buddhism. This inclusivism and the *ris med* outlook, of which Mipham is a major promulgator, permeate his writings and their impact on his thoughts is evident in the efforts he makes to bring the divergent Buddhist traditions and interpretations into harmony.

This, for instance, is demonstrated in the course of his debates in two notable cases: (1) Unlike other critics of Hwashang, Mipham does not dismiss Hwashang's quietism as nihilism. He reasons that Hwashang's practice of non-mentation is not nihilistic, instead, it is an expedient way of calming the mind and through it some persons of sharp faculty can easily give birth to proper insight when inspired by the instruction of a skilful teacher; (2) Similarly, Mipham does not accuse the Gelukpas, as other opponents did, of espousing a nihilist view. He acknowledges that their absence of hypostatic existence is a provisional Emptiness, which helps overcome an intense sense of substantiality and ultimately conduces to the understanding of the final ultimate.

Mipham's reconciliatory tone is heard best in his repeated approbation of Tsongkhapa and his final understanding of Emptiness. This reconciliation through an inclusivistic and *ris med* approach however was not his main motive for writing his works on Madhyamaka which triggered the polemical controversies. The main purpose of his exposition of Madhyamaka was to give Nyingmapas, who were then heavily relying on other schools for *sūtra* studies, an independent philosophical system. By doing so, he also perhaps intended to counteract the proliferation of the Gelukpa scholasticism embodied in their *yig cha* curriculum and eristic mode of study, which he despised for its casuistry and verbosity.

His irenic hopes of finding religious and philosophical harmony may not have been fully realized, but Mipham has certainly succeeded in giving Nyingmapas a Mādhyamika hermeneutic of their own and in raising a major alternative voice on Emptiness besides the Gelukpa tradition dominant in his day. His works on Madhyamaka thus represent the crowning glory of his remarkable contributions to learning in Tibet and it will surely be for this legacy that Mipham will be best remembered and most studied for generations to come.

APPENDIX I

brGal lan nyin byed snang ba
(MGS, vol. Ca, pp. 99–190)

Reply to Trewo Drakar Trulku Lobzang Paldan Tenzin Nyandra's *Zab mo dbu ma'i gnad cung zad brjod pa blo gsal dga' ba'i gtam zhes bya ba mi pham rnam rgyal la klan ka gyis pa dang po*

Mipham wrote his commentary on the ninth chapter of the *Bodhicaryāvatāra* entitled the *Shes rab le'u'i tshig don go sla bar rnam par bshad pa nor bu ke ta ka* in 1878. This he did in 13 days, requested by one Sukama, after he had received the exegetical transmission of the root text from his teacher Paltrul Ugyen Jigme Chökyi Wangpo and read all Indian and Tibetan commentaries available. In his commentary, he reinforced the Ngarabpa interpretations of Mādhyamika philosophy, and argued against certain interpretations which are associated with the Gelukpas. Mipham does not name his opposition but most of his criticisms were clearly targeted at Gelukpa authors. These criticisms, he explains later, were not deliberate polemical attacks, but enquiries he had to make in the course of clarifying his own positions.

His criticism soon provoked counter-criticisms from several contemporary Gelukpa scholars including Drakar Trulku Paldan Tenzin Nyandra of Drepung monastery, who is said to have written his first rejoinder, *Zab mo dbu ma'i gnad cung zad brjod pa blo gsal dga' ba'i gtam*, at the age of twenty-three in 1888/89(?). The rejoinder seems to have reached Mipham relatively quickly as he wrote his rebuttal, *brGal lan nyin byed snang ba*, in 1889. This reply to Drakar Trulku was finished in ten days during the recesses of a meditation retreat and has 46 folios or 92 pages in the MGS version and 112 pages in the recent Sichuan edition.

Mipham begins by mentioning that he is not undertaking this work with sectarian prejudice and hatred towards his opponent although he admits his loyalty to the Ngarabpa tradition. He stresses the importance of an unprejudiced outlook and adherence to rational argument. He says that he is engaging in inter-school debate not because he wishes to arouse controversy but to elucidate the difference in understanding Emptiness between the Ngarabpas and the Chirabpas and to establish the correct understanding.

Major Mādhyamika issues discussed in the Drakar Trulku's criticism and Mipham's reply are:

- the definition of hypostatic existence and grasping at hypostatic existence in Mādhyamika and other schools;
- the issue of all phenomena being superimpositions of the mind;
- definition of individually characterized existents;
- grasping at self and grasping at hypostatic existence;
- whether Śrāvaka and Pratyekabuddha *arhat*s give up grasping;
- whether *arhat*s are liberated from *saṃsāra*;
- defining the 'craving' in the BA, IX/47;
- on grasping at self as particular kind of grasping at phenomena;
- the realization of Non-self and the *arhat*s;
- the typology of the two truths and the nature of the ultimate;
- Reflexive Cognition (*svasaṃvedana, rang rig*);
- unique tenets of Prāsaṅgikas and the two ultimates.

Mipham ends his work urging that religious discussion must not be conducted with bigotry and malice but with sound arguments so that it will contribute to the furtherance of the Buddha's teachings. Drakar Trulku wrote two more criticisms of Mipham. The second one *'Jam dbyangs rnam rgyal gyis 'dod tshul la klan ka bgyis pa zab mo'i gtam* was a revised version of the first one and the third, *Mi pham rnam rgyal gyis rtsod pa'i yang lan log lta'i khong khrag 'don pa'i skyug sman*, was written in reply to Mipham's rebuttal. Mipham wrote no further response and it is not clear whether Mipham did not receive these two or he avoided replying to them. Since writing his *brGal lan nyin byed snang ba*, Mipham mentions receiving two polemical rejoinders from Lhasa, one from Jangkha and a fourth one from Pari Rabsal. He says that he did not take the trouble to write replies to the first three as they lacked philosophical depth. However it is not clear if the two from Lhasa are the same as the ones Drakar Trulku wrote.

APPENDIX II

gZhan gyis brtsad pa'i lan mdor bsdus pa rigs lam rab gsal de nyid snang byed

(MGS, vol. Ca, pp. 191–474)

Mipham's reply to Pari Lobzang Rabsal's *'Jam dbyangs dgongs rgyan rigs pa'i gzi 'bar gdong lnga'i sgra dbyangs*

After the dissemination of his commentary on the ninth chapter of the BA, in which he elucidated the Ngarabpa line of interpretation and argued against certain Gelukpa positions, Mipham received polemical rejoinders from a few Gelukpa scholars. One of them was Pari Lobzang Rabsal of Kubum Jampaling, who was one of the renowned Gelukpa scholars of his day. Among those from whom he received polemical rejoinders, Mipham regarded Pari Rabsal as a scholar whose criticisms contained profound arguments and deserved to be carefully studied and answered.

Pari Rabsal's work was written in 1897 but Mipham got it only in 1902. By then, Mipham's health was deteriorating and he also seems to have become very disheartened by sectarian reaction to his writings. His earlier reply to Drakar Trulku, *brGal lan nyin byed snang ba*, for instance, appears to have provoked more sectarian reaction instead of conducing a non-sectarian dialogue. He was worried that philosophical dialogues were being misconstrued as sectarian attacks and fueling unnecessary anger and ill feeling. So he did not wish to write this reply to Pari Rabsal, but it was the persistent request of his students, such as Kathog Situ and Golog Lingtrul, which led to the writing of this 'brief' rebuttal. The work was written in 18 days in the middle of 1903 with Khenpo Kunzang Paldan as scribe and consists of 142 folios and 283 pages in the MGS version and 316 pages in the recent Sichuan edition.

Mipham begins by showing his strong approval of Pari Rabsal's praise of Tsongkhapa. Both in the beginning and the end, Mipham explains how Tsongkhapa is an outstanding master and how his ultimate view is consonant with that of the Ngarabpas. He also points out that most of the followers of Tsongkhapa misunderstood and misinterpreted Tsongkhapa's teachings on the ultimate Emptiness, although he quotes Changkya and says that many Gelukpa masters knew that Tsongkhapa's understanding of ultimate Emptiness was the same as the Ngarabpa understanding.

The actual answer to the refutation of Pari Rabsal begins with the discussion on the first verse of the ninth chapter. The major topics of their discussions are:

- the terms '*yan-lag*' and '*don*' in the BA, IX/1;
- the typology and definition of the two truths;
- dualistic thinking and the Buddha's gnosis;
- the modes of grasping, meditative equipoise and post-equipoise period;
- the grasping at self and grasping at existent objects;
- conventional reality and the Buddha;
- Emptiness and the ultimate nature of mind;
- the two sets of two truths;
- Śrāvaka and Pratyekabuddha realization of Emptiness;
- the nature of Emptiness free from all elaborations;
- coalescence (*yuganaddha, zung 'jug*);
- the notational and the non-notational ultimates;
- the middle way;
- the ineffability and inexpressibility of the ultimate;
- on Hwashang and non-conceptuality;
- on theses and assertions;
- Prāsaṅgika and Svātantrika differences;
- reflexive awareness and store consciousness;
- difference of philosophical view in the *sūtra* and *mantra* schools.

The bulk of the book is on the theory of Emptiness and on the nature of the realization of Emptiness, his main qualm being the Gelukpa understanding of absence of hypostatic existence as the ultimate Emptiness. He devotes over half of his book to this issue; elaborating on how the ultimate Emptiness is not a mere negation of hypostatic existence but a reality, free from all elaborations.

Throughout his work, Mipham says that this work is written neither with a sectarian prejudice nor with any intention to provoke anger and conflict between the different schools. He frequently reminds his opponent that the argument should be based on reasoning and the debate should not become a worldly quarrel with censorious remarks on one's opponent or a mere quibble. Despite the frequent use of sarcastic language by his opponent, Mipham shows respect to his opponent and carries on his arguments calmly. Mipham and Pari Rabsal later came to share mutual admiration and exchanged not only polemical letters but eulogies praising each other.

APPENDIX III

rDo grub pa dam chos zhes pas gzhan gyi zer sgros bsdus nas mkhas su re ba'i 'khyal ngag de dag mi mkhas mtshang phung du kho rang nas bskul ba bzhin nyams mtshar du bkod pa

(MGS, vol. Nga, pp. 359–415)

Mipham's reply to queries of Dodrub Damchö Zangpo

Mipham wrote in 1876 an extensive commentary on the *Madhyamakālaṃkāra* of Śāntarakṣita entitled *dBu ma rgyan gyi rnam bshad 'jam dbyangs bla ma dgyes pa'i zhal lung* at the behest of his master Jamyang Khyentsei Wangpo. In it, he elucidated most of his Mādhyamika theories and the work soon received criticism even from within the Nyingma circles. The *Dam chos dogs sel* is a work of 28 folios and 55 pages, written as an answer to the queries of Dodrub Damchö Zangpo, a Nyingmapa, who criticized Mipham's commentary on the *Madhyamakālaṃkāra*. It is unique in that it was written for a critic from his own tradition and, unlike the two other polemical replies, the opponent seems to have requested Mipham to dispel his doubts. Strangely, Mipham also makes more impolite and sarcastic remarks here than in his two other replies. Damchö seems initially to have attacked Mipham and also challenged Mipham to a debate, but subsequently he seems to have accepted Mipham's authority and entreated him to write this work.

Mipham begins with some pejorative verses about the kind of work (perhaps the refutation of his commentary on *Madhyamakālaṃkārakārikā*) Damchö has written. Topics discussed here are mostly related to interpretation of the *Madhyamakālaṃkāra*. Major points are:

- the definition of ground, path and resultant middle way;
- the sub-schools of Svātantrika Mādhyamika;
- on how *Madhyamakālaṃkāra* is the ornament of all Mādhyamika schools;
- acceptance of a shared subject for debate in the two Mādhyamika schools;
- the usage of terms 'ultimate' and 'hypostatic existence' with the negandum;
- external entities and the Mind Only assertions;

- reflexive awareness;
- Tsongkhapa's theory of *zhig pa dngos po*;
- *Arhat*s and non-self of phenomena;
- Candrakīrti's three apagogic reasonings;
- Tsongkhapa's assertion of all grasping at hypostatic existence (*bden 'dzin*) to be obscuration of afflictive emotions (*nyon mongs pa'i sgrib pa*).

In this text, Mipham also takes the *gzhan stong* stance, although he declares that it is not his own position, and defends the *gzhan stong* view against the offhanded criticism of Damchö. Throughout his work, Mipham strives to interpret the teachings of great Indian masters such as Maitreya and Nāgārjuna, Dharmakīrti and Candrakīrti without contradiction. Mipham ends by saying that he did not write this to bring conflict between schools and that he avoided writing in detail for fear of offending people. The work was completed within two days.

APPENDIX IV

Tibetan names

Akhu Sherab Gyatsho	A khu Shes rab rGya mtsho
Akyā Yongzin Lobzang Dondrub	A kyā Yongs 'dzin Blo bzang Don grub
Amdo Gedun Chöphel	A mdo dGe 'dun Chos 'phel
Balmang Konchog Gyaltshan	dBal mang dKon mchog rGyal mtshan
Barawa Gyaltshan Palzang	'Ba' ra ba rGyal mtshan dPal bzang
Bodong Paṇchen Chogle Namgyal	Bo dong Paṇ chen Phyogs las rNam rgyal
Bodong Jigdrel/Jigdrak	Bo dong 'Jigs bral/'Jigs grags
Bodpa Trulku Dongag Tanpai Nyima	Bod pa sPrul sku mDo sngags bsTan pa'i Nyi ma
Bumsar Geshe	Bum gsar dGe bshes
Butön Rinchen Drub	Bu ston Rin chen Grub
Chag Lotsāwa Chöje Pal	Chag Lo tsā ba Chos rje dPal
Changkya Ngawang Lobzang Chödan	lCang skya Ngag dbang Blo bzang Chos ldan
Changkya Rolpai Dorje	lCang skya Rol pa'i rDo rje
Chapa Chökyi Seṅge	Cha pa/Phya pa Chos kyi Seṅge
Chari Kalzang Thogme	Cha ris sKal bzang Thogs med
Chim Jampaiyang	mChims 'Jam pa'i dByangs
Chim Lobzang Drak	mChims Blo bzang Grags
Chogro Lüi Gyaltshan	Cog ro Klu'i rGyal mtshan
Chogjur Lingpa	mChog gyur Gling pa
Chomdan Rigpai Raldi	bCom ldan Rig pa'i Ral gri
Chone Jetsün Drakpa Shedrub	Co ne rJe btsun Grags pa bShad grub
Chungtrug Jampa Tashi	Khyung phrug Byams pa bKra shis
Chukye Samten	Chu skyes bSam gtan
Dagpo Tashi Namgyal	Dwags po bKra shis rNam rgyal
Danbag Nechung	Dan bag gNas chung
Danma Lobzang Chöying	lDan/'dan ma Blo bzang Chos dbyings

Derge/Derge Chözod Chenmo	sDe dge/sDe dge Chos mdzod Chen mo
Desi Sangye Gyatsho	sDe srid Sangs rgyas rGya mtsho
Dodrak Rigzin Ngagi Wangpo	rDo brag Rig 'dzin Ngag gi dBang po
Dodrub Jigme Thinley Özer	rDo grub Jigs med 'Phrin las 'Od zer
Dodrub Tanpai Nyima	rDo grub bsTan pa'i Nyi ma
Dokhar Tshering Wangyal	mDo mkhar Tshe ring dBang rgyal
Dolpopa Sherab Gyaltshan	Dol po pa Shes rab rGyal mtshan
Dorje Shugdan	rDo rJe Shugs ldan
Dowa/Dodrub Damchö	rDo ba/rDo grub Dam chos
Drajor Sherab	Grags 'byor Shes rab
Drakar Trulku Paldan Tenzin Nyandra	Brag dkar sPrul sku dPal ldan bsTan 'dzin sNyan Grags
Drathang Khenpo	Grwa thang mKhan po
Drechenpo Sherab Bar	'Bre Chen po Shes rab 'Bar
Drepung/Loseling/Gomang	'Bras spungs/Blo gsal Gling/sGo mang
Drigung Palzin	Bri gung dPal 'dzin
Drigung Kyobpa Jigten Gonpo	Bri gung sKyobs pa 'Jig rten mGon po
Dromtön Gyalwai Jungne	'Brom ston rGyal ba'i 'Byung gnas
Drogmi Lotsāwa Śākya Yeshe	'Brog mi lo tsā ba Śākya Ye shes
Drolungpa Lodoe Jungne	Gro lung pa Blo gros 'Byung gnas
Drubthob Ugyenpa	Grub thob O rgyan pa
Drukpa Pema Karpo	'Brug pa Padma dKar po
Drusha Sonam Seṅge	Bru sha bSod nams Seṅ ge
Dzogchen Pema Rigzin	rDzogs chen Padma Rig 'dzin
Gadan/Jangtse/Shartse	dGa' ldan/Byang rtse/Shar rtse
Gadan Chökhorling	dGa' ldan Chos 'khor Gling
Gadan Phodrang	dGa' ldan Pho brang
Gampopa Sonam Rinchen	sGam po pa bSod nams Rin chen
Gedun Drub	dGe 'dun Grub
Gelukpa/Gedanpa	dGe lugs pa/dGe ldan pa
Getse Paṇḍita Gyurme Tshewang Chogdrub	dGe rtse Paṇḍita 'Gyur med Tshe dbang mChog grub
Geuteng/Giteng Lobzang Paldan	sGe'u sting/sGis steng Blo bzang dPal ldan
Gö Lotsāwa Khugpa Lhatse	'Gos Lo tsā ba Khug pa lHa btsas
Gö Lotsāwa Zhönu Pal	'Gos Lo tsā ba gZhon nu dPal
Gomde Namkha Gyaltshan Zangpo	sGom sde Nam mkha' rGyal mtshan bZang po
Gönpo Chab	mGon po skyabs
Gönpo Namgyal	mGon po rNam rgyal
Gorampa Sonam Seṅge	Go rams pa bSod nams Seṅge
Gungruwa Gyaltshan Zangpo	Gung ru ba rGyal mtshan bZang po
Gungthang Jampaiyang	Gung thang 'Jam pa'i dByangs

Gungthang Konchog Tanpai Drönme	Gung thang dKon mchog bsTan pa'i sGron me
Guru Chöwang	Guru Chos dbang
Gyalrong Namkha Lhundrub	rGyal rong Nam mkha' lHun grub
Gyaltshab Je/Dharma Rinchen	rGyal tshab rJe/Dharma Rin chen
Gyalse Zhanphan Thaye	rGyal sras gZhan phan mTha' yas
Horkhang Sonam Palbar	Hor khang bSod nams dPal 'bar
Hwashang Mohoyen	Hwashang Mohoyen
Jadul Tsöndrü Bar	Bya 'dul brTson 'grus 'Bar
Jamyang Chöje	'Jam dbyangs Chos rje
Jamyang Gawai Lodoe/Legpa Chöjor	'Jam dbyangs dGa' ba'i Blo gros/Legs pa Chos 'byor
Jamyang Zhadpai Lodoe	'Jam dbyangs bZhad pa'i Blo gros
Jamyang Zhadpa Ngawang Tsöndrü	'Jam dbyangs bZhad pa Ngag dbang brTson 'grus
Jampa Lingpa	Byams pa Gling pa
Jamyang Khyentsei Wangpo	'Jam dbyangs mKhyen brtse'i dBang po
Jangdagpo	Byang bdag po
Japa [Alag] Dongag	'Gya pa/'Ja' pa [A lags] mDo sngags
Jatong Chingrupa	rGya stong Phying ru pa
Jedrung Gyurme	rJe drung 'Gyur med
Je Khenpo	rJe mkhan po
Jigme Lingpa	'Jigs med Gling pa
Jonang Chogle Namgyal	Jo nang Phyogs las rNam rgyal
Jonang Kunga Drolchog	Jo nang Kun dga' Grol mchog
Ju Mipham Namgyal Gyatsho	'Ju Mi pham rNam rgyal rGya mtsho
Jula Rinchen Gönpo	'Ju bla Rin chen mGon po
Jumo Hor Sa-ngag Choling	'Ju mo Hor gSang sngags Chos gling
Kadampa	bKa' gdams pa
Kagyu	bKa'/dKar brgyud
Kamtshangpa Palkhang Chözod	Kam tshang pa dPal khang Chos mDzod
Karma Konchog Zhönu	Karma dKon mchog gZhon nu
Karmapa Mikyod Dorje	Karma pa Mi bskyod rDo rje
Karmapa Rolpai Dorje	Karma pa Rol pa'i rDo rje
Karmapa Rangjung Dorje	Karma pa Rang 'byung rDo rje
Kathogpa Dampa Desheg	Kaḥ thog pa Dam pa bDe gshegs
Kathog Rigzin Tshewang Norbu	Kaḥ thog Rig 'dzin Tshe dbang Nor bu
Kawa Paltseg	Ka ba dPal brtsegs
Khangmar Rinchen	Khang dmar Rin chen
Khedrub Je/Geleg Palzang	mKhas grub rJe/dGe legs dPal bzang
Khedrub Tanpa Dargye	mKhas grub bsTan pa Dar rgyas

Khenchen Pema Dorje	mKhan chen Padma rDo rje
Khenpo Jigme Phuntsho	mKhan po 'Jigs med Phun tshogs
Khenpo Zhanga/Zhanphan Chökyi Nangwa	mKhan po gZhan dga'/gZhan phan Chos kyi sNang ba
Khon Konchog Gyalpo	mKhon dKon mchog rGyal po
Khu Dode Bar	Khu mDo sde 'Bar
Khujug	Khu byug
Konchog Jigme Wangpo	dKon mChog 'Jigs med dBang po
Kongtrul Lodoe Thaye	Kong sprul Blo gros mTha' yas
Kunkhyen Lodoe Rinchen Seṅge	Kun mkhyen Blo gros Rin chen Seṅge
Kunpal/Kunzang Paldan	Kun dpal/Kun bzang lPal ldan
Kunzang Chödrak	Kun bzang Chos grags
Kunga Drak	Kun dga' Grags
Labrang Tashikhyil	Bla brang bKra shis 'khyil
Lama Dampa Sonam Gyaltshan	Bla ma Dam pa bSod nams rGyal mtshan
Langnak Sonam Tanpa	Glang nag bSod nams brTan pa
Lithang Khenchen Lobzang Chödrak	Li thang mKhan chen Blo bzang Chos grags
Lobzang Phuntsho	Blo bzang Phun tshogs
Lochen Chabchog	Lo chen sKyabs mchog
Lodrenpa Darma Seṅge	lHo bran pa Dar ma Seṅge
Longchen Rabjampa Drime Özer	Klong chen Rab 'byams pa Dri med 'Od zer
Longdol Lama Ngawang Lobzang	Klong rdol Bla ma Ngag dbang Blo bzang
Lubum/Dobi Geshe Sherab Gyatsho	Klu 'bum/rDo sbis dGe shes Shes rab rGya mtsho
Lüga	Klu dga'
Machig Labdön	Ma gcig Lab sgron
Maja Jangchub Tsöndrü	rMa bya Byang chub brTson 'grus
Marpa Chökyi Lodoe	Mar pa Chos kyi Blo gros
Milarepa	Mi la ras pa
Minling Terchen Gyurme Dorje	sMin gling gTer chen 'Gyur med rDo rje
Möndropa	sMon gro pa
Müchen Konchog Gyaltshan	Mus chen dKon mchog rGyal mtshan
Nagtsho Tshultrim Gyalwa	Nag mtsho Tshul khrims rGyal ba
Naljor Seṅge	rNal 'byor Seṅge
Naro Bonchung	Na ro Bon chung
Ngaban Kunga	rNga ban Kun dga'
Ngaga/Ngawang Palzang	Ngag dga'/Ngag dbang dPal bzang
Ngagyur Nyingma/Nyingmapa	sNga 'gyur rNying ma/rNying ma pa

Ngari Paṇchen Padma Wangyal	mNga' ris Paṇ chen Padma dBang rgyal
Ngawang Chödrak	Ngag dbang Chos grags
Ngawang Lobzang Gyatsho	Ngag dbang Blo bzang rGya mtsho
Ngawang Tashi Namgyal	Ngag dbang bKra shis rNam rgyal
Ngog Lotsāwa Loden Sherab	rNgog Lo tsā ba Blo ldan Shes rab
Ngog Lekpai Sherab	rNgog Legs pa'i Shes rab
Ngorchen Konchog Lhundrub	Ngor chen dKon mchog lHun grub
Ngorchen Kunga Zangpo	Ngor chen Kun dga' bZang po
Ngulchu Dharmabhadra	dNgul chu Dharmabhadra
Norbu Tenzin	Nor bu bsTan 'dzin
Nub Sangye Yeshe	gNubs Sangs rgyas Ye shes
Nya Ön Kunga Pal	Nya dbon Kun dga' dPal
Nyaltön Paljor Lhundrub	gNyal ston dPal 'byor lHun grub
Nyangral Nyima Özer	Nyang ral Nyi ma 'Od zer
Nyedo Mrawai/Tsöndrü Seṅge	sNye mdo sMra ba'i/brTson 'grus Seṅge
Paltrul Ugyen Jigme Chökyi Wangpo	dPal sprul O rgyan 'Jigs med Chos kyi dBang po
Paṇchen Delek Nyima	Paṇchen bDe legs Nyi ma
Paṇchen Lobzang Chökyi Gyaltshan	Paṇ chen Blo bzang Chos kyi rGyal mtshan
Pagsam Wangpo	dPag bsam dBang po
Pang Lotsāwa Lodoe Tanpa	dPang Lo tsā ba Blo gros brTan pa
Pari Lobzang Rabsal	dPa' ris Blo bzang Rab gsal
Patshab Nyima Drak	Pa tshab Nyi ma Grags pa
Pawo Tsuglag Trengwa	dPa' bo gTsug lag Phreng ba
Pha Dampa Sangye	Pha Dam pa Sangs rgyas
Phagpa Lodoe Gyaltshan	'Phags pa Blo gros rGyal mtshan
Phagmo Drupa	Phag mo Gru pa
Phodrang Zhiwa Ö	Pho brang Zhi ba 'Od
Phurchog Jampa Gyatsho	Phur lcog Byams pa rGya mtsho
Rangtongpa	Rang stong pa
Redawa Zhönu Lodoe	Red mda' ba gZhon nu Blo gros
Rigzin Kunzang Sherab	Rig 'dzin Kun bzang Shes rab
Rinchen Zangpo	Rin chen bZang po
Rinpungpa	Rin spungs pa
Rongtön Sheja Kunrig/Śākya Gyaltshan	Rong ston Shes bya Kun rig/Śākya rGyal mtshan
Rongzom Chözang	Rong zom Chos bzang
Rudam Dzogchen Samtan Chöling	Ru dam rDzog chen bSam gtan Chos gling
Serdog/Zilung pa Śākya Chogdan	gSer mdog/Zi lung pa Śākya mChog ldan

Śākya Dorje	Śākya rDo rje
Śākya Zhonu	Śākya gZhon nu
Sakya/Sakyapa	Sa skya/Sa skya pa
Sakya Paṇḍita Kunga Gyaltshan	Sa skya Paṇḍita Kun dga' rGyal mtshan
Sera Jay/May	Se ra Byes/sMad
Sera Jetsün Chökyi Gyaltshan	Se ra rJe btsun Chos kyi rGyal mtshan
Śāntipa Lodoe Gyaltshan	Śāntipa Blos gros rGyal mtshan
Shenchen Kargyal	gShen chen dKar rgyal
Shenyen Maryulwa	bShes gnyen dMar yul ba
Sherab Seṅge	Shes rab Seṅge
Situ Paṇchen Chökyi Jungne	Si tu Paṇ chen Chos kyi 'Byung gnas
Sogdogpa Lodoe Gyaltshan	Sog zlog pa Blo gros rGyal tshan
Sonam Drakpa	bSod nams Grags pa
Sonam Chab	bSod nams sKyabs
Sonam Tsemo	bSod nams rTse mo
Sumpa Khenpo Yeshe Paljor	Sum pa mKhan po Ye shes dPal 'byor
Taglung Drakpa Pal	sTag lung Grags pa dPal
Tagtshang Lotsāwa Sherab Rinchen	sTag tshang Lo tsā ba Shes rab Rin chen
Tandar Lharampa	bsTan dar lHa rams pa
Tāranātha Kunga Nyingpo	Tāranātha Kun dga' sNying po
Tenzin Chögyal	bsTan 'dzin Grags pa
Tenzin Drakpa	bsTan 'dzin Grags pa
Tharpa Lotsāwa Nyima Gyaltshan	Thar pa Lo tsā ba Nyi ma rGyal mtshan
Throshul Jamdor/Jampal Dorje	Khro shul 'Jam rdor/'Jam dpal rDo rje
Thubtan Chödrak	Thub bstan Chos grags
Tölung Jamarwa	sTod lung rGya dmar ba
Trisong Detsan	Khri srong lDe btsan
Tri Ralpachen	Tri Ral pa can
Tshandrok Khenpo	mTshan sgrog mKhan po
Tsangnagpa Tsöndrü Seṅge	gTsang nag pa brTson 'grus Seṅge
Tsang pa	gTsang pa
Tsag/Tseg Wangchuk Seṅge	rTsag/brTsegs dBang phyug Seṅge
Tsan Khawoche	bTsan Kha bo che
Tshonawa Sherab Zangpo	mTsho sna ba Shes rab bZang po
Tsongkhapa Lobzang Drakpa	Tsongkhapa Blo bzang Grags pa
Thuken Chökyi Nyima	Thu'u kwan Chos kyi Nyi ma
Ugyen Lingpa	O rgyan Gling pa
Üepa Losal	dBus pa Blo gsal
Umapa Tsöndrü Seṅge/Pawo Dorje	dBu ma pa brTson 'grus Seṅge/dPa' bo rDo rje
Yagde Paṇchen	gYag sde Paṇ chen
Yagtrugpa Sangye Pal	gYag phrug pa Sangs rgyas dPal

Yeshe Ö	Ye shes 'Od
Yongzin Yeshe Gyaltshan	Yongs 'dzin Ye shes rGyal mtshan
Khenpo Yonga/Yontan Gyatsho	mKhan po Yon dga' or Yon tan rGya mtsho
Yumowa Mikyod Dorje	Yu mo ba Mi bskyod rDo rje
Zhang Yeshe De	Zhang Ye shes sDe
Zamthang Ngawang Lodoe Drakpa	'Dzam thang pa Ngag dbang Blo gros Grags pa
Zangring Drakpa Darma Tshultrim	Zang rings Grags pa Dar ma Tshul khrims
Zhabdrung Ngawang Namgyal	Zhabs drung Ngag dbang rNam rgyal
Zhamar Tenzin	Zhwa dmar bsTan 'dzin
Zhangthang Sagpa Jungne Yeshe	Zhang thang Sag pa 'Byung gnas Ye shes
Zhanphan Chökyi Lodoe	gZhan phan Chos kyi Blo gros
Zhantongpa	gZhan stong pa
Zhechen Drungyig Tenzin Gyaltshan	Zhe chen Drung yig bsTan 'dzin rGyal mtshan
Zhechen Gyaltshab Pema Namgyal	Zhe chen rGyal tshab Padma rNam rgyal
Zhechen Gyaltshab Kunzang Namgyal	Zhe chen rGyal tshab Kun bzang rNam rgyal
Zhechen Tannyi Dargyeling	Zhe chen bsTan gnyis Dar rgyas Gling
Zhuchen Tshultrim Rinchen	Zhu chen Tshul khrims Rin chen
Zu Gawai Dorje	gZu dGa' ba'i rDo rje

NOTES

INTRODUCTION

1 Russell (1998), p. 1087.
2 Quine (2000), p. 2.
3 *Sūtta Nipāta*, verses 9–13, 1119; *Dhammapada*, XX/7, and so on. See Chapter 2, n. 1.
4 MK, XXIV/14; *Vigrahavyāvartanī*, p. 70.
5 MA, VI/23.
6 See Chapter 3, p. 82.
7 See Chapter 4, n. 89 on the two ultimates.
8 Carroll (1998), p. 198.
9 Seyfort Ruegg (1967), p. 5.
10 *Catuḥśataka*, VIII/7.
11 Dreyfus (1997), p. 4.
12 See Dreyfus (2003) and Phuntsho (2004).
13 See Chapter 2, pp. 50–1.
14 Smith (1969) and (2001), pp. 227–33; Goodman (1981); Pettit (1998), pp. 32–64; Pettit (1999a), pp. 19–39; Dieter Schuh (1973), vol. XI/5.
15 MGS, vols Ae and Waṃ.
16 MGS, vol. Na, pp. 650–780. On Gesar, see also Stein (1959).
17 MGS, vol. Ja.
18 MGS, vol. Dhī, pp. 771–1118.
19 Ibid., pp. 89–253.
20 MGS, vol. Ka, pp. 71–138; Mipham Gyatsho (1993).
21 MGS, vol. Nga, pp. 525–90; Amdo Gedun Chöphel and Mipham (1996).
22 Traditional scholars such as Khenpo Jigme Phuntsho have it that Mipham composed his *Nges shes sgron me* when he was seven years old with Jula Rinchen Gönpo (*c.*1850–1920) as the scribe. See Jigme Phuntsho (2002), vol. iii, p. 184. The book does not however have a proper colophon and is not datable. In his commentary on *Nges shes sgron me*, Khenpo Kunpal (1872–1943), one of the well-known disciples of Mipham, provides us with a colophon written by Mipham when he was fifty-seven. Mipham says,

> Although this *Nges shes rin po che'i sgron me* was written as it fortuitously came to my mind in one session when I was very young and a beginner in my studies, there is no contradiction in its content and it holds pithy meaning. Therefore, I leave it as it is, without correction. This [colophon] is written by Mipham at [the age of] fifty-seven.

See Mipham Gyatsho and Kunzang Paldan (1997), p. 256. John Pettit's conjecture that the text probably was written when Mipham was seventeen seems to have no basis either. See Pettit (1998), p. 44. The earliest datable text is a prayer in Mipham's Gesar cycle written in 1859.

23 Smith (1969), p. 8 and (2001), p. 231.
24 MGS, vol. Om, pp. 497–837 and vol. Om, pp. 203–495.
25 Primordial Purity (*Ka dag*) is the term for the empty nature of all things in Dzogchen philosophy.
26 For Ngarabpas, see Chapter 2, n. 72.
27 For *rang stong* and *gzhan stong* controversy, see Chapter 2, n. 62 and Chapter 3, n. 107.
28 See Smith (2001), p. 231; Hookham (1991), p. 176; Streans (1999), p. 77; Williams (1998b), pp. 199–216 and (1999), pp. 1–5.
29 See Samuel (1993), pp. 465, 537; Kapstein (2000b), pp. 119–23.
30 Pettit (1999a), p. 112 and (1999b), pp. 1–4.
31 Kapstein (2000b), pp. 119–23.
32 Wangchuk, 'The Rnying ma Interpretation of the *Tathāgatagarbha* Theory', (forthcoming in the Proceedings of 10th Seminar of International Association of Tibetan Studies).
33 *gSung sgros*, 450: *rang lugs rab lan du gsal te rang stong smra ba'i lugs so//*
34 MGS, vol. 24, pp. 353–774.
35 MGS, vol. Ga, pp. 277–96.
36 Ibid., pp. 322–23.
37 MGS, vol. Ga, pp. 297–323.
38 For the *Ral gri rnam lnga* and *Utpal rnam lnga* see MGS, vol. 27, pp. 467–94; MGS, vol. 23, pp. 319–28; MGS, vol. Pa, pp. 787–820; MGS, vol. Kha, pp. 533–49.
39 MGS, vol. 22, pp. 427–710.
40 Pettit (1998 and 1999a).
41 Lipman (1981) and Doctor (2004).
42 Ehrhard (1998).
43 Mimaki (1982).
44 Mipham Gyatsho (1997b).
45 Kapstein (1988) and (2001), pp. 317–43.
46 Williams (1998b) and see Kapstein (2000b) for his critical review.
47 Padmakara Translation Group (2002) and Scott (2004).
48 *Nges shes sgron me*, Question IV/9: *ka dag bdar sha chod pa la// thal 'gyur lta ba mthar phyin dgos//* MGS, vol. Śrī, p. 88. See also, *Nges shes sgron me*, chapter III/8: *don dam rang ngo shes pa la// bden stong phu thag chod pa dgos//* In order to realize the self-nature of the ultimate, [one] must have fathomed the lack of hypostatic existence.
49 MGS, vol. Om, p. 813: *snang stong mnyam par nges shes rdzogs pa che// klu sgrub gzhung lugs bzang po kho nas mthong//*
50 Tagtshang Sherab Rinchen is perhaps the first to use this allegorical concept. See Tagtshang Lotsāwa (1999), p. 155.
51 *rGyan 'grel*, p. 321.

1 EMPTINESS: ITS SOTERIOLOGICAL, DOCTRINAL, ONTOLOGICAL AND HISTORICAL SIGNIFICANCE IN BUDDHISM

1 View, *darśana* or *dṛṣṭi* in Sanskrit and *lta ba* in Tibetan, covers both philosophically correct and erroneous viewpoints. However, in the context of this bifurcation, it refers to the right view *qua* correct understanding of reality.
2 MA, I/3. *dang po nga zhes bdag la zhen gyur cing// bdag gi 'di zhes dngos la chags skyes pa// zo khyun 'phyen ltar rang dbang med pa yi//*

3 PV, Pramāṇasiddhi/221: *ātmani sati parasaṃjñā svaparavibhāgāt parigrahadveṣau/ anayoḥ sampratibaddhāḥ sarve dośāḥ prajāyante// bdag yod na ni gzhan du shes// bdag gzhan cha las 'dzin dang sdang// de dag dang ni yongs 'brel las// nyes pa thams cad 'byung bar 'gyur//*

4 Ignorance equivalent to the grasping of 'I' and 'my/mine' is identified with the first link of the twelve links of the dependent origination. It is therefore the ignorance which is cause of rebirth in *saṃsāra*. It falls within the obscuration of defiling emotions (*kleśāvaraṇa, nyon mongs pa'i sgrib pa*) of the two obscurations and pertains to the defiling one (*kliṣṭa, nyon mongs can*) of the two kinds of ignorance known to later Indian commentarial literature.

5 Ibid., 215: *tanmūlāśca malāḥ sarve, sa ca satkāyadarśanam/ nyes kun de yi rtsa ba can// de yang 'jig tshogs lta ba yin//* See also verse 198: *mohaś ca mūlaṃ doṣāṇāṃ sa ca sattvagraho vinā/ gti mug nyes pa'i rtsa ba yin// de yang sems can 'dzin pa yin//*

6 Ibid., 215–6. Dharmakīrti argues against the proponents of *abhidharma* who assert that ignorance and view of substantiality are different *caitasikas*. On the relation between *'jig lta* and *ma rig pa/rmongs pa/gti mug* in Tsongkhapa's thought, see *Lam rim*, 234–5, 655–7 and in Mipham's, see MGS, vol. 20, p. 354. Both agree with Dharmakīrti in accepting that the *'jig lta* is a particular *ma rig pa*.

7 Āryadeva, *Catuḥśataka*, VI/10.

8 MA, VI/120: *nyon mongs skyon rnams ma lus 'jig tshogs la// lta las byung ba blo yis mthong 'gyur nas// bdag ni 'di yi yul du rtogs byas nas// rnal 'byor pa yis bdag ni 'gog par byed//*

9 PV, Pramāṇasiddhi/217, 224.

10 Ibid., 214: *mohāvirodhān maitryader nātyantaṃ doṣanigrahaḥ/ byams sogs rmongs dang 'gal med phyir// shin tu nyes pa tshar gcod min//*

Cutting across this general view, many Tibetan masters have accorded ethical values such as Bodhicitta and compassion the pivotal role in Mahāyāna soteriology. One such master is Paltrul Rinpoche, the famous exponent of *Bodhicaryāvatāra* and teacher of Mipham, who even went on to claim that Bodhicitta alone is sufficient to attain Buddhahood. Although this may not be taken literally, the emphasis on Bodhicitta is quite clear. Gombrich, in a recent work on the soteriological role of loving-kindness and compassion in early Buddhism, has also argued that these ethical principles have salvific efficacy on their own. See Gombrich (1997b).

11 Ibid., 255: *muktiastu śūnyatādṛṣṭes tadarthāḥ śeṣabhāvanāḥ/ stong nyid lta bas grol 'gyur gyi// sgom pa lhag ma de don yin//*

12 Āryadeva, *Catuḥśataka*, XII/13: *zhi sgo gnyis pa med pa dang// lta ba ngan rnams 'jig byed pa// sangs rgyas kun gyi yul gyur pa// bdag med ces ni bya bar brjod//*

13 Nāgārjuna, *Ratnāvalī*, I/29–36. Nāgārjuna's statements in these verses have become a hot topic of commentarial exposition and debate in Indo-Tibetan Mādhyamika studies. The verses, 35–7, which Candrakīrti cites to prove that Śrāvaka and Pratyekabuddhas also understand the Non-self of phenomena, is to become a major point of debate.

14 Ibid., I/30: *phung po de ltar mi bden par// mthong nas ngar 'dzin spong bar 'gyur// ngar 'dzin pa dag spangs nas ni// phyis ni phung po 'byung mi 'gyur//*

15 MK, XVIII/4: *mamety aham iti kṣīṇe bahirdhādhyātmam eva ca/ nirudhyata upādānaṃ tatkṣayāj janmanaḥ kṣayaḥ// nang dang phyi rol nyid dag la// bdag dang bdag gi snyam zad na// nye bar len pa 'gag 'gyur zhing// de zad pas na skye ba zad//*

16 Nāgārjuna, *Śūnyatāsaptatikārikā*, 62.

17 MK, XVIII/5: *karmakleśakṣayān mokṣaḥ, karmakleśā vikalpataḥ/ te prapañcāt prapañcas tu śūnyatāyāṃ nirudhyate// las dang nyon mong zad pas thar// las dang nyon mong rnam rtog las// de dag spros pas spros pa ni// stong pa nyid kyis 'gag par 'gyur//*

18 Āryadeva, *Catuḥśataka*, XIV/25.
19 BA, IX/26.
20 *Ketaka*, pp. 49–55, *rGyan 'grel*, pp. 313–21, *Nges shes sgron me*, Question II.
21 Candrakīrti (1912), pp. 19–23.
22 Ibid., p. 302.
23 The eighteen Emptinesses according to Candrakīrti are: 1. Emptiness of the internal, 2. Emptiness of the external, 3. Emptiness of both external and internal, 4. Emptiness of Emptiness, 5. Emptiness of the great, 6. Emptiness of the ultimate, 7. Emptiness of the conditioned, 8. Emptiness of the unconditioned, 9. Emptiness of the limitless, 10. Emptiness of the beginningless and endless, 11. Emptiness of the indisposable, 12. Emptiness of aseity, 13. Emptiness of all phenomena, 14. Emptiness of individual characteristics, 15. Emptiness of the unapprehended and 16. Emptiness of the unsubstantial nature. Candrakīrti summarizes them into four: 1. Emptiness of the substantial, 2. Emptiness of the unsubstantial, 3. Emptiness of the own being, 4. Emptiness of other being. The last two added to the first enumeration of sixteen makes it eighteen or this category of four added to the previous category makes the list of twenty Emptinesses.
24 Nāgārjuna, *Lokātītastava*, 27: *mtshan ma med pa ma rtogs par// khyod kyis thar pa med par gsungs//* Lack of characteristics (*animitta, mtshan ma med pa*), generally understood as a synonym of lack of elaborations (*aprapañca, spros pa med pa*), is another designation for Emptiness in Mahāyāna philosophy. However, this term as one of the three *vimokṣamukha*s, known from very early period of Buddhism, predates Mahāyāna tradition.
25 BA, IX/55: *kleśajñeyāvṛtitamaḥ pratipakṣo hi śūnyatā/ śīghraṃ sarvajñatākāmo na bhāvayati tāṃ katham// nyon mongs shes bya'i sgrib pa yi// mun pa'i gnyen po stong pa nyid// myur du thams cad mkhyen 'dod pas// de ni ci phyir sgom mi byed//*
26 MA, VI/79: *slob dpon klu sgrub zhabs kyi lam las ni// phyi rol gyur la zhi ba'i thabs med do//*
27 Dignāga, *Prajñāpāramitāpiṇḍārthasaṃgrahaḥ*, verse 1.
28 *smra bsam brjod med shes rab pha rol phyin//*
ma skyes ma 'gag nam mkha'i ngo bo nyid//
so so rang rig ye shes spyod yul ba//
dus gsum rgyal ba'i yum la phyag mtshal lo//

Although this popular verse is attributed to Rāhulabhadra by Tibetan scholars, it does not appear in the *Prajñāpāramitāstotra*, which is found at beginning of the *Suvikrāntavikrāmiparipṛcchā, Aṣṭasāhasrikā* and *Pañcaviṃśatisāhasrikā-prajñāpāramitāsūtra*s and commonly said to be by Rāhulabhadra. Moreover, the Tibetan *bstan 'gyur* attributes the *Prajñāpāramitāstotra* to Nāgārjuna.
29 *Saṃcayagāthā*, II/4; *Aṣṭasāhasrikā*, XIII/281.
30 Maitreya, *Abhisamayālaṃkārānāmaprajñāpāramitopadeśaśāstra*, verse 1. The *Prajñā- pāramitāstotra* also assert Prajñāpāramitā to be the sole path to liberation. See Rāhulabhadra, *Prajñāpāramitāstotra*, verse 17.
31 BA, IX/1: *imaṃ parikaraṃ sarvaṃ, prajñārthaṃ hi munir jagau/ tasmād utpādayet prajñāṃ duḥkhanivṛttikāṅkṣayā// yan lag 'di dag thams cad ni// thub pas shes rab don du gsungs// de yi phyir na sdug bsngal dag// zhi bar 'dod pas shes rab bskyed//*
32 Tsongkhapa (1980), *sPyod 'jug shes rab le'u'i ṭīkā blo gsal ba*, p. 652. The argument is also reproduced verbatim in *rGyal sras 'jug ngogs*, p. 363. *Rab gsal*, pp. 357–61.
33 *Ketaka*, pp. 4–5, 138–41.
34 *Saṃcayagāthā*, VII/1.
35 MK, I/Preliminary verses: *anirodham anutpādam/ anucchedam aśāśvatam/ anekār- tham anānārtham, anāgamam anirgamam// yaḥ pratītyasamutpādaṃ prapañcopaśamaṃ śivam/ deśayāmāsa sambuddhas taṃ vande vadatāṃ varam// gang gis rten cing 'brel bar byung// 'gag pa med pa skye med pa// chad pa med pa rtag*

pa med pa// 'ong ba med pa 'gro med pa// tha dad don min don cig min// spros pa nyer zhi zhi ston pa// rdzogs pa'i sangs rgyas smra rnams kyi// dam pa de la phyag 'tshal lo//

36 MK, XXIV/18: *yaḥ pratītyasamutpādaḥ śūnyatāṃ tāṃ pracakṣmahe/ rten cing 'brel bar byung ba gang// de ni stong pa nyid du bshad//*

37 MK, XXIV/19: *apratītyasamutpanno dharmaḥ kaścin na vidyate/ yasmāt tasmād aśūnyo hi dharmaḥ kaścin na vidyate// gang zhig rten 'brel ma yin pa'i// chos 'ga' yod pa ma yin no// de phyir stong nyid ma yin pa'i// chos 'ga' yod pa ma yin no//*

38 Nāgārjuna, *Vigrahavyāvartanī*, p. 22: *yaś ca pratītyabhāvo bhāvānāṃ śūnyateti sā proktā/ rten nas 'byung ba'i dngos rnams gang// de ni stong nyid ces brjod de//*

39 MK, XVIII/6–8, *Yuktiṣaṣṭikākārikā*, pp. 31–6, *Ratnāvalī*, IV/95.

40 Āryadeva, *Catuḥśataka*, VII/20, VII/15.

41 BA, II/57.

42 MA, VI/94–7.

43 MA, VI/80: *upāyabhūtaṃ vyavahārasatyam upeyabhūtaṃ paramārthasatyam/ tayor vibhāgaṃ na paraiti yo vai mithyāvikalpaiḥ sa kumāragayātaḥ// tha snyad bden pa thabs su gyur pa dang// don dam bden pa thabs byung gyur pa ste// de gnyis rnam dbye gang gis mi shes pa// de ni rnam rtog log pa'i lam ngan zhugs//*

44 BA, IX/3–4.

45 AK, VI/67: *anutpādakṣayajnāne bodhih . . . / zad dang mi skye shes pa ni// byang chub . . . //*

46 Maitreya, *Mahāyānasutrālaṃkāra*, VI/2: *tataś ca mokṣo bhramamātrasaṃkṣayaḥ/ de phyir thar pa nor tsam zad pa yin//*

47 MK, XVIII/5: *karmakleśakṣayān mokṣaḥ/ las dang nyon mongs zad pas thar//*

48 Gombrich (1997a), pp. 67–70. Gombrich also mentions that *nirvāṇa* is synonymous to *bodhi* but Mahāyānists later restricted the use to Hināyāna liberation and looked down on it. However, Nāgārjuna's theory and many other Mahāyāna treatment of *nirvāṇa* seem to suggest otherwise.

49 BA, IX/104.

50 MK, XXV/3: *aprahīṇam asaṃprāptam anucchinnam aśāśvatam/ aniruddham anutpannam etan nirvāṇam ucyate// spangs pa med pa thob med pa// chad pa med pa rtag med pa// 'gag pa med pa skye med pa// de ni mya ngan 'das par brjod//*

51 Ibid., XXV/13: *asaṃskṛtaṃ hi nirvāṇaṃ bhāvābhāvau ca saṃskṛtau/ dngos dang dngos med 'dus byas yin// mya ngan 'das pa 'dus ma byas//*

52 Nāgārjuna, *Ratnāvalī*, I/42: *dngos dang dngos po med 'dzin pa// zad pa mya ngan 'das zhes bya//*

53 Nāgārjuna, *Yuktiṣaṣṭikākārikā*, verse 36.

54 MK, XXV/24: *sarvopalambhopaśamaḥ prapañcopaśamaḥ śivaḥ/ dmigs pa thams cad nyer zhi zhing// spros pa nyer zhi zhi ba ste//*

55 Āryadeva, *Catuḥśataka*, XII/23: *chos ni mdor na mi 'tshe bar// de bzhin gshegs pa rnams kyis gsungs// stong nyid mya ngan 'das pa ste// 'dir ni de gnyis 'ba' zhig go //*

56 BA, IX/111: *nirāśritatvan nodeti tvac ca nirvānam ucyate// rten med phyir na mi skye ste// de yang mya ngan 'das par brjod//*

57 I owe this idiomatic presentation to Isabelle Onians.

58 MK, XXV/19.

59 Ibid., XXV/20: *nirvāṇasya ca yā koṭiḥ koṭiḥ saṃsārṇaasya ca/ na tayor antaraṃ kiṃcit susūkṣamam api vidyate// mya ngan 'das mtha' gang yin pa// de ni 'khor ba'i mtha' yin te// de gnyis khyad par cung zad ni// shin tu phra ba'ang yod ma yin//*

60 Nāgārjuna, *Yuktiṣaṣṭikākārikā*, verse 7: *srid pa yongs su shes pa ni// mya ngan 'das pa zhes byar brjod//*

61 Stcherbatsky (1996), p. 56. See also Fatone (1981), p. 2.

62 Later Mahāyāna hermeneuticians classified *nirvāṇa* into the innate *nirvāṇa* (*rang bzhin myang 'das*) and resultant *nirvāṇa*, which include the three traditional categories of *nirvāṇa* with residue. (*sopadhiśeṣanirvāṇa, lhag bcas myang 'das*), *nirvāṇa* without

residue (*nirupadhiśeṣanirvāṇa, lhag med myang 'das*) and non-abiding *nirvāṇa* (*apratiṣṭhitanirvāṇa, mi gnas myang 'das*) and argued that the ontological *nirvāṇa qua* Emptiness taught by Nāgārjuna and others concerns the innate *nirvāṇa*. Thus, it is understood to be different from the *nirvāṇa* which is the result. Others however saw *nirvāṇa* both as ontological truth and soteriological goal equating it with Emptiness in the first case and with enlightenment in the second. Taking the *nirvāṇa* as ontological truth, they formulated that the state of *nirvāṇa qua* enlightenment is just to be in the state of *nirvāṇa qua* Emptiness. This became particularly important to the Vajrayāna schools who professed the identity of the ontological ground and the soteorological result.

63 Murti (1998), p. vii.
64 Stcherbatsky (1996), p. 42.
65 Seyfort Ruegg (1981), p. 7.
66 Stcherbatsky (1996), pp. 43–4.
67 Murti (1998), pp. 8–9.
68 Hopkins (1996), p. 9.

2 THE BIG FUSS ABOUT EMPTINESS: AN OUTLINE OF THE HISTORY OF DEBATES ON EMPTINESS

1 In the Pali canon, there is 'Mogharāja's Questions' in the *Sūtta Nipāta* (SN), v, 16 (verse 1119) where the Buddha describes the world as empty. *Sūtta Nipāta*, verses 9–13 describe things as unreal. The *Cūḷasuññatasutta* in the MN, iii, 104–9 = pp. 965–70 gives a detailed presentation of Emptiness where Emptiness of *x* means absence of *y* in *x* but not of *x* itself. The *Mahāsuññatasutta* in MN does not touch upon the current concept of Emptiness despite its title. See also MN, i, 297 = p. 394; i, 302 = p. 400; ii, 265 = p. 871; iii, 294 = p. 1143. MN, i, 65 = p.160–1 on the views of being and non-being and proliferation may perhaps have had significant bearing on Nāgārjuna's theory of Emptiness transcending entity (*bhāva*) and non-entity (*abhāva*). SN, ii, 17 = vol. I, p. 544 contains the discourse to Kaccānagotta, which Nāgārjuna cites in MK, IX/7. SN, iii, 140–2 = vol. I, pp. 951–3 contains the discourse on similes of the five aggregates, which Candrakīrti later cites in his *Prasannapadā*, p. 15 and *Madhyamakāvatārabhāṣya*, p. 22, most likely from a Sarvāstivādin *Saṃyuktāgama*. See also SN, ii, 267 = vol. I, p. 709; iv, 54 = vol. II, pp. 1163–4; iv, 175 = vol. II, pp. 1238; iv, 297 = vol. II, pp. 1325–6; v, 407 = vol. II, p. 1834; AN, i, 73 = vol. I, p. 68; i, 286 = vol. I, p. 265; i, 297 = vol. I, p. 276; ii, 106 = vol. III, p. 85; DN, xxxiii. 1. 10 = vol. III, p. 219, see *Patisambhidāmagga*, i, 39, 317, 327, 435, 439, 446, 514–15, iii, 200, v, 3, 55, 67, 69, 94, xx, 1–26. The term *suññata* in these sources mainly appears among the triad of Signlessness, Emptiness and Desirelessness and is often glossed as 'empty of self and of what belongs to self'.

The Sarvāstivādin canon contains among Mahāsūtras, the *Śūnyatānāmamahāsūtra* and *Mahāśūnyatānāmamahāsūtra* which corresponds to the *Cūḷasuññatasutta* and *Mahāsuññatasutta* in MN. See *Mahāsūtras*, vol. I, pp. 146–87, 188–263. The former one seems to have been used by the Cittamātra philosophers to support their interpretation of Emptiness and later by the Jonangpa proponents of *gZhan stong* philosophy, who seem to have included both *Śūnyatānāmamahāsūtra* and *Mahāśūnyatānāmamahāsūtra* among the thirty definitive *sūtras* (*nītārthasūtra, nyes don gyi mdo*) according to a list by a certain Jamyang Zhadpai Lodoe. See *Mahāsūtras*, vol. I, pp. 343–4. The *Mahājālamahāsūtra* also discusses, using similes, how the sense objects of three times lack permanent (*rtag pa*), eternal (*brtan pa*), absolute (*ther zug*) and hypostatic (*bden pa*) nature. It is comparable to the SN, iii, 140–2, which Candrakīrti cited to prove that Śrāvaka also understood *dharmanairātmya*. The

Suvarṇabhāsottamasūtra contains a chapter on Emptiness, comparing the body to an empty village and senses to six village thieves. See *The Sūtra of Golden Light*, pp. 21–4 and SN, iv, 175. Emptiness is also treated in Nidāna Saṃyukta of the Sarvāstivādin in the context of *pratītyasamutpāda* and *madhyamā pratipad*. See Tripāṭhī (1962), pp. 152–7. Vasubandhu gives two citations, one from an unidentified sūtra and the other from Kṣudra Āgama, which explain Emptiness in terms of absence of a person. See *Abhidharmakoṣabhāṣya*, Pudgalaviniścaya, pp. 1202–3. In considering the content of Sarvāstivādin canon, it may be notable that with the addition of the Mahāyāna and Vajrayāna literature to the canon, the original Sarvāstivādin doctrine, except for the *vinaya* section, seems to have got immensely eclipsed by the Mahāyāna thought. This is more so because it was passed down through Mahāyāna persons, who did not advocate the Sarvāstivadin philosophical viewpoints. On the matter of Emptiness in the canons, see also Gómez (1976), pp. 137–65; Seyfort Ruegg (1981), p. 7; Mun-Keat (2000), pp. 92–7.

2 While most Mahāyāna and Vajrayāna *sūtra*s deal with Emptiness to some degree, the following are some of the *sūtra*s which, beside the *Prajñāpāramitāsūtra*s, formed important sources for the philosophy of Emptiness and for the Mādhyamika system: the *Kaśyapaparivarta*, the *Daśabhūmika*, the *Vimalakīrtinirdeśa*, the *Śūraṃgamasamādhi*, the *Ākṣayamatinirdeśa*, the *Tathāgataguhyaka*, the *Pitāputrasamāgama*, the *Mañjuśrīparipṛcchā*, the *Upāliparipṛcchā*, the *Satyadvayāvatāra*, the *Samādhirāja*, the *Lalitavistara*. The *Ratnakūta*, the *Avataṃsaka*, the *Saddharmapuṇḍarīka* and the *Laṅkāvatāra* are also major canonical sources for Mahāyāna philosophy. Among them, the *Laṅkāvatāra* form an important source for the Cittamātra understanding of Emptiness. See also Seyfort Reugg (1981), p. 7.

3 Major *Prajñāpāramitāsūtra*s are the *Śatasāhasrikāprajñāpāramitā*, the *Pañcaviṃśatisāhasrikāprajñāpāramitā*, the *Aṣṭādaśasāhasrikāprajñāpāramitā*, the *Daśasāhasrikāprajñāpāramitā*, the *Aṣṭasāhasrikāprajñāpāramitāsūtra* and the *Prajñāpāramitāratnaguṇasaṃcayagāthā*. These six are known as the six mothers (*yum drug*). The first two and the fifth are also respectively known as the three extensive, medium and condensed mothers (*yum rgyas 'bring bsdus gsum*). There are other *sūtra*s such as the, *Suvikrāntavikrāmiparipṛcchaprajñāpāramitā*, the *Saptaśatikāprajñāpāramita*, the *Pañcaśatikaprajñāpāramitā*, the *Vajracchedikāprajñāpāramitā*, the *Prajñāpāramitāpañcāśikā*, the *Prajñāpāramitāhṛdaya*, the *Adhyardhaśatikāprajñāpāramitā*, the *Svalpākṣarāprajñāpāramitā*, the *Kauśikaprajñāpāramitā*, the *Pancaviṃśatiprajñāpāramitā* and the *Bhagavatīprajñāpāramitāsarvatathāgatamātāek ākṣarānāma*. These eleven are known as eleven sons (*sras bcu gcig*) totalling seventeen mother and son *Prajñāpāramita* (*sher phyin yum sras bcu bdun*) literature known among commentators of Maitreya's *Abhisamayālaṃkāra*. See Butön (1989), p. 216. There are also other *Prajñāpāramitāsūtra*s not included in this enumeration or translated into Tibetan. Conze considers the *Aṣṭasāhasrikāprajñāpāramitāsūtra* to be the earliest, parts of it dating back to 100 BC and the 100,000 lines, 25,000 lines, 18,000 lines to be expansions of it around the beginning of Christian era. The short *sūtra*s, among them the *Heart Sūtra* and *Diamond Sūtra*, are dated before 400 AD. Among the verses, he conjectures that the first two chapters of *Ratnaguṇasaṃcayagāthā* may form the original dating back to 100 BC. See Conze (1973) and (1978).

4 See, for instance, the *Heart Sūtra* and the *Ratnaguṇasaṃcayagāthā*. The *Aṣṭasāhasrikāprajñāpāramitā*, ii, 40 depicts even *nirvāṇa* as illusory. See *Rab lan*, pp. 233, 259, where Mipham cites *Susthitamatidevaputraparipṛcchāsūtra* and *Mañjuśrīvihārasūtra* giving accounts of how several monks rejected Mañjusrī's understanding of Emptiness. See *rGyan 'grel*, p. 267 where he mentions debate between the Buddha and Mañjusrī in one of the past lifetimes.

5 See also *Milindapañha*, pp. 25, 54 and *Katthāvatthu*, i, 1; xix, 2, 5. See Lamotte (1988), pp. 605–7.
6 *Patisambhidāmagga*, i, 514–15 and xx, 3.
7 *Kathāvatthu*, i, 1; xix, 2; xvii, 6.
8 Ibid., xvii, 6; xviii, 1, 2. The debate between Theravādins and Vetulayakas however is not on Emptiness.
9 The relationship between Sarvāstivāda and Vaibhāṣika is not clearly defined although many scholars, both traditional and modern, are inclined to regard them as one or at least doctrinally very similar. However, it appears that Vaibhāṣika developed as an intellectual school like Sautrāntika, Yogācāra and Mādhyamika, albeit wide spread among Sarvāstivādin monks, while Sarvāstivāda was primarily a monastic order, a major *nikāya*, although it professed unique doctrinal viewpoints. For Sarvāstivādin and Vaibhaṣika connexion, see also Paul Williams in Craig (1998), vol. 2, p. 77 and C. Lindtner in Carr and Mahalingam (1997), p. 330.
10 See Chapter 2, n. 1.
11 *Vibhāṣā*, TD 27, p. 37a12.
12 The Sarvāstivāda–Vaibhāṣika philosophers classified things into substantially existent (*dravyasat, rdzas yod*) and imputedly existent (*prajñaptisat, btags yod*). All things with discrete existence possessing general and specific characteristics (such as impermanence and audibility of sound) are substantial and real whereas things such as forest, stream, which are made up of basic *dharma*s and are thus not perceivable on their own only have a mentally constructed existence. However, the word 'empty' is rarely used and even the insubstantiality of the *prajñaptisat*, which from the Mahāyāna viewpoint can be understood to be *dharmanairātmya* and therefore Emptiness, is not described as empty. The Sarvāstivādin did not seem to make any distinction of two truths but the Vaibhāṣikas delineated a theory of two truths in which only partless atoms and moments of consciousness and unconditioned things are ultimate entities and all the rest are relatively existent. See AK, VI/4.
13 See Bareau (1955), pp. 76, 82, 84–5; Dutt (1978), p. 127; Conze (1978), p. 1; Williams (1989); Ramanan (1998), p. 53–62; who bases their study on the accounts of eighteen *nikāya*s by Bhavya, Vasumitra and in the *Kathāvatthu*. Venkata Ramanan divides the early *nikāya* into three broad lines of doctrinal philosophy. The pluralistic line included the Sarvāstivādin and its sub-schools who held the view that substances and elements are real and absolute, and that Emptiness in the *sūtra* only referred to the absence of an absolute self. The Sthavira seceded from Sarvāstivādin and formed the second line, which also included other *nikāya*s such as Saṃmitīya, Vatsīputrīya, Mahīśāsaka and the Sautrāntika. They too held the real existence of fundamental substances or *dharma* but differed from the Sarvāstivādin in taking them as being more conditioned, changing and in the process of becoming. They laid more emphasis on the meaningfulness of the subjectivity in contrast to the extreme objectivism of the Sarvāstivādin. His third line, called the absolutist line, covers the philosophical thought of the Mahāsāṅghika and its offshoots. Of them he says:

> The credit of keeping alive the emphasis on the ultimacy of the unconditioned reality by drawing attention to the non-substantiality of the basic elements of existence (*dharma–śūnyatā*) belongs to the Mahāsāṅghikas. Every branch of these clearly drew the distinction between the mundane and the ultimate, came to emphasize the non-ultimacy of the mundane and thus facilitated the fixing of attention on the ultimate. The Bahuśrutīyas distinguished the mundane from the transmundane teachings of the Buddha and held that the

> latter directly lead one to freedom from defilements. These were the teachings of the impermanence of the composite, the painful nature of the defiled, *śūnyatā* of the composite as well as the incomposite, the absence of self-being in things and the peace of Nirvāṅa. The Prajñaptivādins maintained that the *skandhas* in their true nature do not constitute pain, that they are conditionally named 'pain' only when they combine to constitute the complexes of defiled entities. They maintained also that the twelve *āyatanas* are not real entities. It is in the Ekavyāvahārikas however, that one finds the full-fledged doctrine of the non-substantiality of elements. They maintained that all things, mundane as well as transmundane, the self as well as the elements, are only derived names and devoid of substantiality. Ekavyavāhārikas were the first to branch off from their main stem, the Mahāsāṅghikas, perhaps only geographically and not doctrinally, for Vasumitra puts them along with the latter and not separately. The Lokottaravādins maintained the distinction between mundane and the transmundane and held the former as unreal and the latter as real.

Nalinaksha Dutt, following Paramārtha, states 'the Prajñaptivādin held the view that the twelve *āyatana* are not real and like the Mahāyānists held that Buddha's teachings as embodied in the *Pitaka* should be distinguished as nominal (*prajñapti*), conventional (*saṃvṛti*) and causal (*hetuphala*)'. Edward Conze states that doctrines which the *Kathāvatthu* attributes to the Andhakas are so much akin to the Mahāyāna doctrine that the latter may well have developed from them. Paul Williams discusses the *Lokānuvartanasūtra*, which, he says, Candrakīrti quotes as a *sūtra* of Pūrvaśaila, and which teaches both the doctrine of supramundane Buddha and the absence of ultimate, inherent existence in all things, including *dharmas*. 'Thus', he adds, 'not only is the emptiness of *dharmas* found in non-Mahāyāna text (the same is also found in the non-Mahāyāna *Satyasiddhiśāstra* of Harivarman), but this *sūtra* was later accepted into the Mahāyāna.'

However, Williams argues that Buddhist monastic schism happened due to discrepancies in monastic practice and that philosophical dissension did not play any role in the division of *sangha*. Although one's philosophical and ideological stance did not hinder one's affiliation to a certain monastic lineage, it is hard to rule out any monastic split through philosophical differences. It is true that intellectual schools like the Sautrāntika only existed as a school of thought without any monastic base, and that a monastery could also harmoniously host monks of conflicting philosophical viewpoints. Yet, both the Theravādin and Sarvāstivādin *vinaya* discuss disputes happening within the *sangha* due to disparities in philosophical assertions. The records of the second and third councils also mention the doctrinal disputes as well as laxity in monastic discipline. Thus, it would be presumptuous to say that none of the monastic divisions resulting in some eighteen different groups has occurred through philosophical differences. Doctrinal differences, particularly the understanding of what is real and unreal, seem to have had considerable significance in the formation of diverging denominations.

14 SN, iii, 25; see Bareau (1955), pp. 114–26.

15 For the presentation of *pudgala* theory and refutations, see *Saṃmitīyanikāyaśāstra*, T 1649; *Kathāvatthu*, i, 1; *Vibhāṣā*, T 1545, chapter 9; *Abhidharmakoṣabhāṣya*, IX.

16 Roger Jackson uses Sautrantika to refer to (1) An anti-*abhidharma* school, (2) School reflected in Vasubandhu's criticism of *abhidharma* and (3) Pramāṇa School of Dignāga and Dharmakīrti. See Carr and Mahalingam (1997), p. 332. The division however is inaccurate as the second one cannot be considered separate from the first because Vasubandhu's criticisms are the most well-known refutations of Sarvāstivādin

abhidharma by a non-Mahāyānist. Moreover, the first is clearly an overstatement as not all anti-*abhidharma* schools are Sautrāntika. Tibetan scholars refer to two kinds of Sautrāntika: those following scriptures (*lung gi rjes 'brangs*) and those following reasons (*rigs pa'i rjes 'brangs*). The former adheres to Sautrāntika tenets presented in *Abhidharmakoṣa* and its *bhāṣya*, and latter to the Sautrāntika philosophy in Dharmakīrti's seven logico-epistemological treatises. This classification introduced by Tibetan doxographers, or at the earliest by some late Indian scholars, do not clarify the historical sources of Sautrāntika. They only show the works which contain Sautrāntika thoughts and are available to us.

17 MGS, 21, p. 30 and MGS, 22, p. 51. The Gelukpas, however, take not only unassociated conditioned factors but also some universals, which Mipham take to be nominal, to be substantial according to Sautrāntika.

18 Tāranātha (1986), chapter 15, p. 95 mentions a refutation of Mahāyāna in 12,000 verses by a certain bDe byed.

19 See *Ratnāvalī*, IV/68–100, *Mahāyānasaṃgraha*, Prastāvanā; *Mahāyānasutrālaṃkāra*, II; *Madhyamakahṛdaya*, III; BA, IX/41–52.

20 *Ratnāvalī*, IV/86: *Theg chen las ni skye med bstan// gzhan gyis zad pa stong pa nyid// zad dang mi skye don du ni// gcig pas de phyir bzod par gyis//*

Nāgārjuna observes that the Emptiness *qua* non-production in Mahāyāna is the same as Emptiness understood to be cessation/extinction by others (i.e. Śrāvakas. Some versions read 'khyod kyis' – by you – instead of 'gzhan gyis' – by others – in the second line). For this reason, he argues that they should accept Emptiness taught in the Mahāyāna.

BA, IX/41: *satyadarśanato muktiḥ śūnyatādarśanena kiṃ/ bden pa mthong bas grol 'gyur gyi// stong nyid mthong bas ci zhig bya//*

Śāntideva presents this objection from his opponents, thought to be Śrāvakas by his commentators, that seeing the four noble truths is sufficient for liberation and there is no need for seeing Emptiness. Śāntideva replies in detail. This and verses after this were to become a topic of intense debate among his commentators in Tibet concerning the Śrāvaka soteriology. The *Ratnāvalī* mentions Śāriputra and the BA Mahākāśyapa both to argue that Mahāyāna understanding cannot be invalidated just because Śrāvaka figures such as these did not comprehend it.

21 On Nāgārjuna and summary of his works, see Seyfort Ruegg (1981), pp. 4–49; Lindtner (1982).

22 For specific presentation of these schools, see for instance, MK, I/5, XVII/4 for Sarvāstivāda–Vaibhāṣika, VII/4, XVII/13–5 for Saṃmitīya, IX/1 for Vātsīputrīya and XVII/7 for Sautrāntika. MK, XXIV/1–9 gives a general opposition of the Buddhist substantialist and most of his work consists of thorough criticism of Buddhist and non-Buddhist substantialism in general.

23 Traditional historians credited Nāgārjuna with three classes of writings: the scholastic (*rigs tshogs*), hymnic (*bstod tshogs*) and homiletic (*gtam tshogs*) corpuses, to use Seyfort Ruegg's translation. The scholastic *rigs tshogs* or Yukti corpus includes the MK, *Yuktiṣaṣṭika*, *Śūnyatāsaptati*, *Vigrahavyāvartanī*, *Vaidalyasūtra* and certain lost **Vyavahārasiddhi* according to Butön, Longchenpa, Maja Jangchub Tsöndrü, Jigme Lingpa among many others. Tsongkhapa and his followers enumerated six in this corpus but substituted *Vyavahārasiddhi* by *Ratnāvalī*. Gorampa Sonam Seṅge is ambiguous saying five or six texts but Mipham classes *Ratnāvalī* in the homiletic corpus and thus enumerates only five texts in the Yukti corpus. There are a few other works ascribed to Nāgārjuna which would belong to this corpus but are often not enumerated. In the homiletic *gTam tshogs* or Parikathā corpus, the most well known is the *Suhṛllekha*. The hymnic *bsTod tshogs* or Stava corpus includes the *Dharmadhātustava*

and the collection of four *stavas*. See Seyfort Ruegg (1981) for the treatment of the three corpuses.

24 Due to the significant difference in presentation of the concept of the ultimate in the scholastic corpus and the hymnic corpus, some modern scholars questioned Nāgārjuna who has composed MK to have also composed the latter. Seyfort Ruegg observes that it is a convenient way for historians to take MK together with any other texts ascribed to Nāgārjuna that are doctrinally related as a standard point of reference to describe Nāgārjuna's philosophy. However, it is not an adequate determinant to decisively resolve all problems surrounding Nāgārjuna's authorship of works which tradition ascribe to him. According to him, the Yukti corpus delineate a negative theory of the *paramārtha* using an apophatic approach and the hymnic corpus delineate a positive theory employing a cataphatic approach. To these two, he also adds a third 'epochistic' approach connected with the inconceivability and ineffability of Emptiness. See Seyfort Ruegg (1981), pp. 8–9, 33–5. See Chapter 3, n. 1.

25 The *Hastavālaprakaraṇa*, its *vṛtti* and the *Jñānasārasamuccaya* are ascribed to him by the Indo-Tibetan tradition and the *Śata(ka)śāstra* (Pai/Po-lun) and *Akṣaraśataka* and its *vṛtti* by the Chinese tradition. Several tantric works are also ascribed to him.

26 See for instance, his refutation of caste system in chapter VI, atomism in chapter IX, eternal self or soul in chapter X and the concept of time and the Sarvāstivādin acceptance of existence of phenomena in three times in chapter XI, besides his general critical investigation.

27 Tāranātha (1986), chapter 17, pp. 110–12; Butön (1989), p. 149.

28 The historicity of Maitreya is a complicated issue and has been raised by many modern scholars. Tradition has it that he is the same person as the future Buddha who is right now in Tuṣita heaven. His five works became the cornerstone of later Mahāyāna philosophy, particularly the Yogācāra school. The classification of his works between Mādhyamika and Yogācāra has also been a debated topic. Some scholars have considered all five to be Mādhyamika in their content while others took them to be of Cittamātra. The most common tradition seems to be to take, as the Gelukpas do, the *Abhisamayālaṃkāra* and *Ratnagotravibhāga* as Mādhyamika in their content and other three as Cittamātra. Mipham however argues that except for *Sūtralaṅkāra*, there is no reason why the *Madhyāntavibhāga* and *Dharmadharmatavibhāga* have to be classified exclusively as Cittamātra texts. He says that while *Madhyāntavibhāga* teaches the vast aspect of Mahāyāna, the *Dharmadharmatavibhāga* teaches the profound aspect of Mahāyāna in general. Thus, he considers both texts as general Mahāyāna works, which should not be confined to either the Mādhyamika or the Yogācāra.

29 The *sūtra*s teaching mind-only (*sems tsam bstan pa'i mdo*) include according to Mipham's enumeration, *Laṅkāvatārasūtra*, *Ghanavyūhasūtra*, *Sandhinirmocanasūtra*, *Pitāputrasamāgamasūtra*, *Samadhirājasūtra*, *Hastikakṣyasūtra*, *Akṣayamatinirdeśasūtra*, *Dharmasaṃgītisūtra*, *Sāgaranāgarājaparipṛcchāsūtra* and *Ratnameghasūtra*. They should not, however, be seen as *sūtra*s accepted only by the Yogācāra school. Cittamātra, in this case, connotes the idealist tendency of Mahāyāna Buddhism in general rather than the tenets exclusive to the Yogācāra school. In this respect, Mipham refers to two kinds of Cittamātra: the Cittamātra of canonical teachings (*bka'i sems tsam*) and the Cittamātra of the tenet system (*grub mtha'i sems tsam*). The first refers to the canonical teachings dealing with idealism or subjectivism and the latter with the Yogācāra philosophical school that developed through Maitreya, Asaṅga and Vasubandhu. Mipham argues that even the Mādhyamika should be considered to be the proponent of first Cittamātra, as they too must accept the *sūtra*s mentioned.

30 See *Madhyāntavibhāga*, chapter I and *Mahāyānasutrālaṃkāra*, chapter XI for presentation of the triad natures. See also *Mahāyānasutrālaṃkāra*, chapter VI on the ultimate reality.

31 The concept of luminous nature of mind is found in AN, I, 10; *Śatasāhasrikā*, III, 495–502; *Dharmadhātustava*, 12, 19, 21; *Mahāyānottaratantra*, I/63 and *Pramāṇavārttika*, Pramāṇasiddhi/210 and Vasumitra's treatise on the Buddhist schools. See De Jong (1979), pp. 48–9. The Yogācāra thinkers dissented from Mādhyamika in hypostasizing the luminous nature of mind, which they called the dependent consciousness (**paratantravijñāna, gzhan dbang gi rnam shes*). According to them, denying this fundamental consciousness would leave no basis or cause for the empirical world and consequently lead to the extreme of annihilation. They categorized mind, the dependent nature, into eight kinds of consciousnesses: the store-consciousness (*ālayavijñāna, kun gzhi*) which serves as the basis for all experiences, the defiled mind (*kliṣṭamanas, nyon yid*), which is an introvert 'I' clinging, and one mental and five sensory consciounesses, which are known as the engaging consciousnesses (*pravṛttivijñāna, 'jug pa'i rnam shes*).

The eight consciousnesses of the three realms are dualistic cognition. They apprehend external objects and mistake them for real. Because their objects do not exist, they are ultimately deluded and false. On the contrary, the substructural aspect of these consciousnesses, the pure essence of the mind, is ultimately existent. Mind, in its innate form, is pristine and luminous awareness free from the delusion of dual grasping. The eight peripheral consciousnesses, which are deluded and discursive are called impure dependent nature (*ma dag gzhan dbang*) while this pure essence of mind is called the pure dependent nature (*dag pa gzhan dbang*).

This concept of the self-conscious awareness (*shes pa rang rig rang gsal*) lies at the heart of later Yogācāra epistemology, ontology and soteriology. Through making this self-conscious awareness the pivot of their philosophy, the Yogācāra thinkers delineated a highly hypostasized theory of the dependent nature. All constructed things are not real as they seem to be, because they are mere projections of the discursive mind. Discursive mind in turn is not ultimately real because its objects and referents do not exist. Thus, the discursive mind too is negated and only its innate nature, the self-conscious awareness, is established to be ultimately existent. Although this concept of the self-conscious awareness is a cardinal point, it seems to have developed among later Yogācāra thinkers as it is not explicitly mentioned in the early works such as *Mahāyānasutrālaṃkāra* and *Madhyāntavibhāga*. The Mādhyamika including Candrakīrti and Śāntideva found this as the greatest flaw in the Yogācāra/Cittamātra philosophy and undertook rigorous refutation of this concept. See MA, VI/45–7, 72ab for his *pūrvapakṣa* presentation and VI/48–97 and BA, IX/17–33 for their refutations.

32 See *Madhyāntavibhāga*, I/6d, I/14, and *Mahāyānasutrālaṃkāra*, XI/13.

33 It is clear that the Yogācāra thinkers accepted the authority of the Mahāyāna *sūtra*s including the *Prajñāpāramitasūtra*s. However, they interpreted the *sūtra*s in the context of their idealist theory using the stratagem of the three natures. The concept of how the three natures are void of own-being is a good example of their hermeneutic efforts related to Emptiness. It comes up twice in the *Mahāyānasutrālaṃkāra*; chapter XI, 'Ernest Quest' and again in chapter XII, 'Exposition' while discussing the provisional teachings. They took the *sūtra*s, which taught that everything is empty of own-being as provisional teachings, which must not be taken literally. Interpreting such teachings in the light of the three natures, they argued that the constructed are empty of own-being because they lack real characteristics of being. The dependent are empty of own-being in the sense that they are empty of independent birth and the absolute nature is empty of own-being *qua* substantiality. Mipham states this very clearly while discussing the Cittamātra tenet system in his *Grub bsdus*:

> Therefore, all statements that 'all phenomena are without own-being' in the *sūtra* refer to (*dgongs*) the objects of the subject-object superimposition. They refer to the three characteristics separately; the imputed being without

the own-being of charactersitics, the dependent being without the own-being of arising from oneself and the absolute being without the own-being of substantiality. Because just the self-luminous consciousness exists as the basis of *saṃsāra* and *nirvāṇa*, it is not negated. Thus, they assert that no [schools] other than the Cittamātra tradition have (understood) the ultimate intent (*dgongs pa mthar thug*) of the Victorious One.

See MGS, 21, p. 474.

34 Asaṅga, Sthiramati, Gunamati are known to have commented on MK and Dharmapāla wrote a commentary on Āryadeva's *Catuḥśataka*. See Seyfort Ruegg (1981), p. 49.

35 See Bhāvaviveka, *Madhyamakahṛdaya*, V; MA, VI/45–97; BA, IX/17–33. Tāranātha mentions that Candrakīrti and Candragomin, maintaining the Mādhyamika and Yogācāra positions respectively, debated for seven years. See Tāranātha (1986), p. 190.

36 *Madhyamakālaṃkāra*, verse 92–3, See Seyfort Ruegg (1981), pp. 87–100.

37 Of the early commentaries on MK, Bhavya was critical of Buddhapālita and also of the commentary by Sthiramati's (*c*.510–70) teacher, Guṇamati. He approved Devaśarman's commentary. See Seyfort Ruegg (1981), p. 62.

38 Although the terms *prasaṅga* for apagogic reasoning and *svatantra* for autonomous inference were well known among Indian Buddhist logicians and the Mādhyamika school clearly diverged into two distinct lines in India, the name *Prāsaṅgika* is not attested in any known Indian sources or early Tibetan sources. The term Svātantrika is used by late Indian scholar Jayānanda. See Seyfort Ruegg (1981), p. 58 and (2000), pp. 20–1, 240–1, on this. In Tibet, these two lines of interpretation came to be recognized as two different schools with distinct philosophical positions and scholars showed preference to one over the other. However, some Tibetan scholars such as Butön are said to have rejected the distinction of these two Mādhyamika as a Tibetan creation (*bod kyi rtog bzo*). Tsongkhapa states that the designation of the two lines as Svātantrika and Prāsaṅgika by scholars of Later Propagation of Buddhism in Tibet is justified as it accords with Candrakīrti's *Prasannapadā*. See *Lam rim*, p. 573.

Mipham also argues that the two groups are distinguished as different by their logical procedure and exegetic emphasis (such as Buddhapālita's interpretation being refuted by Bhāvaviveka for not supplying the qualifier 'ultimately' and Candrakīrti rebutting Bhāvaviveka's arguments) although they are same in their understanding of the final ultimate. To him, the main difference between Prāsaṅgika and Svātantrika is in the emphasis laid on the two ultimates. The Svātantrikas, as gradualists methodologically, stressed the provisional notational ultimate and thus employed more autonomous inference, supplied qualifiers such as 'ultimately' to the negandum, and accepted individually characterized entities on conventional level. In contrast, the Prāsaṅgikas, as simultaneists insofar as their methodology of establishing Emptiness was concerned, put emphasis on the final Emptiness *qua* non-notational ultimate by using apagogic reasoning. See Chapter 4, pp. 142–6. See *Ketaka*, p. 9. *rGyan 'grel*, p. 64.

Karmapa Mikyod Dorje also argues that all Mādhyamika masters are same in understanding and differ in presentation. See Karmapa Mikyod Dorje (1996), pp. 5–6. See also Śākya Chogdan (1975b), f. 8b = p. 224, arguing that both Svātantrika and Prāsaṅgika equally negate all fabrications ultimately. Along the same line, Seyfort Ruegg observes that the names have 'sometimes been used by Tibetan doxographers not as the name of an immutable and monolithic school corresponding to an essentialist definition of the term; for "Svātantrika" appear to cover works and masters, linked as much by certain common features, or "family resemblances," as by immutably fixed and uniform content . . .'. See Seyfort Ruegg (2000), p. 21.

The division of Mādhyamika into two schools with the names Prāsaṅgika and Svātantrika, it is clear, became established during the Later Propagation of Buddhism in Tibet. Among the late Indian Mādhyamikas, Bodhibhadra is said to mention the Mādhyamika of Bhāvaviveka and Śāntarakṣita, Advayavajra is said to divide Mādhyamika into Māyopamādvayavādin and Sarvadharmāpratiṣṭhānavādin. See Seyfort Ruegg (2000), p. 34 and Changkya (1988), pp. 198–9 for more discussion. Among early Tibetan scholars, Paltseg in his *lTa ba'i rim pa'i man ngag* and Yeshe De in his *lTa ba'i khyad par* mention the bifurcation of Mādhyamikas into *mDo sde spyod pa'i dbu ma* (Sautrāntika-Madhyamaka) of Bhāvaviveka and *rNal sbyor spyod pa'i dbu ma* (Yogācāra-Madhyamaka) of Śāntarakṣita. See Seyfort Ruegg (1981), pp. 58–9 and (2000), p. 23. Similar distinction is made of the 'external' Mādhyamika (*phyi'i dbu ma*) and the 'internal' Mādhyamika (*nang gi dbu ma*). See Seyfort Ruegg (2000), p. 24; Karmay (1988), pp. 150–1. Śākya Dorje (twelfth century) divides Mādhyamikas into non-partisan mainstream (*gzhung phyi mo*) and partisan (*phyogs 'dzin pa*) and the latter into those partisan in the theory of conventional truth and in the theory of the ultimate. He then divides the first into Sautrāntika and Yogācāra Mādhyamika and the latter into Māyopamādvayavādin and Sarvadharmāpratiṣṭhānavādin. See Śākya Dorje, *Theg pa'i spyi 'grel gzhi lam 'bras bu'i rnam gzhag gsal bar byed pa chos kyi gter mdzod kun 'dus rig pa'i sgron ma*, ff. 107b–8b. Tsongkhapa later uses the same classification. See *Lam rim*, pp. 571–2.

Most of later Tibetan doxographers divide Mādhyamikas into *Thal 'gyur pa* (Prāsaṅgika) and *Rang rgyud pa* (Svātantrika), the latter of which is also further divided into *mDo sde spyod pa'i dbu ma rang rgyud pa* (Sautrāntika–Svātantrika–Mādhyamika) and *rNal sbyor spyod pa'i dbu ma rang sgyud pa* (Yogācāra-Svātantrika–Mādhyamika). See *Lam rim*, p. 572; Changkya (1988), p. 198; Thuken (1984), pp. 25–6; Tagtshang (1999), pp. 15, 148. Following Longchenpa, Mipham, in his *Grub bsdus*, discusses Mādhyamika under the three categories of *Rang rgyud gong ma* (Upper Svātantrika) and *Rang rgyud 'og ma* (Lower Svātantrika) and *Thal 'gyur pa*. The Lower Svātantrika further divides into *sGyu ma rigs sgrub pa* such as Samudramegha and *sNang stong tha dad pa* such as Srīgupta. The Upper Svātantrika is identified with Jñānagarbha, Śāntarakṣita, Kamalaśīla *et al.* See MGS, vol. 21, pp. 479–81.

In his *Dogs sel*, Mipham refutes Dodrub Damchö, who dismissed the *sGyu ma rigs grub pa* school as fake classification, reasoning that the classification of Mādhyamika into *Zung 'jug rab tu mi gnas pa* and *sGyu ma rigs grub pa* is known in India, notably in Śūra's *Bhāvanakrāma*. See *Dogs sel*, p. 631. Tagtshang Lotsāwa cites Śūra, Jñānavajra, Avadhūtipāda and Jitāri to support the classification of *sGyu ma rigs grub pa* and *Rab tu mi gnas pa* and equates them with Svātantrika and Prāsaṅgika respectively and refutes Ngog Lotsāwa who classified Candrakīrti and Śāntideva as Svātantrika. See Tagtshang (1999), pp. 14, 141–4.

39 These three are known as *Rang rgyud Shar gsum mKhan po* and their works, *Satyadvayavibhaṅga*, *Madhyamakālaṃkāra* and *Madhyamakāloka* are known as *Rang rgyud Shar gsum*.

40 The Gelukpas, Mipham and most other scholars consider Śāntideva to be Prāsaṅgika. Karmapa Mikyod Dorje includes Śāntideva among the *phyi mo'i dbu ma pa*, the non-partisan root Mādhyamikas along with Nāgārjuna, Āryadeva and Śūra. See Karmapa Mikyod Dorje (1996), p. 5.

41 By the middle of eighth century, Buddhism gained royal patronage and began to flourish in Tibet through the influence of great Indian masters like Padmasambhava, and this lead to contentions between the Bonpos and the Buddhists. The conflict is said to have erupted with prominent Bonpo ministers staging protest against the King on the account of his support and allegiance to the foreign religion and with the Buddhist party demanding a ban on the animal sacrifices the Bonpos undertook. The King convened

a contest between the two religions to prove their worth and superiority. The competition is said to have taken the course of both philosophical debates and competitions in spiritual powers, and the victory, the Bon and Buddhist records each claim differently, to have gone to their sides. Nonetheless, the Buddhists are said to have won the favour of the monarch and thus said to have thrived as a royal faith. Contests between the Bonpos and Buddhism continued in the following centuries. Rinchen Zangpo is said to have defeated Lü Kargyal, whom Gene Smith identifies as Shenchen Kargyal or Lüga (996–1035), the first Bonpo *gter ston*, and Milarepa is said to have debated with Naro Bonchung. See Smith (2001), p. 237.

42 Kamalaśīla was invited to represent the Indian gradualist and be the chief opponent/refuter of Hwashang following the will of his teacher, Śāntarakṣita, the Indian abbot who introduced Buddhist monasticism and Mādhyamika in Tibet. Śāntarakṣita is said to have left a prophecy before he died that there will be a serious doctrinal contention among the followers of Buddhism in Tibet and that his student Kamalaśīla should be invited to evince the wrong views.

43 Buddhism in general and Mahāyāna tradition in particular can be roughly divided into the two divergent categories or at least can be said to comprise two divergent tendencies: one which orients towards a quietist and mystical experience with no conceptuality and mentation and the other which associates with rationality and analytical intellection. These two streams, whether seen as complementary strands as Mipham does or as contradictory as the Gelukpas do, both find their origin in the Indian authors and texts, sometimes even in common sources such as *Prajñāpāramitāsūtra*s and Nāgārjuna. In Tibet, the first instance of conflict between these two could be claimed to have occurred in the form of this historic debate of Samye. See Chapter 3, n. 1, Chapter 5, pp. 193–8.

However, some scholars like Herbert Guenther have questioned that this debate ever happened. See Guenther (1989), p. vii. For a general analysis of the simultaneist innatism/gradualist cultivation, quiet/insight and mystical/intellectual trends and the Samye debate, see Seyfort Ruegg (1989); Wangdu and Diemberger (2000); Tucci (1958), pp. 3–154; Stein (1961), II, pp. 3–154; Imeada (1975); Kuijp (1984) and (1986). See also Coseru (2000). See Gombrich (1997), pp. 96–134 and Bronkhorst (1986) for issues relating to the concentration (*śamatha, gzhi gnas*) and insight (*vipassanā, lhag mthong*) in the Pali canon.

The Gelukpa scholars often treated some later Tibetan controversies on Emptiness as being reminiscent of the Samye debate and, associating themselves with the victorious side of rational gradualists represented by Kamalaśīla, dismissed the claims of their opponents as resilient leftovers of Hwashang. However, Mipham and other non-Gelukpa scholars did not equate the later debates on Emptiness with the Samye debate in the manner the Gelukpas did. Although Emptiness, non-conceptuality and non-mentation formed the most significant features of the Samye debate, these themes *per se* were not points of controversy outright rejected by Kamalaśīla's party. The Samye debate was a rebuttal of Hwashang's simultaneist approach of over-emphasis on quietism and non-mentation, which allegedly misled the Buddhists of Tibet by undermining the moral and ethical values.

44 Wangdu and Diemberger (2000), p. 88.

45 It must be noted that the Mādhyamika system was already well developed during the Early Propagation through Indian masters such as Śāntarakṣīta, Kamalaśīla, Jñānagarbha, Jinamitra *et al.* and Tibetan translators such as Kawa Paltseg, Chogro Lüi Gyaltshan and Zhang Yeshe De. During the early part of Later Propagation commencing in eleventh century, most of earlier translations were revised and many new texts were also translated. The translation, particularly of the tantras, from period of Thonmi Sambhoṭa (seventh century) to Rongzom Chözang are termed as Earlier Translation (*sNga 'gyur*) or Old Secret Mantra (*gSang sngags rNying ma*) and those from the

time of Smṛtijñānakīrti and Rinchen Zangpo are known as Later Translation (*Phyi 'gyur*) or New Secret Mantra (*gSang sngags gSar ma*). On the early developments of Mādhyamika in Tibet, Seyfort Ruegg sums up best in the following passage:

> In sum, it appears that by early in the ninth century major works of all three main lines of the Madhyamaka school – Bhavya's Svātantrika, Buddhapālita's and Candrakīrti's Prāsaṅgika and Śāntarakṣita's and Kamalaśīla's Yogācāra-(Svātantrika-)Madhyamaka – were being translated and studied by Tibetan scholars. At this early time in Tibet the Yogācāra-Madhyamaka seems to have occupied the most prominent place, probably in large part because of the presence in that country of Śāntarakṣita and Kamalaśīla who were leading representatives of this current of the Madhyamaka in the second half of the eighth century. Bhavya's Svātantrika branch was well represented in Tibet in both the *sṅa dar* and the early part of the *phyi dar* periods, even though the first reference to it by the term Raṅ rgyud pa is found in Jayānanda's commentary on the *Madhyamakāvatāra*. On the other hand, even though a couple of its main sources were already translated into Tibetan in the *sṅa dar* period, Candrakīrti's current of the Madhyamaka thought does not figure at this time as a clearly distinguished branch of the Madhyamaka separate from Bhavya's; the first Tibetan scholar to distinguish it clearly and explicitly from the Svātantrika school by means of the appellation Prāsaṅgika was reportedly Pa tshab Ñi ma grags.

See Seyfort Ruegg (2000), p. 22. Scholars such as Balmang Konchog Gyaltshan argued that the Prāsaṅgika has come to Tibet in the Earlier Propagation through master like Padmasambhava, who is by philosophical viewpoint a Prāsaṅgika. See *dGag lan phyogs bsgrigs*, p. 649; Khujug (1998), p. 26. Seyfort Ruegg observes that 'such a classification we no doubt have to regard as an example of doxographical and philosophical–systematic categorization'.

46 For more on Ngog, see also Śākya Chogdan (1975c), pp. 443–56; Seyfort Ruegg (2000), pp. 29–40 and on Sangphu Neuthog, see list of references cited in Seyfort Ruegg (2000), p. 28. Ngog and his followers such as Tölung Jamarwa figure as opponents of Gelukpa school later.

47 Chapa is spelt variantly as Cha pa, Phya pa and Phywa pa.

48 Jayānanda worked with Patshab Nyima Drak, Khu Dode Bar, Kunga Drak and Drajor Sherab and has authored a commentary on *Madhyamakāvatāra*. See Seyfort Ruegg (2000), pp. 20–1. Jayānanda is said to have been defeated by Chapa in a debate. When he returned to debate again with Chapa, the latter was dead. See Khujug (1998), p. 35; Śākya Chogdan (1975b), f. 13b = p. 234.

49 See Śākya Chogdan (1975b), f. 13b = p. 234, which states that he wrote a text containing numerous refutation of Candrakīrti. See Śākya Chogdan (1975c), which states that Chapa refuted Candrakīrti pointing out eight major faults. See Seyfort Ruegg (2000), p. 37. Khujug mentions that Tsag (Tseg) Wangchuk Seṅge also refuted Candrakīrti's Prāsaṅgika. See Khujug (1998), p. 35.

50 Tsangnagpa Tsöndrü Seṅge was student of both Chapa and Khu Dode Bar. Seyfort Ruegg mentions he is said to have been disciple of Patshab. Maja Jangchub Tsöndrü was a student of both Chapa and Tsangnagpa. Śākya Chogdan list a Maja Jangchub Tsöndrü who is one of Patshab's disciples among his four sons (*pa tshab bu bzhi*) but wonders if he is the same as Maja who is disciple of Chapa included among the eight great lions (*seng chen brgyad*). Maja is known to have mastered both the Patshab and Khu tradition of Madhyamaka and considered his teacher Chapa to have not gained the ultimate understanding (*dgongs pa thar thug*) of Madhyamaka. See Śākya Chogdan

(1975b), ff. 12b–13a = pp. 232–3; Khujug (1998), p. 35–6; Seyfort Ruegg (2000), p. 39–41.

51 This era marked the introduction of several currents of Tibetan Buddhism. Atiśa's disciple Dromtön Gyalwai Jungne (1004/5–1063/4), founded the Kadampa tradition; Khon Konchog Gyalpo (1034–102), student of Drogmi Lotsāwa Śākya Yeshe (992/3–1073) started the Sakya school; Marpa Chökyi Lodoe (1012–97), his disciple Milarepa (1040–123) and his pupil Gampopa Sonam Rinchen (1079–153) established the Kagyu lineage, Pha Dampa Sangye (eleventh century) started the *Zhi byed* and Machig Labdön (b. 1031) *gCod* practice in Tibet. At the same time, the adherents of the ancient teachings of Early Propagation such as Rongzom Chözang systematized and redefined the Ngagyur teachings thus forming the Ngagyur Nyingma tradition.

52 See *sNgags log sun 'byin* of Gö Khugpa Lhatse, of Chag Lotsāwa and *Chos log sun 'byin* attributed to Butön Rinchen Drub, published at Gadan Chökhorling, n.d. These refutations are not only targeted at tantras such as Vajrakīlaya (*rDo rje phur pa*) and Māyā (*sGyu 'phrul*) cycles but also at *gter ma*, particularly that of Guru Chöwang. Because of Butön's antipathy towards Nyingma tantras, the Nyingma tantras are said to have been left out from the *bKa' 'gyur* and *bsTan 'gyur*. Thuken Chökyi Nyima rejects that the *Chos log sun 'byin* is by Butön and that Butön objected to certain Nyingma tantras. Thuken also mentions, as does Sapaṇ, Rinchen Zangpo's *Chos dang chos min rnam 'byed* among refutations of Nyingma tantras. See Thuken (1984), pp. 73–4, 76–7. See also 'The Ordinance of lHa Bla-ma Ye-shes-'od' and 'An Open Letter by Pho-brang Zhi-ba-'od' in Karmay (1998). Both prince-monks were deeply saddened by the open abuse of tantras in their days and criticized the malpractice of the village tantrics. Yeshe Ö explicitly disapproves the practice of *sbyor ba* and *sgrol ba* and teachings going under the name of Dzogchen but does not mention any tantras in particular although Karmay conjectures Yeshe Ö to be criticizing *Guhyagarbhatantra* of the Nyingma tradition. Dorji Wangchuk disagrees. See Wangchuk (2002), p. 274. Phodrang Zhiwa Ö lists over seventy texts that are spurious. Other critics also include Drigung Palzin, Drigung Kyobpa Jigten Gonpo, Sumpa Khenpo Yeshe Paljor and Kamtshangpa Palkhang Chözod. See Kapstein (2000), pp. 121–37 for discussion of Sumpa Khenpo's criticism, *gSung rab rnam dag chu'i dri ma sel byed nor bu ke ta ka* and Thuken's reply, *Nor bu ke ta ka'i byi dor*.

53 Among defenders are figures such as the Nyingma scholars, Rongzom Chözang and Longchenpa Drime Özer, the Kadampa master Chomdan Rigpai Raldi, the translator, Tharpa Lotsāwa Nyima Gyaltshan, the famous historians Gö Lotsāwa Zhönu Pal and Pawo Tsuglag Trengwa, the yogi Drubthob Ugyenpa, Serdog Paṅchen Śākya Chogdan, the third Longchenpa Ngawang Tashi Namgyal, Jigme Lingpa and most prominently the scholar–physician Sogdogpa Lodoe Gyaltshan. The last produced a detailed rebuttal of refutations against Nyingma tantras. See Lodoe Gyaltshan (1998). The most recent defence was undertaken by Dudjom Rinpoche. See Dudjom Rinpoche (1991), Part VII. See also Smith (2001), pp. 16–7, 238 and Wangchuk (2002). Mipham touches on the issue very briefly in his *gSung sgros*, pp. 671–3.

Besides the controversy on certain Nyingma tantras and *gter mas*, which culminated in considerable polemical exchanges, criticism of tantras belonging to other traditions appears to have been a common practice among many scholars throughout the Later Propagation. Balmang Konchog Gyaltshan reports that Ngog refuted *Lam 'bras* of Sakya in his treatise *rDo rje tshig rkang*, Nya Ön Kunga Pal refuted Kagyupa mind-pointing instructions, *gtum mo* practice and *Ra li so gnyis*, Butön to have refuted Sakya tantras and Redawa to have refuted *Kālacakra* and instructions of *ṣaḍaṅgayoga*. See *dGag lan phyogs bsgrigs*, p. 652. See also Stearns (1999) who mentions that Redawa first wrote an objection to *Kālacakra* entitled *Nor bu'i phreng ba* and later wrote a reply to his own objection called *Nor bu'i phreng ba'i rang lan*. Dudjom Rinpoche also gives a long list of criticism and counter-criticism. See Dudjom Rinpoche (1991), pp. 929–31. Seyfort Ruegg also cites Ngawang Chödrak who observes that Redawa only rejected the modernists version of Kālacakra and *ṣaḍaṅgayoga* practice like Sapaṇ's criticism of the Neo-Mahāmudrā or Chinese style Dzogchen. Butön and Ngorchen Konchog Lhundrub are also said to have criticized the modernist Mahāmudrā. See Seyfort Ruegg (2000), p. 64. Smith observes that Chomdan Rigpai Raldi objected to the *Kālacakra* cycle. See Smith (2001), p. 313. Ngorchen Kunga Zangpo refuted Tsongkhapa on many points relating to tantric practice to which Khedrub Geleg Palzang wrote the reply *Phyin ci log gi gtam gyi 'byor ba la zhugs pa'i smra ba ngan pa rnam par 'thag pa'i bstan bcos gnam lcags 'khor lo*. See *dGag lan phyogs bsgrigs*, pp. 1–69.

54 Sakya Paṇḍita Kunga Gyaltshan (1992), vol. iii, pp. 68–9. The practice of non-mentation (*amanasikāra, yid la mi byed pa*) is considered to be a form of Madhyamaka practice promulgated by Maitripāda who was an exponent of Nāgārjuna's Mādhyamika and is said to have defeated the Yogācāra master Śāntipa in a debate. However, Ngog's disciple Drolungpa Lodoe Jungne and many other Kadampas are also said to have argued that the practice of non-mentation is not consonant with Mādhyamika. Karmapa Mikyod Dorje observes that the refuters of Kagyupa practice of non-mentation are opposing Indian masters such as Maitripāda and Saraha. He defends the Kagyupa Mahāmudrā and *amanasikāra*. See Karmapa Mikyod Dorje (1996), pp. 7–13, 36.

55 Ibid., p. 51: *da lta'i phyag rgya chen po dang// rgya nag lugs kyi rdzogs chen la// yas bab dang ni mas 'dzegs gnyis// rim gyis pa dang gcig car bar// ming 'dogs bsgyur ba ma gtogs pa// don la khyad par dbye ba med// . . . phyi las rgyal khrims nub pa dang// rgya nag mkhan po'i gzhung lugs kyi// yi ge tsam la rten nas kyang// de yi ming 'dogs gsang nas ni// phyag rgya chen por ming bsgyur nas// de (sic) lta'i phyag rgya chen po ni// phal cher rgya nag chos lugs yin//* See also Jackson (1994).

56 See *dGag lan phyogs bsgrigs*, p. 651.

57 Although the precise application of the designations *Tshad ma snga rabs pa* and *Tshad ma phyi rabs pa* are vague, later Tibetans scholars generally associated the first with Chapa and his realist interpretation of Dharmakīrti's logico-epistemology. Sapaṅ's criticism of this realist interpretation and his nominalist/conceptualist understanding of Dharmakīrti constitutes the latter. On differences and conflicts in interpretation of Dharmakīrti's logico-epistemological tradition in Tibet, see Dreyfus (1997).

58 Other centres included centres at Sakya founded by Khon Konchog Gyalpo, Nenying founded by Drechen Sherab Bar, college at Zulphu founded by Jadul Tsöndrü Bar, Nyethang Dewachen founded by Jatong Chingrupa, college at Trophu founded by Zangring Drakpa Darma Tshultrim, Tshal Chökhorling founded by Śākya Zhonu, at Danbag Nechung and Nganlam Tshulchen founded by Lodrenpa Darma Seṅge and college at Narthang founded by Drusha Sonam Seṅge. See Śākya Chogdan (1975b), f. 12b–16b = pp. 232–40.

59 The second half of thirteenth century seems to have been relatively quiet in terms of Mādhyamika scholarly activity. Prominent masters at that time include Sakyapa Phagpa Lodoe Gyaltshan (1235–80), who became the tutor to Kublai Khan defeating his non-Buddhist opponents in debate, Drubthob Ugyenpa (1230–1309), Taglung Drakpa Pal (1251–96), Pang Lotsāwa Lodoe Tanpa (1276–1342), Üepa Losal (*c.*1300), among others.

60 See Khujug (1996), p. 38.

61 See n. 52 for Butön and refutation of Nyingma tantras. See also Seyfort Ruegg (1966) and (1973). Mipham claims that Butön rejected the Svātantrika and Prāsaṅgika classification as a Tibetan fiction. See *Ketaka*, p. 9.

62 The *gzhan stong* theory based on sources such as *Tathāgatagarbhasūtras*, *Kālacakra* and Maitreya's *Ratnagotravibhāga* centred on the absolute and hypostatic nature of *tathāgatagarbha* which is inherently endowed with the enlightened qualities of the Buddha but empty (*stong*) of all other (*gzhan*) accidental phenomena, which are illusory and defiled. Early propagators of this school include Zu Gawai Dorje (early eleventh century), Tsan Khawoche (b. 1021) and Yumowa Mikyod Dorje (eleventh century). Among Dolpopa's followers were his contemporaries Jonang Chogle Namgyal (1306–86) and Nya Ön Kunga Pal (1345–1439), both of who taught Tsongkhapa. Chogle Namgyal is said to have been a Rangtongpa who went to debate with Dolpopa on *gzhan stong* and got converted by the latter. Dolpopa, prior to his advocacy of *gzhan stong* is also said to have debated with Karmapa Rangjung Dorje (1284–1339) who prophesied that Dolpapa will embrace *gzhan stong* in the future. Dolpopa's main writings on *gzhan stong* are *Ri chos nges don rgya mtsho* and *bKa' bsdu bzhi pa*. Zilungpa Śākya Chogdan, Jonang Kunga Drolchog (1495–1566) and his reincarnate Tāranātha (1575–1634) are eminent ones among later Zhantongpas. During the last one, Jonang school thrived, supported by the Tsangpa government but temporarily declined facing persecution during the fifth Dalai Lama's reign over Tibet. It revived soon after. For history of *gzhan stong*, see Zamthang Ngawang Lodoe Drakpa, *dPal ldan jo nang pa'i chos byung rgyal ba'i chos tshul gsal byed zla ba'i sgron me*; Thuken (1984), pp. 218–32; Kongtrul, *Shes bya kun khyab mdzod* and his commentary on *Mahāyānottaratantraśāstra*; Seyfort Ruegg (1963) and (2000), pp. 78–81; S. Hookham (1991); Stearns (1999).

63 For a list of early works containing refutations of *gzhan stong* absolutism, see Thuken (1984), p. 230.

64 Longchenpa's major works comprise the *mDzod chen bdun* (Seven Great Treasures), the *Rang grol skor gsum* (Trilogy of Self-Liberation), *Ngal gso skor gsum* (The Trilogy of Relaxation) and their commentaries.

65 Longchenpa Drime Özer, *Yid bzhin rin po che'i mdzod*, vol. II, p. 659.

66 See *dGag lan phyogs bsgrigs*, p. 665.

67 Thuken reports that both Yagde Paṇchen and Rongtön were defeated by Bodong in debate but Bodong himself was vanquished by young Khedrub rJe for criticizing *Tshad ma rigs gter*. See Thuken (1984), p. 234. Balmang Konchog Gyaltshan mentions that Bodong Jigdrel (perhaps Bodong Paṇchen Chogle Namgyal, who is sometimes known as Bodong Jigdrak) refuted Yagtrugpa and his student Sonam Chab by showing twenty-five internal contradictions in their understanding of classification of apapogic reasoning in *Tshad ma rigs gter*. See *dGag lan phyogs bsgrigs*, p. 665; Khujug (1996), pp. 47–8.

68 See Thuken (1984), p.189; Khujug (1996), p. 43; Chari Kalzang Thogme (2000), vol. i, pp. 111–2. All cite Karma Konchog Zhönu, the fourteenth-century teacher of Karmapa Rolpai Dorje, saying that the credit of having Madhyamaka that Tibetan scholars talk about so much now goes to Redawa: *da lta gangs can pa rnams kha dbu ma sna dbu ma zer ba 'di red mda' ba'i bka' drin yin/ de'i gong thang sag na dbu ma shi ba'i ro gcig yod/* See also Seyfort Ruegg (2000), pp. 62–3. Tagtshang (1999), p. 170 also mentions that Madhyamaka was about to disappear when Redawa and Lochen Chabchog revived. Tibetan scholars also say that Madhyamaka came to Re (*dbu ma red la babs*) through Redawa just as *abhidharma* came to Chim (*mngon pa mchims la babs*) through Chim Jampaiyang and Chim Lobzang Drak, and *vinaya* came to Tsho (*'dul ba mtsho la babs*) through Tshonawa Sherab Zangpo. Redawa was, however, very critical of the Jonangpa *gzhan stong* theory. Hence, later Jonangpas

branded Redawa as an 'evil demon who would spread the nihilistic view'. See Stearns (1999), p. 56.

69 On the names Gadanpa (*dGa' ldan pa*) and Gelukpa (*dGe lugs pa*), see Seyfort Ruegg (2000), pp. 5–6. On Gelukpas and Geluk position, see also Newland (1992), p. 22 and Napper (1989), p. 14.

70 On Tsongkhapa's arrival at his Madhyamaka theory, see Seyfort Ruegg (2000), pp. 88–103.

71 Tsongkhapa's main contribution to Madhyamaka are his *Lam rim*, vol. pa and *Drang nges*, vol. pha, his commentary on MK, *Rigs pa'i rgya mtsho*, vol. ba and his commentary on MA, *dGongs pa rab gsal*, vol. ma. Minor works include his *rTen 'brel stod pa legs bshad snying po*, vol. kha, *Byang chub lam rim chung ba*, vol. pha, *rJe red mda' ba'i gsung lan*, vol. kha, *rJe btsun 'jam pa'i dbyangs kyi lam gyi gnad red mda' bar shog dril du phul ba*, vol. pha, *Bla ma dbu ma pa la mdo khams su phul ba*, vol. kha, *sPyod 'jug shes rab le'u'i ṭikka blo gsal ba*, vol. ma, *rTsa ba shes rab kyi dka' gnas chen po brgyad kyi brjed byang*, vol. ba, *dBu ma thal gyur pa'i lugs kyi zab lam dbu ma'i lta khrid*, vol. tsha, *dBu ma'i lta khrid bsdus pa*, vol. tsha, *dGe sbyor gyi gnad la dri ba snyan bskul ba lhag bsam rab dkar*, vol. kha. Tsongkhapa's authorship of the last five are sometimes questioned as they appear to be compilations of Tsongkhapa's notes and lectures by his students, by Gyaltshab Je in the case of first two and Khedrub Je for the next two. Thuken argues that attribution of authorship of the last one, *Dri ba lhag bsam rab dkar*, to Tsongkhapa is questionable for the reasons that Paṇchen Jampa Lingpa considered it to be not by Tsongkhapa, the syntactical composition does not agree with other works of Tsongkhapa, the epithet used in the colophon is unknown and his students did not include it within the writings of Tsongkhapa. However most took it as Tsongkhapa's criticism of Kagyupa meditators and this led to a series of polemical exchanges. Jinpa (1999) gives a thorough treatment to argue that this is by Tsongkhapa and that it reflects Tsongkhapa's dissatisfactoriness about the intellectual and philosophical climate prevailing then.

For Tsongkhapa's philosophy of Emptiness and Mādhyamika procedure, see also Tsongkhapa (1978), Hopkins (1983), Napper (1989), Thurman (1984), Tauscher (1995), Seyfort Ruegg (1991, 2000 and 2002). See also Tatz (1989), Matsumoto (1990) and Seyfort Ruegg's criticism in Seyfort Ruegg (2000), pp. 87–8.

72 'Ngarabpa' (*sNga rabs pas*), literally, 'those of previous era' appears mainly in the context of Mādhyamika and Pramāṇa exegesis. For application in Pramāṇa context, see n. 57. Although the precise application of the designation in Mādhyamika context is not clear, Ngarabpas roughly included the scholars belonging to the lineage of Ngog, Thangsag, Sakya, Kagyu and Nyingma traditions. They are distinguished by doctrinal positions such as the delimitation of Mādhyamika negandum to all phenomena, understanding of Emptiness as neither existent, nor non-existent, both and neither, the unknowability of Emptiness, the absence of apprehension and subjectivity in the cognition of the ultimate, the ineffability of Emptiness, etc. As mentioned earlier, Mādhyamikas in Tibet have already been divided between Rangtongpa and Zhantongpa since Dolpopa's time. With Tsongkhapa's interpretation, the Rangtongpas further split into two groups of those following the Ngarabpa interpretation and those following the new Gelukpa interpretation. The latter is sometimes referred to as 'Chirabpa' (*Phyis rabs pa*) or *phyis kyi dbu ma*. Mipham calls Longchenpa *et al.*, Ngarabpas and Tsongkhapa *et al.* Chirabpas and observes that he belongs to the Ngarabpa group. See *Dogs sel*, p. 413. Śākya Chogdan, Gorampa and Karmapa Mikyod Dorje, Amdo Gedun Chöphel and Gelukpa polemicists also make the distinction of the two in similar manner. Thus, I shall use 'Ngarabpa' as a blanket term for those who held the mainstream *rang stong* position before Tsongkhapa and was opposed by Tsongkhapa and other Gelukpa scholars. Even scholars after Tsongkhapa, who held the

same position as regards Emptiness, fall into this category and are sometimes referred to as Ngarabpas. Conversely, 'Chirabpa' refers to those of Tsongkhapa's time and post-Tsongkhapa period and are mainly those who adhered to the Gelukpa viewpoint.

73 Je Tsongkhapa, Gyaltshab Je and Khedrub Je are known as *rJe yab sras gsum* and form the most important trio of Gelukpa heirarchs.

74 See Khujug (1996), pp. 46–9. An oral story has it that Rongton defeated Gyaltshab Je in debate but backed off when Khedrub Je challenged him to a debate. Zhang Yi Sun (1993), *Bod rgya tshig mdzod chen mo*, p. 3247, however dates Khedrub Je's debate with Rongtön to have happened in 1427. It also dates Khedrub's defeat of Bodong Paṇchen in 1400 which suggests that the debate was not a major intellectual encounter between two established scholars as Bodong was then twenty-five and Khedrub who was only fifteen.

75 Although not much is known about him and his viewpoint, he is said to have presented a two-fold method of maintaining (*skyong tshul lugs gnyis*) the view. Thuken also reports that he misunderstood Tsongkhapa's final view with Tsongkhapa's premature view and to have understood Tsongkhapa's view to be a presuppositional or implicative negation. Whatever be the case, he was scolded by Khedrub Je, the then head of Gelukpa school, for his [mis]understanding of the view. Following this, he is known to have lamented: *Blo bzang grags pa dga' ldan gnas su gshegs// byams chen chos rje mi dbang gtsug na mdzes// rgyal mtshan bzang po gangs ri'i khrod du lus//* ... His writings are believed to have been burnt during the time of the fifth Dalai Lama. See Thuken (1984), pp. 316, 323–4; Khujug (1996), pp. 48–9; Balmang Konchog Gyaltshan in *dGag lan phyogs bsgrigs*, p. 716. Akhu Sherab Gyatsho lists seven works by him. See Akhu Sherab Gyatsho in Lokesh Chandra (1981), no. 11389–95. Jamyang Chöje of Drepung is said to have professed a view akin to *gzhan stong* school and Kunkhyen Lodoe Rinchen Seṅge of Sera is also considered to have dissented from Tsongkhapa in view. See Thuken (1984), p. 324.

76 *dGag lan phyogs bsgrigs*, p. 652.

77 See Tagtshang (1999), p. 15. In this doxographical work he criticizes the four mistaken Mādhyamikas: *gnyis stong bden smra rnam rig dbu ma pa// snang la skur bdebs snang sel dbu ma pa// tha snyad tshad 'jal rigs grub dbu ma pa// stong nyid bden grub gzhan stong dbu ma pa'o//* See H. Tauscher (1992). Tagtshang's criticism of Tsongkhapa was rebutted by Paṇchen Lobzang Chökyi Gyaltshan, Gyalrong Namkha Lhundrub and Lithang Khenchen Lobzang Chödrak and by Jamyang Zhadpa Ngawang Tsöndrü. See Akhu Sherab Gyatsho in Lokesh Chandra (1981), no. 11453–4.

78 See Gorampa (1999). Refuting the two traditions which he associates with two extremes, he adopts the tradition espousing Madhyamaka to be free from extremes (*mtha' bral la dbu mar smra ba*), which is passed down from the lineage of Ngog, Sakya, Kagyu, Patshab and Thangsag through Yagtrugpa and Redawa. This Madhyamaka, he explicitly mentions, is free from all extremes of existence and non-existence, is and is not (*yod med yin min gyi mtha' thams cad dang bral ba*).

79 Gorampa (1968). Gorampa's criticisms have been replied to by Jamyang Zhadpa, Sera Jetsün Chökyi Gyaltshan, Paṇchen Delek Nyima and Jamyang Gawai Lodoe. Gorampa is said to have also written a refutation of certain *rNam bzhag rim pa'i ṭīkka*. See *dGag lan phyogs bsgrigs*, p. 665.

80 Sākya Chogdan (1975a). The work, made up of twelve chapters, sets at the beginning as one of its purpose the refutation of mistaken interpretation in Tibet held by a certain later important master, that is, Tsongkhapa. Counter-refutation against Śākya Chogdan has been written by Sera Jetsün.

81 See Thuken (1984), p. 159; *dGag lan phyogs bsgrigs*, p. 665. A response to this is said to have been written by Paṇchen Lobzang Chökyi Gyaltshan. Śākya Chogdan embraced *gzhan stong* absolutism toward the end of his life and wrote his

Lugs gnyis rnam 'byed. The writings of Śākya Chogdan were suppressed in Tibet along with works of other Zhantongpas such as Jonang Tāranātha. The suppression however did not happen in Bhutan and Śākya Rinchen (1710–59), the ninth Je Khenpo of Bhutan and putative reincarnate of Śākya Chogdan had the works of Śākya Chogdan produced as manuscripts in Phajoding. See also Tillemans and Tomabechi (1995).

82 The work is entitled *lTa ba ngan pa tshar gcod pa'i bstan bcos gnam lcags 'khor lo*, and Galo refutes Gorampa accusing him of not being skilled in presenting the opposition, in criticizing the opposition, in presenting his own position and ends with an admonition. See *dGag lan phyogs bsgrigs*, pp. 519–605. Galo has also authored a polemical text entitled *dBu ma'i brgal lan theg chen lhun po*.

83 Sera Jetsün's rebuttal, *Zab mo stong pa nyid kyi lta ba la log rtog 'gog par byed pa'i bstan bcos lta ba ngan pa'i mun sel* finished by Paṇchen Delek Nyima, confutes Śākya Chogdan's *Tsod yig tshigs bcad ma, dBu ma rnam gnes* and Gorampa's criticism in *lTa ba ngan sel* in detail. See *dGag lan phyogs bsgrigs*, pp. 176–518. Paṇchen Delek Nyima is also attributed with another polemical tract, *Kar lan gyi yang lan*. See Akhu Sherab Gyatsho in Lokesh Chandra (1981), no. 11435.

84 Thuken (1984), p. 324.

85 He is said to have written a reply to Karmapa Mikyod Dorje's criticism of Tsongkhapa according to Akhu Sherab Gyatsho in Lokesh Chandra (1981), no. 11433. See also Sonam Drakpa (1973b).

86 Karmapa Mikyod Dorje (1996).

87 *rNam rdzun pa'i dbu ma*, also known as *rNam rig dbu ma* (Vijñapti Madhyamaka), is a current of Vijñānavada and Madhyamaka synthesis which was associated with the *gzhan stong* viewpoint. It was also known as the *dbu ma chen po*. This tradition maintained the ultimate existence of an absolute gnosis which is termed as *gzhan ma yin pa'i de bzhin nyid*, the quiddity that is not other.

88 See *dGag lan phyogs bsgrigs*, pp. 69–173. Sera Jetsün attacked both Karmapa and Śākya Chogdan for espousing the ultimate existence of absolute gnosis. Karmapa however appears to have given up the viewpoint in the commentary on *Sphuṭārtha* when he wrote his *Dwags brgyud grub pa'i shing rta*. In latter text, he criticizes Śākya Chogdan's differentiation between the Yogācāra Alīkākāravādin school and Mādhyamika Alīkākāravādin school and refutes the whole concept of absolute gnosis in the Mādhyamika system. See Karmapa Mikyod Dorje (1996), pp. 16, 20–43.

89 Akhu Sherab Gyatsho in Lokesh Chandra (1981), no. 11433. See Seyfort Ruegg (1986a) and Williams (1983).

90 Pema Karpo (1999).

91 For the polemical tracts, see vol. Kha/ya-ki of his works. For *Klan ka gzhom pa'i gtam*, see vol. Kha/ha of his works.

92 See 'Shar rtse gzal ngo'i brgal lan' in *Klan ka gzhom pa'i gtam*, vol. Kha/ya, ff. 14–20. Gomde Namkha Gyaltshan wrote a commentary on the *Bodhicittavivaraṇa*, to which he appended his refutation, the *'Brug mi pham padma dkar pos phyag chen gyi bshad sbyar rgyal ba'i gan mdzod ces par rje tsong kha pa la dgag pa mdzad pa'i gsung lan*. See *dGag lan phyogs bsgrigs*, pp. 607–45. The 'Shar rtse gzal ngo'i brgal lan' is an answer to Gomde Namkha Gyaltshan's arguments. Among other scholars, Padma Karpo replies to one Drathang Khenpo, Shagpa, Jedrung Gyurme, Nalanḍa Khenpo, Ngamring Khenpo, Shenyen Maryulwa, Tshandrok Khenpo and Jangdagpo on *Kālacakra*, *saḍaṅgayoga*, Mahāmudrā, *He Vajra*, etc. See also Broido (1985).

93 See Thuken (1984), pp. 157–8 which quotes Paṇchen Lobzang Chökyi Gyaltshan: *lhan cig skyes pa'i gwa'u ma// lnga ldan ro snyoms yi ge bzhi// zhi byed gcod yul rdzogs chen dang// dbu ma'i lta khrid la sogs pa// so sor ming 'dogs mang na yang//*

nges don lung rigs la mkhas shing// nyams myong can gyi rnal 'byor pas// dpyad na dgongs pa gcig tu bab//. See Smith (2001), pp. 119–31.

94 See vol. Nga of his works. See also Lokesh Chandra (1981), no. 815–6; Cabezón (1995).

95 See Thuken (1984), p. 216. Jonangpa works are confiscated and banned and their monasteries converted to Gelukpa centres during the reign of the great fifth Dalai Lama. Tagten Phuntsholing, Tāranātha's seat, was changed to Gadan Phuntsholing. Similarly, several of the Karma Kagyupa monasteries were changed to Gelugpa monasteries.

96 His antipathy towards the Kagyupas and Jonangpas were repercussions of Kagyupa hostility to Gelukpas during the Tsangpa rule. Gene Smith blames Möndropa, the poetry teacher of the fifth Dalai Lama, for slandering against Jonangpas, which led to the persecution. See Smith (2001), p. 95. The fifth Dalai Lama's writings such as *Snyan nag me long gi dka' 'grel dbyangs can dgyes pa'i glu dbyangs*, contain sarcastic remarks about Kagyupas lack of erudition and reflect his ridicule, or at least dissatisfaction, of the Kagyupas. See Phuntsho (1999).

97 His support to the Sakya and Nyingma was so strong that the fifth Dalai Lama even came to be considered Geluk externally, Sakya internally and Nyingma secretly. The Nyingmapas saw during this period the foundation of five major monasteries, Thubtan Dorje Drak in 1635, Palyul Jangchubling in 1665, Ugyen Mindrolling in 1676, Rudam Dzogchen Samtan Chöling in 1685/6 and Zhechen Tannyi Dargyeling in 1734 through masters such as Minling Terchen Gyurme Dorje, Lochen Dharmaśrī, Dodrak Rigzin Ngagi Wangpo, Dzogchen Pema Rigzin, Rigzin Kunzang Sherab and Zhechen Gyaltshab Gyurme Kunzang Namgyal. The northern Drukpa order also enjoyed support because Pagsam Wangpo, their candidate for Pema Karpo's incarnation and rival of Zhabdrung Ngawang Namgyal of southern Drukpa line, was his cousin.

98 *Tshig gsal stong thun gyi tshad ma'i rnam bshad zab rgyas kun gsal tshad ma'i 'od brgya 'bar ba skal bzang snying gi mun sel*, vol. da of his works. For Jamyang Zhadpa on Madhyamaka, see, Yoshimizu (1996); Seyfort Ruegg (2000), pp. 187–95.

99 See the Mādhyamika chapter in his *Grub mtha'i rnam bshad rang gzhan grub mtha' kun dang zab don mchog tu gsal ba kun bzang zhing gi nyi ma lungs rigs rgya mtsho skye dgu'i re ba kun skong.*

100 Paṇchen Lobzang Chögyan wrote the *dGe ldan bka' brgyud rin po che'i phyag chen rtsa ba rgyal ba'i gzhung lam* and *dGe ldan bka' brgyud rin po che'i bka' srol phyag rgya chen po'i rtsa ba rgyas par bshad pa yang gsal sgron me.* See vol. Nga of his writings and Lokesh Chandra (1981), no. 802–3.

101 Changkya (1988), p. 204; Thuken (1984), pp. 156–8.

102 See Smith (2000), pp. 133–46. For Changkya Rolpai Dorje on Madhyamaka, see Hopkins (1987). Changkya criticizes the Jonangpas and Tagtshang harshly. See Changkya (1988), p. 206.

103 See MGS, vol. Pa, pp. 821–67.

104 Thuken (1984). See also Smith (2001), pp. 147–70.

105 See n. 52 for his polemic on tantra.

106 See Smith (2001), pp. 171–6.

107 See *dGag lan phyogs bsgrigs*, pp. 649–743. The full title appears *bDen gtam snying rje'i rol mtsho las zur du phyung ba sa rnying bka' brgyud sogs kyi rnam bzhag mgo smos tsam mu to'i rgyang 'bod kyi tshul du bya gtong snyan sgron bdud rtsi'i bsang gtor.*

108 The *yig cha* of Sera Jay consists mainly of works by Jetsün Chökyi Gyaltshan and Gomde Namkha Gyaltshan, of Sera May by Khedrub Tanpa Dargye (1493–1568), Chone Jetsün Drakpa Shedrub (1675–1748), of Drepung Loseling by Paṇchen Sonam Drakpa, of Drepung Gomang by Jamyang Zhadpa, of Gadan Jangtse by Sera Jetsün, Gomde Namkha Gyaltshan and Chungtrug Jampa Tashi, of Gadan Shartse by Sonam Drakpa and of Tashi Lhunpo by masters such as Śāntipa Lodoe Gyaltshan.

109 See Smith (2001), pp. 87–96. Situ's time saw a cultural revival of interest in Sanskrit, linguistics and history through famous virtuosi such as Situ Pañchen, Zhuchen Tshultrim Rinchen, Dokhar Tshering Wangyal, Zhechen Drungyig Tenzin Gyaltshan, Ngulchu Dharmabhadra and Akyā Yongzin Lobzang Dondrub. Historians included Changkya Rolpai Dorje, Thuken Chökyi Nyima, Kathog Rigzin Tshewang Norbu, Tenzin Chögyal of Bhutan and Gönpo Chab of Üjümüjin.

110 See Smith (2001), p. 90.

111 On Jigme Lingpa, see Gyatso (1998).

112 Smith (2001), pp. 22–3.

113 Not all masters of Nyingma renaissance were in favour of the *ris med* movement. Gene Smith reports that Dzogchen Khenchen Pema Dorje was one of the greatest scholars of the 'pure' Nyingma tradition. He expressed doubts that the eclecticism that was in vogue might ultimately be destructive of his beloved tradition. He wrote a number of refutations and counter-refutations including one against the Sakya scholar Langnak Sonam Tanpa, entitled *Snga 'gyur rnying ma'i gzhung la brgal ba'i lan lung dang rigs pa'i skya rengs dang po*. See Smith (2001), p. 327.

114 Smith (2001), pp. 24–5, 248–9 for more details on the religious conflicts and individual experiences leading to the development of *ris med* movement.

115 The Gelukpa tradition has long been established in places such as Lithang, Bathang and Chamdo.

116 Paltrul and Kongtrul, and Khyentse to an extent, took great interest in both learning and teaching the important texts of all traditions. Kongtrul's ecumenism, like Mipham's, extended even to the Bonpos that his inclusion of Bonpo *gter mas* in his *Rin chen gter mdzod* collection even earned him protests from Nyingmapas such as Tenzin Drakpa. Khyentse and some of his numerous incarnations were considered as masters both of Sakya and Nyingma while Kongtrul was respected as both Kagyu and Nyingma master and Paltrul excercised some spiritual influence among the Gelukpas.

The reorientation of Buddhist learning to Indian originals can be best seen in the efforts of Khenpo Zhanga or Zhanphan Chökyi Nangwa who compiled into interlinear annotations the Indian commentaries on the thirteen great treatises. These thirteen great treatises and their annotated commentaries formed the fundamental academic curriculum of most Sakya, Nyingma and Kagyu colleges in the twentieth century.

117 Throughout his writings, Mipham revers the thoughts and writings of Rongzom and Longchenpa much more than any of his teachers or contemporaries and holds them as supreme authorities in Nyingma scholarship.

118 Mipham is said to have received no systematic education. The only proper lessons he is said to have had are lectures on chapter 9 of BA from Paltrul who is well known for his specialization and repeated exposition of this text. See Kunzang Chödrak (1987), p. 635; Dudjom Rinpoche (1991), vol. i, p. 872. Apart from the influence on Mipham's thought by Rongzom and Longchenpa, which Mipham happily acknowledges, the only minor influences that may be detected is from the Sakya scholars such as Sapaṇ in Pramāṇa theories and Gorampa and Śākya Chogdan in Mādhyamika arguments. However, it is difficult to tell, particularly in the latter case, whether the similarities are merely coincidental as they were using the same sources and reading along the same lines for a similar conclusion or are influences received through Mipham's exposure to and familiarity with their writings.

119 Mipham persistently professes the inclusivism that all understanding of Emptiness, including the Gelukpa understanding of Emptiness, form different stages of a coherent process of realizing Emptiness. This is seen as consistent also with the *ekayāna* inclusivism and with the much more elaborate Dzogchen inclusivism.

120 Many Nyingmapas appear to have relied on the Gelukpa text books for training in *sūtra* as it is suggested by the use of Gelukpa works in Dodrub monastery. Dodrub

Damchö stands out as Nyingma scholar who adhered to Gelukpa interpretation and challenged Mipham until later. Such was the Gelukpa influence that even later commentaries after Mipham written by Nyingma heirarchs such as Khenpo Zhanga and Ngaga contain positions generally ascribed to the Gelukpas while others such as Thubtan Chödrak wholely adopted a Gelukpa Madhyamaka interpretation. Attention must also be brought to the Jigme Lingpa's exposition in his autocommentary on *Yon tan rin po che'i mdzod* of the unique characteristics of Prāsaṅgika Mādhyamika which are identical with those Tsongkhapa and his followers formulated. This has recently given rise to much enquiry among the Nyingmapas and some Khenpos have even ventured to explain it as confusion caused by a typographic error between understanding the passage as an exposition of Jigme Lingpa's own viewpoint and as a citation of the Gelukpa viewpoint.

121 See Introduction, p. 19.

122 MGS, vol. Nga, pp. 359–415. See Appendix III.

123 Mipham mentions that he received two refutations from Lhasa and one from Jangkha in addition to Pari Rabsal's refutation. It is not clear whether the ones from Lhasa include Drakar Trulku's refutations or not. Mipham says the first three were not worth replying. This might suggest that Drakar's refutation, to which Mipham replied, is not among the first two from Lhasa. See *Rab lan*, pp.135–6.

124 His main rebuttal of Pari Rabsal is the *gZhan gyis rtsad pa'i lan mdor bsdus pa rigs lam rab gsal de nyid snang byed*, MGS, Ca, pp. 191–474. This is reprinted in *Ketaka*, pp. 135–451. See Appendix II. There are also two other short replies to Pari Rabsal. One contains some philosophical discussions but the other is verse reply to a letter received from Pari Rabsal. See *Rab lan*, pp. 451–63. The reply to Drakar Trulku is *brGal lan nyin byed snang ba*, MGS, vol. Ca, pp. 99–190 and also reprinted in *Ketaka*, pp. 467–579. See Appendix I.

125 Kunzang Chödrak (1987), p. 644; Dudjom Rinpoche, (1991), vol. i, p. 876.

126 Jigme Phuntsho, *Kun mkhyen mi pham rgya mtsho la gsol ba 'debs tshul g.yul las rnam par rgyal ba'i rnga sgra*, ff. 13a, 15b. Lobzang Phuntsho is said to have considered Mipham as Mañjuśrī and composed a eulogy to Mipham.

127 Kapstein (2002), p. 315.

128 MGS, vol. Śrī, pp. 71–123; Mipham and Kunzang Paldan (1997).

129 MGS, vol. Pa, pp. 563–608.

130 MGS, vol. 22, pp. 427–710.

131 MGS, vol. Om, pp. 497–837. For the criticisms see pp. 526–618.

132 See *Rab gsal*.

133 The subsequent ones include *Rigs 'phrul dpyid kyi pho nya*, a verse composition and a shorter verse letter. See Pari Lobzang Rabsal (1991), pp. 350–3.

134 See Khujug (1998), p. 76.

135 Drakar Trulku Tenzin Nyandra (2001a).

136 Drakar Trulku Tenzin Nyandra (2001b).

137 Drakar Trulku Tenzin Nyandra (2001c).

138 Smith (2001), p. 328.

139 *gSung sgros*, pp. 550–74.

140 Jigme Phuntsho, *Kun mkhyen mi pham rgya mtsho la gsol ba 'debs tshul g.yul las rnam par rgyal ba'i rnga sgra*, ff. 15–16.

141 Geuteng Lobzang Paldan (1998), vol. i, pp. 347–591 and vol. ii, pp. 3–186.

142 Lubum/Dobi Geshe Sherab Gyatsho (1982), vol. i, pp. 137–309.

143 Ibid., vol. iii, pp. 1–245.

144 Bodpa Trulku (1996).

145 On Amdo Gedun Chöphel, see Sherab Gyatsho (1998); Horkhang Sonam Palbar (1999); pp. 523–70; Stoddard (1985) and Mengele (1999).

146 Amdo Gedun Chöphel (1994), vol. ii, pp. 271–376.
147 Chukye Samten (1997).
148 The latest and the most heated religious controversy among Tibetans is certainly the Dorje Shugdan issue. A lot of polemical tracts have been written on this including writings by the Dalai Lama and objections to him. See Kapstein (2000), p. 254; Dreyfus (1998); Lopez Jr (1998), pp. 181–207.
149 Newland (1992), p. 33.

3 WHAT IS NEGATED BY ULTIMATE ANALYSIS? DEBATES ON THE DELIMITATION OF THE MĀDHYAMIKA NEGANDUM

1 Mahāyāna thought can be generally classified into two trends: one inclined to an analytic/apophatic approach and other to a romantic/cataphatic approach to Emptiness *qua* ultimate. The Mādhyamika system, as presented in the major Indian Mādhyamika treatises, can be said to fall within the first trend while other Mahāyāna traditions such as the Dzogchen, Mahāmudrā and Soto Zen traditions, broadly speaking, belong to the latter trend as they engage in a cataphatic treatment of Emptiness *qua* ultimate and in the generation of the experience of Emptiness through yogic practices, quintessential oral instructions, symbolic gestures and contemplative meditation rather than just ratiocination. However, there are cases where both approaches are adopted by the same author or in the same text. For the two approaches in Nāgārjuna, see Seyfort Ruegg (1981), pp. 33–4. See Chapter 2, n. 24.

In Mipham's Mādhyamika and Dzogchen thought, the two approaches are different but complementary ways of approaching Emptiness although both cataphaticism and apophaticism are to be eschewed in the final realization of Emptiness. See *Nges shes sgron me*, Question I/2–3; *rGyan 'grel*, pp. 58, 259. See also *Nges shes sgron me*, Question III/8 and Question IV/9. See Chapter 2, n. 43 for the two tendencies of quietist/mystical and analytical/intellectual.

2 Mādhyamika reasonings are numerous in number but Tibetan scholars often speak of the five great Mādhyamika reasonings (*dbu ma'i gtan tshigs chen po lnga*). For Mipham's categorization, see MGS, 21, p. 484. In his *mKhas 'jug*, p. 385, he discusses four major reasonings.
3 MK, XVIII/5. See Chapter 1, p. 26–7.
4 See Chapter 2, n. 1.
5 Magee (1999), pp. 64–5.
6 *Lam rim*, p. 579: *dper na/ gang zag mi 'dug snyam du nges pa la med rgyu'i gang zag de shes dgos pa ltar/ bdag med pa dang rang bzhin med pa nges pa la'ang med rgyu'i bdag dang rang bzhin de legs par ngos 'dzin dgos te/ dgag par bya ba'i spyi legs par ma shar na de bkag pa'ang phyin ci ma log par mi nges pa'i phyir . . .*
7 *Drang nges*, p. 152.
8 *dGongs pa rab gsal*, pp. 123–4 = f. 71: *med rgyu'i bden grub dang/ gang gis stong pa'i dgag bya'i rnam pa blo yul du ji lta ba bzhin ma shar na/ bden med dang stong pa'i ngo bo legs par nges pa mi srid do// de yang grub mtha' smra bas 'phral du kun brtags pa'i bden grub dang/ bden 'dzin ngos zin pa tsam gyis mi chog pa'i phyir/ thog ma med pa nas rjes su zhugs pa/ grub mthas blo bsgyur ma bsgyur gnyis ga la yod pa'i lhan skyes kyi dben 'dzin dang/ des bzung ba'i bden grub legs par ngos 'dzin pa ni gnad shin tu che ste/ de ngos ma 'dzin par rigs pas dgag bya bkag kyang thog ma med pa nas zhugs pa'i bden zhen la ci yang mi gnod pas skabs don stor bar 'gyur ba'i phyir ro//*
9 *Lam rim*, pp. 579–80.
10 See Hopkins (1983 and 1987), Thurman (1984), Wayman (1978), Napper (1989), Newland (1992), Magee (1999) and Lopez (2001). See also Tauscher (1995), Seyfort Ruegg (1991 and 2000), Tatz (1989), Williams (1998b) and Matsumoto (1990).

11 See Śākya Chogdan (1975a), chapter VIII and Amdo Gedun Chöphel (1994), pp. 289, 369.
12 See MGS, vol. Ga, pp. 359–78; *Dogs sel* and Pettit (1999), pp. 415–27.
13 On this binary, see *gSung sgros*, pp. 603–8, 658–61; *Lam rim*, p. 650; Sera Jetsün (1973), pp. 275–8.
14 *gSung sgros*, p. 603.
15 On cognitive negandum, see Chapter 3, pp. 159–67.
16 *Lam rim*, p. 651. See also *Drang nges*, p. 175, where he stresses that the inborn grasping at self and its object are the main neganda of reasoning and *dGongs pa rab gsal*, p. 123 = f. 71, where he mentions both hypostatic existence and grasping at it in his discussion of dialectical negandum.
17 Magee (1999), p. 76–8.
18 Changkya (1988), p. 288; Sera Jetsün (1973), pp. 275–8. They seem to have understood 'this' in 'this negandum has to be non-existent' to refer to the objective inherent existence, and not to dialectical negandum as others understood.
19 *dGag lan phyogs bsgrigs*, p. 524; See Gorampa (1999), p. 11.
20 A genre of logic manuals containing a wide range of dialectical topics, *bsdus grwa* texts are said to have originated with Chapa Chökyi Seṅge. They make up the curriculum of the initial years of training in Gelukpa monasteries.
21 Dealing with the taxonomy of autonomous inference in Tibetan dialectics, *rtag rigs* form a section of the Tibetan *bsdus grwa* text books.
22 *Lam rim*, p. 652.
23 Longchenpa and Mipham, unlike most of other Nyingma masters were familiar with the *bsdus grwa* logic that was propagated by Chapa and his disciples in Tibet. Longchenpa had his training in Sangphu Neuthog seminary while Mipham went to Gadan monastery very briefly. Both these were schools, which excelled in *bsdus grwa* logic, albeit at different times.
24 BA, IX/140ab: *kalpitaṃ bhāvam aspṛṣṭvā tadabhāvo na gṛhyate/ brtag bya'i dngos la ma reg par// de yi dngos med 'dzin ma yin//*
25 Ibid., IX, 139–41: *pramāṇam apramāṇam cen nanu tatpramitam mṛṣā/ tattvataḥ śūnyatā tasmād bhāvānāṃ nopapadyate/ kalpitaṃ bhāvam aspṛṣṭvā tadabhāvo na gṛhyate/ tasmād bhāvo mṛṣā yo hi tasyābhāvaḥ sphutaṃ mṛṣā// tasmāt svapne sute naṣṭe sa nāstīti vikalpanā/ tad bhāvakalpan otpādaṃ vibadhnāti mṛṣā ca sā// gal te tshad ma tshad min na// des gzhal rdzun par mi 'gyur ram// de nyid du na stong pa nyid// sgom pa de phyir mi 'thad 'gyur// brtag bya'i dngos la ma reg par// de yi dngos med 'dzin ma yin// de phyir rdzun pa'i dngos gang yin// de yi dngos med gsal bar rdzun// des na rmi lam bu shi la// de med snyam pa'i rnam rtog ni// de yod rnam par rtog pa yi// gegs yin de yang brdzun pa yin//*
26 Williams (1998b), pp. 64–103: Williams' work on this is very meticulous and insightful although it must be mentioned that his translation of *abhāva* as negation throughout the chapter is ambiguous and imprecise. First, *abhāva* can be misunderstood as the dialectical process of negating something instead of understanding it as the state of lacking entity (*bhāva*), which is what it is supposed to mean in this context. Second, rendering *abhāva* as negation has a misleading connotation that *bhāva*, as the negandum, is being negated. Although one could argue that this verse deals with the process of negation, and that *bhāva* is the negandum, as did the Gelukpas, Śāntideva does not explicitly say that. He only plainly states that without recourse to entity, its non-entity cannot be apprehended and that because the entity is false, the corresponding non-entity is also false.
27 Mipham is reading *brtag bya'i* (= *kalpitavyam*) instead of *brtags pa'i* (*kalpitam*) and glossing *brtag bya'i* as *brtag par bya ba'i*. This reading is not attested by the Sanskrit version and is likely a misprint or mistranslation in the root text Mipham is using. He

seems to be taking the word *brtags bya* in the sense of 'to be examined/analyzed', in other words, the object of examination, although *brtag* on its own can mean examine as well impute or construct by the conceptual mind. Semantically, it would be odd to read *brtags bya* as 'to be imputed' in this case as it would have the connotation of something impending to be imputed instead of referring to an entity that is already imputed. From the context, it can be seen that Mipham is reading *brtag bya'i dngos po* to mean 'the entity to be examined/analyzed'. In his *rGyan 'grel*, he cites these verses and has it *brtag pa'i dngos po*. See MGS, Nga/13, p. 258. Tsongkhapa's *dGongs pa rab gsal*, p. 123 = f. 71 and *rGyal sras 'jug ngogs*, p. 441 and most Gelukpa texts read *brtags pa'i dngos la* (*kalpitaṃ bhāvam*) in verse 140a while *Lam rim* has *btags pa'i dngos la*. These variants do not however effect the reading much and such variations in reading have been properly appraised in Williams (1998b), p. 64–103.

28 *Ketaka*, p. 118: *'dir bdag cag gis tshad mas grub don stong nyid ces dmigs gtad kyi yul bden grub cig la grub mtha' 'cha' ba ni med de/ gang gi phyir na/ brtag par bya ba'i dngos po bum sogs lta bu de la ma reg pa'am ma brten par ni bum med lta bu dngos po de yi dngos med yan gar du nam yang 'dzin pa ma yin te/ de phyir bum med dang bum pa'i stong pa lta bu rnam grangs pa'am nyi tshe ba'i stong pa de'ang gzhan dngos po de bkag pa'am bsal ba'i cha yin pas/ 'di ltar rang bzhin gyis rdzun pa'i dngos po gang yin pa de'i dngos med kyang gsal bar te nges par rdzun pa yin par 'dod do// 'o na dngos po kun med ces bsgoms pas ci bya ste/ dngos yod dang dngos med gnyis ka rdzun par mgo mnyam zhing gnyis ka yang dag pa min pa'i phyir zhe na/ re zhig thog med nas goms pa'i dngos zhen gyis srid par 'ching bar byed pa de'i gnyen por dngos po rang bzhin med par goms pa tsam ste/ dngos dngos med gnyis char rdzun pa des na ji ltar rmi lam du bu byung nas shi ba rmis te sdug bsnyal ba na/ bu med snyam pa'i rnam rtog ni/ bu de yod snyam pa'i rnam rtog gi gegs yin la de'ang rdzun pa yin pa bzhin no// des na shing gnyis zung du brdar ba'i mes shing gnyis ka bsregs pa bzhin du dngos kun bden med du rnam par dpyad pa'i shes rab kyi mes dngos dngos med du bzhag pa'i dmigs pa'i gtad so thams cad kyi nags 'thib po ma lus pa bsregs nas spros pa thams cad zhi ba'i ye shes la gnas pa'i tshe na khas len thams cad dang bral ba'i dbu ma chen po yin no//*

29 *Madhyamakālaṃkāra*, 71ab: *skye la sogs pa med pa'i phyir// skye ba med la sogs mi srid//*

30 *rGyan 'grel*, pp. 257–8. See also Mipham's citation of this verse and *Satyadvayavibhāga*, p. 9 in his *Ketaka*, p. 7.

31 Williams (1998b), pp. 91, 98.

32 *rGyal sras 'jug ngogs*, pp. 441–2: *kho bo cag la stong nyid 'jal ba'i tshad ma rdzun pa dang des bzhag pa'i stong pa nyid kyang rdzun pa yin par ches 'thad de/ rtog pas bden pa'i dngos po bkag pa'i dgag pa nges pa de dgag bya'i rnam pa shar ba la rag las pa'i phyir/ der thal/ brtags pa'i dngos po bden grub la rtog pas ma reg par te bden grub kyi rnam pa ma shar bar bden stong de'i dngos por bden med de rtog pas 'dzin pa ma yin pa'i phyir/ de'i phyir dgag bya rdzun pa'i dngos po gang yin pa de mi srid pas dgag bya de bkag pa de 'di dngos med gsal bar rdzun no// snga ma'i dpe ni rtog pa la mo gsham bu'i rnam pa ma shar bar mo gsham bu shi ba'i rnam pa mi shar ba bzhin no//... de bkag pa'i bden stong yang rdzun pa yin gyi bden par ma grub bo// de ni rtsa she las/ gal te mi stong cung zad yod// ces sogs kyi don ston pa yin no// bden grub kyi spyi ma shar bar bden stong legs par mi nges pas stong nyid nges pa dgag bya'i tshad 'dzin la mkhas dgos pa yin no/ rgyu mtshan des na dper na rmi lam du bu shi ba dmigs pa la bu de med snyam pa'i rnam rtog ni bu de yod snyam pa'i rnam par rtog pa'i gegs yin yang/ rmi lam gyi spang gnyen gnyis po de yang rdzun pa yin pa de bzhin du gnyen po rdzun pas spang bya rdzun pa 'joms pa dang/ tshad ma rdzun pas gzhal bya rdzun pa 'jal ba mi 'gal la ...//*

33 Ibid., p. 390, *Ketaka*, p. 37.

34 Williams (1998), p. 102.

35 *Lam rim*, p. 580.
36 Ibid., pp. 582–90.
37 Ibid., p. 584.
38 MK, I/1: *na svato nāpi parato na dvābhyāṃ nāpy ahetutaḥ/ utpannā jātu vidyante bhāvāḥ kva cana kecana// bdag las ma yin gzhan las min // gnyis las ma yin rgyu med min// dngos po gang dag gang na yang // skye ba nam yang yod ma yin//*
39 *Lam rim*, pp. 582–90.
40 Ibid., pp. 592–3.
41 MK, XXIV/7–40.
42 *Lam rim*, pp. 590–1.
43 Ibid., p. 589.
44 'All phenomena from matter to omniscience' is a phrase used frequently in Tibetan literature to sum up all existent things. It is derived from the *abhidharma* and *Prajñāpāramitā* categorization of all phenomena where the phenomenology begins with matter and ends with omniscient gnosis of the Buddha. Tsongkhapa, in *Lam rim*, p. 580, uses this phrase and says some Mādhyamika argued all phenomena from matter to omniscience are negated.
45 *Vigrahavyāvartanī*, verse 1. See Johnston and Kunst (1990), pp. 3, 42, 95.
46 *Lam rim*, p. 584.
47 *Vigrahavyāvartanī*, verses 21–3.
48 *rGyan 'grel*, p. 27: *dper na bden grub ces pa'ang/ don dam dpyod pas dpyad bzod du grub pa la grags che bas phal cher de ltar go ba yin gyi/*; p. 60: *don dam dpyod pas dpyad nas mi bzlog pa'am mi khegs pa zhig yod na bden grub tu 'gyur bas . . . /*
49 Ibid., p. 109.
50 *'Jug 'grel*, pp. 535, 548, 609; *gSung sgros*, p. 619.
51 Ibid., p. 535: *don dam dpyod byed kyis mthun snang kun rdzob kyi bum pa de la dpyad na/ dpyad bzod gang yang ma rnyed pa'am/ ma dmigs pa de la/ don dam dpyod byed kyi tshad mas ma dmigs pa dang/ don dam par med pa dang/ ngo bo stong pa nyid dang/ dpyad bzod du grub pa'i bden grub med pa zhes btags pa yin gyi/ de las gzhan pa'i bden grub 'jog byed dang/ bden med 'jog byed cung zad kyang med do//*
52 *dGongs pa rab gsal*, pp. 125 = f. 72a: *de ltar byas na blo la snang ba'am blo'i dbang gis bzhag pa min par don gyi sdod lugs su yod pa ni/ bden pa dang don dam dang yang dag par yod pa dang der 'dzin pa ni dben 'dzin lhen skyes so//*
See also *Drang nges*, pp. 156–8.
53 Ibid., p. 146, *Drang nges*, p. 269. In his *dGongs pa rab gsal*, pp. 125–6 = f. 72b, p. 134 = f. 77b, Tsongkhapa explains the application of the term 'ultimate' to a negandum in two different ways: (1) The 'ultimate' refers to the cognition based on ultimate analysis. To exist ultimately in this case is to be found by such ultimate cognition. The cognition itself and its object are obtained by the ultimate cognition, so they exist ultimately in this sense. (2) The 'ultimate' refers to an objective reality which, if existent, would exist without being posited by thought or through appearance to subjective thought. There is nothing which exists ultimately in this sense. In the *Lam rim*, p. 669–70 and the *Drang nges*, p. 153, he explains three referents of the term 'ultimate': (1) the ultimate truth, which is the object of ultimate cognition, (2) the non-conceptual gnosis (*rnam par mi rtog pa'i ye shes*) of the sublime beings which directly discern the ultimate and (3) the concordant ultimate *qua* cognition of the ultimate through analytic intellect (*shes rab*). An ultimately existent thing, if possible, is what would be found by the analytic intellect. See also Changkya (1988), p. 237. See Chapter 4, p. 136–42 for the theory of concordant and final ultimates.
54 *Drang nges*, p. 157.
55 *dGongs pa rab gsal*, p. 134 = f. 77b: *sngar bshad pa'i ming gi tha snyad kyi dbang tsam gyis bzhag pa min pa'i yod par 'dzin pa ni/ bden pa dang don dam par dang*

yang dag tu grub pa dang/ rang gi ngo bos dang rang gi tshan nyid kyis dang rang bzhin gyis yod par 'dzin pa lhen skyes yin la/ des bzung ba'i zhen yul ni brtag pa mtha' bzung gi bden tshad do//

56 *dGongs pa rab gsal*, p. 125 = f. 72, p. 134 = f. 77b. See Changkya (1988), p. 284.

57 *Drang nges*, pp. 166–77. Tsongkhapa notes that own/individual characteristics in this context has to be understood differently from the concept of own/individual characteristics discussed in the *abhidharma* and *pramāṇa* literature.

58 *Drang nges*, p. 269.

59 *Lam rim*, p. 661: *des na nang gi blo'i dbang gis bzhag pa min par rang gi ngo bo'i sgo nas yul gi steng du grub pa de la bdag gam rang bzhin zhes zer la/*

60 Drakar Trulku Tenzin Nyandra (2001a), p. 471.

61 *Nyi snang*, pp. 473–4.

62 Ibid., p. 476.

63 Ibid., p. 477.

64 For the three types of conceptual thought in Mipham's epistemological theory, see Chapter 5, pp. 189–91.

65 *Nyi snang*, pp. 477–80. The criticism of the Gelukpa theory of conventionality presented here and in other writings of Mipham behoves further study, but it exceeds the aim of this book.

66 *dGongs pa rab gsal*, p. 134 = f. 77b; *Lam rim*, p. 662; *Drang nges*, p. 175; *Ketaka*, p. 49.

67 The antinomical presentation, which Tsongkhapa and Mipham made in their commentaries on MK, XV/2, of Emptiness *qua* lack of inherent nature as inherent nature with three attributes, is most likely influenced by Candrakīrti's reading of the verse in similar manner. Thus, while most traditional scholars following Candrakīrti understand the verse as discussing inherent nature *qua* reality of Emptiness (*chos nyid stong pa nyid*), modern scholars such as Richard Hayes, Richard Robinson, Seyfort Ruegg and Jay Garfield have taken it as a description of the inherent nature, which is denied by the Mādhyamikas. For a study of this verse, see Ames (1982) and Magee (1999), who following Candrakīrti and Tsongkhapa discusses two kinds of inherent natures, one which is the negandum and the other which is reality.

68 *Lam rim*, p. 607.

69 Ibid., p. 607.

70 Ibid., pp. 607, 612.

71 Ibid., p. 607.

72 Ibid., pp. 607–8.

73 *gSung sgros*, p. 444.

74 *Lam rim*, p. 652.

75 *dGag lan phyogs bsgrigs*, pp. 85–6: *bden par yod pa ma yin, tha snyad du med pa ma yin/*; *dGongs pa rab gsal*, p. 203 = f. 117b: *bum pa bum pas mi stong bum pa bden grub kyis stong/*; *gSung sgros*, p. 441: *bum pa bum pas mi stong/ bum pa bden grub kyis stong/* See also *'Jug 'grel*, p. 533, etc.

76 Amdo Gedun Chöphel (1994), vol. ii, p. 288.

77 *'Jug 'grel*, p. 610; *gSung sgros*, pp. 529–30.

78 *Nges shes sgron me*, Question I/13; *Rab lan*, p. 318; *rGyan 'grel*, pp. 61–2, 64; *gSung sgros*, pp. 487, 529.

79 *Rab lan*, pp. 136, 318; *gSung sgros*, p. 505; *'Jug 'grel*, pp. 595–6.

80 *Prasannapadā*, pp. 10–11 (B 26–27); MA, VI/36. See Seyfort Ruegg (2000), p. 230.

81 *Lam rim*, p. 668; *dGongs pa rab gsal*, p. 148 = f. 86a, p. 208 = f. 120b; *Drang nges*, p. 221. Seyfort Ruegg remarks in his introduction to *The Great Treatise on the Stages of the Path to Enlightenment* that, 'following Candrakīrti, Tsong-kha-pa rejects the addition of the specification "in the ultimate sense" (*don dam par, paramārthatas*)

before the four great propositions with which Nāgārjuna has begun his *Madhyamaka-kārikā*, and which proclaim the non-production of a self-existent entity (*dngos po, bhāva*) from (i) itself, (ii) another such entity, (iii) both, and (iv) neither (i.e. from no cause at all)'. See Tsongkhapa (2000), p. 24. However, it must be clarified that Tsongkhapa, as discussed earlier, does not totally reject the general application of the specification. Neither does he associate the rejection with Candrakīrti. In his *Lam rim*, *dGongs pa rab gsal* and *Drang nges*, he emphatically argues that Candrakīrti only rejected the application of the specification to the production from itself because such production did not occur even conventionally.

82 Ibid., p. 665; *dGongs pa rab gsal*, p. 208 = f. 120b.

83 Ibid., p. 665; See also *Drang nges*, p. 246: Tsongkhapa uses the example of the *Heart Sūtra*. In the beginning of Avalokiteśvara's answer to Śāriputra, Avalokiteśvara says, 'Śāritputra! The noble son or noble daughter who wishes to engage in the practice of profound Prajñānapāramitā must view likewise; [he/she] must view five aggregates as being empty of inherent nature', thus applying the qualifier 'inherent' to the negandum. For the rest of the text the qualifier is not used. Tsongkhapa says that one must understand the insertion of the qualifier from the context.

84 Ibid., p. 664–5.

85 *Rab lan*, pp. 319, 305–6.

86 MA, VI/38.

87 *'Jug 'grel*, p. 549.

88 *Nges shes sgron me*, Question I/12–17.

89 *dGongs pa rab gsal*, p. 134 = f. 77b, pp. 208–9 = f. 120b; *Lam rim*, p. 619; *rGyan 'grel*, p. 64.

90 *Madhyamakāvatārabhāṣya*, p.117–23.

91 MA, VI/34–6, *Madhyamakāvatārabhāṣya*, p. 123. The main refutations of Svātantrika acceptance of entities with own characteristics are the three apagogic reasoning Candrakīrti mentions in his *Madhyamakāvatāra*. If conventional things have own characteristics, (1) it follows that Emptiness is the cause of destruction of conventional entities (*stong nyid dngos po 'i 'jig rgyur thal ba*), because in the state of Emptiness as actualized by the meditative equipoise of the sublime beings, conventionally real and existent things are not perceived. Emptiness would be accountable for the destruction if such real entities existed until Emptiness was realized and not after that; (2) it follows that conventional truths are immune to analysis (*tha snyad bden pa rigs pas dpyad bzod du thal ba*) because conventional entities retain their own characteristics and endure even under the scrutiny of ultimate reasoning. If they exist, either ultimately or conventionally, when being examined by ultimate analysis, they must be immune to the analysis; (3) it follows that production cannot be negated even ultimately (*don dam par yang skye ba mi khegs par thal ba*) because its own being can be found when an examination of it is undertaken. If a conventional rational enquiry into the own characteristics or own being of production can find own characteristics of production, even an ultimate analysis would not be able to negate it. See *dGongs pa rab gsal*, pp. 201–14 = ff. 115–20; *Rab lan*, p. 307; *'Jug 'grel*, pp. 592–618; *gSung sgros*, pp. 562–3; Karma Phuntsho (1997), pp. 244–9. Gorampa however regards this to be a refutation of the proponents of Cittamatra. See Gorampa (1968), pp. 616–17.

92 *'Jug 'grel*, p. 592; *rGyan 'grel*, p. 64; *gSung sgros*, p. 505.

93 *Rab lan*, p. 136; *gSung sgros*, pp. 505, 562. See Chapter 3, p. 75.

94 Ibid.

95 *gSung sgros*, p. 477.

96 Ibid., p. 604.

97 Ibid., pp. 478–9.

98 Ibid., p. 473.

99 Amdo Gedun Chöphel (1994), vol. ii, pp. 287–8.
100 *rGyan 'grel*, pp. 63, 237.
101 Other works where Mipham touches on this include his Mādhyamika writings such as *sTong thun seng ge'i nga ro, mKhas 'jug* and his annotative commentary on MK.
102 An absolute negation in Tibetan dialectics is one in which, having negated the negandum, nothing is either directly or indirectly affirmed. It is like the negation in the statement 'there is no vase'. An implicative negation is one in which, after negating the negandum, something is affirmed or implied, as in the statement, 'this is not a golden vase'. A golden vase is negated but something else is being confirmed. See *dGongs pa rab gsal*, pp. 142–3 = ff. 82–3; *Drang nges*, p. 278–81; *rGyan 'grel*, p. 229 and Karma Phuntsho (1997), p. 45–48. See also Seyfort Ruegg (2000), pp. 224–6.
103 *Prasannapadā*, p. 7 (B. 13).
104 For Mipham, see *Nges shes sgron me*, Question I/3; *gSung sgros*, p. 486. For Geluk source, see *dGongs pa rab gsal*, pp. 140–1 = ff. 81–2; *Drang nges*, p. 282.
105 *Rab lan*, p. 136; *'Jug 'grel*, p. 539; *gSung sgros*, p. 487; *mKhas 'jug*, p. 385.
106 Ibid., p. 537; *Nges shes sgron me*, Question I/8–16; *gSung sgros*, pp. 438, 471.
107 The general *rang stong* and *gzhan stong* controversy deals with the nature of *tathāgatagarbha*. Zhantongpas such as the Jonangpas, based on sources such as *Tathāgatagarbhasūtra*s, *Ratnagotravibhāga* and *Kālacakra*, argued that the *tathāgatagarbha* is an absolute reality inherently endowed with the qualities of the Buddha. It is therefore not empty of its nature but only of other things, that is, the adventitious defects of *saṃsāra*. Karmapa Mikyod Dorje in some of his works and Śākya Chogdan toward the end of his life advocated a version of *gzhan stong* asserting the sublime gnosis to be innate and absolute, thus not empty of its own nature but of impure defects. Rangtongpas such as Gelukpas and Mipham, based primarily on the Mādhyamika treatises, argued that the *tathāgatagarbha*, like all other phenomena, is empty of its own being. Hence, it is not absolute. However, even among the Rangtongpas, there are two currents of thought with regard to the intrinsic presence of the Buddha's qualities in the *tathāgatagarbha*. On the one hand are those who profess a soteriological process of gradual acquisition and progressive cultivation, and on the other, those advocating an innatism, in which the soteriological thrust is in revealing the latent qualities through elimination of the obscurations. The Gelukpas and most Sakyapas belonged to the first, viewing the *tathāgatagarbha* as the seed of Buddhahood and denying that it is endowed with the qualities of the Buddha. Other Rangtongpas such as Mipham, like the Zhantongpas, professed the innatist theory by accepting the latency of the qualities of the Buddha in the *tathāgatagarbha*. Mipham criticizes both the *gzhan stong* absolutists, who assert the *tathāgatagarbha* to be absolute and established with own being even on the ultimate level, as well as the Rangtongpas who argue that the *tathāgatagarbha* is empty not only of own being but also of the latent qualities of enlightenment. See Introduction, p. 16–17; Chapter 2, n. 62. Mipham's accusation of Gelukpas of having to espouse *gzhan stong* viewpoint in the current context is however not particularly related to the theory of *tathāgatagarbha* but to their theory of Emptiness *qua* absence of hypostatic existence.
108 *gSung sgros*, pp. 445, 545; *sTong thun seng ge'i nga ro*, p. 590.
109 Ibid., p. 437.
110 Ibid., pp. 548–9: Mipham remarks that if the extrinsic Emptiness of a vase being not empty of itself but of hypostatic existence is acceptable, the Gelukpas should also embrace the extrinsic Emptiness of the ultimate being not empty of itself but of dualistic conventional phenomena. He further remarks that people of Tibet should assess which of these two *gzhan stong* concepts is better. See *Nges shes sgron me*, I/9.
111 *dGongs pa rab gsal*, p. 203 = f. 117b.

112 *mKhas 'jug*, p. 385.
113 *gSung sgros*, pp. 436–7; *'Jug 'grel*, pp. 545, 607.
114 Ibid., p. 438.
115 Ibid., p. 440.
116 *Nges shes sgron me*, Question I/9; *'Jug 'grel*, p. 537.
117 Ibid., Question I/10.
118 Ibid., Question I/12.
119 *'Jug 'grel*, p. 607.
120 *Rab lan*, p. 258.
121 *Nges shes sgron me*, Question I/18–19.
122 Ibid., Question I/20–2.
123 *'Jug 'grel*, pp. 541–2.
124 Ibid., p. 603.
125 Ibid., p. 541; *mKhas 'jug*, p. 385; *gSung sgros*, p. 537.
126 *Nges shes sgron me*, Question I/8–18; *'Jug 'grel*, p. 541.
127 *gSung sgros*, p. 531.
128 *'Jug 'grel*, p. 541.
129 Ibid., p. 537–9.
130 *gSung sgros*, p. 438: *don dpyod kyis bum pa med par ma 'grub na/ bden grub ji ltar khegs/ med par grub na de nyid don dam par stong pa yin gyi/ de las gzhan pa'i bden grub yan gar ba 'gog pa'i rigs pa ci/*
131 *'Jug 'grel*, pp. 544–5: *de'i phyir bum pa bden grub gzhan gyis stong pa'i lugs 'di'i ltar na/ bum par snang ba nyid rang gi ngo bos mi stong par 'dod pas bum pa bden grub tu 'gyur te/ don dpyod kyis dpyad na chos rang gi ngo bo nyid med par ma rtogs pa de las bden grub gzhan med do//*
132 Ibid., pp. 541, 545.
133 Ibid., p. 547.
134 Ibid., pp. 595–6; *rGyan 'grel*, pp. 64–5.
135 *gSung sgros*, pp. 504–5.
136 *'Jug 'grel*, pp. 547–9.
137 *dGongs pa rab gsal*, pp. 201–14 = ff. 115–20; *Drang nges*, pp. 166–7.
138 Ibid., p. 156.
139 *'Jug 'grel*, p. 601; *gSung sgros*, pp. 509–10. See Chapter 1, n. 23.
140 *Ratnāvalī*, I/35: *skandhagrāho yāvad asti tāvad evāhamityapi/ ji srid phung por 'dzin yod pa// de srid de la ngar 'dzin yod//*
141 *'Jug 'grel*, p. 601.
142 *Rab lan*, pp. 261, 296; *gSung sgros*, p. 481.
143 *gSung sgros*, pp. 431–2: *spyir 'khor 'das gnyis kyi snang ba ni nam yang rgyun chad mi srid la/ snang ba yod na de stong pa la stong nyid du btags kyi/ snang ba med pa ri bong gyi rwa la sogs pa ni stong pa nyid kyi don ma yin te/ tha snyad du med pa yin pas/ ri bong gi rwa rwa stong gi tha snyad sbyar yang gtan med kyi don yin no// stong pa nyid ni tha snyad du yod pa'i chos rnams kyis chos nyid yin te/ . . . des na stong pa nyid 'di tha snyad du yod pa'i chos thams cad kyi rang bzhin nam gnas lugs su bsgrub par bya ba yin gyi/ tha snyad du med pa zhig gi chos nyid du bsgrub bya ni gtan min no//*
144 Ibid., p. 432: *de'i phyir stong nyid zhes pa tha snyad du yod pa'i chos rnams kyi chos nyid yin la/ stong nyid yan gar du gnas pa dngos po la mi srid do/*
145 *gSung sgros*, pp. 447–8.
146 Ibid., pp. 542–9.
147 It might perhaps be clearer to render *bden grub* as truly existent to understand this particular reasoning. He argues that the vase being not empty of vase conventionally would mean that it has a true conventional existence. Hence, it would contradict to say

that it is not truly existent. His point is that if the statement is taken on the conventional level, the vase should either have no true existence conventionally by being empty of itself or be truly existent.

148 *Rab lan*, p. 262; *'Jug 'grel*, p. 595; *gSung sgros*, p. 504.
149 Ibid., p. 261.
150 *gSung sgros*, p. 444.
151 *'Jug 'grel*, p. 543.
152 Ibid., p. 544.
153 *gSung sgros*, pp. 438–9.
154 MA, VI/141: *rang khyim rtsig phug sbrul gnas mthong bzhin du// 'di na glang chen med ces dogs bsal te// sbrul gyi 'jigs pa'ang spong bar byed pa ni// kye ma gzhan gyi gnam por 'gyur nyid do//* Tsongkhapa cites this in his *Lam rim*, p. 645 against those whose delimitation of negandum are over-narrow. Mipham cites this against the Gelukpas in his *gSung sgros* by rephrasing it likewise: *tha snyad dngos po mi stong 'dzin bzhin du// chos gzhan stong pa yin ces dogs bsal bas// dngos zhen mtha' dag 'jig par 'dod pa ni// kye ma gtan gyi gnam por 'gyur nyid do//*
155 *Rab lan*, p. 137: *da lta rang re yi blo gsal 'ga' zhig// snang ba lang ling de rang sar bzhag nas// dgag bya rwa can zhig tshol bar 'dug kyang// a ma rgan mo de bros dogs 'dug go//.* The term *rwa can* or 'possessing horn' is a metaphor for a non-existent thing and mother is an epithet of Prajñānapāramitā.
156 Amdo Gedun Chöphel (1994), vol. ii, pp. 292, 311; Bodpa Trulku (1996), p. 158.
157 Ibid., pp. 291–2.
158 Ibid., p. 290.
159 Ibid., p. 292: *'ga' zhig gis/ bum pa/ ka ba sogs rigs pas 'gag na thams cad med par lta ba'i chad lta skye snyam nas 'jigs pa ni don med pa'i sems khral te/ mdun na mthong bzhin pa'i bum pa 'di gtan med do snyam pa'i chad lta zhig so skye rang ga ba la skye bar ga la srid/ gal te de 'dra'i blo zhig skyes na bum pa mthong rgyu yod/ reg rgyu yod pa dngos su shes pas/ bum pa 'di nga la snang rgyu 'dug kyang snang bzhin du gtan nas med do snyam pa'i blo rang shugs kyis skyes pas blo de 'dra ni snang ba ltar du med par 'dzin pa'i snang stong gnyis tshogs kyi dbu ma'i lta ba de yin gyi/ chad lta ga la yin/*
160 Hopkins (1983), p. 544.
161 Napper (1989), p. 147.
162 Newland (1992), p. 18.
163 *Rab lan*, pp. 256, 261; *gSung sgros*, pp. 479–82.
164 *Saṃcayagāthā*, I/13; *Samādhirājasūtra*, IX/27; *Kaśyapaparivarta*, p. 56; MK, XV/7, XV/10, XXII/11–2, XXII/14; *Catuḥśataka*, VIII/20, XVI/25; *Jñānasārasamuccaya*, 11, 29. See Seyfort Ruegg (1977) and Seyfort Ruegg (2000), pp. 139–47.
165 Seyfort Ruegg (1977), p. 9.
166 Sera Jetsün Chökyi Gyaltshan (1989), vol. i. p. 178–9: *de ltar ma yin na/ chos thams cad chos can/ yod pa yin par thal/ med pa ma yin pa'i phyir/ ... gzhan yang/ chos thams cad yod pa yang yin/ med pa yang yin/ gnyis ka yang yin/ gnyis ka ma yin pa yang yin par thal/ chos thams cad yod pa yang ma yin/ med pa yang ma yin/ gnyis ka yang ma yin/ gnyis ka ma yin pa yang ma yin pa'i phyir/ rtags khas/*
167 'Reversion of is and reversion of is-not' or *yin log min log* is a topic in *bsdus grwa*, that is roughly the law of double negation. The basic rules are: reversion of x = non-x and reversion of reversion of $x = x$. Thus, any odd number of reversion of x = non-x and any even number of reversion of $x = x$. However the reversion of non-$x = x$, and any number of reversion of non-x shall amount to x. See Phurchog Jampa Gyatsho (1993), pp. 32–7.
168 *Rab gsal*, p. 386: *'dir dgag pa gnyis kyis rnal ma go zhes rgya bod kyi mkhas pa'i rigs pa yang khas che mod/ rang gsod pa'i mtshon cha rang gis brdar ba ste/ bden med du med na bden grub dang/ bden grub ma yin pa min na'ang bden grub tu 'gyur ba'i*

phyir/ blo gsar bu ba rnams kyi spyod yul yin log min log gi bsdus tshan la yang rgyus med pa'i rang chos te/ grub mtha'i kha 'dzin ni tshegs che bar snang ngo//

169 *dGongs pa rab gsal*, p. 140 = f. 81; *Drang nges*, p. 282. See also Seyfort Ruegg (1991).
170 *Lam rim*, pp. 599–600.
171 *dGongs pa rab gsal*, p. 141 = f. 81b.
172 *Drang nges*, p. 286.
173 Ibid., pp. 286–7.
174 *Lam rim*, pp. 599–600.
175 Ibid.
176 *Vigrahavyāvartanī*, verse 26: *naiḥsvābhāvyānāṃ cennaiḥsvābhāvyena vāranaṃ yadi hi/ naiḥsvābhāvyanivṛttau svābhāvyaṃ hi prasiddhaṃ syāt// gal te rang bzhin med nyid kyis// ci ste rang bzhin med pa bzlog// rang bzhin med pa nyid log na// rang bzhin nyid du rab grub 'gyur//* See *Lam rim*, p. 599; *dGongs pa rab gsal*, pp. 141–2 = ff. 81–2; *Drang nges*, p. 286; *Rab gsal*, p. 386.
177 *Rab lan*, p. 267.
178 Ibid., p. 269.
179 Ibid., pp. 265–6.
180 Ibid., p. 267: *bsdus tshan gyi gzhung gis sangs rgyas kyi bka' sun 'byin dgos pa ni ha cang yang thal ma ches sam/*
181 Ibid., p. 268.
182 Tibetans disagreed on whether or not Nāgārjuna accepted the law of logical bivalence, excluded middle and non-contradiction. The Gelukpas clearly endorsed these rules in Nāgārjuna's system while others rejected that Nāgārjuna maintained such assertions. Yet some others argued that Nāgārjuna would not accept the viability of such rules himself but employ them while dialoguing with those who accept them. In the West, Seyfort Ruegg, rejecting the opinion that Nāgārjuna's thought is anti-rational and anti-philosophical, considers the logical rules such as excluded middle, logical bivalence and non-contradiction as rational underpinning of Nāgārjuna's system. See Seyfort Ruegg (1977, pp. 5, 52, 53; 1981, pp. 93, 41 and 2000, p. 221).
183 See Chapter 4, p. 122–3; *Nges shes sgron me*, Question VII for his position on thesis. See Seyfort Ruegg (2000), pp. 105–232 for a detailed discussion of various stances on Mādhyamika assertion of theses.
184 See Seyfort Ruegg (1991) and (2000), pp. 232–304.
185 *Rab lan*, pp. 256–8.
186 Sera Jetsün Chökyi Gyaltshan (1989), vol. i, p. 178. See also Tillemans (1999), p. 135–7, where he discusses Sera Jetsün's glosses and *catuṣkoṭi* but mistranslates Sera Jetsün in some cases.
187 *gSungs sgros*, p. 481.
188 *Rab lan*, p. 261; *rGyan 'grel*, p. 60; *'Jug 'grel*, p. 562; *gSung sgros*, p. 476.
189 See Chapter 3, n. 91.
190 *rGyan 'grel*, p. 60: *de ltar na don dam dpyod pa'i rigs pas bden grub ces bya de kho na 'gog gi chos can gcig kyang mi khegs la/ de'i yul can 'dzin pa mtha' dag kyang mi bzlog na/ gzung 'dzin gyi spros pa mtha' dag stong nyid kyis mi khegs la/ gzhan yang 'phags pa'i mnyam gzhag dngos po'i 'jigs rgyur thal ba sogs gsum po 'jug cing/ don dam dpyod pas dpyad nas mi bzlog pa'am mi khegs pa zhig yod na bden grub tu 'gyur bas na/ skye med la sogs pa'i tshig gis spros pa mtha' dag zhi ba'i don la 'jug par bya'o//*
191 See Chapter 4, p. 155–6; *Rab lan*, pp. 296–7, 341; *gSung sgros*, pp. 478–9; *'Jug 'grel*, p. 562.
192 See *Nges shes sgron me*, Question I/3–4.
193 *Lam rim*, p. 590.
194 Ibid., pp. 594–5.

195 *Lam rim*, pp. 598–9: *chos 'di rnams rang gis ngo bos grub par 'dod na/ dngos por smra ba'am yod pa'i mthar ltung ba yin gyi/ de dag yod pa tsam smra ba ni dngos por smra ba'am yod par smra ba ma yin no// de bzhin du phyi nang gi dngos po rnams don byed pa'i nus pas stong pa'i dngos med du 'dod na dngos po med par smra ba'am med mthar ltung ba yin gyi/ de dag rang bzhin med par smra bas med mthar ltung ba min no// de ltar ye med pa dang rang bzhin med pa dang rang gis ngo bos grub pa dang yod pa tsam gyi khyad ma phyed par yod med kyi mthar ltung ba 'gog pa na kho bo cag med par mi smra yi yod pa ma yin zhes zer ro// yod par mi smra yi med pa ma yin zhes zer ba yin no zhes smra ba tsam la re bas ni 'gal 'du sha stag smra zhing dbu ma'i don yang cung zad kyang mi shod de/*

196 *'Jug 'grel*, pp. 532–3.

197 Ibid., p. 535: *de la bsam nas/ don dam dpyod byed kyis bum pa mi 'gog bden grub 'gog zer ba'i khas len de byung ba yin kyang don dam dpyod byed kyis bum pa ma bkag par/ bden grub yan gar ba 'gog tshul gyi rigs pa yod na de ltar grub mod kyang/ don dam par bum pa mi dmigs par ma grub kyi bar du/ de'i bden med kyang mi grub ste/ don dam dpyod byed kyis mthun snang kun rdzob kyi bum pa de la dpyad na/ dpyad bzod gang yang ma rnyed pa'am/ ma dmigs pa de la/ don dam dpyod byed kyi tshad mas ma dmigs pa dang/ don dam par med pa dang/ ngo bo stong pa nyid dang/ dpyad bzod du grub pa'i bden grub med pa zhes btags pa yin gyi/ de las gzhan pa'i bden grub 'jog byed dang/ bden med 'jog byed cung zad kyang med do//*

198 Ibid., p. 557.

199 Ibid, p. 558.

200 *gSung sgros*, p. 528.

201 See also *'Jug 'grel*, p. 558: *don gyi steng na chos can dang de'i chos tha dad du grub pa mi srid do//* Ontologically, the subject and its property are not established as different.

202 *'Jug 'grel*, pp. 534–5.

203 Ibid., p. 543.

204 Ibid., pp. 533, 536; *rGyan 'grel*, p. 27.

205 Ibid., p. 545.

206 *'Jug 'grel*, p. 539: *des na skabs 'dir stong mi stong zhes pa ni/ tha snyad du stong mi stong ma yin gyi/ don dam par yod med la/ mi stong pa dang/ stong pa'i tha snyad byed pa'i skabs yin pas/ don dam par mi stong pa'i chos ni rnam pa kun tu med nges su go bar bya'o// tha snyad kyi dbang du byas na/ bum pa bum pas mi stong par 'dod de/ tha snyad du de stong na bum pa med par 'gyur/*

207 I render *bden grub* as 'truly existent' instead of 'hypostatic existence' here. In this usage, Mipham does not understand by *bden grub* a reified entity but rather an empirically true and real existence. See Chapter 3, n. 147.

208 *'Jug 'grel*, p. 540.

209 Ibid., p. 555.

210 *gSung sgros*, p. 436; *Rab lan*, pp. 426–7.

211 Ibid., pp. 448–9.

212 Gomde Namkha Gyaltshan cites MA, VI/113 and well known passage from *Trisaṃvaranirdeśa* to support this theory in his rebuttal of Pema Karpo. See *dGaglan phyogs bsgrigs*, p. 615. See also Seyfort Ruegg (2000), p. 112.

213 *gSung sgros*, pp. 448–9.

214 Amdo Gedun Chöphel (1994), vol. ii, pp. 309–10.

215 *gSung sgros*, p. 450: *rang lugs rab lan du gsal te rang stong smra ba'i lugs so//*

216 *Rab lan*, p. 426: *snga rabs pa phal ches tha snyad du yod pas yod go mi chod la/ don dam par med pas med go chod ces 'dzer/ phyi rabs pa phal gyis kun rdzob tu yod pas yod go chod la/ don dam par med pas med go mi chod zer/ bdag cag gis ni de gnyis ka ltar mi smra ste/ tha snyad du yod pas tha snyad du yod pa'i go chod la don dam par yod pa'i go mi chod/ don dam par med pas don dam par med pa'i go chod la tha*

snyad du med pa'i go mi chod/ don dam par med pa dang tha snyad du yod pa gnyis dngos po rnams kyi steng na 'gal med don gcig tu 'char ba'i go tshul yod par smra'o//

217 *'Jug 'grel*, p. 554.

218 *Nges shes sgron me*, Question V.

219 See Chapter 4, pp. 123–4.

220 *Lam rim*, p. 654.

221 Ibid., pp. 655–7.

222 Ibid., p. 659. See Chapter 3, pp. 70–2.

223 *Rab gsal*, p. 384.

224 Ibid., p. 392.

225 *dGongs pa rab gsal*, p. 137 = f. 79b. He discusses the same triad in his *Lam rim*, pp. 703–4. See also Seyfort Ruegg (2000), pp. 276–7.

226 Ibid., p. 160.

227 *Lam rim*, pp. 703–6. See also Seyfort Ruegg (2000), pp. 276–9.

228 *gSung sgros*, p. 603.

229 Ibid., pp. 604–5.

230 Ibid., p. 608.

231 Ibid., pp. 605–6.

232 Ibid., p. 509.

233 Ibid., pp. 510–11.

234 *Ratnāvalī*, I/35: *skandhagrāho yāvad asti tāvad evāhamityapi/ ji srid phung por 'dzin yod pa// de srid de la ngar 'dzin yod//.*

235 *dGongs pa rab gsal*, p. 57 = f. 33b; *Nyi snang*, p. 480.

236 *dBu ma rtsa ba'i 'chan 'grel gnas lugs rab gsal klu dbang dgongs rgyan*, MGS, vol. Om, pp. 369–70.

237 *Rab lan*, p. 261.

238 *gSung sgros*, p. 477.

239 *dBu ma rtsa ba'i 'chan 'grel gnas lugs rab gsal klu dbang dgongs rgyan*, MGS, vol. Om, p. 370.

240 *Nyi snang*, p. 549.

241 Amdo Gedun Chöphel (1994), vol. ii, pp. 290–1; Lopez (2001), pp. 73–9.

242 Ibid., p. 291: *rang cag la ni bden 'dzin gyi blo 'di thog med nas goms pa yin pas/ bum pa mthong tshe thog mar skye ba'i blo de ni/ bum par bden 'dzin yin par thag chod/ de'i phyir rigs pa'i dgag bya la kha nas khyad ci tsam phye yang don la 'gog rgyu de/ bum pa 'gog dgos/ ka ba 'gog dgos/ yod pa 'gog dgos/ med pa 'gog dgos kyi/ bum pa bzhag nas bum pa bden grub bya ba zhig zur du 'gog rgyu ga la yod/*

243 BA, IX/26: *yathā dṛṣṭaṃ śrutaṃ jñātaṃ naiveha pratiṣidhyate/ satyataḥ kalpanā duḥkhahetur nirvāyate// ji ltar mthong thos shes pa dag// 'dir ni dgag par bya min te// 'dir ni sdug bsngal rgyur gyur pa// bden par rtog pa bzlog bya yin//*

244 *rGyal sras 'jug ngogs*, p. 384: *ci ste rang rig med na dran pa med pas yul myong ba dang mthong thos sogs med par 'gyur ro zhe na/ ji ltar mig shes kyis mthong ba dang nyan shes kyis thos pa dang yid kyis shes pa la sogs pa dag kun rdzob 'dir ni dgag par bya ba min te/ de dgag mi dgos te de tsam gyis sdug bsngal mi skyed cing dgra bcom pa rnams la yang tha snyad de yod pa'i phyir ro// dgag mi nus te 'gog na lung rigs kyis 'gog dgos na de 'gog na lung rigs la yang mtshungs pa'i phyir ro// bkag na skyon yod de chad lta can du 'gyur ba'i phyir ro// des na 'dir ni sdug bsngal rgyur gyur pa yul de dag bden par rtog pa ldog bya yin te de nyid 'khor ba'i rtsa ba yin pa'i phyir/ 'khor ba'i rtsa ba ma log na 'khor ba mi ldog cing gzugs sgra sogs bden 'dzin 'khor ba'i rtsa bar bstan pas nyan rang la chos kyi bdag med rtogs pa yod pa gsal bar bzhed pa yin no// kha rag pa la sogs pa dbang shes la snang tsam dgag bya min la de la rtag mi rtag dang yod med sogs gang du gzung yang dgag bya yin no zhes zer ba ni rgya nag gi mkhan po slar 'ongs pa yin no//*

245 '*ma brtag nyams dga' ba'*, is a phrase that Mipham uses to denote the conventional mode of thinking where things are not analyzed and their existence accepted without critical enquiry. The term '*ma brtag gcig pu nyams dga' ba'* (**akalpita ekarāmaṇīya*) originally appears in Śāntarakṣita's description of conventional truth in his *Madhyamakālaṃkāra*, 64.

246 *Ketaka*, p. 30: *ji ltar mthong thos dang shes pa 'di dag ma brtags nyams dga' ba tsam gyi dbang du byas te brjod na ni/ 'dir dgag pa min te de dgag mi nus la dgag kyang mi dgos pa'i phyir/ 'o na ci zhig 'gog ce na/ 'dir sdug bsngal gyi rgyur gyur pa dngos po kun la der zhen gyi bden par rtog pa bzlog bya yin no// 'dir mthong ba mngon sum dang/ thos pa gang zag gzhan nam lung las dang/ shes pa rjes dpag tshad ma'i sgo nas bzhag pa'i tha snyad la 'grel pas bshad do// mdor na rang rig pa 'gog pa ni don dam par 'gog pa yin gyi bem po las log tsam la tha snyad du rang rig par 'dogs pa'i tshul de 'gog pa ma yin te/...*

247 *Ketaka*, p. 82.

248 Ibid., p. 102.

249 See Williams (1998a) for Mipham on reflexive awareness and Pettit (1999) for Mipham and the Gelukpas on the *śrāvaka* and *pratyekabuddha* realization of selflessness. See also Kapstien (2000b).

250 See Chapter 2, p. 44.

251 *Rab gsal*, p. 385: *de ltar na/ khyed cag gis bdag med par bzung na med mtha' dang yod par bzung na yod mthar lhung bar bshad pas de lta na gnyis ka min par bzung na gnyis min gyi mthar ltung ba'i phyir/ de'i phyir gang du'ang 'dzin pa med pas hwa shang mahāyāna'i rjes su song ba la the tshom med de/ lham lus pa bgo skal du thob pa'i phyir le lan bda' ba'ang med do//* The last sentence is a satirical allusion to the myth that Hwashang left his shoe when he left Tibet and interpreted it as a sign that his tradition would come back to Tibet. Pari Rabsal is suggesting that Mipham is now upholding the Hwashang position, thus symbolically inheriting the shoe left behind. See Chapter 3, n. 254.

252 *Rab gsal*, p. 392: *Hwa shang gi lta bar smad khul gyi zhob che na yang/ des rgyab rten du drangs pa'i lung rnams sems kyi gtad sor 'cha' zhing/ yod med dang blang dor shes dang shes bya gang yid la byed kyang bdag 'dzin lam la gegs byed kyi sgrib par 'dod pa'i phyir na khyed rgya nag nas da lta rab byung gi gzugs kyis byon pa gor ma chag go//*

253 See *dGongs pa rab gsal*, p. 118 = f. 68a; *Lam rim*, p. 643; *dGag lan phyogs bsgrigs*, p. 385.

254 The account of Hwashang leaving or forgetting his shoe seems to be a mistaken case. *dBa' bzhed* reports that the Hwashang, who was chased from Tibet after Me Ag Tshom died, left his shoe prophesying that his followers will someday return to Tibet. Thus, it is not the Hwashang (Mohoyen) who was involved in debate with Kamalaśīla. *rGyal rabs gsal ba'i me long* however attributes this account to the Hwashang Mohoyen and his departure after he was defeated in the debate.

255 See Chapter 3, pp. 75–7.

256 *Samādhirājasūtra*, IX/23: *na cakṣuḥ pramāṇaṃ na śrotra ghrāṇaṃ na jihva pramāṇaṃ na kāya cittam/ pramāṇa yadyeta bhaveyur īndriyā kasyā ryāmargena bhaveta kāryam// mig dang rna ba sna yang tshad ma min// lce dang lus dang yid kyang tshad ma min// gal te dbang po 'di dag tshad yin na// 'phags pa'i lam gyis su la ci zhig bya//* Tsongkhapa cites this as a support used by his opponents in his *Lam rim*, p. 581. See also *rGyal sras 'jug ngogs*, p. 373.

257 *rGyal sras 'jug ngogs*, p. 373; *Lam rim*, p. 614.

258 *Lam rim*, pp. 616–7.

259 *rGyan 'grel*, p. 67.

4 THE FULLY EMPTY: MIPHAM'S THEORY OF THE ULTIMATE REALITY

1 See Seyfort Ruegg (1986, 1991, 2000); Hopkins (1983, 1986, 1997); Thurman (1984); Wayman (1978), Newland (1992); Napper (1989) and Cabezón (1992). There are also, in other languages, works such as Tauscher (1995) and Yoshimizu (1996).

2 See MK, XXIV/8; MA, VI/23; BA, IX/2; *Satyadvayavibhaṅga*, 3.

3 I am rendering the term *saṃvṛti(kun rdzob)* as convention and *vyavahara (tha snyad)* as transaction.

4 *Rab lan*, p. 304: *gzhung chen po rnams su bden pa gnyis kyi 'jog tshul mi 'dra ba gnyis bshad pa'i dang po gnas tshul skye med la don dam dang/ snang tshul tha snyad la kun rdzob kyi ming gis bstan pa de yin la/ gnyis pa gnas snang mthun par gyur pa'i yul dang yul can gnyis ka la don dam dang/ mi mthun par gyur pa'i yul and yul can gnyis ka la kun rdzob kyi ming gis bstan pa ni tha snyad nye bar bzung ba'i dbang du yin la/ lugs 'di'i dbang du byas na mdo sngags gang yin kyang yul can la'ang don dam gyi ming 'jug pa dang/ rtogs pa po gang zag la yang rnam grangs yin min gyi skyes bu dam par gdags rung bar 'gyur ro// lugs de gnyis kun rdzob dang don dam zhes ming mthun yang don gyi rnam gzhag byed tshul mi 'dra bas so so'i lugs kyi dgongs pa phye nas 'chad ma shes na gzhung chen po rnams khab mig ltar dog pa'i blos nam mkha' gzhal bas 'jal re zad par 'gyur ro//*

5 MGS, vol, Pa, p. 800.

6 Ibid., p. 800; *gSung sgros*, p. 450.

7 Ibid., p. 801.

8 *gSung sgros*, p. 450: *'di gnyis ka kun rdzob dpyod byed kyi tshad ma yin gyi/ rang gi ngo bo mi stong par sgrub pa min no//*

9 Longchenpa Drime Özer, *Grub mtha' rin po che'i mdzod*, pp. 125–6: *mtshan nyid la gnyis las kun rdzob kyi mtshan nyid gzung 'dzin spros pa dang bcas pa'i rnam par snang ba/ . . . don dam pa'i bden pa'i mtshan nyid ni gzung 'dzin spros pa dang bral ba'i ngo bo ste/*

10 Longchenpa Drime Özer, *Yid bzhin rin po che'i mdzod*, vol. II, p. 653.

11 *dGongs pa rab gsal*, pp. 167–8 = ff, 96–7.

12 *Rigs pa'i rgya mtsho*, pp. 474–6.

13 Tsongkhapa (1980a), p. 657: *des na don dam rtogs pa'i tshad ma'i yul du gyur pa ni don dam bden pa'i mtshan nyid do// . . . kun rdzob yin par brjod pa ni mtshon bya'o// blo ni mtshan nyid de snga ma'i stobs kyis tha snyad pa'i blo'i yul lo//*

14 *Rigs pa'i rgya mtsho*, p. 475; *dGongs pa rab gsal*, p. 167 = f. 96b.

15 Sonam Drakpa (1973a), p. 191: *gzhung 'dis chos thams cad kyi steng na tha snyad dpyod byed kyi tshad ma tha snyad dpyod byed kyi tshad mar song ba'i rnyed don dang/ mthar thug dpyod byed mthar thug dpyod byed kyi tshad mar song ba'i rnyed don gnyis su phye nas/ snga ma kun rdzob bden pa'i mtshan nyid dang/ phyi ma don dam bden pa'i mtshan nyid yin par bstan pa'i phyir te/*

16 Sera Jetsün (1973), p. 405: *mthar thug dpyod pa'i rigs shes kyi rnyed don gang zhig/ mthar thug dpyod pa'i rigs shes de khyod la mthar thug dpyod pa'i rigs shes su song ba khyod don dam bden pa yin pa'i mtshan nyid/ . . . tha snyad tshad ma'i rnyed don gang zhig/ de khyod la tha snyad pa'i tshad mar song ba khyod kun rdzob bden pa yin pa'i tshan nyid/*

17 Newland (1992), pp. 95–110.

18 *rGyal sras 'jug ngogs*, p. 368: *gang zag dang phung po rang bzhin gyis dben pa mtshan gzhi/ don dam bden par mtshon la/ rang nyid dngos su rtogs pa'i blo mngon sum tshad ma de la rang nyid gnyis su snang ba'i sgo nas de'i spyod yul du 'gyur ba min pa gang zhig/ rang 'jal ba'i mngon sum tshad ma des shes par bya ba yin pa'o// . . . gang zag dang phung po mtshan gzhi/ kun rdzob bden pa yin par brjod de/ rang nyid dngos su*

rtogs pa'i blo mngon sum tshad ma de la rang nyid gnyis su snang ba'i sgo nas rtogs par bya ba'o//

19 Drakar Trulku Tenzin Nyandra (2001a), p. 411.

20 *Ketaka*, p. 6.

21 MGS, vol. 21, p. 486: *mtshan nyid ni/ kun rdzob blo yi yul las ma 'das pa'i chos dpyad mi bzod pa/ don dam blo'i yul las 'das pa'i chos nyid dmigs pa nye bar zhi ba'o//*

22 Kunzang Paldan (1995), p. 624: *blo 'das smra bsam brjod med don dam bden pa'i mtshan nyid/ blo 'khrul pa yul dang bcas pa kun rdzob bden pa'i mtshan nyid/*

23 Bodpa Trulku (1996), p. 130: *rang lugs kyi bden pa gnyis po so so'i mtshan nyid bzhed tshul ni/ ji lta ba'i gnas lugs gang zhig mnyam gzhag blo 'das ye shes kyi yul du gyur pa dang/ ji snyad pa'i snang tshul gang zhig mthong ba tha snyad pa'i blo yi yul du gyur pa de/ rim bzhin don dam dang/ kun rdzob bden pa'i mtshan nyid du 'jog pa lags so//*

24 Ibid., p. 131.

25 *gSung sgros*, p. 452: *snang ba kun rdzob kyi phyogs su gtogs pa'i chos la'ang/ 'khrul ma 'khrul bslu mi bslu'i khyad phyed dgos kyi/ kun rdzob yin tshad 'khrul snang yin mi dgos so// don dam pa'i ming btags tshad stong rkyang yin mi dgos te/ kun rdzob dang don dam la gzhal lugs kyi ming so sor 'ong ba'i tshul gnyis 'di mdo dang bstan bcos chen po rnams la yongs su grags pa yin no//* See also pp. 465–6.

26 For definition of two negations, see *dGongs pa rab gsal*, p. 142 = f. 82a; *Drang nges*, pp. 278–80; Phurchog Jampa Gyatsho (1993), pp. 227–8; Karma Phuntsho (1997), pp. 45–6.

27 *Lam rim*, p. 639: *kho bo cag ni myu gu la rang gi ngo bos grub pa'i rang bzhin bkag pa na rang bzhin med do snyam du nges par 'gyur la/ de nas blo gzhan zhig gis rang bzhin med pa nyid yod do snyam du 'dzin pa na'ang de'i yul rigs pas 'gog pa min gyi/ stong nyid de rang gi ngo bos grub par 'dod na 'gog pa yin no//*

28 *rGyal sras 'jug ngogs*, p. 384; *Rab gsal*, p. 384.

29 *Drang nges*, p. 281: *'di la sngon gyi kha cig dbu ma pa la rang bzhin 'gog pa'i rtags dang rjes dpag yod kyi/ rang bzhin med pa sgrub pa'i 'di gnyis med . . . //*

30 Ibid., p. 283.

31 Ibid., p. 284: *de'i phyir rigs pas rang bzhin bkag tsam yin te/ rang bzhin med pa bsgrubs pa min zhes smra ba ni dbu tshad gang gi yang rigs par mi snang ngo//*

32 *Lam rim*, p. 680, *dGongs pa rab gsal*, pp. 141–2 = ff. 164b–65a.

33 See Chapter 3. pp. 91–3.

34 *Drang nges*, p. 286.

35 *Saṃcayāgātha*, III/25: *gang zhig yod pa ma yin de ni med ces bya//*

36 See Chapter 3, pp. 92–3.

37 See Chapter 3, pp. 93–4.

38 *Rab lan*, p. 269.

39 Longchenpa Drime Özer, *Yid bzhin rin po che'i mdzod*, vol. II, pp. 658–660.

40 *Nges shes sgron me*, VII/4–7.

41 *rGyan 'grel*, pp. 63–4.

42 *Rab lan*, pp. 253–4.

43 *rGyan 'grel*, p. 255.

44 See *Drang nges*, p. 284: Bhāvaviveka cites this in his *Prajñāpradipa* and Tsongkhapa mentions in his *Drang nges*, p. 285 that Avalokitavrata reports this verse is in *Lokaparīkṣa*. Thurman conjectures that this is from a work by Nāgārjuna known to Bhāvaviveka but now lost.

45 *dGag lan phyogs bsgrigs*, pp. 334–6.

46 For the analogy of pointing the moon, see *rGyan 'grel*, pp. 59, 259, *Rab lan*, pp. 276, 424.
47 Maitreya, *Ratnagotravibhāga*, I/154 and *Abhisamayālaṃkāra*, V/21: *nāpaneyamataḥ kiṃcit prakṣeptavyaṃ na kiṃcana/ dṛṣṭavyaṃ bhūtato bhūtaṃ bhūtadarśī vimucyate// 'di la bsal bya ci yang med// gzhag par bya ba cung zad med// yang dag nyid la yang dag lta// yang dag mthong ba rnam par grol//*
48 *Nges shes sgron me*, I/3: *de gnyis blo yis brtags pa tsam// don la gnyis kar khas mi len// dgag sgrub gnyis dang bral ba yi// blo 'das 'dod ma'i chos nyid yin//*
49 *rGyan 'grel*, p. 58: *ji srid dgag sgrub kyi 'dzin stangs dang bcas pa de srid du rnam par rtog pa'i spros pa mtha' bzhi dang bral ba'i rang bzhin ma yin no//*
50 For the analogy of space, see *rGyan 'grel*, pp. 17, 36, 235; *Ketaka*, p. 39.
51 *rGyan 'grel*, p. 261: *stong pa nyid ni ci yang ma mthong ba'i tshig bla dags so//*
52 Ibid., pp. 57, 58.
53 MGS, Om, p. 338: *mdor na rang bzhin yod pa dgag gi// rang bzhin med pa kho na mi sgrub bo//*
54 *Prasannapadā*, p. 168 (B. 393): *na vayam asyāsattvaṃ pratipādayāmaḥ kiṃ tarhi paraparikalpitaṃ sattvam asya nirākurmaḥ/ evaṃ na vayam asya sattvaṃ pratipādayāmaḥ kiṃ tarhi paraparikalpitam asattvam asya apakūrmaḥ/ antadvaya parihārena madhyamāyāh pratipādayitum iṣṭatvād/ kho bo cag ni 'di med par sgrub pa ma yin gyi/ 'o na ci zhe na/ 'di gzhan gyis yod pa nyid du yongs su brtags pa 'gog pa yin no// de bzhin du kho bo cag ni yod pa nyid du sgrub pa ma yin te/ 'o na ci zhe na/ 'di gzhan gyis med pa nyid du brtags pa sel ba yin te/ mtha' gnyis bsal nas dbu ma'i lam sgrub par 'dod pa'i phyir ro//*
55 *Drang nges*, p. 286.
56 *dGag lan phyogs bsgrigs*, p. 336: *tshig gsal gyi don ni/ kho bo cag don dam par yod pa dang tha snyad du med par mi sgrub ste/ gzhan gyis yod par btags pa'i bden grub dang/ gzhan gyis med par btags pa'i tha snyad du med pa gsal nas/ mtha' de gnyis dang bral ba'i dbu ma'i lam bsrgub par 'dod pa'i phyir zhes pa'i don no//*
57 Ibid., pp. 339–41: *da ni ye shes snying po kun las btus pa dang/ 'jug pa sogs las gsungs pa'i mtha' bzhi spros bral gyi don rje tsong kha pa'i dgongs pa dang mthun par kho bos bshad par bya ste/ de yang chos thams cad yod pa min zhes pa/ chos thams cad don dam par yod pa min zes pa'i don dang/ chos thams cad med pa min zhes pa/ chos thams cad gtan med pa min zhes pa'i don dang/ gnyis ka min zhes pa chos thams cad yod med gnyis ka min zhes pa'i don dang/ gnyis ka min pa min zhes pa'i don ni/ yod pa dang med pa gang rung min pa min zhes pa'i don yin no//. . . mdor na lung de rnams kyi don bsdus ste bshad na/ chos thams don dam par yod pa min gtan nas med pa min yod med gnyis ka min yod med gang rung min pa min zhes pa'i don yin te/*
58 *Rab lan*, p. 211.
59 *rGyan 'grel*, pp. 55–6, 255; *Nges shes sgron me*, III/8; *Ketaka*, p. 7.
60 Ibid., p. 261.
61 See Chapter 5, n. 165.
62 *Rab lan*, p. 245: *de kho na nyid ni bden med do zhes dri med grags pas brjod mi dgongs pa ga la yin/*
63 Ibid., p. 266.
64 *gSung sgros*, p. 599.
65 *rGyan 'grel*, p. 255; *Nges shes sgron me*, V/5–6, VII/18–26.
66 *Rab lan*, p. 261.
67 *Nges shes sgron me*, VII/17.
68 See *rGyan 'grel*, pp. 264–70 and *Rab lan*, pp. 211–52.
69 See *Rab gsal*, pp. 384–5.
70 *rGyan 'grel*, pp. 59–60: *'di ltar skye med la sogs pa'i tshig gis dmigs pa'i spyod yul mtha' dag stong par ston cing/ chos gang stong pa de la der zhen ldog pas na dmigs*

pa med par bstan par zad do// des na bden med ces pa'i tshig gis dngos po rnams dpyad na ma grub pa tsam zhig ston gyi/ bden grub ces dgag rgyu gzhan zhig gis bum sogs stong pa lta bu min zhing/ . . . skye med la sogs pa'i tshig gis spros pa mtha' dag zhi ba'i don la 'jug par bya'o//

71 Cited in *rGyan 'grel*, p. 261.

72 Ibid., pp. 261–2; *Rab lan*, p. 243; See also Seyfort Ruegg (2000), pp. 134, 176–7 for this analogy.

73 *rGyan 'grel*, p. 262.

74 *gSung sgros*, p. 489: *bden par grub pa'ang tha snyad du tha snyad tshad ma'i ngor mi slu bar grub pa la'ang go rung/ ngo bo nyid/ rang mtshan/ rang bzhin sogs la'ang/ tha snyad du bum pa lto ldir ba sogs kyi rnam par snang ba'i ngo bo sogs la'ang go rung/* See Chapter 3, n. 147.

75 *rGyan 'grel*, p. 28.

76 BA, IX/31–32.

77 Ibid., IX/33–35: *śūnyatāvāsanā dhānād dīyate bhāvavāsanā/ kiṃ cin nāstīti cābhyāsāt sāpi pāścāt prahīyate// yadā na labhyate bhāvo yo nāstīti prakalpyate/ tadā nir āśrayo 'bhāvaḥ kathaṃ tiṣṭhen mateḥ puraḥ// yadā na bhāvo nābhāvo mateḥ saṃtiṣṭhate puraḥ/ tadānya gatya bhāvena nirālambhā praśāmyati// stong nyid bag chags goms pas ni// dngos po'i bag chags spong 'gyur zhing// ci yang med ces goms pas ni// de yang phyis nas spong bar 'gyur// gang tshe gang zhig med do zhes// brtag pa'i dngos po mi dmigs pa// de tshe dngos med rten bral ba// blo yi mdun na ji ltar gnas// gang tshe dngos dang dngos med dag// blo yi mdun na mi gnas pa// de tshe rnam pa gzhan med pas// dmigs pa med par rab tu zhi//*

78 Butön (1989), p. 167; Tāranātha (1986), p. 203.

79 *Ketaka*, p. 36.

80 Ibid., pp. 37–8: *re zhig thog med nas goms pa'i dngos po yod pa nyid du zhen pa de'i ngor byas nas med pa nyid du sgrub cing goms par byed de/ dngos po rang bzhin med par ma shes na gnas lugs mtha' bral la nges pa skye ba'i skabs gtan nas med pas so// 'on kyang med pa nyid de tsam kho na gnas lugs mthar thug ni ma yin te/ gang tshe gzugs sogs dngos po gang zhig med do zhes brtag bya'i dngos po de tha snyad du rang gi ngo bos skye ba sogs su mi dmigs na/ de tshe de la brten pa'i dngos med kyang rten dngos po dang bral bas na/ blo yi mdun na dmigs gtad kyi yul du ji ltar gnas te gnas mi srid de mo sham gyi bu skye ba med na de shi ba'ang mi dmigs pa bzhin no// des na med pa ni yod pa la brten nas bzhag pa tsam ltos med du ngo bos grub pa ni med do// 'o na yod pa bkag nas med pa sgrub/ slar yang med pa'ang bkag nas yod pa sgrub/ de gnyis res mos spel bas ci zhig bya zer na/ rnam shes la rton cing tshur mthong rtog ge'i dbang du byas pa dag la glang chen gyi khrus dang 'dra ba'i kun rtog 'di lta bu byung ba ni shin tu bden te bsam gyis mi khyab pa'i chos nyid ni skal dman rnams skrag pa'i gnas che ba'i rab yin pas de'i tshul ni mi shes shing/ dngos med du bstan na chad stong du bzung/ snang bcas su bstan na bden grub tu bzung/ zung 'jug ces brjod na tha gu dkar nag bsgril ba lta bu'i don du bzung/ bsam gyis mi khyab ces brjod na cang med ci med hwa shang gi lta ba lta bu zhig las mi 'char ba yin te/ zab mo'i mthar thug pa'i chos 'di kun gyis bde blag tu shes nus na/ de dag 'jig rten mtha' dag las 'das shing 'phags pa'i spyod yul lta dka' zhing shes par dka' ba bsam gyis mi khyab pa zhes ji ste gsung/*

81 Ibid., p. 39: *de ltar na gang gi tshe dngos po dang dngos po med pa dag gang yang blo yi mdun na mi gnas pa de'i tshe/ de las gzhan bden par grub pa'i rnam pa gzhan med pas na bden 'dzin gyi dmigs pa'i gtad so mtha' dag med par spros pa ma lus pa rab tu zhi ba yin te/ so so rang rig pa'i ye shes tsam gyis rab tu phye ba smra bsam brjod du med pa nam mkha'i dkyil lta bu'i mnyam pa nyid do//*

82 *Saṃcayagāthāsūtra*, I/9: *imi skandha śūnya parikalpayi bodhisattvo/ carati nimitti anupādapade asakto// phung 'di stong zhes rtog na'ang byang chub sems dpa' ni// mtshan ma la spyod skye med gnas la dad ma yin//*

83 Also included among Tsongkhapa's works is the annotative commentary, *rGyal tshab chos rjes rje'i drung nas gsan pa'i shes rab le'u'i zin bris*, which is said to be Tsongkhapa's notes inscribed by Gyaltshab. This and the ninth chapter of Gyaltshab's commentary on the ninth chapter are almost identical.

84 *rGyal sras 'jug ngogs*, pp. 387–9.

85 Ibid., pp. 389–90: *stong nyid bag chags goms pa ste dngos po rang bzhin gyis stong par rtogs na dngos po bden par 'dzin pa'i bag chags spong bar 'gyur zhing/ ci yang med ces pa ste bden med nyid kyang bden med du rtogs pa goms pas ni bden med bden 'dzin de yang phyis nas spong bar 'gyur ro// . . . gang gi tshe dngos po gang zhig bden par med do zhes brtag bya'i dngos po bden par yod na dmigs su rung ba las bden par mi dmigs pas/ bden med du rtogs pa de'i tshe bden pa'i dngos med rten chos can bden grub dang bral ba'i phyir bkag pa bden grub blo de'i mdun du ji ltar gnas te chos can dang bral ba'i chos nyid med pas bden stong bden par grub na/ chos can de'i rang bzhin du grub pa dgos la de bden pa'i rang bzhin du grub pa sngar nas khegs pa'i phyir/ des na gang gi tshe dngos po dang dngos med dag bden grub gang yang blo yi mdun na mi gnas pa de'i tshe bden par grub pa'i rnam pa gzhan med pas/ bden 'dzin gyi dmigs pa'i gtad so mtha' dag med par rtogs pas spros pa mtha' dag rab tu zhi ba yin te/ stong nyid mngon sum du rtogs pa'i gang zag gis don stong nyid la gnyis snang gi spros pa yang zhi la stong nyid don spyi'i tshul gyis rtogs pa la ni gnyis snang ma khegs kyang des don bden pa'i spros pa khegs pa yin no//*

86 See *rGyan 'grel*, pp. 21–25; *mKhas 'jug*, pp. 147–51 and *Grub bsdus*, pp. 456–90.

87 MGS, Pa, p. 707: Mipham discusses the three ultimates of reality (*don gyi don dam*), of attainment (*thob pa don dam*) and of practice (*sgrub pa don dam*). They respectively correspond to the ground (*gzhi*), fruition (*'bras bu*) and path (*lam*). He also comments that all ultimates can be included within the *'gyur med yongs grub* and *phin ci ma log pa'i yongs grub* which are the objective reality and subjective gnosis. Following this, he states that all objects and subjects of which the ontic and appearing modes are consonant could be called ultimate.

88 See Mipham Gyatsho, *gSang snying spyi don 'od gsal snying po*, MGS, vol. 19, p. 37.

89 Kapstein renders *paryāyaparamārtha/ rnam grangs pa'i don dam* and *aparyāyaparamārtha/ rnam grangs min pa'i don dam* as denotational and non-denotational ultimate in Kapstein (1988), but in Kapstein (2001, pp. 317–43), he uses the terms denotable and undenotable absolute. See p. 328. Pettit translates them loosely as conceptual/ nominal and non-conceptual/final ultimates. See Pettit (1999), p. 53, *passim*. Similarly, Tauscher translates them as 'konzeptuelle absolute' and 'nichtkonzeptuelle absolute' [Wirklichkeit] but the same terms, *rnam grangs pa/ rnam grangs ma yin pa* in connection with *saṃvṛti*, he renders as 'entsprechende' and 'eigentliche' *saṃvṛti*. Tauscher (1995), pp. 53, 238, 294, *passim*. Seyfort Ruegg describes *saparyāyaparamārtha/ rnam grangs dang bcas pa'i don dam* as 'notional', conceptualised and discursive *paramārtha* while *aparyāya/ rnam grangs ma yin pa* as being beyond conceptual thinking and language. See Seyfort Ruegg (2001), pp. 97–9, 229–30. Dreyfus translates them as figurative and actual ultimates and Padmakara Translation Group as approximate ultimate and the ultimate in itself. See Dreyfus (2003), pp. 323, 334, *passim* and Padmakara Translation Group (2002), p. 39. None of these translations including 'notational and non-notational ultimates', which I use here, satisfactorily convey the original Sanskrit and Tibetan terms as used in the present context. However, I have chosen, having considered the meanings of 'notation' in the *Oxford English Dictionary*, to translate *rnam grangs pa'i don dam* as notational ultimate because (1) it can be verbally and conceptually noted or marked, (2) it is *paramārtha/ don dam* [merely] in the etymological sense of the word and (3) it is a conceptual representation or notation of the real ultimate. *rNam grangs ma yin pa'i don dam* is non-notational for being otherwise.

I have not used other translations such as conceptual, notional, nominal, figurative and denotational and non-conceptual, absolute, actual, non-denotational to avoid confusion as some of these words are often used, as I myself do, to translate other terms and concepts such as *rtog bcas/ rtog med* (conceptual/non-conceptual), *ming tsam, btags yod* (nominal/notional), *mthar thug* (final), while others such as 'denotational' and 'denotable' are used for applications of *brda/ mtha' snyad* in semasiological contexts.

90 *Ketaka*, p. 9.

91 *Madhyamakahṛdayavṛttitarkajvālā*, p. 117, *Satyadvayavibhāga*, p. 9, *Madhyamakālaṃkāra*, p. 71. Seyfort Ruegg mentions that clear mention of this division is also found in the *Madhyamakārthasaṃgraha* ascribed to Bhavya although it is not certain whether this Bhavya is identical with the author of *Prajñāpradīpa*. See Seyfort Ruegg (2000), p. 229. He in fact claims it to be the earliest mention but does not say how this would be earlier than the one in *Tarkajvālā*.

92 Lopez (1987), p. 135; *Madhyamakahṛdayavṛttitarkajvālā*, p. 117: *don dam pa zhes bya ba la don zhes bya ba ni shes par bya ba yin pa'i phyir don te/ brtag par bya ba dang go bar bya ba zhes bya ba'i tha tshig go// dam pa zhes bya ba ni mchog ces bya ba'i tshig gi sgra yin te/ don dam pa zhes bsdu ba ni de don yang yin la dam pa yang yin pas don dam pa'o// yang na dam pa'i don te rnam par mi rtog pa'i ye shes dam pa'i don yin pas dam pa'i don to// yang na don dam pa dang mthun pa ste don dam pa rtogs pa dang rjes su mthun pa'i shes rab la don dam pa yod la de yod pas don dam pa dang mthun pa'o//*

93 *Madhyamakahṛdayavṛttitarkajvālā*, p. 120: *don dam pa ni rnam pa gnyis te/ de la gcig ni mngon par 'du byed pa med par 'jug pa 'jig rten las 'das pa zag pa med pa spros pa med pa'o// gnyis pa ni mngon par 'du byed pa dang bcas par 'jug pa bsod nams dang ye shes kyi tshogs kyi rjes su mthun pa dag pa 'jig rten pa'i ye shes zhes bya ba spros pa dang bcas pa ste//*

94 Lopez (1987), p. 139.

95 *Madhyamakālaṃkāravṛtti*, pp. 89–91 and *Satyadvayavibhāgavṛtti*, p. 194.

96 *Madhyamakālaṃkāra*, p. 70 and *Satyadvayavibhāga*, p. 9.

97 Ibid., p. 71: *skye la sogs pa med pa'i phyir// skye ba med la sogs mi srid//*

98 *Satyadvayavibhāga*, p. 9: *dgag bya yod pa ma yin pas// yang dag tu na bkag med gsal//*

99 *Lam rim*, p. 669–70. See Chapter 3, p. 75–6, *passim* for the use of the term ultimate by Tsongkhapa.

100 Ibid., p. 572.

101 Napper (1989), pp. 429–40; Newland (1992), pp. 161–2.

102 Changkya (1988), p. 244.

103 Ibid., *mdor bsdu na yul chos nyid don dam bden pa dngos dang/ yul can gyi shes pa don dam bden pa dngos ma yin mod kyang gzhung las bshad tshod la de yang don dam par bshad pa dang/ de dag re re la yang dngos dang rjes mthun pa gnyis gnyis kyi rnam bzhag yod par shes par bya'o//*

104 Napper (1989), pp. 438–9.

105 *Rab lan*, p. 304.

106 *Ketaka*, p. 10.

107 *Rab lan*, p. 304.

108 *Nyi snang*, p. 542–3: *de la don dam pa ni gnyis te/ rnam grangs pa dang rnam grangs min pa'i don dam mo// dang po ni rnam pa kun tu blo'i yul te/ de ni bden stong gi ldog pa tsam yin pas blo'i bye brag yid rtog bcas kyi yul tsam mo// de don dam mtshan nyid pa min kyang don dam rtogs pa'i sgor gyur pa'i phyir mthun pa'i don dam mam rnam grangs pa'i don dam zhes gzhung rnams su brda gdags par mdzad do//*

109 *Ketaka*, p. 7: *don dam de la'ang skye ba dang gnas pa sogs bkag pa'i skye med dang gnas med sogs med dgag tsam gyi stong pa ni stong pa chen po mtha' bzhi dang bral ba la 'jug pa'i sgo tsam yin pas rnam grangs pa'i don dam mam/ mthun pa'i don dam zhes brda mdzad de/*

110 *rGyan 'grel*, p. 61: *des na yod par zhen pa dgag p'ai don du phyi stong pa nyid la sogs pa dang/ de ltar bkag pa'i dngos med la zhen pa dgag pa'i ched du stong pa nyid stong pa la sogs pa ji skad gsungs pa'i tshul gyis mtha' kun dang bral ba'i rnam grangs min pa'i don dam 'di yin no//*

111 *Ketaka*, p. 7; *rGyan 'grel*, pp. 55, 60.

112 *rGyan 'grel*, p. 255: *de ltar yod med kyi zlas phye ba'i dgag bya bden grub bkag pa'i med rkyang 'di ni nges pa'i don du tha snyad dam kun rdzob tu gtogs pa yin gyi// gnas lugs mthar thug pa yin kyang/ dam pa'i don nam gnas lugs mthar thug pa'i don dam mtshan nyid pa de dang mthun pa'i phyir/ 'bras ming rgyu la btags pa'i tshul du bden yod kyi ldog phyogs bden med rkyang pa 'di 'la'ang ni dam pa'i don zhes bya bar brjod na'ang rnam grangs pa'i don dam mam btags pa ba yin no// de la don dam pa mtshan nyid pa ni med rkyang tsam ma yin te/ mtha' bzhi'i spros bral yin na'ang gzhan sel gyi rtog pa'i blo yul na gnas pa'i dngos po'i bden med tsam po ba rnam grangs pa'i don dam 'di med na don dam chen po rtogs pa'i thabs med la/ de rtogs byed kyi thabs sam rgyu yin cing de la gtogs pa yin pas don dam zhes brda sbyar ba yin te/*

113 *Rab gsal*, pp. 384–5. See also *Rab lan*, pp. 205–10.

114 *Rab lan*, pp. 210–11: *'dus byas 'dus ma byas kyi chos thams cad rang bzhin med par shes nas dmigs pa'i spros pa kun las 'das pa'i de kho na nyid kyi yul can rnam par mi rtog pa'i ye shes la reg pa dang/ der ma son par bden grub tsam khegs kyang de nyid la dngos po med pa'i mtshan mar zhen nas spros pa nyi tshe ba bkag tsam gyi stong nyid la stong nyid mthar thug tu 'dzin pa'i go tshul gnyis yod pas na/ spyir bden med dang stong nyid dang bdag med kyi don gnas lugs ma yin no zhes nam yang mi brjod kyang/ spros pa mtha' dag ma khegs pa'i spros pa can gyi lta ba de dag yum nas bshad pa'i stong pa nyid mthar thug pa ma yin zhes bdag cag gis gsar du smras pa ma yin te/*

115 Ibid., *ston pa bcom ldan 'das rjes 'brangs dang bcas pas gsungs pa yin pas bdag cag ston pa'i rjes su 'brangs nas de ltar smra'o//*

116 *Nges shes sgron me*, VII/33–4.

117 *Rab lan*, p. 64: *des na rnam grangs pa'i don dam khas len dang bcas pa de rtsal du bton nas 'chad pa rang rgyud pa'i mtshan nyid yin la/ rnam grangs ma yin pa'i don dam khas len kun bral rtsal du bton nas 'chad pa thal 'gyur ba yin pa shes par bya'o//*

118 Ibid.

119 *rGyan 'grel*, pp. 66, 80, 262.

120 Ibid., p. 80.

121 *Ketaka*, p. 9.

122 *Madhyamakahṛdaya*, III/12: *yang dag kun rdzob rnams kyi skas// med par yang dag khang chen gyi// steng du 'gro bar bya ba ni// mkhas la rung ba ma yin no//*

123 *Madhyamakālaṃkāravṛtti*, 89 and see *rGyan 'grel*, p. 255, *Ketaka*, p. 8 and *Rab lan*, p. 301. See also *Rab lan*, p. 255 where *bdag med* is considered a correct conventional truth. Mipham also mentions in his *Nges shes sgron me*, VII/40 that notational ultimate is conventional truth.

124 See *Madhyamakahṛdayavṛttitarkajvālā*, 111–2.

125 MK, XXIV/10: *vyavahāram anāśritya paramārtho na deśyate/ tha snyad la ni ma brten par// dam pa'i don ni bstan mi nus//*

126 MA, VI/80: *tha snyad bden pa thabs su gyur pa dang// don dam bden pa thabs byung gyur pa ste//*

127 *rGyan 'grel*, pp. 81–2.

128 Ibid.

129 Ibid., p. 67.

130 Ibid., p. 62.

131 Ibid. On Mipham's distinction of the two schools, see also Dreyfus (2003). Dreyfus correctly demonstrates that the Svātantrika and Prāsaṅgika distinction, according to

Mipham, is more pragmatic and procedural than substantive and ontological. However, Dreyfus's concluding observation that Mipham puts emphasis on the notational ultimate in his Madhyamaka writings and may therefore himself fall within the Svātantrika camp despite claiming to be a Prāsaṅgika smacks of inadequate reading of Mipham. Throughout his Madhyamaka writings including *Nges shes sgron me*, Mipham underscored, as this book seeks to show, the delineation of the non-notational ultimate free from all extremes. Dreyfus's misunderstanding seems to have primarily arisen from Mipham's liberal use of terms such as *bden stong* and *skye med*, which I have already discussed. Furthermore, Dreyfus's interpretation that Mipham uses tantric 'luminosity' to dispel the negative extreme seems arbitrary and exaggerated. Mipham, like other Mādhyamikas, accepts that the Mādhyamika reasoning can eliminate all extremes. Hence, there is no need in the Madhyamaka context to rely on the tantric 'luminosity' to dispel the second negative extreme of non-existence. Mipham claims to establish the final Emptiness free all elaborations through a purely Mādhyamika procedure. Moreover, he also criticizes the Gelukpa for relying on conventional existence to dispel the extreme of non-existence.

132 Ibid., p. 63.

133 Ibid., p. 71, *Rab lan*, p. 400.

134 Tsongkhapa, *Lam gtso rnam gsum*, 11–2: *snang ba rten 'byung bslu ba med pa dang// stong pa khas len bral ba'i go ba gnyis// ji srid so sor snang ba de srid du// da dung thub pa'i dgongs pa rtogs pa med// nam zhig re 'jog med par cig car du// rten 'brel mi bslur mthong ba tsam nyid nas// nges shes yul gyi 'dzin stang kun zhig na// de tshe lta ba'i dpyad pa rdzogs pa lags//*

135 *Rab lan*, p. 247: *rje tsong kha pas red mda' bar phul ba'i shog dril du/ thal 'gyur ba'i 'phags pa rnams mnyam bzhag na khas len thams cad med pa'i rnam grangs min pa'i don dam la mnyam par bzhag nas/ rjes thob tu rten 'brel gzugs brnyan lta bu rnam grangs pa'i don dam bden pa 'gog med du 'char bar gsungs pas rnam grangs min pa'i don dam spros bral mtshan nyid pa 'phags pa'i spyod yul du gsungs pas spros bral nyid gnas lugs mthar thug tu bzhed par gsal lo//*

136 *rGyan 'grel*, p. 262.

137 Ibid., pp. 27, 291.

138 Nāgārjuna, *Pañcakrama*, V/13: *saṃvṛtim paramārthaṃ pṛthagjñatvā vibhāgataḥ/ saṃmīlanaṃ bhaved yatra yuganaddhaṃ tad ucyate// snang ba dang ni stong pa (kun rdzob dang ni don dam) dag// so so'i char ni shes gyur nas// gang du yang dag 'dres gyur pa// zung du 'jug par de bshad do//*

139 *Ketaka*, p. 10: *'dir stong nyid ston pa'i skabs su gzugs la sogs pa med par dgag pa ni med dgag kho na yin te/ ma yin par dgag kyang mthar gtugs na dngos por zhen pas stong nyid kyi don du mi rung bas med dgag yin bzhin du/ rten 'byung bslu med du snang bas snang stong zung du 'jug pas na dgag sgrub kyi 'dzin stangs zhig gzhig dgos te/ ji skad du/ chos rnams stong pa 'di shes nas// las dang 'bras bu rten pa gang// ngo mtshar bas kyang 'di ngo mtshar// rmad byung bas kyang 'di rmad byung// zhes dang/ rim lnga las/ snang ba dang ni stong pa dag// so so'i char ni shes gyur nas// gang du yang dag 'dres gyur pa// zung du 'jug par de bshad do//*

140 *rGyan 'grel*, p. 271.

141 *Nges shes sgron me*, V/14–20.

142 *rGyan 'grel*, p. 291.

143 *Nges shes sgron me*, VII/30.

144 *rGyan 'grel*, pp. 61, 292–3.

145 '*Char* literally means to appear or arise. I am not using the word appear here for *'char* as *snang* is rendered by appear. Arise does not translate well, so I am using a loose translation of experience. Experience here does not necessarily denote a direct

empirical feeling (*mngon sum myong ba*) but is more than a pure intellectual thinking (*rtog dpyod kyi bsam pa*).

146 *rGyan 'grel*, p. 293: *de ltar stong pa dang/ zung 'jug dang/ spros bral dang/ mnyam nyid de/ dbu ma'i 'char rim bzhi po de dag snga ma snga ma rim bzhin goms pa la brten nas/ phyi ma phyi ma'i tshul nges pa skye ba nyid de/ 'di dag ni shin tu gal che ba'i man ngag gi gnad dam pa'o//*

147 *Nges shes sgron me*, I/7: *ka ba khegs pa'i stong pa dang// shul na lus pa'i snang ba gnyis// stong dang mi stong zung 'jug tu// mi rung sred bu sgrim pa bzhin//* The first line on negation of the pillar reads slightly odd here. The context requires it to read as negation of hypostatic existence or hypostatic pillar and not negation of the pillar because Mipham is refuting the Gelukpa interpretation that pillar is not being negated but hypostatic existence is. The commentaries also take it to be negation of the hypostatic pillar. If the pillar itself is negated, such Emptiness can, according to Mipham, coalesce with the interdependent appearance of the pillar. The coalescence would then be genuine and not like twisting two threads. Perhaps, Mipham was not quite careful with syntactical structure of his words or assumed it can be understood to be hypostatic pillar from the context.

148 *Ketaka*, p. 38.

149 *dGongs pa rab gsal*, pp. 165–6 = f. 95b; *Rigs pa'i rgya mtsho*, p. 475.

150 *Ketaka*, p. 8: *'on kyang gnas lugs mthar thug pa'i dbang du na kun rdzob tu yod pa dang/ don dam par med pa zhes yod pa dang med pa'i mtshan nyid so sor phyogs su chad de gnas pa ma yin te/ gang snang ba'i gzugs la sogs pa 'di nyid stong zhing/ gang stong bzhin pa de nyid gzugs sogs su snang ba yin pas na snang stong zung du 'jug pa'i chos kyi dbyings sgro 'dogs so gnyis dang bral ba mngon du ma byas pa de srid sher phyin mtshan nyid pa ma yin pas/*

151 *rGyan 'grel*, p. 63.

152 *Nges shes sgron me*, VII/22: *stong pa 'ba' zhig yul byed pa'i// lam de bden gnyis phyogs gcig la// ltung phyir nyi tshe'i lta ba de// zung 'jug dang ni spros bral min// zung 'jug yod dang med pa pa'am// snang dang stong pa mnyam nyid kyang// 'di ni don dam stong pa'i dbyings// 'ba' zhig yul can yin phyir ro// spros pa yod med la sogs pa'i// dmigs pa'i rnam pa thams cad de// 'di ni med pa'i spros pa dang// ma bral de la dmigs pa'i phyir//*

153 *rGyan 'grel*, p. 256.

154 *Nges shes sgron me*, I/19–23: *spyir na gzhan gyis stong pa des// stong go nges par mi chod de// rta la ba lang ma grub kyang// rta de stong par ga la nges// rta mthong de yis ba lang la// ci zhig phan te ci zhig gnod// de phyir mi stong myang 'das dang// 'khor ba'ang chos dang chos nyid du// mi rung snang stong zung 'jug dang// srid zhi mnyam nyid 'di la med// chu zla zla ba min no zhes// gnam zlas stong dang chu zla rang// snang de zung 'jug yin na ko// zung 'jug rtogs pa sus kyang sla// ba lang rta min kun gyis shes// ba lang snang bar mgon sum mthong// de rtogs ngo mtshar che bo zhes // bdag nyid chen po ci ste gsungs// des na rang gi lugs la ni // chu zla brtags na chu zla nyid// cung zad mi rnyed med bzhin du// chu zla snang bar mngon sum tshe// med dgag yin kyang snang rung ba// stong dang yod pa so kye'i blor// 'gal yang 'dir ni mngon sum du// zung 'jug 'di la rmad byung zhes// ngo mtshar tshig gis mkhas rnams bsngags//*

155 The Omniscient One here refers to Longchenpa.

156 *Nges shes sgron me*, VII/18: *des na kun mkhyen bzhed pa bzhin// rang lugs 'di ltar shes par bya// dbu ma mtshan nyid pa yin na// zung 'jug dbu ma chen po 'am// spros bral dbu ma yin dgos te//*

157 *Ketaka*, p. 40.

158 *Rab lan*, pp. 254–5.

159 Ibid., p. 284.

160 *Lam rim*, p. 598.

161 Tsongkhapa, *Lam gtso rnam gsum*, 13: *gzhan yang snang bas yod mtha' sel ba dang// stong pas med mtha' sel zhing stong pa nyid// rgyu dang 'bras bur 'char ba'i tshul shes na// mthar 'dzin lta bas 'phrog par mi 'gyur ro//*
162 *Rab lan*, pp. 296–7; *gSung sgros*, pp. 478–9; *'Jug 'grel*, p. 562.
163 Ibid., pp. 297, 341–3.
164 Ibid., pp. 284, 296.
165 Ibid., p. 285.
166 Ibid., pp. 285, 291.
167 *Rab gsal*, p. 387.
168 Ibid., p. 387–9.
169 *Rab lan*, pp. 255–6, 274.
170 Ibid., p. 278.
171 Ibid., p. 283.
172 Pema Karpo accuses the Gelukpas of falling to the extreme of nihilism with regard to their understanding of ultimate truth and of falling to the extreme of eternalism with regard to their understanding of conventional truth. See *dGag lan phyogs bsgrigs*, p. 611. Gorampa Sonam Seṅge accuses the Gelukpas of espousing a nihilistic understanding of Emptiness. See Gorampa (1999), p. 41.
173 *rGyan 'grel*, p. 57.
174 *Rab lan*, pp. 283–5.
175 Ibid., pp. 274, 283; MGS, Om, pp. 337–8.
176 *Samādhirājasūtra*, IX/27: *astīti nāstīti ubhe pi antā, śuddhī aśuddhīti ime pi antā/ tasmād ubhe anta vivarjayitvā, madhye pi sthānaṃ na karoti paṇḍitaḥ// yod dang med ces bya ba gnyis ka mtha'// gtsang dang mi gtsang 'di yang mtha' yin te// de phyir gnyis ka'i mtha' ni rab spangs nas// mkhas pa dbus la'ang gnas par yongs mi byed//*
177 *Rab lan*, p. 284: *gang la mtha' ni yod min pa// de la dbus kyang ga la yod//* This varies slightly from MK, XI/2: *naivāgraṃ nāvaraṃ yasya tasya madhyaṃ kuto bhavet/ gang la thog med mtha' med par// de la dbus ni ga la yod//* How could there be a middle for that which has neither beginning nor end?
178 *Jñānasārasamuccaya*, p. 11: *de phyir dngos yod mi bya zhing// dngos po med pa'i yid kyang spangs// kun mkhyen go 'phang 'dod rnams kyis// de bzhin bar du'ang gnas mi bya//*
179 *Āryaratnakūṭa: Kāśyapaparivarta*, pp. 56–60: *nityam iti kāśyapa ayam eko ntaḥ anityam iti kāśyapa ayaṃ dvitīyo ntaḥ yad etayor dvayo nityānityayor madhyaṃ tad arūpy anidarśanam anābhāsam avijñaptikam apratiṣṭham aniketam iyam ucyate kāśyapa madhyamā pratipad dharmāṇāṃ bhūtapratyavekṣā/ ātmeti kāśyapa ayam eko ntaḥ nairātmyan ity ayaṃ dvitīyo ntaḥ yad ātmanerātmyayor madhyaṃ tad arūpy anidarśanam anābhāsam avijñaptikam apratiṣṭham aniketam iyam ucyate kāśyapa madhyamā pratipad dharmāṇāṃ bhūtapratyavekṣā/ . . . astīti kāśyapa ayam eko ntaḥ nāstīty ayaṃ dvitīyo ntaḥ etayor dvayor antayor madhyam iyam ucyate kāśyapa madhyamā pratipad dharmāṇāṃ bhūtapratyavekṣā/ 'od srung rtag ces bya ba 'di ni mtha' gcig go// mi rtag ces bya ba 'di ni mtha' gnyis so// mtha' gnyis kyi dbus gang yin pa de ni/ dpyad du med pa/ bstan du med pa/ rten ma yin pa/ snang ba med pa/ rnam par rig pa med pa/ gnas pa med pa/ 'od srung 'di ni dbu ma'i lam chos rnams la yang dag par so sor rtog pa zhes bya'o// 'od srung bdag ces bya ba 'di ni mtha' gcig go// bdag med ces bya ba 'di ni mtha' gnyis so// mtha' gnyis kyi dbus gang yin pa de ni dpyad du med pa/ bstan du med pa/ rten ma yin pa/ snang ba med pa/ rnam par rig pa med pa/ gnas pa med pa/ 'od srung 'di ni dbu ma'i lam chos rnams la yang dag par so sor rtog pa zhes bya'o// . . . 'od srung yod ces bya ba 'di ni mtha' gcig go/ med ces bya ba 'di ni mtha' gnyis so// mtha' 'di gnyis kyi dbus gang yin pa de ni dbu ma' lam chos rnams la yang dag par so sor rtog pa zhes bya'o//*

180 *Rab lan*, p. 291: *gzhung de dag gis khyed cag ltar dbus zhes pa ka ba gnyis bsgrig gi bar mtshams lta bu dmigs pa can zhig la gnas par bya ba'i yul du ngos ma bzung ste/*. . . pp. 294–5: *des na dbus zhes pa mtha' gang la'ang mi dmigs pa la brjod kyi dmigs pa can gyis gnas par bya ba'i yul la 'dzin dgos na/ stong pa nyid ji tsam bstan kyang rnam par rtog pa dang spros pa las 'das pa gtan mi srid pas//*

181 Ibid., VII/18–19: *des na kun mkhyen bzhed pa bzhin// rang lugs 'di ltar shes par bya// dbu ma mtshan nyid pa yin na// zung 'jug dbu ma chen po'am// spros bral dbu ma yin dgos te// 'phags pa'i mnyam bzhag ye shes dang// rjes su mthun par gtan phabs nas// yod med la sogs mtha' rnams kun// nyer zhi'i rang bzhin yin phyir ro//*

182 *Nges shes sgron me*, VII/33–34.

183 Ibid., VII/82–3, VII/ 85–6, VII/81.

184 Ibid., VII/73: *de phyir bden gnyis so so yi// khas len dang bcas dbu ma de// 'bras ming rgyu la btags pa yi// res 'jog dbu ma chung ngu yin//*

185 Ibid., VII/82–84.

186 Ibid., VII/85–6: *bden gnyis shes rab dri med kyis// drangs pa zung 'jug ye shes che// yod med yin min la sogs pa// mtha' bzhi'i spros kun nyer zhi ba'i// 'phags pa'i mnyam gzhag ye shes nyid// zung 'jug 'bras bu'i dbu mar bzhag//*

187 MK, XIII/8: *śūnyatā sarvadṛṣṭīnāṃ proktā niḥsaraṇaṃ jinaih/ yeṣāṃ tu śūnyatādṛṣtis tān asādhyān babhāṣire// rgyal ba rnams kyis stong pa nyid// lta kun nges par 'byin par gsungs// gang dag stong pa nyid lta ba// de dag sgrub tu med par gsungs//*

188 MK, XIII/7.

189 See Chapter 4, pp. 130–1.

190 *Lam rim*, p. 640.

191 See *Rab lan*, pp. 211, 238, 243, 332; *rGyan 'grel*, p. 269; *Ketaka*, p. 39.

192 MK, XXIV/11: *vināśayati durdṛṣṭā śūnyatā mandamedhasaṃ/ sarpo yathā durgṛhīto vidyā vā duṣprasādhitā// stong pa nyid la lta nyes na// shes rab chung rnams phung bar 'gyur// ji ltar sbrul la gzung nyes dang// rig sngags nyes par bsgrubs pa bzhin//*

193 MK, XXIV/12: *ataś ca pratyudāvṛttaṃ cittaṃ deśayituṃ muneḥ / dharmaṃ matvāsya dharmasya mandair duravagāhatāṃ// de phyir gzhan pas chos 'di ni// gting dpog dka' bar mkhyen gyur nas// thub pa'i thugs ni chos ston las// rab tu log par gyur pa yin//*

194 *rGyan 'grel*, p. 55.

195 *Ketaka*, p. 38; *rGyan 'grel*, p. 56.

196 Ibid., p. 38; *rGyan 'grel*, p. 56; *Rab lan*, p. 210.

5 IS EMPTINESS KNOWABLE AND EFFABLE?

1 This sequential link between linguistic communication, realization and *nirvāṇa* is nicely summed up in MK, XXIV/10.

2 See Chapter 2, n. 43. Seyfort Ruegg discusses two currents pertaining to the knowability and expressibility of the absolute *qua tathāgatagarbha*, which, though not identical with the division here, directly impinges on the current issue. See Seyfort Ruegg (1971) and also (1973), p. 59–61.

3 Hopkins (1983), p. 406; Napper (1989), pp. 711–2. Seyfort Ruegg mentions Ngog, Tsangnagpa and Butön among those who held the absolute *qua tathāgatagarbha* to be beyond words and discursive thought and even cognitive judgement. See Seyfort Ruegg (1971), p. 492 and also (1973), p. 60. In his *Theg chen rgyud bla ma'i don bsdus*, Ngog does not explicitly say that the ultimate is not knowable but describes it to be beyond conceptual thought and therefore not an object of speech. See Ngog Loden Sherab (1993), p. 11.

4 *rGyal sras 'jug ngogs*, p. 366. Newland conjectures Tölung Jamar to be an early twelfth century master. See Newland (1992), p. 44.

5 See Sakya Paṇḍita Kunga Gyaltshan (1992), vol. i, p. 383.

6 *Vajracchedikāprajñāpāramitāsūtra*, p. 26: *dharmatā ca na vijñeyā na sā śakyā vijānitum// chos nyid shes par bya min pas// de ni rnam par shes mi nus//* Reality is not knowable, it can never be known.

7 MK, XVIII/7: *nivṛttam abhidhātavyaṃ nivṛttaś cittagocaraḥ/ anutpannāniruddhā hi nirvāṇam iva dharmatā// brjod par bya ba ldog pa ste// sems kyi spyod yul ldog pas so// ma skyes pa dang ma 'gags pa// chos nyid mya ngan 'das dang mtshungs//* Reality is like nirvāṇa, unborn and unceasing. It defies being an object of expression because it defies being in the sphere of mind.

8 *dGongs pa rab gsal*, p. 168 = f. 97a. See also *rGyal sras 'jug ngogs*, pp. 365–7 and Tsongkhapa (1978c), *rGyal tshab chos rjes rje' i drung nas gsan pa'i shes rab le'u'i zin bris*, p. 59. See Newland (1992), pp. 39–50 and Hopkins (1983), pp. 405–21 for detailed presentation of Gelukpa basis of classification of two truths. See also Napper (1989), pp. 126–33.

9 Ibid., pp. 168–9 = f. 97a. The same argument is almost verbatim reproduced in *rGyal sras 'jug ngogs*, 365–7 and *rGyal tshab chos rjes rje'i drung nas gsan pa'i shes rab le'u'i zin bris*, p. 59.

10 Ibid., p. 167 = f. 97a: *bden pa gnyis kyi dbye gzhi la 'dod tshul mi 'dra ba mang mod kyang/ 'dir shes bya la bya ste/*

11 Ibid., p. 168 = 97a: *'di ltar de bzhin gshegs pas kun rdzob dang don dam pa gnyis thugs su chud de/ shes par bya ba yang kun rdzob dang don dam pa'i bden pa 'dir zad de/ de yang bcom ldan 'das kyis stong pa nyid rab tu gzigs/ rab tu mkhyen/ legs par mngon du byas pas de'i phyir thams cad mkhyen pa zhes bya'o//*

12 MK, XV/2: *akṛtrimaḥ svabhāvo hi nirapekṣaḥ paratra ca// rang bzhin dag ni bcos min dang // gzhan la ltos pa med pa yin//* Inherent nature is that which is uncontrived and non-dependent on another.

13 *Rigs pa'i rgya mtsho*, pp. 322–3. See also Napper (1989), pp. 127–9.

14 Jinpa (1999), p. 9.

15 *Ketaka*, p. 12: *de la 'dir chos nyid shes bya min par brjod pa ni/ chos nyid spros pa thams cad las 'das pas na/ de ni blos dmigs par byar med pas yin te/ gang yul dang yul can du ma gyur cing mtshan ma gang du'ang ma grub pa de la yang dag par na ji ltar shes bya zhes brjod de/*

16 *Nyi snang*, p. 541.

17 Ibid.

18 Ibid., p. 545.

19 See Chapter 4, n. 50 for space analogy.

20 *Ketaka*, p. 12; *Nyi snang*, p. 546.

21 Ibid., p. 13: *don dam par gzung 'dzin med pa'i mnyam bzhag gis 'di gzung bya'am shes bya yin zer na tshig de dngos shugs mi 'gal lam/*

22 Ibid.

23 MA, XI/13: *gang tshe skye med de nyid yin zhing blo yang skye ba dang bral ba// de tshe de rnam brten las de yis de nyid rtogs pa lta bu ste// ji ltar sems ni gang gi rnam pa can du gyur pa de yis yul// de yongs shes pa de bzhin tha snyad nye bar brten nas rig pa yin//* This verse is an answer to a question that if reality is peace and the intellect cannot engage in it as a subjective cognition, there cannot be knowledge or knower of the reality.

24 *Nyi snang*, p. 541: *tha snyad du don dam rtogs pa'i blo zhig su'i lugs la'ang yod pa smos ma dgos la/*

25 Ibid., p. 545.

26 Ibid., p. 542: *de'i phyir mdo dang bstan bcos kun na tha snyad kyi dbang du byas te don dam shes bya yin pa dang yul yin pa sogs ji snyed gsungs pa dang/ mnyam bzhag mi rtog pa'i ye shes kyis ji ltar rtogs pa dang rjes su mthun par shes dang shes bya*

yul dang yul can la sogs pa'i spros pa'i drwa ba gang yang med par brjod bral so so rang gis rig par bya ba'i don zab mo bstan pa/

27 BA, IX/2: *saṃvṛtiḥ paramārthaś ca satyadvayam idam matam/ buddher agocaras tattvaṃ buddhiḥ saṃvṛtir ucyate// kun rdzob dang ni don dam pa// 'di ni bden pa gnyis su 'dod// don dam blo yi spyod yul min// blo ni kun rdzob yin par 'dod//*

28 See *rGyal sras 'jug ngogs*, p. 366; Newland (1992), pp. 43–4.

29 *Ngog Loden Sherab* (1993), p. 11: *rnam par rtog pa ni kun rdzob yin pas don dam pa rtog pa'i yul ma yin//*

30 *rGyal sras 'jug ngogs*, p. 367.

31 Gyaltshab Je, *Theg pa chen po rgyud bla ma'i tikka*, p. 9.

32 Newland (1992), pp. 45–6.

33 *dGongs pa rab gsal*, p. 168 = f. 97a: *des na don dam bden pa shes bya ma yin pa dang/ blo gang gis kyang ma rtogs pa spyod 'jug gi dgongs par 'chad pa ni/ log par 'chad pa'o//* This is reproduced verbatim in *rGyal sras 'jug ngogs*, pp. 365–6 and *rGyal tshab chos rjes rje'i drung nas gsan pa'i shes rab le'u'i zin bris*, p. 59.

34 Tsongkhapa (1980a), p. 656.

35 *Ketaka*, p. 12.

36 Ibid., p. 11: *de'i phyir dngos po'i gnas tshul don dam pa ni yod pa dang/ med pa dang/ gnyis ka dang/ gnyis min gyi mtha' kun dang bral bas na blo yi spyod yul min te/ blo dang sgra ni kun rdzob yin gyi don dam pa ma yin pa'i phyir ro// blos 'di dang 'di'o zhes dmigs shing 'du byed pa dang/ sgras 'di dang 'di'o zhes gang brjod pa sems dang ngag gi spyod yul du gyur pa'i chos de ni brtags na rnam par dben pas sgyu ma bzhin du stong pa yin gyi dpyad bzod pa nam yang mi srid do//*

37 *Āryasaṃvṛtiparamārthasatyanirdeśasūtra: lha'i bu gal te don dam pa'i bden pa ni lus dang ngag dang yid kyi spyod yul du gyur na de don dam pa'i grangs su mi 'gro zhing/ kun rdzob kyi bden pa nyid du 'gyur ro// lha'i bu 'on kyang don dam pa'i bden pa ni tha snyad thams cad las 'das pa dang/ bye brag med pa/ ma skyes pa/ ma 'gags pa/ brjod par bya ba dang/ rjod par byed pa dang/ shes bya dang/ shes pa dang bral ba yin te/ ji srid du rnam pa thams cad kyi mchog dang ldan pa'i thams cad mkhyen pa'i ye shes kyi yul las 'das pa yin te/ ji ltar don dam pa'i bden pa'o zhes brjod pa ltar ni ma yin no//*

38 *Ketaka*, p. 11; *rGyan 'grel*, p. 271; *Rab lan*, p. 375; *Nyi snang*, pp. 550, 554.

39 Ibid., p. 12.

40 *dGongs pa rab gsal*, pp. 194–5 = f. 112a; *Rigs pa'i rgya mtsho*, p. 485.

41 *rGyan 'grel*, p. 229: *rang min bsal ba'i tshul gyis de'i ngo bo shes par bya ba rnam bcad dang/ rang gi ngo bo sgrub pa'i tshul gyis rang min mtha' dag bsal ba yongs gcod/*

42 *Ketaka*, p. 13.

43 *Rab gsal*, p. 399.

44 *Ketaka*, p. 5 commenting on the BA, IX/1.

45 Ibid., p. 13 commenting on the BA, IX/3.

46 Ibid., 11; See Chapter 5, n. 36.

47 Ibid., p. 3. Mipham mentions that profound Emptiness is difficult to fathom by even diligent men of great learning if not for the blessing of the Buddha and one's acquaintance with it in the past.

48 *Rab gsal*, p. 399–403.

49 Drakar Trulku Tenzin Nyandra (2001a, p. 412; 2001b, p. 435).

50 *Bodhicittavivaraṇa*, p. 68: *kun rdzob stong pa nyid du bshad// stong nyid kho na kun rdzob ste// med na mi 'byung nges pa'i phyir// byas dang mi rtag ji bzhin no//* Drakar Trulku, like most other Tibetan commentators, use this verse to substantiate the argument that the two truths, that is conventional truth and the ultimate truth *qua* Emptiness, are of identical nature, just like impermanence and causation.

51 Drakar Trulku Tenzin Nyandra (2001b), p. 436: *gzhan yang de chos can/ blo yi yul yin par thal/ 'phags pa'i mnyam bzhag ye shes kyis gzhal bya yin pa'i phyir/*

52 Drakar Trulku Tenzin Nyandra (2001a, pp. 414–5; 2001b, p. 436).
53 *Rab lan*, pp. 372, 378–9.
54 Ibid., pp. 372–3.
55 Ibid., *de yang khyod ni don dam pa ni dmigs pa'i spyod yul can du rtogs bya min pa dang kun rdzob tha snyad kyi dbang du byas te rtogs pa yod pa'i don gnyis kyi dbang du byas pa'i khas len tshul shan ma phyed par bab col du rgol ba'i tshig gis rang tshang ston pa la mkhas pa zhig ste/*
56 *Rab gsal*, p. 404.
57 Drakar Trulku Tenzin Nyandra (2001a), p. 414.
58 *Rab lan*, pp. 428–9.
59 *Nyi snang*, p. 541.
60 Hopkins (1983), p. 409.
61 Newland (1992), p. 214.
62 Ibid., p. 553.
63 *Rab lan*, p. 376.
64 Ibid., p. 550.
65 *Nyi snang*, 548.
66 See Chapter 4, pp. 114–6.
67 *Rab lan*, p. 374: *de ltar na dmigs pa med pa'i blo ni gnas snang mthun par gyur pa'i phyir don dam gyi yul can yin la/ dmigs pa can gyi blo ni gnas snang mi mthun par gyur pa'i phyir kun rdzob kyi yul can yin pas/ 'di skabs su bshad pa'i yul can kun rdzob des don dam mi rtogs zhes rgyu mtshan du bkod rung ste/ gnas snang mi mthun pa'i blo des don dam dngos su nam yang rtogs mi nus so// des na rnal 'byor pa de dag yul gyi ngos nas snang phyogs la kun rdzob bden par bzhag pa'i kun rdzob bden pa yin kyang des mi rtogs zhes rgyu mtshan du bkod pa ma yin te/ bden gnyis 'jog tshul gnyis yod pa gong du bshad zin pa de'i phyi ma ltar gnas snang mthun mi mthun gyi sgo nas 'jog tshul don gyis song ba'i gnad phra mo ma shes par kun rdzob ces pa'i ming tsam las don gyi shan ma phyed pa'i rtsod par song ngo//*
68 Ibid., pp. 372–5.
69 *Nyi snang*, pp. 549–50.
70 Ibid., p. 550.
71 *Rab lan*, p. 373: *sgra blo'i yul min par bsgrub pa'i blo de dmigs pa can yin la/ don dam bden pa rtogs pa'i blo de dmigs pa med pa can yin pas blo'i ming tsam la brten nas don gyi gnad ma go ba tshig gi rtsod pa tsam du zad do//*
72 Ibid., p. 377.
73 Ibid., p. 373; *Nyi snang*, p. 541.
74 Ibid., p. 378: *sgra blo'i yul yin pa'i lung dang rigs pa dang pha rol gyi khas len gnod byed du bkod nas 'gal ba ji ltar bsgrub kyang sun 'byin ltar snang las rnam pa kun tu mi 'da' ste/ don dam pa'i bden pa dmigs pa can gyi spyod yul zhig tu ni 'grub pa mi srid la/ sgra blo'i spyod yul las 'das pa so so rang rig pa'i spyod yul du gyur pa'i dmigs med spros bral gyi don rtogs pa la tha snyad du don dam bden pa rtogs zhes phyogs snga ma pa rnams kyis 'dod cing/ de gnyis kyi dgongs don so sor bshad du yod cing don 'gal med du sgrub pa'i rigs pa yang dag yod pa'i phyir/*
75 Ibid., p. 387.
76 *Nyi snang*, pp. 551–2.
77 *Rab lan*, pp. 380–2; *Nyi snang*, p. 543.
78 Hopkins (1983), p. 406.
79 *Rab lan*, pp. 411–2.
80 *dGongs pa rab gsal*, p. 166 = f. 96.
81 *Rab lan*, pp. 411–2.
82 Ibid., p. 373.

83 Ibid., p. 374: *gzung 'dzin med pa'i blo zhes pa'ang yul gang du dmigs pa med pa dang/yul can dmigs pa can gyi 'dzin pa med pa la 'chad dgos shing/*
84 See Chapter 4, p. 132.
85 See Chapter 4, n. 51, pp. 130–1.
86 Candrakīrti (1912), p. 110.
87 *dGongs pa rab gsal*, pp. 193–5=ff. 91a–92a; *Rigs pa'i rgya mtsho*, pp. 323–4.
88 *rGyan 'grel*, p. 259: *ci yang ma mthong zhes pa mthong ba dgag pa'i tshul gyis brjod pa dang/ ci'ang med par mthong zhes mthong ba sgrub pa lta bu'i tshig gnyis la khyad par med do//*
89 *Nges shes sgron me*, III/2, 5–6.
90 This saying appears in the instruction on freeing from four kinds of clinging (*zhen pa bzhi bral gyi gdams ngag*): *'dzin pa byung na lta ba min/*
91 Jinpa (1999), p. 9 and (2002), p. 25.
92 *Lam rim*, pp. 564–6.
93 Ibid., pp. 582–3.
94 Ibid., pp. 626–7.
95 *Rab lan*, p. 400; *rGyan 'grel*, p. 71.
96 See Chapter 4, p. 147.
97 *Rab lan*, p. 400: *nam zhig snang stong res 'jog gi tshul du 'dzin ma dgos par/ bden gnyis ye nas 'du 'bral med pa'i gnad kyis/ rten 'byung bslu med kyi snang ba yin par mthong tsam nas/ zung 'jug mtha' bral gyi gnas lugs la nges shes skyes te/ stong mi stong sogs dmigs pa'i gtad gso'i yul gyi 'dzin stangs thams cad zhig pa'i spros bral rjes mthun pa de lta bu go na lta ba'i dpyad pa rdzogs pa yin gyi/ de bas lhag por dpyad du med de gnas lugs zung 'jug gi don go ba yin pas/ de'i ngang du goms pas 'phags pa'i ye shes 'dren par 'gyur ba nyid du gsungs pa gor ma chag snyam du sems . . . /*
98 Ibid., p. 401.
99 *Lam rim*, pp. 779–80.
100 Ibid., pp. 783–90.
101 Ibid., p. 789: *gang zhig shes rab kyis dngos po'i ngo bo nyid so sor brtags nas mi sgom gyi/ yid la byed pa yongs su spangs pa tsam 'ba' zhig sgom par byed pa de'i rnam par rtog pa mi ldog cing ngo bo nyid med pa nam yang rtogs par mi 'gyur ste/ shes rab kyi snang ba med pa'i phyir//*
102 Ibid., pp. 788–90.
103 Ibid., p. 788. It may be noted that this analogy of two twigs dissolving in the fire that is produced by rubbing them is used profusely by Mipham in his writings to illustrate the nature of coalescence of two truths in the ultimate.
104 *Ketaka*, pp. 10–11; *Rab lan*, pp. 386–7.
105 *Rab lan*, pp. 387: *so skye rnams kyis spros bcas dang dmigs pa can 'ba' zhig bsgom pas/ 'phags pa'i ye shes dmgis med spros bral 'byung na/ de 'dra'i ye shes de tshogs sbyor du sgom pa sngon song gi rgyu med pas/ nas las 'bras skye ba ltar 'gyur ro . . . //*
106 Ibid., p. 294.
107 *Ketaka*, p. 11.
108 *Vajragarbhaṭīkā*: *Kodrava yi sa bon las// sā lu'i 'bru ni 'byung ba med// rnam rtog sa bon las byung ba'i// 'bras bu rnam rtog bcas par 'gyur// rnam par mi rtog las skyes pa'i// 'bras bu rnam par mi rtog 'gyur//* See *Rab lan*, pp. 251, 387 for the citation. *Kodrava* is identified in Monier Monier-Williams, *A Sanskrit-English Dictionary*, p. 313, as species of grain eaten by the poor (*Paspalum Scrobikulatum*). *Bod rgya tshig mdzod chen mo*, p. 28 has the name *koṭa* which it describes as poor quality grain like buckwheat.
109 *Rab lan*, p. 341.

110 Mipham Gyatsho, *Legs bshad snang ba'i gter*, p. 470; *Tshad ma kun las btus pa'i mchan 'grel rigs lam rab gsal snang ba*, MGS, Hung, p. 477; *Nyi snang*, p. 477.
111 Dignāga, *Pramāṇasamuccaya*, I/3cd and PV, Pratyakṣa, 287.
112 Asaṅga and Vasubandhu in the *Abhidharmasamuccaya* and *Abhidharmakośa* respectively present a classification of *vikalpa* into *svabhāvavikalpa, abhinirupaṇavikalpa* and *anusmaraṇavikalpa*. Asaṇga further divides them into seven types of *vikalpas*. See MGS, Ga, p. 406 and *Abhidharmakośa*, I/33.
113 Maitreya, *Madhyāntavibhāga*, I/9ab; Jñānagarbha, *Satyadvayavibhaṅga*, 33ab. Although the same name *svabhāvavikalpa* is used, Mipham's concept of *svabhāvavikalpa* differs from the *svabhāvavikalpa* in Asaṅga's and Vasubandhu's classification. Mipham includes in it all cognitive processes of ordinary beings involving reification and dualistic grasping. In the latter case, *svabhāvavikalpa* is equated with *vitarka*, which is the third type in Mipham's classification.
114 AK, II/33.
115 *Rab gsal*, p. 393.
116 See Chapter 4, pp. 155–8. where he argues that Emptiness *qua* mere absolute negation and the middle way formed conjoining lack of hypostatic existence and conventional existence cannot be object of a non-conceptual awareness.
117 *Rab lan*, p. 341–4.
118 *rGyan 'grel*, p. 57; *Rab lan*, p. 405.
119 Maitreya, *Dharmadharmatavibhāga*, p. 55: *yid la mi byed yang dag 'das// nye bar zhi dang ngo bo'i don// mngon rtags 'dzin pa rnam pa lnga// spangs ba'i rang gi mtshan nyid do//*
120 *Rab lan*, pp. 406–7. See also his commentary on *Dharmadharmatavibhāga*, *Ye shes snang ba rnam 'byed*, MGS, Pa, pp. 645–6.
121 Ibid., p. 384: *bden med med dgag rtogs pa'i blo ni sems byung shes rab yin la/ bden gnyis dbyer med kyi chos dbyings rtogs pa ni gzung 'dzin med pa'i ye shes yin te/*
122 *Nges shes sgron me*, VI/34–5, VII/62–4, 90. It must however be noted that Mipham does not use the term non-conceptual gnosis (*rnam par mi rtog pa'i ye shes*) in his *Nges shes sgron me*. Here, he uses the term coalescent gnosis (*zung 'jug ye shes*) very frequently and other descriptions such as gnosis of equality free from apprehension (*mi dmigs mnyam pa'i ye shes*).
123 Nub Sangye Yeshe, in his *bSam gtan mig sgron*, ranked Hwashang's simultaneist system above the gradualists but below Vajrayāna. Nyangral Nyima Özer describes Hwashang's system as simlutaneism meant for persons of sharp calibre in his *Chos 'byung me tog snying po* while Ugyen Lingpa's *Blon po bka' yi thang yig* gives a detailed treatment of Hwashang's simultaneism in a positive light. It was however Longchenpa who referred to Hwashang's remark on how both virtuous and evil thoughts bind us just as gold and iron chains, and treated it almost on par with Dzogchen in his *sDe gsum snying po*. Jigme Lingpa, in his *Kun mkhyen zhal lung*, also considered Hwashang's practice suitable for sharpest faculties although he distinctly marked the difference between it and the *sNying thig* meditation of Dzogchen. Kathog Tshewang Norbu doing a historical study in his *rGya nag hwa shang gi byung tshul grub mtha'i phyogs snga bcas sa bon tsam smos pa* rejects any affinity between Dzogchen and Hwashang's Chan system and even questions the authenticity of the distinction of simultaneists and gradualists. Some later Nyingmapas seem to include Hwashang's system in the mind (*sem sde*) section of Dzogchen. See Sam van Schaik (2003).
124 See Chapter 4, pp. 110–1.
125 *Rab lan*, pp. 337–8: *de'i phyir sngon gyi rgya nag dge slong gis ci yang yid la mi byed pa'i rgyab brten du mdo sde brgyad bcu khungs su byas zhes grags pa'i gtam rgyun tsam las/ mdo sde'i lung drangs pa dang/ de'i don ji ltar gtan la phab pa'i yig cha*

gang yang deng sang mi snang bas/ de dang gzhan 'dra mi 'dra yang ji ltar shes nus te/ 'dra gzhi ma nges pa'i phyir ro// gal te des rnam par mi rtog pa'i ye shes mdo dang bstan bcos chen po rnams nas ji skad gsungs pa ltar gtan la phab yod na/ sbyin sogs thabs kyi cha bkag pa 'ba' zhig tu bstan pa skad du deng sang bshad pa'i rna thos gtam rgyun 'di yang mi bden par nges te/ thabs tshul rigs pa de thams cad rnam par mi rtog pa'i ye shes bskyed pa'i sgo dang/ rnam par mi rtog pa'i ye shes kyis zin pas sbyin sogs thabs kyi cha dang ldan pa'i rnam kun mchog ldan gyi stong nyid rgyal ba sras dang bcas pas bgrod gcig lam ji bzhin gtan la phab yod na de la de 'dra'i lugs ngan pa 'dzin pa'i smra ba 'byung mi rigs la/ Kamalaśīla sogs kyis dgag par yang mi rigs te/ rgyal ba'i lam yang dag pa 'gog pa'i nang pa'i mkhas pa su yang mi srid do// gal te mdo sde khungs su drangs kyang mdo sde'i don ji bzhin ma shes par log par bshad na des rgyab brten du drangs pa tsam gyis lung de dag la da lta gtad so cha ba thams cad de'i lugs su ga la 'gyur te/ des rang blo'i dri mas sangs rgyas kyi bka'i don bslad kyang/ sangs rgyas kyi bka' ni bka' ma yin par mi 'gyur bas . . . //

126 Ibid., p. 338.

127 *Nges shes sgron me*, III/1–3: *lta ba'i dngos gzhi skyong ba'i dus// kha cig cir yang mi 'dzin zer// cir yang mi 'dzin zhes pa'i don// legs par rtogs dang log rtog gnyis// dang po mtha' bzhi spros bral ste// 'phags pa'i ye shes kyi mdun na// gang yang gnas pa med mthong bas// 'dzin stang ngang gis zhig pa ste// stong gsal mkha' la lta dang mtshungs// gnyis pa dran med hwa shang lugs// ma dpyad ce nar bzhag pa yis// lhag mthong gsal ba'i cha med par// mtsho gting rdo bzhin tha mal gnas//*

128 Ibid., III/4–6.

129 *rGyan 'grel*, p. 58.

130 Ibid., p. 57.

131 *Rab lan*, p. 405.

132 Ibid., p. 403.

133 Ibid., p. 404.

134 *Nges shes sgron me*, IV/8. The analysis of arising, abiding, coming and going (*'byung gnas 'gro 'ong brtag pa*) is a Dzogchen technique of analysing the mind by searching for its arising, abiding, coming and going. This and the instruction 'dismantling the structure of mind' (*sems kyi khang bu bshig pa'i man ngag*) through searching for the shape, colour, size and location of mind are two basic Dzogchen mind-pointing instructions.

135 Ibid., III/36, *Ketaka*, p. 10.

136 Ibid., III/8, IV/9; See Introduction, p. 18.

137 Ibid., III/38–41.

138 *Zhen yul* in Tibetan epistemology generally refers to the final object (*gzhal bya mthar thug*) of conceptual thought as opposed to the apparent object (*snang yul*) which is the conceptually constructed universal image (*don spyi*). Here, I am rendering *zhen yul* as referential object, as in the current context, it denotes the referent of language and conceptual thought.

139 Ngog Loden Sherab (1993), p. 11: *don dam pa ni ngag gi yul ma yin pa'i phyir te/ rnam par rtog pa ni kun rdzob yin pas don dam pa rtog pa'i yul ma yin pa'i phyir ro// ngag gis brjod du med pa'i don yang 'dir sgra dang rtog pa'i zhen yul ma yin pa la dgongs te/*

140 Ibid., *sgra rtog gi zhen yul ma yin pa yang mtshan nyid mtha' dag dang bral ba'i phyir ro//*

141 Seyfort Ruegg (1971), p. 492. See also Seyfort Ruegg (1973), p. 60.

142 See Chapter 1, n. 28.

143 Seyfort Ruegg (1973, p. 60).

144 Candrakīrti (1912), p. 109.

145 *dGongs pa rab gsal*, pp. 189–90 = f. 109b; *Rigs pa'i rgya mtsho*, p. 387.

146 *Gyaltshab Je, Theg pa chen po rgyud bla ma'i ṭīkā*, f. 9: *chos nyid sgra rtog gis ji ltar ji ltar brjod cing yid la byas kyang 'phags pa'i mnyam gzhag gis rtogs pa ltar mi nus pa'i don yin gyi don dam pa'i bden pa sgra dang rnam par rtog pa'i yul du cung zad kyang bya bar mi nus pa'i don ma yin te/*

147 *Rab gsal*, p. 401: *blo'i yul du khas ma blangs pa'i 'gal khur ma bzod pa'i steng du/ slar yang sgra'i yul du khas ma blangs pa'i 'gal 'du spos kyi glang pos theg tshad cig kyang 'gel te/ kye ma rgan bu lnga pa'i lam du btang na dge sbyong gi tshul 'jig mod/ da res 'dzam gling gi mkhas mi mkhas grangs yas pas sdig chen khur du 'khyer ba'i grogs dan byed par 'dug pas mi skyon snyam nas sems dpa' bskyed de smras pa/*

148 *Ketaka*, pp. 8, 16, 45, 125. For the last reference, also see the last verse of BA/IX.

149 The passage is from *Tathāgataguhyasūtra*, quoted in *Prasannapadā*, p. 155 (B. 366), p. 237 (B. 539): *yāṃ ca śāntamate rātriṃ tathāgato 'nuttaram samyaksambodhim abhisambuddho yāṃ ca rātriṃ anupādāya, parinirvāsyati asminn antare tathāgatenaikam apy akṣaram nodāhṛtaṃ nāpi pravyāharati nāpi pravyāhariṣyati/* See Seyfort Ruegg (2001), p. 113.

150 MA, VI/97: *stong nyid don can nges don shes par gyis//*

151 *Rab lan*, pp. 416–25.

152 Ibid., p. 418.

153 *Rigs pa'i rgya mtsho*, pp. 383, 530–3. See also Mipham's commentary on MK, XVIII/7 and XXV/24 taking them on the level of ultimate truth. MGS, vol. Om, pp. 374, 470–1.

154 *Rab lan*, p. 424.

155 Ibid., p. 542, *Ketaka*, p. 11.

156 Ibid., p. 419: *dmigs pa med pa'i stong nyid ston pa de dag nges don gyi mdo sde yin la/ dmigs pa can kun rdzob ston pa drang don . . . /*

157 *Rab lan*, pp. 420–1; Mipham Gyatsho, *Tshad ma kun las btus pa'i mchan 'grel rigs lam rab gsal snang ba*, MGS, Hung, p. 593; *Tshad ma rnam 'grel gyi 'grel pa legs bshad snang ba'i gter*, MGS, 20, pp. 62, *passim*; *brDa shan 'byed the tshom drwa ba gcod pa'i ral gri*, MGS, Kha, pp. 538–9. See also Dignāga, *Pramāṇsamuccaya*, chapter V; PV, Svārthānumāna/91, 138; Dharmakīrti, *Nyāyabindhu*, I/12–14.

158 Ibid., p. 421; *Tshad ma rnam 'grel gyi 'grel pa legs bshad snang ba'i gter*, MGS, 20, p. 61; *mKhas 'jug*, MGS, 22, p. 32; *Rigs gter mchan 'grel phyogs las rnam par rgyal ba'i ru mtshon*, MGS, Kha, 604.

159 PV, Svārthānumāna/213–14: *nāntarīyakatā 'bhāvāc chabdānāṃ vastubhis saha/ nārthasiddhis tatas te hi vaktrabhiprāyasūcakaḥ// sgra rnams dngos dang lhan cig tu// med na mi byung nyid med phyir// de las don sgrub min de dag// smra po'i bsam pa ston par byed//* See *Prasannapadā*, p. 9 (B. 24): *na hi śabdāḥ dāṇḍapāśikā iva vaktārama svatantrayanti, kiṃ tarhi? satyāṃ śaktau vaktur vivakṣām anuvidhīyante/*

160 *Rab lan*, p. 420.

161 Gyaltshab Je, *Theg pa chen po rgyud bla'i ṭīkā*, f. 9a: *rang mtshan sgra'i brjod bya ma yin pa dang/ don dam bden pa sgras brjod du med pa gnyis mi 'dra ste/ sgras brjod bya rang mtshan gyi rang bzhin la ma zhugs kyang gnyis su snang ba'i tshul gyis de'i rtogs tshul yongs su rdzogs la/ chos nyid sgra rtog gis ji ltar brjod cing yid la byas kyang 'phags pa'i mnyam gzhag gis rtogs pa ltar mi nus . . . /*

162 Ngog Loden Sherab (1993), p. 11: *ngag gis brjod du med pa'i don yang 'dir sgra dang rtog pa'i zhen yul ma yin pa la dgongs te/ dngos su sgra'i shes pa la mi snang ba tsam ma yin no// 'di ltar yin na ni kun rdzob pa bum pa la sogs pa yang de ltar thal ba'i phyir ro//*

163 *Rab lan*, pp. 421–2: *'o na ci zhe na/ bum sogs dngos po dang/ mkha' sogs dngos med de dngos dngos med kyi chos su gtogs pa'am/ dgag pa dang sgrub pa'i tshul gyis rtogs par bya ba'i chos thams cad la rang rang gi ngo bo de dang der dmigs shing brjod par nus pa/ de'i phyir rnam par rtog pa'i spyod yul du gyur pa yin no// nges don gnas lugs stong pa nyid ni/ dngos dngos med dam dgag sgrub kyi mtha' gang rung ngam/*

gnyis yin gnyis min gang du'ang brtag pa dang brjod par mi nus pa'i phyir brjod du med pa dang rnam par rtog pa'i yul ma yin pa nyid du brjod pa yin no//

164 Ibid., pp. 394–5, See also *gSung sgros*, pp. 499–500.

165 See Chatper 1, n. 28.

166 *Satyadvayavibhaṅga*, 11cd: *'jam dpal gyis ni yang dag dri// rgyal ba'i sras po mi gsung gzugs//* This is in reference to the episode in *Vimalakīrtinirdeśasūtra*, where Mañjuśrī asks Licchavi Vimalakīrti to explain non-dual reality and Vimalakīrti remains silent to indicate that words do not apply to this reality. For this Mañjuśrī applauds Vimalakīrti. See Eckel (1987), p. 78; See Chapter 4, n. 62

167 *Rab lan*, p. 422.

168 Ibid., p. 424.

169 Ibid., p. 382: *don dam la dngos su 'jug pa'i sgra rtog med pas sgra rtog gi dngos yul ma yin la/ bstan pa dang dper bya ba sogs las 'das par gsungs pa ltar yin kyang/ brgyud nas 'jug pa'i sgra rtog med pa ma yin te/ don dam spros bral gtan la 'beb byed kyi lung rigs dri ma med pa rnams kyis brjod med so so rang rig pa'i don la nges pa drangs nas goms par byas pa'i mthus don dam pa mngon sum rtogs par 'thad do//*

170 *Rab lan*, pp. 374–6.

171 *Akṣayamatinirdeśasūtra*: *don dam pa'i bden pa ni gang la sems kyi rgyu ba yang med na yi ge rnams lta ci smos//* The ultimate truth is that in which there is not even mental activity; why mention about letters? This is quoted in Jñānagarbha's commentary on *Satyadvayavibhaṅga*, partially in *Prasannapadā* and in Bhāvaviveka's commentary on MK. See Eckel (1987), pp. 74, 121.

172 See Chapter 5, n. 37.

173 Candrakīrti (1912), p. 139: *de ni spros pa thams cad kyi yul ma yin pa'i rang bzhin can yang yin te/ mngon par brjod pa ni btags pa'i rnam pa 'dzin pa'i phyir te/ ji srid mngon par brjod pa de srid du dngos po brjod pa ma yin no//* Beside, that is by nature not within the scope of all elaborations [such as expression] for expression apprehends the aspect which is imputed. As long as [it] is being expressed, the real thing is not being expressed.

174 Gyaltshab Je, *Theg pa chen po rgyud bla ma'i ṭīkā*, f. 9a.

175 *Rab lan*, p. 377.

BIBLIOGRAPHY

Primary sources

Aṅguttara Nikāya (*The Book of Gradual Sayings*), F. L. Woodward (tr.) (1932/6), 5 vols, London: Pali Text Society.

Āryasaṃvṛtiparamārthasatyanirdeśasūtra, DK, mDo sde, vol. Ma, Tohoku No. 179.

Aṣṭādaśasāhasrikāprajñāpāramitāsūtra, DK, Sher phyin, vol. Ka, Tohoku No. 10.

Aṣṭasāhasrikāprajñāpāramitāsūtra, DK, Sher phyin, vol. Ka, Tohoku No. 12.

Dhammapada (*The Word of the Doctrine*), K. R. Norman (tr.) (1997), Oxford: Pali Text Society.

Dīgha Nikāya, J. Estlin Carpenter (ed.) (1911), London: Pali Text Society.

Fünfundzwanzig Sūtras des Nidānasaṃyukta, Chandrabhal Tripāṭhi (ed. tr.) (1962), Berlin: Akademie Verlag.

Kāśyapaparivartasūtra, (in the *Ratnakūta* collection), DK, dKon brtsegs, vol. Cha, Tohoku No. 87, *The Kāśyapaparivarta*, Baron von Staël-Holstein (ed.) (1933), Harvard: Yenching Institute.

Kathāvatthuppakaraṇa-Aṭṭhakathā (*The Debates Commentary*), Bimala Churn Law (tr.) (1940), London: Oxford University Press.

Mahāsūtras: Great Discourses of the Buddha, Peter Skilling (ed.) (1994), 2 vols, Oxford: Pali Text Society.

Majjhima Nikāya (*The Middle Length Discourses of the Buddha*), Bhikkhu Ñāṇamoli and Bhikkhu Bodhi (trs) (1995), Boston: Wisdom Publications.

Paṭisambhidāmagga (*The Path of Discrimination*), Bhikkhu Ñāṇamoli (tr.) (1997), Oxford: Pali Text Society.

Pitāputrasamāgamanasūtra, (in the *Ratnakūta* collection), DK, dKon brtsegs, vol. Nga, Tohoku No. 60.

Prajñāpāramitāhṛdaya, DK, Sher phyin, vol. Ka, Tohoku No. 21.

Prajñāpāramitāratnaguṇasaṃcayagāthā, Akira Yuyama (ed.) (1976), London: Cambridge University Press, DK: Sher phyin, vol. Ka, Tohoku No. 13.

Samādhirājasūtra, DK, mDo sde, vol. Da, Tohoku No. 127, chapter I–IV also in Gomez and Silk (ed.) (1989), *Studies in the Literature of the Great Vehicle*, Ann Arbor: The University of Michigan, chapter IX in Christoph Cüppers (ed.) (1990), *The IXth Chapter of the Samādhirājasūtra*, Stuttgart: Franz Steiner Verlag.

Saṃyutta Nikāya, (*Connected Discourses of the Buddha*), Bhikkhu Bodhi (tr.) (2000), Oxford: Pali Text Society.

Sutta Nipāta (*The Group of Discourses*), K. R. Norman (tr.) (1992), Oxford: Pali Text Society.

Suvikrāntavikramiparipṛcchāprajñāpāramitāsūtra, Ryusho Hikata (ed.) (1958), Fukuoka: Kyushu University, DK, Sher phyin, vol. Ka, Tohoku No. 14.

Tathāgatajñānamudrāsamādhisūtra, DK, mDo sde, vol. Da, Tohoku No. 131.

The Sūtra of Golden Light, R. E. Emmerick (ed. and tr.) (1996), Oxford: Pali Text Society.

Amdo Gedun Chöphel (1994), *dGe 'dun chos 'phel gyi gsung rtsom*, 3 vols, Lhasa: Bod ljongs Bod yig dPe rnying dPe skrun khang.

—— and Mipham (1996), *'Dod pa'i bstan bcos*, Dharamsala: Sherig Parkhang.

Āryadeva, *Catuḥśataka*, DT, dBu ma, vol. Tsa, Tohoku No. 3846.

—— (?) *Jñānasārasamuccayakārikā*, DT, dBu ma, vol. Tsa, Tohoku No. 3851.

Bhāvaviveka, *Prajñāpradīpamūlamadhyamakavṛtti*, DT, dBu ma, vol. Tsha, Tohoku No. 3853.

—— (2001), *Madhyamakahṛdaya*, in Chr. Lindtner (ed.), *Madhyamakahṛdayam of Bhavya*, Chennai: Adyar Library and Research Centre, DT, dBu ma, vol. Dza, Tohoku No. 3855.

——, *Madhyamakahṛdayavṛttitarkajvālā*, DT, dBu ma, vol. Dza, Tohoku No. 3856.

Bodpa Trulku Dongag Tanpai Nyima (1996), *lTa grub shan 'byed gnad kyi sgron me'i rtsa 'grel*, Chengdu: Si khron Mi rigs dPe skrun khang.

Butön Rinchen Drub (1989), *bDe bar gshegs pa'i bstan pa gsal bar byed pa'i chos kyi 'byung gnas gsung rab rin po che'i mdzod*, Beijing: Krung go Bod kyi Shes rig dPe skrun khang.

Candrakīrti (1912a), *Madhyamakāvatāra*, La Vallée Poussin (ed.), St. Petersbourg: Commissionnaires de l'Académie Imperiale des Sceinces. Also DT, dBu ma, vol. 'A, Tohoku No. 3861.

—— (1912b), *Madhyamakāvatārabhāṣya*, in La Vallée Poussin (ed.), *Madhyamakāvatāra*, St. Petersbourg: Commissionnaires de l'Académie Imperiale des Sceinces. Also DT, dBu ma, vol. 'A, Tohoku No. 3862.

—— (1989), *Prasannapadā, Mādhyamakaśāstra*, Swami Dwarika Das Shastri (ed.), Varanasi: Bauddha Bharati.

——, *Madhyamakaprajñāvatārakārikā*, DT, dBu ma, vol. 'A, Tohoku No. 3863.

Chandra, Lokesh (1981), *Materials for a History of Tibetan Literature*, Kyoto: Rinsen Book.

Changkya Rolpai Dorje (1988), *Grub mtha' thub bstan lhun po'i mdzes rgyan*, Beijing: Krung go Bod kyi Shes rig dPe skrun khang.

Chari Kalzang Thogme (2000), *gZhung pod lnga'i spyi bshad*, Lanzhou: Kansu Mi rigs dPe skrun khang, vols I and II.

Chukye Samten (1997), *Log lta'i tshang tshing sreg pa'i lung rigs rdo rje me lce*, Lanzhou: Kansu Mi rigs dPe skrun khang.

Dharmakīrti (1989), *Pramāṇavārttikam*, Ram Chandra Pandeya (ed.), Delhi: Motilal Banarsidass.

Dignāga (1959), *Prajñāpāramitāpiṇḍārthasaṃgrahaḥ*, E. Fraulwallner (ed.), Wiener Zeitschrift für die Kunde Süd- und Ostasiens und Archiv für indische Philosophie 3, pp. 140–4.

Dobi Geshe Sherab Gyatsho (1982), *rJe btsun shes rab rgya mtsho 'jam dpal dgyes pa'i blo gros kyi gsung rtsom*, Xining: mTsho sngon Mi rigs dPe skrun khang.

Drakar Trulku Paldan Tenzin Nyandra (2001a), *Zab mo dbu ma'i gnad cung zad brjod pa blo gsal dga' ba'i gtam zhes bya ba mi pham rnam rgyal la klan ka gyis pa dang po'o* in *Brag dkar blo bzang dpal ldan bstan 'dzin snyan grags kyi gsung 'bum*, Chengdu: dMangs khrod dpe dkon sdud sgrig khang, vol. Na, pp. 397–432 (Copy in the Library of IsMEO, Rome, No. 277/5).

——(2001b), *'Jam dbyangs rnam rgyal gyis 'dod tshul la klan ka bgyis pa zab mo'i gtam* in *Brag dkar blo bzang dpal ldan bstan 'dzin snyan grags kyi gsung 'bum*, Chengdu: dMangs khrod dpe dkon sdud sgrig khang, vol. Na, pp. 433–48 (Copy in the Library of IsMEO, Rome, No. 277/6).

——(2001c), *Mi pham rnam rgyal gyis rtsod pa'i yang lan log lta'i khong khrag 'don pa'i skyug sman zhes bya ba* in *Brag dkar blo bzang dpal ldan bstan 'dzin snyan grags kyi gsung 'bum*, Chengdu: dMangs khrod dpe dkon sdud sgrig khang, vol. Na, pp. 449–742 (Copies in Oslo University Library and Library of IsMEO, Rome, No. 277/7).

Giteng Lobzang Paldan (1998), *Blo bzang dpal ldan gyi ljags rtsom phyogs bsgrigs*, 3 vols, Beijing: Krung go Bod kyi Shes rig dPe skrun khang.

Gomde Sharchen Namkha Gyaltshan, *Byang chub sems 'grel gyi rnam par bshad pa'i zhar byung 'brug pa mi pham padma dkar pos phyag chen rgyal ba'i gan mdzod ces par rje tshong kha pa la dgag pa mdzad pa'i gsung lan zhes bya ba* in *dGag lan phyogs bsgrigs*, pp. 607–45.

Gorampa Sonam Seṅge (1968), *dBu ma la 'jug pa'i dkyus kyi sa bcad pa dang gzhung so so'i dka' ba'i gnas la dpyad pa lta ba ngan sel*, in *The Complete Works of the Great Master of the Sa skya Sect of Tibetan Buddhism*, Tokyo: The Toyo Bunko, vol. 13, pp. 24–84.

——(1999), *lTa ba'i shan 'byed theg mchog gnad kyi zla zer*, Sarnath: Sakya Student's Union.

Gyaltshab Je / Dharma Rinchen (1994), *sPyod 'jug 'grel pa rgyal sras 'jug ngogs*, Xining: mTsho sngon Mi rigs dPe skrun khang.

——(n.d.) *Theg pa chen po rgyud bla ma'i ṭīkā*, in *The Collected Writings of rGyal tshab rJe*, Shigatse: Tashi Lhunpo, vol. Ga.

Horkhang Sonam Palbar (1999), *Hor khang bsod nams dpal 'bar gyi gsung rtsom*, Beijing: Krung go Bod kyi Shes rig dPe skrun khang.

Jamyang Gawai Lodoe, *lTa ba ngan pa thams cad tshar gcod pa'i bstan bcos gnam lcags 'khor lo zhes bya ba* in *dGag lan phyogs bsgrigs*, pp. 519–605.

Jangchub Gyatsho (2001), *Brag dkar gsung 'bum gyi dkar chag*, Chengdu: dMangs khrod dpe dkon bsdu sgrig khang.

Jigme Phuntsho (2002), *Chos rje dam pa yid bzhin nor bu 'jigs med phun tshogs 'byung gnas dpal bzang po'i gsung 'bum*, Serta: gSer ljongs Bla ma rung lNga rig Nang bstan Slob gling.

——(n.d.) *Kun mkhyen mi pham rgya mtsho la gsol ba 'debs tshul g.yul las rnam par rgyal ba'i rnga sgra*, n.p.

Jñānagarbha, *Satyadvayavibhaṅgakārikā*, in Malcolm Eckel (1992), *Jñānagarbha on the Two Truths*, Delhi: Motilal Banarsidass, 1989. Also DT, dBu ma, vol. Sa, Tohoku No. 3881.

Karma Phuntsho (1997), *Tshad ma rigs pa'i them skas*, Bylakuppe: Ngagyur Nyingma Institute.

Karmapa Mikyod Dorje (1996), *dBu ma la 'jug pa'i kar ṭīk dwags brgyud grub pa'i shing rta*, Seattle: Nitartha International.

Khedrub Geleg Palzang, *Phyin ci log gi gtam gyi sbyor ba la zhugs pa'i smra ba ngan pa rnam par 'thag pa'i bstan bcos gnam lcags 'khor lo zhes bya ba* in *dGag lan phyogs bsgrigs*, pp. 1–68.

Khedrub Geleg Palzang, Sera Jetsün, Jamyang Galo, Gomde Namkha Gyaltshan and Balmang Konchog Gyaltshan (1997), *dGag lan phyogs bsgrigs*, Chengdu: Si khron Mi rigs dPe skrun khang.

Khujug alias Kagon (1998), *dBu ma'i gtan tshigs kyi go don rin chen phreng ba*, Beijing: Mi rigs dPe skrun khang.

—— (n.d.) *Grub mtha' rin po che'i mdzod*, Thimphu: National Library.

Kunzang Chödrak (1987), *Gangs ri'i khrod kyi smra ba'i sen ge gcig pu 'jam mgon mi pham rgya mtsho'i rnam thar snying po bsdus pa*, MGS, vol. Hung, pp. 621–732.

Kunzang Paldan (1995), *Byang chub sems dpa'i spyod pa la 'jug pa'i tshig 'grel 'jam dbyangs bla ma'i zhal lung bdud brtsi'i thig pa*, Chengdu: Si khron Mi rigs dPe skrun khang.

Lodoe Gyaltshan, [Sog zlog pa] (1998), *gSang sngags snga 'gyur la bod du rtsod pa snga phyir byung ba rnams kyi lan du brjod pa nges pa don gyi 'brug sgra*, Chengdu: Si khron Mi rigs dPe skrun khang.

Lodoe Gyatsho (1987), *sMra ba'i seng ge mi pham phyogs las rnam par rgyal ba'i gsung rab rnams kyi bzhugs byang ngo mtshar nor bu'i me long*, MGS, vol. Śrī, pp. 641–76.

Longchenpa Drime Özer (n.d.), *Yid bzhin rin po che'i mdzod*, Thimphu: National Library.

Maitreya (1970), *Mahāyānasūtrālaṃkāra*, S. Bagchi (ed.), Darbhanga: The Mithila Institute, 1970. Also in *Byams chos sde lnga*, Beijing: Mi rigs dPe skrun khang, 1993, pp. 27–107.

—— (1993a), *Abhisamayālaṃkārānāmaprajñāpāramitopadeśaśāstra*, Ramshankar Tripathi (ed.), Sarnath: Central Institute of Higher Tibetan Studies. Also in *Byams chos sde lnga* (1993), Beijing: Mi rigs dPe skrun khang, pp. 1–26.

—— (1993b), *Dharmadharmatavibhāgaśāstra*, in *Byams chos sde lnga*, Beijing: Mi rigs dPe skrun khang, pp. 150–6.

—— (1994), *Madhyāntavibhāgaśāstra*, Swami Dwarikadas Shastri (ed.), Varanasi: Bauddha Bharati. Also in *Byams chos sde lnga*(1993), Beijing: Mi rigs dPe skrun khang, pp. 157–65.

—— (1997), *Ratnagotravibhāgamahāyānottaratantraśāstra*, H. S. Prasad (ed.), Delhi: Sri Satguru Publications. Also in *Byams chos sde lnga* (1993), Beijing: Mi rigs dPe skrun khang, pp. 108–49.

Mipham [Jamyang Namgyal] Gyatsho (1987), *Mi pham rgya mtsho'i gsung 'bum* (The Collected Works of Mipham Gyatsho), Kathmandu: Zhechen Monastery, 1987. This collection, compiled by H. H. Dilgo Khyentse Rinpoche, consists of twenty-seven volumes as of 1998. The redaction was based on the Derge collection of Mipham's writings and those printed in other monasteries are added to it. The volumes are marked: Om, A, Ra, Pa, Tsa, Na, Dhī, Śrī, Hung, E, Waṃ, Ka, Kha, Ga, Nga, Ca, Cha, Ja, 19, 20, 21, 22, 23, 24, 25, 26 and 27.

——, *rDo grub pa dam chos zhes pas gzhan gyi zer sgros bsdus nas mkhas su re ba'i 'khyal ngag de dag mi mkhas mtshang phung du kho rang nas bskul ba bzhin nyams mtshar du bkod pa*, MGS, vol. Nga, pp. 359–415.

——, *Nges shes rin po che'i sgron me*, MGS, vol. Śrī, pp. 71–123.

——, *dBu ma rgyan gi rnam bshad 'jam dbyang bla ma dgyes pa'i zhal lung*, MGS, vol. Nga, pp. 1–358.

——, *Yid bzhin mdzod kyi grub mtha' bsdus pa*, MGS, vol. 21, pp. 439–500.

——, *dBu ma rtsa ba'i mchan 'grel rab gsal klu dbang dgongs rgyan*, MGS, vol. Om, pp. 203–495.

——, *dBu ma 'jug pa'i 'grel pa zla ba'i zhal lung dri med shel phreng*, MGS, vol. Om, pp. 497–837.

——, *bDe gshegs snying po'i stong thun seng ge'i nga ro*, MGS, vol. Pa, pp. 563–608.

——, *Theg pa chen po rgyud bla ma'i mchan'grel ma pham zhal lung*, MGS, vol. Pa, pp. 349–561.

——, *gZhan stong mkhas lan seng ge'i nga ro*, MGS, vol. Ga, pp. 359–78.

——, *gZhung spyi'i dka' gnad gsung gros phyogs bsdus rin po che'i za ma tog*, MGS, vol. 22, pp. 427–710.

——(1984), *Cintāmaṇi: Tibetan Manuscripts on Buddhist Meditation of the Great Perfection School*, Varanasi: Sanskrit University.

——(1993a), *sPyod 'jug sher 'grel ketaka*, Chengdu: Si khron Mi rigs dPe skrun khang, pp. 1–130. Also in MGS, vol. Ca, pp. 1–98.

——(1993b), *gZhan gyis brtsad pa'i lan mdor bsdus pa rigs lam rab gsal de nyid snang byed* in *sPyod 'jug sher 'grel ketaka*, Chengdu: Si khron Mi rigs dPe skrun khang, pp. 133–464. Also in MGS, vol. Ca, pp. 191–474.

——(1993c), *brGal lan nyin byed snang ba* in *sPyod 'jug sher 'grel ketaka*, Chengdu: Si khron Mi rigs dPe skrun khang, pp. 467–679. Also in MGS, vol. Ca, pp. 99–190.

——(1993d), *bZo gnas nyer mkho'i za ma tog*, Xining: mTsho sngon Mi rigs dPe skrun khang.

——and Kunzang Paldan (1997), *Nges shes sgron me rtsa 'grel*, Chengdu: Si khron Mi rigs dPe skrun khang.

——(2000), *bKa' brgyad rnam bshad dang spyi don 'od gsal snying po yang dag grub pa'i tshig 'grel bcas*, Chengdu: Si khron Mi rigs dPe skrun khang.

Nāgārjuna (1986), *Lokātītastava* in Chr. Lindtner (tr.), *Master of Wisdom*, Berkeley: Dharma Publishing, pp. 1–11.

——(1991), *Bodhicitta-Vivaraṇa and Bodhicitta-Bhāvanā*, Ācārya Gyaltsen Namdol (tr. and ed.), Sarnath: Central Institute of Higher Tibetan Studies.

——(1994), *Pañcakrama*, Katsumi Mimaki and Tôru Tomabechi (eds), Tokyo: The Toyo Bunko.

——(1996a), *Ratnāvalī* in *dBu ma rigs tshogs drug*, Lanzhou: Kan su Mi rigs dPe skrun khang, pp. 74–124. Also in Heramba Chatterjee Shastri (ed.) (1997), *The Philosophy of Nāgārjuna as contained in the Ratnāvalī*, Calcutta: Saraswati Library.

——(1996b), *Śūnyatāsaptatikārikā* in *dBu ma rigs tshogs drug*, Lanzhou: Kan su Mi rigs dPe skrun khang, pp. 54–61; Also in Sempa Dorje (ed.) (1996), *Śūnyatāsaptati*, Sarnath: Central Institute of Higher Tibetan Studies.

——(1996c), *Vigrahavyāvartanīkārikā* in *dBu ma rigs tshogs drug*, Lanzhou: Kan su Mi rigs dPe skrun khang, pp. 46–53. Also in Bhattacharya (tr.) and Johnston and Kunst (eds) (1990), *The Dialectical Method of Nāgārjuna: Vigrahavyāvartanī*, Delhi: Motilal Banarsidass.

——(1996d), *Yuktiṣaṣṭikākārikā* in *dBu ma rigs tshogs drug*, Lanzhou: Kan su Mi rigs dPe skrun khang, pp. 62–8. Also in Cristina Anna Scherrer Schaub (ed. and tr.) (1991), *Yuktiṣaṣṭikāvṛtti*, Bruxelles: Mélanges Chinois et Bouddhiques.

——(1997), *Mūlamadhyamakakārikāḥ*, J. W. de Jong (ed.), Madras: The Adyar Library and Research Centre. Also Swami Dwarika Das Shastri (ed.) (1989), *Mādhyamakaśāstra*, Varanasi: Bauddha Bharati and in *dBu ma rigs tshogs drug* (1996), Lanzhou: Kan su Mi rigs dPe skrun khang, pp. 1–45.

Ngog Loden Sherab (1993), *Theg chen rgyud bla ma'i don bsdus*, Dharamsala: LTWA.

Padma Karpo, [Drukpa] (1999), *Phyag rgya chen po'i man ngag gi bshad sbyar rgyal ba'i gan mdzod*, in *The Collected Writings of Kun mkhyen Padma dKar po*, Thimphu: National Library, vol. Ta/dza.

Pari Lobzang Rabsal (1991), *'Jam dpal dbyangs kyi dgongs rgyan rigs pa'i gzi 'bar gdong lnga'i sgra dbyangs* in *Yongs rdzogs bstan pa'i mnga' bdag sudhīsara'i gsung 'bum*, Beijing: Krung go Bod kyi Shes rig dPe skrun khang, pp. 354–412.

Phurchog Jampa Gyatsho (1993), *Tshad ma'i gzhung don 'byed pa'i bsdus grwa dang blo rtags kyi rnam gzhag rigs lam 'phrul gyi lde mig*, Lanzhou: Kan su Mi rigs dPe skrun khang.

Prajñākaramati (1989), *Bodhicaryāvatārapañjikā*, P. L. Vaidya and Sridhar Tripathi (eds), Darbhanga: The Mithila Institute. Also *Bodhisattvacaryāvatārapañjikā*, DT, dBu ma, vol. La, Tohoku No. 3872.

Rāhulabhadra (1958), *'Prajñāpāramitāstotra'* in *Suvikrāntavikramiparipṛcchā prajñāpāramitāsūtra*, Ryusho Hikata (ed.), Fukuoka: Kyushu University.

Śākya Chogdan (1975a), *dBu ma rnam par nges pa'i chos kyi bang mdzod lung dang rigs pa'i rgya mtsho*, in *The Complete Works of gSer mdog Paṇ chen Śākya mChog ldan*, Thimphu: Kunzang Tobgey, vol. 14 and 15.

—— (1975b), *dBu ma'i byung tshul rnam par bshad pa'i gtam yid bzhin lhun po*, in *The Complete Works of gSer mdog Paṇ chen Śākya mChog ldan*, Thimphu: Kunzang Tobgey, vol. 4, pp. 209–48.

—— (1975c), *rNgog lo tstsha ba chen pos bstan pa ji ltar bskyangs pa'i tshul*, in *The Collected Writings of gSer mdog Pat chen Śākya mChog ldan*, Thimphu: Kunzang Tobgey, vol. 16, pp. 443–56.

Śākya Dorje (n.d.), *Theg pa'i spyi 'grel gzhi lam 'bras bu'i rnam gzhag gsal bar byed pa chos kyi gter mdzod kun 'dus rig pa'i sgron ma*, n.p.

Sakya Paṇḍita Kunga Gyaltshan (1992), *Sa paṇ kun dga' rgyal mtshan gyi gsung 'bum*, 3 vols, Lhasa: Bod ljongs Bodyig dPe rnying dPe skrun khang.

Śāntarakṣita, *Madhyamakālaṃkārakārikā*, DT, dBu ma, vol. Sa, Tohoku No. 3884. Also Masamichi Ichigo (ed. and tr.) (1989), 'Śantarakṣita's *Madhyamakālaṃkāra*', in Gómez and Silk (eds), *Studies in the Literature of the Great Vehicle*, Ann Arbor: The University of Michigan Press.

——, *Madhyamakālaṃkāravṛtti*, DT, dBu ma, vol. Sa, Tohoku No. 3885.

Śāntideva (1998), *Bodhicaryāvatāra*, P. L. Vaidya and Sridhar Tripathi (eds), Darbhanga: The Mithila Institute. Also (1990), *Byang chub sems dpa'i spyod pa la 'jug pa*, Xining: mTsho sngon Mi rigs dPe skrun khang.

Sera Jetsün Chökyi Gyaltshan, *Zab mo stong pa nyid kyi lta la log rtog 'gog par byed pa'i bstan bcos lta ba ngan pa'i mun sel zhes bya ba*, in *dGag lan phyogs bsgrigs*, pp. 175–518.

—— *gSung lan klu grub dgongs rgyan zhes bya ba* in *dGag lan phyogs bsgrigs*, pp. 89–173.

—— (1973), *dBu ma'i rnam bshad legs bshad skal bzang mgul rgyan*, New Delhi: Lha mkhar Yongs 'dzin bsTan pa rGyal mtshan, Madhyamaka Text Series, vol. 4, pp. 1–561.

—— (1989), *rGyan 'grel spyi don rol mtsho*, Beijing: Krung go Bod kyi Shes rig dPe skrun khang.

Sherab Gyatsho (1988), 'A mdo ba dge 'dun chos 'phel gyi mdzad rnam', *dGe 'dun chos 'phel gyi gsung rtsom*, Bir: Dzongsar Shedra, vol. ii, pp. 375–82.

Sonam Drakpa (1973a), *dBu ma'i spyi don zab don gsal ba'i sgron me*, New Delhi: Lha mkhar Yongs 'dzin bsTan pa rGyal mtshan, Madhyamaka Text Series, vol. 6, pp. 1–331.

—— (1973b), *dBu ma 'jug pa'i brgal lan zab don yang gsal sgron me*, New Delhi: Lha-dkhar Yoṅs-'dzin bstan-pa-rgyal-mtshan, Madhyamaka Text Series, vol. 6, pp. 333–586.

Tagtshang Lotsāwa (1999), *Grub mtha' kun shes rtsa 'grel*, Beijing: Mi rigs dPe skrun khang.

Tāranātha (1986), *rGya gar chos byung*, Chengdu: Si khron Mi rigs dPe skrun khang.

Thuken Lobzang Chökyi Nyima (1984), *Grub mtha' thams cad kyi khung dang 'dod tshul ston pa legs bshad shel gyi me long*, Lanzhou: Kan su Mi rigs dPe skrun khang.

Tsongkhapa Lobzang Drakpa (1973), *dBu ma dgongs pa rab gsal*, Bylakuppe: Sera-mey Computer Centre. Also *bsTan bcos chen mo dbu ma 'jug pa'i rnam bshad dgongs pa rab gsal* in *The Collected Works of Tsoṅ kha pa Blo bzaṅ Grags pa* (1980), New Delhi: Ngawang Gelek Demo, vol. Ma, pp. 1–535.

——(1975), *dBu ma rtsa ba tshig le'ur byas pa shes rab ces bya ba'i rnam bshad rigs pa'i rgya mtsho*, in *The Collected Works of Tsoṅ kha pa Blo bzaṅ Grags pa*, New Delhi: Ngawang Gelek Demo, vol. Ba, pp. 1–566.

——(1978a), *sPyod 'jug shes le'u'i ṭīka blo gsal ba*, in *The Collected Works of rJe Tsoṅ kha pa Blo bzaṅ Grags pa*, New Delhi: Ngawang Gelek Demo, vol. Ma, pp. 650–722.

——(1978b), *rJe btsun 'jam pa'i dbyangs kyi lam gyi gnad red mda' bar shog dril du phul ba* in *The Collected Works of rJe Tsoṅ kha pa Blo bzaṅ Grags pa*, New Delhi: Ngawang Gelek Demo, vol. Pha, pp. 1–12.

——(1978c), *rGyal tshab chos rjes rje'i drung nas gsan pa'i shes rab le'u'i zin bris* in *The Collected Works of rJe Tsoṅ kha pa Blo bzaṅ Grags pa*, New Delhi: Ngawang Gelek Demo, vol. Ma, pp. 53–151.

——(1978d), *dGe sbyor gyi gnad la dri ba snyan skul ba lhag bsam rab dkar* in *The Collected Works of rJe Tsoṅ kha pa Blo bzaṅ Grags pa*, New Delhi: Ngawang Gelek Demo, vol. Kha.

——(1978e), *Lam gyi gtso bo rnam gsum* in *The Collected Works of rJe Tsoṅ kha pa Blo bzaṅ Grags pa*, New Delhi: Ngawang Gelek Demo, vol. Kha, pp. 142–3.

——(1997), *Byang chub lam rim che ba*, Xining: mTsho sngon Mi rigs dPe skrun khang.

——(n.d.), *Drang ba dang nges pa'i don rnam par phye ba'i bstan bcos legs bshad snying po*, Bylakuppe: Sermey Monastery.

Vasubandhu (1981), *Abhidharmakoṣa & bhāṣya*, Swāmī Dwārikādās Śastri (ed.), Varanasi: Bauddha Bharati.

Zhang Yi Sun (ed.) (1993), *Bod rgya tshig mdzod chen mo*, Beijing: Mi rigs dPe skrun khang.

Western and secondary sources

Ames, William (1982), 'The Notion of *Svabhāva* in the Thought of Candrakīrti', *JIP*, 10, pp. 161–77.

Bareau, André (1955), *Les Sectes Bouddhiques du Petit Véhicule*, Saïgon: École Française d'Extrême-Orient.

Blackburn, Simon (1994), *Oxford Dictionary of Philosophy*, Oxford: Oxford University Press.

Broido, M. (1985), 'Padma dkar po on the two *satyas*', *JIABS*, 8/2, pp. 7–59.

Burnouf, E. (1844), *Introduction a l'Histoire du Buddhisme Indien*, Paris: Imprimerie Royale.

Cabezón, José Ignacio (1992), *A Dose of Emptiness: An Annotated Translation of the sTong thun chen mo of mKhas grub dGe legs dpal bzang*, Albany: State University of New York Press.

——(1994), *Buddhism and Language: A Study of Indo-Tibetan Scholasticism*, Albany: State University of New York Press.

Cabezón, José Ignacio (1995), 'On the sGra pa Shes rab rin chen pa'i rtsod lan', *Asiatische Studien/Études Asiatique*, 49, pp. 643–69.

Carr, Brian and Indira Mahalingam (eds) (1997), *Companion Encyclopedia of Asian Philosophy*, London: Routledge.

Carroll, Lewis (1998), *Alice's Adventures in Wonderland and Through the Looking-Glass*, Oxford: Oxford University Press.

Conze, Edward (1973), *The Perfection of Wisdom in Eight Thousand Lines and its Verse Summary*, Bolinas: Four Seasons Foundation.

——(1978), *The Prajñāpāramitā Literature*, Tokyo: The Reiyukai.

Cooper, David (1999), *Epistemology, The Classic Readings*, Oxford: Blackwell.

——(2000), *Metaphysics, The Classic Readings*, Oxford: Blackwell.

Coseru, Christian (2000), *Sudden/Gradual Approaches to Enlightenment in Indian Mahāyāna Buddhism with Reference to Abhisamayālaṃkāloka of Haribhadra*, PhD thesis, Australian National University, available in 2001 at <http://www.anu.edu.au/asianstudies/ahcen/coseru.html>

Craig, Edward (ed.) (1998), *Routledge Encyclopedia of Philosophy*, London: Routledge.

De Jong, J. W. (1979), *Buddhist Studies*, Gregory Schopen (ed.), Berkeley: Asian Humanities Press.

Doctor, Thomas (2004), *Speech of Delight: Mipham's Commentary on Shantarakshita's Ornament of the Middle Way*, Ithaca: Snow Lion Publications.

Dreyfus, George (1997), *Recognizing Reality, Dharmakīrti's Philosophy and its Tibetan Interpretations*, Albany: State University of New York Press.

——(1998), 'The Shuk-den Affair: History and Nature of a Quarrel', *JIABS*, 21/2, pp. 227–70.

——(2003), 'Would the True Prāsaṅgika Please Stand?' in George Dreyfus and Sara McClintock (eds), *The Svātantrika-Prāsaṅgika Distinction, What Difference Does a Difference make?*, Boston: Wisdom Publications, pp. 317–47.

Dudjom Rinpoche (1991), *The Nyingma School of Tibetan Buddhism*, Gyurme Dorje and Mathew Kapstein (trs), Boston: Wisdom Publications.

Dutt, Nalinaksha (1978), *Mahāyāna Buddhism*, Delhi: Motilal Banarsidass.

Eckel, Malcolm David (1992), *Jñānagarbha on the Two Truths*, Delhi: Motilal Banarsidass.

Ehrhard, Franz-Karl (1988), 'Observations on Prāsaṅgika Madhyamaka in the rÑiṅ-ma-pa-school' in Helga Uebach and Jampa Panglung (eds), *Tibetan Studies: Proceedings of the 4th Seminar of the IATS*, Munich: Schloss Hohenkammer, pp. 139–47.

Eliade, Mircea and Iaon Couliano with Hillary Wiener (1999), *The Eliade Guide to World Religions*, San Francisco: Harper Collins.

Fatone, Vincente (1981), *The Philosophy of Nāgārjuna*, Delhi: Motilal Banarsidass.

Gombrich, Richard F. (1991), *Buddhist Precept and Practice*, Delhi: Motilal Banarsidass.

——(1997a), *How Buddhism Began: The Conditioned Genesis of the Early Teachings*, New Delhi: Munshiram Manoharlal.

——(1997b), *Kindness and Compassion as Means to Nirvana*, Amsterdam: Royal Netherlands Academy of Arts and Sciences.

Gómez, L. (1976), 'Proto-Mādhyamika in Pāli canon', *Philosophy East and West*, XXVI, pp. 137–65.

Goodman, Steven M. (1981), 'Mi-Pham rgya-mtsho: An Account of His Life, the Printing of his Works, and the Structure of his Treatise Entitled *mKhas-pa'i tshul la 'jug-pa'i sgo*', in Ronald M. Davidson (ed.), *Wind Horse: Proceedings of the North American Tibetological Society*, Berkeley: Asian Humanities Press, pp. 58–78.

Guenther, Herbert V. (1971), *Buddhist Philosophy in Theory and Practice*, Baltimore: Penguin Books.
——(1989), *Tibetan Buddhism in Western Perspective*, Berkeley: Dharma Publishing.
Gyatso, Janet (1998), *Apparitions of the Self*, New Jersey: Princeton University Press.
Hirakawa, Akira and Paul Groner (eds and tr) (1990), *A History of Indian Buddhism: From Śākyamuni to Early Mahāyāna*, Honolulu: University of Hawaii Press.
Hookham, S. K. (1991), *The Buddha Within*, Albany: State University of New York Press.
Hopkins, Jeffrey (1976), *Practice and Theory of Tibetan Buddhism*, London: Rider.
——(1989) 'A Tibetan delineation of different views of Emptiness in the Indian Middle Way School', *The Tibet Journal*, 14/1, pp. 10–43.
——(1996), *Meditation on Emptiness*, Boston: Wisdom Publications.
——(1997), *Emptiness Yoga, The Tibetan Middle Way*, New Delhi: Motilal Banarsidass.
Huntington, C. W., Jr (1983), 'The System of the Two Truths in the Prasannapadā and the Madhyamakāvatāra: A Study in Mādhyamika Soteriology', *JIP*, 2/1, pp. 77–106.
——and Geshe Namgyal Wangchen (1992), *The Emptiness of Emptiness*, Delhi: Motilal Banarsidass.
Jackson, David (1994), *Enlightenment by a Single Means: Tibetan Controversies on the "Self-Sufficient White Remedy"*, Wien: Verlag der Österreichischen Akademie der Wissenschaften.
Jackson, Roger (1982), 'Sa-skya Paṇḍita's Account of the bSam yas Debate: History as Polemic', *JIABS*, 5/1, pp. 89–99.
Jinpa, Thupten (1999), 'Tsongkhapa's Qualms about Early Tibetan Interpretations of Madhyamaka Philosophy', *The Tibet Journal*, 24/2, pp. 1–28.
——(2002), *Self, Reality and Reason in Tibetan Philosophy: Tsongkhapa's Quest for the Middle Way*, London: RoutledgeCurzon.
Johnston, E. H. and Kunst, Arnold (eds) (1990), *The Dialectical Method of Nāgārjuna*, Delhi: Motilal Banarsidass.
Kalupahana, David (1986), *Mūlamadhyamakakārikā of Nāgārjuna*, New York: State University of New York.
Kapstein, Matthew (1988), 'Mi-pham's Theory of Interpretation' in Donald S. Lopez Jr (ed.), *Buddhist Hermeneutics*, Honolulu: University of Hawaii Press, pp. 149–74.
——(1999), 'Buddhist Perspectives on Ontological Truth', in Eliot Deutsch and Ron Bontekoe (eds), *A Companion to World Philosophies*, Oxford: Blackwell Publishers, pp. 420–33.
——(2000a), *The Tibetan Assimilation of Buddhism*, Oxford: Oxford University Press.
——(2000b), "We Are All Gzhan stong pas", *Journal of Buddhist Ethics*, 7, pp. 105–25.
——(2001), *Reason's Traces*, Boston: Wisdom Publications.
Karmay, Samten (1988), *The Great Perfection*, Leiden: E. J. Brill.
——(1998), *The Arrow and the Spindle*, Kathmandu: Mandala Book Point.
Katz, Nathan, (1976), 'An Appraisal of the Svātantrika-Prāsaṅgika Debates', *Philosophy East and West*, 26/3, pp. 253–66.
Kawamura, Leslie S. (1981a), 'An Analysis of Mi-pham's *mKhas-'jug*', in Ronald M. Davidson (ed.), *Wind Horse: Proceedings of the North American Tibetological Society*, Berkeley: Asian Humanities Press, pp. 112–26.
——(1981b), 'An Outline of *Yāna-Kauśalya* in Mi-pham's *mKhas-'jug*', *Indogaku Bukkyōgaku Kenkyū*, 29/1, pp. 956–61.
——(1982), 'An Analysis of *Yānā-Kauśalya* in Mi-pham's *mKhas-'jug*', *Bulletin of Institute of Buddhist Cultural Studies*, Ryukoku University, 20, pp. 1–19.

Kawamura, Leslie S. (1983), 'The *Akṣayamatinirdeśasūtra* and Mi-pham's *mKhas-jug*', *Contributions on Tibetan and Buddhist Philosophy*, Wiener Studien zur Tibetologie und Buddhismuskunde, Heft 11, 2, pp. 131–45.

Keith, A. Berriedale (1963), *Buddhist Philosophy in India and Ceylon*, Varanasi: Chowkhamba Sanskrit Series Office.

Kuijp, Leonard W. J. van der (1984), 'Miscellanea to a Recent Contribution on/to the bSam-yas Debate', *Kailash*, XI, 3–4, pp. 149–84.

—— (1986), 'On the Sources for Sakya Pat ḍita's Notes on the bSam-yas Debate', *JIABS*, 9.2, pp. 147–153.

Lamotte, Étienne (1962), *L'Enseignement de Vimalakīrti*, Louvian: Publications Universitaires.

—— (1988), *History of Indian Buddhism*, Louvain-la-Neuve: Institut Orientaliste.

Lancaster, Lewis (1977), *Prajñāpāramitā and related systems: Studies in Honour of Edward Conze*, Berkeley: Buddhist Studies Series.

La Vallée Poussin, Louis de (1932–33), 'Réflexions sur le Madhyamka', *Mélanges chinois et bouddhiques*, II, pp. 4–59.

Lindtner, Christian (1982), *Nāgārjuniana: Studies in the Writings and Philosophy of Nāgārjuna*, Copenhagen: Akademisk Forlag.

Lipman, Kennard (1981), 'A Controversial Topic from Mi-pham's Analysis of Śāntarakṣita's *Madhyamakālaṃkāra*', in Ronald M. Davidson (ed.) *Wind Horse*, Berkeley: Asian Humanities Press, pp. 40–57.

Lopez, Donald S., Jr (1987), *A Study of Svātantrika*, Ithaca: Snow Lion Publications.

—— (1998a), *The Heart Sūtra Explained: Indian and Tibetan Commentaries*, Albany: State University of New York Press.

—— (1998b), *Elaborations on Emptiness*, New Delhi: Munshiram Manoharlal.

—— (2001), 'Painting the Target: The Identification of the Object of Negation (dgag bya), in Newland (ed.), *Changing Minds: Contributions to the Study of Buddhism and Tibet in Honor of Jeffrey Hopkins*, Ithaca: Snow Lion Publications, pp. 63–81

Magee, William (1999), *The Nature of Things: Emptiness and Essence in the Geluk World*, Ithaca: Snow Lion Publications.

Mathes, Klaus-Dieter (1996), *Unterscheidung der Gegebenheiten von ihrem wahren Wesen*, Swisttal-Odendorf: Indica et Tibetica Verlag.

Matilal, Bimal Krishna (1986), *Perception: An Essay on Classical Indian Theories of Knowledge*, Oxford: Clarendon Press.

Matsumoto, S. (1990), 'The Madhyamika philosophy of Tsong-kha-pa', *Memoirs of the Research Department of the Toyo Bunko*, 48, pp. 17–47.

May, Jacques (1959), *Candrakīrti Prasannapadā Madhyamakavṛtti*, Paris: Adrien-Maisonneuve.

Mimaki, Katsumi (1982), 'Le commentaire de Mipham sur le *Jñānasārasamuccaya*', in L.A. Hercus, *Indological and Buddhist Studies: Volume in Honour of Professor J. W. De Jong on his Sixtieth Birthday*, Canberra: Australian National University, pp. 353–76.

Mipham [Namgyal] Gyatsho, Nāgārjuna and Tsongkhapa (1978), *Stanzas for a Novice Monk*, Glenn Mullin (tr.), Dharamsala: LTWA.

—— (1986a), *Great Gift and the Wishfulling Gem*, Berkeley: Dharma Publishing.

—— (1986b), *Fish King's Power of Truth*, Berkeley: Dharma Publishing.

—— (1990), Jay Goldberg and Doya Nardin (trs), *MO: Tibetan Divination System*, Ithaca: Snow Lion Publications.

——(1997a), Erik Pema Kunzang (tr.), *Gateway to Knowledge*, 3 vols, Hong Kong: Rangjung Yeshe Publications.

——(1997b), *Calm and Clear*, Tarthang Tulku and Tibetan Nyingma Meditation Center (tr. and comm.), Berkeley: Dharma Publishing.

Monier-Williams, Monier (1986), *A Sanskrit–English Dictionary*, Tokyo: Meicho Fukyukai.

Moore, G. E. (1953), *Some Main Problems of Philosophy*, London: George Allen & Unwin.

Mun-Keat, Choong (2000), *The Fundamental Teachings of Early Buddhism: A Comparative Study based on the Sūtrāṅga portion of the Pali Saṃyutta Nikāya and the Chinese Saṃyuktāgama*, Wiesbaden: Harrassowitz.

Murti, T. R. V. (1998), *The Central Philosophy of Buddhism*, New Delhi: Munshiram Manoharlal.

Nāgārjuna and Lama Mi-pham (1975), *Golden Zephyr: Instructions from a Spiritual Friend*, Leslie Kawamura (tr.), Berkeley: Dharma Publishing.

Napper, Elizabeth (1989), *Dependent Arising and Emptiness*, Boston: Wisdom Publications.

Newland, Guy (1992), *Two Truths*, Ithaca: Snow Lion Publications.

——(ed.) (2001) *Changing Minds: Contributions to the Study of Buddhism in Tibet in Honour of Jeffrey Hopkins*, Ithaca: Snow Lion Publications.

Padmakara Translation Group (2002), *Introduction to the Middle Way: Chandrakirti's Madhyamakavatara with Commentary by Jamgön Mipham*, Boston: Shambala Publications.

Palden Dragpa, Geshe (1996), 'The Four Theses of Negation of Prāsaṅgika Mādhyamika', *Indo-Tibetan Mādhyamika Studies*, New Delhi: Tibet House.

Pettit, John W. (1998), 'Theory, Practice and Ultimate Reality in the Thought of Mipham Rinpoche', PhD thesis, Columbia University.

——(1999a), *Mipham's Beacon of Certainty*, Boston: Wisdom Publications.

——(1999b), 'Review of Altruism and Reality', *Journal of Buddhist Ethics*, 6, pp. 1–14.

Phuntsho, Karma (1998), *The Strengths and Weaknesses of the Tibetan Buddhist Traditions: A Satirical Text by Mipham*, paper read at the 8th Seminar of IATS, Bloomington.

——(2004), 'Nominal Persons and the Sound of Their Hands Clapping', *Buddhist Studies Review*, 21/2, pp. 225–40.

Plato (1964), *The Republic*, Desmond Lee (tr.), Harmondsworth: Penguin Books.

Quine, W. V. (2000), 'On What There Is', in Kim and Sosa (eds), *Metaphysics*, Oxford: Blackwell.

Ramanan, K. Venkata (1998), *Nāgārjuna's Philosophy*, Delhi: Motilal Banarsidass.

Robinson, Richard (1978), *Early Mādhyamika in India and China*, Delhi: Motilal Banarsidass.

Russell, Bertrand (1998), 'The Problems of Philosophy' in Louis Pojman (ed.), *Classics of Philosophy*, Oxford: Oxford University Press, pp. 1086–134.

Samuel, Geoffrey (1993), *Civilized Shamans: Buddhism in Tibetan Societies*, Washington DC: Smithsonian Institution Press.

Schayer, Stanislaw (1931), *Ausgewählte Kapitel aus der Prasannapadā*, Krakow: Naktadem Polskiej Akademji Umiejętności.

Schuh, Dieter (1973), *Tibetische Handschriften und Blockdrucke*, Wiesbaden: Franz Steiner, IX/5.

Scott, Jim (2004), *Maitreya's Distinguishing Phenomena and Pure Being*, Ithaca: Snow Lion Publications.

Seyfort Ruegg, David (1963), 'The Jo naṅ pas, a school of Buddhist ontologist according to the Grub mtha' šel gyi me loṅ', *Journal of American Oriental Society*, 83, pp. 73–91.
——(1966), *Life of Bu ston Rin po che*, Rome: IsMEO.
——(1967), *The Study of Indian and Tibetan Thought: Some Problems and Perspectives*, Leiden: E. J. Brill
——(1971), 'On the Knowability and Expressibility of Absolute Reality in Buddhism', *Indogaku Bukkyōgaku Kenkyū*, 20/1, pp. 1–7.
——(1973), *Le traité du tathāgatagarbha de Bu ston Rin chen grub*, Paris: École Française d'Extrême-Orient.
——(1977), 'The Uses of the Four Positions of the *catuṣkoṭi* and the Problem of the Description of Reality in Mahāyāna Buddhism', *Journal of Indian Philosophy*, 5, pp. 1–71.
——(1979), 'On the Reception and Early History of the dBu-ma (Madhyamaka) In Tibet', in Aris and Suu Kyi (eds) *Tibetan Studies in Honour of Hugh Richardson: Proceedings of the International Seminar on Tibetan Studies*, Warminster: Aris & Philips, pp. 277–79.
——(1981), *The Literature of the Madhyamaka School of Philosophy in India*, Wiesbaden: Otto Harrassowitz.
——(1983), 'On the Thesis and Assertion in the Madhyamaka/Dbu ma', *Contributions on Tibetan and Buddhist Religion and Philosophy* (Wiener Studien zur Tibetologie und Buddhismuskunde Heft) 11, pp. 205–33.
——(1986a), 'A Karma bKa' brgyud Work on the Lineages and Traditions of the Indo-Tibetan dbu ma', in Gnoli and L. Lanciotti (eds) *Orientalia Iosephi Tucci Memoriae Dicata*, Rome: Istituto per il Medio ed Estremo Oriente, pp. 1249–80.
——(1986b), 'Does the Madhyamaka have a Thesis and Philosophical Position?', in Bimal K. Matilal (ed.) *Buddhist Logic and Epistemology: Studies in the Buddhist Analysis of Inference and Language*, Lancaster: Reidel, pp. 229–37.
——(1989a), *Buddha-nature, Mind and the Problem of Gradualism in a Comparative Perspective: On the Transmission and Reception of Buddhism in India and Tibet*, London: School of Oriental and African Studies.
——(1989b), 'On the Tibetan Historiography and Doxography of the 'Great Debate of Samyas'', *Tibetan Studies: Proceedings of the 5th Seminar of International Association of Tibetan Studies*, Narita, pp. 237–44.
——(1991), 'On Pramāṇa Theory in Tsongkhapa's Madhyamaka Philosophy', *Studies in the Buddhist Epistemological Tradition*, Wien: Verlag der Österreichischen Akademie der Wissenschaften.
——(2000), *Three Studies in the History of Indian and Tibetan Madhyamaka Philosophy*, Wien: Arbeitskreis für Tibetische und Buddhistische Studien.
——(2002), *Two Prolegomena to Madhyamaka Philosophy: Candrakīrti's Prasannapadā Madhyamakavṛtti on Madhyamakakārikā, I. 1 and Tsoṅ kha pa blo bzaṅ grags pa/ rGyal tshab dar ma rin chen's dka' gnad/gnas brgyad kyi zin bris*, Wien: Arbeitskreis für Tibetische und Buddhistische Studien.
Skilling, Peter (1994) (ed.), *Mahāsūtras: The Great Discourses of the Buddha*, 2 vols, Oxford: Pali Text Society.
Smart, Ninian (1999), *World Philosophies*, London: Routledge.
Smith, Gene E. (1969), 'Introduction' to 'Jam-mgon Mi-pham rGya-mtsho, *gZhan-gyis brtsad-pa'i lan mdor-bsdus-pa rigs-lam rab-gsal de-nyid snang-byed*, Gangtok: Ngagyur Nyingmay Sungrab.
——(2001), *Among Tibetan Texts*, Boston: Wisdom Publications.

Stcherbatsky, Th. (1996), *The Conception of Buddhist Nirvāṇa*, Delhi: Motilal Banarsidass.

Stearns, Cyrus R. (1999), *The Buddha from Dolpo*, Boston: Wisdom Publications.

Stein, R. A. (1959), *Recherches sur l'Épopée et le Barde au Tibet*, Paris: Presses Universitaires.

——(1961), *Une Chronique ancienne de bSam yas: sBa-bźed*, Paris: Publications de l'Institut des Hautes Études Chinoises.

Stoddard, Heather (1985), *Le mendiant de l'Amdo*, Paris: Société d' ethnographie.

Streng, Federick J. (1967), *Emptiness: A Study in Religious Meaning*, New York: Abingdon Press.

Tatz, Mark (1982), 'Who is Tsong-kha-pa Refuting in his *Basic Path to Awakening?*', in Lawrence Emstein and Richard Sherburne (eds) *Reflections on Tibetan Culture: Essays in memory of Turrell V. Wylie*, New York: The Edwin Mellen Press, pp. 149–63.

Tauscher, Helmut (1992), 'Controversies in Tibetan Madhyamaka exegesis: sTag tshaṅ Lo tsāba's critique of Tsoṅ kha pa's assertion of validly established phenomena', *Asiatische Studien/ Etudes Asiatique* 46/1, pp. 411–36.

——(1995), *Die Lehre von den zwei Wirklichkeiten in Tsoṅ kha pas Madhyamaka-Werken*, Wien: Arbeitskreis für Tibetische und Buddhistische Studien.

Thurman, Robert (1984), *Tsongkhapa's Speech of Gold in the Essence of True Eloquence*, Princeton: Princeton University Press.

Tillemans, Tom J. F. (1999), *Scripture, Logic, Language: Essays on Dharmakīrti and his Tibetan Successors*, Boston: Wisdom Publications.

——and Toru Tomabechi (1995), 'Le *dBu ma'i byung tshul* de Śākya mchog ldan', *Asiatische Studien/ Etudes Asiatique*, 49/4, pp. 853–89.

Tola, Fernando and Dragonetti, Carmen (1995), *On Voidness: Study on Buddhist Nihilism*, Delhi: Motilal Banarsidass.

Tripāṭhī, Chandrabhāl (ed.) (1962), *Fünfundzwanzig Sūtras des Nidānasaṃyukta*, Berlin: Akademie Verlag.

Tsongkhapa Lobzang Drakpa (1978), *Calming the Mind and Discerning the Real: Buddhist Meditation and the Middle View*, Alex Wayman (tr.), New York: Columbia University Press.

——(2000), *The Great Treatise on the Stages of the Path to Enlightenment*, Joshua Cutler and Guy Newland (eds), Ithaca: Snow Lion Publications, vol. I

——(2002), *The Great Treatise on the Stages of the Path to Enlightenment*, Joshua Cutler and Guy Newland, (eds), Ithaca: Snow Lion Publications, vol. III

——(2004), *The Great Treatise on the Stages of the Path to Enlightenment*, Joshua Cutler and Guy Newland (eds), Ithaca: Snow Lion Publications, vol. II

Tucci, Giuseppe (1958), 'Minor Buddhist Texts', Part II, Rome: IsMEO, 9/2.

Van Schaik, Sam (2003), 'The Great Perfection and the Chinese Monk: Rnyingmapa defences of Hwa-shang Mahāyāna in the Eighteenth Century', *Buddhist Studies Review*, 20/2, pp. 189–204.

Vasubandhu (1990), *Abhidharmakoṣabhāṣya*, La Vallée Poussin (French tr.), Leo Pruden (English tr.), Berkeley: Asian Humanities Press.

Wangchuk, Dorji (2002), 'An Eleventh Century Defence of the Authenticity of the *Guhyagarbha Tantra*', in Eimer and Germano (eds), *The Many Canons of Tibetan Buddhism*, Leiden: E. J. Brill, pp. 265–91.

Wangdu and Diemberger (trs and eds) (2000), *dBa bzhed*, Wien: Verlag der Österreichischen Akademie der Wissenschaften.

Warder, A. K. (1970), *Indian Buddhism*, Delhi: Motilal Banarsidass.

Williams, Paul (1979), 'Tsong-kha-pa on Kun-rdzob bden-pa', in Aris and Suu Kyi (eds) *Tibetan Studies in Honour of Hugh Richardson: Proceedings of the International Seminar on Tibetan Studies*, Warminster: Aris & Philips Ltd, pp. 277–9.

——(1983), 'A Note on Some Aspects of Mi Bskyod Rdo Rje's Critique of Dge Lugs Pa Madhyamaka', *JIP*, II, pp. 125–45.

——(1989), *Mahāyāna Buddhism*, London: Routledge.

——(1998a), *Altruism and Reality: Studies in Philosophy of the Bodhicaryāvatāra*, Richmond: Curzon.

——(1998b), *The Reflexive Nature of Awareness: A Tibetan Madhyamaka Defence*, Richmond: Curzon.

——(1999), 'A Response to John Pettit', *Journal of Buddhist Ethics*, 6, pp. 1–11.

Yoshimizu, Chizuko (1996), *Die Erkenntnislehre des Prāsaṅgika-Madhyamaka*, Wien: Arbeitskreis für Tibetische und Buddhistische Studien.

Zimmer, Heinrich (1951), *Philosophies of India*, London: Routledge and Kegan Paul.

NAME AND PLACE INDEX

SUBJECT INDEX